mind-altering
drugs

the science of
subjective experience

Edited by

Mitch Earleywine

OXFORD
UNIVERSITY PRESS

2005

OXFORD
UNIVERSITY PRESS

Oxford University Press, Inc., publishes works that further
Oxford University's objective of excellence
in research, scholarship, and education.

Oxford   New York
Auckland   Cape Town   Dar es Salaam   Delhi   Hong Kong   Karachi
Kuala Lumpur   Madrid   Melbourne   Mexico City   Nairobi
New Delhi   Shanghai   Taipei   Toronto

With offices in
Argentina   Austria   Brazil   Chile   Czech Republic   France   Greece
Guatemala   Hungary   Italy   Japan   Poland   Portugal   Singapore
South Korea   Switzerland   Thailand   Turkey   Ukraine   Vietnam

Copyright © 2005 by Oxford University Press, Inc.

Published by Oxford University Press, Inc.
198 Madison Avenue, New York, New York 10016

www.oup.com

Oxford is a registered trademark of Oxford University Press

Library of Congress Cataloging-in-Publication Data
Mind-altering drugs : the science of subjective experience / edited by Mitch Earleywine.
p. cm.
Includes bibliographical references and index.
ISBN-13 978-0-19-516531-9
ISBN 0-19-516531-4
1. Substance abuse.   2. Reinforcement (Psychology)   3. Individual differences.
I. Earleywine, Mitch.
RC564.M557 2005
616.86—dc22   2004010568

9 8 7 6 5 4 3 2 1

Printed in the United States of America
on acid-free paper

Preface

A parsimonious and intuitive theory of substance abuse relies on the idea that drugs create changes in subjective states that users find reinforcing. A clear understanding of individual differences in these subjective changes can help researchers investigate the etiology of substance abuse. Links between subjective and neurological changes during intoxication also reveal valuable information about the brain mechanisms involved in alterations of consciousness. In addition, frank discussions of these changes in mood, sensations, and consciousness can help substance abusers sort the pros and cons of their drug consumption in therapeutic ways. Nevertheless, researchers and clinicians familiar with drugs often do not know the best way to describe or quantify their subjective effects.

At least a third of Americans have used an illicit drug at least once. Drugs attract considerable attention in science, legislation, and the media. Nevertheless, people develop their attitudes about drugs and drug users based on limited information. Government policies form without a complete picture of the intoxication experience, too. Researchers often find themselves divided into camps based on the drug they study most often (e.g., the Research Society on Alcoholism), limiting their ability to benefit from important work done on other drugs.

A thorough and accessible review of the subjective effects of drugs and the dominant theories behind these effects will help inform readers about the experience of intoxication and help researchers learn from studies in other disciplines. I sincerely hope that readers will finish this book with a clear sense of the theories and techniques behind the investigations of intoxication and how subjective experiences relate to addictive potential. This work should help people make educated decisions about drug use. It will also help researchers identify ideal ways to assess a drug's subjective effects.

In addition, clinicians may understand their substance-abusing clients better once they gain insight into the intoxication that they seek. The chapters here reveal that each drug of abuse has its own unique properties, creating novel sensations, thoughts, emotions, and experiences. In addition, these changes in subjective states appear to motivate consumption in a way that may help explain problematic use. In addition, the final chapter shows an alternative technique (neurofeedback) that can create comparable changes in subjective state. Each chapter describes the relevant research and explains its limitations. These concise descriptions of select studies will also help readers understand the complex interaction of societal, biological, social, and psychological factors in the creation of altered states of consciousness.

Contents

Contributors

Sandy M. Comer
New York State Psychiatric Institute
College of Physicians and Surgeons of Columbia University

Travis A. R. Cook
University of California, San Diego

Christopher J. Correia
Auburn University

Harriet de Wit
University of Chicago

Mitch Earleywine
University of Southern California

Suzette M. Evans
New York State Psychiatric Institute
Department of Psychiatry, College of Physicians and Surgeons
of Columbia University

Susan C. Han
New York State Psychiatric Institute
Department of Psychiatry, College of Physicians and Surgeons
of Columbia University

Kristina M. Jackson
University of Missouri–Columbia and the Midwest Alcoholism
Research Center

Scott Kollins
Duke University

David Lenson
University of Massachusetts–Amherst

Ralph Metzner
California Institute of Integral Studies

Norman Miller
University of Southern California

Siegfried Othmer
EEG Institute

Vicki Pollock
EEG Institute

Alison E. Richardson
University of Missouri–Columbia and the Midwest Alcoholism Research Center

Kenneth J. Sher
University of Missouri–Columbia and the Midwest Alcoholism Research Center

Rick Strassman
University of New Mexico School of Medicine

Diana J. Walker
University of Chicago

Tamara L. Wall
University of California, San Diego

Mark D. Wood
University of Rhode Island

James P. Zacny
University of Chicago

mind-altering
drugs

1

Behavioral Theories of Choice

Understanding the Relationship Between Drug Use and Drug-Free Reinforcement

CHRISTOPHER J. CORREIA

Drugs are highly reinforcing, and under certain conditions drug use can become an organism's dominant response. However, under different conditions, organisms show a greater preference for drug-free behaviors and experiences. The present chapter provides an overview of empirical research and clinical theory that attempts to explain the relationship between drug use, drug-related reinforcement, and drug-free reinforcement. The purpose of this chapter is to review how theories on choice behavior have contributed to our understanding of drug use. The review will include a brief history of the theoretical and empirical underpinnings of the behavioral choice perspective, a sample of laboratory and "real world" research studies that highlight the interplay between drug use and drug-free alternatives, and a discussion of some of the clinical implications of this research. The overarching goal of the chapter is for all readers to come away with a better understanding of how an individual's pattern of drug use is tied to the broader environment. But, first, a series of familiar questions.

Why Do People Use Drugs?

For as long as recorded history, and probably longer, humans have self-administered psychoactive substances (the terms *substance* and *drug* are used generically to refer to all abused drugs, both licit and illicit). Behavioral theories of drug use tend to focus on the reinforcing properties of psychoactive substances. Evidence for the ability of drug use to serve as a positive reinforcer is widely available. Experimental research has repeatedly demonstrated that nondependent humans and animals will self-administer a variety of substances (e.g., nicotine, alcohol, and cocaine), and that these substances can maintain high rates of operant behavior (Brady & Lukas, 1984; Griffiths, Bigelow, & Henningfield, 1980; Johanson, 1978). Under certain conditions, drug-taking behavior develops into the subject's dominant response. In one early laboratory study, rhesus monkeys preferred cocaine over food, and the study had to be terminated after eight days to save the subjects from starvation (Aigner & Balster, 1978). Other laboratory studies have demonstrated that primates will voluntarily self-administer fatal amounts of cocaine (Deneau, Yanagita, & Seevers, 1969). While animal drug self-administration studies typically do not expose subjects to such dangerous levels of drug use, they do highlight the notion that, under certain circumstances, animals find certain drugs highly reinforcing.

The drugs that promote high levels of responding and self-administration in laboratory animals are the same drugs that humans tend to use in their natural environment. The majority of substance users experience minimal negative consequences, but some humans self-administer dangerously high levels of their preferred drug. Each year in the United States, approximately 440,000 deaths are attributed to cigarette smoking (Centers for Disease Control and Prevention [CDC], 2002a); 110,000 deaths are attributed to alcohol (National Institute of Alcohol Abuse and Alcoholism, 2001); and 20,000 deaths are attributed to illicit drug use (CDC, 2002b). It has been estimated that Americans spent $64 billion on illicit drugs in one year (Office of National Drug Control Policy, 2001). Clearly, animals are not alone in their sometimes dangerous susceptibility to the reinforcing effects of drugs.

The fact that drug use serves as a powerful reinforcer for humans and animals suggests that substance-related reinforcement has a strong biological underpinning. Indeed, all reinforcers appear to operate through a common neural mechanism. In other words, the biological mechanisms that allow us to experience substance use as a reinforcing behavior are similar to those that allow us to experience eating a good meal, having sex, and other substance-free behaviors as reinforcing (Wise, 1998). However, as summarized by McKim (2003), the drug-related reinforcement differs from these drug-free examples in several important ways. First, whereas food consumption and sexual behavior are regulated by natural satiation mechanisms, most drugs do not appear to have any natural limits to their reinforcing ability. Second, most drugs work by quickly flooding the brain's reward system, making drug reinforcement stronger and more immediate than drug-free reinforcers. Third, and finally, our brain's reward system is designed, through the principles of evolution and natural selection, to "enjoy" behaviors that increase our chance of survival. However, our brain may not be equipped to deal with the reinforcing properties and addictive potential that come with the introduction of synthetic drugs and more immediate delivery systems (intravenous injections, freebasing). To summarize, humans share a powerful, species-wide, biologically determined affinity toward a variety of psychoactive drugs. In many ways, drug use is the quickest, most efficient, and most reliable way to experience pleasure.

Why Don't We All Use Drugs?

The powerful reinforcing properties of many psychoactive substances have been well established, and the human central nervous system is genetically engineered to experience drug use as rewarding and pleasurable. After considering these two important factors, Chilcoat and Johanson (1998) made the following observation about cocaine abuse:

> At the most radical level, we would suggest that the accumulation of evidence of the normalcy of cocaine reinforcement changes the question that epidemiologists should ask from "What are the risk factors for cocaine abuse?" to "Why aren't we all abusing cocaine?" A more reasonable conclusion is not that we are all inherent cocaine abusers but that the probability of drug-seeking behavior is far greater than most epidemiologists ever consider. Said another way, we are all at some risk and this risk is not trivial. (p. 326)

Neurobiological and operant-based experimental research has advanced our understanding of substance abuse and dependence by establishing the consumption of psychoactive substances as a positive reinforcer. But these perspectives alone do not tell the whole story. How do we explain individual differences in the decision to abstain from, use, or abuse psychoactive drugs? Simply put, if we all share similar brains, and all of our brains are programmed to experience drug use as highly reinforcing, then why aren't we all hopelessly addicted?

The Behavioral Choice Perspective

Drug use is just one of many activities available to an individual. Thus, along with working, watching television, and interacting with other people, substance use is one of several activities to which an individual may choose to distribute his or her behavior and derive reinforcement. In psychology and the behavioral sciences, a variety of theories have attempted to understand the choices that people make. The behavioral choice perspective is a collection of operant-based research and theory utilized to explain the establishment of preferences among available reinforcers. Behavioral theories of choice have been applied to a broad range of behaviors, including the prediction of cigarette smoking, eating and physical activity, and drug and alcohol abuse (Bickel, DeGrandpre, Higgins, & Hughes, 1990; DeGrandpre & Bickle, 1996; Epstein, Bulik, Perkins, Caggiula, & Rodefer, 1991; Epstein, Smith, Vara, Rodefer, 1991; Vuchinich & Tucker, 1983, 1988). What follows is a brief history of the behavioral choice perspective, followed by an extended discussion of how that framework has been able to advance our understanding of drug use.

A Brief History

Behavioral theories of choice draw from a rich foundation of empirically supported principles. Traditional theories of reinforcement have tended to focus on the relationship between an individual reinforcer and behavior (e.g., Skinner, 1938). Behaviors that result in reinforcing consequences tend to be repeated, and changes in the frequency or intensity of the reinforcement lead to predicable changes in the behavior. However, as reinforcement theory has developed over time, there has been a tendency to focus less on individual reinforcers and more on the context within which reinforcement occurs. Thus, in addition to considering how behavior is influenced by one particular reinforcer, behavioral theorists began to ask how an individual establishes preferences and allocates his or her behavior among an array of simultaneously available reinforcers.

Premack (1965) operationally defined a preference as the ordering a participant gives to a set of stimuli, suggesting that preferences for a particular stimulus are determined in the context of all other competing stimuli. Herrnstein (1970) formalized the relationship between reinforcers with the matching law, a mathematical account of choice behavior particularly well suited to understanding preference selection in a broader environmental context. The theory and accompanying equations specify that an individual's behavior is distributed across concurrently available options in proportion to the amount of reinforcement received for engaging in each behavior. Simply put, the frequency of a given behavior is a function of its reinforcement, relative to the reinforcement obtained from all other possible activities. Thus, the amount of reinforcement received from a behavior *relative to other options* is viewed as more predictive of choice behavior than the *absolute amount* of reinforcement received. It follows that the amount of behavior allocated to a given behavior will decrease if the reinforcement associated with competing behaviors in the environments is increased. Reviews of the literature suggest that the matching law can adequately describe human choice behavior in both controlled and natural environments (cf. McDowell, 1988). The work of Premack and

Herrnstein revealed that behavior allocation is affected by environmental conditions and, more specifically, the reinforcement associated with all of the activities available within the environment.

Behavioral Theories of Choice and Substance Use

Vuchinich and Tucker (1983) proposed the behavioral theories of choice as a framework for understanding the environmental context surrounding substance use and abuse. These authors described the behavioral choice perspective as a molar account of how organisms allocate their behavior among a set of available activities, with the full set of available activities constituting the surrounding context. Thus, the behavioral choice perspective recognizes that preferences for substances arise within a broader environmental context that includes the availability or utilization of competing reinforcers and their associated environmental constraints. In other words, decisions to use drugs are the result of an interaction between the reinforcing properties of the drug, the availability of the drug, and the availability of alternative, drug-free activities. Analyses emerging from this perspective aim to identify the variables that control the reinforcing value of substance use relative to the reinforcing value of other available activities (Vuchinich & Tucker, 1988).

After reviewing the work of Premack (1965), Herrnstein (1970), and other behavioral choice researchers, Vuchinich and Tucker (1983) proposed the following generalization: If constraints on a particular reinforcer are increased, there is a tendency for its consumption to be reduced and for behavior to be reallocated among the other available reinforcers. When applied to the use of psychoactive substances, the generalization suggests that the environmental context surrounding drug use can be investigated as a function of two classes of variables: (a) the direct constraints imposed on access to substance use and (b) reinforcers other than substance use that are available and the constraints imposed on access to them.

Investigating the Drug-Taking Environment

What follows is a review of studies that use the behavioral choice perspective to better understand the relationship between drug use and the broader environmental context. The review begins by looking at the effect direct constraints can have on drug use and then moves on to look at the relationship between drug use and alternative, drug-free reinforcers.

Direct Constraints on Access to Substances

Constraints usually refer to changes in the price of a substance, but they can include any factor that limits the availability of or devalues substance use, including the introduction of negative consequences contingent on substance use. Constraints can be the result of an experimental manipulation, such as the response required to obtain a substance, or conditions existing in the natural environment.

Laboratory Studies

In one early study (Liebson, Cohen, Faillace, & Ward, 1971), alcoholics receiving inpatient treatment earned credits by doing laundry work, tutoring other patients, and performing other types of service. The credits could then be exchanged for a variety of goods and services, including health care, entertainment, and alcohol. The token economy allowed the researchers to manipulate the price of alcohol and the amount of operant behavior required to obtain alcohol. Increasing the amount of work required to obtain alcohol resulted in decreased alcohol consumption. Subsequent experimental conditions within the same study demonstrated that making positive reinforcement (opportunity to work, money) contingent on consuming less than a predetermined limit could effectively maintain moderate drinking and abstinence. These results were later replicated in a study of alcohol self-administration in moderate drinkers (Van Etten, Higgins, & Bickel, 1995). Three male volunteers could earn a designated amount of beer (2 oz or 4 oz) by pulling a lever a designated number of times (100, 200, 400, 800, or 1,600). Thus, the experimenters manipulated both the available dose and the response requirement. As in the earlier study with alcoholics, moderate drinkers showed decreased alcohol consumption as schedule requirements increased.

Bigelow, Griffiths, and Liebson (1976) demonstrated that the relationships between response requirement and self-administration generalized beyond alcohol to other psychoactive drugs. Five men with a documented history of sedative abuse resided on a behavioral research ward and were given the opportunity to earn tokens by riding a stationary bicycle; the tokens could be exchanged for doses of either diazepam or sodium pentobarbital, other ward privileges (e.g., use of recreational equipment), or money. The number of tokens required to earn a single dose of drug was varied across days in a mixed order among 1, 3, 5, 8, or 10 tokens per dose. The variation of the response cost per dose had a similar effect on self-administration for all participants, with drug intake decreasing as a function of increased cost. More generally, Griffiths et al. (1980) reviewed the experimental literature on the relationship between drug self-administration and response requirement. These authors concluded that the "results have shown a relationship which is remarkably generalizable across species, across drugs, and across settings; as response requirement increases, the amount of drug self-administered typically decreases" (p. 30).

Population Studies

Results from studies conducted in the natural environment complement the results of the laboratory-based studies. Population-based studies relate constraints such as price increases to aggregated indexes of alcohol use (i.e., beverage sales) and related negative consequences. Ornstein (1980) reviewed studies on the relationship between price and demand for beverages containing alcohol. In doing so, Ornstein synthesized the results of 22 studies covering 13 countries and spanning the years 1870–1970. He concluded that demand for beer, wine, and distilled spirits decreases as price increases. A more recent review concluded that increases in the total price of alcohol can reduce drinking and driving and other alcohol-related crimes and can lower the frequency of diseases, injuries, and deaths related to alcohol use and abuse (Chaloupka, Grossman, & Saffer, 2002).

Alternative Reinforcers and Drug Use

Direct constraints on access to substances can have a powerful effect on substance use. However, direct constraints alone can not sufficiently control the availability and use of drugs. The United States' experiment with alcohol prohibition revealed that the total costs of constraining access to alcohol (i.e., enforcement costs, health costs associated with home-brewed alcohol, corrosion of respect for laws and government) were simply too high. More recently, the "war on drugs" has been unable to eliminate the availability of illicit drugs. Indeed, in 2002, more than 85% of U.S. 12th graders report that marijuana is "fairly easy" or "very easy" to obtain, and approximately 50% reported similar availability for cocaine, MDMA, and amphetamines (Monitoring the Future, 2002).

Thus, when constraints are unable to eliminate the availability of drugs, alternative reinforcers may be the more salient determinants of actual consumption. In other words, decisions to *not* use drugs are usually the result of competition from substance-free alternatives rather than from the effects of prohibitive constraints (Vuchinich and Tucker, 1988). Carroll (1996b) proposes two additional reasons for taking a systematic approach to studying the effects of alternative reinforcers on substance use, abuse, and dependence. First, humans and animals in laboratory studies given equal access to a substance will not consume at the same level, even when variables affecting constraints on access to the substance (e.g., dose, schedule of access) are held constant. In other words, availability alone does not explain the variation in drug self-administration. Second, despite the control it affords, the laboratory is unable to replicate the rich environmental context that surrounds drug use. Failure to account for the effects of substance-free alternatives may partially explain why techniques capable of markedly reducing drug use in the laboratory—such as punishment, contingent time out from other reinforcers, and other forms of treatment—tend to demonstrate diminished effects when applied in the natural environment. Thus, a better understanding of the effects of alternative reinforcers may lead to improved models of substance use and treatment efficacy. What follows is a review of studies that demonstrate the inverse relationship between substance use and alternative reinforcers.

Laboratory Studies

Several laboratory paradigms have been used to demonstrate a relationship between the reinforcing effects of drugs and the presence of an alternative reinforcer. The dependent variable is typically a measure of substance use preference, such as the amount of the substance consumed, the amount of effort devoted to obtaining a substance, or the number of times substance use is chosen over an alternative reinforcer. Independent variables involve manipulations of the availability and magnitude of an alternative reinforcer.

Vuchinich and Tucker (1983) studied preference for alcohol consumption among nonalcoholic males as a function of the value and delay of an alternative reinforcer. Participants could earn points by responding with button presses, and the points could be redeemed for either money or alcohol. The investigators manipulated the monetary value of the points (2¢ or 10¢) and the delay before money was received (no delay, 2-week delay, or 8-week delay). As predicted, participants showed greater preference for alcohol under the low money condition, and participants in both delay conditions preferred alcohol more than participants in the no-delay condition. Preference for alcohol is also responsive to changes in the price of access to an alternative. In one study (Landau, 1986), nonalcoholic participants could earn points on a button-pressing task, and points could be used to gain access to either alcohol or video game playing. The price, in terms of points, remained constant for alcohol throughout the course of the study, while the price of video game playing was manipulated by the investigator. When the price of access to video game playing increased, four of the six participants showed an increased preference for alcohol relative to video game playing. The remaining two participants showed exclusive preference for video game playing throughout the study.

Higgins, Bickel, and Hughes (1994) examined the influence of an alternative reinforcer on cocaine use among four adult humans. During eleven controlled laboratory sessions, participants made repeated choices between cocaine versus placebo or between cocaine versus varying amounts of money (0–$2.00). Subjects always chose cocaine rather than placebo, indicating that the drug served as a reinforcer. When subjects were asked to choose between cocaine and money, the amount of cocaine consumed decreased as the amount of concurrently available money increased. These results are similar to other laboratory studies showing that the presence of an alternative reinforcer can decrease cocaine (Hart, Haney, Foltin, & Fischman, 2000; Higgins, Roll, & Bickel, 1996) and heroin self-administration (Comer et al., 1998). Several laboratory studies have also demonstrated an inverse relationship between cigarette smoking, the magnitudes of an alternative reinforcer, and the delay associated with the alternative reinforcer (e.g., Bickel, Madden, & DeGrandpre, 1997; Shahan, Bickel, Badger, & Giordano, 2001; Roll, Reilly, & Johanson, 2000).

Across these laboratory studies, participants showed a greater preference for substance use when the value of the alternative reinforcer was small, the alternative reinforcer was delayed, or the price of the alternative reinforcer was increased. In summarizing the literature on substance use and alternative reinforcers, Vuchinich and Tucker (1988) concluded that substance use may emerge as a highly preferred activity when constraints on psychoactive substances are minimal and alternative reinforcers either are sparse or constraints on their access make them difficult to acquire. Carroll (1996b) conducted a more comprehensive review of human and animal laboratory self-administration studies in which the availability of nondrug reinforcers was manipulated. Carroll concluded that the availability of nondrug alternative reinforcers reliably and effectively reduces drug-self administration, can slow or prevent acquisition of drug self-administration, and may suppress withdrawal under some conditions. Findings tend to generalize across species (humans, baboons, monkeys, and rats); drugs of abuse (heroin, ethanol, amphetamine, morphine, phencyclidine, cocaine, and cigarettes); types of alternative reinforcers (food, sucrose, carbohydrates, money, and video game playing); and route of administration (intravenous, oral).

Natural Environment Studies

Laboratory studies have repeatedly demonstrated that, under controlled conditions, the magnitude or immediacy of alternative drug-free reinforcers influences drug use. A growing literature has documented an inverse relationship between substance use and alternative reinforcers in the natural environment. The findings of these studies are very consistent with those reported in the experimental literature: drug use occurs within a broader context, and the drug-free elements of that context impact patterns of drug use. The studies reviewed in the following highlight the diverse methodologies and samples that have been employed in this literature.

POPULATION STUDIES

Large-scale epidemiological studies have also demonstrated that alternative reinforcers can reduce drug use. One study investigated drug use and involvement in various activities among 1,516 urban middle school students. Students with high levels of religious involvement (praying, reading the Bible, frequenting religious services and revivals) were substantially less likely to have initiated drug use (Johanson, Duffy, & Anthony, 1996). Kandel & Raveis (1989) reported that adoption of conventional social roles (e.g., getting married, having children) and existing in a social context that did not favor drug use were among the factors that predicted cessation among a longitudinal cohort of 1,222 drug-using young adults.

BEHAVIORAL ALLOCATION

Correia and colleagues conducted a series of studies on how individuals allocate their time and derive reinforcement from substance-related and substance-free activities. All these studies used the Pleasant Events Schedule (PES; MacPhillamy & Lewinsohn, 1982) to measure behavioral allocation and obtained positive reinforcement; the PES was modified to allow participants to distinguish between behaviors engaged in while sober (substance-free reinforcement) and those engaged in while using or under the influence of alcohol and other drugs (substance-related reinforcement). An initial study with college undergraduates (Correia, Simons, Carey, & Borsari, 1998) demonstrated that predictions of substance use improved when both substance-free and substance-related reinforcement were taken into account. Specifically, a negative relationship was observed between substance-free reinforcement and the frequency of substance use, indicating that as reinforcement from substance-free activities decreased, the frequency of substance use increased. The addition of a reinforcement ratio, based on Herrnstein's (1970) matching law equations and designed to measure reinforcement received from substance-related activities relative to total reinforcement, accounted for additional unique variance. A related study (Correia & Carey, 1999) reported similar relationships between the frequency of substance use and substance-free reinforcement in a sample of substance-using psychiatric outpatients. A third study (Correia, Carey, & Borsari, 2002) extended the research by demonstrating a relationship between substance-related reinforcement and measures of substance use quantity and related negative consequences.

Van Etten, Higgins, Budney, and Badger (1998) used the PES to compare the density of naturally occurring positive reinforcement experienced by cocaine abusers with the density experienced by a matched control group. Cocaine abusers reported a lower frequency of engagement in nonsocial, introverted, passive outdoor, and mood-related activities relative to the control group. Similar findings were reported in a study of college student binge drinkers (Correia et al., 2003). Relative to the comparison group of lighter drinking undergraduates, students who engaged in frequent binge drinking derived less reinforcement from a variety of substance-free activities.

SOCIAL SUPPORT AND CIGARETTE SMOKING

Social support has been linked to physical health and emotional well-being. Recent studies have reported that positive role models, community involvement, and spending time with organized groups serve as protective factors against cigarette smoking (Atkins, Oman, Vesely, Aspy, & McLeroy, 2002; Elder et al., 2000). Earlier studies had reported that increased rates of smoking are associated with divorce, separation, single marital status, widowhood, and lack of a confidant (Fisher, 1996). Although these results can be interpreted in a variety of ways, they are consistent with Fisher's (1996) view that social support is rewarding and reinforcing, and that it can function as a substitute for smoking in certain contexts. The following quotation summarizes his proposition:

> The review of [social supports] effects and those of nicotine suggests that social support and nicotine may be substitutable for each other. Both (a) appear to enhance task performance, (b) have positive benefits on mood, and (c) appear to have enhanced utility in the face of distress. These similar values of social support and nicotine might be the basis for their serving as substitutes for each other in times of stress, low mood, and desire for energized performance. (Fisher, 1996, p. 215)

Thus, behaviors that garner social support can be viewed as alternatives to drug use. Environments that provide high levels of social support should protect individuals from high levels of drug use; conversely, high levels of drug use would be expected in environments where social support is sparse or unavailable. The commodity view of social support has been applied to other forms of substance use (Rachlin, 2000) and might prove useful in understanding a variety of other addictive behaviors.

RELAPSE

Building on their earlier laboratory findings, Vuchinich and Tucker (1996) tested an application of the behavioral choice perspective to the problem of alcohol relapse. The decision to consume alcohol after treatment was likened to choosing an immediate but small reward over delayed but larger rewards that are often contingent on maintaining abstinence, such as improved health, work performance, and family relations. Participants were 26 male veterans in an aftercare program following inpatient treatment for alcohol dependence. They provided daily records of alcohol consumption and an explanation for why they drank. Participants also recorded significant positive and negative life events and a rating of their impact on mood. As predicted, drinking episodes preceded by negative events were more severe. The authors proposed that certain life events (e.g., separation from a spouse) led to a reduction in the future availability of nondrinking reinforcement, thus increasing the relative reinforcing value of alcohol consumption.

DRUG-FREE ATTITUDES AND EXPECTANCIES

Numerous studies have demonstrated that positive attitudes and expectancies toward drug use consistently predict drug consumption and drug-related behaviors (Petraitis, Flay, & Miller, 1995; Stacy, Widaman, & Marlatt, 1990). However, from a behavioral choice perspective, attitudes toward sobriety and drug-free alternatives should also be predictive of drug use. Simons and Carey (2000) examined the effect of attitudes toward drug-free experience on marijuana use in a sample of college undergraduates. They found that less favorable attitudes toward drug-free experience were related to higher reports of marijuana use. A positive attitude toward drug-free experience, however, was related to less frequent marijuana use, even among those with a positive attitude toward marijuana. Levy and Earleywine (2000) reported similar results, where expectancies for drug-free activities were inversely related to alcohol consumption among college students. These data are consistent with the behavioral choice perspective in suggesting that drug use is not simply a function of having a positive attitude toward drugs but also involved a context involving the availability of and attitudes toward potentially rewarding alternative activities.

All the studies reviewed in this section are consistent with previous experimental research and further highlight the connection between substance-related behaviors and alternative reinforcers. Thus, in both the laboratory and the natural environment, the frequency, quantity, and negative consequences of substance use are tied to the broader environmental context. These studies do not suggest that alternative reinforcers directly change the reinforcing properties of drugs or make the human brain less susceptible to their reinforcing effects. However, one clear implication is that drugs exert less control over behavior when viable alternatives are readily available. Drug use thrives in environments where alternative reinforcers are sparse. When alternatives are present, dangerous patterns of drug use are less likely to develop. Certainly, more research is needed to determine both the extent to which drug-free alternatives can substitute for drug use and which types of activities protect individuals from initiating harmful patterns of substance abuse. Indeed, most people do in fact have ample alternatives to drug use, insofar as drug use is never the only available option. But for some individuals, due to either a lack of alternatives or an inability to utilize the alternatives that are available, drug use becomes the preferred source of reinforcement. The final section of this chapter reviews some of the clinical implications of the behavioral choice research. Embedded in this review is a discussion of various strategies for shifting the balance of behavioral allocation away from drug-related reinforcers and toward drug-free alternatives.

Treatment Implications

Thus far, this chapter has presented the behavioral choice perspective as a theory capable of understanding some of the individual differences in drug use. The theoretical foundations of the behavioral theories on choice were presented, and a diverse group of empirical studies demonstrating the connection between drug use and alternative reinforcers was reviewed. The chapter now turns to the clinical utility of the behavioral choice perspective. Two treatment approaches, contingency management and cognitive-motivational treatment, will be discussed. Although different in may ways, these approaches were chosen because they both attempt to decrease drug use by increasing the reinforcement associated with drug-free behaviors.

Contingency Management Approaches

The behavioral choice perspective has informed interventions for a number of substances, including alcohol (Hunt & Azrin, 1973; Petry, Martin, Cooney, & Kranzler, 2000); benzodiazepines (Stitzer, Bigelow, & Liebson, 1979); cocaine (Higgins et al., 1993); marijuana (Sigmon, Steingard, Badger, Anthony, & Higgins, 2000); opiates (Silverman et al., 1996); and tobacco (Corby, Roll, Ledgerwood, & Schuster, 2000). An early application, termed the *community reinforcement approach*, was implemented for alcoholics admitted to a public hospital for inpatient treatment (Hunt & Azrin, 1973). Treatment was designed to replace reinforcement received from drinking with reinforcement received from more socially appropriate sources. Community reinforcement participants were provided with counseling designed to improve employment prospects, marital and family relationships, and nondrinking social interactions. Some community reinforcement participants with limited financial resources were provided with radios or televisions, subscriptions to local newspapers, telephones, and fees to obtain a driver's license. These goods and services were provided to help clients access alternative sources of reinforcement by providing entertainment or facilitating communication with employers and social partners. The results indicated that the mean percentage of time spent drinking, unemployed, away from home, and institutionalized was more than twice as high for the "usual care" control group participants than for the community reinforcement participants. These results persisted across a 6-month posthospitalization assessment period (Hunt & Azrin, 1973).

Higgins and colleagues developed a similar approach, termed the *abstinence reinforcement procedure,* for the treatment of clients diagnosed with cocaine dependence. The conceptual framework for the treatment, based on the drug self-administration literature, calls for changes in the user's environment so that (a) drug use and abstinence are readily detected, (b) drug abstinence is readily reinforced, (c) drug use results in a loss of reinforcement, and (d) the density of reinforcement derived from nondrug sources is increased to compete with the reinforcing effects of drug use. To achieve these aims, the treatment combined elements of the community reinforcement approach with a contingency management program. In the original study (Higgins et al., 1991), urine specimens were screened four times per week, and vouchers used to make retail purchases were awarded for each clean urine specimen. Vouchers were awarded according to an escalating schedule; the value of the first cocaine-free urine sample was worth $1.50, and the value of consecutive cocaine-free urine samples increased by $0.65. To encourage continuous abstinence, $10.00 bonuses were awarded for each set of four consecutive negative specimens, and a cocaine-positive urine sample reset the value of the vouchers back to $1.50. An individual who remained abstinent throughout the 12-week treatment program could earn up to $1,038, which could be used for purchase of retail items (e.g., ski lift passes, camera equipment, and continuing education materials) that facilitated the treatment goal of increasing drug-free activities. Treatment retention rates were higher in the contingency management program (11 of 13 participants completed) than in the comparison group, a 12-week 12-step program (5 of 12 completed). When urine specimens were examined, 92% of those provided by members of the contingency management group were negative for cocaine, compared with 78% negative for the 12-step group. Results were later replicated (Higgins et al., 1993) using a similar treatment and a more stringent random assignment procedure.

Since the two seminal studies by Higgins and his colleagues, contingency management procedures have been used to reduce the use of a variety of substances. A study by Iguchi, Belding, Morral, Lamb, and Husband (1997) demonstrated the effectiveness of a 12-week contingency management program in the treatment of opioid dependence. Participants were randomly assigned to one of three treatment conditions: urinalysis-based reinforcement (UA), treatment-plan-based reinforcement condition (TP), and standard care (STD). Participants in the UA and TP conditions could earn vouchers, described as treatment assistance coupons, redeemable for expenses linked to a treatment plan (e.g., clothing for a job interview). Participants in the UA condition earned vouchers for opioid-negative urine specimens. Vouchers were awarded to the TP participants for meeting objectively defined, clearly verifiable, individually tailored treatment plan tasks. Despite the fact that only the UA participants were directly reinforced for abstaining, the TP condition participants were more than twice as likely to produce negative urine specimens. This study demonstrates the power of not only of reinforcing drug abstinence but also of reinforcing behaviors that will contribute to broader behavioral changes that promote a healthier lifestyle.

A recent and novel application of contingency management can be seen in Silverman's therapeutic workplace (Silverman, Svikis, Robles, Stitzer & Bigelow, 2001; Silverman et al., 2002), which has been used to help drug-abusing pregnant and postpartum women achieve abstinence by paying them a salary to work and/or acquire job skills related to data entry. Each day, when a participant reports to the workplace, she is required to provide a urine sample, and if the sample is drug free, she is allowed to work that day. After completing a 3-hour work shift, she receives a payment voucher. Patients can earn additional vouchers for appropriate professional demeanor, and bonuses based on productivity are also provided. Thus, salary is linked to abstinence and job performance. Over the initial 6 months of the study, 59% of the urine samples from the women assigned to the workplace were drug-free, compared with 33% of the samples from the women in the control group. Therapeutic workplace participants continued to provide significantly more cocaine- and opiate-free urine samples than did the controls throughout the 3-year study period.

As summarized by Wong, Jones, and Stitzer (in press), the community reinforcement approach and abstinence reinforcement procedure share some core elements. The primary conceptual framework goal of both treatments is that drug-free reinforcers can compete with the pharmacological and nonpharmacological reinforcement associated with drug use. Thus, both attempt to decrease drug use by increasing the density of positive reinforcement garnered from drug-free, alternative behaviors. Both treatments are derived from principles of operant conditioning and behavioral pharmacology, and both enjoy empirical support from applied studies (for a more comprehensive review, see Higgins & Silverman, 1999).

Cognitive-Motivational Treatments

Marlatt and Kilmer (1998) suggested that treatment strategies derived from the behavioral choice perspective could emerge as effective components in broader cognitive-motivational treatments for substance use. These authors specifically mentioned motivational interviewing (Miller & Rollnick, 2002), which uses feedback regarding substance-related behaviors and consequences to promote contemplation or initiation of behavior change. For example, one study with college students (Kilmer, Larimer, Alexander, & Marlatt, 1998) used time-allocation data to assess the relationship between drinking and environmental constraints limiting engagement in preferred activities. The results revealed a positive relationship between perceived constraints and time engaged in drinking, such that perceived constraints on preferred activities were associated with increased drinking. The authors suggested that information regarding constraints on access to valued substance-free activities could be used as sources of motivational feedback. Thus, patients could be encouraged to consider how constraints on preferred activities could be reduced, and on how alcohol use imposed additional constraints on other potentially rewarding activities. As a second example, Marlatt and Kilmer (1998) observed that many relapse-prevention programs are designed to teach patients alternative coping behaviors that will replace drug use (see Carroll, 1996a; Marlatt & Gordon, 1985), and that a functional analysis of drug-taking behavior often yields useful information about alternative activities that may be substituted for drug use.

Parallels can also be drawn between motivational counseling and the behavioral choice perspective (Correia, in press). Motivational counseling (Cox & Klinger, in press; Cox, Klinger, & Blount, 1991, 1999), a treatment specifically designed to increase a patient's motivation to change maladaptive patterns of behavior, explicitly recognizes the importance of alternative reinforcers. Cox and Klinger's (1988) model of alcohol use, for example, suggests that drinking occurs when the expected utility of alcohol use outweighs the expected utility of not drinking. For alcoholics, repeated decisions to drink alcohol are often linked to an inadequate number of drug-free incentives and goals. It follows that a major component of motivational counseling for alcohol abuse is helping patients increase the degree to which drug-free sources of reinforcement can foster emotional satisfaction and replace the reinforcement gained from drinking. Indeed, one of the tenets of motivational counseling for alcoholism is that "any treatment technique will be doomed to failure if it enables the alcoholic to stop drinking but does not provide them with alternative sources of satisfaction" (Cox & Klinger, 1988, p. 176).

Motivational counseling uses a number of techniques to increase engagement in alternative sources of reinforcement (Cox et al., 1991, 1999). One strategy involves shifting from negative goals that require a decrease in behavior ("eat less so I can lose weight") to goals that promote engagement in more attractive alternative behaviors ("become more physically fit and attractive through increased exercise and good nutrition"). Other strategies help patients identify new goals and incentives that might take the place of alcohol abuse and other unwanted behaviors. The previously described Pleasant Events Schedule (PES; MacPhillamy & Lewinsohn, 1982; see also Correia et al., 2002) is one tool that could be used to identify new goals or incentives. The PES is a self-report measure of the frequency and subjective pleasure of potentially reinforcing events and activities, which could be used, for example, to help clients identify activities that are highly pleasurable but engaged in infrequently, and these activities could then be targeted as possible substitutes for unwanted behaviors. Alternatively, people with very few or no highly pleasurable activities could benefit from treatment programs that expose them to novel sources of reinforcement, such as activity-oriented groups. The PES could also be used to empirically demonstrate the relationship between unhealthy behaviors such as substance use and other sources of reinforcement such as family relations or occupational success. To achieve this goal, clients could complete one reinforcement survey to document their actual activities and another to document the sources of reinforcement that would be available to them if they reduced or eliminated their substance use (see MacPhillamy & Lewinsohn, 1974, for a similar strategy used in depression research). This type of information, if presented early in treatment, may help motivate clients who are reluctant to give up the reinforcement derived from substance use by making them more aware of underutilized substance-free sources of reinforcement.

Summary and Conclusions

This chapter began with some questions and observations regarding the highly reinforcing nature of drug use and drug-related behaviors. Despite the fact that all humans have the potential to experience drug use as highly pleasurable and reinforcing, most individuals do not develop debilitating addictions. We have yet to formulate a theory that perfectly predicts who will and who will not become drug abusers. However, a number of theories have advanced our understanding of drug use. The goal of the current chapter was to review the behavioral choice perspective on drug use. The behavioral theories on choice provide a set of empirically validated concepts and research procedures that have proved very useful in understanding how drug use and drug-related reinforcement are related to a broader environmental context that includes the availability and utilization of drug-free alternatives. Numerous studies have reported that individuals who experience their drug-free behaviors as reinforcing are less likely to initiate drug use, use drugs less frequently, and are less likely to experience the negative consequences typically associated with drug use. As discussed in the second half of this chapter, the behavioral choice perspective provides a number of direct clinical applications. Studies have repeatedly demonstrated that drug use can be reduced, both in the laboratory and in the real world, by providing alternatives reinforcers that compete for behavior. While it is important to continue to understand the reinforcing properties of drugs, this chapter demonstrates that equal attention should be paid to better understanding the context in which drug use occurs.

References

Aigner T. G., & Balster, R. L. (1978). Choice behavior in rhesus monkeys: Cocaine versus food. *Science, 11*, 534–535.

Atkins, L. A., Oman, R. F., Vesely, S. K., Aspy, C. B., & McLeroy, K. (2002). Adolescent tobacco use: The protective effects of developmental assets. *American Journal of Health Promotion, 16*, 198–205.

Bickel, W. K., DeGrandpre, R. J., Higgins, S. T., & Hughes, J. R. (1990). Behavioral economics of drug self-administration. I. Functional equivalence of response requirement and drug dose. *Life Science, 47*, 1501–1510.

Bickel, W. K., Madden, G. J., & DeGrandpre, R. J. (1997). Modeling the effects of combined behavioral and pharmacological treatment on cigarette smoking: Behavioral-economic analyses. *Experimental and Clinical Psychopharmacology, 5*, 334–343.

Bigelow, G. E., Griffiths, R. R., & Liebson, I. A. (1976). Effects of response requirement upon human sedative self-administration and drug-seeking behavior. *Pharmacology, Biochemistry and Behavior, 5*, 681–685.

Brady, J. V., & Lukas, S. E. (Eds.). (1984). *Testing drugs for physical dependence and abuse liability* (NIDA Research Monograph No. 52). Rockville, MD: Department of Health and Human Services, National Institute of Drug Abuse.

Carroll, M. E. (1996a). Reducing drug abuse by enriching the environment with alternative non-drug reinforcers. In L. Green & J. Kagel (Eds.), *Advances in behavioral economics* (Vol. 3, pp. 37–68). Norwood, NJ: Ablex.

Carroll, M. E. (1996b). Relapse prevention as a psychosocial treatment: A review of controlled clinical trials. *Experimental and Clinical Psychopharmacology, 4*, 46–54.

Centers for Disease Control and Prevention. (2002a). Annual smoking-attributable mortality, years of potential life lost, and economic costs—United States, 1995–1999. *MMWR: Morbidity and Mortality Weekly Report, 51*, 300–303.

Centers for Disease Control and Prevention. (2002b). Death: Final data for 2000. *National Vital Statistics Report, 50*, 1–120.

Chaloupka, F. J., Grossman, M., & Saffer, H. (2002). The effects of price on alcohol consumption and alcohol-related problems. *Alcohol Research and Health, 26*, 22–34.

Chilcoat, H. D., & Johanson, C. E. (1998). Vulnerability to cocaine abuse. In S. T. Higgins & J. L. Katz (Eds.), *Cocaine abuse: Behavior, pharmacology, and clinical applications* (pp. 313–342). New York: Academic Press.

Comer, S. D., Collins, E. D., Wilson, S. T., Donovan, M. R., Foltin, R. W., & Fischman, M. W. (1998). Effects of an alternative reinforcer on intravenous heroin self-administration by humans. *European Journal of Pharmacology, 345*, 13–26.

Corby, E. A., Roll, J. M., Ledgerwood, D. M., & Schuster, C. R. (2000). Contingency management interventions for treating the substance abuse of adolescents: A feasibility study. *Experimental and Clinical Psychopharmacology, 8,* 371–376.

Correia, C. J. (in press). Behavioral economics: Basic concepts and clinical applications. In W. M. Cox & E. Klinger (Eds.), *International handbook of motivational counseling.* West Sussex, England: Wiley.

Correia, C. J., & Carey, K. B. (1999). Applying behavioral theories of choice to drug use in a sample of psychiatric outpatients. *Psychology of Addictive Behaviors, 13,* 207–212.

Correia, C. J., Carey, K. B., & Borsari, B. E. (2002). Measuring substance-free and substance-related reinforcement in the natural environment. *Psychology of Addictive Behavior, 16,* 28–34.

Correia, C. J., Carey, K. B., Simons, J., & Borsari, B. (2003). Relationships between binge drinking and substance-free reinforcement in a sample of college students: A preliminary investigation. *Addictive Behaviors, 28,* 361–368.

Correia, C. J., Simons, J., Carey, K. B., & Borsari, B. E. (1998). Predicting drug use: Application of behavioral theories of choice. *Addictive Behaviors, 23,* 705–709.

Cox, W. M., & Klinger, E. (1988) A motivational model of alcohol use. *Journal of Abnormal Psychology, 97,* 168–180.

Cox, W. M., & Klinger, E. (in press). *International handbook of motivational counseling.* West Sussex, England: Wiley.

Cox, W. M., Klinger, E., & Blount, J. P. (1991). Alcohol use and goal hierarchies: Systematic motivational counseling for alcoholics. In W. R. Miller & S. Rollnick (Eds.), *Motivational interviewing* (pp. 260–271). New York: Guilford.

Cox, W. M., Klinger, E., & Blount, J. P. (1999). *Systematic motivational counseling: A treatment manual.* Unpublished manuscript, University of Wales, Bangor.

DeGrandpre, R. J., & Bickel, W. K. (1996). Drug dependence as consumer demand. In L. Green & J. Kagel (Eds.), *Advances in behavioral economics* (Vol. 3, pp. 1–36). Norwood, NJ: Ablex.

Deneau, G., Yanagita, T., & Seevers, M. H. (1969). Self-administration of psychoactive substances by the monkey. *Psychopharmacologia, 16,* 30–48.

Elder, J. P., Campbell, N. R., Litrownik, A. J., Ayala, G. X., Slymen, D. J., Parra-Medina, D., & Lovato, C. Y. (2000). Predictors of cigarette and alcohol susceptibility and use among Hispanic migrant adolescents. *Preventative Medicine, 31,* 115–123.

Epstein, L. H., Bulik, C. M., Perkins, K. A., Caggiula, A. R., & Rodefer, J. (1991). Behavioral economic analysis of smoking: Money and food as alternatives. *Pharmacology Biochemistry, and Behavior, 38,* 715–721.

Epstein, L. H., Smith, J. A., Vara, L. S., & Rodefer, J. S. (1991). Behavioral economic analysis of activity choice in obese children. *Health Psychology, 10,* 311–316.

Fisher, E. B., Jr. (1996). A behavioral-economic perspective on the influence of social support on cigarette smoking. In L. Green and J. H. Kagel (Eds.), *Advances in behavioral economics* (Vol. 3, pp. 207–236). Norwood, NJ: Ablex.

Griffiths, R. R., Bigelow, G. E., & Henningfield, J. E. (1980). Similarities in animal and human drug-taking behavior. In N. K. Mello (Ed.), *Advances in substance abuse: Behavioral and biological research* (Vol. 1, pp. 1–90). Greenwich, CT: JAI Press.

Hart, C. L., Haney, M., Foltin, R. W., & Fischman, M. W. (2000). Alternative reinforcers differentially modify cocaine self-administration by humans. *Behavioral Pharmacology, 11,* 87–91.

Herrnstein, R. J. (1970). On the law of effect. *Journal of the Experimental Analysis of Behavior, 13,* 243–266.

Higgins, S. T., Bickel, W. K., & Hughes, J. R. (1994). Influence of an alternative reinforcer on human cocaine self-administration. *Life Sciences, 55,* 179–187.

Higgins, S. T., Budney, A. J., Bickel, W. K., Hughes, J. R., Foerg, B. A., & Badger, G. (1993). Achieving cocaine abstinence with a behavioral approach. *American Journal of Psychiatry, 150,* 763–769.

Higgins, S. T., Delaney, D. D., Budney, A. J., Bickel, W. K., Hughes, J. R., Foerg, F., et al. (1991). A behavioral approach to achieving initial cocaine abstinence. *American Journal of Psychiatry, 148,* 1218–1224.

Higgins, S. T., Roll, J. M., & Bickel, W. K. (1996). Alcohol pretreatment increases preference for cocaine over monetary reinforcement. *Psychopharmacology, 123,* 1–8.

Higgins, S. T., & Silverman, K. (Eds.). (1999). *Motivating behavior change among illicit-drug abusers: Research on contingency management interventions.* Washington, DC: American Psychological Association.

Hunt, G. M., & Azrin, N. H. (1973). A community reinforcement approach to alcoholism. *Behavior Research and Therapy, 11,* 91–104.

Iguchi, M. Y., Belding, M. A., Morral, A. R., Lamb, R. J., & Husband, S. D. (1997). Reinforcing operants other than abstinence in drug abuse treatment: An effective alternative for reducing drug use. *Journal of Consulting and Clinical Psychology, 65,* 421–428.

Johanson, C. E. (1978). Drugs as reinforcers. In D. E. Blackman & D. J. Sanger (Eds.), *Contemporary research in behavioral pharmacology* (pp. 325–390). New York: Plenum.

Johanson, C. E., Duffy, F. F., & Anthony, J. C. (1996). Associations between drug use and behavioral repertoire in urban youths. *Addiction, 91,* 523–534.

Kandel, D. B., & Raveis, V. H. (1989). Cessation of illicit drug use in young adulthood. *Archives of General Psychiatry, 46,* 109–116.

Kilmer, J. R., Larimer, M. E., Alexander, E. N., & Marlatt, G. A. (1998, November). Bait for the hook in motivation enhancement programs: Contributions from molar behavioral theory of choice. In J. R. Kilmer (Chair), *Interventions with college student drinkers: Reducing alcohol-related harm.* Symposium conducted at the meeting of the 32nd annual convention of the Association for the Advancement of Behavior Therapy, Washington, DC.

Landau, D. (1986). *The effects of changes in constraints on access to video game playing on alcohol consumption.* Unpublished doctoral dissertation. University of Florida, Gainesville.

Levy, B., & Earleywine, M. (2000, November). *Studying expectancies predict problem drinking among college students: Approaching problem drinking from an expectancies choice perspective.* Poster session presented at the annual meeting for the Association for Advancement of Behavior Therapy, New Orleans, LA.

Liebson, I. A., Cohen, M., Faillace, L. A., & Ward, R. F. (1971). The token economy as a research method in alcoholics. *Psychiatric Quarterly, 45,* 574–581.

MacPhillamy, D. J., & Lewinsohn, P. M. (1974). Depression as a function of desired and obtained pleasure. *Journal of Abnormal Psychology, 83,* 651–657.

MacPhillamy, D. J., & Lewinsohn, P. M. (1982). The pleasant events schedule: Studies on reliability, validity, and scale intercorrelation. *Journal of Consulting and Clinical Psychology, 50,* 363–380.

Marlatt, G. A., & Gordon, J. R. (Eds.). (1985). *Relapse prevention: Maintenance strategies in the treatment of addictive behaviors.* New York: Guilford.

Marlatt, G. A., & Kilmer, J. R. (1998). Consumer choice: Implications of behavioral economics for drug use and treatment. *Behavior Therapy, 29,* 567–576.

McDowell, J. J. (1988). Matching theory in natural human environments. *Behavior Analyst, 11,* 95–109.

McKim, W. A. (2003). *Drugs and behavior: An introduction to behavioral pharmacology.* Upper Saddle River, NJ: Prentice Hall.

Miller, W. R., & Rollnick, S. (2002). *Motivational interviewing* (2nd ed.). New York: Guilford.

Monitoring the Future (n.d.). *Data tables and figures.* Retrieved March 10, 2003, from http://www.monitoringthefuture.org/data/data.html

National Institute of Alcohol Abuse and Alcoholism. (2001). *Number of deaths and age-adjusted death rates per 100,000 population for categories of alcohol-related mortality, United States and States, 1979–96.* Retrieved March 10, 2002, from http://www.niaaa.nih.gov/databases/armort01.txt

Office of National Drug Control Policy. (2001). *What America's users spend on illegal drugs.* Washington, DC: Author.

Ornstein, S. I. (1980). Control of alcohol consumption through price increase. *Journal of Studies on Alcohol, 41,* 807–818.

Petraitis, J., Flay, B. R., & Miller, T. Q. (1995). Reviewing theories of adolescent substance use: Organizing pieces in the puzzle. *Psychological Bulletin, 117,* 67–86.

Petry, N. M., Martin, B., Cooney, J. L., & Kranzler, H. R. (2000). Give them prizes, and they will come: Contingency management for the treatment of alcohol dependence. *Journal of Consulting and Clinical Psychology, 68,* 250–257.

Premack, D. (1965). Reinforcement theory. In D. Levine (Ed.), *Nebraska symposium on motivation* (pp. 123–180). Lincoln: University of Nebraska Press.

Rachlin, H. (2000). The lonely addict. In W. K. Bickel & R. E. Vuchinich (Eds.), *Reframing health behavior change with behavioral economics* (pp. 145–166). Mahwah, NJ: Erlbaum.

Roll, J. M., Reilly, M. P., & Johanson, C. E. (2000). The influence of exchange delays on cigarette versus money choice: A laboratory analog of voucher-based reinforcement therapy. *Experimental and Clinical Psychopharmacology, 8,* 366–370.

Shahan, T. A., Bickel, W. K., Badger, G. J., & Giordano, L. A. (2001). Sensitivity of nicotine-containing and de-nicotinized cigarette consumption to alternative non-drug reinforcement: A behavioral economic analysis. *Behavioral Pharmacology, 12,* 277–284.

Sigmon, S. C., Steingard, S., Badger, G. J., Anthony, S. L., & Higgins, S. T. (2000). Contingent reinforcement of marijuana abstinence among individuals with serious mental illness: A feasibility study. *Experimental and Clinical Psychopharmacology, 8,* 509–517.

Silverman, K., Svikis, D., Robles, E., Stitzer, M. L., & Bigelow, G. E. (2001). A reinforcement-based therapeutic workplace for the treatment of drug abuse: Six-month abstinence outcomes. *Experimental and Clinical Psychopharmacology, 9,* 14–23.

Silverman, K., Svikis, D., Wong, C. J., Hampton, J., Stitzer, M. L., & Bigelow, G. E. (2002). A reinforcement-based therapeutic workplace for the treatment of drug abuse: Three-year abstinence outcomes. *Experimental and Clinical Psychopharmacology, 10,* 228–240.

Silverman, K., Wong, C. J., Higgins, S. T., Brooner, R. K., Montoya, I. D., Contoreggi, C., et al. (1996). Increasing opiate abstinence through voucher-based reinforcement therapy. *Drug and Alcohol Dependence, 41,* 157–165.

Simons, J., & Carey, K. B. (2000). Attitudes toward marijuana use and drug-free experience: Relationships with behavior. *Addictive Behaviors, 25,* 323–331.

Skinner, B. F. (1938). *The behavior of organisms: An experimental analysis.* Englewood Cliffs, NJ: Prentice-Hall.

Stacy, A. W., Widaman, K. F., & Marlatt, G. A. (1990). Expectancy models of alcohol use. *Journal of Personality and Social Psychology, 58,* 918–928.

Stitzer, M. L., Bigelow, G. E., & Liebson, I. (1979). Reducing benzodiazepine self-administration with contingent reinforcement. *Addictive Behaviors, 4,* 245–252.

Van Etten, M. L., Higgins, S. T., & Bickel, W. K. (1995). Effects of response cost and unit dose on alcohol self-administration in moderate drinkers. *Behavioural Pharmacology, 6,* 754–758.

Van Etten, M. L., Higgins, S. T., Budney, A. J., & Badger, G. J. (1998). Comparison of the frequency and enjoyability of pleasant events in cocaine abusers vs. non-abusers using a standardized behavioral inventory. *Addiction, 93,* 1669–1680.

Vuchinich, R. E., & Tucker, J. A. (1983). Behavioral theories of choice as a framework for studying drinking behavior. *Journal of Abnormal Psychology, 92,* 408–416.

Vuchinich, R. E., & Tucker, J. A. (1988). Contributions from behavioral theories of choice to an analysis of alcohol abuse. *Journal of Abnormal Psychology, 97,* 181–195.

Vuchinich, R. E., & Tucker, J. A. (1996). Alcohol relapse, life events, and behavioral theories of choice: A prospective analysis. *Experimental and Clinical Psychopharmacology, 4,* 19–28.

Wise, R. A.(1998). Drug-activation of brain reward pathways. *Drug and Alcohol Dependence, 51,* 12–22.

Wong, C. J., Jones, H. E., & Stitzer, M. L. (in press). Community reinforcement and contingency management interventions for substance abuse. In W. M. Cox & E. Klinger (Eds.), *International handbook of motivational counseling.* West Sussex, England: Wiley.

2

Psychedelic, Psychoactive, and Addictive Drugs and States of Consciousness

RALPH METZNER

In this chapter, I propose to examine the states of consciousness induced by hallucinogens or psychedelic drugs in the framework of a general model of altered states of consciousness (ASCs). Although modern science, construed in a strict sense within a materialist worldview, cannot deal adequately with subjective states of consciousness, I argue that a return to William James's philosophy of radical empiricism can provide an appropriate epistemological underpinning for the empirical study of consciousness. According to the general model of ASCs, the content of a state of consciousness is a function of the internal set and external setting; regardless of the catalyst or trigger, which might be a drug, hypnotic induction, shock, rhythmic sounds, music, and so forth. Altered states of consciousness, whether induced by drugs or other means, differ energetically on the dimensions of (a) arousal versus sedation, (b) pleasure versus pain, and (c) expansion versus contraction. I argue that the classical hallucinogenic or psychedelic drugs are consciousness expanding and therefore opposite in effect to drugs, such as the opiates, alcohol, cocaine, and amphetamines, that can lead to addicted, fixated, contracted states of consciousness. I call psychoactive (or "mood regulating") those drugs, such as the stimulants and depressants in moderate dosages, that affect primarily the dimensions of arousal and pleasure-pain, without significant expansion of consciousness. Finally, the implications for applications in psychotherapy are also discussed.

Radical Empiricism as the Epistemology
for the Study of Consciousness

It is only recently, in rereading William James's writings on his philosophy of radical empiricism, that I came to realize that this philosophy actually provides the epistemology of choice for the study of states of consciousness, ordinary or altered. Within the materialistic paradigm still ruling in scientific circles, any insights or learning gained from dreams, drug experiences, trances, intuitions, mystical ecstasies, or the like are seen as "merely subjective" and limited to those states, that is, not having general applicability or "objective reality." The psychologist Charles Tart (1972), in an essay on "state-specific sciences," attempted to break the conceptual stranglehold of this paradigm by suggesting that observations made in a given state of consciousness could only be verified or replicated in that same state. This solution seems theoretically valid but attended with practical difficulties.

William James started with the basic assumption of the empirical ("experience-based") approach: All knowledge is derived from experience. Radical empiricism applies this principle inclusively, not exclusively. James writes:

> I give the name of "radical empiricism" to my *Weltanschauung*. . . . To be radical an empiricism must neither admit into its construction any element that is not directly experienced, nor exclude from them any element that is directly experienced. For such a philosophy, the relations that connect experiences must themselves be experienced relations, and any kind of relation experienced must be accounted as "real" as anything else in the system. (James, 1912/1996, p. 42)

This view can provide a philosophical foundation for a scientific psychology of consciousness. All knowledge must be based on observation, that is, experience; so far this view coincides with the empiricism of the natural and social sciences. It is the second statement that is truly "radical" and that explains why James included religious and paranormal experiences in his investigations. The experiences in modified states of consciousness are currently excluded from materialistic, reductionistic science, as are all kinds of anomalous experiences, such as shamanic journeys, near-death experiences, and mystical or paranormal experiences. They need not and should not be excluded in a radical empiricism.

Western psychology finally may be coming around to the views expressed by William James, after his personal research with the psychedelic anesthetic nitrous oxide, almost 100 years ago, in his book *The Varieties of Religious Experience*:

> Our normal waking consciousness, rational consciousness as we call it, is but one special type of consciousness, whilst all about it, parted

from it by the filmiest of screens, there lie potential forms of consciousness entirely different. . . No account of the universe in its totality can be final which leaves these other forms of consciousness quite disregarded. (James, 1901/1958, p. 228)

From the perspective of radical empiricism, it is not where or how observations are made that makes a field of study "scientific"; it is what is done with the observations afterward. Repeated systematic observations from the same observer, and replicating observations from others, is what distinguishes the scientific method from casual or haphazard observations, or those made with intentions other than gathering knowledge. Whereas the ideology of fundamentalist scientism does not permit the objective investigation of subjective experience, the epistemology of radical empiricism posits that it is possible to be objective about subjective experience, using the accepted canons of the scientific method. The methodology of systematic introspection as well as phenomenology serve as beginnings of such a more inclusive approach.

Altered States of Consciousness (ASCs) as a Paradigm for the Study of Consciousness

The discovery of psychedelics and the kind of time-limited, profoundly altered states of consciousness they induced led to a significant reexamination and evaluation of all states of consciousness, both those ordinarily experienced by all, such as waking, sleeping, and dreaming, and those deliberately or spontaneously induced. There are those altered states generally considered positive, healthy, expansive, associated with increased knowledge and moral value, such as religious or mystical experience, ecstasy (literally "ex-stasis"), transcendence, hypnotherapeutic trance, creative inspiration, tantric erotic trance, shamanic journey, cosmic consciousness, *samadhi*, nirvana, or satori; and those considered negative, unhealthy, contractive, associated with delusion, psychopathology, destructiveness, and even crime, such as depression, psychosis, madness, hysteria, mania, dissociative disorders, substance addictions (alcohol, narcotics, stimulants), and behavioral addictions and fixations (sexuality, violence, gambling, spending).

A brief personal note might be permitted: As a psychologist, I have been involved in the field of consciousness studies, including altered states induced by drugs, plants, and other means, for more than 40 years. In the 1960s I worked at Harvard University with Timothy Leary and Richard Alpert (later known as Ram Dass), doing research on the possible applications of psychedelic drugs, also called "consciousness-expanding," such as psilocybin, mescaline, and LSD (Leary, Litwin, & Metzner, 1963; Leary, Metzner, & Alpert, 1964). Later, during the 1970s, the focus of my work shifted to the exploration of nondrug methods for the transformation of consciousness, such as are found in Eastern and Western traditions of yoga, meditation, and alchemy (Metzner, 1971). I also studied intensively the newer psychotherapeutic methods, many deriving from the work of pioneers such as Wilhelm Reich, that involve deep altered states induced by breath- and bodywork. During the 1980s I came into contact with the work of Michael Harner (1973), Joan Halifax (1982), Peter Furst (1976), Terence McKenna and Dennis McKenna (1975), and others who have studied shamanic teachings and practices around the globe. These shamanic traditions involve what are called "non-ordinary states of consciousness" induced by a variety of methods, including hallucinogenic plants but also drumming, fasting, wilderness vision questing, sweat lodge, and others. This work allowed me to see certain consistent patterns in altered states of consciousness, regardless of the technique or catalyst used to induce them.

The key to understanding the content of a psychedelic experience as formulated by Timothy Leary, Frank Barron, and colleagues in the early days of the Harvard Psilocybin Research Project was the "set-and-setting" hypothesis: that the content of a psychedelic experience is not so much a function of pharmacology, that is, a "drug effect," but rather a function of the *set*, which is all the internal factors of expectation, intention, mood, temperament, and attitude; and *setting*, which is the external environment, both physical and social, and including the attitudes and intentions of whoever provides or initiates the experience. The drug is regarded as a trigger, or catalyst, propelling the individual into a different field or state of consciousness, in which the vividness and contextual qualities of sense perceptions are greatly magnified.

This hypothesis helps one to understand how it is possible that the very same drug was studied and interpreted as a model psychosis (*psychotomimetic*), an adjunct to psychoanalysis (*psycholytic*), a treatment for addiction or a stimulus to creativity (*psychedelic*), a facilitator of shamanic spiritual insight (*entheogenic*), or even, as by the U.S. Army and the Central Intelligence Agency, as a truth serum type of tool for obtaining secrets from enemy spies. Of the two factors of set and setting, set or intention is clearly primary, since it ordinarily determines what kind of setting one will choose for the experience. In fact, it has been shown experimentally in small groups that asking people to pay close attention to their inner experience, with nothing else to occupy their attention, itself is sometimes sufficient to induce a mild altered state (Hunt & Chefurka, 1976).

In my classes on altered states of consciousness, I have extended the set and setting hypothesis to all alterations of consciousness, no matter by what trigger they are induced (drugs, foods, fasting, hypnotic inductions, sounds, drumming, breathing methods, movement as in trance dance, wilderness isolation, and many others), and even those states that recur cyclically and regularly, such as sleeping and waking (Metzner, 1989). In those cyclic alterations of consciousness, one may say that internal biochemical events normally trigger the transition to sleeping or waking consciousness, but external factors may provide an additional catalyst. For example, lying in bed, in darkness, may trigger changes in melatonin levels in the pineal gland, which in turn trigger falling asleep; brighter light, or the sounds of an alarm, can be the trigger for awakening, again mediated by cyclical biochemical changes. There may be, in addition, external factors such as stimulant or sedative drugs, which trigger those alterations. Figure 2.1 is a representation of this general model of altered states. I call it *heuristic*, rather than explanatory, since it can serve as a framework for discovery and understanding rather than explaining changes in consciousness by reference to events at another level, such as brain function.

In classes I have often asked students to choose one positive and one negative altered state from their recent experience and to then analyze it and determine what was the trigger, what the set, and what the setting. This is usually quite revealing, in the sense of heightening one's awareness of the impact of one's own inner set and intention on the quality of experience.

Clearly, for example, the content of our dreams can be analyzed as a function of set—internal factors in our consciousness during the day— as well as the environment in which we find ourselves. Some writers on what is called "dream incubation" make deliberate use of this principle, consciously formulating certain questions related to their inner process or outer situation, as they enter the world of sleep dreaming.

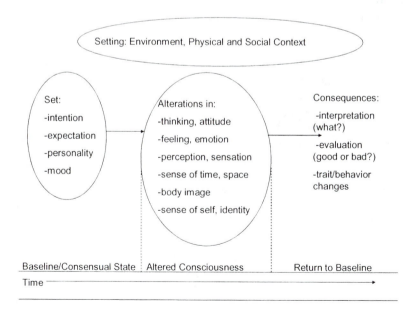

Figure 2.1. General Heuristic Model of Altered States of Consciousness

In hypnotherapy, as in any form of psychotherapy, we always start with the intention or question that the client brings, using that to direct the movement into and through the trance state. In shamanic practice, whether with rhythmic drumming as the catalyst or using entheogenic plant concoctions like ayahuasca or conscious nighttime dreaming as the preferred method of the practitioner, one always comes initially with a question or intention. Even one's experience in the ordinary waking state, such as that of the reader perusing this chapter, is a function of the internal factors of intention or interest and of the setting where the reading is taking place.

Some researchers, notably Stanislav Grof (1985), in his cartography of altered states, whether induced by psychedelics or by holotropic breathing, have categorized the different states by content, such as perinatal memories, identifications with animals or plants, experiences beyond the ordinary framework of time and space, and so on. Others have taken a somewhat different approach, focusing on the energetics of altered states, apart from content. An early paper by Roland Fischer (1971), published in *Science*, arranged various states of consciousness on a continuum of arousal, or what he called *ergotrophic* versus *trophotropic* activation (roughly equivalent to sympathetic and parasympathetic nervous system activation).

Because such a scheme involves placing schizophrenia and creative inspiration in the same general category, both being "high-energy" states, I thought a second dimension of pain versus pleasure, or what I call the *hedonic continuum,* should be added. The term *high* can mean high arousal or stimulation, such as an amphetamine jag, or it can mean highly pleasurable, such as sexual ecstasy. Figure 2.2 shows an orthogonal mapping of these two dimensions of states of consciousness, with possible placements for psychoactive stimulant and sedative drug effects. In general, I would say the psychoactives (stimulants and depressants) differ from the classical psychedelics in that (a) the pharmacological trigger effect is dominant, and the set-setting content variables less so; and (b) they are not consciousness-expanding (see later in the chapter for further discussion). It is difficult to place psychedelic drug experiences on the coordinate axes of this model because their energetics can be "all over the map," including high and low arousal, and heavenly as well as hellish components.

I have also developed a graphic rating scale (Metzner, 1986), in which the continua are shown with each of the two dimensions converted to a 7-point scale, for self-rating. This Altered State Graphic Profile (ASGP) can be and has been used to compare different states of consciousness within an individual's experience or different people's experience of a particular kind of state, drug or nondrug. The ASGP has been designed to assess and display two major dimensions of altered states of consciousness, the level of arousal or wakefulness and the pleasure-pain (hedonic) continua.

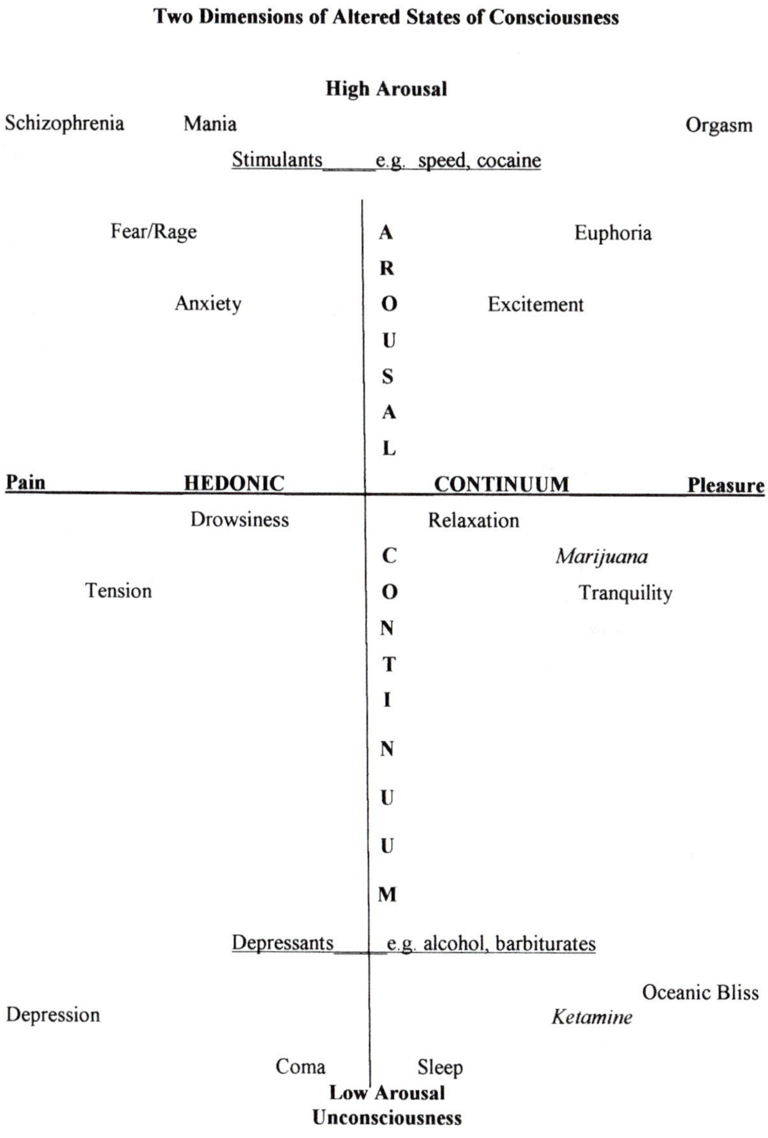

Two Dimensions of Altered States of Consciousness

High Arousal

Schizophrenia   Mania   Orgasm

                Stimulants_____e.g. speed, cocaine

Fear/Rage   **A**   Euphoria

                   R

    Anxiety   **O**   Excitement

                   U

                   S

                   A

                   L

Pain_____**HEDONIC**_____**CONTINUUM**_____**Pleasure**

     Drowsiness   Relaxation

                 C   *Marijuana*

   Tension   **O**   Tranquility

                 N

                 T

                 I

                 N

                 U

                 U

                 M

    Depressants_____e.g. alcohol, barbiturates

                          Oceanic Bliss

Depression   *Ketamine*

     Coma | Sleep

Low Arousal
Unconsciousness

Figure 2.2. Two Dimensions of Altered States of Consciousness

It has been found that individuals can, with a little advance preparation, give numerical estimates of these two aspects of awareness, regardless of the content of the experience or how the altered state is induced. The purpose of this kind of measurement of subjective experience is twofold: First, it can facilitate the individual's own observation, reflection, and recollection of states of consciousness; experience has shown that doing the rating helps ground one during new and confusing experiences. The second purpose is to permit comparative research on the states of consciousness induced by different drugs or other kinds of "triggers" such as hypnosis, meditation, sound, music, sensory deprivation, breathing, sex, or movement. Research on how other variables, such as personality, might affect altered states would also be possible with the ASGP.

The ASGP has two separate scales: the upper one for the arousal continuum and the lower one for the hedonic (pleasure-pain) continuum (see figure 2.3). Every 15 minutes, assign a numerical value from +3 to –3 to your subjective sense of these two dimensions. The ratings can, of course, be done at less frequent intervals, but both scales should always be scored. The actual clock time can be entered beneath each scale. It is best to obtain at least an hour's worth of readings prior to the trigger event (e.g., drug ingestion); these will then serve as the baseline, to which the altered state values can be compared. The space between the two scales can be used to indicate the time and nature of triggers and other external stimuli that presumably affect the altered state. These might include 150 mg MDMA, one glass of wine, 3 lungsful of marijuana, hypnotic induction, zazen sitting, listening to symphonic music, chanting "om," watching a sunset, relating to one's partner, and so forth. The ratings can be entered personally by the experiencer, or else the guide, sitter, therapist, or friend can obtain the ratings.

The ratings called for are numerical estimates of one's own experience. The descriptive adjectives are rough indications only, whose meaning will vary from person to person. It is assumed that both these dimensions vary from the presumed "normal," "usual," or "baseline" midpoint of 0. The arousal continuum is a measure of wakefulness and attentiveness; it should be distinguished from the active-passive and tension-relaxation dimension. The –1 point would correspond to EEG alpha waves and "light" hypnotic trance; the –2 point corresponds to theta waves, twilight imagery with some drowsy shifting, and moderate trance; and –3 corresponds to deep trance or sleep or complete dissociation from the environment. On the hedonic continuum, the negative part of the scale would include negative emotional states such as anxiety, depression, anger, sickness, and the like. What is being assessed is only the intensity and the pleasure or discomfort, not the specific emotion involved. It is possible to indicate more specific information about the content of the experience in the space provided for listing trigger events.

The arousal or wakefulness continuum has a zero or neutral point, "awake & calm," and then goes to "alert/attentive" (+1), "stimulated" (+2), and "aroused/excited" (+3); in the opposite direction, it is "alpha/ meditative" (–1), "drifting/twilight" (–2), and "deep trance/sleep" (–1). The hedonic or pleasure-pain continuum has a zero or neutral point and goes to "pleasant" (+1), "elated/euphoric" (+2) and "ecstatic/ heaven" (+3); in the opposite direction, it is "unpleasant" (–1), "painful/disturbing" (−2), and "agony/hell" (−3). On the hedonic continuum, the negative part of the scale includes such generally unpleasant emotional states as anxiety, depression, anger, sickness, and the like. What is being assessed is only the affective intensity and discomfort involved, neither the specific emotion involved nor the underlying thought content.

The two continua are displayed with a time line: Depending on the particulars of the altered state, this can be calibrated for longer or shorter periods and intervals. The individual can be asked to place a check mark at the appropriate point on the two scales, say, every 15 or 30 minutes, as was done in an unpublished study of the effects of MDMA; the resulting graphs of subjective intensity can then also be compared to graphs of levels of biochemical markers, such as serotonin levels. It is best to obtain readings of the two continua for at least an hour prior

AROUSAL CONTINUUM

Aroused/excited +3																
Stimulated +2																
Alert/attentive +1																
Awake and calm 0																
Alpha/meditative −1																
Drifting/twilight −2																
Deep trance/sleep −3																
CLOCK TIME																

INDICATE TRIGGER
AND OTHER EVENTS I

HEDONIC CONTINUUM

Ecstatic/"heaven" +3																
Elated/euphoric +2																
Pleasant +1																
Neutral 0																
Unpleasant −1																
Painful/disturbing −2																
Agony/ "hell" −3																
CLOCK TIME																

Figure 2.3. Altered States Graphic Profile

to the trigger event (e.g., drug ingestion) to establish a baseline in the "ordinary" state. Specific triggering events that presumably affect the altered state can also be indicated at the time they occurred. These might include 100 mg MDMA, one glass of wine, 3 inhalations of cannabis, hypnotic induction, begin zazen meditation, begin symphonic music, chanting, watching sunset, and so forth. Whereas in many kinds of studies, individuals can readily assess their subjective state while "in" it, we have also found that for many kinds of experiences, the ASGP can be filled out retrospectively, from memory.

A third purely formal or energetic dimension of altered states, irrespective of content, is *expansion* versus *contraction*. Psychedelic drugs were originally called "consciousness-expanding": In such states, one does not see hallucinated, illusory objects; rather, one sees the ordinary objects but also sees, knows, and feels associated patterns and aspects that one was not aware of before. In such states, in addition to perception, there is *apperception*—the reflective awareness of the experiencing subject and understanding of associated elements of context. Another way of saying this is that an objective observer or witness consciousness is added to the subjective experiencing. This expanded, aware apperceptive element is generally absent in the psychoactive stimulants and depressants, which simply move consciousness either "up" or "down" on the arousal dimension and away from pain or discomfort. The observer witness consciousness is also notoriously absent in the addictive state induced by narcotics, which is typically described as "uncaring," "cloudy," or "sleep-like."

A note on the term *hallucinogenic*: This is the term most often used in the psychiatric research literature for these substances, called *psychedelic* (mind-manifesting) in the subculture of those interested in conscious self-exploration. The main objection to the term is that these drugs and plants do not in fact induce hallucinations, in the sense of "illusory perceptions." Nevertheless, the term *hallucinogen* deserves to be rehabilitated. The original meaning of the Latin *alucinare*, from which it is derived, is to "wander in one's mind," and traveling or journeying in inner space is actually quite an appropriate descriptive metaphor for such experiences, which are referred to colloquially as "trips." Another term, *entheogen*, proposed by R. Gordon Wasson and Jonathan Ott, has the same root as *enthusiasm* and means "releasing or expressing the divine within" (Ott, 1995, p 126). This was suggested as an appropriate term for plant-derived substances used in shamanic spiritual healing rituals in indigenous cultures, such as ayahuasca, for which the term *psychedelic* might seem too much tied to modern Western culture and history (Metzner, 1999).

To return for a moment to nondrug alterations of consciousness, waking up, both the ordinary kind and the metaphoric kind referred to in spiritual texts, is an experience of expanded consciousness: I become aware of the fact that it is I who is lying in this bed, in this room, having just had this particular dream, and the rest of the world outside, with all the relations of family and work, community and cosmos. To *transcend* means to "go beyond"; therefore, transcendent experiences, variously referred to in the spiritual traditions as enlightenment, ecstasy, liberation, and revelation, all involve an expansion of consciousness, in which the previous field of consciousness is then seen as more limited (e.g., "that was only a dream"), but included in a greater context, providing insight.

In the essay "Addiction and Transcendence as Altered States of Consciousness" (Metzner, 1994), I proposed that whereas psychedelic and other forms of transcendent experiences can be regarded as prototypical expansions of consciousness, the prototypical contracted states of consciousness are found in the fixations of addictions, obsessions, compulsions, and attachments.

Addictions and Compulsions as Contracted States of Consciousness

A useful book that summarizes and integrates sociopsychological research on addiction is Stanton Peele's *The Meaning of Addiction* (1985), in which the author identifies the main features of what he calls "addictive experience" or "involvement." In other words, this is an analysis in terms of the state of consciousness of the addicted person. Addictive experiences or involvements are defined as "potent modifications of mood and sensation." When a drug or behavior has the ability to produce an immediate, effective, and powerful modification of mood and sensation, then there is the potential for developing an addictive or compulsive involvement. This definition identifies an addictive experience as a particular variety of altered consciousness. An altered state of consciousness may be defined as a time-limited state in which the patterns of thought, of feeling or mood, or of perception and sensation are altered from the ordinary or baseline condition.

The relative role of genetic, biochemical, sociocultural, personality, and situational factors in the development of addictive involvements is still a matter of considerable controversy. Some believe that genetic, biochemical conditions create a predisposition to become addicted, and that personality and situational factors act as triggers or catalysts. Others argue that the addiction is completely learned and that biochemical and genetic factors only predispose the particular choice of the addictive object or behavior. Much more research is obviously needed to sort out the relative contributions of these different contextual factors. In this chapter I am focusing on the experience, the phenomenology of addiction.

If we examine addictive experience as an altered state of consciousness of a certain kind, we can compare it with other kinds of altered states of consciousness (see figure 2.4). I propose that addictive experiences, compulsions, and attachments involve a fixation of attention and a narrowing of perceptual focus—in other words, a contracted state of consciousness. This is in contrast to transcendent, ecstatic, or mystical states, which involve mobility of attention and a widening of perceptual focus—in other words, the classic expanded state of consciousness (see figure 2.5). *Transcendent* means "above and beyond," and *ecstasy* means "ex-stasis"—out of the static condition, out of the usual state of consciousness. Addiction and attachment, on the other hand, involve the opposite direction: fixation, repetition, narrowing, and selectivity of attention and awareness.

Sentience, awareness, or attention can be thought of as a kind of beam that can be focused on a very narrow point or band, or that can take in much wider arcs and areas of the total circle of potential awareness. This beam changes its focus and range constantly, and narrowing and widening it are obviously normal and natural capacities.

As the psychologist Frank Barron (1963) pointed out in his studies of creative individuals, creativity involves a preference for the complexity found in expanded states of consciousness. "Waking up" is an experience of moving into an expanded state of consciousness with more complex information; "falling asleep," in contrast, involves a reduction and narrowing of awareness—facilitated by a closing of the eyes, a quieting of body movements, and so forth. Sometimes expansions of consciousness themselves may function as catalysts for a reactive contraction, as the brain-mind struggles to interpret the increased flow of information and stimuli. This is perhaps part of what happens in a psychotic "break," in which the brain is no longer able to integrate the complexity of sensory input. A defensive strategy would then be to reduce and simplify the focus of attention. It is easy to see the short-term adaptive advantages of simplification and contraction of attention in states of fear or rage: the focussing of attention on the stimuli of threat or danger helps to mobilize energy for the appropriate "flight-or-fight" response. We are "hardwired" to have survival needs and strategies take precedence over creative impulses or mystical yearnings.

If we think of consciousness as a spherical field of perceptual awareness that surrounds us and moves with us wherever we go, we can create a graphic model by taking a horizontal plane section of this sphere; we then have a circle of 360° as the potential field of awareness and attention. In any given state of consciousness, we could say attention is selectively focused on a 30° arc or segment of the circle. In an expanded state of consciousness, we could say the arc of attention expands to 90° or more; in a contracted state, attention is selectively focused on only 15° or less.

In an addictive trance it is just the object of desire, the craved sensation, the liquor bottle, or the crack pipe, that captures the attention, to the exclusion of other aspects of reality, other segments of the total

Baseline sense of consciousness   **Contracted state—fixation**

Figure 2.4. Contraction of Consciousness

circle of potential awareness. The comedian Richard Pryor did a routine about his cocaine addiction that was filmed and can be seen on video *(Richard Pryor—Live on Sunset Strip)*. It is an awesome performance in which he describes a lifestyle that became more and more restricted, until he was isolated from all other relationships except the one with his crack pipe, which had become repetitive and ritualistic. He did not work or socialize or communicate with anyone—only the pipe, with which he talked and which told him: "This is all you need." One smoke after another, and nothing else mattered; nothing else could capture his interest or attention. Awareness and attention were completely contracted, fixated, and simplified.

Another, very different, area of human experience in which selective narrowing of attention also occurs is in the mother-infant bonding situation. The linguistic affinity of the words *bonding, attachment,* and *addiction* already points to the psychological similarity. This was brought home to me in a vivid way when I was watching my infant daughter and her attachment behavior toward the maternal breast. She would be moving around, gurgling and wiggling her limbs, and then suddenly she would start focusing on the breast. She would start to cry, and all her movements were toward the mother, with her attention completely zeroed in on the breast. I then lost the ability to distract her or capture her attention. I could no longer say, "Here, look at this," and have her follow me with eye and hand movements. I realized that this was exactly the same kind of narrowing of awareness and attention as would occur in a drinker, focusing only on the bottle, or the crack addict on the pipe, or anyone focusing on the object of craving.

The attachment or addiction process, then, involves an immediate or very rapid alteration of mood and sensation, in the direction of need satisfaction, anxiety reduction, and cognitive simplification. When we focus on the object or experience we are craving or wanting, awareness ceases to be engaged with other aspects of our experienced reality, particularly pain, fear, or anxiety. There is a genuine need to reduce pain and fear, and this need is immediately and effectively satisfied. There is a narrowed focus, a fixation of attention. Then there is repetition of these steps, and gradually, over time, a kind of ritual may develop.

The ritual aspect of addictions and compulsions is very significant. I once worked with a man with a self-described sexual addiction that involved compulsive viewing of pornography and visits with prostitutes in which he always placed himself in submissive and degrading positions. It was extremely repetitive and ritualistic behavior—and no other kind of sexual activity or experience held any attraction for him. Even the orgasmic sexual fulfillment seemed to be secondary to the peculiar satisfaction gained from ritualistic repetition of certain symbolic actions.

The ingestion of drugs that produce dependency always seems to become associated with ritualistic behavior, which is repeated compulsively in the same way over and over. This is true of the narcotic drugs such as the opiates, depressants such as the barbiturates, psychiatric tranquilizers and antidepressants, and stimulants such as amphetamine and cocaine. Ritualistic ingestion is quite obvious and well known in the case of the socially sanctioned and commercially promoted addictive substances, including alcohol, tobacco, and coffee: In these situations the ingestion ritual forms part of the advertising message promoting consumption. Ingestion rituals are also evident in the case of food addictions, especially those involving sugar, wheat products, and meat. Food ingestion rituals become painfully distorted in the binge and purge behaviors of those with "eating disorders," who may be, among other things, trying to forcefully control their addictions.

The immediate or very rapid modification of mood and sensation produced by such drugs and foods is one of the factors facilitating the development of dependency. Alcoholics often remark on the empowerment they feel when their chosen drink first hits the stomach: immediately the anxiety or frustration is lifted, one experiences relief from the pain or, in the case of stimulants, relief from the feelings of impotence and inadequacy. The sense of power comes from the immediacy of the change of state. Any unpleasant aftereffects, which may be well known to the addict, are too far removed in future time to override the immediate feedback of satisfaction.

The power to instantly alter one's state of consciousness, especially to move it from painful to pleasurable or even neutral, may generalize from the physiological drug effect to the ritualistic behavior surrounding it. For the smoker, just pulling out the cigarette and preparing it for lighting may already have some anxiety-reducing effects. Similar considerations apply in the case of the activity addictions, including compulsive sexuality, gambling, shopping, or working, where the ritualistic repetition of certain behaviors in itself seems to be able to reduce anxiety and change one's consciousness. By becoming absorbed in routine tasks, one can avoid dwelling on anxiety-provoking aspects of life. The fact that "working hard" is an essential ingredient of the American (especially Protestant) work ethic, and that obvious social rewards are associated with it, does not alter the basic dynamics. When "working hard" is associated with an extreme narrowing and fixation of attention, to the exclusion of other pursuits and interests, it becomes compulsive "workaholism." Family and other social relationships may be impaired, and even work productivity and resourcefulness can decline—as corporate managers have begun to recognize.

Transcendent experiences, expansions of consciousness, also powerfully modify mood and sensation, but in a way that is quite different: The entire range of experience, the continuum of sensation and perception, is extended and made more fluid. Terminal cancer patients who were given LSD and compared its pain-reducing effect to that of morphine said that with the psychedelic they still felt the pain but it was not as painful anymore, and there were many other more differentiated experiences that occupied their attention. Generally, the consciousness-expanding psychedelics have not led to addiction, and narcotics addicts tend not to like them. The effects are too unpredictable, too varied, too subtle, and too delayed to allow the kind of immediate pain relief or tension relief the addict is seeking.

Nevertheless, there is some evidence to suggest that in rare circumstances transcendent experiences themselves, whether induced by drugs, meditation, or physical practices such as running, can also become the objects of addiction. If someone is taking psychedelic drugs, such as LSD, or empathogens, such as MDMA, repetitively, with a similar kind of change of state involved, to the exclusion of other interests and the eventual neglect of family and other responsibilities, this again is the classic pattern of addiction and abuse. The pattern has even been observed with some meditators, who may avoid dealing with intrapsychic or interpersonal conflict by constantly and obsessively meditating. Teachers in the Asian spiritual traditions talk about the possibility of spiritual addiction, or "spiritual materialism," and warn of becoming attached or too fascinated by unusual, ecstatic, or visionary experiences—which are disparaged as "illusions."

The compulsive meditator or user of psychedelics may become addicted to that transcendent experience itself, so that he or she just wants to keep repeating the transcendent experience over and over, which of course is not possible. There is an inherent self-limiting factor in these kinds of experiences: You cannot keep transcending; you have to have something to transcend from. Or, the ego first has to build some boundaries, before they can dissolve in unitive states of consciousness.

Psychedelics and Transcendence as Expanded States of Consciousness

In terms of the 360° circle of potential awareness, in transcendence and ecstasy, awareness and attention expand from the normal or usual baseline, which might be an arc of 30° or 60°, to a wider arc of 90°, 120°, or 180°,—that is, a fuller, more complex range of perceptual awareness. Individuals who take LSD, the prototypical consciousness-expanding experience, often report that their range of visual perception had expanded to 360°—so that they felt they could see out of the backs of their heads. This could be considered a metaphor for an experience of expanded, all-around sentience. The individual may actually become more aware of what was happening all around—a form of sense perception not necessarily limited to psychedelic drug states.

Transcendent or ecstatic experiences, like the classic accounts of mystical or cosmic consciousness, involve a widening of the focus of attention, an expansion of awareness beyond the boundaries of the ordinary or baseline state. Barron's research on creativity also demonstrated that creative inspiration involves complex, expanded states of awareness. The "empathogenic" psychedelics, such as MDMA, apparently produce an expansion and deepening of the field of emotional awareness (while not altering perceptual awareness), which probably accounts for their value as an adjunct to psychotherapy (Metzner & Adamson, 2001). Expansions of consciousness generally involve detachment, a "rising above" the attachments of cravings and addictions. In alchemical language, they involve the operation of *solutio*, the dissolving of obsessive fixations and defensive rigidities. Meditation practices, including transcendental meditation (TM) also clearly aim to produce a kind of unitive state of consciousness, in which the conflicts and dualisms of ordinary consciousness are dissolved or transcended.

Two analogies or metaphors for the drug experience have been used repeatedly by writers in the field of psychedelic consciousness studies.

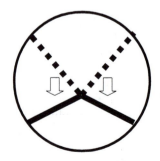

Baseline sense of consciousness   **Expanded state—transcendence**

Figure 2.5. Expansion of Consciousness

One is the *amplifier analogy*, according to which the drug functions as an amplifier of sense perception, both interior and exterior. The amplification may occur in part as a result of a lowering of sensory thresholds, a cleansing of the "doors of perception"—to use the phrase of William Blake that Aldous Huxley used to describe his mescaline experience. The other analogy most often used is the *microscope*: It has repeatedly been said that psychedelics could play the same role in psychology as the microscope does in biology. This, too, is a metaphor of expanded consciousness: The psychedelic microscope opens up to direct, repeatable, verifiable observation realms and processes of the human mind that have hitherto been largely hidden or inaccessible.

That mystical and spiritual experiences can and do often occur with psychedelics was recognized early on by most researchers in this field, thereby posing both a challenge and a promise to the psychological disciplines and professions. Albert Hofmann (1983), who discovered the unusual properties of LSD "by accident," testified that his ability to recognize the consciousness-expanding nature of the LSD experience was based on its similarity to his childhood mystical experiences in nature. Stanislav Grof (1985) found that after resolving biographical childhood issues, and then perinatal traumas, individuals would often find themselves in realms of consciousness completely transcendent of time, space, and other parameters of our ordinary worldview. He gave the name *transpersonal* to these realms of consciousness and *holotropic* (seeking the whole) to the predominant quality of consciousness in these realms, as well as to other means of accessing these realms, such as certain breathing methods (holotropic breathwork).

Timothy Leary, stimulated no doubt by his association with Aldous Huxley, Huston Smith, and Alan Watts, devoted considerable time and energy to exploring and describing the spiritual and religious dimensions of psychedelic experience. This work resulted in adaptations of the Tibetan Buddhist Bardo Thödol and the Chinese Taoist Tao Te Ching as guidebooks for psychedelic experience (Leary et al. 1964; Leary, 1997).

Synchronistically with the revelations and insights emerging from psychedelic research in psychology and religion, a generation of students and researchers in anthropology and ethnobotany was inspired to explore the roots of humankind's involvement with psychoactive plants in shamanism. In shamanic rituals of healing or divination (obtaining knowledge from spiritual realms) there is also an expanded state of consciousness, called a *shamanic journey*. This journey state may be induced by hallucinogenic plant substances or through techniques of rhythmic drumming (Harner, 1980). Shamanic rituals involving hallucinogens are the intentional arrangement of the set and the setting for purposes of healing and divination. Traditional Western psychotherapy, with or without psychedelics, can also appropriately be seen as a ritual, that is, an experience formally structured according to the intention of healing or problem solving.

The Use of Psychedelics in Psychotherapy
and the Treatment of Addictions

The first research papers that came out of the Sandoz labs where Albert Hofmann had synthesized LSD and accidentally discovered its astounding properties described it as bringing about "psychic loosening or opening" (*seelische Auflockerung*). This was the *psycholytic* concept that became the dominant model for LSD-assisted psychotherapy in Europe. In psycholytic therapy, neurotic patients suffering from anxiety, depression, or obsessive-compulsive or psychosomatic disorders were given LSD in a series of sessions at gradually increasing doses, while undergoing more or less standard analytic interactions using a Freudian perspective (Passie, 1985; Grof, 1980). The rationale was that through the *psycholysis* (the alchemical *solutio* metaphor), the loosening of defenses, the patient would become more vividly aware of his or her previously unconscious emotional dynamics and reaction patterns (presumably acquired in early family interactions), and such insight would bring about a resolution of inner conflicts. The Czech psychiatrist Stanislav Grof, working within this model, made the startling discovery that in such a series (involving increasing doses) there could be an even deeper psychic opening—to birth and prenatal memories. After resolving the conflicts stemming from the Freudian dynamics of early childhood, patients would find themselves reliving the significant sensory-emotional features of their birth experience—patterns to which Grof (1985) gave the name *perinatal matrices*.

More or less simultaneously with the psycholytic approach being developed in Europe, the *psychedelic* model became the preferred approach in Anglo-American psychological and psychiatric circles. The English psychiatrist Humphrey Osmond, who worked in Canada with Abram Hoffer on the treatment of alcoholism with LSD, and who provided Aldous Huxley with his first mescaline experience (immortalized in *The Doors of Perception*), introduced this term in an exchange of letters with Huxley. First used in the treatment of alcoholics, where it was thought to simulate the often life-changing "bottoming out" experience, psychedelic therapy usually involved one or a small number of high-dose sessions, during which the contents of the unconscious mind would be manifested in the form of vivid hallucinatory imagery, leading to insight and transformation (Passie, 1985).

The understanding of the dynamics of contractions and expansions of consciousness offered here supports and extends the applications of consciousness-expanding psychedelics, particularly in the treatment of consciousness-contracting compulsions and addictions (Halpern, 1996). LSD found one of its principal early uses in the treatment of alcoholism (Mangini, 1998). Native American participants in the peyote rituals of the Native American Church have been consistently successful in recovery from alcoholism (McClusky, 1997; Horgan, 2003). Ayahuasca, or *hoasca*, an Amazonian hallucinogenic concoction, has been used in the treatment of alcoholism and other addictions (Grob, McKenna, & Callaway, 1996). Ibogaine, a derivative from an African religious hallucinogen, has been researched for its use in the treatment of cocaine addiction (Mash & Kovera,. 1998). Psilocybin, the psychoactive principle of Mexican visionary mushrooms, was tried in the treatment of recidivist offenders (Leary & Metzner, 1965) and is currently being tested as a treatment for obsessive-compulsive disorders (Delgado & Mereno, 1998).

It should be pointed out that in proposing the use of consciousness-expanding substances in the treatment of addictions, we are not suggesting a "magic bullet" pharmacological "cure" for addiction, a drug effect to counteract a drug effect. Rather, the treatment with psychedelic substances, in traditional shamanistic societies, as well as in innovative Western therapy settings, involves a prolonged guided experience of self-confrontation, participation in shared group ritual experiences, and the acceptance of and support by a community of like-minded individuals.

Not only certain drugs but also cognitive processes that lead to expanded awareness, such as mindfulness meditation, can be used to counteract the fixations and attachments found in psychopathology. Indeed, mindfulness awareness practice as the antidote to the attachments and cravings inherent in everyday existence has been a key element of Buddhist and other yogic teachings for thousands of years. Western physicians have also begun to utilize those kinds of meditative methods to alleviate suffering and increase recovery for a wide variety of medical conditions.

Psychoactive Drugs and Alterations of Consciousness

Examination of the 360° circle model of the field of consciousness reveals a third kind of possible alteration that is neither an expansion nor a contraction of attentional focus but merely the redirection of attention to another part of the total spectrum. In figure 2.6, the hypothetical 30° arc of attention is moved away from, dissociated, from the previous baseline to some other part of the sensorium, not expanded and perhaps not contracted either, just different. We could call this kind of alteration of consciousness *channel switching,* to use an analogy from television.

If the focus of attention is on some object or event in the exterior or interior world, the analogy would be that it is like looking at a program on a TV channel. The focus of attention and perception is on the images being presented to the viewer. We might call this the normal "attachment mode" of perception. If I am depressed, or sad, or watching some exterior event or activity, I am perceptually attached, or

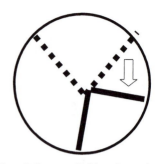

Baseline sense of consciousness   **Dissociation—switching channels**

Figure 2.6. Alteration of Consciousness

focused or fixated, on that depression, sadness, or perceived event. The analogy to compulsive, fixated consciousness would be if the individual becomes so totally absorbed by the program being watched that he or she is oblivious to what is going in the immediate environment and even recklessly ignoring of the real needs of others, such as children. For true transcendence, with consciousness expansion, the analogy would be that you would still be seeing the TV images, but you step back from it and also see what is around you in the room, and through the window, outside the house. The transcendent state always includes the former narrower focus of attention, and adds to it. You get the bigger picture, as it were, the differentiated context, the more complex awareness that there is a whole world out there, and that you have a choice as to where to direct your attention.

Now, switching the channel is a kind of transcendence, in the sense that you are no longer watching the program to which you were previously attending. If you are depressed, and you are able to "switch channels" somehow, you would have "gone beyond" the depression. Antidepressant drugs could be considered "channel-switching" drugs; probably most psychiatric mood-altering drugs function in this way. Some forms of psychotherapy, such as the use of affirmations, and some kinds of interventions or distractions by friends, what the French call "changer les idées," could be understood in this way. You are able to change the focus of your attention away from the distressing or painful contents that were preoccupying you. Such redirection of attention can have definite therapeutic value.

The effect of the psychoactive, mood-altering drugs can, I believe, best be understood in terms of this channel-switching analogy. They are consciousness-altering, whereas the psychedelic drugs are truly consciousness-expanding. Alcohol, for example, just switches your channel of attention and awareness, plus moving your consciousness downward on the arousal continuum, toward greater relaxation. It does not expand your awareness or your perception. It switches the focus of your attention, so that instead of feeling tense or anxious, you feel relaxed and euphoric, at least for a while, until the depressant effect spreads to more and more aspects of cognitive and sensory-motor function. The same is true of the other depressant drugs: They shift the focus of attention from anxiety to relaxation. Because they bring about this change of mood-state effectively and rapidly, we learn that we can "escape" painful inner states in that way—a fixation-addiction can easily develop.

The stimulant drugs, including cocaine, the amphetamines, and caffeine, also trigger a shift of the focus of attention, without an expansion of awareness, and a movement "upward" along the arousal continuum. With these drugs there is a switch from feelings of powerlessness, inadequacy, and impotence to feelings of powerfulness, competence, and sexual arousal. The cocaine "rush," or the amphetamine "speed" feeling is the sensation of being "on top of the world," full of competence and power, immediately after ingestion. There is the fantasy illusion of personal power, which is inevitably followed by deflation and "letdown" as the pharmacological "high" wears off.

One may wonder whether the pervasive and spreading attraction of cocaine and other stimulants, as well as of nicotine, a comparatively mild stimulant, is not in some way a reflection of the increasing sense of powerlessness and helplessness that so many people feel in our fragmented society, marked by profound social inequities and dislocations. Perhaps, too, there is a personality or temperament difference between those who are drawn to the depressants to escape anxiety in a passive manner and those who are drawn to the stimulants, and the activity addictions, for switching to a state of feeling powerful and competent.

Rage addiction, or compulsive violence, which is often, though not always, associated with sexual aggression and abuse, may also be understood as a learned fixated response to early and repeated feelings of inadequacy and powerlessness. Assaultive and destructive behavior temporarily switches the perpetrator's attention and awareness away from painful feelings of inadequacy and impotence, and fear of even deeper helplessness. Having once learned a "way out" of extraordinarily painful feeling-states, it becomes easy to follow the road to addiction and compulsive repetition.

The addictions to shopping and gambling may develop because these activities momentarily shift attention away from feelings of worthlessness. Where a great deal of identity and self-esteem is tied up with how many material possessions one owns or how much money one has to spend, shopping gives one the momentary illusion of an increase in possession and greater self-worth based on spending. The advertising media know this "consumer complex" and play on it to maximal effect, as one can readily observe in any suburban shopping mall, where the powerful, constantly repeated subliminal message is "buying is good," "you are good and beautiful when you buy." Compulsive gamblers likewise can toy with the illusion, and the possibility, of suddenly winning large sums. Having material possessions, or even being close to the possibility of monetary wealth, gives a feeling of worth, prosperity, and social esteem.

The process I am describing as channel switching, a pseudo-transcendent method of altering one's consciousness, may also be involved in what is popularly referred to as "head-tripping." This is the kind of compulsive intellectualizing that has also been characterized as a "thinking addiction." If I am "tripping" in my head, in the realm of thoughts, ideas, and books, I can avoid really feeling and learning from my own emotions and bodily sensations. For many, this is the simplest form of escape, the easiest and least noticed form of addictive fixation. Freud called it *sublimation* (an alchemical metaphor) and stated that it was the one defense mechanism that "really worked." Perhaps because the head is spatially located above the rest of the body, the notion of transcending or "climbing above," by directing attention to the head, comes easily to mind.

Channel switching is probably also the appropriate analogy to use in describing spiritual addiction or compulsive meditation practice. I once had a client who was a former practitioner of TM. She was quite nervous and anxious all the time, except when she was meditating, which she did twice a day for 20 minutes. In TM, the individual concentrates on a specific, selected mantra—and the mind can exclude all other thoughts. While this client was meditating, she was not anxious—when she was not meditating, she was anxious. So meditation was a shift in focus, in attention, a channel switching, not a true transcendence, not an expansion of consciousness.

True transcendence dissolves fixations and expands contracted forms of perception. The "doors of perception" are cleansed, as William Blake put it, with the phrase that Aldous Huxley used as the title for his book on his mescaline experiences. Mindfulness meditation (*vipassana*) produces true transcendence because in mindfulness meditation, you do not try to hold concentration on some chosen object or subject. You simply observe and note the continuous stream of sensations, feelings, and thoughts. Whatever comes up, you just note it. You just observe it. You do not go away from, or try to leave it, or try to concentrate on something else. You also do not analyze or interpret it, as you would in psychotherapy. Just let it come up and pass away. Thoughts arise and pass. All aspects of experience are included; none are excluded. That is why mindfulness meditation produces a gradual transcendence, a gradual, progressive detachment and disidentification, that includes the former contents of consciousness as elements of a larger whole.

In the addiction-recovery movement, as exemplified in the writings and seminars of teachers such as John Bradshaw, as well as in the basic 12-step teaching, tremendous importance is given to acknowledging and validating the horrible and painful experiences that one has had:

the pain, shame, guilt, grief, loneliness, abandonment, abuse, humiliation, despair, and so on. This acknowledgment of the pain and shame is seen as essential to freeing oneself from the addiction. We can see this from the point of view of the process of true transcendence, where everything is included, with all its often terrifying complexities, as compared with channel switching, as usually occurs in the addictions, where we simply try to escape from the difficulties and demons.

References

Adamson, S., & Metzner, R.(1988). The nature of the MDMA experience and its role in healing, psychotherapy and spiritual practice. *ReVision, 10*, 59–72.

Barron, F. (1963/1990). *Creativity and psychological health*. Buffalo, NY: Creative Education Foundation.

Delgado, P., & Mereno, F. (1998). Hallucinogens, serotonin and obsessive-compulsive disorder. *Journal of Psychoactive Drugs, 30*, 359–366.

Fischer, R. (1971). A cartography of the ecstatic and meditative states. *Science, 174*, 897–904.

Furst, P. (1976). *Hallucinogens and culture*. San Francisco: Chandler and Sharp.

Grob, C., McKenna, D., & Callaway, J. C. (1996). Human pharmacology of hoasca, a plant hallucinogen used in ritual context in Brazil. *Journal of Nervous and Mental Disease, 184*, 86–94.

Grof, S. (1980). *LSD psychotherapy*. Pomona, CA: Hunter House.

Grof, S. (1985). *Beyond the brain: Birth, death and transcendence in psychotherapy*. Albany: State University of New York Press.

Halifax, J. (1982). *Shaman: Wounded healer*. New York: Crossroad.

Halpern, J. (1996). The use of hallucinogens in the treatment of addiction. *Addiction Research, 4*, 177–189.

Harner, M. (Ed.). (1973). *Hallucinogens and shamanism*. New York: Oxford University Press.

Harner, M. (1980). *The way of the shaman*. San Francisco: Harper and Row.

Hofmann, A. (1983). *LSD: My problem child*. Los Angeles: Tarcher.

Horgan, J. (2003). Peyote on the brain. *Discover, 24*, 68–74.

Hunt, H. T., & Chefurka, C. M. (1976) A test of the psychedelic model of altered states of consciousness. *Archives of General Psychiatry, 33*, 867–876.

James, W. (1901/1958). *Varieties of religious experience*. New York: New American Library.

James, W. (1912/1996). *Essays in radical empiricism*. Lincoln: University of Nebraska Press.

Leary, T. (1997). *Psychedelic prayers and other meditations*. Berkeley: Ronin.

Leary, T., Litwin, G., & Metzner, R. 1963. Reactions to psilocybin administered in a supportive environment. *Journal of Nervous and Mental Diseases, 137*, 561–573.

Leary, T., & Metzner, R. (1965). A new behavior change program using psilocybin. *Psychotherapy: Theory, Research and Practice, 2*, 61–72.

Leary, T., Metzner, R., & Alpert, R. (1964). *The psychedelic experience: A manual based on the Tibetan Book of the Dead*. New Hyde Park, NY: University Press Books.

Mangini, M. (1998). Treatment of alcoholism using psychedelic drugs: A review of the program of research. *Journal of Psychoactive Drugs, 30*, 381–418.

Mash, D. C., & Kovera, C. A. (1998). Medication development of ibogaine as a pharmacotherapy for drug dependence. *Annals of New York Academy of Sciences, 844*, 274–292.

McClusky, J. (1997). Native American Church peyotism and the treatment of alcoholism. *MAPS Bulletin, 7*(4), 3–4.

McKenna, T., & McKenna, D. (1975). *The invisible landscape.* New York: Seabury Press.

Metzner, R. (1971). *Maps of consciousness.* New York: Collier-Macmillan.

Metzner, R. (1986). *The Altered States Graphic Profile (ASGP).* One page, with instructions on the reverse side. Copies may be obtained gratis from the author.

Metzner, R. (1989). States of consciousness and transpersonal psychology. In R. Vallee & S. Halling (Eds.), *Existential and phenomenological perspectives in psychology.* (pp. 227–329) New York: Plenum.

Metzner, R. (1994). Addiction and transcendence as altered states of consciousness. *Journal of Transpersonal Psychology,* 1–17.

Metzner, R. (Ed.). 1999. *Ayahuasca: Human consciousness and the spirits of nature.* New York: Thunder's Mouth Press.

Metzner, R. (2002). The role of psychoactive plant medicines. In C. S. Grob (Ed.), *Hallucinogens: A reader.* (pp. 23–37) New York: Tarcher/Putnam.

Metzner, R., & Adamson, S. (2001). Using MDMA in healing, psychotherapy and spiritual practice. In J. Holland (Ed.), *Ecstasy: The Complete Guide* (pp. 182–207) Rochester, VT: Park Street Press.

Ott, J. (1995). *The age of entheogens and the angels' dictionary.* Kennewick, WA: Natural Products.

Passie, T. (1985). *Psycholytic and psychedelic therapy research: An international bibliography.* New York: Laurentius.

Peele, S. (1985). *The meaning of addiction.* Lexington, MA: Heath.

Tart, C. T. 1972. States of consciousness and state-specific science. *Science 176*, 1203–1210.

3

Hallucinogens

RICK STRASSMAN

The *psychedelics* or *hallucinogens* probably are the most complex and controversial, and in many ways the most fascinating, group of psychoactive compounds in our pharmacopoeia. Humans have used these agents, which are found in plants, fungi, and other animals for millennia (Grinspoon & Bakalar, 1979; Ott, 1993; Schultes, Hofmann, & Rätsch, 1998). There is little indication that contemporary civilization seeks out their effects any less than did our ancestors (Pinchbeck, 2002; Pope, Ionescu-Pioggia, & Pope, 2001; Stafford, 1992). In addition, the presence of endogenous hallucinogens in the human body continues to challenge us in ways we barely have begun to explore (Strassman, 2001).

History

Both LSD (lysergic acid diethylamide-25) and the neurotransmitter serotonin were discovered at nearly the same time, in the middle to late 1940s. It soon became apparent that they shared basic pharmacological and physiological properties, thus leading to theories relating serotonin to mental illness (Cerletti & Rothlin, 1955; D. X. Freedman, 1961; Gaddum & Hameed, 1954; Woolley & Shaw, 1954). At the same time, chlorpromazine's antipsychotic effects also began being demonstrated. Psychedelics thus occupy a position of fundamental importance, equivalent to those of serotonin and chlorpromazine, in the birth and development of contemporary biological psychiatry and psychopharmacology.

The hallucinogens subsequently garnered a tremendous amount of research interest and funding for more than two decades. Studies included basic explorations of the psychopharmacology of mental states (Sokoloff, Perlin, Kornetsky, & Kety, 1957) and of the nature of psychoses (Rinkel, DeShon, Hyde, & Solomon, 1952) and religious experience (Pahnke & Richards, 1966). Psychedelics were used as adjuncts in the psychotherapy of intractable psychiatric (Simmons, Leiken, Lovaas, Schaeffer, & Perloff, 1966), alcohol-related (Kurland, Unger, Shaffer, & Savage, 1967), and other substance abuse disorders (Savage & McCabe, 1973), and to reduce the pain and suffering associated with terminal cancer (Kast & Collins, 1964; Pahnke, Kurland, Goodman, & Richards, 1969). They also were used in the training of psychiatric clinicians (MacDonald & Galvin, 1956; Rinkel, 1956) and for enhancement of creativity (Harman, McKim, Mogar, Fadiman, & Stolaroff, 1966).

The legitimate study of these agents ended nearly as quickly as it began (Ulrich & Patten, 1991). The massive social and political unrest associated with the Vietnam War, Tim Leary's highly publicized flouting of academic propriety while studying these drugs at Harvard, and public health concerns over widespread out-of-control abuse of the psychedelics resulted in enactment of the federal Controlled Substances Act of 1970, which strictly regulated possession of psychedelics even for research purposes (Controlled Substances Act, 1970; Lee & Shlain, 1986; Stevens, 1998). These onerous regulatory burdens, and the stigma associated with the drugs, effectively ended funding, approval, and performance of any new human studies for more than 20 years.

Despite this hiatus in human studies, basic research continued apace. Such preclinical activity using LSD and related compounds has led to many fundamental discoveries related to the role of serotonin and serotonergic drugs in the treatment of psychiatric conditions. These include the development of more effective and specific antidepressants, antipsychotics, and antianxiety agents.

Within the last decade, European (Oepen, Fuengeld, Harrington, Hermle, & Botsch, 1989) and American (Strassman, 1991) research communities have resumed clinical studies with psychedelics, and these drugs once more may occupy an important place in psychopharmacology and pharmacotherapy.

Nomenclature

If one's appreciation for the complex nature of a family of drugs is determined by the number of names it has received, clearly these compounds exist in a class by themselves. *Psychedelic* is the most popular name and refers to their "mind-manifesting" properties. *Hallu-*

cinogen is more common within a medicolegal context; however, hallucinations are not an invariant or even distinguishing feature of the intoxication.

For those who wish to emphasize particular characteristics of these drugs, there is no dearth of other names. However, the more narrowly these terms focus on specific qualities, the more one loses an appreciation for the wide spectrum of effects the drugs characteristically produce. We have, for example, *psychotomimetic* and *psychotogen*, mimicking or generating psychosis; *entheogen*, eliciting the divine; *mysticomimetic*, mimicking mystical states; *phanerothyme*, making feelings visible; *psychotoxin* or *schizotoxin*, a psychosis- or schizophrenia-producing metabolic product; *psychodysleptic*, mind-disrupting; *oneirogen*, producing dreams; and *phantasticant*, stimulating fantasy. In this chapter, I will use interchangeably the two most accepted terms, *psychedelic* and *hallucinogen*, loosely depending upon the context in which they are discussed.

Chemistry and Pharmacology

The "typical" or "classical" psychedelics include two major chemical families (Nichols, 1997; Shulgin & Shulgin, 1991, 1997). Mescaline, from the peyote cactus, is the most well-known member of the *phenethylamines*. The popular drug MDMA belongs in this family, too, but its effects are not typically psychedelic. The *tryptamines* contain the *simple tryptamines*: DMT (N,N-dimethyltryptamine) and psilocybin (found in psychedelic mushrooms), as well as the *ergolines*, in which is included the prototypical psychedelic LSD.

Effects are rather similar among the various classical psychedelics, and more germane in describing differences are those related to temporal course: time to onset, peak, and resolution of effects. For example, responses to parenterally administered (smoked or injected) tryptamines such as DMT and 5-MeO-DMT (5-methoxy-DMT) begin within a minute or less, peak within 2 to 15 minutes, and are negligible by 30 to 60 minutes. Orally administered psilocybin begins exerting it effects within 15 to 30 minutes; its effects peak at 3 to 5 hours and resolve by 6 to 8 hours. Those of LSD and mescaline begin within 20 to 45 minutes, peak at 4 to 6 hours, and continue 10 to 14 hours after ingestion.

The preponderance of animal (Nichols, 1997) and the little available human (Vollenweider, Vollenweider-Scherpenhuyzen, Babler, Vogel, & Hell, 1998) data support a primary role of serotonin receptors in mediating the effects of classical hallucinogens, especially as partial agonists of the $5\text{-HT}_{2A/2C}$ sites. In addition, the role of the 5-HT_{1A} site remains controversial (Winter, Filipink, Timineri, Helsley, & Rabin, 2000). Modifications of dopamine (Hoch, 1956; Vollenweider et al.,

1998; Vollenweider, Vontobel, Hell, & Leenders, 1999), N-methyl-D-aspartate (NMDA)/glutamate (Gewirtz & Marek, 2000), acetylcholine (Haubrich & Wang, 1977), and norepinephrine (McCall & Aghajanian, 1980) systems also occur but are less well understood.

Psychophysiological effects of hallucinogens in humans have also been assessed, particularly during the first wave of research. These include alterations in visual function (Fischer, Hill, Thatcher, & Scheib, 1970; Gouzoulis-Mayfrank et al., 2002; Krus, Resnick, & Raskin, 1966); taste sensitivity (Fischer & Warshay, 1968); reaction time (Edwards & Cohen, 1961); sense of time passage (Aronson, Silverstein, & Klee, 1959); and prepulse inhibition of startle reflex (Gouzoulis-Mayfrank, Heekeren, 1998). Brain imaging studies have begun to localize effects of psychedelics in humans. Mescaline appears to reduce blood flow to the right hemisphere in resting (Oepen et al., 1989) or challenged (Hermle, Gouzoulis-Mayfrank, & Spitzer, 1998) conditions.

These studies have generated data providing an interface between human and lower animal electrophysiological data and in some cases provide a bridge between endogenous psychopathological states and hallucinogen intoxication, as, for example, when invoking the "psychotomimetic" model. However, they approach the study of "subjective" effects of these drugs at least one step removed from the immediately experienced phenomena.

Additional drugs possess definite psychedelic properties, at least within specific dose ranges. What distinguishes them from typical agents are differences regarding their clinical pharmacology and mechanisms of action. For example, ketamine, an *arylcycloalkylamine*, and the closely related drug phencyclidine (PCP) elicit a syndrome very similar to that of more typical agents (Bowdle et al., 1998; Jansen, 2001). However, they produce general anesthesia at higher doses and primarily blockade brain NMDA receptors (Tamminga, 1999).

Ibogaine, an especially long-acting (approximately 24 hour) compound, elicits a profoundly psychedelic syndrome. It appears significantly more toxic than typical hallucinogens (Vastag, 2002), and basic research suggests a complex interaction of serotonergic and opioid receptor modification (Helsley, Rabin, & Winter, 2001; Pablo & Mash, 1998). Clinical and preclinical data concerning ibogaine and its less toxic metabolite, noribogaine, indicate an easing of withdrawal from opiates and longer term protective effects against relapse (Alper, Lotsof, Frenken, Luciano, & Bastiaans, 1999).

Salvinorin A, the active ingredient of the "diviner's sage," *Salvia divinorum*, also produces robust hallucinogenic effects at rather low doses (Siebert, 1994), but it seems to do so via kappa opioid mechanisms (Roth et al., 2002).

Although these nontypical agents are clearly of interest, in this chapter I will focus on the more typical ones because they are by far the most commonly used, and nearly all published clinical research data exist for them.

Set and Setting

In the case of the psychedelics, perhaps more so than for any other psychoactive drugs (Eisner, 1997; Sjoberg & Hollister, 1965), set and setting play a crucial role in the subjective experience, as well as the objective interpretation, of drug effects (Naditch, Alker, & Joffe, 1975). *Set* in this context refers to the subject's expectations and mental and physical state. *Setting* partakes of both the physical and the psychological environment, including the expectations and behavior (set) of the research team.

With respect to set, subjects to whom hallucinogens have been administered in clinical research cover a wide range: well-educated, nonpatient, mostly professional normal volunteers (Boszormenyi, 1960; Harman et al., 1966); drug-naive undergraduates (Bottrill, 1969); investigators themselves performing "auto-experimentation" (MacDonald & Galvin, 1956; Shulgin, Shulgin, & Jacob, 1986; Szara, 1957); patients with schizophrenia (Denber & Merlis, 1955; Turner & Merlis, 1959), depression (Savage, 1952; Sloane & Doust, 1954), neuroses (Brandup & Vanggard, 1977; Pauk & Shagass, 1961; Sandison, Spencer, & Whitelaw, 1954), character disorders (Buckman, 1969; Savage, 1959; Vanggaard, 1964), sociopathy (Shagass & Bittle, 1967), childhood psychosis or severe autism (Bender, 1966; A. M. Freedman, Ebin, & Wilson, 1962; Simmons et al., 1966), drug or alcohol addiction (Abramson, 1967; Abuzzahab & Anderson, 1971; MacLean, MacDonald, Byrne, & Hubbard, 1961), and cancer (Cohen, 1965; Kast & Collins, 1964; Pahnke et al., 1969); and prisoners (Isbell, 1959). Subjects' preparation for drug effects can range from extensive (Strassman, Qualls, Uhlenhuth, & Kellner, 1994) to minimal (Hill, Haertzen, Wilbach, & Miner, 1963a; Linton & Langs, 1962).

Regarding setting, as alluded to earlier, this also partakes of the reasons one is administering a psychedelic drug to an individual and the types of expected effects that are more or less overtly encouraged. Thus, a psychedelic drug could be given to produce a mystical state or a schizophrenic psychosis, as an adjunct to individual or group psychotherapy, or for less clinical psychological or psychophysiological investigations.

Physical surroundings in psychedelic research settings vary dramatically. Volunteers may be given these drugs in groups (Jarvik, Abramson, & Hirsch, 1955; Lennard, Jarvik, & Abramson, 1956; MacLean et al., 1961; Slater, Morimoto, & Hyde, 1957) or, most commonly, individually. The clinical environment has ranged from being strapped down into one's bed in a locked room (Smart, Storm, Baker, & Solursh, 1966) to a cozy and homey consultation suite (Kurland et al., 1967).

Considering these factors, it is possible to imagine two polar situations in which the exact same dose of the same hallucinogen is administered to a "human research subject" and widely disparate subjective effects data are generated because of set and setting factors. At one end are responses seen in a well-functioning normal volunteer with extensive hallucinogen experience, prepared in previous nondrug sessions by the experimenters to have a "mystical" experience. The session takes place in a comfortable ground-level consulting room with a garden just steps outside, using eyeshades and provocative music, attended upon by a nondirective, friendly clinician wearing street clothes and no heavy fragrances or makeup.

At the other end of this spectrum might be a hallucinogen-naive, unprepared, regressed, strapped-down, psychotic patient, in a bare seclusion room without windows on the 20th floor of a state hospital locked ward, studied by experimenters in white hospital uniforms, heavily perfumed and made-up, who expect a worsening of the subject's condition. The examiners are placing and removing electrodes onto the patient's scalp and checking rectal temperature periodically during acute intoxication.

In which set of circumstances would 200 µg of LSD produce an "entheogenic" effect, and in what situation might we see "psychotomimetic" responses?

Typical Effects

It is useful to attempt a description of a "generic" psychedelic experience before discussing some of the salient issues concerning measurement of these effects. At the same time, we must appreciate that it is impossible to accurately predict what any given drug session will be like in any individual on any particular day, because of set and setting issues.

Drawing upon my reading of the lay and scientific literature, as well as interviews and conversations with thousands of people who have taken these drugs in recreational, shamanic, therapeutic, spiritual, and clinical research settings, I will paint a broad picture of a full psychedelic experience. By "full," I mean to distinguish a typical high-dose experience from low, subpsychedelic doses of typical drugs. Furthermore, this description does not apply to nonpsychedelic psychoactive drugs, such as MDMA, other amphetamines, or average-strength marijuana or hashish.

Psychedelics affect all those aspects of consciousness that, melded together, make us uniquely human. These include our senses of self and body awareness and our thoughts, emotions, and perceptions.

Perceptual effects are quite frequent but not invariant. Visual effects usually predominate. With eyes open or shut, more or less brightly colored, rapidly swirling and crawling geometric patterns appear in space and may overlay objects in the environment. Those physical objects themselves may melt or fragment visually, shrink or expand. Drug-induced de novo patterns may coalesce into formed visual images, consisting of familiar or unfamiliar objects, in various stages of movement. Colors may be the brightest and most saturated one has ever seen.

Auditory effects are relatively frequent and consist of sounds becoming softer, louder, harsher, or gentler. Sometimes new sounds, including music or song, emerge, as might previously absent rhythms in preexisting sounds. "Voices," as such, are generally rare.

Tactile sensitivity may increase or decrease. Tastes and smells may become more or less acute, or may even be experienced with no objective basis. Emotional effects are common and marked. Empathy for others can take on cosmic proportions or can shrink to nothingness in a nearly autistic self-absorption. Anxiety, terror, pleasure, tension, relaxation, and ecstasy all may be extreme, rapidly fluctuate, or coexist. No feelings at all may be experienced. Acceptance of emotional pain and conflict, or the emergence of new and poignant emotional issues, may emerge.

Thoughts vary in rate from the norm, and time passes more swiftly or slowly. Thinking becomes clearer or more muddled. No thoughts may exist, or our minds burst with new ideas. Insights into the past, present, and future appear, or a pervading sense of hopelessness and helplessness takes over. Cognitive freshness and novelty overlay our experience, and the significance of everyday reality takes on a new dimension.

The sense of self undergoes an alteration in the feeling of "control" by inner and outside forces. Boundaries between self and others become firmer or looser, and our personal identity can fill the entire universe or be absolutely negated. Psychedelics affect our sense of volitional efficacy—as we feel more or less acutely our own free will or, contrariwise, our inexorable predestination.

Physically, there are fluctuations in body temperature and in the sense of weight, size, and proportion. One feels movement through space, sometimes at dizzying speed, or a powerful experience of somatic inertia and torpor. Body and mind may feel as if they have separated.

Hallucinogens and Endogenous Altered States of Consciousness

Similarities among different naturally occurring unusual states of consciousness and the altered mental states brought on by psychedelics have been noted and discussed since the discovery of exogenous hallucinogens. Such conditions include near-death experiences (NDEs), psychoses (most often schizophrenia but sometimes mania), and mystical experiences. Most of these discussions relate to the psychotic and mystical states, but mystical and near-death experiences also share many features.

Psychosis

One area of investigation relates to the etiology of endogenous psychoses. That is, do endogenous compounds mediate any of the symptoms of psychosis? For many years, studies consistently demonstrated the presence of DMT in human body tissues and fluids, and increasing refinement in elucidating DMT's biosynthetic pathways impelled intensive investigation into its role as an endogenous "schizotoxin" (Gillin, Kaplan, Stillman, & Wyatt, 1976). Unfortunately, this was another area of research that ended prematurely as much because of political concerns as scientific ones (Strassman, 2001, pp. 48–52).

Nevertheless, DMT was the first, and remains the best, candidate for a naturally occurring compound in humans that has psychedelic/psychotomimetic properties. Our recent discovery that DMT cannot induce tolerance to its own effects, even with frequent, closely spaced injections (Strassman, Qualls, & Berg, 1996), strengthens even further its ranking as the prime candidate in this field.

Hallucinogens also have been used to generate clinical models for endogenous psychoses. There clearly are some similarities between the effects of LSD and schizophrenia (Bowers & Freedman, 1966; Hollister, 1962; Langs & Barr, 1968; Vardy & Kay, 1983; Young, 1974). The terms *model psychosis* and *experimental schizophrenia* were coined to describe these time-limited imitations of endogenous mental illness (Bercel, Travis, Olinger, & Dreikurs, 1956; Luby, Gottlieb, Cohen, Rosenbaum, & Domino, 1962; Rinkel et al., 1952).

The greatest similarities between hallucinogen-generated and endogenous psychoses appear to exist between the acute psychedelic state and the acute and/or prodromal symptoms of schizophrenia and acute mania. Such overlapping symptoms include a sense of oversignificance to everyday thoughts, perceptions, and feelings; a heightening of sensory acuity; and ideas of overinclusiveness, leading to ideas of reference or frank paranoia. Thus, acutely ill patients with many positive symptoms resemble normal volunteers undergoing a dysphoric psychedelic experience more than the latter resemble patients with chronic, undifferentiated syndromes with prominent negative symptoms.

Administering psychedelics to psychotic patients and asking them to make comparisons between drug-induced and endogenous symptoms would provide a crucial "within-subjects" design. However, previous such studies were limited by impressionistic assessments of subjective effects and by poorly communicative patients. Some studies reported a qualitative difference between states (Cholden, Kurland, & Savage, 1955; Fink, Simeon, Haque, & Itil, 1966), and others described a worsening of preexisting psychotic symptomatology (Hoch, Cattell, & Pennes, 1952; MacDonald & Galvin, 1956). Those patients who could adequately relate their experiences did note a difference between drug-induced and spontaneous symptoms (Turner & Merlis, 1959; Turner, Almudevar, & Merlis, 1959).

The regulatory difficulties involved in clinical research with hallucinogens also brought this fruitful area of research to an end in the early 1970s. However, with the recent resumption of human studies, the psychotomimetic model is being used again as a way to understand the psychedelic state (Gouzoulis-Mayfrank et al., 1998; Vollenweider & Geyer, 2001). In the United States, ketamine is being employed for these purposes as much for its more accessible regulatory status than for its ability to induce a clinically relevant, NMDA receptor–mediated, model psychosis (Tamminga, 1999). Our European colleagues also are using the classical agents, specifically psilocybin, in Switzerland and Germany (Spitzer, Thimm, Hermle, Holzmann, Kovar, Heinmann, et al., 1996; Vollenweider et al., 1997).

Psychotomimetic research in the 1950s and 1960s used clinical impressions to the detriment of objective data. We now must avoid the opposite tendency, and not focus on rating scale or psychophysiological similarities to the detriment of commonsense clinical similarities and differences between the syndromes.

A logical consequence of the psychotomimetic model is the blockade or reversal of the model psychosis in normal volunteers with drugs that might then have efficacy in treating endogenous conditions. These studies were attempted during the first phase of human psychedelic research (Fabing, 1955; Isbell, Miner & Logan, 1959; Meltzer et al., 1982) and are being pursued in contemporary studies (Vollenweider et al., 1998).

Mystical Experience

Mystical states of consciousness are characterized by profound alterations in one's sense of self, and in the experiences of time and space. Merging into a white light, a sense of timelessness within the eternal present, and a powerful interconnectedness of all existence are hallmarks of this state. In addition, powerful emotions are associated with these cognitive and perceptual effects. There is the unshakable conviction that consciousness is not dependent upon the body and, subsequently, that death is not the end of consciousness.

The striking similarities between high-dose, or "peak," psychedelic experiences and mystical ones are alluded to by the titles of some books that discuss these resemblances: *Entheogens and the Future of Religion* (Forte, 1997) and *The Varieties of Psychedelic Experience* (Master &

Houston, 2000) (a reference to William James's *Varieties of Religious Experience* [1997]).

In addition, experimental studies have attempted to utilize these similarities for beneficial effects by turning the positive impact of religious experience toward a variety of clinical conditions. These include the pain and anguish associated with terminal illness (Cohen, 1965; Grof, Goodman, Richards, & Kurland, 1973; Kast & Collins, 1964) and with drug and alcohol abuse (Pahnke, Kurland, Unger, Savage, & Grof, 1970; Savage & McCabe, 1973).

Although substantial time and energy were expended in both theoretical discussions and applied studies of "experimental mysticism," almost no attempts were made to relate mystical states to endogenous hallucinogens. The existence of DMT and 5-MeO-DMT as endogenous human hallucinogens clearly has relevance to this issue and was a major consideration in the development of our studies in New Mexico.

Near-Death Experiences

Those who have nearly died frequently have what are referred to as *near-death experiences* (Moody, 1988; Ring, 1980), another highly altered endogenous state quite similar to that brought on by exogenous psychedelics, as well as observed in mystical states. There is the sensation of rapid movement, sometimes through a tunnel; accompanying music, songs, or voices; the presence of "beings" such as friends, angels, or spirits; and the realization that one is dead. There also are powerful emotional concomitants to these experiences, a review of one's life in rapid sequence, and sometimes the feeling of being commanded to return to life because the time to die has not yet come. Some NDEs may climax in a state indistinguishable from a mystical experience brought on by drug or natural causes.

Even less experimental data exist for an endogenous "NDE-ogen," but, as noted earlier, there are endogenous hallucinogens that may be considered likely candidates for mediating such naturally occurring experiences (Jansen, 1997; Strassman, 1997).

Adverse Effects Literature

Data gathered from individuals who have had acute or delayed adverse reactions to hallucinogens have been used to characterize these drugs' effects. The presentation of acute and chronic reactions runs the gamut of psychiatric symptomatology and includes anxiety, mood, and psychotic syndromes. Issues that reduce the utility of these data include the fact that the identity and purity of drugs consumed are almost always unknown. Several others drugs and/or alcohol may have been ingested concurrently. Little or no premorbid data or characterization of these individuals is available, and drug effects occurred in an unsupervised setting.

Often, the reaction to the drug effects, rather than the effects themselves, is the focus of clinical attention. In this case the psychedelic drug effect may be conceptualized as a nonspecific psychic trauma akin to leaving home for the first time, the breakup of an important relationship, sleep deprivation, or a physical assault. Although such acute and longer-term data are of clinical relevance, they do not provide especially accurate or useful information regarding acute effects of these drugs (Strassman, 2001).

Rating Scales

Clinical observations by skilled clinicians were among the first attempts to describe a general pattern of hallucinogens' effects in humans. These observations were conceptualized using behavioral/descriptive (Klee, Bertino, Weintraub, & Callaway, 1961; Lennard et al., 1956; Rinkel et al., 1952) and psychodynamic (Bercel et al., 1956; Denber & Merlis, 1955) perspectives. They provided colorful and provocative accounts, but it was difficult to transfer observational techniques and data generated from one research center to another.

A parallel course of research used preexisting psychological tests or inventories of mental states and traits to assess hallucinogenic drug intoxication. These included, for example, the MMPI (Belleville, 1956), Rorschach tests (Wertham & Bleuler, 1932), Wechsler intelligence tests (Kurland, Savage, Pahnke, Grof, & Olsson, 1971), and the Clyde Mood Scale (Hollister, Macnicol, & Gillespie, 1969).

This type of research compares hallucinogens' effects with previously defined psychopathological syndromes, as well as assessing how they modify well-characterized psychological functions. However, none of these tests was originally developed specifically to quantify the characteristic hallucinogenic drug intoxication. As with the psychophysiological studies referred to earlier, they do not directly contact the subjective realm, the actual immersion in, and palpability of, the psychedelic state itself, but rather describe indirect effects, less truly subjectively felt.

Self-report-based, introspectively derived observational data, based upon a conscious recognition of what is passing through one's mind, are the materials that one should mine to best describe the effects of these drugs. This is the gold standard, and quantitative research, to be successful in assessing these effects, should more or less operationalize those internally derived and experienced data.

During the first stage of human psychedelic research, three rating scales were most frequently used to quantify the psychological effects of these drugs. Two were developed specifically using LSD: the Linton-Langs Inventory and the Abramson et al. questionnaire. The Addiction Research Center Inventory (ARCI) was developed to assess the characteristics of several test drugs, one of which was LSD.

Recently, with new human studies taking place in Europe and the United States, the ARCI is again being used, as are two newer instruments, the Hallucinogen Rating Scale (HRS), developed by our New Mexico group, and the APZ, a Swiss instrument.

Linton-Langs Scale

The Linton-Langs scale (Linton & Langs, 1962) was drafted by reviewing the LSD literature and papers on the psychoanalytic theory of altered states of consciousness. A preliminary version of the scale was administered to the researchers and their colleagues who took LSD. The scale was modified based upon their experiences.

Experimental subjects were male professional actors with no previous hallucinogen experience, who were told neither what drug they were to receive nor what the effects might be. Thirty subjects received 100 µg LSD, and 20 separate subjects received placebo. The questionnaire was administered by the research team the day before, several times during, and the day after the drug/placebo session. There were 74 response items, scored 0 (*no*), ½ (*somewhat* or *a little*), or 1 (*yes*). Disagreements between raters were settled by discussion.

Sixty-three of the 74 questions significantly discriminated between LSD and placebo. A priori scales were developed, clustering items that were thought relevant to the same psychic area of function. These 16 scales were labeled, for example, "distortions of visual perception," "disturbance of time sense," "body image change," "somatic symptoms," and "suspiciousness." Four "empirical" scales were then developed from the experimental data, factoring questions that showed a high degree of correlation. These four factors, or "scales," were a heterogeneous collection of items labeled "A," "B," "C," and "D." For example, Scale A contained items related to "impaired control of attention," "loss of inhibition," "elation," and "subjective feelings of having new powers of insight."

This scale was used by other investigators with LSD (Johnson, 1969) and for other hallucinogens (Faillace, Vourlekis, & Szara, 1967).

Abramson et al. Scale

The Abramson et al. questionnaire (Abramson et al., 1955) was developed in 1955 by reviewing the literature on LSD. It contained 47 items and was administered to subjects by a member of the experimental team several times during drug sessions. Responses initially were scored 0–5, but for data analytic purposes were later converted to 0 or 1, indicating the presence or absence of a given symptom.

Twenty-six men and women paid volunteer "nonpsychotic" adult subjects were used in the development of the questionnaire. Subjects received saline placebo, 25 to 75 µg LSD (low dose) or 100 to 225 mcg LSD (high dose). Sessions took place in groups of two to four subjects, with different doses the rule among subjects; that is, placebo subjects might be in the same room with high-dose subjects.

Questions focused primarily on subjective somatic and perceptual symptoms, such as dizziness, unsteadiness, sweating, paresthesias, blurred vision, inner trembling, and weakness. Only 5 of their 47 questions differentiated between the high dose and placebo, perhaps due to the unusual nature of the placebo group interacting with high-dose subjects (Cheek & Holstein, 1971).

Groups of questions were clustered in an a priori manner among "physiological," "perceptual," and "cognitive" categories. No attempt was made to generate factors by factor analytic methods. Subsequent papers by these investigators (Jarvik et al., 1955) modified the questionnaire, using a 0–3 scoring system (but still scoring all "positive" answers equally) and adding 12 questions.

This rating scale was used at the Addiction Research Center in Kentucky (Isbell & Logan, 1957), where several questions were included in the development of the Addiction Research Center Inventory.

Addiction Research Center Inventory

The most frequently used rating scale for drug effects is the Addiction Research Center Inventory (Haertzen & Hickey, 1987; Haertzen, Hill, & Belleville, 1963; Hill et al., 1963a; Hill, Haertzen, Wolbach, & Miner, 1963b). This is a 550-item, true-false test whose development began in 1958. The scale was drafted from data obtained from detoxified opiate addicts serving prison terms for violations of narcotics laws.

The results of 200 sentence completion responses made under no-drug, placebo, and various drug states, some MMPI questions, and items from other contemporary rating scales generated 3,300 questions. Treatments in the initial ARCI study included no-drug, saline placebo, two doses of LSD, chlorpromazine, amphetamine, pentobarbital, two doses of pyrahexyl (a marijuana-like compound), morphine, and alcohol. A "judgment process" reduced the number of items to 550 (Haertzen & Hickey, 1987).

A priori "general" categories were first developed, consisting of "interests and drives," "sensation and perception," "bodily symptoms and processes," and "feelings and attitudes." "Empirical drug" scales were then developed by assessing which items generated significantly more positive responses for each drug compared with placebo. These scales had the disadvantage of showing extensive overlap among items; that is, they indicated more of a general drug effect than being able to discriminate among different drugs. For this purpose, "group variability" scales were then generated (Haertzen, 1966).

Data were examined for all items over the 11 conditions just described, and five patterns emerged. Questions were chosen that typified these five patterns, and these were placed into the group variability scales. These were named "morphine-Benzedrine (MBG)," "pentobarbital-chlorpromazine-alcohol (PCAG)," "LSD (LG)," "alcohol (AG)," and "Benzedrine (BG)."

The MBG scale concerns euphoria; the PCAG scale, fatigue and decreased motivation; the LG scale, anxiety, tension, depersonalization, and changes in perception and sensation (the "dysphoria" items); the AG scale, "high" feelings; and the BG scale, a sense of enhanced intellectual efficiency. These group variability scales therefore reflect effects of specific drugs, or features shared by certain drugs, rather than effects on particular psychological functions such as cognition or perception. For example, drugs are more or less "morphine-like" or "LSD-like."

Several short forms of the ARCI are more commonly used than the full version and are capable of distinguishing among drugs if adequate doses are given (Sullivan et al., 1992). The ARCI has been used to characterize the effects of other hallucinogens besides LSD, including DMT (Rosenberg, Isbell, Miner, & Logan, 1964).

APZ Scale

The Swiss APZ (Abnormer Psychischer Zustände; altered states of consciousness) scale was developed to test the hypothesis that altered states of consciousness possess etiology-independent invariant elements. Eight hundred original questions were formulated based on previously existing rating scales for altered states, "free reports," other psychiatric rating scales, and the author's personal experience with altered states. These were reduced to 158 items, with a yes-no choice, and pilot data generated in a series of experiments using four drug- and nondrug induction methods:

1. "Hallucinogens of the first order": oral THC (tetrahydrocannabinol—one of the most psychoactive constituents of marijuana/hashish), 0.25 mg/kg; intramuscular DMT, 0.25 mg/kg; and oral psilocybin.
2. Inhaled nitrous oxide, a "hallucinogen of the second order."
3. "Psychological deprivation in a broader sense," including "perceptual deprivation" (presumably in an isolation apparatus), "hypnagogic" states, autogenic training, and hypnosis.
4. "Sensory overload," sensory bombardment with extremely variable stimuli.

A total of 393 normal volunteers generated pilot data for the APZ, which was self-administered before and after an altered state or control treatment. Several factor analytic methods were applied to these data, and 72 items were found to significantly differentiate all four treatments from control conditions. A general altered state of consciousness factor, Veränderter Wachbewusstseinszustand (VWB), was generated. Three subscales emerged from further factor analytic processing of the data and are most commonly used in reporting data.

These subscales are Ozeanische Selbstentgrenzung (OSE; Oceanic Boundlessness), which measures pleasant ecstatic experiences and feelings of eternity and unity; Angstvolle Ichauflösung (AIA; Dread of Ego Dissolution), reflecting a disintegrative anxious state, thought to correspond to what is commonly referred to as a "bad trip"; and Visionäre Umstrukturierung (VUS; Visionary Restructuralization), hallucinatory phenomena, as well as nonvisual experiences of altered meaning and significance (Dittrich, 1994).

Although these subscales were derived factor analytically rather than clinically, a content analysis of randomly selected clinical reports, using blind raters, demonstrated significant correlations between clinical reports and APZ scores.

A larger study of 1,133 normal volunteers in six countries was performed in subjects recruited by asking if they had experienced an altered state of consciousness within the past 12 months. They were asked to answer the APZ recollecting their most recent altered state. This was marijuana/hashish for 44% of the subjects; LSD, 8.5%; meditation, 7.6%; and hypnagogic states, 5.6%. Similar results to those from the pilot study emerged with respect to a single "altered state" factor, as well as confirming the existence of the three subscales.

A German-language psychometrically improved version of the APZ has been reported, as has another instrument by the same author that measures Vigilance Reduction and Auditive Alteration (Dittrich, 1998).

Hallucinogen Rating Scale

We developed the Hallucinogen Rating Scale, a self-administered instrument, for our studies in New Mexico. A preliminary version was drafted based on interviews with 19 experienced psychedelic users who had also used DMT, usually in the smoked freebase form. These individuals were familiar with the full range of the psychedelic experience, including their positive, sought-after aspects. This was important because older rating scales, including the benchmark ARCI, give little reason to expect that these drugs are at all reinforcing, contrary to thousands of years of field data and more than a hundred years of clinical data to the contrary. During pilot work with the HRS, we added and dropped various questions from the original items developed from the interviews with our DMT informants.

The first version of the HRS consisted of 126 items, many of which were repeated in the instrument to assess effects during the initial, middle, and late stages of the DMT intoxication. This repetition, resulting in a required 233 responses, made answering the questionnaire laborious and confusing and made analyses unduly complex. We therefore analyzed the initial data using the highest score for each item among these three stages. In addition, subsequent versions of the HRS present items only once and request respondents to answer for the most intensely they experienced any particular descriptor. Questions are answered using a 0–4 scale (*not at all* to *extremely*).

The original HRS data were generated during our DMT dose-response study. In this experiment, 12 volunteers with a history of previous psychedelic use, who were otherwise physically and psychiatrically normal, received four doses of DMT and saline placebo in a double-blind, randomized design. The rating scale was administered after DMT effects had resolved, usually 30 to 60 minutes after administration.

We studied experienced hallucinogens users, who were well-prepared and highly motivated to receive DMT in a clinical research environment. We believed that those who are familiar with these drugs could best observe and describe their effects utilizing previous experiences to fully fill out the nuances of their psychological properties. We also knew how extraordinarily rigorous it would be to take psychedelic doses of DMT on a busy hospital research ward, as well as needing to provide biological samples and fill out a rating scale. Experienced users, especially those we determined by history capable of managing dysphoric reactions in previous informal use, also would be less likely to panic in the noxious clinical research environment.

The doses of DMT were 0.05, 0.1, 0.2, and 0.4 mg/kg administered intravenously. Clinically, the 0.2- and 0.4-mg/kg doses were uniformly experienced by our sophisticated group of volunteers as fully hallucinogenic, the 0.4-mg/kg dose usually being the most intense psychedelic experience of the volunteer's life. The 0.1-mg/kg dose was subhallucinogenic, but it elicited physical and emotional symptoms that were usually somewhat dysphoric. The 0.05-mg/kg dose was occasionally mistaken for placebo and, at most, generated mild and pleasant emotional and somatic effects.

Before volunteers entered into the full dose-response study, they first received low and high doses, nonblind, on consecutive days, to screen out volunteers who found the setting or drug effect aversive. During these preliminary sessions, volunteers and the research team spent as much time as necessary reviewing the questionnaire to clarify any ambiguities or questions the volunteer might have in answering items. Once familiar with it, volunteers required less than 10 minutes to fill it out. The most recent version of the HRS (3.06) contains 100 questions, as well as several additional items being tested for inclusion to subsequent versions.

Using data from the DMT dose-response study, 75 of the 126 items demonstrated a significant drug effect compared with placebo. We then clustered these 75 items into six groups using two a priori methods. One was based on a clinical mental status approach, along the lines of what students are taught in their medical school psychiatry clerkships:

questions assessing mood and affect, thought processes and content, and sensory experiences. This model was substantially influenced by a system of Buddhist psychology known as Abhidharma (Strassman & Galanter, 1980).

Abhidharma can be translated as "collection of states." This system of Buddhist theory and practice focuses on mental states: positive, neutral, and negative ones, how they can be modified by particular meditation practices, and the role and qualities of a suitable meditation teacher. One of the most useful teachings of this field is its deconstruction of conscious experience into what are called *skandhas*, or "heaps," the constituents of that ongoing experience. There are five *skandhas*, seamlessly sewn together in such a way as to produce the impression of a separate, cohesive self with its own unique subjective reality.

These are form, which refers to the experience of the body; feeling, referring to emotional/affective factors; consciousness, which refers to cognitive faculties; perception, referring to all sensory modalities; and habitual tendencies, or volition, that which we experience as free will but that more accurately relates to the accumulation of past causes and effects that results in a sense of efficacy in decision making.

We placed groups of HRS items into these five categories, naming them Somaesthesia, Affect, Consciousness, Perception, and Volition, respectively. To these we added a sixth, "Intensity," a global measure of how powerfully modified was the overall state of consciousness. We called these groupings "clinical clusters." We also performed various factor analyses on the data and found that a principal components factor analysis with a VARIMAX rotation, setting the factors to six (corresponding in number to the clinical clusters described previously), provided the best fit.

A comparison of results generated by using either the clinical clusters or the principal components factors showed comparable sensitivity in distinguishing among various doses of DMT and placebo. The principal components factors accounted for only a slightly greater amount of the variability in the data set than did the clinical clusters. Because the clinical clusters provided conceptually meaningful sets of items with a goodness of fit comparable to the principal components factors, we decided to utilize the clinical clusters method of scoring the HRS (Strassman et al., 1994).

The HRS has been used to study several different drugs: MDMA (Tancer & Johanson, 2001); the MDMA-congener MDE (Gouzoulis-Mayfrank et al., 1999); methamphetamine (Gouzoulis-Mayfrank et al., 1999); the DMT-containing brew ayahuasca (Riba, Rodriguez-Fornells, Urbano, et al., 2001; Riba, Rodriguez-Fornells, Strassman, et al., 2001); the serotonin agonist *m*-CPP (Tancer & Johanson, 2001); psilocybin (Gouzoulis-Mayfrank et al., 1999); and ketamine (Bowdle et al., 1998; Krupitsky, Burakov, Romanov, Grinenko, & Strassman, 2001).

The HRS has several features that support its value in characterizing and quantifying hallucinogenic drug effects.

1. It was drafted from informal reports of, and research data generated from, experienced hallucinogen users who found these drugs reinforcing. The Abramson et al. and Linton-Langs instruments were designed using results obtained from drug-naive controls, and the ARCI studied narcotics-preferring prisoners. Neither of these groups can provide as detailed a picture of psychedelics' effects as those individuals with extensive and generally ego-syntonic experiences with them. In addition, our volunteers were well prepared for the effects of DMT. This allowed subjects to carefully observe and report on drug effects rather than utilizing all their psychological resources to maintain equilibrium in the face of an unexpected and unusual experience.
2. The HRS was designed specifically to assess psychedelic effects, similar to the Linton-Langs and Abramson et al. scales. The ARCI used several different drugs, and the APZ also employed various methods for inducing altered states. In the case of the APZ, some of the drugs, while referred to as hallucinogenic, may not have been so because doses were too low. In addition, it was designed to assess altered states in general rather than those produced by hallucinogens in particular. Thus, the HRS encompasses the fullest range of possible psychedelic experiences.
3. HRS data were generated from four doses of DMT and placebo. This provides greater sensitivity to subtle dose effects than scales derived from one or two doses of drug.
4. The use of a mental status, meditation-based approach places drug effects on consciousness into a value-free but clinically relevant context, with wide generalizability. That is, instead of metadescriptors, such as "oceanic boundlessness" or "loss of inhibition," responses are measured within the basic building blocks of mental states, which, when blended together, produce the full spectrum of ongoing subjective experience.

There have been several studies using the HRS in combination with either the APZ or the ARCI. Riba, Rodriguez-Fornells, Strassman, et al. (2001) compared the HRS and ARCI in assessing ayahuasca effects in normal volunteers. There were significant but modest correlations between the Perception and Somaesthesia HRS clinical clusters with the ARCI LSD scale. In addition, the HRS Intensity cluster correlated positively with the ARCI stimulant (MBG) scale.

Tancer and Johanson (2001) used the HRS and ARCI to assess effects of MDMA and *m*-CPP, with the HRS yielding what appears to be greater sensitivity to drug effects than the ARCI. One anomalous finding is that the middle dose of MDMA, 110 mg/70 kg, elicited fewer significant effects on HRS clinical clusters than did the lowest, 75 mg/70 kg, dose.

Gouzoulis-Mayfrank et al. (1999) used both the APZ and the HRS to assess subjective responses to MDE, psilocybin (0.2 mg/kg, most likely a subpsychedelic dose), and methamphetamine. Correlations between scores of the two scales were not performed. Five of six HRS scales demonstrated significant differences between psilocybin and placebo, and between MDE and placebo, and Perception differentiated between psilocybin and MDE. The total APZ score, and each subscale, differentiated between psilocybin and placebo, and between MDE and placebo; total score and "bad trip" subscale differentiated between psilocybin and MDE. No subscale of either instrument satisfactorily distinguished between methamphetamine and any other condition, including placebo.

Subjective Effects of DMT:
Results of New Mexico Studies

We gave a solution of DMT fumarate by means of a 30-second infusion, followed by a 15-second flush of the line with sterile saline. Psychological responses to DMT peaked at about 2 minutes after completing the saline flush, began resolving thereafter, and were barely noticeable by 30 minutes.

Quite marked was the "rush" of IV DMT. Nearly all subjects reported this within 5 to 10 seconds from the beginning of the infusion. This was an overwhelming torrent of experience that completely replaced previously held mental contents. A sense of mounting inner tension and vibration, accompanied by a high-pitched sound, was associated with intense visual hallucinatory effects. This rush climaxed in the feeling that consciousness had separated from the body. Once the rush began resolving, DMT effects were rather similar to those reported in the literature and described by our initial cohort of DMT respondents.

In addition to using the HRS, we also found it of interest to classify sessions using three clinically descriptive categories—personal, invisible, and transpersonal—to capture the most salient content of the sessions. Personal sessions primarily stayed within the realm of body-based feelings and mind-based thoughts. They were qualitatively not much different than what one might see in effective depth psychotherapy: abreaction; enhanced recall of, and emotional responses to, memories; controlled regression; magnified transference feelings and thoughts; and the working through of present-day or historical conflicted material.

Transpersonal sessions contained near-death and mystical experiences. These were the types of effects both the volunteers and the research team were expecting and seeking, but they were relatively uncommon, at least in "pure culture." That is, they rarely occurred alone or as the predominant material in drug sessions. When they were experienced, they were part of the more complex "invisible" sessions.

Invisible sessions tapped into some of the most fascinating, but at the same time most perplexing, findings of our research. Volunteers reported what they believed were "freestanding" realities, "more real than real," an apperception of planes of existence coexisting with this one. Most unsettling, for both us and our volunteers, were descriptions of contact with "beings"—conscious, intelligent, interactive entities that, no matter how hard we tried to interpret as "something else," remained fixed in the subjects' minds as undeniably existent as such. In fact, some of the "alien abduction" literature is extraordinarily similar to these types of DMT experiences (Mack, 1994).

More than half of our 60 volunteers experienced at least some "invisible" material. This was a quite unexpectedly high prevalence, despite my having some forewarning from our preliminary interviews with DMT informants that they might occur. Some of the most speculative and far-reaching conclusions we arrived at regarding DMT's properties revolve around explicating the frequency, intensity, and "reality" of these types of sessions. For example, if these "encounters" are perceptions of freestanding, independent phenomena, rather than being "only" brain generated, this suggests a "receiving" rather than solely "data-generating" role of the brain in its relationship to consciousness. In addition, we considered possible "locations" of the content of these experiences and refer to contemporary cosmological theories regarding parallel universes and dark matter.

The occurrence of "invisible" sessions actually is described in the older DMT literature (Boszormenyi & Szara, 1958; Turner & Merlis, 1959) and contrasts with published reports of the effects of other hallucinogens. This suggests a unique pharmacology of DMT.

In addition, the intravenous route, which caused reactions to DMT to develop so swiftly, may have played a role in the our seeing a high prevalence of these experiences in our studies. Volunteers were unable to manipulate effects through their will, thus producing a more "pure" pharmacological effect, rather than one modified even minimally by personal psychology.

Finally, we used high doses, ones that bordered on inducing a delirium in some of our volunteers. However, few subjects, in retrospect, would have preferred lower doses, and some even suggested a higher dose would have been welcome.

Future Directions

It does not seem as if there are an especially large number of questions remaining in the area of methodology of assessing subjective effects of psychedelics. Rather, it is the application of these unique states that is the next frontier in clinical research.

Available rating scales, especially the newer and less biased HRS and APZ, along with careful clinical observation, now can adequately describe and measure effects of both newer and older psychedelics. Many tryptamine and phenethylamine analogs were administered in previous human studies, but sample sizes were small and a wide variety of rating scales used (Angrist, Rosen, & Gershon, 1974; Cholden et al., 1955; Eisner & Cohen, 1958; Isbell, Miner, et al., 1959; Jarvik et al. 1955). Quantifying effects of these psychedelic congeners will generate a more usable database for subsequent research.

For these normative data, it is necessary to recruit volunteers that are healthy, stable, and experienced with hallucinogens. It is also crucial to provide an optimal setting, or psychological and physical environment, to allow the full development of drug effects. To ignore the setting factor is to disregard much of what was learned from the first 30 years of clinical investigations.

Once characterization of subjective effects of particular compounds is available, it will be possible to proceed to correlative and mechanism-of-action studies that elucidate biological underpinnings of these effects. These data will aid structure-activity research for development of drugs with unique effects on consciousness. Such investigations will help us understand better the nature and structure of brain-consciousness dynamics.

Current clinical research emphasizing the "psychotomimetic" effects of psychedelics may be better served by reporting effects on, for example, cognitive, emotional, or volitional faculties rather than attempting to force a complex syndrome into a mold ("model psychosis") that may not be an exact fit. This approach would be more scientifically honest and would lessen unnecessary contentiousness between proponents of any particular model.

We ought to begin considering the application of the psychological effects of psychedelics to human conditions. Psychopathological syndromes with defects in particular mental constructs might be modifiable through psychedelic psychopharmacotherapies. Post-traumatic stress disorders, to use one example, may benefit from psychotherapeutic treatments that adjunctively utilize the ability of psychedelics to de-repress memories and generate visual symbolization of conflicts and affects in ways that are interpretable and manageable. The treatment of psychosomatic disorders, in which the body nonverbally and unconsciously absorbs and holds onto psychic conflicts, also may benefit from psychedelic-enhanced mental imagery, abreaction, and associative cognitive processes.

The unique properties of psychedelics also could be applied to problem solving, as was done in previous creativity research. The loosening of associative processes seen with low to medium doses of psychedelics, visualization of conceptual problems, and general sense of "inspiration" all may reliably stimulate the imagination.

Although there exists substantial resistance on the part of both religious and scientific communities to "clinical spirituality" research, there clearly are significant overlapping characteristics of the mystical, near-death, and psychedelic states. Determining what are the psychedelic aspects of the mystical and near-death experiences, as well as the mystical and near-death aspects of the psychedelic experience, could provide valuable leverage in studying, understanding, and reliably inducing particularly useful and desired experiences in those with an interest and context for supporting them.

In this era of "cosmetic psychopharmacology," where feeling better than normal is increasingly acceptable, the "recreational," or "ludibund" properties of the psychedelics are of great interest. With the ever-increasing threats associated with world travel, ways in which we can inwardly journey to highly exotic inner landscapes may take on growing importance.

Finally, the "entity contact" experiences of our volunteers, their resemblance to "endogenous" contact experiences in popular literature and in older, more mythological and legendary literature may shed light on a particularly enigmatic phenomenon, one that certainly predates the age of spaceships and aliens. The ability to induce such experiences may allow us to begin developing a consensus about their characteristics, their cross-cultural generalizability, and the development of models to understand them.

We are poised at a particularly exciting moment in the resumption of clinical research with psychedelics. I hope we have learned from the mistakes of the first wave of research and will build upon its successes. Many of the questions that could not be adequately answered before clinical research with these drugs ceased can be revisited, and more sophisticated tools and concepts applied to them. It will be extraordinarily important to keep the actual subjective effects of these drugs in the forefront of any new research models and to avoid the premature closure that accompanies inflexible insistence on what those effects represent. In this way, it will be easier to maintain focus on how best to study psychedelics and apply their effects to some of our most difficult theoretical and clinical concerns.

Appendix: Hallucinogen Rating Scale

1. Amount of time between when the drug was administered and feeling an effect:
   Not applicable, no effect 0–5 secs 5–15 secs 15–30 secs 30–60 secs
   More 1 minute

2. A "rush"
Not at all slightly Moderately Very Much Extremely

2a. Location of rush:

3. Change in salivation
Not at all slightly Moderately Very Much Extremely

3a. Drier, wetter, or both (circle one)
Not at all slightly Moderately Very Much Extremely

4. Body feels different
Not at all slightly Moderately Very Much Extremely

4a. Please describe
Not at all slightly Moderately Very Much Extremely

5. Change in sense of body weight
Not at all slightly Moderately Very Much Extremely

5a. Lighter, heavier, or both (circle one)
Not at all slightly Moderately Very Much Extremely

6. Feel as moving/falling/flying through space
Not at all slightly Moderately Very Much Extremely

7. Change in body temperature
Not at all slightly Moderately Very Much Extremely

8. Electric/tingling feeling
Not at all slightly Moderately Very Much Extremely

9. Pressure or weight change in chest or abdomen
Not at all slightly Moderately Very Much Extremely

10. Shaky feelings inside
Not at all slightly Moderately Very Much Extremely

11. Feel body shake/tremble
Not at all slightly Moderately Very Much Extremely

12. Feel heart beating
Not at all slightly Moderately Very Much Extremely

13. Feel heart skipping beats or irregular
Not at all slightly Moderately Very Much Extremely

14. Nausea
Not at all slightly Moderately Very Much Extremely

15. Physically comfortable
Not at all slightly Moderately Very Much Extremely

16. Physically restless
Not at all slightly Moderately Very Much Extremely

17. Flushed
Not at all slightly Moderately Very Much Extremely

18. Urge to urinate
Not at all slightly Moderately Very Much Extremely

19. Urge to move bowels
Not at all slightly Moderately Very Much Extremely

20. Sexual feelings
Not at all slightly Moderately Very Much Extremely

21. Feel removed, detached, separated from body
Not at all slightly Moderately Very Much Extremely

22. Change in skin sensitivity
Not at all slightly Moderately Very Much Extremely

22a. More sensitive, less sensitive, or both

23. Sweating
Not at all slightly Moderately Very Much Extremely

24. Headache
Not at all slightly Moderately Very Much Extremely

25. Anxious
Not at all slightly Moderately Very Much Extremely

26. Frightened
Not at all slightly Moderately Very Much Extremely

27. Panic
Not at all slightly Moderately Very Much Extremely

27a. Self-accepting
Not at all slightly Moderately Very Much Extremely

27b. Forgiving your self or others
Not at all slightly Moderately Very Much Extremely

28. At ease
Not at all slightly Moderately Very Much Extremely

29. Feeling like laughing
Not at all slightly Moderately Very Much Extremely

30. Excited
Not at all slightly Moderately Very Much Extremely

31. Awe, amazement
Not at all slightly Moderately Very Much Extremely

31a. Understanding other's feelings
Not at all slightly Moderately Very Much Extremely

32. Safe
Not at all slightly Moderately Very Much Extremely

33. Feel presence of numinous force, higher power, God
Not at all slightly Moderately Very Much Extremely

34. Change in feeling about sounds in room
Not at all slightly Moderately Very Much Extremely

34a. More pleasant, less pleasant, or both (circle one)

35. Happy
Not at all slightly Moderately Very Much Extremely

36. Sad
Not at all slightly Moderately Very Much Extremely

36a. Loving
Not at all slightly Moderately Very Much Extremely

37. Euphoria
Not at all slightly Moderately Very Much Extremely

38. Despair
Not at all slightly Moderately Very Much Extremely

39. Feel like crying
Not at all slightly Moderately Very Much Extremely

40. Change in feeling of closeness to people in room
Not at all slightly Moderately Very Much Extremely

40a. Less close, more close, or both (circle one)

41. Change in "amount" of emotions
Not at all slightly Moderately Very Much Extremely

41a. Less emotional, more emotional, or both (circle one)

42. Emotions seem different from usual
Not at all slightly Moderately Very Much Extremely

43. Feel at one with universe
Not at all slightly Moderately Very Much Extremely

44. Feel isolated from people/things
Not at all slightly Moderately Very Much Extremely

45. Feel reborn
Not at all slightly Moderately Very Much Extremely

46. Satisfaction with the experience
Not at all slightly Moderately Very Much Extremely

47. Like the experience
Not at all slightly Moderately Very Much Extremely

48. How much would you like to repeat the experience
Never again slightly Moderately Very Much Extremely

49. Desire for the experience regularly
Not at all slightly Moderately Very Much Extremely

50. An odor
Not at all slightly Moderately Very Much Extremely

50a. Please describe:

51. A taste
Not at all slightly Moderately Very Much Extremely

51a. Please describe:

52. A sound or sounds accompanying the experience
Not at all slightly Moderately Very Much Extremely

52a. Please describe:

53. Sense of silence or deep sleep
Not at all slightly Moderately Very Much Extremely

54. Sounds in room sound different
Not at all slightly Moderately Very Much Extremely

55. Change in distinctiveness of sounds
Not at all slightly Moderately Very Much Extremely

55a. Less distinct, more distinct or both (circle one)

56. Auditory synesthesia ("hearing" visual or other nonauditory perception)
Not at all slightly Moderately Very Much Extremely

57. Visual effects
Not at all slightly Moderately Very Much Extremely

58. Room looks different
Not at all slightly Moderately Very Much Extremely

59. Change in brightness of objects in room
Don't know, eyes closed Not at all slightly Moderately Very Much
Extremely

59a. Brighter, duller, or both (circle one)

60. Change in visual distinctness of objects in room
Don't know, eyes closed Not at all slightly Moderately Very Much
Extremely

60a. Sharper, blurrier or both (circle one)

61. Room overlaid with visual patterns
Don't know, eyes closed Not at all slightly Moderately Very Much
Extremely

62. Eyes open visual field vibrating or jiggling
Don't know, eyes closed Not at all slightly Moderately Very Much
Extremely

63. Visual synesthesia ("seeing" sound or other nonvisual perception)
Not at all slightly Moderately Very Much Extremely

64. Visual images, visions, or hallucinations (can include only geometric
abstract patterns)
Not at all slightly Moderately Very Much Extremely

65. Kaleidoscopic nature of images/visions/hallucinations
Not applicable, none seen Not at all slightly Moderately Very Much
Extremely

66. Difference in brightness of visions compared to usual daylight vision
Not applicable, none seen Not at all slightly Moderately Very Much
Extremely

67. Dimensionally of images/visions/hallucinations
Not applicable, none seen Not at all slightly Moderately Very Much
Extremely

68. Movement within visions/hallucinations
Not applicable, none seen Not at all slightly Moderately Very Much
Extremely

69. White light
Not at all slightly Moderately Very Much Extremely

70. Feel as if dead or dying
Not at all slightly Moderately Very Much Extremely

71. Sense of speed
Not at all slightly Moderately Very Much Extremely

72. Déjà vu (that you have experienced this *exact* situation, even with no
real memory of it)
Not at all slightly Moderately Very Much Extremely

73. Jemais vu (that you experience this exact situation in the future)
Not at all slightly Moderately Very Much Extremely

74. Contradictory feelings at the same time (happy and sad; hopeful and
hopeless)
Not at all slightly Moderately Very Much Extremely

75. Sense of chaos
Not at all slightly Moderately Very Much Extremely

76. Change in strength of sense of self
Not at all slightly Moderately Very Much Extremely

76a. More strongly, less strongly, or both (circle one)

77. New thoughts of insights
Not at all slightly Moderately Very Much Extremely

78. Memories of childhood
Not at all slightly Moderately Very Much Extremely

79. Feel like a child
Not at all slightly Moderately Very Much Extremely

80. Change in rate of thinking
Not at all slightly Moderately Very Much Extremely

80a. Faster, slower, or both (circle one)

81. Change in quality of thinking
Not at all slightly Moderately Very Much Extremely

81a. Sharper, duller, or both (circle one)

82. Difference in feeling of reality of experiences compared to everyday experience
Not at all slightly Moderately Very Much Extremely

83. Dreamlike nature of the experiences
Not at all slightly Moderately Very Much Extremely

84. Thoughts of present or recent past personal life
Not at all slightly Moderately Very Much Extremely

85. Insights into personal or occupational concerns
Not at all slightly Moderately Very Much Extremely

86. Change in rate of time passing
Not at all slightly Moderately Very Much Extremely

86a. Passing faster, slower, or both (circle one)

87. Unconscious
Definitely not Not sure Definitely yes

87. Change in sense of sanity
Not at all slightly Moderately Very Much Extremely

88a. More sane, less sane, or both (circle one)

89. Urge to close eyes
Not at all slightly Moderately Very Much Extremely

90. Change in effort breathing
Not at all slightly Moderately Very Much Extremely

90a. Breathing more relaxed, more difficult, or both (circle one)

91. Able to follow the sequence of effects
Not at all slightly Moderately Very Much Extremely

92. Able to "let go"
Not at all slightly Moderately Very Much Extremely

93. Able to focus attention
Not at all slightly Moderately Very Much Extremely

94. In control
Not at all slightly Moderately Very Much Extremely

95. Able to move around if asked to do so
Not at all slightly Moderately Very Much Extremely

96. Able to remind yourself of being in a research room,
being administered a drug, the temporary nature of the experience
Not at all slightly Moderately Very Much Extremely

97. Waxing and waning of the experience
Not at all slightly Moderately Very Much Extremely

98. Intensity
   Not at all slightly Moderately Very Much Extremely

99. High
   Not at all slightly Moderately Very Much Extremely

100. Dose you think you received
   Not at all slightly Moderately Very Much Extremely

Any other comments?

References

Abramson, H. A. (Ed.). (1967). *The use of LSD in psychotherapy and alcoholism*. New York: Bobs-Merrill.

Abramson, H. A., Jarvik, M. E., Kaufman, M. R., Kornetsky, C., Levine, A., & Wagner, M. (1955). Lysergic acid diethylamide (LSD-25). I. Physiological and perceptual responses. *Journal of Psychology, 39*, 3–60.

Abuzzahab, F. S., Sr., & Anderson, B. J. (1971). A review of LSD treatment in alcoholism. *International Pharmacopsychiatry, 6*, 223–235.

Aghajanian, G. K., & Bing, O. H. L. (1964). Persistence of lysergic acid diethylamide in the plasma of human subjects. *Clinical Pharmacology and Therapeutics, 5*, 611–614.

Alper, K. R., Lotsof, H. S., Frenken, G. M. N., Luciano, D. J., & Bastiaans, J. (1999). Treatment of acute opioid withdrawal with ibogaine. *American Journal on Addictions, 8*, 234–242.

Angrist, B., Rosen, J., & Gershon, S. (1974). Assessment of tolerance to the hallucinogenic effects of DOM. *Psychopharmacology, 36*, 203–207.

Aronson, H., Silverstein, A. B., & Klee, G. D. (1959). Influence of lysergic acid diethylamide (LSD-25) on subjective time. *Archives of General Psychiatry, 1*, 469–472.

Belleville, R. (1956). MMPI score changes induced by lysergic acid diethylamide. *Journal of Clinical Psychology, 12*, 279–282.

Bender, L. (1966). D-lysergic acid in the treatment of the biological features of childhood schizophrenia. *Diseases of the Nervous System, S22*, 43–46.

Bercel, N. A., Travis, L. E., Olinger, L. B., & Dreikurs, E. (1956). Model psychoses induced by LSD-25 in normals. II. Rorschach test findings. *Archives of Neurology and Psychiatry, 75*, 612–618.

Boszormenyi, Z. (1960). Creative urge as an after effect of model psychoses. *Confinia Psychiatrica, 3*, 117–126.

Boszormenyi, Z., & Szara, S. I. (1958). Dimethyltryptamine experiments with psychotics. *Journal of Mental Science, 104*, 445–453.

Bottrill, J. H. (1969). Personality change in LSD users. *Journal of General Psychology, 80*, 157–161.

Bowdle, T. A., Radant, A. D., Cowley, D. S., Kharasch, E. D., Strassman, R. J., & Roy-Byrne, P. P. (1998). Psychedelic effects of ketamine in healthy volunteers: Relationship to steady-state plasma concentrations. *Anesthesiology, 88*, 82–88.

Bowers, M. B., Jr., & Freedman, D. X. (1966). "Psychedelic" experiences in acute psychoses. *Archives of General Psychiatry, 15*, 240–248.

Brandup, E., & Vanggard, T. (1977). LSD treatment in a severe case of compulsive neurosis. *Acta Psychiatrica Scandinavica, 55*, 127–141.

Buckman, J. (1969). Psychedelic drugs as adjuncts to analytic psychotherapy. In R. E. Hicks, P. J. Fink, & V. B. O. Hammett (Eds.), *Psychedelic drugs* (pp. 210–216). New York: Grune and Stratton.

Cerletti, A., & Rothlin, E. (1955). Role of 5–hydroxytryptamine in mental diseases and its antagonism by lysergic acid derivatives. *Nature, 176*, 785–786.

Cheek, F. E., & Holstein, C. M. (1971). Lysergic acid diethylamide tartrate (LSD-25) dosage levels, group differences, and social interaction. *Journal of Nervous and Mental Disease, 153*, 133–147.

Cholden, L. S., Kurland, A. A., & Savage, C. (1955). Clinical reactions and tolerance to LSD in chronic schizophrenia. *Journal of Nervous and Mental Disease, 122*, 211–221.

Cohen, S. (1965, November). LSD and the anguish of dying. *Harper's*, 69–78.

Controlled Substances Act, Public Law 91–153, 21 U.S.C. 801 et seq (1970).

Denber, H. C. B., & Merlis, S. (1955). Studies on mescaline. VI. Therapeutic aspects of the mescaline-chlorpromazine combination. *Journal of Nervous and Mental Disease, 122*, 463–469.

Dittrich, A. (1994). Psychological aspects of altered states of consciousness of the LSD type: Measurement of their basic dimensions and prediction of individual differences. In A. Pletscher & D. Ladewig (Eds.), *Fifty years of LSD: Current status and perspectives of hallucinogens* (pp. 101–118). New York: Parthenon.

Dittrich, A. (1998). The standardized psychometric assessment of altered states of consciousness (ASCs) in humans. *Pharmacopsychiatry, S2*, 80–84.

Edwards, A., & Cohen, S. (1961). Visual illusion, tactile sensibility and reaction time under LSD-25. *Psychopharmacology, 2*, 297–303.

Eisner, B. G. (1997). Set, setting, and matrix. *Journal of Psychoactive Drugs, 29*, 213–216.

Eisner, B. G., & Cohen, S. (1958). Psychotherapy with lysergic acid diethylamide. *Journal of Nervous and Mental Disease, 127*, 528–539.

Fabing, H. D. (1955). New blocking agent against the development of LSD-25 psychosis. *Science, 121*, 208–210.

Faillace, L. A., Vourlekis, A., & Szara, S. I. (1967). Clinical evaluation of some hallucinogenic tryptamine derivatives. *Journal of Nervous and Mental Disease, 145*, 306–313.

Fink, M., Simeon, J., Haque, W., & Itil, T. (1966). Prolonged adverse reactions to LSD in psychotic subjects. *Archives of General Psychiatry, 15*, 450–454.

Fischer, R., & Warshay, D. (1968). Psilocybin-induced autonomic, perceptual, and behavioral change. *Pharmakopsychiatrie Neuro-Psychopharmakologie, 1*, 291–302.

Fischer, R., Hill, R., Thatcher, K., & Scheib, J. (1970). Psilocybin-induced contraction of nearby visual space. *Agents and Actions, 1*, 190–197.

Forte, R. (Ed.). (1997). *Entheogens and the future of religion.* San Francisco: Council on Spiritual Practices.

Freedman, A. M., Ebin, E. V., & Wilson, E. A. (1962). Autistic schizophrenic children: An experiment in the use of D-lysergic acid diethylamide (LSD-25). *Archives of General Psychiatry, 6*, 203–213.

Freedman, D. X. (1961). Effects of LSD-25 on brain serotonin. *Journal of Pharmacology and Experimental Therapeutics, 134*, 160–166.

Gaddum, J. H., & Hameed, K. A. (1954). Drugs which antagonize 5–hydroxytryptamine. *British Journal of Pharmacology, 9*, 240–248.

Gewirtz, J. C., & Marek, G. J. (2000). Behavioral evidence for interactions between a hallucinogenic drug and group II metabotropic glutamate receptors. *Neuropsychopharmacology, 23*, 569–576.

Gillin, J. C., Kaplan, J., Stillman, R., & Wyatt, R. J. (1976). The psychedelic model of schizophrenia: The case of N,N-dimethyltryptamine. *American Journal of Psychiatry, 133*, 203–208.

Gouzoulis-Mayfrank, E., Habermeyer, E., Hermle, L., Steinmeyer, A. M., Kunert, H. J., & Sass, H. (1998). Hallucinogenic drug induced states resemble acute endogenous psychoses: Results of an empirical state. *European Psychiatry, 18*, 399–406.

Gouzoulis-Mayfrank, E., Heekeren, K., Thelen, B., Lindenblatt, H., Kovar, K. A., Sass, H., et al. (1998). Effects of the hallucinogen psilocybin on habituation and pre-pulse inhibition of the startle reflex in humans. *Behavioural Pharmacology, 9*, 561–566.

Gouzoulis-Mayfrank, E., Thelen, B., Habermeyer, E., Kunert, H. J., Kovar, K.-A., Lindenblatt, H., et al. (1999). Psychopathological, neuroendocrine and autonomic effects of 3,4–methylenedioxyethylamphetamine (MDE), psilocybin and *d*-methamphetamine in healthy volunteers. *Psychopharmacology, 142*, 41–50.

Gouzoulis-Mayfrank, E., Thelen, B., Maier, S., Heekeren, K., Kovar, K. A., Sass, H., et al. (2002). Effects of hallucinogen psilocybin on covert orienting of visual attention in humans. *Neuropsychobiology, 45*, 205–212.

Grinspoon, L., & Bakalar, J. B. (1979). *Psychedelic drugs reconsidered.* New York: Basic Books.

Grof, S., Goodman, L. E., Richards, W. A., & Kurland, A. A. (1973). LSD-assisted psychotherapy in patients with terminal cancer. *International Pharmacopsychiatry, 8*, 129–144.

Haertzen, C. A. (1966). Development of scales based on patterns of drug effects, using the Addiction Research Center Inventory (ARCI). *Psychological Reports, 18*, 163–194.

Haertzen, C. A., & Hickey, J. E. (1987). Addiction Research Center Inventory (ARCI): Measurement of euphoria and other drug effects. In J. A. Bozarth (Ed.), *Methods of assessing the reinforcing properties of abused drugs* (pp. 489–524). New York: Springer-Verlag.

Haertzen, C. A., Hill, H. E., & Belleville, R. E. (1963). Development of the Addiction Research Center Inventory (ARCI): Selection of items that are sensitive to the effects of various drugs. *Psychopharmacology, 4*, 155–166.

Harman, W. W., McKim, R. H., Mogar, R. E., Fadiman, J., & Stolaroff, M. J. (1966). Psychedelic agents in creative problem solving: A pilot study. *Psychological Reports, 19*, 211–227.

Haubrich, D. R., & Wang, P. F. L. (1977). N,N-Dimethyltryptamine lowers rat brain acetylcholine and dopamine. *Brain Research, 131*, 158–161.

Helsley, S., Rabin, R. A., & Winter, J. C. (2001). Drug discrimination studies with ibogaine. *Alkaloids Chemistry and Biology, 56*, 63–77.

Hermle, L., Gouzoulis-Mayfrank, E., & Spitzer, M. (1998). Blood flow and cerebral laterality in the mescaline model of psychosis. *Pharmacopsychiatry, S31*, 85–91.

Hill, H. E., Haertzen, C. A., Wolbach, A. B., Jr., & Miner, E. J. (1963a). The Addiction Research Center Inventory: Appendix. I. Items comprising empirical scales for seven drugs. II. Items which do not differentiate placebo from any drug condition. *Psychopharmacologia, 4*, 184–205.

Hill, H. E., Haertzen, C. A., Wolbach, A. B., Jr., & Miner, E. J. (1963b). The Addiction Research Center Inventory: Standardization of scales which evaluate subjective effects of morphine, amphetamine, pentobarbital, alcohol, LSD-25, pyrahexyl and chlorpromazine. *Psychopharmacologia, 4*, 167–183.

Hoch, P. H. (1956). Studies in routes of administration and counteracting drugs. In L. Cholden (Ed.), *Lysergic acid diethylamide and mescaline in experimental psychiatry* (pp. 8–12). New York: Grune and Stratton.

Hoch, P. H., Cattell, J. P., & Pennes, H. H. (1952). Effects of mescaline and lysergic acid diethylamide (d-LSD-25). *American Journal of Psychiatry, 108*, 579–584.

Hollister, L. E. (1962). Drug-induced psychoses and schizophrenic reactions: A critical comparison. *Annals of the New York Academy of Science, 96*, 80–92.

Hollister, L. E., Macnicol, M. F., & Gillespie, H. K. (1969). An hallucinogenic amphetamine analog (DOM) in man. *Psychopharmacology, 14*, 62–73.

Isbell, H. (1959). Comparison of the reactions induced by psilocybin and LSD-25 in man. *Psychopharmacology, 1*, 29–38.

Isbell, H., & Logan, C. R. (1957). Studies on the diethylamide of lysergic acid (LSD-25). II. The effects of chlorpromazine, azacyclonol, and reserpine on the intensity of the LSD reaction. *Archives of Neurology and Psychiatry, 77*, 350–358.

Isbell, H., Logan, C. R., & Miner, E. J. (1959). Studies on lysergic acid diethylamide (LSD-25). III. Attempts to attenuate the LSD-reaction in man by pretreatment with neurohumoral blocking agents. *Archives of Neurology and Psychiatry, 81*, 20–27.

Isbell, H., Miner, E. J., & Logan, C. R. (1959). Relationships of psychotomimetic to anti-serotonin potencies of congeners of lysergic acid diethylamide (LSD-25). *Psychopharmacology, 1*, 20–28.

James, W. (1997). *The varieties of religious experience*. New York: Macmillan.

Jansen, K. L. R. (1997). The ketamine model of the near-death experience: A central role for the N-methyl-D-aspartate receptor. *Journal of Near-Death Studies, 16*, 5–26.

Jansen, K. L. R. (2001). *Ketamine: Dreams and realities*. Sarasota, FL: Multidisciplinary Association for Psychedelic Studies.

Jarvik, M. E., Abramson, H. A., & Hirsch, M. W. (1955). Comparative subjective effects of seven drugs including lysergic acid diethylamide (LSD-25). *Journal of Abnormal and Social Psychology, 51*, 657–662.

Johnson, F. G. (1969). LSD in the treatment of alcoholism. *American Journal of Psychiatry, 126*, 481–487.

Kast, E. C., & Collins, V. J. (1964). Lysergic acid diethylamide as an analgesic agent. *Anesthesia and Analgesia, 43*, 285–291.

Klee, G. D., Bertino, J., Weintraub, W., & Callaway, E. (1961). The influence of varying dosage on the effects of lysergic acid diethylamide (LSD-25) in humans. *Journal of Nervous and Mental Disease, 132*, 404–409.

Krupitsky, E. M., Burakov, A. M., Romanov, T. N., Grinenko, A. Y., & Strassman, R. J. (2001). Ketamine-assisted psychotherapy (KPT) of heroin addiction: Immediate effects and six month follow-up. *Heffter Review of Psychedelic Research, 2*, 88–101.

Krus, D. M., Resnick, O., & Raskin, M. (1966). Apparent eye level test: Its background and use in psychopharmacology. *Archives of General Psychiatry, 14*, 419–427.

Kurland, A. A., Savage, C., Pahnke, W. N., Grof, S., & Olsson, J. E. (1971). LSD in the treatment of alcoholics. *Pharmakopsychiatrie Neuro-Psychopharmakologie, 4*, 83–94.

Kurland, A. A., Unger, S., Shaffer, J. W., & Savage, C. (1967). Psychedelic therapy using LSD in the treatment of the alcoholic patient: A preliminary report. *American Journal of Psychiatry, 123*, 1202–1209.

Langs, R. J., & Barr, H. L. (1968). Lysergic acid diethylamide (LSD-25) and schizophrenic reactions: A comparative study. *Journal of Nervous and Mental Disease, 147*, 163–172.

Lee, M. A., & Shlain, B. (1986). *Acid dreams: The complete social history of LSD, the CIA, the sixties, and beyond* (Rev. ed.). New York: Grove.

Lennard, H., Jarvik, M. E., & Abramson, H. A. (1956). Lysergic acid diethylamide (LSD-25). XII. A preliminary statement of its effects upon interpersonal communication. *Journal of Psychology, 41*, 185–198.

Linton, H. B., & Langs, R. J. (1962). Subjective reactions to lysergic acid diethylamide (LSD-25). *Archives of General Psychiatry, 6*, 352–368.

Luby, E. D., Gottlieb, J. S., Cohen, B. D., Rosenbaum, G., & Domino, E. F. (1962). Model psychoses and schizophrenia. *American Journal of Psychiatry, 119*, 61–67.

MacDonald, J. M., & Galvin, J. A. V. (1956). Experimental psychotic states. *American Journal of Psychiatry, 112*, 970–976.

Mack, J. E. (1994). *Abduction.* New York: Ballantine.

MacLean, J. R., MacDonald, D. C., Byrne, U. P., & Hubbard, A. M. (1961). The use of LSD-25 in the treatment of alcoholism and other psychiatric problems. *Quarterly Journal of Studies on Alcohol, 22*, 34–45.

Master, R., & Houston, J. (2000). *The varieties of the psychedelic experience.* Rochester, VT: Park Street Press.

McCall, R. B., & Aghajanian, G. K. (1980). Hallucinogens potentiate responses to serotonin and norepinephrine in the facial motor nucleus. *Life Sciences, 26*, 1149–1156.

Meltzer, H. Y., Wiita, B., Tricou, B. J., Simonovic, M., Fang, V. S., & Manov, G. (1982). Effects of serotonin precursors and serotonin agonists on plasma hormone levels. In B. T. Ho, J. C. Schoolar, & E. Usdin (Eds.), *Serotonin in biological psychiatry* (pp. 117–139). New York: Raven.

Moody, R. A. (1988). *Life after life* (Rev. ed.). New York: Bantam Books.

Naditch, M. P., Alker, P. C., & Joffe, P. (1975). Individual differences and setting as determinants of acute adverse reactions to psychoactive drugs. *Journal of Nervous and Mental Disease, 161*, 326–335.

Nichols, D. E. (1997). Role of serotonergic neurons and 5-HT receptors in the action of hallucinogens. In H. G. Baumgarten & M. Göthert (Eds.), *Handbook of experimental pharmacology: Serotoninergic neurons and 5-HT receptors in the CNS* (pp. 563–585). Heidelberg, Germany: Springer-Verlag.

Oepen, G., Fuengeld, M., Harrington, A., Hermle, L., & Botsch, H. (1989). Right hemisphere involvement in mescaline-induced psychosis. *Psychiatry Research, 29*, 335–336.

Ott, J. (1993). *Pharmacotheon*. Kennewick, WA: Natural Products.

Pablo, J. P., & Mash, D. C. (1998). Noribogaine stimulates naloxone-sensitive[35S]GTPgammaS binding. *NeuroReport, 9*, 109–114.

Pahnke, W. N., Kurland, A. A., Goodman, L. E., & Richards, W. A. (1969). LSD-assisted psychotherapy with terminal cancer patients. In R. E. Hicks, P. J. Fink, & V. B. O. Hammett (Eds.), *Psychedelic drugs* (pp. 33–42). New York: Grune and Stratton.

Pahnke, W. N., Kurland, A. A., Unger, S., Savage, C., & Grof, S. (1970). The experimental use of psychedelic (LSD) psychotherapy. *Journal of the American Medical Association, 212*, 1856–1863.

Pahnke, W. N., & Richards, W. A. (1966). Implications of LSD and experimental mysticism. *Journal of Religion and Health, 5*, 175–208.

Pauk, Z. D., & Shagass, C. (1961). Some test findings associated with susceptibility to psychosis induced by lysergic acid diethylamide. *Comprehensive Psychiatry, 2*, 188–195.

Pinchbeck, D. (2002). *Breaking open the head: A psychedelic journey into the heart of contemporary shamanism*. New York: Broadway Books.

Pope, H. G., Jr., Ionescu-Pioggia, M., & Pope, K. W. (2001). Drug use and life style among college undergraduates: A 30–year longitudinal study. *American Journal of Psychiatry, 158*, 1519–1521.

Resnick, O., Krus, D. M., & Raskin, M. (1964). LSD-25 action in normal subjects treated with a monoamine oxidase inhibitor. *Life Sciences, 3*, 1207–1214.

Riba, J., Rodríguez-Fornells, A., Strassman, R. J., & Barbanoj, M. J. (2001). Psychometric assessment of the Hallucinogen Rating Scale. *Drug and Alcohol Dependence, 62*, 215–223.

Riba, J., Rodríguez-Fornelis, A., Urbano, G., Morte, A., Antonijoan, R., Montero, M., et al. (2001). Subjective effects and tolerability of the South American psychoactive beverage *Ayahuasca* in healthy volunteers. *Psychopharmacology, 154*, 8–95.

Ring, K. (1980). *Life at death: A scientific investigation of the near-death experience*. New York: Coward, McCann, and Geoghegan.

Rinkel, M. (1956). Biochemical reflections on the psychosis problem. In L. Cholden (Ed.), *Lysergic acid diethylamide and mescaline in experimental psychiatry* (pp. 13–18). New York: Grune and Stratton.

Rinkel, M., DeShon, H. J., Hyde, R. W., & Solomon, H. C. (1952). Experimental schizophrenia-like symptoms. *American Journal of Psychiatry, 108*, 572–578.

Rosenberg, D. E., Isbell, H., Miner, E. J., & Logan, C. R. (1964). The effect of N,N-dimethyltryptamine in human subjects tolerant to lysergic acid diethylamide. *Psychopharmacology, 5*, 217–227.

Roth, B. L., Baner, K., Westkaemper, R., Siebert, D., Rice, K. C., Steinberg, S., et al. (2002). Salvinorin A: A potent naturally occurring non-nitrogenous kappa opioid selective agonist. *Proceedings of the National Academy of Sciences USA, 99*, 11934–11939.

Sandison, R. A., Spencer, A. M., & Whitelaw, J. D. A. (1954). The therapeutic value of lysergic acid diethylamide in mental illness. *Journal of Mental Science, 100*, 491–507.

Savage, C. (1952). Lysergic acid diethylamide (LSD-25): A clinical-psychological study. *American Journal of Psychiatry, 108*, 896–900.

Savage, C. (1959). The resolution and subsequent remobilization of resistance by LSD in psychotherapy. *Journal of Nervous and Mental Disease, 125*, 434–437.

Savage, C., & McCabe, O. L. (1973). Residential psychedelic (LSD) therapy for the narcotic addict: A controlled study. *Archives of General Psychiatry, 28*, 808–814.

Schultes, R. E., Hofmann, A., & Rätsch, C. (1998). *Plants of the gods*. Rochester, VT: Healing Arts Press.

Shagass, C., & Bittle, R. M. (1967). Therapeutic effects of LSD: A follow-up study. *Journal of Nervous and Mental Disease, 144*, 471–478.

Shulgin, A. T., & Shulgin, A. (1991). *PIHKAL*. Berkeley, CA: Transform Press.

Shulgin, A. T., & Shulgin, A. (1997). *TIHKAL*. Berkeley, CA: Transform Press.

Shulgin, A. T., Shulgin, L. A., & Jacob, P., III. (1986). A protocol for the evaluation of new psychoactive drugs in man. *Methods and Findings in Experimental and Clinical Pharmacology, 8*, 313–320.

Siebert, D. J. (1994). Salvia divinorum and salvinorin a: New pharmacologic findings. *Journal of Ethnopharmacology, 43*, 53–56.

Simmons, J. Q., III, Leiken, S. J., Lovaas, O. I., Schaeffer, B., & Perloff, B. (1966). Modification of autistic behavior with LSD-25. *American Journal of Psychiatry, 122*, 1201–1211.

Sjoberg, B. M., Jr., & Hollister, L. E. (1965). The effects of psychotomimetic drugs on primary suggestibility. *Psychopharmacology, 8*, 251–262.

Slater, P. E., Morimoto, K., & Hyde, R. W. (1957). The effect of group administration upon symptoms formation under LSD. *Journal of Nervous and Mental Disease, 125*, 312–315.

Sloane, B., & Doust, J. W. L. (1954). Psychophysiological investigations in experimental psychoses: Results of the exhibition of d-lysergic acid diethylamide to psychiatric patients. *Journal of Mental Science, 100*, 129–144.

Smart, R. G., Storm, T., Baker, E. F. W., & Solursh, L. (1966). A controlled study of lysergide in the treatment of alcoholism. I. The effects on drinking behavior. *Quarterly Journal of Studies on Alcohol, 27*, 469–482.

Sokoloff, L., Perlin, S., Kornetsky, C., & Kety, S. S. (1957). The effects of d-lysergic acid diethylamide on cerebral circulation and over-all metabolism. *Annals of the New York Academy of Science, 66*, 468–477.

Spitzer, M., Thimm, M., Hermle L., Holzmann, P. Kovar, K. A. Heinmann, H., et al. (1996). Increased activation of indirect semantic associations under psilocybin. *Biological Psychiatry, 39*, 1055–1057.

Stafford, P. (1992). *Psychedelics encyclopedia* (3rd ed.). Berkeley, CA: Ronin.

Stevens, J. (1998). *Storming heaven: LSD and the American dream*. New York: Grove.

Strassman, R. J. (1991). Human hallucinogenic drug research in the United States: A present-day case history and review of the process. *Journal of Psychoactive Drugs, 23*, 29–38.

Strassman, R. J. (1997). Endogenous ketamine-like compounds and the NDE: If so, so what? *Journal of Near-Death Studies, 16*, 27–41.

Strassman, R. J. (2001). *DMT: The spirit molecule*. Rochester, VT: Park Street Press.

Strassman, R. J., & Galanter, M. (1980). The Abhidharma: A cross-cultural application of meditation. *International Journal Social Psychiatry, 26,* 283–290.

Strassman, R. J., Qualls, C. R., & Berg, L. M. (1996). Differential tolerance to biological and subjective effects of four closely-spaced doses of N,N-dimethyltryptamine in humans. *Biological Psychiatry, 39,* 784–795.

Strassman, R. J., Qualls, C. R., Uhlenhuth, E. H., & Kellner, R. (1994). Dose-response study of N,N-dimethyltryptamine in humans. II. Subjective effects and preliminary results of a new rating scale. *Archives of General Psychiatry, 51,* 98–108.

Sullivan, J. T., Preston, K. L., Testa, M. P., Busch, M., & Jasinksi, D. R. (1992). Psychoactivity and abuse potential of sumatriptan. *Clinical Pharmacology and Therapeutics, 52,* 635–642.

Szara, S. I. (1957). The comparison of the psychotic effects of tryptamine derivatives with the effects of mescaline and LSD-25 in self-experiments. In W. Garattini & V. Ghetti (Eds.), *Psychotropic drugs* (pp. 460–467). New York: Elsevier.

Tamminga, C. (1999). Glutamatergic aspects of schizophrenia. *British Journal of Psychiatry, S37,* 12–15.

Tancer, M. E., & Johanson, C. E. (2001). The subjective effects of MDMA and mCPP in moderate MDMA users. *Drug and Alcohol Dependence, 65,* 97–101.

Turner, W. J., Jr., Almudevar, M., & Merlis, S. (1959). Chemotherapeutic trials in psychosis. III. Addendum. 2–Brom-D-lysergic acid diethylamide (BOL). *American Journal of Psychiatry, 116,* 261–262.

Turner, W. J., Jr., & Merlis, S. (1959). Effect of some indolealkylamines on man. *Archives of Neurology and Psychiatry, 81,* 121–129.

Ulrich, R. F., & Patten, B. M. (1991). The rise, decline, and fall of LSD. *Perspectives in Biology and Medicine, 34,* 561–578.

Vanggaard, T. (1964). Indications and counter-indications for LSD treatment. *Acta Psychiatrica Scandinavica, 40,* 426–435.

Vardy, M. M., & Kay, S. F. (1983). LSD psychosis or LSD-induced schizophrenia? A multi-method inquiry. *Archives of General Psychiatry, 40,* 877–883.

Vastag, B. (2002). Addiction treatment strives for legitimacy. *Journal of the American Medical Association, 288,* 3096–3101.

Vollenweider, F. X., & Geyer, M. A. (2001). A systems model of altered consciousness: Integrating natural and drug-induced psychoses. *Brain Research Bulletin, 56,* 495–507.

Vollenweider, F. X., Leenders, K. L., Scharfetter, C., Leenders, K., Maguire, P., Stadelmann, O., & Angst, J. (1997). Positron emission tomography and fluorodeoxyglucose studies of metabolic hyperfrontality and psychopathology in the psilocybin model of psychosis. *Neuropsychopharmacology, 16,* 357–372.

Vollenweider, F. X., Vollenweider-Scherpenhuyzen, M. F., Babler, A., Vogel, H., & Hell, D. (1998). Psilocybin induces schizophrenia-like psychosis in humans via a serotonin-2 agonist action. *NeuroReport, 9,* 3897–3902.

Vollenweider, F. X., Vontobel, P., Hell, D., & Leenders, K. L. (1999). 5-HT modulation of dopamine release in basal ganglia in psilocybin-induced psychosis in man: A PET study with [11C]raclopride. *Neuropsychopharmacology, 20,* 424–433.

Wertham, F., & Bleuler, M. (1932). Inconstancy of the formal structure of the personality. *Archives of Neurology and Psychiatry, 28,* 52–70.

Winter, J. C., Filipink, R. A., Timineri, D., Helsley, S. E., & Rabin, R. A. (2000). The paradox of 5–methoxy-N,N-dimethyltryptamine: An indoleamine hallucinogen that induces stimulus control via 5–HT$_{1A}$ receptors. *Pharmacology, Biochemistry and Behavior, 65,* 75–82.

Woolley, D. W., & Shaw, E. N. (1954). A biochemical and pharmacological suggestion about certain mental disorders. *Science, 119,* 587–588.

Young, B. G. (1974). A phenomenological comparison of LSD and schizophrenic states. *British Journal of Psychiatry, 124,* 64–74.

4

Subjective Effects of Alcohol I

Effects of the Drink
and Drinking Context

KENNETH J. SHER, MARK D. WOOD,
ALISON E. RICHARDSON,
AND KRISTINA M. JACKSON

The subjective effects of alcohol are varied, and the purported effects on mood, arousal, cognition, and behavior are so well known in most cultures that they are commonly referenced in popular music, literature, film, and the fine arts. The Old Testament refers to alcohol as both a "gift" from God (Genesis 27:28) and the means that permitted Lot's daughters to seduce him (Genesis 19:33). It appears that, for millennia, alcohol consumption has generated considerable ambivalence in many cultures for both its desired and disastrous effects.

If there is one "fact" that we can state strongly about the subjective effects of alcohol, it is that these effects are highly conditional on a number of interacting factors. These factors encompass parameters such as beverage dose, aspects of the drinking context, and an array of person variables, acting alone and in interaction with each other. In this chapter and the next, we survey the putative subjective effects of alcohol, focusing on presumably *positively reinforcing* effects (e.g., euphoria, stimulation/arousal), presumably *negatively reinforcing* (e.g., anxiolytic, antidepressant) effects, and apparently *punishing* subjective effects, such as nausea and hangover.

The chapter is organized as follows. After a brief overview of the categories of subjective effects just detailed, we consider the role of subjective effects from the context of prominent contemporary theories of alcohol use and misuse. Building on this conceptual foundation, we next discuss important features of beverage and dose and characteristics of the setting (including the concurrent use of other psychoactive drugs) that affect the subjective experience of drinking. We then consider what is known based on the various methodological approaches used to investigate subjective effects—including survey research on alcohol expectancies and drinking motives, ecological momentary assessment—with a particular emphasis on experimental research. In a companion chapter (chapter 5, this volume), we consider the critical role of individual differences in alcohol effects.

Toward a Taxonomy of Subjective Effects

Here we classify alcohol effects on the basis of three general stimulus classes: positive reinforcement, negative reinforcement, and punishment. It is important to note, however, that various effects of alcohol (e.g., sexual arousal, sedation) can be evaluated differently across people (e.g., Leigh, 1989). That is, although it is possible to generally classify subjective responses to alcohol such as perceived sexual arousal as positively reinforcing and sedation as presumably negative, ultimately these effects may be experienced differently across individuals, and even within the same individuals as a function of context or setting. Accordingly, here we qualify our description with the adverb *presumably* in recognition of these sources of variability.

Presumably Positively Reinforcing Effects

Presumably positively reinforcing responses to alcohol ingestion are among the most well known and fundamental motives for human drinking behavior (Cooper, Frone, Russell, & Mudar, 1995; Cox & Klinger, 1988). As discussed in detail later, the subjective experience of euphoria is quite common among self-report measures assessing expected effects of alcohol (e.g., Brown, Christiansen, & Goldman, 1987), amply understood with respect to its occurrence during the ascending limb of the blood alcohol curve (Martin, Earleywine, Musty, Perrine, & Swift, 1993) and well characterized with respect to neuropsychopharmacological mechanisms (Fromme & D'Amico, 1999). Additionally, alcohol's general stimulation/arousal properties, also linked to the ascending limb of the blood alcohol curve, have long been recognized. For example, Levine noted that drinking modest amounts throughout the day was a common occurrence in colonial America, with workplace consumption viewed as an invigorating and presumably productive practice

(Levine, 1978). Social facilitation and sexual arousal are also frequently ascribed subjective effects of drinking, although as noted in subsequent sections, these subjective effects are likely determined, at least in part, by the negatively reinforcing (e.g., disinhibitory, anxiolytic) effects of alcohol.

Presumably Negatively Reinforcing Effects

It is undoubtedly the case that most people believe that alcohol consumption results in anxiety or stress reduction, and that relief of aversive affective states is a common motive for drinking (Cox & Klinger, 1988; Greeley & Oei, 1999; Sher, 1987). As demonstrated in studies with animal and human populations reviewed later, these beliefs are largely understood as having a neuropsychopharmacological basis, with GABA (gamma aminobutyric acid), the main inhibitory neurotransmitter of the central nervous system (CNS), identified as a primary mechanism of this effect. Likewise, antidepressant subjective effects of drinking are well known and widely endorsed, as discussed in more detail with reference to both correlational and experimental studies. Indeed, evidence exists linking subjective expectations that alcohol is useful for relief of negative affect to more problematic drinking styles (Cooper et al., 1995), and a proneness to affective disturbance has been a ubiquitous feature of most alcohol use disorders from the earliest (e.g., R. Knight, 1937) to more recent (e.g., Babor et al., 1992; Cloninger, 1987; Zucker, 1986) alcohol use disorder typologies.

Presumably Punishing Effects

A number of presumably punishing subjective effects are sometimes associated with alcohol, the occurrence of which also varies according to drug (e.g., dosage, timing), setting (e.g., social vs. solitary), and person (e.g., genetic) parameters. These include a potential increase in negative affective states such as anger, depressant effects such as sedation or sadness, as well as nausea, light-headedness, vertigo, and hangovers (e.g., Schuckit & Gold, 1988). Because aversive subjective effects, such as hangover, are not widely studied and therefore are not included elsewhere in our discussion, we conclude this section with a brief consideration of this phenomenon.

Hangover

Hangover is generally understood to be an aversive subjective state commonly experienced in the hours following alcohol ingestion. Although there is no strict definition of hangover identified in the research literature, it is commonly assumed to encompass a set of characteristic "morning-after" symptoms (Slutske, Piasecki, & Hunt-Carter, 2003).

These include physical symptoms, such as headache, fatigue, nausea, thirst, and diarrhea; cognitive and mood disturbances, such as anxiety, irritability, and decreased ability to concentrate; and associated autonomic nervous system changes, including increased blood pressure and heart rate, sweating, and tremor (Swift & Davidson, 1998).

Hangover is arguably the most common negative consequence associated with alcohol use (Wechsler, Davenport, Dowdall, Moeykens, & Castillo, 1994; Wiese, Shlipak, & Browner, 2000). In light of this, it is surprising that research on hangover is limited. Prevalence data suggest that 75% of those who drink to intoxication report experiencing hangover at least some of the time (Harburg, Gunn, Gleiberman, DiFranceisco, & Schork, 1993). In a sample of college students, 90% of drinkers reported experiencing at least one hangover symptom during their first few drinking episodes, and 87% reported experiencing one symptom in the past year (Slutske et al., 2003).

Given the prevalence of hangover, it seems clear that this phenomenon may be an important motivator, and thus a potential determinant of subsequent drinking behavior of the individual. Two competing theories of hangover's motivational impact have been proposed (Span & Earleywine, 1999). The traditional-punishment model suggests that hangover may act as a punisher, making subsequent drinking less likely. Alternatively, the withdrawal-relief model suggests that hangover may actually encourage heavy drinking by setting the stage for negative reinforcement. This model proposes that individuals who experience severe hangover will drink to relieve their hangover symptoms (e.g., the "hair of the dog" phenomenon), resulting in increased drinking. Available data lend credence to the latter, suggesting that hangover is associated with increased risk for alcohol use disorder (AUD). For instance, correlational data suggest that those who are at increased risk for AUD experience greater hangover frequency (Newlin & Pretorius, 1990). In an alcohol challenge paradigm, Span and Earleywine (1999) demonstrated that sons of alcoholics experience greater hangover symptoms than sons of nonalcoholics.

Theoretical Perspectives on Alcohol Effects

The subjective and objective acute effects of alcohol are multiply determined, resulting from a complex set of interactions between physiological, psychological, and socioenvironmental factors (Wood, Vinson, & Sher, 2001). Regardless of their determinants, the subjective effects of alcohol are well known to the drinker and are arguably among the primary motivations for the use of alcohol. Accordingly, either directly or indirectly, these phenomenological experiences of the drinker constitute important components of theories of alcohol use and misuse. Here we briefly consider subjective effects from the context of several prominent conceptual viewpoints: neuropsychopharmacology, cognitive theories (e.g., alcohol myopia), expectancy theory, and other aspects of social learning theory.

Because our focus is on the role of subjective effects within these larger theories, our coverage is selective. Additionally, although we examine these viewpoints separately for ease of illustration, we note that there is a great deal of conceptual overlap among the broad theoretical distinctions covered here and that, for the most part, they form complementary rather than competing explanations for the complex effects of alcohol on human behavior.

Neuropsychopharmacology

Alcohol interacts both acutely and chronically with most of the CNS neurotransmitter systems that have been identified as playing a critical role in regulating cognition, affect, and behavior (Fromme & D'Amico, 1999). In this section, we draw on both human and animal studies to categorize subjective effects along positive and negative reinforcement dimensions with an emphasis on acute rather than chronic effects of alcohol use.

The positively reinforcing subjective effects of alcohol such as euphoria and increased arousal are thought to be largely associated with enhanced monoaminergic (e.g., dopamine, serotonin, norepinephrine) and opioid peptide activity (National Institute on Alcohol Abuse and Alcoholism [NIAAA], 1997). Through both direct and indirect (i.e., neuromodulation of other neurotransmitters) effects, dopamine is implicated in both the locomotor stimulation and euphoric effects of stimulants (Wise & Bozarth, 1987) and possibly alcohol (Weiss & Koob, 1991). As noted by Fromme and D'Amico (1999), more recent research has investigated dopamine's mediational role in euphoria, forwarding the alternate hypotheses that enhanced dopaminergic activity serves attention-orienting (Wickelgren, 1997) and/or memory consolidation (Otmakhova & Lisman, 1998) functions. Opioid peptides, with putative analgesic, reward, and reinforcement functions in the CNS, are thought to also partially mediate alcohol's positively reinforcing effects (Kranzler & Anton, 1994; Nevo & Hamon, 1995). The subjective experience of arousal in response to alcohol consumption has been linked to norepinephrine. Enhanced norepinephrine activity is linked to increased arousal and attention functions (Wolkowitz, Tinklenberg, & Weingartner, 1985) and may underlie the stimulant effects of alcohol observed at low doses and on the ascending limb of the blood alcohol curve (Earleywine & Erblich, 1996; Fromme & D'Amico, 1999).

The negatively reinforcing acute subjective effects of alcohol, including anxiolysis and possibly some antidepressant effects, are thought to be mediated by alcohol's effects on the gamma-aminobutyric acid (GABA$_A$) receptor. Multiple experimental approaches suggest that alcohol's effects on the $GABA_A$ receptor may be a mechanism for alcohol's anxiolytic, sedative, and motor-impairing effects. For example, drugs that facilitate gabaergic activity via their actions on various sub-units of the $GABA_A$ complex (e.g., benzodiazepines, alcohol, and other sedative drugs) have been shown to increase sedative and motor im-pairment effects in animals and to decrease passive avoidance (i.e., reduce conditioned inhibition or conflict; e.g., see Fromme & D'Amico, 1999, for a review). Drugs that act as "inverse agonists" and antago-nists at the $GABA_A$ receptor have demonstrated the ability to counter-act anxiolytic and impairing psychomotor effects of alcohol (Liljequist & Engel, 1982; Samson & Harris, 1992; Suzdak et al., 1986; Wood et al., 2001) and to reduce alcohol intake (see Fromme & D'Amico, 1999). Additionally, neurochemical analyses have found that alcohol consump-tion resulted in enhanced GABA-mediated inhibition of neurons (Mihic & Harris, 1997).

Although most rewarding effects of alcohol are viewed as being centrally mediated, it is possible that some effects can be mediated peripherally. For example, alcohol has been shown to have beta-blocking activity and consequently could reduce peripheral arousal (e.g., heart palpitation, tachycardia) in stressful situations, especially where physiological arousal itself is likely to lead to an escalating cycle of arousal/anxiety (e.g., performance anxiety; Cummings & Marlatt, 1983; Dai, Thavundayil, & Gianoulakis, 2002; Levenson, Sher, Grossman, Newman, & Newlin, 1980; Lewis & Vogeltanz-Holm, 2002; Sher & Levenson, 1982; Sinha, Robinson, & O'Malley, 1998; Wilson, Abrams, & Lipscomb, 1980; Zeichner, Feuerstein, Swartzman, & Reznick, 1983). Also, some of alcohol's most punishing acute subjective effects (e.g., flushing) appear to be due to intermediary by-products of ethanol metabolism, specifically acetaldehyde, which is a toxic metabolite of alcohol (Eriksson, 1983; Eriksson, Mizoi, & Fukunaga, 1982).

Although the chapter's focus on subjective effects leads to a primary consideration of acute effects, such effects are experienced in the con-text of an ongoing pattern of use (except in those cases where we are focusing on an individual's initial experiences with alcohol). In recent years, there has been increasing research and theoretical emphasis on acute effects in relation to chronic effects. As noted by Fromme and D'Amico (1999), the chronic effects of alcohol on various neurotrans-mitter systems (e.g., GABA, dopamine, norepinephrine, serotonin, opiate peptides) tend to be opposite in direction to the acute effects. Some neuroscientists believe these chronic effects represent a form of neuroadaption that underlies the development of alcohol dependence. That is, repeated acute doses lead to neuropharmacological changes in the opposite direction of the acute effects. For example, Koob and Le Moal (2001) have advanced the theory of *allostasis* to explain the relation between acute drug effects and dependence. Basically, this theory posits that, over time, compensatory (homeostatic) adaptations to acute drug administration alter the natural homeostatic set point so that these compensatory responses no longer serve to restore homeostasis. For example, the profile of neuropharmacological activity and associated effects during withdrawal is often opposite in direction to the corresponding profile of acute effects. This suggests that in early stages of alcohol involvement, reinforcement from use may predominate, but with chronic exposure, negative affect starts to develop, setting up a "spiraling addiction cycle" (Koob & Le Moal, 1997, p. 56). That is, chronic use leads to dependence phenomena that provide further motivation for use. Thus, it is important when conceptualizing the subjective effects of alcohol to consider the drinking history and chronic adaptations to alcohol because they affect not only tolerance but also the underlying affective state and therefore the stimulus value of alcohol. For example, effects that can be viewed as positively reinforcing early in the course of drinking (e.g., euphoria) because they reflect an increase in positive affect from a neutral state could, over time, induce a chronically dysthymic state that is then relieved by alcohol—in effect becoming negatively reinforcing. The fact that some mood and anxiety disorders appear to be "substance induced" and remit with a period of abstinence is becoming increasingly recognized in the clinical literature (e.g., Preuss, Schuckit, Smith, Barnow, & Danko, 2002; Schuckit & Hesselbrock, 1994) and is consistent with the notion that some chronic adaptations to heavy alcohol use induce prolonged, negative subjective states.

Cognitive Theories

Contemporary theories of alcohol use and misuse have invoked cognitive processes to help understand why the pharmacological effects of alcohol on intrapersonal (e.g., euphoria, anxiety) and interpersonal (e.g., aggression, risky sex) processes are highly variable across persons and situations (Sayette, 1999). The most influential of these models is Steele and Josephs's (1990) "alcohol myopia" theory, which proposes that alcohol's effects are contingent upon information processing with regard to more or less salient features of the drinking context. Specifically, they propose that alcohol consumption results in a narrowing of the ability to process a range of relevant situational cues to those most immediate and salient in a given situation. Thus, alcohol myopia would postulate that the effects of alcohol consumption vary according to the salience of particular environmental cues. As described in both this chapter and the next, this hypothesis has received support across multiple domains and can be invoked to provide a coherent explanation for how alcohol can lead either to an animated, euphoric, celebratory experience or to a depressive "crying in one's beer" experience. In several studies, Steele and colleagues have shown that alcohol consumption followed by distracting pleasant or neutral stimuli can attenuate stress responses, but when no distraction is present, alcohol consumption either no longer reduces anxiety or produces anxiogenic effects (Josephs & Steele, 1990; Steele & Josephs, 1988; Steele, Southwick, & Pagano, 1986). Likewise, in two studies MacDonald and colleagues found that alcohol consumption interacted with cue saliency in ways consistent with alcohol myopia theory. MacDonald, MacDonald, Zanna, and Fong (2000) observed that arousal cues interacted with dose condition such that participants who were both intoxicated and more highly aroused reported stronger intentions to engage in unprotected sex than those who were sober, presumably because the latter participants were capable of considering both salient (e.g., arousal) and inhibiting (e.g., fear of AIDS) cues. In a second study, MacDonald, Fong, Zanna, and Martineau (2000) made inhibiting cues more salient by stamping bar patrons' hands with a threatening message ("AIDS Kills") and observed that this manipulation "canceled out" tendencies among intoxicated participants to report greater intentions to engage in risky sex. Additionally, effects consistent with alcohol myopia theory have also been observed with respect to drinking and driving (MacDonald, Zanna, & Fong, 1995) and aggressive behavior (Leonard, 1989).

Sayette (1993) proposed a cognitive model of alcohol effects on stress response that has also been examined with respect to aggressive behavior and is presumably related to a range of alcohol effects where cognitive appraisal of a given situation is a key determinant of affective state. Briefly, Sayette hypothesized that stress responses to alcohol are mediated by disruptions in the ability to appraise stressful information as a result of cognitive impairment. If a stressor is sufficiently appraised, alcohol's effects will be anxiogenic; but if encoding is disrupted, alcohol will be anxiolytic. Consistent with this hypothesis, using multiple measures of stress response, Sayette, Martin, Perrott, Wertz, and Hufford (2001) found greater anxiolytic effects when the stress manipulation followed rather than preceded alcohol consumption.

As noted by Sayette (1999), research is needed that directly links cognitive and affective processing. Strong support for the hypothesis that "alcohol attenuates fear and impairs response inhibition via its effects on cognitive processing" comes from a recent study by Curtin, Patrick, Lang, Cacioppo, and Birbaumer (2001, p. 527). Attentional processing was assessed using event-related potential (i.e., P3 component) to conditions where threat cues were presented in isolation versus divided attention (visual-motor task plus threat cues), and fear was assessed using fear-potentiated startle and response latency measures. During the divided attention task (but not during the threat cue only condition), individuals receiving alcohol (approximately .08% BAC) had both attenuated P3 responses and attenuated fear indices relative to the no-alcohol condition. These results provide strong evidence that alcohol can impair cognitive functioning during threat conditions.

Moreover, impairments in cognitive processes seem to account for reductions in fear responses and behavioral inhibition.

In sum, although alcohol myopia theory and the attention disruption model differ with respect to the particular mechanisms by which alcohol's cognitive impairment effects occur, they both propose that alcohol's effects on affect (e.g., stress) or behavior (e.g., risky sex, aggression) will vary according to the salience of the situational cues. From this perspective, alcohol consumption can be either euphoric or depressogenic, anxiolytic or anxiogenic, disinhibiting or inhibiting, all because of the nature of the context of the drinking experience. In contrast to neuropsychopharmacological theories that tend to promote the notion that subjective effects are a mechanistic by-product of alcohol's direct and indirect effects on the brain systems underlying motivation, cognitive theories such as Steele and Josephs's and Sayette's provide a strong theoretical basis for understanding why alcohol (and other drug) effects appear to be so highly conditional upon the context of the drinking experience.

Expectancy Theory

Although expectancy theory can be viewed as a component of more general cognitive and social learning approaches, it warrants special emphasis because it has been a prominent conceptual framework for understanding the subjective effects of alcohol use for more than two decades. The importance of individually held beliefs regarding the effects of alcohol as important determinants of subjective effects of alcohol has been demonstrated in numerous studies using the so-called balanced placebo design (e.g., Hull & Bond, 1986; Marlatt & Rohsenow, 1980; Vogel-Sprott & Fillmore, 1999), which experimentally manipulates the belief that an individual is getting alcohol independently of whether or not he or she is actually getting alcohol. This is typically accomplished by using four experimental conditions: (a) told alcohol—get alcohol, (b) told alcohol—not get alcohol, (c) told nonalcoholic beverage—get alcohol, and (d) told nonalcoholic beverage—not get alcohol. (Note that this design differs from the traditional placebo-controlled design, which typically includes only conditions 1 and 2 and thus permits only an assessment of the effect of alcohol given the expectation that alcohol is being consumed.

Although three decades of using the balanced-placebo design in alcohol research have helped to identify those areas where one's beliefs appear to affect his or her subjective experiences and behaviors (i.e., primarily mood and social behavior; see Hull & Bond, 1986), these findings only suggest that there is something "in the mind" of the drinker that is important in determining subjective effects of alcohol. Over the past 20 years, research on the nature of alcohol expectancies has begun to characterize these cognitive structures and processes that are critical in determining human response to alcohol.

Note that although we are presenting expectancy theory as a largely cognitive explanation for some types of alcohol effects, it is increasingly clear that these models are compatible, if not converging, with neurobiological explanations (Goldman, Del Boca, & Darkes, 1999; McCarthy, Wall, Brown, & Carr, 2000) in that they reflect, in part, a summary of an individual's pharmacological experience with alcohol. Here we use the term *outcome* expectancy, defined as beliefs that people have about the affective, cognitive, and behavioral effects of drinking alcohol (Goldman, Brown, & Christiansen, 1987). (Expectancy notions are also compatible with basic notions of classical conditioning, which has become increasingly "cognitive" in recent years; Rescorla, 1988.)

What types of expectancies do individuals hold about the effects of alcohol? Varying psychometric methods (e.g., exploratory and confirmatory factor analysis, multidimensional scaling) have been employed in the development of a number of self-report expectancy measures designed to assess particular types of beliefs about drinking and examine their relations with alcohol use and problems (Fromme, Stroot, & Kaplan, 1993; George, Frone, et al., 1995; Goldman, Brown, Christiansen, & Smith, 1991; Leigh, 1989; Leigh & Stacy, 1991; Martin et al., 1993). Although the specific content of empirically derived factors varies across methods and measures, factors related to "tension reduction," "social and/or sexual facilitation," and "enhanced cognitive or motor performance" have been replicated across studies. Goldman et al. (1999) suggest that outcome expectancies can be categorized along three basic dimensions: (a) positive versus negative expected outcomes (e.g., increased sociability vs. increased aggressiveness); (b) positive versus negative reinforcement (e.g., social facilitation vs. tension reduction); and (c) arousal versus sedation (e.g., stimulant vs. depressant effects). A growing body of research utilizing implicit assessment of outcome expectancies has also demonstrated associations with alcohol use (Palfai & Wood, 2001; Stacy, 1997; Wiers, van Woerden, Smulders, & de Jong, 2002). The fact that these "implicit" expectancies are measured unobtrusively and independently of typical explicit expectancy measures suggests that some aspects of expectancies are not easily articulated by the drinker but can still be shown to affect his or her behavior.

The bulk of outcome expectancy research is cross-sectional, with consistent demonstration of robust associations between outcome expectancies and measures of alcohol use and problems across drinking patterns ranging from abstention to alcohol dependence and among diverse subject populations, including adolescents, college students, and adults (e.g., Brown, Goldman, & Christiansen, 1985; Connors, O'Farrell, Cutter, & Thompson, 1986; Earleywine & Erblich, 1996;

Fromme et al., 1993; Leigh, 1987; Leigh & Stall, 1993; Mann, Chassin, & Sher, 1987; Wood, Nagoshi, & Dennis, 1992; Wood, Sher, & Strathman, 1996). Research with children and adolescents has demonstrated that outcome expectancies antedate actual drinking experience and become more well defined and more likely to reflect social facilitation and arousal dimensions (Dunn & Goldman, 1996; Miller, Smith, & Goldman, 1990) with increasing drinking experience.

Prospective studies are comparatively few, but they are consistent with the notion of etiologic relevance of outcome expectancies in the initiation and maintenance of alcohol use, and perhaps in its escalation to problem levels. Outcome expectancies assessed prior to the onset of drinking have been found to predict alcohol use onset and subsequent use (Christiansen, Smith, Roehling, & Goldman, 1989; Newcomb, Chou, Bentler, & Huba, 1988; Stacy, Newcomb, & Bentler, 1991). In contrast to mean level increases demonstrated over 3 years of early adolescence noted by Smith, Goldman, Greenbaum, and Christiansen, (1995), Sher and colleagues (Sher, Wood, Wood, & Raskin, 1996) observed significant decreases in outcome expectancies over 4 years in a college student sample. Piecing together these two longitudinal studies spanning early to late adolescence suggests that outcome expectancies, at least for certain forms of reinforcement from alcohol (e.g., social facilitation) increase over the course of early to middle adolescence, then plateau and begin to moderate in late adolescence and early adulthood. Likewise, outcome expectancies have also been shown to be predictive of response to alcoholism treatment (B. T. Jones & McMahon, 1994), decreases in abstinence among alcoholics following treatment (Connors, Tarbox, & Faillace, 1993), and, at least over short follow-up periods, response to experimental manipulations in predictable ways (Darkes & Goldman, 1993, 1998; Roehrich & Goldman, 1995).

Research has suggested that outcome expectancies associated with arousal are more likely to be salient to heavier drinkers, whereas lighter drinkers are more likely to endorse sedating effects (Rather, Goldman, Roehrich, & Brannick, 1992). Moreover, there is some evidence that outcome expectancies related to enhanced cognitive or motor performance appear to be particularly prognostic of problematic alcohol use (Brown, Creamer, & Stetson, 1987; Mann et al., 1987; Sher et al., 1996), at least in adolescence and early adulthood (Sher & Gotham, 1999).

In sum, outcome expectancies, as indices of expected subjective effects from alcohol use, appear to be etiologically relevant for understanding alcohol use and misuse. Contemporary research in this area has moved beyond static models and univariate prediction to modeling dynamic associations and consideration of outcome expectancies and alcohol use in relation to neurobiological factors such as responses to alcohol (McCarthy et al., 2000) and personality (Henderson, Goldman, Coovert, & Carnevalla, 1994; Sher, Walitzer, Wood, & Brent, 1991). Perhaps most important, beliefs about the effects of alcohol have been cast as important components of more comprehensive biopsychosocial models of alcohol use and misuse (Sher, 1991), as well as prominent psychosocial theories of behavior that have been applied to alcohol use (Bandura, 1986). Despite the large body of studies showing the importance of expectancies as determinants and consequences of drinking behavior, there are relatively few studies that directly link individually held expectancies to subjective effects observed under controlled laboratory studies.

Fillmore and Vogel-Sprott (1995) assessed the effect of impairment expectancies on response to alcohol and placebo. They found that expected impairment did predict performance on a motor skills task, such that those who expected to experience greater impairment performed worse on the task (Fillmore & Vogel-Sprott, 1995). However, when subjects were told to expect that their performance on the task would suffer while they were under the influence of alcohol, impairment was reduced and performance on the task improved (Fillmore, Mulvihill, & Vogel-Sprott, 1994; Fillmore & Vogel-Sprott, 1996). Fillmore and colleagues suggest that this improvement in performance may be a compensatory reaction, intended to counteract the expected impairment (Fillmore & Blackburn, 2002). In our own work, expectancies for reinforcement did predict subjective responses to both placebo and alcoholic beverages, but the effects were short-lived and dependent upon a social drinking context (Sher, 1985). These latter findings indicate that individuals do bring differing expectations to their drinking experiences, but the extent to which individual differences in alcohol outcome expectancies determine alcohol effects is highly conditional upon type of effect, stage of intoxication, and environmental context.

Other Social Learning Theory Perspectives

As noted by Maisto, Carey, and Braddiza (1999), many versions and aspects of social learning theory (SLT) have been examined along a continuum of alcohol use, ranging from consumption (e.g., quantity-frequency) to alcohol abuse and dependence. Nonetheless, the basic notion that alcohol use and misuse are shaped by both direct (e.g., differential reinforcement) and indirect (e.g., vicarious) learning in response to socioenvironmental influences is a core feature of SLT-based approaches and has clear relevance for consideration of the subjective effects of alcohol. Here we consider the role of subjective effects with reference to the four major principles of SLT articulated by Bandura (1969): differential reinforcement, vicarious learning, cognitive processes, and reciprocal determinism with particular emphasis on studies examining mediational or moderational relations between SLT variables and alcohol use and misuse.

The SLT concept of differential reinforcement is invoked to explain the variability in expected outcomes of drinking across different settings or situations. For example, as noted by Maisto et al. (1999), whereas anticipated outcomes such as social or sexual facilitation are more likely to be considered by drinkers in social settings (e.g., parties), the same individuals are likely to expect different outcomes in situations less supportive of alcohol use (e.g., the workplace). Indeed, in Bandura's (1969) original formulation, the development of alcoholism is hypothesized to result from the development of less adaptive (i.e., less diffuse) reinforcement contingencies associated with alcohol use.

Vicarious learning refers to the ability to assimilate beliefs, attitudes, and behaviors indirectly, based on the observation of others and the response contingencies associated with their behavior (Abrams & Niaura, 1987). As noted previously, this aspect of SLT has been well supported in studies examining the existence of beliefs about the subjective effects of alcohol that antedate actual experience with drinking (Dunn & Goldman, 1996; Miller et al., 1990). Modeling as a result of vicarious learning may be direct, as in the imitation of drinking behavior, or, more relevant to our focus here, indirect, through the adoption of attitudes or expectations about alcohol's effects (Maisto et al., 1999). These learned attitudes and expectations play an important mediating role (e.g., Sher et al., 1991; Wood, Read, Palfai, & Stevenson, 2001) through which, consistent with SLT, more distal psychosocial factors influence alcohol use and problems.

Cognitive processes, such as accessing and retrieving encoded information in response to environmental cues, represent a third principle of SLT. Both outcome and efficacy expectations are thought to be cued in response to environmental stimuli and serve to guide behavioral choices in a given situation. Overall, although outcome expectancies have demonstrated more robust associations with alcohol use than efficacy expectations, studies jointly examining both constructs have observed significant relations between each and drinking behavior (Aas, Klepp, Laberg, & Aaro, 1995; Baldwin, Oei, & Young, 1993).

As noted by the fourth principle of SLT, relations between cognitive and behavioral variables are thought to be *reciprocally determined*; that is, behaviors influence cognitive factors, which in turn serve to influence future behavior. The notion of reciprocal determinism as applied to alcohol use–outcome expectancy relations has been supported in longitudinal studies of both early (Smith et al., 1995) and late (Sher et al., 1996) adolescents.

The SLT-based hypothesis that deficits in coping skills, particularly in combination with positive outcome expectancies, are important psychosocial determinants of alcohol use and misuse has also received support across a number of studies. For example, Cooper, Russell, and George (1988) found that both emotion-focused coping and outcome expectancies predicted greater levels of drinking to cope, and that this relationship was stronger for those who held more positive alcohol expectancies. These results were subsequently replicated in a college student sample (Evans & Dunn, 1995). Likewise, Kushner, Sher, Wood, and Wood (1994) found that, among men, positive relations between anxiety and alcohol use were more robust among those with stronger tension-reduction outcome expectancies. Additionally, Cooper, Russell, Skinner, Frone, and Mudar (1992) observed that among men with more positive outcome expectancies, negative life events demonstrated stronger positive associations with alcohol use than those observed among men with less positive outcome expectancies.

Summary of Theoretical Perspectives

As a psychoactive drug, alcohol exerts important effects on most of the major neurotransmitter systems that affect behavior, in particular, those involved in reward, arousal, and inhibition. However, it is clear that even as our knowledge of the neuropharmacological basis of alcohol effects progresses, a purely molecular account will be insufficient for accounting for the variety of alcohol effects. In particular, the individual's drinking history will have profound effects on the nature of the subjective effects in as many as three ways: (a) It can affect tolerance, (b) it can affect the tonic, underlying hedonic state of the individual, and (c) it will shape the individual's beliefs regarding how alcohol will affect him or her (which in turn will shape the subjective response to alcohol). Additionally, the immediate context where drinking takes place both internally (e.g., the mental set, concerns, goals) and externally (e.g., the physical setting, the behaviors of others) will further condition the nature of alcohol effects. It is critically important to bear this in mind when we consider laboratory-based studies of alcohol effects, where much of the natural variation in both drinking histories and immediate drinking contexts is highly constrained.

Aspects of Beverage and Dose

It goes without saying that the effects of alcohol must be understood on the basis of the nature of the drink. Although there is relatively little in the way of empirical evidence pointing to different subjective effects of different types of beverages (e.g., wine, beer, distilled spirits), popular beliefs often promote the idea that some types of beverages are more likely than others to have certain desired or undesired effects. Marketers, although explicitly banned from advertising alcohol on the basis of strength or specific subjective or behavioral effects (Bureau of Alcohol, 1999), clearly try to promote various beverages as producing camaraderie, sexual potency, or power (Finn & Strickland, 1982; Grube, 1993; Pinsky & Silva, 1999; Slater, Rouner, Murphy, Beauvais, Van Leuven & Domenech Rodriguez, 1996; Strickland, Finn, & Lambert, 1982). However, the possible differential effects of beverage type (i.e., beer, wine, spirits) on physiological, behavioral, emotional, and social outcomes have received relatively little empirical attention compared with studies of the effects of alcohol in general (Smart, 1996). (A major exception to this generalization is research on the health-promoting and health-damaging effects of beer, wine, and distilled spirits with respect to all-cause mortality and cardiovascular disease [e.g., Ellison, 2002; Rosenberg et al., 1981; Sacco et al., 1999].) Indeed, there has definitely been a bias among investigators studying alcohol effects to use a limited range of alcoholic drinks in studying alcohol effects, presumably for practical concerns (e.g., dosing, developing credible placebos). This point is well illustrated by a recent meta-analysis of balanced-placebo design studies (McKay & Schare, 1999), which found that the overwhelming majority of investigations (55 of 64) included only tonic/vodka, and there was little evidence to suggest that beverage type moderated the alcohol effects under investigation. Systematic studies of the behavioral effects of substances with differing congener contents in rodents (e.g., York, 1984) have failed to reveal major differences attributable to beverage type. Still, differences in potentially pharmacologically active components of alcoholic beverages (e.g., differences in the congener content of distilled and fermented beverages) have been implicated in some negative symptoms associated with intoxication, such as hangover (Swift & Davidson, 1998), and further clarification of this issue seems warranted. However, in the absence of strong evidence to the contrary, it is probably reasonable to assume that the major differences among beverages with respect to effects are attributable to differences in alcohol concentration, which range from under 5% for many beers to more than 75% for some types of distilled spirits (although distilled spirits are often consumed in diluted form because they are combined with various mixers).

Do Vehicles (Mixers) Make a Difference?

Because of their effects on absorption, various mixers can possibly affect how alcohol is experienced. Alcohol's effect may be influenced by the contents of the vehicle with which it is administered. Certain vehicles, such as seltzer, tonic, colas, and other carbonated beverages, facilitate absorption of alcohol into the bloodstream. These effervescent beverages move alcohol through the stomach and to the small intestines, where the alcohol is absorbed into the bloodstream (Roueche, 1960). Conversely, vehicles high in food content delay absorption. Mixers such as milk (as in eggnog) and butter (as in hot buttered rum) are digested in the stomach, hindering alcohol's progression to the small intestines and delaying its absorption into the bloodstream (Roueche, 1960).

Similarly, alcohol's effect can be moderated by the contents of the stomach. When alcohol is ingested in the presence of food, absorption into the bloodstream is delayed (Fraser, Rosalki, Gamble, & Pounder,

1995; A. W. Jones & Jonsson, 1994). Although some reports suggest the type of food makes little difference (e.g., Kalant, 1971), there is some support for the important role of dietary fats in slowing alcohol absorption (A. W. Jones, Jonsson, & Neri, 1991).

Expected Beverage Content

More than 30 years ago, Marlatt, Demming, and Reid (1973) introduced the balanced-placebo design into alcohol research and dramatically demonstrated that putative pharmacological effects of alcohol might, in fact, represent effects attributable to the belief that one has consumed alcohol. Although there are several slight variations, as noted in the earlier section on expectancy theory, in its most basic form the balanced-placebo design independently manipulates the pharmacological agent (i.e., alcohol) and the expectation that one is receiving alcohol (Marlatt & Rohsenow, 1980; Martin & Sayette, 1993; Rohsenow & Marlatt, 1981; Sayette, Breslin, Wilson, & Rosenblum, 1994).

Although dozens of studies conducted in the 1970s and 1980s employed the balanced-placebo design, it appears that the initial enthusiasm it engendered among researchers waned for both substantive and methodological reasons. Substantively, it appears that for many alcohol effects, expectancy effects were far less important than some of the initial results suggested. For example, in Hull and Bond's (1986) influential meta-analytic review of balanced-placebo design studies, across 14 studies the mean effect for expectancy on mood (the domain closest to the focus of this chapter) was very small and not significant. Hull and Bond (1986) concluded that "expectancy increases the incidence of illicit social behaviors and has few effects on nonsocial acts . . . consistent with the hypothesis that expectancy provides an attributional excuse to engage in desired but socially prohibited acts" (p. 358).

Methodological criticism has focused on the difficulty of successfully executing the deceptions involved in the design, especially in the antiplacebo condition, where subjects are told they will not receive alcohol but then have it administered to them in an ostensibly nonalcoholic beverage. It is simply difficult to give an intoxicating dose of alcohol to someone and have the person not recognize an altered state, and so the design can be difficult to implement successfully at high doses (Martin, Earleywine, Finn, & Young, 1990). Similarly, but somewhat less so, it is also difficult to administer an ostensibly large dose of alcohol in the placebo condition and maintain the deception for an extended period. Although manipulation checks conducted at the end of the experiment typically reveal some degree of deception, participants' reports of the alcoholic content of their drinks are subject to self-report biases, and some data suggest that participants exhibit strong demand effects in this situation (L. Knight, Barbaree, & Boland, 1986;

Lyvers & Maltzman, 1991; Martin et al., 1990). Thus, although the balanced-placebo design has been important historically in demonstrating that beliefs the drinker brings to the study can be important (especially in studying disinhibition), its utility in studying subjective effects is clearly less than was commonly believed 20 years ago. Despite this, cross-sectional and prospective data have consistently shown that expectations about the beverage are robust predictors of alcohol consumption and problems (e.g., Goldman et al., 1999) and highlight the importance of individuals' *perceived* or at least *anticipated* effects of alcohol as a determinant of drinking even in those situations in which it is not a critical determinant of the actual experience of intoxication.

Dose

Most, if not all, of alcohol's effects are dose responsive (although not necessarily monotonically so). Indeed, it can be argued that the dose-response effect of alcohol is the primary determinant of the individual's experience of stimulation or sedation (Marlatt, 1976). Holdstock and de Wit (1998) provided an excellent overview of studies that investigated how dose influences the subjective effects of alcohol. In summarizing the literature, they note, "At high doses, and during the descending limb of the alcohol dose-response curve, ethanol typically produces sedative-like effects. . . . However, at low doses, and during the ascending limb, ethanol often has stimulant-like effects" (p. 1903). These patterns for high and low doses are consistent with the biphasic relation between alcohol and subjective effects discussed later in this chapter. Importantly, Holdstock and de Wit (1998) also highlight studies that are inconsistent with the general, biphasic trend. For example, they discuss results that suggest the subjective effects of alcohol (e.g., activation) change with dose monotonically (e.g., Persson, Sjöberg, & Svensson, 1980). One explanation for the inconsistent findings is that individual differences related to the subjective effects of alcohol often are not considered (Holdstock & de Wit, 1998).

To examine this possibility, Holdstock and de Wit (1998) conducted a randomized, double-blind study with 49 healthy men and women. Participants were randomly assigned to a low (0.2 g/kg), medium (0.4 g/kg), or high (0.8 g/kg) alcohol condition. Findings indicated that: (a) a low dose (0.2 g/kg) of ethanol had neither stimulant-like nor sedative-like effects, (b) a medium dose (0.4 g/kg) had only sedative-like effects that occurred during the descending limb of the alcohol dose response, and (c) at the highest dose, ethanol had both stimulant-like and sedative-like subjective effects during the ascending limb and sedative-like effects during the descending limb. Given the somewhat puzzling nature of the later findings (i.e., inconsistent with the biphasic pattern), these results were considered further. Findings indicate that approximately "half of the subjects reported typical 'biphasic' effects after ethanol, (e.g., stimulant-like effects during the ascending limb and sedative-like effects during the descending limb). The other half of the subjects did not report any stimulant-like effects, regardless of limb, after 0.8g/kg of ethanol" (Holdstock & de Wit, 1998, p. 1908). These results suggest that more complex models (compared with the biphasic framework) are needed that account for both dose-related and individual differences in the subjective effects of alcohol. With respect to mood, at low or moderate doses of alcohol, mood and physiological systems are stimulated to levels above those obtained at the predrinking state. However, at very high doses of alcohol, mood and associated systems can be depressed to levels below baseline.

The nature of dose responsivity undoubtedly varies across different types of alcohol effects. Tiplady et al. (1998) studied the effect of two doses of alcohol on performance and found a dose effect in a digit/symbol substitution task but not for a 4-choice reaction time task. Research conducted by Mills and Bisgrove also illustrates the variable nature of dose-response effects. These authors report no gender difference in cognitive impairment at a low alcohol dose but significantly more impairment in females, compared with males, at a high dose (Mills & Bisgrove, 1983). Although some have argued that many dose effects persist across a drinking episode (Tucker, Vuchinich, & Sobell, 1982), there is increasing recognition that for many if not most alcohol effects, there is considerable variability as a function of rising and falling blood alcohol concentration.

Route of Administration

In humans, as opposed to laboratory animals, alcohol is almost always consumed via an oral route. However, there have been studies that have examined intravenous alcohol administration in humans. These studies, in principle, might be able to shed light on what types of alcohol effects are more basic (i.e., due to the direct pharmacological effects of alcohol) and not dependent on drinking rituals and taste cues that could confound drug effects with expectancy effects (Hartocollis, 1963; Warren & Raynes, 1972). For example, in an early study of intravenous injection compared with social and isolated drinking, Warren and Raynes (1972) found that subjects' mood did not differ significantly across routes of administration. More recently, Morzorati and colleagues (e.g., Morzorati, Ramchandani, Flury, Li, & O'Connor, 2002) have used a breath alcohol clamp technique to gain better experimental control over rate of breath alcohol concentration change and to study acute tolerance processes. This methodology utilizes intravenous alcohol infusions in combination with estimates of each individual's pharmacokinetic distribution and elimination rates to hold breath alcohol concentration (BrAC) steady, and thus minimize variance in BrAC (Froehlich et al., 2001; Morzorati et al., 2002; Subramanian et al., 2002). Experiments using non-oral routes of alcohol administration, although arguably providing less ecological validity for understanding naturalistic drinking experience, can offer insights into effects of alcohol that are possibly not as highly mediated by expectancies, as well as providing exquisite control over the rate of change in BAC in order to better characterize limb and acute tolerance effects (see later discussion).

Limb of the Blood Alcohol Curve

As just discussed, in characterizing the subjective effects of alcohol, it is critical to consider the limb of the blood alcohol concentration (BAC) curve. Simply put, the *ascending limb* of the BAC refers to the period that immediately begins with the ingestion or administration of alcohol and ends with the peak BAC. During the ascending limb, alcohol is absorbed from the gastrointestinal tract into the bloodstream Because, under normal drinking situations, alcohol is absorbed at a rate faster than the body can eliminate it (through catabolic breakdown into acetaldehyde and acetate and, to a lesser extent, excretion through expired air, sweat, and urine), there is an increase in the amount of alcohol in the bloodstream and a corresponding increase in BAC (Kalant, 1971). Depending on the rate of consumption and type of alcoholic beverage consumed (and controlling for gender, body mass, liver size, amount and type of stomach content, etc.), the slope of the BAC curve during the ascending limb can vary substantially, with faster drinking and drinking of more concentrated forms of ethanol leading to steeper positive BAC slopes. For example, a 180-lb man who consumes 6 standard drink equivalents (i.e., a 4-oz glass of wine, a 12-ounce can of beer, or an ounce of distilled spirts) in a half hour may be estimated to reach an (approximate) peak BAC of .125%; if the same amount was consumed at a slower rate, say over 3 hours, the peak BAC would be closer to .08%. During the period when BAC is rising, individuals commonly report experiencing stimulant-like effects of the drug, such as elation, stimulation, vigor, loquaciousness, sociability, and euphoria (e.g., Connors & Maisto, 1979; Ekman, Frankenhaeuser, Goldberg, Hagdahl, & Myrsten, 1964; Martin et al., 1993).

The *descending limb* refers to the subsequent period of time when the BAC is decreasing, primarily due to metabolic breakdown (although, again, some alcohol is excreted in sweat, breath, and urine; Kalant, 1971). In contrast to the slope of the ascending limb, which can vary dramatically as a function of dosing parameters, the slope of the descending limb is less variable. For most individuals, alcohol is eliminated at about .01 to .02% per hour, with the midpoint of this range, .015% per hour, the constant most often used as a reference (Wallgren & Barry, 1970). Consequently, if someone were to reach a BAC of .08% (the legal limit for driving in most jurisdictions in the United States), it would take 4 to 8 hours for him or her to completely eliminate alcohol from the bloodstream. (In contrast, the .08% BAC could be achieved by drinking heavily over a relatively short period of time.)

During the descending limb of the BAC curve, individuals' reports of subjective experience often reflect the sedative-like effects of alcohol, including feelings of sluggishness, sedation, difficulty concentrating, and slowed thinking (Erblich, Earleywine, Erblich, & Bovbjerg, 2003; Holdstock, King, & de Wit, 2000; Martin et al., 1993). These effects are often visible on the ascending limb as well but tend to have a later onset and to be more persistent than stimulating effects; thus, they tend to be overshadowed by stimulating effects on the ascending limb but predominate on the descending limb.

These biphasic effects can be observed objectively under controlled laboratory conditions but are also well known to drinkers who, when sober, report they anticipate that alcohol will be more stimulating on the ascending limb and more sedating on the descending limb (Earleywine, 1994; Earleywine & Martin, 1993). Not only do drinkers think about subjective effects as consisting of both of these types of effects, but the relative salience of stimulating versus sedating effects appears to differ as a function of drinking pattern, with heavier drinkers being more likely to have strong associations with stimulant effects relative to sedative effects and lighter drinkers showing the opposite pattern (Earleywine, 1994). This suggests a bias toward either experiencing or recalling stimulating versus sedating effects, and this bias may have motivational relevance for drinking. The extent to which the biphasic effects of alcohol are observed is moderated by a number of factors related both to the drink itself and to characteristics of the drinker. With respect to drink, the factor that has been the most studied is dose of alcohol, with higher doses showing a combination of both greater stimulation and greater sedation than lower doses (King, Houle, de Wit, Holdstock, & Schuster, 2002).

Regardless of whether true biphasic effects are observed, it is often the case that subjective and behavioral effects occurring during the ascending limb of the BAC curve are attenuated on the descending limb. That is, a given BAC is usually associated with a muted profile of effects depending on whether it is obtained when the BAC is rising or falling (Hiltunen, 1997; Hiltunen, Saxon, Skagerberg, & Borg, 2000; Niaura, Nathan, Frankenstein, Shapiro, & Brick, 1987). This general phenomenon is known as *acute tolerance*, a rapid homeostatic adjustment to the direct stimulus effect of alcohol. Although acute tolerance is most obvious when we document a smaller alcohol effect in an individual at a given BAC (say, .06) when the blood alcohol level is falling as opposed to rising, it is reasonable to speculate that acute tolerance processes are induced immediately with the initiation of drinking but are largely masked by an increasing BAC.

The biphasic nature of many alcohol effects, including arousal (e.g., Earleywine & Erblich, 1996; Holdstock & de Wit, 1998), cognitive functioning (e.g., B. M. Jones & Vega, 1972; Pihl, Paylan, Gentes-Hawn, & Hoaken, 2003), and aggression and behavioral undercontrol (e.g., Erblich et al., 2003; Giancola & Zeichner, 1997), and the more general phenomenon of acute tolerance highlight the notion that temporal parameters of drinking beyond simple dose and even BAC are critical determinants of alcohol effects. Thus, in considering the subjective effects of alcohol, the limb of the BAC must be taken into account.

A number of explanations for acute tolerance effects may also, in part, be applicable to understanding biphasic effects of alcohol. Perhaps the most influential explanation at the behavioral level is known as *opponent process theory* (Solomon, 1980; Solomon & Corbitt, 1974). Solomon and Corbit's (1974) opponent-process theory posits that a positive (or negative) hedonic state (or A-State) elicits a countervailing negative (or positive) hedonic state (or B-State) that serves to counteract the initial state as part of a natural homeostatic mechanism. That is, the positive stimulating effect of alcohol is thought to reflect the A-state that elicits a compensatory B-state. Opponent-process theory has been used to explain not only biphasic effects of alcohol but also the development of tolerance. Shipley (1987) provides an overview of this model and summarizes existing empirical support (e.g., Rosellini & Lashley, 1982; Solomon & Corbit, 1973; Starr, 1978).

The opponent-process theory of tolerance posits that a drug, such as alcohol, produces an A-state that is followed by a counterdirectional B-state, bringing the drug-induced perturbance back to baseline. Over time, the B-state strengthens, thereby reducing the reaction to the drug (i.e., the opponent B-state reduces the initial A-state; chronic tolerance). Siegel and colleagues (e.g., Siegel, Baptista, Kim, McDonald, & Weise-Kelley, 2000) have extended this model to a conditioning model where Solomon's B-state is evoked not by the unconditioned effect of the drug (i.e., A-state) but by cues accompanying the drug. Recent evidence suggests that in addition to external cues associated with the drug, interoceptive cues associated with drug administration also play an important role in acquisition of tolerance and withdrawal; that is, the immediate effects of the drug can themselves serve as cues. From this perspective, processes related to acute tolerance could be induced in the absence of the drug itself if sufficient drug cues are present.

Not surprisingly, because of ethical issues, studies of the development of chronic tolerance in humans are rare. However, based on rodent studies, there is strong evidence that acute and chronic tolerance are related, with acute tolerance increasing with the development of chronic tolerance (e.g. Bell et al., 2001; Tampier, Quintanilla, & Mardones, 2000).

Consequently, recent data and theory point to temporal factors as being critical in determining subjective effects. Subjective effects vary as a function of dose, the limb of the blood alcohol curve, and the drinking history and amount of chronic adaptation to alcohol that has occurred in the drinker. As we discuss in the next section, multiple other factors regarding the setting further determine the subjective nature of the drinking experience.

Setting

A relatively small number of laboratory-based studies have examined how the presence of other people can influence the subjective effects of alcohol (Doty & de Wit, 1995; Pliner & Cappell, 1974; Sher, 1985; Warren & Raynes, 1972). This type of research typically compares participants assigned to a drink-alone condition with those assigned to a social drinking condition (groups of two or more people) across a range of subjective experiences (e.g., mood). Findings consistently indicate that individuals in social drinking conditions report more positive subjective effects of alcohol, including higher scores on measures of euphoria and pleasure, compared with those in drink alone conditions. For example, Doty and de Wit (1995) studied social drinkers who were randomly assigned to one of four groups that differed on the dose received (0.5 g/kg or 0.8 g/kg) and drinking context (isolated or in a social group). Regardless of dose, participants in the social drinking conditions reported increased levels of positive mood, elation, and friendliness, whereas, participants in the isolated drinking condition reported increased levels of dysphoria. Taken together, these studies indicate that in laboratory settings the subjective effects of ethanol can be influenced by social context (Doty & de Wit, 1995) and that laboratory-based observations of subjective effects are invariably constrained. Cognitive theories (e.g., Steele & Josephs, 1990) provide a strong conceptual foundation for understanding the role of context in determining the nature of alcohol's subjective effects by emphasizing how positive and negative stimuli can condition alcohol's subjective effects.

When considering the role of context, it is important to remain mindful that it can affect the nature of the dosing that an individual will self-administer, as can the perceived environment in which the individual is drinking. Extensive research on modeling effects in ad-lib alcohol consumption has shown powerful effects on the rate and amount of alcohol consumed. For example, Lindman (1982) found that subjects who drank in a barlike laboratory setting with drinking companions consumed nearly twice as much alcohol as those who were isolated, and other naturalistic observations support this basic finding (Rosenbluth, Nathan, & Lawson, 1978). Various experimental studies investigating the role of the drinking companion's rate of consumption exemplify the importance of peer modeling on consumption and suggest that social influence plays an important part in determining volume consumed and/or rate of consumption (e.g., Caudill & Marlatt, 1975; Dericco & Garlington, 1977; Lied & Marlatt, 1979; Strickler, Dobbs, & Maxwell, 1979). Additionally, there is some evidence to support the idea that the specific relationship of the drinker to his or her companions is a critical determinant of how much an individual consumes. Those in groups drink faster than those in pairs, mixed-gendered pairs of drinkers consume alcohol faster than same-sex pairs, and among males, drinking in all-male groups is associated with greater consumption than in mixed-gendered groups (e.g., Mayer, Forster, Murray, & Wagenaar, 1998; Rosenbluth et al., 1978; Senchak, Leonard, & Greene, 1998). Survey data also suggest that consumption of alcohol is greater in groups than in isolation, and that more drinking occurs when an individual is in the presence of friends than when surrounded by family members or significant others (Harford, 1983). Thus, context appears critical with respect to both ad-lib dosing (i.e., drug administration) and independently affecting the nature of subjective experience given a specific dose. These context effects place important boundary conditions on what can be learned from controlled experimentation and highlight the need for alternative approaches (see later section on nonexperimental approaches to studying subjective experience).

Other Important Moderators of the Subjective Effects of Alcohol

Coadministration of Alcohol with Other Psychoactive Substances

Alcohol is frequently used in conjunction with other licit (e.g., tobacco, caffeine) and illicit (e.g., marijuana, cocaine) psychoactive drugs. Thus, characterizing the subjective effects of alcohol in the natural environment requires us to consider additionally how concurrent administration of alcohol with other substances might lead to subjective states that differ either qualitatively or quantitatively from those associated with alcohol intoxication alone.

SMOKING

There is a strong association between alcohol use and cigarette smoking in the general population, with 37% of regular drinkers reporting that they smoke on a regular basis (Bobo & Husten, 2000). The population correlation between smoking and drinking is perhaps at its most extreme when considering those who are alcoholic, as many as 90% of alcoholics are reported to smoke (Istvan & Matarazzo, 1984). Although the proportion of alcoholics who smoke appears to be somewhat smaller during the past two decades, it is still found to be more than 70% in recent studies (Madden, Bucholz, Martin, & Heath, 2000). For the present purposes, it is especially important to note not only that drinkers frequently smoke but that they tend to smoke more when drinking (e.g., Griffiths, Bigelow, & Liebson, 1976). Both controlled laboratory studies and correlational field studies document that alcohol consumption increases smoking intensity (Griffiths et al., 1976; Mintz, Boyd, Rose, Charuvastra & Jarvik, 1985; Mitchell, de Wit, & Zacny, 1995; Nil, Buzzi, & Baettig, 1984; Perkins, Fonte, & Grobe, 2000). Though the subjective effects of alcohol (e.g., Sher, 1985) and nicotine (e.g., Duka, Seiss, & Tasker, 2002; Scheitrum & Akillas, 2002) are greatly influenced by the contexts of their use, in general, nicotine is characterized as a stimulant, and alcohol as a biphasic drug, showing stimulant-like qualities initially and sedative-like qualities later in the course of action. Experimental studies have shown that nicotine administration following alcohol exposure does attenuate some of the acute subjective effects of alcohol consumption. Perkins et al. (1995) found that smokers who received nicotine after consuming alcohol reported lower levels of both subjective intoxication and sedation than those who did not receive nicotine. Lyon, Tong, Leigh, and Clare (1975) reported improvement in decision time in a choice reaction time task after smokers received both alcohol and nicotine, as compared with alcohol alone. Michel and Battig (1989) also reported that among smokers, administration of one cigarette following alcohol ingestion attenuated the depressant effects of alcohol, resulting in alertness and cognitive ability scores comparable to those of the control group, and superior to those who received only alcohol. Kerr, Sherwood, and Hindmarch (1991) reported further evidence of nicotine's antagonistic effect on alcohol by demonstrating improvements on memory and psychomotor performance following alcohol and nicotine administration versus alcohol alone. Overall, the general effect of coadministration of alcohol and nicotine appears to be one of blunting alcohol's effects, perhaps due to acute cross-tolerance between these two substances, a phenomenon clearly demonstrated in various animal studies (e.g., A. C. Collins, Burch, de Fiebre, & Marks, 1988), or because of competing, opposing effects (e.g., Perkins, 1997). Although the majority of findings on alcohol-nicotine interaction suggest blunted alcohol effects, some data suggest that certain sensations of intoxication might actually be increased by coadministration, suggesting acute sensitization (e.g., Rose et al., 2002; Little, 2000); however, here the data are much more preliminary. Regardless, Alcohol × Tobacco/Nicotine interactions indicate substantial moderation of alcohol effects by smoking (or direct administration of nicotine via other routes; Perkins et al., 1995) and highlight the need to consider co-occurring smoking that frequently accompanies drinking alcohol.

CAFFEINE

The nature of alcohol-caffeine coadministration is often different in form than alcohol-tobacco coadministration. Although caffeine is sometimes administered at the same time as alcohol in beverages using colas (e.g., rum and Coke) or coffee (e.g., Irish coffee), more typically caffeine is used by intoxicated individuals as an amethystic (i.e., sobering agent; Alkana & Noble, 1979; Nash, 1966; Newman & Newman, 1956) after consumption has terminated and the drinker wants to curb the effects of alcohol.

It may be surprising that experimental investigations of caffeine's antagonistic action are less common than those employing nicotine, given that caffeine is widely assumed to offset the behavioral and sedating effects of alcohol intoxication. Kerr et al. (1991) suggest that a combination of alcohol and caffeine does improve performance on a short-term memory task and a compensatory tracking task, and elevates critical flicker fusion threshold above levels obtained during both placebo and alcohol-alone trials. Azcona, Barbanoj, Torrent, and Jane (1995) report a decrease in reaction time after administration of alcohol and caffeine, as compared with alcohol alone, though they did not find a difference in ratings of drunkenness between the two groups. Liguori and Robinson (2001) studied the effect of a caffeine and alcohol combination on braking latency in a simulated driving task and on a choice reaction time task. Although they found caffeine attenuated the decrement in braking latency induced by alcohol, it did not improve choice reaction time. Of particular relevance for the current discussion, mood reports were not statistically different for the alcohol and caffeine group compared with those who received alcohol alone. Franks, (1975) found that while caffeine did antagonize alcohol-induced decrements on tests of simple reaction time, it did not have an antagonistic effect on other cognitive and psychomotor tasks; similar nonsignificant effects were reported by Nuotto, Mattila, Seppala, and Konno. (1982). Furthermore, Oborne and Rogers (1983) found evidence for a decrement in performance on a memory scan task when caffeine and alcohol were administered together, relative to alcohol alone. As is evidenced by these reports, the findings in this field suffer from considerable variability. Despite the variability in the literature regarding effects of caffeine on alcohol intoxication, null effects regarding conjoint caffeine and alcohol effects on mood suggest that, at the least, the putatively sobering effect of caffeine on alcohol intoxication is, at best, less than is usually assumed.

ALCOHOL AND ILLICIT SUBSTANCES

Not surprisingly, because of practical constraints of administering illegal substances to human research participants, there has been considerably less research conducted on the conjoint effects of alcohol and illicit drugs such as marijuana and cocaine, despite the fact that individuals frequently report co-occurring use of alcohol with both of these substances. For example, estimates suggest that nearly one third of young adults in the general population have used both alcohol and

SUBJECTIVE EFFECTS OF ALCOHOL I   111

marijuana during the previous six months, and more than one quarter have used alcohol and other illicit drugs simultaneously (Earleywine & Newcomb, 1997). Despite the relative dearth of human research on this topic, some brief comments on existing research are warranted.

COCAINE

Concurrent alcohol and cocaine use is widespread; estimates of comorbidity suggest more than 90% of cocaine users also use alcohol (Grant & Harford, 1990). The physiological and subjective effects of these drugs, alone and in combination, have received some empirical study and point to unique pharmacological consequences of combined cocaine and alcohol use.

Specifically, the combined use of these two drugs results in the production of cocaethylene, a metabolite of cocaine synthesized when alcohol is ingested in the presence of cocaine (e.g., Perez-Reyes & Jeffcoat, 1992; Rafla & Epstein, 1979;). The euphoriant effects of cocaethylene have led some researchers to hypothesize that this metabolite may be a reinforcer, perhaps facilitating concurrent use of these drugs. Existing data do, in fact, show that simultaneous alcohol and cocaine use is associated with increased ratings of positive subjective experience (i.e., "feeling good") compared with administration of either alcohol or cocaine alone (Farre et al., 1993). Similar results were found for ratings of subjective "high" after a combination of alcohol and cocaine (McCance-Katz et al., 1993; Perez-Reyes & Jeffcoat, 1992). Evidence regarding the extent to which cocaine attenuates subjective feelings of drunkenness per se is mixed (Farre et al., 1997; Farre et al., 1993; Higgins et al., 1993), although combined alcohol and cocaine use apparently can lead to lower levels of alcohol-related psychomotor impairment (Farre et al., 1993; Higgins et al., 1993).

MARIJUANA

High base-rate use of marijuana in the general population suggests the coadministration of this drug with alcohol may be common. In their study of polydrug use, Earleywine and Newcomb (1997) found that 31% of their sample reported using both alcohol and marijuana during the past 6 months, and 28% reported using the two drugs simultaneously during that period. Empirical evidence suggests that administration of alcohol in combination with marijuana leads to intoxicating effects greater than those of either drug administered singularly (Chait & Perry, 1994; Lukas & Orozco, 2001). Although the combination of marijuana and alcohol can sometimes lead to increased negative subjective effects, most findings indicate this increase is additive and does not represent an interaction between the two drugs (e.g., Chait & Perry, 1994; Perez-Reyes, Hicks, Bumberry, Jeffcoat, & Cook, 1988).

Lukas and Orozco (2001) found that plasma THC levels were higher in the presence of alcohol than when marijuana was used alone. This increase in plasma THC may contribute to the increase in subjective experience of intoxication. There is little evidence to suggest that the reverse is true; THC does not appear to have an effect on blood alcohol level (Chait & Perry, 1994). It is critical to note that alcohol-marijuana interactions appear to be very important from the standpoint of human performance and traffic safety, since combined use appears to show synergistic effects of alcohol and marijuana on driving ability (Lamers & Ramaekers, 2001) that could substantially increase the driver's risk for crashes and other driving-related mishaps.

Summary

Most research on the subjective effects of alcohol has tended to view "alcohol effects" in isolation from other drugs (especially tobacco but also caffeine, cocaine, and marijuana) that are frequently taken on the same occasions that alcohol is consumed. Depending on the nature of the drug, these effects could either blunt or increase reinforcing and punishing effects. The basic phenomenon of Alcohol × Other Drug interactions has not been studied extensively in humans despite the fact that these interactions are likely to be important from the standpoint of both motivation and behavioral impairment. An adequate understanding of "real life" alcohol effects requires consideration of these complex interactions.

Studies of Disinhibition

Although, by definition, disinhibition is viewed as a behavioral effect of alcohol and not a subjective effect, consideration of disinhibition is highly relevant here because subjective effects are commonly hypothesized to mediate disinhibition via alcohol's effect on affect (e.g., anger, sadness) and cognition (e.g., alcohol myopia). Thus, alcohol's effects on behavior thought to be under some degree of inhibition under most circumstances (e.g., aggression, sexual assault, high-risk sex) can be used to infer underlying changes in subjective state. Moreover, the centrality of the construct of disinhibition (with respect to appraisal and reappraisal processes) initially proposed for alcohol-related aggression by Taylor and Leonard (1983) and later generalized to an array of alcohol-related social behaviors (e.g., Steele & Josephs, 1990; Steele & Southwick, 1985) further underscores its perceived importance in understanding alcohol's subjective effects.

Whereas alcohol consumption is linked anecdotally to presumably punishing subjective effects such as anger, laboratory studies, such as those examining alcohol-related aggression, tend to place greater emphasis on behavioral measures of what is typically labeled "affective" or "angry," as opposed to "instrumental" aggression (Geen, 1990). The majority of laboratory studies of alcohol and *aggression* have used a procedure developed and refined by Taylor and colleagues (Taylor, 1967). Results from a large body of research conducted within this paradigm over the past four decades indicate that alcohol has a strong but not invariant facilitative effect on the expression of aggressive behavior. In a meta-analysis of laboratory studies of alcohol and aggression, average effect size estimates (d) were .61 for alcohol versus placebo (i.e., expect alcohol, receive placebo) condition comparisons and .25 for alcohol versus control (i.e., neither expect nor receive alcohol) group comparisons (Bushman & Cooper, 1990). Earlier meta-analyses on alcohol and social behavior that included examinations of laboratory alcohol-aggression studies yielded similar effect size estimates (Hull & Bond, 1986; Steele & Southwick, 1985).

Although studies with women are much less common, it appears that observed effects are moderated by gender (Bushman, 1997; Giancola et al., 2002), as well as by a number of situational factors such as provocation (Taylor, Schmutte, Leonard, & Cranston, 1979) and an array of other variables such as stated pacifistic intentions by an opponent (Taylor, Gamman, & Capasso, 1976), self-awareness (Bailey, Leonard, Cranston, & Taylor, 1983), and social norms (Jeavons & Taylor, 1985). Dispositional factors such as empathy (Giancola, 2003), trait aggression (Giancola, 2002a), and trait anger (Giancola, 2002b) have also been shown to moderate the alcohol-aggression relation. Of particular note with respect to disinhibition, it appears easier to initially inhibit the expression of aggression from intoxicated participants than it is to decrease it once instigated, as Taylor and Gammon (1976) found that third-party intervention (i.e., experimental confederates encouraging moderate responses) did little to decrease aggressive responses. Laplace, Chermack, and Taylor (1994) found that inexperienced drinkers demonstrated significantly higher levels of aggression than individuals with moderate and high drinking experience, with other studies indicating moderation by beverage factors such as the type (e.g., Gustafson, 1988, 1990) and quantity of alcohol consumed (Taylor & Gammon, 1975), as well as the limb of the blood alcohol curve (Giancola & Zeichner, 1997). Like general theories of alcohol effects, neuropharmacological, expectancy, and cognitive theories have been invoked to explain alcohol's effects on aggression (Bushman, 1997; Giancola, 2002b; Taylor & Chermack, 1993).

Like aggressive behavior, the presumed causal link between acute intoxication and the increased likelihood of *sexual behavior*, including high-risk sexual behavior, is widely held and deeply ingrained across both cultures and time. Empirically, methodological limitations and the inherent difficulty of conducting research in this area make causal inferences about alcohol's relations with risky sex exceedingly difficult

(Leigh & Stall, 1993). A comprehensive review of empirical approaches and theoretical explanations for the purported link between alcohol use and sexual behavior is beyond the scope of this chapter (see Cooper, 2002; Crowe & George, 1989; Leigh & Stall, 1993; Wilson, 1977). Rather, here we consider laboratory studies that have examined subjective and objective arousal, perceived risk perceptions, and perceived likelihood of engaging in sexual behaviors in response to actual or expected alcohol ingestion. Again, consistent with our focus in this section, these findings are largely examined in the context of psychopharmacological and information-processing explanations of the mediational role of disinhibition in the expression of alcohol's subjective effects.

Although experimental investigations of the effect of alcohol and sexual responsiveness date back to the 1950s, methodological short-comings severely limit the conclusions that can be drawn from these studies. Two early studies examined the effects of various doses of alcohol on both objective (plethysmographically assessed) and subjective (self-report assessed) sexual arousal in response to erotic stimuli in samples of men and women (Briddell & Wilson, 1976; Wilson & Lawson, 1976a). While parallel findings of significant negative linear dose effects were found for men and women for objective sexual arousal, men's subjective reports mirrored objective data, but women reported *enhanced* sexual arousal in contrast to observed decrements in their objective arousal levels.

In the 1970s, researchers began to disentangle pharmacological and expectancy set effects through the use of the balanced placebo design (Marlatt & Rohsenow, 1980). Findings from these studies suggest that, at least at lower doses, expectations regarding alcohol's effects on sexuality are more powerful than are pharmacological effects (Abrams & Wilson, 1983; Briddell et al., 1978; George & Marlatt, 1986; Lang, Searles, Lauerman, & Adesso, 1980; Wilson & Lawson, 1976b, 1978). It is also important to note that although relatively few studies have been conducted, expectancy set effects observed in men have not been replicated in samples of women (Norris, 1994).

More recent research has combined expectancy set manipulation (expect alcohol, expect no alcohol) with both questionnaire and vignette methods in an attempt to better explicate the expected and pharmacological effects of alcohol. For example, these studies have demonstrated that both expectancy set (George, Derman, & Nochajski, 1989) and perceived alcohol ingestion within the context of a vignette (George, Cue, Lopez, Crowe & Norris, 1995) moderated the influence of preexisting outcome expectancies on responses to sexually explicit stimuli or perceived likelihood of the occurrence of sex. George, Stoner, Norris, Lopez, and Lehman (2000) replicated and extended these findings in a study examining direct and indirect relations of preexisting sexual facilitation outcome expectancies, expectancy set, sexual arousal, and sexual disinhibition with erotica viewing behavior among dyads. In this study, a priori sexual facilitation expectancies moderated the relation between expectancy set and perceived sexual arousal, which, in turn, predicted perceived sexual disinhibition of a coparticipant, which was associated with increased time spent viewing erotica. These findings, all obtained in lieu of actual alcohol ingestion, in conjunction with studies reviewed earlier, provide strong evidence for expectancy-based theories of alcohol's effects on sexual behavior. However, data consistent with pharmacological disinhibition via impaired cognitive processing also exist.

McCarty, Diamond, and Kaye (1982), using the balanced-placebo design in a study examining sexual arousal in response to erotic images, found the strongest effects for subjective effects of sexual arousal and fantasy among individuals who did not know they were drinking alcohol (i.e., participants who were told that their alcoholic drinks did not contain alcohol). In four studies, Fromme and colleagues (Fromme, D'Amico, & Katz, 1999; Fromme, Katz, & D'Amico, 1997) examined the effects of alcohol and expectancy set on sexual risk taking and found consistent evidence for alcohol-induced impairment rather than expectancy set, with those receiving alcohol reporting fewer perceived negative consequences from risky sex and a greater perceived likelihood of engaging in risky sex. As discussed earlier in this chapter, MacDonald and colleagues (MacDonald, Fong, et al., 2000; MacDonald, MacDonald, et al., 2000) conducted a series of studies examining the effect of intoxication on intentions for risky sexual behavior from the perspective of alcohol myopia theory (Steele & Josephs, 1990). As noted by MacDonald, Fong, et al. (2000), the likelihood of risky sexual behavior may increase or decrease depending on whether impelling (e.g., sexual arousal) or inhibiting (e.g., fear of contracting AIDS) cues are most salient in the situation. They found that dose and arousal interacted such that only participants who were both intoxicated and aroused reported stronger intentions to have unprotected sex, presumably because arousal cues were more salient than inhibiting cues, whereas sober participants were able to weigh both impelling and inhibiting cues. When MacDonald, Fong, et al. (2000) made inhibiting cues more salient by stamping the hands of college student bar patrons with a message highlighting the threat of AIDS, they found that this "canceled out" the tendency of intoxicated participants to report greater intentions for risky sex.

At first glance it would seem that expectancy theory and alcohol myopia offer opposing predictions of the likely relation between alcohol consumption and risky sex. However, George et al. (2000), in an attempt to reconcile their findings with pharmacologically driven cognitive impairment models, suggest the possibility that these two processes may both be operative, with ascendancy dependent on the level of situational conflict and, particularly, level of intoxication. Specifically, they propose that expectancy may lead to alcohol consumption in sexual situations to attain disinhibitory outcomes and, consistent with their data (George et al., 2000), may guide immediate postconsumption perceptions and behavior. However, at higher blood alcohol levels, cognitive impairment resulting from the pharmacological effects of alcohol may then preclude consideration of more distal (e.g., inhibitory) cues. These findings highlight the importance of considering the precise nature of the situation (such as the drinker's goals, active conflicts, etc.) in determining the nature of the alcohol effect.

Nonexperimental Approaches to Studying Subjective Experience

To a large degree, measures of alcohol outcome expectancies (Brown, Goldman, Inn, & Anderson, 1980; Fromme et al., 1993) provide straightforward answers to the general question of how alcohol affects subjective experience and behavioral experience and the extent that these are viewed as motives for drinking. That is, individuals commonly report that alcohol increases sociability, feeling "high," and feeling "more sexy" and decreases feelings of anxiety and depression. In addition to these positive experiences, people also frequently report negative subjective effects such as being sedated, made ill, and becoming disinhibited in undesired ways. Moreover, these same types of positive effects are reflected in the stated reasons for drinking (e.g., Cooper et al., 1992) and negative effects reflected in reasons for not drinking (e.g., Greenfield, Guydish & Temple, 1989). Although both expectancies and reasons for drinking tend to be strong correlates of drinking and predict drinking prospectively, it is never clear to what extent they mirror the actual experience of the drinker.

Owing to limitations of the restricted contexts imposed by laboratory experimentation and the vagaries of survey-based, retrospective self-reports of subjective effects of alcohol, there has been a recent interest in so-called diary-based approaches to assess subjective effects of alcohol in the natural environment. These daily process methods, which sample ongoing experience in everyday life, have been used to examine the association between mood and stress and drinking on a daily basis. These methods are often referred to as Ecological Momentary Assessment (EMA; Stone & Shiffman, 1994) or experience sampling (Reis & Gable, 2000).

Daily process data minimize biases (e.g., current state of the person, reconstruction bias, retroactive reconstruction) that are inherent to retrospective recall and are more representative of respondents' experiences in real-world drinking contexts, and the collection of repeated assessments adds to the reliability of the data (Shiffman & Hufford, 2002; Shiffman & Stone, 1998; Stone & Shiffman, 1994). The value of diary-based methods in the alcohol literature was first demonstrated in basic assessments of quantity and frequency of consumption; individuals reported more drinking via daily diary assessment than with retrospective methods (e.g., Carney, Tennen, Affleck, del Boca, & Kranzler, 1998; Webb, Redman, Sanson-Fisher, & Gibberd, 1990), particularly for those who reported heavy drinking. Recent studies highlight the advantages of this approach for examining subjective effects of alcohol.

Most data on subjective states and consumption have focused on the role of positive and negative affect on subsequent drinking. Overall, existing studies have tended to show that both positive emotions (Armeli, Tennen, Affleck, & Kranzler, 2000; R. Collins et al., 1998; Litt, Cooney, & Morse, 2000; Steptoe & Wardle, 1999; Swendsen et al., 2000) and negative emotions (Armeli et al., 2000; Litt et al., 2000) are associated with greater consumption and with the desire or urge to drink, but these studies also make clear the contextual constraints on the affect-drinking relationship.

To date, EMA and experience sampling approaches have not been employed extensively to study the effects of alcohol on subjective state. R. Collins et al. (1998) documented that whereas positive mood at the beginning of a drinking episode increased excessive (5+ drinks/occasion) drinking, at the end of a reported drinking episode, positive mood was negatively associated with excessive drinking, suggesting either that excessive drinking actually reduces a positive mood or that individuals in a positive mood feel the need to discontinue drinking. Hussong, Hicks, Levy, and Curran (2001) failed to detect any within-time associations between alcohol use and positive or negative affect once they controlled for lagged reciprocal effects between alcohol consumption and affect (although they did find that greater weekday drinking predicted greater weekend positive affect, and greater weekend drinking predicted greater weekday negative affect). Although the use of EMA is still in its infancy in the study of alcohol effects, it holds great promise in that, at least in principle, it will allow assessment of intoxication in natural contexts, with coadministered substances, and in underage drinkers—all things that are difficult to do in the laboratory. These types of studies can provide the critical linkages between epidemiological surveys and behavioral pharmacological investigations.

Concluding Comments

Perhaps more so than any other psychoactive substance, alcohol is consumed for an extraordinarily broad range of effects (e.g., from stimulation to sedation, for positive reinforcement and for negative reinforcement). The determinants of the nature of the effect are highly conditional upon the beliefs individuals bring to the drinking situation, their history of consumption, their current mood states, their drinking contexts, and the nature of the drinking episode. Additionally, as discussed in chapter 5, a host of additional factors related to the characteristics of the drinker further qualify subjective effects. Moreover, for many drinkers, alcohol is often consumed with other substances (notably tobacco but also illicit drugs and caffeine); this concurrent use of alcohol and other drugs further qualifies the nature of the drinking experience. The subjective effects obtained from alcohol, or at least the individual's beliefs about alcohol's effects on him- or herself, appear to be important determinants of the drinking pattern. Characterizing this nexus of determinants of drinking experience is important if we wish to be able to fully understand the uses of alcohol and the determinants of drinking in both alcohol-dependent and nondependent drinkers.

The authors want to thank Gilbert Parra and Amee Epler for their help in the preparation of the manuscript.

References

Aas, H., Klepp, K. I., Laberg, J. C., & Aaro, L. E. (1995). Predicting adolescents' intentions to drinking alcohol: Outcome expectancies and self-efficacy. *Journal of Studies on Alcohol, 56,* 293–299.

Abrams, D. B., & Niaura, R. S. (1987). Social learning theory. In H. T. Blane & K. E. Leonard (Eds.), *Psychological theories of drinking and alcoholism* (pp. 131–178). New York: Guilford.

Abrams, D. B., & Wilson, G. (1983). Alcohol, sexual arousal, and self-control. *Journal of Personality and Social Psychology,* 188–198.

Alkana, R. L., & Noble, E. P. (1979). Amethystic agents:Reversal of acute ethanol intoxication in humans. In E. Majchrowicz & E. P. Noble (Eds.), *Biochemistry and pharmacology of ethanol* (Vol. 2, pp. 349–374). New York: Plenum.

Armeli, S., Tennen, H., Affleck, G., & Kranzler, H. R. (2000). Does affect mediate the association between daily events and alcohol use? *Journal of Studies on Alcohol, 61,* 862–871.

Azcona, O., Barbanoj, M. J., Torrent, J., & Jane, F. (1995). Evaluation of the central effects of alcohol and caffeine interaction. *British Journal of Clinical Pharmacology, 40,* 393–400.

Babor, T. F., Hofmann, M., DelBoca, F. K., Hesselbrock, V. M., Meyer, R. E., Dolinsky, Z. S., et al. (1992). Types of alcoholics. I. Evidence for an empirically derived typology based on indicators of vulnerability and severity. *Archives of General Psychiatry, 49,* 599–608.

Bailey, D. S., Leonard, K. E., Cranston, J. W., & Taylor, S. P. (1983). Effects of alcohol and self-awareness on human physical aggression. *Personality and Social Psychology Bulletin, 9,* 289–295.

Baldwin, A. R., Oei, T. P., & Young, R. (1993). To drink or not to drink: The differential role of alcohol expectancies and drinking refusal self-efficacy in quantity and frequency of alcohol consumption. *Cognitive Therapy and Research, 17,* 511–530.

Bandura, A. (1969). Social learning of moral judgments. *Journal of Personality and Social Psychology, 11,* 275–279.

Bandura, A. (1986). *Social foundations of thought and action: A social cognitive theory.* Upper Saddle River, N.J.: Pearson Education.

Bell, R. L., Stewart, R. B., Woods, J. E., Lumeng, L., Li, T.-K., Murphy, J. M., et al. (2001). Responsivity and development of tolerance to the motor impairing effects of moderate doses of ethanol in alcohol-preferring (P) and -nonpreferring (NP) rat lines. *Alcoholism: Clinical and Experimental Research, 25,* 644–650.

Bobo, J. K., & Husten, C. (2000). Sociocultural influences on smoking and drinking. *Alcohol Health and Research World, 24,* 225–232.

Briddell, D. W., Rimm, D. C., Caddy, G. R., Krawitz, G., Sholis, D. & Wonderlin, R. J. (1978). Effects of alcohol and cognitive set on sexual arousal to deviant stimuli. *Journal of Abnormal Psychology, 87,* 418–430.

Briddell, D. W., & Wilson, G. (1976). Effects of alcohol and expectancy set on male sexual arousal. *Journal of Abnormal Psychology, 85,* 225–234.

Brown, S. A., Christiansen, B. A., & Goldman, M. S. (1987). The Alcohol Expectancy Questionnaire: An instrument for the assessment of adolescent and adult alcohol expectancies. *Journal of Studies on Alcohol, 48,* 483–491.

Brown, S. A., Creamer, V. A., & Stetson, B. A. (1987). Adolescent alcohol expectancies in relation to personal and parental drinking patterns. *Journal of Abnormal Psychology, 96,* 117–121.

Brown, S. A., Goldman, M. S., & Christiansen, B. A. (1985). Do alcohol expectancies mediate drinking patterns of adults? *Journal of Consulting and Clinical Psychology, 53,* 512–519.

Brown, S. A., Goldman, M. S., Inn, A., & Anderson, L. R. (1980). Expectations of reinforcement from alcohol: Their domain and relation to drinking patterns. *Journal of Consulting and Clinical Psychology, 48,* 419–426.

Bureau of Alcohol, Tobacco, and Firearms. (1999, October 22). *Health Claims and Other Health-Related Statements in the Labeling and Advertising of Alcohol Beverages.* Retrieved December 18, 2003, from http://www.atf.gov/press/fy00press/102299healthclm.htm

Bushman, B. J. (1997). Effects of alcohol on human aggression: Validity of proposed explanations. In M. Galanter (Ed.), *Recent developments in alcoholism: Vol. 13: Alcohol and violence: Epidemiology, neurobiology, psychology, family issues* (pp. 227–243). New York: Kluwer.

Bushman, B. J., & Cooper, H. M. (1990). Effects of alcohol on human aggression: An integrative research review. *Psychological Bulletin, 107,* 341–354.

Carney, M. A., Tennen, H., Affleck, G., del Boca, F. K., & Kranzler, H. R. (1998). Levels and patterns of alcohol consumption using timeline followback, daily diaries and real-time "electronic interviews." *Journal of Studies on Alcohol, 59,* 447–454.

Caudill, B. D., & Marlatt, G. (1975). Modeling influences in social drinking: An experimental analogue. *Journal of Consulting and Clinical Psychology, 43,* 405–415.

Chait, L., & Perry, J. (1994). Effects of alcohol pretreatment on human marijuana self-administration. *Psychopharmacology, 113,* 346–350.

Christiansen, B. A., Smith, G. T., Roehling, P. V., & Goldman, M. S. (1989). Using alcohol expectancies to predict adolescent drinking behavior after one year. *Journal of Consulting & Clinical Psychology, 57,* 93–99.

Cloninger, C. R. (1987). A systematic method for clinical description and classification of personality variants. *Archives of General Psychiatry, 44*, 573–588.

Collins, A. C., Burch, J. B., de Fiebre, C. M., & Marks, M. J. (1988). Tolerance
to and cross tolerance between ethanol and nicotine. *Pharmacology, Biochemistry and Behavior, 29*, 365–373.

Collins, R., Morsheimer, E. T., Shiffman, S., Paty, J. A., Gnys, M., & Papandonatos,
G. D. (1998). Ecological momentary assessment in a behavioral drinking
moderation training program. *Experimental and Clinical Psychopharmacology, 6*, 306–315.

Connors, G. J., & Maisto, S. A. (1979). Effects of alcohol, instructions, and
consumption rate on affect and physiological sensations. *Psychopharmacologia, 62*, 261–266.

Connors, G. J., O'Farrell, T. J., Cutter, H. S., Thompson, D. L. (1986). Alcohol
expectancies among male alcoholics, problem drinkers, and nonproblem
drinkers. *Alcoholism: Clinical and Experimental Research, 10*, 667–671.

Connors, G. J., Tarbox, A. R., & Faillace, L. A. (1993). Changes in alcohol
expectancies and drinking behavior among treated problem drinkers. *Journal of Studies on Alcohol, 54*, 676–683.

Cooper, M. (2002). Alcohol use and risky sexual behavior among college
students and youth: Evaluating the evidence. *Journal of Studies on Alcohol, 63(Suppl. 14)*:101–117.

Cooper, M., Frone, M. R., Russell, M., & Mudar, P. (1995). Drinking to regu-
late positive and negative emotions: A motivational model of alcohol use.
Journal of Personality and Social Psychology, 69, 990–1005.

Cooper, M., Russell, M., & George, W. H. (1988). Coping, expectancies, and
alcohol abuse: A test of social learning formulations. *Journal of Abnormal
Psychology, 97*, 218–230.

Cooper, M., Russell, M., Skinner, J. B., Frone, M. R., Mudar, P. (1992). Stress
and alcohol use: Moderating effects of gender, coping, and alcohol expectancies. *Journal of Abnormal Psychology, 101*, 139–152.

Cox, W., & Klinger, E. (1988). A motivational model of alcohol use. *Journal
of Abnormal Psychology, 97*, 168–180.

Crowe, L. C., & George, W. H. (1989). Alcohol and human sexuality: Review
and integration. *Psychological Bulletin, 105*, 374–386.

Cummings, C. C., & Marlatt, G. A. (August, 1983). *Stress induced alcohol consumption.* Paper presented at the 91st annual convention of the American
Psychological Association, Anaheim, CA.

Curtin, J. J., Patrick, C. J., Lang, A. R., Cacioppo, J. T., & Birbaumer, N. (2001).
Alcohol affects emotion through cognition. *Psychological Science, 12*, 527–
531.

Dai, X., Thavundayil, J., & Gianoulakis, C. (2002). Differences in the responses
of the pituitary beta-endorphin and cardiovascular system to ethanol and
stress as a function of family history. *Alcoholism: Clinical and Experimental Research, 26*, 1171–1180.

Darkes, J., & Goldman, M. S. (1993). Expectancy challenge and drinking reduction: Experimental evidence for a mediational process. *Journal of Consulting and Clinical Psychology, 61*, 344–353.

Darkes, J., & Goldman, M. S. (1998). Expectancy challenge and drinking reduction: Process and structure in the alcohol expectancy network. *Experimental and Clinical Psychopharmacology, 6*, 64–76.

Dericco, D. A., & Garlington, W. K. (1977). The effect of modeling and disclosure of experimenter's intent on drinking rate of college students. *Addictive Behaviors, 2* (Suppl. 3), 135–139.

Doty, P., & de Wit, H. (1995). Effect of setting on the reinforcing and subjective effects of ethanol in social drinkers. *Psychopharmacology, 118,* 19–27.

Duka, T., Seiss, E., & Tasker, R. (2002). The effects of extrinsic context on nicotine discrimination. *Behavioural Pharmacology, 13,* 39–47.

Dunn, M. E., & Goldman, M. S. (1996). Empirical modeling of an alcohol expectancy memory network in elementary school children as a function of grade. *Experimental and Clinical Psychopharmacology, 4,* 209–217.

Earleywine, M. (1994). Anticipated biphasic effects of alcohol vary with risk for alcoholism: A preliminary report. *Alcoholism: Clinical and Experimental Research, 18,* 711–714.

Earleywine, M., & Erblich, J. (1996). A confirmed factor structure for the Biphasic Alcohol Effects Scale. *Experimental and Clinical Psychopharmacology, 4,* 107–113.

Earleywine, M., & Martin, C. S. (1993). Anticipated stimulant and sedative effects of alcohol vary with dosage and limb of the blood alcohol curve. *Alcoholism: Clinical and Experimental Research, 17,* 135–139.

Earleywine, M., & Newcomb, M. D. (1997). Concurrent versus simultaneous polydrug use: Prevalence, correlates, discriminant validity, and prospective effects on health outcomes. *Experimental and Clinical Psychopharmacology, 5,* 353–364.

Ekman, G., Frankenhaeuser, M., Goldberg, L., Hagdahl, R., & Myrsten, A. L. (1964). Subjective and objective effects of alcohol as functions of dosage and time. *Psychopharmacologia, 6,* 399–409.

Ellison, R. C. (2002). Balancing the risks and benefits of moderate drinking. *Annals of the New York Academy of Sciences, 957,* 1–6.

Erblich, J., Earleywine, M., Erblich, B., & Bovbjerg, D. H. (2003). Biphasic stimulant and sedative effects of ethanol: Are children of alcoholics really different? *Addictive Behaviors, 28,* 1129–1139.

Eriksson, C. J. (1983). Human blood acetaldehyde concentration during ethanol oxidation (update 1982). *Pharmacology, Biochemistry and Behavior, 18*(Suppl, 1), 141–150.

Eriksson, C. J., Mizoi, Y., & Fukunaga, T. (1982). The determination of acetaldehyde in human blood by the perchloric acid precipitation method: The characterization and elimination of artifactual acetaldehyde formation. *Analytical Biochemistry, 125,* 259–263.

Evans, D., & Dunn, N. J. (1995). Alcohol expectancies, coping responses and self-efficacy judgments: A replication and extension of Cooper et al.'s 1988 study in a college sample. *Journal of Studies on Alcohol, 56,* 186–193.

Farre, M., de la Torre, R., Gonzalez, M. L., Teran, M. T., Roset, P. N., Menoyo, E., et al. (1997). Cocaine and alcohol interactions in humans: Neuroendocrine effects and cocaethylene metabolism. *Journal of Pharmacology and Experimental Therapeutics, 283,* 164–176.

Farre, M., de la Torre, R., Llorente, M., Lamas, X., Ugena, B., Segura, J., et al. (1993). Alcohol and cocaine interactions in humans. *Journal of Pharmacology and Experimental Therapeutics, 266,* 1364–1373.

Fillmore, M. T., & Blackburn, J. (2002). Compensating for alcohol-induced impairment: Alcohol expectancies and behavioral disinhibition. *Journal of Studies on Alcohol, 63,* 237–246.

Fillmore, M. T., Mulvihill, L. E., & Vogel-Sprott, M. (1994). The expected drug and its expected effect interact to determine placebo responses to alcohol and caffeine. *Psychopharmacology, 115,* 383–388.

Fillmore, M. T., & Vogel-Sprott, M. (1995). Expectancies about alcohol-induced motor impairment predict individual differences in responses to alcohol and placebo. *Journal of Studies on Alcohol, 56,* 90–98.

Fillmore, M. T., & Vogel-Sprott, M. (1996). Evidence that expectancies mediate behavioral impairment under alcohol. *Journal of Studies on Alcohol, 57,* 598–603.

Finn, T., & Strickland, D. E. (1982). A content analysis of beverage alcohol advertising. II. Television advertising. *Journal of Studies on Alcohol, 43,* 964–989.

Franks, H. M., Hagedorn, H., Hensley, V. R., Hensley, W. J., & Starmer, G. A. (1975). The effect of caffeine on human performance, alone and in combination with ethanol. *Psychopharmacologia, 45,* 177–181.

Fraser, A. G., Rosalki, S. B., Gamble, G. D., & Pounder, R. E. (1995). Inter-individual and intra-individual variability of ethanol concentration-time profiles: Comparison of ethanol ingestion before or after an evening meal. *British Journal of Clinical Pharmacology, 40,* 387–392.

Froehlich, J., Stewart, R., Li, T., Mosemiller, A., McCullough, D., Ho, M., et al. (2001). Introduction of steady-state blood alcohol levels: Application to the study of within-session alcohol tolerance in rats. *Alcoholism: Clinical and Experimental Research, 25,* 370–376.

Fromme, K., & D'Amico, E. J. (1999). Neurobiological bases of alcohol's psychological effects. In K. E. Leonard & H. T. Blane (Eds.), *Psychological theories of drinking and alcoholism* (2nd ed., pp. 422–455). New York: Guilford.

Fromme, K., D'Amico, E. J., & Katz, E. C. (1999). Intoxicated sexual risk taking: An expectancy or cognitive impairment explanation? *Journal of Studies on Alcohol, 60,* 54–63.

Fromme, K., Katz, E., & D'Amico, E. (1997). Effects of alcohol intoxication on the perceived consequences of risk taking. *Experimental and Clinical Psychopharmacology, 5,* 14–23.

Fromme, K., Stroot, E. A., & Kaplan, D. (1993). Comprehensive effects of alcohol: Development and psychometric assessment of a new expectancy questionnaire. *Psychological Assessment, 5,* 19–26.

Geen, R. G. (1990). *Human aggression.* Philadelphia: Open University.

George, W. H., Cue, K. L., Lopez, P. A., Crowe, L. C., & Norris, J. (1995). Self-reported alcohol expectancies and postdrinking sexual inferences about women. *Journal of Applied Social Psychology, 25,* 164–186.

George, W. H., Derman, K. H., & Nochajski, T. H. (1989). Expectancy set, self-reported expectancies and predispositional traits: Predicting interest in violence and erotica. *Journal of Studies on Alcohol, 50,* 541–551.

George, W. H., Frone, M. R., Cooper, M., Russell, M., Skinner, J. B., & Windle, M. (1995). A revised Alcohol Expectancy Questionnaire: Factor structure confirmation and invariance in a general population sample. *Journal of Studies on Alcohol, 56,* 177–185.

George, W. H., & Marlatt, G. (1986). The effects of alcohol and anger on interest in violence, erotica, and deviance. *Journal of Abnormal Psychology, 95,* 150–158.

George, W. H., Stoner, S. A., Norris, J., Lopez, P. A., & Lehman, G. L. (2000). Alcohol expectancies and sexuality: A self-fulfilling prophecy analysis of dyadic perceptions and behavior. *Journal of Studies on Alcohol, 61,* 168–176.

Giancola, P. R. (2002a). The influence of trait anger on the alcohol-aggression relation in men and women. *Alcoholism: Clinical and Experimental Research, 26,* 1350–1358.

Giancola, P. R. (2002b). Alcohol-related aggression during the college years: Theories, risk factors, and policy implications. *Journal of Studies on Alcohol, 63, Suppl. 14,* 129–139.

Giancola, P. R. (2003). The moderating effects of dispositional empathy on alcohol-related aggression in men and women. *Journal of Abnormal Psychology, 112,* 275–281.

Giancola, P. R., Helton, E. L., Osborne, A. B., Terry, M. K., Fuss, A. M., & Westerfield, J. A. (2002). The effects of alcohol and provocation on aggressive behavior in men and women. *Journal of Studies on Alcohol, 63,* 64–73.

Giancola, P. R., & Zeichner, A. (1997). The biphasic effects of alcohol on human physical aggression. *Journal of Abnormal Psychology, 106,* 598–607.

Goldman, M. S., Brown, S. A., & Christiansen, B. A. (1987). Expectancy theory: Thinking about drinking. In H. T. Blane & K. E. Leonard (Eds.), *Psychological theories of drinking and alcoholism* (pp. 181–226). New York: Guilford.

Goldman, M. S., Brown, S. A., Christiansen, B. A., & Smith, G. T. (1991). Alcoholism and memory: Broadening the scope of alcohol-expectancy research. *Psychological Bulletin, 110,* 137–146.

Goldman, M. S., Del Boca, F. K., & Darkes, J. (1999). Alcohol expectancy theory: The application of cognitive neuroscience. In K. E. Leonard & H. T. Blane (Eds.), *Psychological theories of drinking and alcoholism* (2nd ed., pp. 203–246). New York: Guilford.

Grant, B. F., & Harford, T. C. (1990). Concurrent and simultaneous use of alcohol with cocaine: Results of national survey. *Drug and Alcohol Dependence, 25,* 97–104.

Greeley, J., & Oei, T. (1999). Alcohol and tension reduction. In K. E. Leonard & H. T. Blane (Eds.), *Psychological theories of drinking and alcoholism* (2nd ed., pp. 14–53). New York: Guilford.

Greenfield, T. K., Guydish, J., & Temple, M. T. (1989). Reasons students give for limiting drinking: A factor analysis with implications for research and practice. *Journal of Studies on Alcohol, 50,* 108–115.

Griffiths, R. R., Bigelow, G. E., & Liebson, I. (1976). Facilitation of human tobacco self-administration by ethanol: A behavioral analysis. *Journal of the Experimental Analysis of Behavior, 25,* 279–292.

Grube, J. W. (1993). Alcohol portrayals and alcohol advertising on television: Content and effects on children and adolescents. *Alcohol Health and Research World, 17,* 54–60.

Gustafson, R. (1988). Effects of beer and wine on male aggression as measured by a paper-and-pen test. *Psychological Reports, 62,* 795–798.

Gustafson, R. (1990). Wine and male physical aggression. *Journal of Drug Issues, 20*, 75–86.

Harburg, E., Gunn, R., Gleiberman, L., DiFranceisco, W., & Schork, A. (1993). Psychosocial factors, alcohol use, and hangover signs among social drinkers: A reappraisal. *Journal of Clinical Epidemiology, 46*, 413–422.

Harford, T. C. (1983). A contextual analysis of drinking events. *International Journal of the Addictions, 18*, 825–834.

Hartocollis, P. (1963). Drunkenness and suggestion: An experiment with intravenous alcohol. *Quarterly Journal of Studies on Alcohol, 23*, 376–389.

Henderson, M. J., Goldman, M. S., Coovert, M. D., & Carnevalla, N. (1994). Covariance structure models of expectancy. *Journal of Studies on Alcohol, 55*, 315–326.

Higgins, S. T., Rush, C. R., Bickel, W. K., Hughes, J. R., Lynn, M., & Capeless, M. A. (1993). Acute behavioral and cardiac effects of cocaine and alcohol combinations in humans. *Psychopharmacology, 111*, 285–294.

Hiltunen, A. J. (1997). Acute alcohol tolerance in social drinkers: Changes in subjective effects dependent on the alcohol dose and prior alcohol experience. *Alcohol, 14*, 373–378.

Hiltunen, A. J., Saxon, L., Skagerberg, S., & Borg, S. (2000). Acute tolerance during intravenous infusion of alcohol: Comparison of performance during ascending and steady state concentrations—A pilot study. *Alcohol, 22*, 69–74.

Holdstock, L., & de Wit, H. (1998). Individual differences in the biphasic effects of ethanol. *Alcoholism: Clinical and Experimental Research, 22*, 1903–1911.

Holdstock, L., King, A. C., & de Wit, H. (2000). Subjective and objective responses to ethanol in moderate/heavy and light social drinkers. *Alcoholism: Clinical and Experimental Research, 24*, 789–794.

Hull, J. G., & Bond, C. F. (1986). Social and behavioral consequences of alcohol consumption and expectancy: A meta-analysis. *Psychological Bulletin, 99*, 347–360.

Hussong, A. M., Hicks, R. E., Levy, S. A., & Curran, P. J. (2001). Specifying the relations between affect and heavy alcohol use among young adults. *Journal of Abnormal Psychology, 110*, 449–461.

Istvan, J., & Matarazzo, J. D. (1984). Tobacco, alcohol, and caffeine use: A review of their interrelationships. *Psychological Bulletin, 95*, 301–326.

Jeavons, C. M., & Taylor, S. P. (1985). The control of alcohol-related aggression: Redirecting the inebriate's attention to socially appropriate conduct. *Aggressive Behavior, 11*, 93–101.

Jones, A. W., & Jonsson, K. A. (1994). Food-induced lowering of blood-ethanol profiles and increased rate of elimination immediately after a meal. *Journal of Forensic Sciences, 39*, 1084–1093.

Jones, A. W., Jonsson, K. A., & Neri, A. (1991). Peak blood-ethanol concentration and the time of its occurrence after rapid drinking on an empty stomach. *Journal of Forensic Sciences, 36*, 376–385.

Jones, B. M., & Vega, A. (1972). Cognitive performance measured on the ascending and descending limb of the blood alcohol curve. *Psychopharmacologia, 23*, 99–114.

Jones, B. T., & McMahon, J. (1994). Negative and positive alcohol expectancies as predictors of abstinence after discharge from a residential treatment program: A one-month and three-month follow-up study in men. *Journal of Studies on Alcohol, 55*, 543–548.

Josephs, R. A., & Steele, C. M. (1990). The two faces of alcohol myopia: Attentional mediation of psychological stress. *Journal of Abnormal Psychology, 99*, 115–126.

Kalant, H. (1971). Absorption, diffusion, distribution, and elimination of ethanol: Effects on biological membranes. In B. Kiss in & H. Begleiter (Ed.), *The biology of alcoholism* (Vol. 1). New York: Plenum.

Kerr, J., Sherwood, N., & Hindmarch, I. (1991). Separate and combined effects of the social drugs on psychomotor performance. *Psychopharmacology, 104*, 113–119.

King, A. C., Houle, T., de Wit, H., Holdstock, L., & Schuster, A. (2002). Biphasic alcohol response differs in heavy versus light drinkers. *Alcoholism: Clinical and Experimental Research, 26*, 827–835.

Knight, L., Barbaree, H., & Boland, F. (1986). Alcohol and the balanced-placebo design: The role of experimenter demands in expectancy. *Journal of Abnormal Psychology, 95*, 335–340.

Knight, R. (1937). The dynamics and treatment of chronic alcohol addiction. *Bulletin of the Menninger Clinic, 1*, 233–250.

Koob, G. F., & Le Moal, M. (1997). Drug abuse: Hedonichomeostatic dysregulation. *Science, 278*, 52–58.

Koob, G. F., & Le Moal, M. (2001). Drug addiction, dysregulation of reward and allostasis. *Neuropsychopharmacology, 24*, 97–127.

Kranzler, H. R., & Anton, R. F. (1994). Implications of recent neuropsychopharmacologic research for understanding the etiology and development of alcoholism. *Journal of Consulting and Clinical Psychology, 62*, 1116–1126.

Kushner, M. G., Sher, K. J., Wood, M. D., & Wood, P. K. (1994). Anxiety and drinking behavior: Moderating effects of tension-reduction alcohol outcome expectancies. *Alcoholism: Clinical and Experimental Research, 18*, 852–860.

Lamers, C., & Ramaekers, J. (2001). Visual search and urban city driving under the influence of marijuana and alcohol. *Human Psychopharmacology, 16*, 393–401.

Lang, A. R., Searles, J., Lauerman, R., & Adesso, V. J. (1980). Expectancy, alcohol, and sex guilt as determinants of interest in and reaction to sexual stimuli. *Journal of Abnormal Psychology, 89*, 644–653.

Laplace, A. C., Chermack, S. T., & Taylor, S. P. (1994). Effects of alcohol and drinking experience on human physical aggression. *Personality and Social Psychology Bulletin, 20*, 439–444.

Leigh, B. C. (1987). Beliefs about the effects of alcohol on self and others. *Journal of Studies on Alcohol, 48*, 467–475.

Leigh, B. C. (1989). In search of the seven dwarves: Issues of measurement and meaning in alcohol expectancy research. *Psychological Bulletin, 105*, 361–373.

Leigh, B. C., & Stacy, A. W. (1991). On the scope of alcohol expectancy research: Remaining issues of measurement and meaning. *Psychological Bulletin, 110*, 147–154.

Leigh, B. C., & Stall, R. (1993). Substance use and risky sexual behavior for exposure to HIV: Issues in methodology, interpretation, and prevention. *American Psychologist, 48*, 1035–1045.

Leonard, K. E. (1989). The impact of explicit aggressive and implicit non-aggressive cues on aggression in intoxicated and sober males. *Personality and Social Psychology Bulletin, 15,* 390–400.

Levenson, R. W., Sher, K. J., Grossman, L. M., Newman, J., & Newlin, D. B. (1980). Alcohol and stress response dampening: Pharmacological effects, expectancy, and tension reduction. *Journal of Abnormal Psychology, 89,* 528–538.

Levine, H. G. (1978). The discovery of addiction: Changing conceptions of habitual drunkenness in America. *Journal of Studies on Alcohol, 39,* 143–174.

Lewis, B. A., & Vogeltanz-Holm, N. D. (2002). The effects of alcohol and anxiousness on physiological and subjective responses to a social stressor in women. *Addictive Behaviors, 27,* 529–545.

Lied, E. R., & Marlatt, G. (1979). Modeling as a determinant of alcohol consumption: Effect of subject sex and prior drinking history. *Addictive Behaviors, 4,* 47–54.

Liguori, A., & Robinson, J. H. (2001). Caffeine antagonism of alcohol-induced driving impairment. *Drug and Alcohol Dependence, 63,* 123–129.

Liljequist, S., & Engel, J. (1982). Effects of GABAergic agonists and antagonists on various ethanol-induced behavioral changes. *Psychopharmacology, 78,* 71–75.

Lindman, R. (1982). Social and solitary drinking: Effects on consumption and mood in male social drinkers. *Physiology and Behavior, 28,* 1093–1095.

Litt, M. D., Cooney, N. L., & Morse, P. (2000). Reactivity to alcohol-related stimuli in the laboratory and in the field: Predictors of craving in treated alcoholics. *Addiction, 95,* 889–900.

Little, H. J. (2000). Behavioral mechanisms underlying the link between smoking and drinking. *Alcohol Health and Research World, 24,* 215–224.

Lukas, S. E., & Orozco, S. (2001). Ethanol increases plasma Delta-sup-9–tetrahydrocannabinol (THC) levels and subjective effects after marihuana smoking in human volunteers. *Drug and Alcohol Dependence, 64,* 143–149.

Lyon, R., Tong, J., Leigh, G., & Clare, G. (1975). The influence of alcohol and tobacco on the components of choice reaction time. *Journal of Studies on Alcohol, 36,* 587–596.

Lyvers, M. F., & Maltzman, I. (1991). The balanced placebo design: Effects of alcohol and beverage instructions cannot be independently assessed. *International Journal of the Addictions, 26,* 963–972.

MacDonald, T. K., Fong, G. T., Zanna, M. P., & Martineau, A. M. (2000a). Alcohol myopia and condom use: Can alcohol intoxication be associated with more prudent behavior? *Journal of Personality and Social Psychology, 78,* 605–619.

MacDonald, T. K., MacDonald, G., Zanna, M. P., & Fong, G. (2000b). Alcohol, sexual arousal, and intentions to use condoms in young men: Applying alcohol myopia theory to risky sexual behavior. *Health Psychology, 19,* 290–298.

MacDonald, T. K., Zanna, M. P., & Fong, G. T. (1995). Decision making in altered states: Effects of alcohol on attitudes toward drinking and driving. *Journal of Personality and Social Psychology, 68,* 973–985.

Madden, P. A., Bucholz, K. K., Martin, N. G., & Heath, A. C. (2000). Smoking and the genetic contribution to alcohol-dependence risk. *Alcohol Health and Research World, 24,* 209–214.

Maisto, S. A., Carey, K. B., & Bradizza, C. M. (1999). Social learning theory. In K. E. Leonard & H. T. Blane (Eds.), *Psychological theories of drinking and alcoholism* (2nd ed., pp. 106–163). New York: Guilford.

Mann, L. M., Chassin, L., & Sher, K. J. (1987). Alcohol expectancies and the risk for alcoholism. *Journal of Consulting and Clinical Psychology, 55,* 411–417.

Marlatt, G. (1976). Alcohol, stress, and cognitive control. In I. G. Sarason and C. D. Spielberger (Eds.), *Stress and anxiety.* 3, 271–296

Marlatt, G. A., Demming, B., & Reid, J. B. (1973). Loss of control drinking in alcoholics: An experimental analogue. *Journal of Abnormal Psychology, 81,* 233–241.

Marlatt, G. A., & Rohsenow, D. J. (1980). Cognitive processes in alcohol use: Expectancy and the balanced placebo design. In N. K. Mello (Ed.), *Advances in substance abuse: Behavioral and biological research* (pp. 159–199). Greenwich, CT: JAI Press.

Martin, C. S., Earleywine, M., Finn, P. R., & Young, R. D. (1990). Some boundary conditions for effective use of alcohol placebos. *Journal of Studies on Alcohol, 51,* 500–505.

Martin, C. S., Earleywine, M., Musty, R. E., Perrine, M., & Swift, R. M. (1993). Development and validation of the Biphasic Alcohol Effects Scale. *Alcoholism: Clinical and Experimental Research, 17,* 140–146.

Martin, C. S., & Sayette, M. A. (1993). Experimental design in alcohol administration research: Limitations and alternatives in the manipulation of dosage-set. *Journal of Studies on Alcohol, 54,* 750–761.

Mayer, R. R., Forster, J. L., Murray, D. M., & Wagenaar, A. C. (1998). Social settings and situations of underage drinking. *Journal of Studies on Alcohol, 59,* 207–215.

McCance-Katz, E. F., Price, L. H., McDougle, C. J., Kosten, T. R., Black, J. E. & Jatlow, P. I. (1993). Concurrent cocaine-ethanol ingestion in humans: Pharmacology, physiology, behavior, and the role of cocaethylene. *Psychopharmacology. 111,* 39–46.

McCarthy, D. M., Wall, T. L., Brown, S. A., & Carr, L. G. (2000). Integrating biological and behavioral factors in alcohol use risk: The role of ALDH2 status and alcohol expectancies in a sample of Asian Americans. *Experimental and Clinical Psychopharmacology, 8,* 168–175.

McCarty, D., Diamond, W., & Kaye, M. (1982). Alcohol, sexual arousal, and the transfer of excitation. *Journal of Personality and Social Psychology, 42,* 977–988.

McKay, D., & Schare, M. L. (1999). The effects of alcohol and alcohol expectancies on subjective reports and physiological reactivity: A meta-analysis. *Addictive Behaviors, 24,* 633–647.

Michel, C., & Baettig, K. (1989). Separate and combined psychophysiological effects of cigarette smoking and alcohol consumption. *Psychopharmacology, 97,* 65–73.

Mihic, S. J., & Harris, R. A. (1997). Neurotransmitter review: GABA and the GABAA receptor. *Alcohol Health and Research World, 21,* 127–131.

Miller, P. M., Smith, G. T., & Goldman, M. S. (1990). Emergence of alcohol expectancies in childhood: A possible critical period. *Journal of Studies on Alcohol, 51,* 343–349.

Mills, K. C., & Bisgrove, E. Z. (1983). Body sway and divided attention performance under the influence of alcohol: Dose-response differences between males and females. *Alcoholism: Clinical and Experimental Research, 7,* 393–397.

Mintz, J., Boyd. G., Rose. K. E., Charuvastra. V. C., & Jarvik, M. E. (1985). Alcohol increases cigarette smoking: A laboratory demonstration. *Addictive Behaviors, 10,* 203–207.

Mitchell, S., de Wit, H., & Zacny, J. (1995). Effects of varying ethanol dose on cigarette consumption in healthy normal volunteers. *Behavioural Pharmacology, 6,* 359–365.

Morzorati, S. L., Ramchandani, V., Flury, L., Li, T., & O'Connor, S. (2002). Self-reported subjective perception of intoxication reflects family history of alcoholism when breath alcohol levels are constant. *Alcoholism: Clinical and Experimental Research, 26,* 1299–1306.

Nash, H. (1966). Psychological effects and alcohol-antagonizing properties of caffeine. *Quarterly Journal of Studies on Alcohol, 27,* 727–734.

National Institute on Alcohol Abuse and Alcoholism. (1997). *Ninth special report to the U.S. Congress on alcohol and health from the secretary of health and human services.* Washington, D. C.: Author.

Nevo, I., & Hamon, M. (1995). Neurotransmitter and neuromodulatory mechanisms involved in alcohol abuse and alcoholism. *Neurochemistry International, 26,* 305–336.

Newcomb, M. D., Chou, C.-P., Bentler, P., & Huba, G. (1988). Cognitive motivations for drug use among adolescents: Longitudinal tests of gender differences and predictors of change in drug use. *Journal of Counseling Psychology, 35,* 426–438.

Newlin, D. B., & Pretorius, M. B. (1990). Sons of alcoholics report greater hangover symptoms than sons of nonalcoholics: A pilot study. *Alcoholism: Clinical and Experimental Research, 14,* 713–716.

Newman, H. W., & Newman, E. J. (1956). Failure of dexedrine and caffeine as practical antagonists of the depressant effect of ethyl alcohol in man. *Quarterly Journal of Studies on Alcohol, 17,* 406–410.

Niaura, R. S., Nathan, P. E., Frankenstein, W., Shapiro, A. P., & Brick, J. (1987). Gender differences in acute psychomotor, cognitive, and pharmacokinetic response to alcohol. *Addictive Behaviors, 12,* 345–356.

Nil, R., Buzzi, R., & Baettig, K. (1984). Effects of single doses of alcohol and caffeine on cigarette smoke puffing behavior. *Pharmacology, Biochemistry and Behavior, 20,* 583–590.

Norris, J. (1994). Alcohol and female sexuality: A look at expectancies and risks. *Alcohol Health and Research World, 18,* 197–201.

Nuotto, E., Mattila, M. J., Seppala, T., & Konno, K. (1982). Coffee and caffeine and alcohol effects on psychomotor function. *Clinical Pharmacology and Therapeutics, 31,* 68–76.

Oborne, D. J., & Rogers, Y. (1983). Interactions of alcohol and caffeine on human reaction time. *Aviation, Space and Environmental Medicine, 54,* 528–534.

Otmakhova, N., & Lisman, J. (1998). D1/D5 dopamine receptors inhibit depotentiation at CA1 synapses via cAMP-dependent mechanism. *Journal of Neuroscience, 18,* 1270–1279.

Palfai, T., & Wood, M. D. (2001). Positive alcohol expectancies and drinking behavior: The influence of expectancy strength and memory accessibility. *Psychology of Addictive Behaviors, 15,* 60–67.

Perez-Reyes, M., Hicks, R. E., Bumberry, J., Jeffcoat, A., Cook, C. E. (1988). Interaction between marihuana and ethanol: Effects on psychomotor performance. *Alcoholism: Clinical and Experimental Research, 12,* 268–276.

Perez-Reyes, M., & Jeffcoat, A. R. (1992). Ethanol/cocaine interaction: Cocaine and cocaethylene plasma concentrations and their relationship to subjective and cardiovascular effects. *Life Sciences, 51,* 553–563.

Perkins, K. A. (1997). Combined effects of nicotine and alcohol on subjective, behavioral and physiological responses in humans. *Addiction Biology, 2,* 255–267.

Perkins, K. A., Fonte, C., & Grobe, J. (2000). Sex differences in the acute effects of cigarette smoking on the reinforcing value of alcohol. *Behavioural Pharmacology, 11,* 63–70.

Perkins, K. A., Sexton, J., DiMarco, A., Grobe, J., Slierka, A., & Stiller, R. L. (1995). Subjective and cardiovascular responses to nicotine combined with alcohol in male and female smokers. *Psychopharmacology, 119,* 205–212.

Persson, L. O., Sjöberg, L., & Svensson, E. (1980). Mood effects of alcohol. *Psychopharmacology, 68,* 295–299.

Pihl, R. O., Paylan, S. S., Gentes-Hawn, A., & Hoaken, P. N. S. (2003). Alcohol affects executive cognitive function differentially on the ascending versus descending limb of the blood alcohol concentration curve. *Alcoholism: Clinical and Experimental Research, 27,* 773–779.

Pinsky, I., & Silva, M. T. A. (1999). A frequency and content analysis of alcohol advertising on Brazilian television. *Journal of Studies on Alcohol, 60,* 394–399.

Pliner, P., & Cappell, H. (1974). Modification of affective consequences of alcohol: A comparison of social and solitary drinking. *Journal of Abnormal Psychology, 83,* 418–425.

Preuss, U. W., Schuckit, M. A., Smith, T. L., Barnow, S., & Danko, G. P. (2002). Mood and anxiety symptoms among 140 children from alcoholic and control families. *Drug and Alcohol Dependence, 67,* 235–242.

Rafla, F. K., & Epstein, R. L. (1979). Identification of cocaine and its metabolites in human urine in the presence of ethyl alcohol. *Journal of Analytical Toxicology, 3,* 59–63.

Rather, B. C., Goldman, M. S., Roehrich, L., & Brannick, M. (1992). Empirical modeling of an alcohol expectancy memory network using multidimensional scaling. *Journal of Abnormal Psychology, 101,* 174–183.

Reis, H. T., & Gable, S. L. (2000). Event-sampling and other methods for studying everyday experience. In H. T. Reis & C. M. Judd (Eds.), *Handbook of research methods in social and personality psychology* (pp. 190–222). New York: Cambridge University Press.

Rescorla, R. A. (1988). Pavlovian conditioning: It's not what you think it is. *American Psychologist, 43,* 151–160.

Roehrich, L., & Goldman, M. S. (1995). Implicit priming of alcohol expectancy memory processes and subsequent drinking behavior. *Experimental and Clinical Psychopharmacology, 3,* 402–410.

Rohsenow, D. J., & Marlatt, G. (1981). The balanced placebo design: Methodological considerations. *Addictive Behaviors, 6,* 107–122.

Rose, J. E., Brauer, L. H., Behm, F. M., Cramblett, M., Calkins, K., & Lawhon, D. (2002). Potentiation of nicotine reward by alcohol. *Alcoholism: Clinical and Experimental Research, 26,* 1930–1931.

Rosellini, R. A., & Lashley, R. L. (1982). The opponent-process theory of motivation. VIII. Quantitative and qualitative manipulations of food both modulate adjunctive behavior. *Learning and Motivation, 13,* 222–239.

Rosenberg, L., Slone, D., Shapiro, S., Kaufman, D. W., Miettinen, O. S., & Stolley, P. D. (1981). Alcoholic beverages and myocardial infarction in young women. *American Journal of Public Health, 71,* 82–85.

Rosenbluth, J., Nathan, P. E., & Lawson, D. M. (1978). Environmental influences on drinking by college students in a college pub: Behavioral observation in the natural environment. *Addictive Behaviors, 3,* 117–121.

Roueche, B. (1960). *The neutral spirit: A portrait of alcohol.* Boston: Little, Brown.

Sacco, R. L., Elkind, M., Boden-Albala, B., Lin, I. F., Kargman, D. E., Hauser, W. A., et al. (1999). The protective effect of moderate alcohol consumption on ischemic stroke. *Journal of the American Medical Association, 281,* 53–60.

Samson, H. H., & Harris, R. A. (1992). Neurobiology of alcohol abuse [Comment]. *Trends in Pharmacological Sciences, 13,* 206–211.

Sayette, M. A. (1993). An appraisal-disruption model of alcohol's effects on stress responses in social drinkers. *Psychological Bulletin, 114,* 459–476.

Sayette, M. A. (1999). Cognitive theory and research. In K. E. Leonard & H. T. Blane (Eds.), *Psychological theories of drinking and alcoholism* (2nd ed., pp. 247–291). New York: Guilford.

Sayette, M. A., Breslin, F., Wilson, G., & Rosenblum, G. D. (1994). An evaluation of the balanced placebo design in alcohol administration research. *Addictive Behaviors, 19,* 333–342.

Sayette, M. A., Martin, C. S., Perrott, M. A., Wertz, J. M., & Hufford, M. R. (2001). A test of the appraisal-disruption model of alcohol and stress. *Journal of Studies on Alcohol, 62,* 247–256.

Scheitrum, R. R., & Akillas, E. (2002). Effects of personality style, anxiety and depression on reported reasons for smoking. *Journal of Applied Biobehavioral Research, 7,* 57–64.

Schuckit, M. A., & Gold, E. O. (1988). A simultaneous evaluation of multiple markers of ethanol/placebo challenges in sons of alcoholics and controls. *Archives of General Psychiatry, 45,* 211–216.

Schuckit, M. A., & Hesselbrock, V. (1994). Alcohol dependence and anxiety disorders: What is the relationship? *American Journal of Psychiatry, 151,* 1723–1734.

Senchak, M., Leonard, K. E., & Greene, B. W. (1998). Alcohol use among college students as a function of their typical social drinking context. *Psychology of Addictive Behaviors, 12,* 62–70.

Sher, K. J. (1985). Subjective effects of alcohol: The influence of setting and individual differences in alcohol expectancies. *Journal of Studies on Alcohol, 46,* 137–146.

Sher, K. J. (1987). Stress-response dampening. In H. T. Blane & K. E. Leonard (Eds.), Psychological theories of drinking and alcoholism (pp. 227–264). New York: Guilford.

Sher, K. J. (1991). *Children of alcoholics: A critical appraisal of theory and research*. Chicago: University of Chicago.

Sher, K. J., & Gotham, H. (1999). Pathological alcohol involvement: A developmental disorder of young adulthood. *Development and Psychopathology, 11*, 933–956.

Sher, K. J., & Levenson, R. W. (1982). Risk for alcoholism and individual differences in the stress-response-dampening effect of alcohol. *Journal of Abnormal Psychology, 91*, 350–367.

Sher, K. J., Walitzer, K. S., Wood, P. K., & Brent, E. E. (1991). Characteristics of children of alcoholics: Putative risk factors, substance use and abuse, and psychopathology. *Journal of Abnormal Psychology, 100*, 427–448.

Sher, K. J., Wood, M. D., Wood, P. K., & Raskin, G. (1996). Alcohol outcome expectancies and alcohol use: A latent variable cross-lagged panel study. *Journal of Abnormal Psychology, 105*, 561–574.

Shiffman, S., & Hufford, M. (2002). *Methods of measuring patient experience: Paper vs. electronic patient diaries*. Retrieved May 13, 2004 from www.invivodata.com

Shiffman, S. M., & Stone, A. A. (1998). Ecological momentary assessment: A new tool for behavioral medicine research. In D. S. Krantz & A. Baum (Eds.), *Technology and methods in behavioral medicine* (pp. 117–131). Mahwah, N. J.: Erlbaum

Shipley, T. E. (1987). Opponent process theory. In H. T. Blane & K. E. Leonard (Eds.), *Psychological theories of drinking and alcoholism* (pp. 346–383). New York: Guilford.

Siegel, S., Baptista, M. A., Kim, J. A., McDonald, R. V., & Weise-Kelly, L. (2000). Pavlovian psychopharmacology: The associative basis of tolerance. *Experimental and Clinical Psychopharmacology, 8*, 276–293.

Sinha, R., Robinson, J., & O'Malley, S. (1998). Stress response dampening: Effects of gender and family history of alcoholism and anxiety disorders. *Psychopharmacology, 137*, 311–320.

Slater, M. D., Rouner, D., Murphy, K., Beauvais, F., Van Leuven, J. & Domenech Rodriguez, M. (1996). Male adolescents' reactions to TV beer advertisements: The effects of sports content and programming context. *Journal of Studies on Alcohol, 57*, 425–433.

Slutske, W. S., Piasecki, T. M., & Hunt-Carter, E. E. (2003). Development and initial validation of the Hangover Symptoms Scale: Prevalence and correlates of hangover symptoms in college students. *Alcoholism: Clinical and Experimental Research, 27*, 1442–1450.

Smart, R. G. (1996). Behavioral and social consequences related to the consumption of different beverage types. *Journal of Studies on Alcohol, 57*, 77–84.

Smith, G. T., Goldman, M. S., Greenbaum, P. E., & Christiansen, B. A. (1995). Expectancy for social facilitation from drinking: The divergent paths of high-expectancy and low-expectancy adolescents. *Journal of Abnormal Psychology, 104*, 32–40.

Solomon, R. L. (1980). The opponent-process theory of acquired motivation: The costs of pleasure and the benefits of pain. *American Psychologist, 35*, 691–712.

Solomon, R. L., & Corbit, J. D. (1973). An opponent-process theory of motivation. II. Cigarette addiction. *Journal of Abnormal Psychology, 81*, 158–171.

Solomon, R. L., & Corbit, J. D. (1974). An opponent-process theory of motivation. I. Temporal dynamics of affect. *Psychological Review, 81*, 119–145.

Span, S. A., & Earleywine, M. (1999). Familial risk for alcoholism and hangover symptoms. *Addictive Behaviors, 24*, 121–125.

Stacy, A. W. (1997). Memory activation and expectancy as prospective predictors of alcohol and marijuana use. *Journal of Abnormal Psychology, 106*, 61–73.

Stacy, A. W., Newcomb, M. D., & Bentler, P. M. (1991). Cognitive motivation and drug use: A 9-year longitudinal study. *Journal of Abnormal Psychology, 100*, 502–515.

Starr, M. D. (1978). An opponent-process theory of motivation. VI. Time and intensity variables in the development of separation-induced distress calling in ducklings. *Journal of Experimental Psychology: Animal Behavior Processes, 4*, 338–355.

Steele, C. M., & Josephs, R. A. (1988). Drinking your troubles away. II. An attention-allocation model of alcohol's effect on psychological stress. *Journal of Abnormal Psychology, 97*, 196–205.

Steele, C. M., & Josephs, R. A. (1990). Alcohol myopia: Its prized and dangerous effects. *American Psychologist, 45*, 921–933.

Steele, C. M., & Southwick, L. (1985). Alcohol and social behavior. I. The psychology of drunken excess. *Journal of Personality and Social Psychology, 48*, 18–34.

Steele, C. M., Southwick, L., & Pagano, R. (1986). Drinking your troubles away: The role of activity in mediating alcohol's reduction of psychological stress. *Journal of Abnormal Psychology, 95*, 173–180.

Steptoe, A., & Wardle, J. (1999). Mood and drinking: A naturalistic diary study of alcohol, coffee and tea. *Psychopharmacology, 141*, 315–321.

Stone, A. A., & Shiffman, S. (1994). Ecological Momentary Assessment (EMA) in behavorial medicine. *Annals of Behavioral Medicine, 16*, 199–202.

Strickland, D. E., Finn, T., & Lambert, M. (1982). A content analysis of beverage alcohol advertising. I. Magazine advertising. *Journal of Studies on Alcohol, 43*, 655–682.

Strickler, D. P., Dobbs, S. D., & Maxwell, W. A. (1979). The influence of setting of drinking behaviors: The laboratory vs the barroom. *Addictive Behaviors, 4*, 339–344.

Subramanian, M. G., Heil, S. H., Kruger, M. L., Collins, K. L., Buck, P. O., Zawacki, T., et al. (2002). A three-stage alcohol clamp procedure in human subjects. *Alcoholism: Clinical and Experimental Research, 26*, 1479–1483.

Suzdak, P. D., Glowa, J. R., Crawley, J. N., Schwartz, R. D., Skolnick, P., & Paul, S. M. (1986). A selective imidazobenzodiazepine antagonist of ethanol in the rat. *Science, 234*, 1243–1247.

Swendsen, J. D., Tennen, H., Carney, M. A., Affleck, G., Willard, A., & Hromi, A. (2000). Mood and alcohol consumption: An experience sampling test of the self-medication hypothesis. *Journal of Abnormal Psychology, 109*, 198–204.

Swift, R., & Davidson, D. (1998). Alcohol hangover: Mechanisms and mediators. *Alcohol Health and Research World, 22*, 54–60.

Tampier, L., Quintanilla, M. E., & Mardones, J. (2000). Acute tolerance, alcohol sensitivity and drinking pattern in the F2 generation of UChA and UChB rats. *Journal of Studies on Alcohol, 61*, 647–651.

Taylor, S. P. (1967). Aggressive behavior and physiological arousal as a function of provocation and the tendency to inhibit aggression. *Journal of Personality, 35*, 297–310.

Taylor, S. P., & Chermack, S. T. (1993). Alcohol, drugs and human physical aggression. *Journal of Studies on Alcohol 54 Suppl. 11*, 78–88.

Taylor, S. P., & Gammon, C. B. (1975). Effects of type and dose of alcohol on human physical aggression. *Journal of Personality and Social Psychology, 32*, 169–175.

Taylor, S. P., & Gammon, C. B. (1976). Aggressive behavior of intoxicated subjects: The effect of third-party intervention. *Journal of Studies on Alcohol, 37*, 917–930.

Taylor, S. P., Gammon, C. B., & Capasso, D. R. (1976). Aggression as a function of the interaction of alcohol and threat. *Journal of Personality and Social Psychology, 34*, 938–941.

Taylor, S., & Leonard, K. (1983). Alcohol and human physical aggression. In R. Green & E. Donnerstein (Eds.), *Aggression: Theoretical and empirical reviews: Issues in research* (Vol. 2, pp. 77–101). New York: Academic Press.

Taylor, S. P., Schmutte, G. T., Leonard, K. E., & Cranston, J. W. (1979). The effects of alcohol and extreme provocation on the use of a highly noxious electric shock. *Motivation and Emotion, 3*, 73–81.

Tiplady, B., Faineteau, H., Loganathan, A., Spiegelberg, M., Taylor, Z., & Wright, P. (1998). Effects of ethanol and temazepam on performance in memory and psychomotor tasks: A dose-response comparison. *Human Psychopharmacology, 13*, 285–291.

Tucker, J. A., Vuchinich, R. E., & Sobell, M. B. (1982). Alcohol's effects on human emotions: A review of the stimulation/depression hypothesis. *International Journal of the Addictions, 17*, 155–180.

Vogel-Sprott, M., & Chipperfield, B. (1987). Family history of problem drinking among young male social drinkers: Behavioral effects of alcohol. *Journal of Studies on Alcohol, 48*, 430–436.

Vogel-Sprott, M., & Fillmore, M. T. (1999). Learning theory and research. In K. E. Leonard & H. T. Blane (Eds.), *Psychological theories of drinking and alcoholism* (2nd ed., pp. 292–327). New York: Guilford.

Wallgren, H., & Barry, H. (1970). *Actions of alcohol.* New York: Elsevier.

Warren, G. H., & Raynes, A. E. (1972). Mood changes during three conditions of alcohol intake. *Quarterly Journal of Studies on Alcohol, 33*, 979–989.

Webb, G. R., Redman, S., Sanson-Fisher, R. W., & Gibberd, R. W. (1990). Comparison of a quantity-frequency method and a diary method of measuring alcohol consumption. *Journal of Studies on Alcohol, 51*, 271–277.

Wechsler, H., Davenport, A., Dowdall, G., Moeykens, B., & Castillo, S. (1994). Health and behavioral consequences of binge drinking in college: A national survey of students at 140 campuses. *Journal of the American Medical Association, 272*, 1672–1677.

Weiss, F., & Koob, G. F. (1991). The neuropharmacology of ethanol self-administration. In R. E. Meyer, G. F. Koob, M. J. Lewis & S. M. Paul (Eds.), *Neuropharmacology of ethanol* (pp. 125–162). Boston: Birkhauser.

Wickelgren, I. (1997). Getting the brain's attention. *Science, 278*, 35–37.

Wiers, R. W., Van Woerden, N., Smulders, F. T., & De Jong, P. J. (2002). Implicit and explicit alcohol-related cognitions in heavy and light drinkers. *Journal of Abnormal Psychology, 111*, 648–658.

Wiese, J. G., Shlipak, M. G., & Browner, W. S. (2000). The alcohol hangover. *Annals of Internal Medicine, 132*, 897–902.

Wilson, G. (1977). Alcohol and human sexual behavior. *Behaviour Research and Therapy, 15*, 239–252.

Wilson, G., Abrams, D. B., & Lipscomb, T. R. (1980). Effects of intoxication levels and drinking pattern on social anxiety in men. *Journal of Studies on Alcohol, 41*, 250–264.

Wilson, G., & Lawson, D. M. (1976a). Effects of alcohol on sexual arousal in women. *Journal of Abnormal Psychology, 85*, 489–497.

Wilson, G., & Lawson, D. M. (1976b). Expectancies, alcohol, and sexual arousal in male social drinkers. *Journal of Abnormal Psychology, 85*, 587–594.

Wilson, G., & Lawson, D. M. (1978). Expectancies, alcohol, and sexual arousal in women. *Journal of Abnormal Psychology, 87*, 358–367.

Wise, R. A., & Bozarth, M. A. (1987). A psychomotor stimulant theory of addiction. *Psychological Review, 94*, 469–492.

Wolkowitz, O. M., Tinklenberg, J. R., & Weingartner, H. (1985). A psychopharmacological perspective of cognitive functions. II. Specific pharmacologic agents. *Neuropsychobiology, 14*, 133–156.

Wood, M. D., Nagoshi, C. T., & Dennis, D. A. (1992). Alcohol norms and expectations as predictors of alcohol use and problems in a college student sample. *American Journal of Drug and Alcohol Abuse, 18*, 461–476.

Wood, M. D., Read, J. P., Palfai, T. P., & Stevenson, J. F. (2001). Social influence processes and college student drinking: The mediational role of alcohol outcome expectations. *Journal of Studies on Alcohol, 62*, 32–43.

Wood, M. D., Sher, K. J., & Strathman, A. (1996). Alcohol outcome expectancies and alcohol use and problems. *Journal of Studies on Alcohol, 57*, 283–288.

Wood, M. D., Vinson, D. C., & Sher, K. J. (2001). Alcohol use and misuse. In A. Baum, T. Revenson, & J. Singer (Eds.), *Handbook of health psychology* (pp. 281–318). Hillsdale, NJ: Erlbaum.

York, J. L. (1984). The role of congeners in the effects of different alcoholic beverages. *Substance and Alcohol Actions/Misuse, 5*, 123–130.

Zeichner, A., Feuerstein, M., Swartzman, L., & Reznick, E. (1983). Acute effects of alcohol on cardiovascular reactivity to stress in Type A (coronary prone) businessmen. In A. Pohorecky & J. Brick (Eds.), *Stress and alcohol use* (pp. 353–368). New York: Plenum.

Zucker, R. A. (1986). The four alcoholisms: A developmental account of the etiologic process. *Nebraska Symposium on Motivation, 34*, 27–83.

5

Subjective Effects of Alcohol II

Individual Differences

KENNETH J. SHER AND MARK D. WOOD

As noted in our other chapter in this volume (see chapter 4), the subjective effects of alcohol are a complex function of the drink, the current subjective state, and the setting. However, it is also clear that a full understanding of the subjective effects of alcohol requires consideration of the drinker. The idea that there are large individual differences associated with the effects of alcohol is long-standing. More than 100 years ago, Fere (1899) asserted that "all subjects do not offer the same susceptibility to the action of medicaments and poisons" and noted, "Lasegue has specially insisted upon the differences of aptitude for intoxication . . . [and has labeled these individuals] *alcoholizable.*" The idea that some individuals appear relatively impervious (i.e., highly tolerant) to alcohol effects and that others are "good drunks" or "mean drunks" is consistent with everyday observation. Research over the past 25 years points to several types of "alcoholizability," but we are still far from being able to characterize fully, on a priori grounds, how someone is likely to respond to alcohol purely on the basis of these individual difference variables.

Genetics

One of the most robust risk factors for alcoholism is family history of alcoholism (Cotton, 1979; Pollock, Schneider, Gabrielli, & Goodwin,

1987). Several twin and adoption studies (see Heath, 1995; McGue, 1999) have demonstrated that alcohol use patterns and alcohol dependence have a strong genetic component. Given the strong etiological role of genetic factors that have been established by genetic epidemiological studies, it is not surprising that genetic variability in alcohol response has been an intense area of research interest over the past 25 years.

Family History of Alcoholism

Family history of alcoholism is, arguably, the most well-established risk factor for the development of alcohol dependence. Across a variety of studies and depending on how alcoholism is defined in parents and offspring, children of alcoholics are at a 3- to 10-fold risk for the development of alcohol dependence themselves (Cloninger, 1987a; McGue, 1994; Sher, 1991). Familial transmission of alcoholism appears to be due substantially to genetic factors (e.g., Heath, 1995, Heath et al., 1997, McGue, 1994), as well as to environmental factors, with mean estimates of heritability trending about .50 (McGue, 1999) for both men and women. Although there are multiple theories as to why those with a family history of alcoholism tend to develop alcoholism themselves, one class of theories, which we have termed *pharmacological vulnerability,* has received considerable support and is directly relevant to the issue of subjective effects of acute alcohol intoxication (Sher, 1991).

At least three competing alternative hypotheses regarding alcohol's motivational influence on subsequent drinking in children of alcoholics have been formulated (e.g., Schuckit & Smith, 2000; Sher, 1991). First, it may be that individuals with a positive family history experience increased sensitivity to alcohol's positive and negatively reinforcing effects, and that they drink at relatively high levels (as compared with those at low risk) because alcohol is highly rewarding to them. Another hypothesis is that those who are at high risk for alcoholism experience decreased sensitivity to alcohol's punishing effects and are therefore able to drink at relatively high levels because they experience diminished negative effects and/or consequences (relative to those at low risk). Yet another alternative hypothesis is that those at high risk for alcoholism experience decreased sensitivity to alcohol's reinforcing effects and thus must drink at relatively high levels to experience the rewarding effects associated with alcohol consumption. A number of research groups have attempted to evaluate these three ideas by comparing the subjective experience (or presumed correlates of subjective experience) of those at high and low risk for alcoholism. This has generated a large empirical literature on individual differences in alcohol effects as a function of family history.

Before we summarize this body of research, a few major methodological points are in order. First, because typically laboratory studies of alcohol effects must use experienced drinkers who are over the legal drinking age (although see Behar et al., 1983), studies in humans cannot directly assess "initial sensitivity." That is, any observed differences between individuals with and without a positive family history of alcoholism could be due to either innate differences in sensitivity or acquired differences in response (i.e., chronic tolerance [or sensitization]). Second, because individuals who have already experienced serious alcohol-related consequences or severe dependence are screened out of laboratory studies for ethical reasons, participants in these studies probably do not include those most at risk. Thus, existing findings in the literature do not clearly resolve differences associated with innate sensitivity and acquired tolerance, and they may fail to characterize the responses of those individuals with the most morbid alcohol-related trajectories (i.e., those who develop moderate or severe dependence by age 21).

Effects of Alcohol on the Nonstressed Individual

Perhaps the seminal finding in this area comes from Schuckit's early study (1980), which found that, relative to men without a positive family history of alcoholism, men with a positive family history showed a less intense response to a moderate (0.75 ml/kg) dose of alcohol on the Subjective High Assessment Scale (SHAS; Judd et al., 1977). This finding was replicated in a second study by Schuckit (1984) and by several other groups who have documented less intense reactions to alcohol among those with a positive family history as compared with those without (Heath & Martin, 1992; McCaul, Turkkan, Svikis, & Bigelow, 1991; Morzorati, Ramchandani, Flury, Li, & O'Connor, 2002; Moss, Yao, & Maddock, 1989; Neale & Martin, 1989; Pollock, Teasdale, Gabrielli, & Knop, 1986; Pollock, 1992).

In an important extension of this work, Schuckit and Smith (1996) demonstrated the potential etiologic significance of these findings by showing that over a 10-year follow-up period, low subjective response to alcohol predicted the onset of alcohol dependence in this same sample. Although formal tests to evaluate whether low response to alcohol mediated family history risk on later alcohol dependence were inconclusive, the combination of individual differences associated with family history risk and prospective prediction of alcohol dependence strongly implicates an etiologic role for low response to alcohol (Schuckit, 1995; see also Volavka et al, 1996). As noted by Newlin and Thomson (1990), however, it is unclear if the findings by Schuckit and colleagues point more to a difference in positive reinforcement or in punishment because several items on their measure of subjective intoxication appear to implicate decreased sensitivity to aversive effects of alcohol. Additionally, at least one study (Moss et al., 1989) found that decreased sensitivity was limited to the descending limb of the blood alcohol curve.

Despite the replication of decreased response to alcohol among family history–positive participants in subjective report across several labs, the literature has reported several contradictory findings (Conrod, Peterson, Pihl, & Mankowski, 1997; de Wit & McCracken, 1990; Kaplan, Hesselbrock, O'Connor, & Depalma, 1988; McCaul, Turkkan, Svikis, & Bigelow, 1990; Morzorati et al., 2002; Nagoshi & Wilson, 1987) as well as null findings (e.g., Bauer & Hesselbrock, 1993; Heath et al., 1999; Vogel-Sprott & Chipperfield, 1987). It is important to note that de Wit and McCracken's (1990) finding of increased alcohol response was limited to the ascending limb of the blood alcohol curve. Thus, existing literature suggests that those with a family history of alcoholism could show either a decreased or an increased subjective response to alcohol, and there are some intriguing findings that the direction of effect (i.e., increased or decreased alcohol effect) could be conditional upon whether or not the blood alcohol curve is rising or falling. Newlin and Thomson (1990) discuss this issue at length in their "differentiator model," discussed later in this section.

Effects of Alcohol on the Stressed Individual

Most investigations on subjective effects of alcohol in those with and without a family history of alcoholism study individuals who can be characterized as being in a "resting state"—sitting passively in the laboratory or being a participant in a laboratory setting with nonemotional tasks. However, a distinct set of studies have examined the effect of alcohol on response to a discrete stressor in order to examine the stress-response-dampening effects of alcohol. In general, these studies have yielded a more consistent set of findings in the direction of *increased* sensitivity to alcohol. In one of the first studies in this area to examine family history differences in both men and women, Levenson, Oyama, and Meek (1987) found that both men and women with alcoholic fathers showed greater attenuation of the cardiovascular response to a stressor from alcohol than gender-matched controls when measured using physiological data (heart rate, pulse transmission time to the ear, and finger pulse amplitude). However, these results were not replicated in analysis of self-report data. Subsequent studies by Finn, Pihl, and their colleagues (Finn & Pihl, 1987; Finn, Zeitouni, & Pihl, 1990) replicated the enhanced stress-response-dampening effect on cardiovascular measures among men with dense family histories of alcoholism.

Differentiator Model

Evidence suggests that sons of alcoholics experience physiological changes that reflect increased sensitivity to alcohol's reinforcing effects, particularly while blood alcohol concentration is rising (e.g., Conrod et al., 1997). For instance, Cohen and colleagues found that during the ascending limb of the blood alcohol curve, sons of alcoholics experience high levels of low-frequency EEG activity (Cohen, Porjesz, & Begleiter, 1993), which is associated with a euphoric subjective state (Lukas, Mendelson, Benedikt, & Jones, 1986). Interestingly, during the descending limb of the blood alcohol curve, sons of alcoholics experience a decrease in low-frequency EEG activity as compared with controls, again reflecting the important role of time since ingestion when considering these effects. Using the intravenous breath alcohol clamping methodology discussed in chapter 4 of this volume, Morzorati et al. (2002) found that individuals with positive family history for alcoholism report feeling more intoxicated than controls during the period between baseline and the beginning of the clamping interval. However, during the clamping interval (i.e., while breath alcohol concentration is held constant for an extended period), family history–positive subjects' reports of intoxication are not significantly different from those of controls. Gianoulakis, Krishnan, and Thavundayil (1996) have examined the differences in beta-endorphin (an endogenous opioid involved in reinforcement) levels in sons of alcoholics and controls following alcohol ingestion. Their results suggest that after a moderate dose, those at high risk for alcoholism experience higher levels of beta-endorphin than those at low risk.

Taken together, these data on familial risk for alcoholism and ethanol response suggest that those with a family history of alcoholism may be more likely to experience enhanced reinforcement from alcohol early in the course of intoxication. Later on in the drinking episode (when blood alcohol levels are either stable or decreasing, and the profile of reinforcement and punishment shifts), those at high risk seem to either become less sensitive to alcohol than those at lower risk or at least not differ from them in alcohol response.

Newlin and Thomson (1990) synthesize these findings into what they term a *differentiator model*; the subjective effects (and other effects of alcohol) appear to follow the function of the first differential (slope) of the blood alcohol curve, amplifying reinforcing effects (associated with the ascending limb) and dampening punishing effects (associated with the descending limb). Such a model suggests a potent pairing of complementary mechanisms underlying human variability in alcohol response, pronounced reinforcement coupled with diminished punishment. Together these two mechanisms can be viewed as providing a strong motivational basis for consumption. Although this model appears to account for quite a bit of the data, there are still too many inconsistencies in the literature to embrace the model unconditionally.

Allelic Variation and Responses to Alcohol

In order to identify specific genetic mechanisms underlying vulnerability to alcoholism, researchers have increasingly been examining the relation between specific genes and individual differences in response to alcohol. The genes that have, to date, received the most empirical attention are those related to alcohol metabolism. Specifically, research has linked variations in two of the major enzymes involved in alcohol metabolism, alcohol dehydrogenase (ADH) and aldehyde dehydrogenase (ALDH), with variability in subjective and objective responses to alcohol (Chen et al., 1996; Luczak, Elvine-Kreis, Shea, Carr, & Wall, 2002; Nakamura et al., 1996). The most widely researched of these relates to a mutation in the gene that encodes for ALDH2, which results in elevated acetaldehyde levels, leading to an alcohol-induced flushing response (Higuchi, Matsushita, Murayama, Takagi, & Hayashida, 1995). This mutation is present in a large proportion (approximately 40%) of individuals of Asian descent; is associated with a range of presumably punishing effects such as facial flushing, heart palpitations, and nausea; and is theorized to be protective against the development of alcohol dependence (Higuchi et al., 1995; Takeshita, Morimoto, Mao, Hashimoto, & Furuyama, 1994; Wall, Thomasson, Schuckit, & Ehlers, 1992).

Allelic variation in alcohol metabolism genotypes has also demonstrated relations with sensitivity to alcohol's effects. For example, Wall et al. (1992) observed that individuals with at least one *ALDH2*2* allele had higher blood acetaldehyde levels and demonstrated more intense, although not necessarily more aversive, responses to alcohol as assessed by both subjective and physiological measures. Moreover, two recent studies have been conducted in an explicit attempt to link cognitive and neurobiological correlates of alcohol use. McCarthy et al. (2000) examined alcohol expectancies as a mediator of *ALDH2* gene status–drinking quantity relations in a sample of Asian Americans and found support for partial mediation among women but not men. In an alcohol challenge study with the same population, McCarthy, Brown, Carr, and Wall (2001) found that physiological response to alcohol mediated *ALDH2* – expectancy relations among men but not women. Although preliminary, these findings provide intriguing evidence supportive of a role for alcohol expectancies as an important mechanism through which genetic variation influences responses to alcohol, drinking behavior, and potentially the development of alcohol dependence. Findings of significant heritability of alcohol expectancies (or closely related constructs such as attitudes about alcohol) are also consistent with this notion (Perry, 1973; Prescott, Cross, Kuhn, Horn, & Kendler, in press; Vernon, Lee, Harris, & Jang, 1996), although the data are not entirely consistent (Slutske et al., 2002).

Although response to alcohol as a function of variability in ADH genotypes has yet to be explored in alcohol challenge studies, there is evidence suggestive of etiologically relevant variability. Specifically, the presence of the *ADH2*3* allele leads to more rapid metabolism of alcohol to acetaldehyde (Crabb, 1995), potentially also producing an altered subjective response to drinking. The presence of at least one

ADH2*3 allele was also observed to be significantly more prevalent among family history–negative young adult African Americans (Ehlers, Gilder, Harris, & Carr, 2001) and was associated with higher levels of alcohol expectancies in the same population (Ehlers, Carr, Betancourt, & Montane-Jaime, 2003), which could potentially be related to greater subjective responses to alcohol as well.

Motivationally Relevant Candidate Genes

With increasing recognition that responses to alcohol likely vary across multiple genetic loci (McGue, 1999; Schuckit, 1999), along with enhanced understanding of specific neurobiological substrates that may be of particular importance in understanding alcohol's subjective effects (Fromme & D'Amico, 1999), researchers are beginning to test more fine-grained hypotheses in the search for motivationally relevant candidate genes. Consistent with this approach is an emphasis not on broader, heterogeneous phenotypes, such as alcohol abuse or dependence, but on narrower behavioral phenotypes, or "endophenotypes" (Burmeister, 1999; Hill & Neiswanger, 1997) thought to be foundational to the clinical syndrome. Given the putative association of dopamine with drug or drug cue–induced incentive value, arousal, and euphoria (Weiss & Koob, 1991), genes that are polymorphous with respect to dopamine receptors are logical candidates to examine in studies of endophenotypes. Following this logic, in two recent studies Hutchison and colleagues have examined the potential moderating role of the D_4 dopamine receptor gene (DRD4) in relations between craving and responses to alcohol and tobacco (or related cues). For example, Hutchison, McGeary, Smolen, Bryan, and Swift (2002) observed a significant Alcohol × DRD4 polymorphism interaction on drink urge ratings such that individuals with long repeat DRD4 alleles (DRD4-L) demonstrated enhanced urges to drink in the alcohol condition, whereas individuals with short repeat DRD4 alleles (DRD4-S) displayed decreased urges in the alcohol condition. There were significant main effects for DRD4 polymorphism on subjective effect measures of stimulation/arousal and "feeling high," with DRD4-L participants reporting lower levels of both arousal and subjective high. However, the interactions between DRD4 alleles and alcohol were not significant. Somewhat analogous findings were reported by Hutchison, LaChance, Niaura, Bryan, and Smolen (2002) with smoking, suggesting that the effects with alcohol may be generalized to some other psychoactive drugs of abuse. These findings provide intriguing preliminary data on the relevance of specific genes for influencing alcohol (and other drug) seeking. Of particular note are the findings across both studies suggesting that DRD4 polymorphism is implicated in the incentive value of both alcohol and tobacco, but not in the reinforcing or stimulatory effects of either drug. As noted by Hutchison, LaChance, et al. (2002), these findings are consistent with earlier research with dopamine agonists (Hutchison et al., 2001), as well as incentive sensitization models of addiction (e.g., Berridge & Robinson, 1998). More generally, they highlight the importance of genetic variability in determining individual differences in response to alcohol.

Personality

Seventy-five years ago, the noted social psychologist William McDougall (1929) speculated that "the markedly extraverted personality is very susceptible to the influence of alcohol" (p. 301) because such a person was assumed to have lower levels of baseline cortical inhibition. The influential psychiatric theorist Hervey Cleckley (1982, p. 18) asserted that individuals with psychopathic personalities were prone to "fantastic and uninviting behavior after drink" and "quick shifts between maudlin and vainglorious moods"; he noted that such behavior can occur with little or no alcohol as well. Although clinical and anecdotal evidence suggests that some individuals are exquisitely sensitive to disinhibition and mood lability from alcohol, empirical evidence for individual differences in such effects is sparse (Urschel & Woody, 1996). Beginning almost 50 years ago, Eysenck (1957) and his colleagues (e.g., Claridge, 1970; Claridge, Canter, & Hume, 1973; Franks, 1964) examined the effects of alcohol and other drugs on sedation thresholds (i.e., dose of the drug required to induce a behavioral effect related to sedation) and behavioral performance in efforts to test hypotheses concerning the relation between arousal and personality. Recent interest in the neuropharmacological bases of personality variation (e.g., Cloninger, 1987b; Zuckerman, 1991, 1995) has provided further rationale for the study of personality-based individual differences in alcohol sensitivity by refining and providing a neurobiological foundation for the speculations of earlier theorists such as McDougall and Eysenck. That is, if alcohol affects the major neurotransmitter (e.g., dopamine, norepinephrine, serotonin) and hormonal (e.g., testosterone) systems thought to underlie variation in temperament and personality, individual differences in personality could reflect variation in the baseline functioning of these neurotransmitter systems. This baseline functioning could determine, in part, the nature and extent of alcohol's effects on these systems. Such effects could be specific to ethanol acting directly and indirectly on one or more of these neuropharmacological systems or nonspecifically as a response to a novel stimulus (e.g., as any novel, reinforcing, or punishing stimulus).

Impulsivity/Disinhibition

Perhaps the most intriguing findings to date are those showing that individuals who are high on the trait of impulsivity/disinhibition appear to be more sensitive to the stress-reducing properties of alcohol, especially on cardiovascular measures (Levenson et al., 1987; Sher, Bylund, Walitzer, Hartmann, & Ray-Prenger, 1994; Sher & Levenson, 1982; Zeichner, Giancola, & Allen, 1995). For example, in one study, Sher and Levenson (1982) reasoned that individuals who show higher levels of the stress-response-dampening effects of alcohol may be those for whom alcohol's effects are most reinforcing. These authors found that highly impulsive and uninhibited participants (as measured by the MacAndrew Alcoholism scale of the MMPI) showed an increased stress-response-dampening effect from alcohol on cardiovascular measures. In a later study, Sher et al. (1994) reported that individuals with the lowest activity levels of platelet monoamine oxidase (MAO; an enzyme important in the catabolism of the catecholamines and serotonin) had elevated scores on a measure of antisociality and showed stronger stress response dampening on heart rate, as compared with those with high MAO activity. In other studies (e.g., Nagoshi, Wilson, & Rodriguez, 1991), traits related to impulsivity/disinhibition have been found to relate (negatively) to alcohol effects on motor performance. Although these findings are provocative, they have been difficult to replicate on a consistent basis (Niaura, Wilson, & Westrick, 1988; Sher & Walitzer, 1986).

Negative Affectivity

Somewhat analogous findings have been found with respect to coronary-prone (i.e., type A) personalities, who tend to show attenuated cardiovascular reactivity after consuming alcohol (Zeichner, Edwards, & Cohen, 1985). Similarly, those high in trait hostility appear to show pronounced alcohol-related dampening of cardiovascular responses (Zeichner et al., 1995). Further support for differential responsivity to alcohol according to trait negative affectivity comes from both correlational and experimental data assembled in the evaluation of the self-awareness model of alcohol (Hull, 1987). This model is based on the theory that many painful affective states (such as depression over a failure experience) are mediated by a state of self-awareness and that alcohol can reduce this distress by interfering with those cognitive mechanisms that are foundational to self-awareness. Individuals high in private self-consciousness (i.e., the trait counterpart of the state of self-awareness) are particularly vulnerable to experience negative affect when confronted with negative information about the self and are also very likely to obtain relief from alcohol when experiencing negative affect mediated via self-awareness processes (see Hull, 1987).

Another area of personality-related individual differences in alcohol effects concerns aggression-related traits on alcohol-related aggression. In a series of publications based on a single laboratory study, Giancola (2002a, 2002b, 2002c, 2003) found that alcohol-related aggression was more pronounced among those participants (especially men) with lower levels of dispositional empathy, higher levels of trait anger, higher levels of dispositional aggressivity, and higher levels of trait irritability. These findings point to the importance of considering underlying personality traits that are related to the behavior under investigation when considering variability in response to alcohol.

To date, the literature relating basic dimensions of personality to alcohol effects must be considered promising but inconclusive. It is not surprising that a clear pattern of findings has yet to emerge given (a) the relatively small samples that characterize much of this literature, (b) the variability with respect to the measures used to assess personality, (c) the variability in the experimental protocols used to study alcohol effects, and (d) the modest reliability of many of the effects under investigation. We also note that our focus here is on how personality might affect responses to alcohol and not, more broadly, on the etiological significance of personality in alcohol use disorders (see Sher, 1991; Sher, Trull, Bartholow, & Vieth, 1999). For example, as we have noted elsewhere,

> Individuals (especially those who are high on traits related to impulsivity and disinhibition) may develop pathological alcohol involvement because they are particularly sensitive to the pharmacological effects of alcohol, because they are motivated to get high or otherwise seek . . . reinforcement from alcohol, and because their socialization experiences put them on a trajectory for social deviance. (Sher & Trull, 1994, p. 96)

That is, individual differences in alcohol effects represent only one possible mechanism relating personality to alcohol use, alcohol problems, and alcohol dependence.

Alcohol Expectancies

For many years it has been recognized that individuals report consuming alcoholic beverages to alter their mental state, and these motives are strongly related to drinking status (e.g., Cahalan, Cisin, & Crossley, 1969). Similarly, as noted in chapter 4 of this volume, individuals hold a number of beliefs (i.e., alcohol outcome expectancies) concerning the anticipated effects of alcohol consumption. Research on the balanced-placebo design, also discussed in chapter 4 of this volume, clearly indicates that beliefs about drinking, in general, can be important determinants of alcohol effects. Somewhat surprisingly, though, the question of how individual differences in alcohol expectancies relate to individual differences in alcohol effects has not been systematically explored. As noted by Sher et al. (chapter 4, this volume), those studies that have been done suggest some correspondence between what people say they expect from alcohol and what they actually experience but, overall, less than one might expect and in a highly conditional way.

Perhaps it is unreasonable to expect a high level of congruence between anticipated alcohol effects and actual effects. First, the reliability of individual differences in subjective and behavioral effects of alcohol in the laboratory is often low for some measures of intoxication (e.g., Nagoshi & Wilson, 1988, 1989). Perhaps equally important, expectancies are context, dose, and limb dependent, and expectancies derived based on drinking in the natural environment may not be generalizable to the laboratory environment. This speculation is supported by one of our studies that found "more pronounced [subjective] effects among subjects with strong expectancies who drank in group settings" (Sher, 1985, p. 145) as opposed to under solitary conditions. Moreover, the influence of expectancies, context, and temporal aspects of the drinking session varied across different measures of subjective experience. Additionally, there might be some individuals whose expectancies are strongly related to actual alcohol effects and others whose expectancies are not; consequently, overall sample estimates of association obscure these different classes of individuals. This possibility is supported by O'Malley and Maisto's (1985) findings of an association between expectancies and subjective effects in those with a positive family history of alcohol but no association in those without familial risk. Finally, the work of Vogel-Sprott, Fillmore, and their colleagues, discussed in chapter 4 of this volume, also suggests very complex relations between alcohol expectancies and alcohol effects under some conditions. That is, if a person is anticipating negative effects of alcohol (at least on performance) prior to drinking, he or she might make compensatory adjustments to counteract the expected effect. That is, the expectancy itself, under some conditions, could elicit strategies to minimize alcohol effects with the result of attenuating the relationship between alcohol expectancies and alcohol effects. The net effect of these various factors (i.e., the specificity of expectancies with respect to dose, setting, BAC limb; moderation of the expectancy-subjective effect relation; compensatory strategies; low reliability [i.e., repeatability] of alcohol effects) is to attenuate correlations between individual differences in alcohol effects and objectively observed alcohol effects in the laboratory.

Cognitive Functioning

Given that prominent theories of the mechanisms of alcohol-related effects such as Hull's (1981) self-awareness theory and Steele and Josephs's (1990) alcohol myopia model posit a central role of cognitive processing, it is not surprising that researchers have begun to investigate the role of various cognitive abilities in predicting the magnitude of various alcohol effects. That is, if alcohol exerts many of its effects via compromising one or another cognitive function (e.g., attentional capacity, various memory processes), individual differences in baseline cognitive function could be expected to moderate those alcohol effects that are mediated by that function. For example, if alcohol affects mood by restricting attentional capacity, perhaps those with limited attentional capacity (i.e., with little "reserve" capacity) might be especially vulnerable to alcohol effects.

There have not been many studies of subjective experience directly addressing this possibility, but those that have been conducted have yielded provocative findings. For example, Peterson, Finn, and Pihl (1992) showed that various baseline neurocognitive measures of executive functions correlated with alcohol-related dampening of stress reactivity. There are also several studies now showing that individuals with low levels of executive function are particularly prone to react aggressively when intoxicated, especially under conditions of low provocation, and the magnitude of this increased aggression appears to be mediated by changes in alcohol-induced executive functioning (for a recent review, see Pihl, Assaad, & Hoaken, 2003). Recently, Giancola (2000) has elaborated on the role of executive functioning as both a mediator and a moderator of alcohol-related aggression, while noting that direct evidence for either is lacking. The theoretical analysis is restricted to aggression and, thus, focuses on the relation between executive functions and aggressive behavior such as perspective taking, consideration of future consequences, and alternative (i.e., nonaggressive) behavioral alternatives. Nonetheless, it is still informative for present purposes in that it highlights the close interrelation between individual differences in cognitive abilities, the effect of alcohol on those abilities, and the nature of experience while intoxicated.

Concluding Comments

It is abundantly clear that there is wide variability in subjective and other responses to alcohol. The sources of this variability include allelic variation in enzymes responsible for the metabolism of alcoholism, sensitivity (through either initial sensitivity or acquired tolerance), temperament, neurocognitive functioning, and social learning. These sources of heterogeneity in alcohol response appear to be very important not only in understanding the acute effects of alcohol on the individual but also in understanding risk processes underlying the development of alcohol use disorders. Thus, understanding the mechanisms of response heterogeneity could provide the foundation for identifying both those at highest risk for the development of pathological alcohol involvement and preventive and treatment interventions that are tailored to underlying risk mechanisms. Unfortunately, existing research has tended to focus on only one or two domains of individual differences at a time, making it difficult to discern whether ostensibly different domains of individual differences (e.g., genetic variation associated with dopamine neurotransmission, executive function, and temperament/personality) are indexing overlapping or distinct processes. More multivariate investigations on large, heterogeneous samples of drinkers are needed to more fully characterize individual differences in alcohol effects and the underlying mechanisms responsible for them.

The authors want to thank Alison E. Richardson, Kristina M. Jackson, Gilbert Parra, and Amee Epler for their help in the preparation of this manuscript.

References

Bauer, L. O., & Hesselbrock, V. M. (1993). EEG, autonomic and subjective correlates of the risk for alcoholism. *Journal of Studies on Alcohol, 54*, 577–589.

Behar, D., Berg, C. J., Rappaport, J. L., Linnoila, M., Cohen, M., C., B., et al. (1983). Behavioral and physiological effects of ethanol in high-risk and control children: A pilot study. *Alcoholism: Clinical and Experimental Research, 7*, 404–410.

Berridge, K. C., & Robinson, T. E. (1998). What is the role of dopamine in reward: Hedonic impact, reward learning, or incentive salience? *Brain Research–Brain Research Reviews, 28*, 309–369.

Burmeister, M. (1999). Basic concepts in the study of diseases with complex genetics. *Biological Psychiatry, 45*, 522–531.

Cahalan, D., Cisin, I. H., & Crossley, H. M. (1969). *American drinking practices: A national study of drinking behavior and attitudes* (Monograph No. 6). New Brunswick, NJ: Rutgers Center of Alcohol Studies.

Chen, W. J., Loh, E. W., Hsu, Y. P., Chen, C. C., Yu, J. M., & Cheng, A. T. (1996). Alcohol-metabolising genes and alcoholism among Taiwanese Han men: Independent effect of ADH2, ADH3 and ALDH2. *British Journal of Psychiatry, 168*, 762–767.

Claridge, G. (1970). *Drugs and human behavior*. London: Praeger.

Claridge, G., Canter, S., & Hume, W. I. (1973). *Personality differences and biological variations: A study of twins*. New York: Pergamon.

Cleckley, H. M. (1982). *The mask of sanity* (6th ed.). New York: Plume.

Cloninger, C. R. (1987a). Recent advances in family studies of alcoholism. *Progress in Clinical and Biological Research, 241*, 47–60.

Cloninger, C. R. (1987b). A systematic method for clinical description and classification of personality variants. *Archives of General Psychiatry, 44*, 573–578.

Cohen, H. L., Porjesz, B., & Begleiter, H. (1993). The effects of ethanol on EEG activity in males at risk for alcoholism. *Electroencephalography and Clinical Neurophysiology, 86*, 368–376.

Conrod, P. J., Peterson, J. B., Pihl, R. O., & Mankowski, S. (1997). Biphasic effects of alcohol on heart rate are influenced by alcoholic family history and rate of alcohol ingestion. *Alcoholism: Clinical and Experimental Research, 21*, 140–149.

Cotton, N. S. (1979). The familial incidence of alcoholism: A review. *Journal of Studies on Alcohol, 40,* 89–116.

Crabb, D. W. (1995). Ethanol oxidizing enzymes: Roles in alcohol metabolism and alcoholic liver disease. *Progress in Liver Diseases, 13,* 151–172.

de Wit, H., & McCracken, S. (1990). Ethanol self-administration in males with and without an alcoholic first-degree relative. *Alcoholism: Clinical and Experimental Research, 14,* 63–70.

Ehlers, C. L., Carr, L., Betancourt, M., & Montane-Jaime, K. (2003). Association of the ADH2*3 allele with greater alcohol expectancies in African-American young adults. *Journal of Studies on Alcohol, 64,* 176–181.

Ehlers, C. L., Gilder, D. A., Harris, L., & Carr, L. (2001). Association of the ADH2*3 allele with a negative family history of alcoholism in African American young adults. *Alcoholism: Clinical and Experimental Research, 25,* 1773–1777.

Eysenck, H., Casey, S., & Trouton, D. (1957). Drugs and personality. II. The effect of stimulant and depressant drugs on continuous work. *Journal of Mental Science, 103,* 645–649.

Fere, C. (1899). *The pathology of emotions* (R. Park, Trans.). London: University Press.

Finn, P. R., & Pihl, R. (1987). Men at high risk for alcoholism: The effect of alcohol on cardiovascular response to unavoidable shock. *Journal of Abnormal Psychology, 96,* 230–236.

Finn, P. R., Zeitouni, N. C., & Pihl, R. O. (1990). Effects of alcohol on psychophysiological hyperreactivity to nonaversive and aversive stimuli in men at high risk for alcoholism. *Journal of Abnormal Psychology, 99,* 79–85.

Franks, C. M. (1964). The use of alcohol in the investigation of drug-personality postulates. In R. Fox (Ed.), *Alcoholism: Behavioral research, therapeutic approaches* (pp.101–122). New York: Springer.

Fromme, K., & D'Amico, E. J. (1999). Neurobiological bases of alcohol's psychological effects. In K. E. Leonard & H. T. Blane (Eds.), *Psychological theories of drinking and alcoholism* (2nd ed., pp. 422–455). New York: Guilford.

Giancola, P. R. (2000). Executive functioning: A conceptual framework for alcohol-related aggression. *Experimental and Clinical Psychopharmacology, 8,* 576–597.

Giancola, P. R. (2002a). Alcohol-related aggression during the college years: Theories, risk factors, and policy implications. *Journal of Studies on Alcohol. 63 (Suppl 14)* 129–139.

Giancola, P. R. (2002b). Alcohol-related aggression in men and women: The influence of dispositional aggressivity. *Journal of Studies on Alcohol, 63,* 696–708.

Giancola, P. R. (2002c). The influence of trait anger on the alcohol-aggression relation in men and women. *Alcoholism: Clinical and Experimental Research, 26,* 1350–1358.

Giancola, P. R. (2003). The moderating effects of dispositional empathy on alcohol-related aggression in men and women. *Journal of Abnormal Psychology, 112,* 275–281.

Gianoulakis, C., Krishnan, B., & Thavundayil, J. (1996). Enhanced sensitivity of pituitary beta-endorphin to ethanol in subjects at high risk of alcoholism. *Archives of General Psychiatry, 53,* 250–257.

Heath, A. C. (1995). Genetic influences on alcoholism risk: A review of adoption and twin studies. *Alcohol Health and Research World, 19*, 166–171.

Heath, A. C., Bucholz, K., Madden, P., Dinwiddie, S., Slutske, W., Bierut, L., et al. (1997). Genetic and environmental contributions to alcohol dependence risk in a national twin sample: Consistency of findings in women and men. *Psychological Medicine, 27*, 1381–1396.

Heath, A. C., Madden, P., Bucholz, K., Dinwiddie, S., Slutske, W., Bierut, L., et al. (1999). Genetic differences in alcohol sensitivity and the inheritance of alcoholism risk. *Psychological Medicine, 29*, 1069–1081.

Heath, A. C., & Martin, N. G. (1992). Genetic differences in psychomotor performance decrement after alcohol: A multivariate analysis. *Journal of Studies on Alcohol, 53*, 262–271.

Higuchi, S., Matsushita, S., Murayama, M., Takagi, S., & Hayashida, M. (1995). Alcohol and aldehyde dehydrogenase polymorphisms and the risk for alcoholism. *American Journal of Psychiatry, 152*, 1219–1221.

Hill, S. Y., & Neiswanger, K. (1997). The value of narrow psychiatric phenotypes and "super" normal controls. In K. Blum & E. P. Noble (Eds.), *Handbook of psychiatric genetics* (pp. 37–46). Boca Raton, FL: CRC Press.

Hull, J. G. (1981). A self-awareness model of the causes and effects of alcohol consumption. *Journal of Abnormal Psychology, 90*, 586–600.

Hull, J. G. (1987). Self-awareness model. In H. T. Blane & K. E. Leonard (Eds.), *Psychological theories of drinking and alcoholism* (pp. 272–301). New York: Guilford.

Hutchison, K. E., LaChance, H., Niaura, R., Bryan, A., & Smolen, A. (2002). The DRD4 VNTR polymorphism influences reactivity to smoking cues. *Journal of Abnormal Psychology, 111*, 134–143.

Hutchison, K. E., McGeary, J., Smolen, A., Bryan, A., & Swift, R. M. (2002). The DRD4 VNTR polymorphism moderates craving after alcohol consumption. *Health Psychology, 21*, 139–146.

Hutchison, K. E., Swift, R., Rohsenow, D. J., Monti, P. M., Davidson, D., & Almeida, A. (2001). Olanzapine reduces urge to drink after drinking cues and a priming dose of alcohol. *Psychopharmacology, 155*, 27–34.

Judd, L. L., Hubbard, B., Janowsky, D. S., Huey, L. Y., & Attewell, P. A.. (1977). The effect of lithium carbonate on affect, mood, and personality of normal subjects. *Archives of General Psychiatry, 34*, 346–351.

Kaplan, R. F., Hesselbrock, V. M., O'Connor, S., & Depalma, N. (1988). Behavioral and EEG responses to alcohol in nonalcoholic men with a family history of alcoholism. *Progress in Neuro-Psychopharmacology and Biological Psychiatry, 12*, 873–885.

Levenson, R. W., Oyama, O. N., & Meek, P. S. (1987). Greater reinforcement from alcohol for those at risk: Parental risk, personality risk, and sex. *Journal of Abnormal Psychology, 96*, 242–253.

Luczak, S. E., Elvine-Kreis, B., Shea, S. H., Carr, L. G., & Wall, T. L. (2002). Genetic risk for alcoholism relates to level of response to alcohol in Asian-American men and women. *Journal of Studies on Alcohol, 63*, 74–82.

Lukas, S. E., Mendelson, J. H., Benedikt, R. A., & Jones, B. (1986). EEG alpha activity increases during transient episodes of ethanol-induced euphoria. *Pharmacology, Biochemistry and Behavior, 25*, 889–895.

McCarthy, D. M., Brown, S. A., Carr, L. G., & Wall, T. L. (2001). ALDH2 status, alcohol expectancies, and alcohol response: Preliminary evidence for a mediation model. *Alcoholism: Clinical and Experimental Research, 25,* 1558–1563.

McCarthy, D. M., Wall, T. L., Brown, S. A., & Carr, L. G. (2000). Integrating biological and behavioral factors in alcohol use risk: The role of ALDH2 status and alcohol expectancies in a sample of Asian Americans. *Experimental and Clinical Psychopharmacology, 8,* 168–175.

McCaul, M. E., Turkkan, J., Svikis, D., & Bigelow, G. (1991). Familial density of alcoholism: Effects on psychophysiological responses to ethanol. *Alcohol, 8,* 219–222.

McCaul, M. E., Turkkan, J. S., Svikis, D. S., & Bigelow, G. E. (1990). Alcohol and secobarbital effects as a function of familial alcoholism: Acute psychophysiological effects. *Alcoholism: Clinical and Experimental Research, 14,* 704–712.

McDougall, W. (1929). The chemical theory of temperament applied to introversion and extroversion. *Journal of Abnormal and Social Psychology, 24,* 293–309.

McGue, M. (1994). Why developmental psychology should find room for behavioral genetics. In C. A. Nelson (Ed.), *Threats to optimal development: Integrating biological, psychological, and social risk factors: The Minnesota symposia on child psychology* (Vol. 27, pp. 105–119). Minneapolis: University of Minnesota.

McGue, M. (1999). Behavioral genetic models of alcoholism and drinking. In K. E. Leonard & H. T. Blane (Eds.), *Psychological theories of drinking and alcoholism* (2nd ed., pp. 372–421). New York: Guilford.

Morzorati, S. L., Ramchandani, V., Flury, L., Li, T., & O'Connor, S. (2002). Self-reported subjective perception of intoxication reflects family history of alcoholism when breath alcohol levels are constant. *Alcoholism: Clinical and Experimental Research, 26,* 1299–1306.

Moss, H. B., Yao, J. K., & Maddock, J. M. (1989). Responses by sons of alcoholic fathers to alcoholic and placebo drinks: Perceived mood, intoxication, and plasma prolactin. *Alcoholism: Clinical and Experimental Research, 13,* 252–257.

Nagoshi, C. T., & Wilson, J. R. (1987). Influence of family alcoholism history on alcohol metabolism, sensitivity, and tolerance. *Alcoholism: Clinical and Experimental Research, 11,* 392–398.

Nagoshi, C. T., & Wilson, J. R. (1988). One-month repeatability of emotional responses to alcohol. *Alcoholism: Clinical and Experimental Research, 12,* 691–697.

Nagoshi, C. T., & Wilson, J. R. (1989). Long-term repeatability of human alcohol metabolism, sensitivity and acute tolerance. *Journal of Studies on Alcohol, 50,* 162–169.

Nagoshi, C. T., Wilson, J. R., & Rodriguez, L. A. (1991). Impulsivity, sensation seeking, and behavioral and emotional responses to alcohol. *Alcoholism: Clinical and Experimental Research, 15,* 661–667.

Nakamura, K., Iwahashi, K., Matsuo, Y., Miyatake, R., Ichikawa, Y., & Suwaki, H. (1996). Characteristics of Japanese alcoholics with the atypical aldehyde dehydrogenase 2*2. I. A comparison of the genotypes of ALDH2, ADH2, ADH3, and cytochrome P-4502E1 between alcoholics and nonalcoholics. *Alcoholism: Clinical and Experimental Research, 20,* 52–55.

Neale, M., & Martin, N. (1989). The effects of age, sex, and genotype on self-report drunkenness following a challenge dose of alcohol. *Behavior Genetics, 19*, 63–78.

Newlin, D. B., & Thomson, J. B. (1990). Alcohol challenge with sons of alcoholics: A critical review and analysis. *Psychological Bulletin, 108*, 383–402.

Niaura, R., Wilson, G., & Westrick, E. (1988). Self-awareness, alcohol consumption, and reduced cardiovascular reactivity. *Psychosomatic Medicine, 50*, 360–380.

Norris, J. (1994). Alcohol and female sexuality: A look at expectancies and risks. *Alcohol Health and Research World, 18*, 197–201.

O'Malley, S. S., & Maisto, S. A. (1985). Effects of family drinking history and expectancies on responses to alcohol in men. *Journal of Studies on Alcohol, 46*, 289–297.

Perry, A. (1973). The effect of heredity on attitudes toward alcohol, cigarettes, and coffee. *Journal of Applied Psychology, 58*, 275–277.

Peterson, J. B., Finn, P. R., & Pihl, R. O. (1992). Cognitive dysfunction and the inherited predisposition to alcoholism. *Journal of Studies on Alcohol, 53*, 154–160.

Pihl, R. O., Assaad, J. M., & Hoaken, P. N. S. (2003). The alcohol-aggression relationship and differential sensitivity to alcohol. *Aggressive Behavior, 29*, 302–315.

Pollock, V., Teasdale, T., Gabrielli, W., & Knop, J. (1986). Subjective and objective measures of response to alcohol among young men at risk for alcoholism. *Journal of Studies on Alcohol, 47*, 297–304.

Pollock, V. E. (1992). Meta-analysis of subjective sensitivity to alcohol in sons of alcoholics. *American Journal of Psychiatry, 149*, 1534–1538.

Pollock, V. E., Schneider, L. S., Gabrielli, W. F., Jr., & Goodwin, D. W. (1987). Sex of parent and offspring in the transmission of alcoholism. A meta-analysis. *Journal of Nervous and Mental Disease, 175*, 668–673.

Prescott, C. A., Cross, R. J., Kuhn, J. W., Horn, J. L., & Kendler, K. S. (in press). Is risk for alcoholism mediated by individual differences in drinking motivations? *Alcoholism: Clinical and Experimental Research*.

Schuckit, M. A. (1980). Self-rating of alcohol intoxication by young men with and without family histories of alcoholism. *Journal of Studies on Alcohol, 41*, 242–249.

Schuckit, M. A. (1984). Subjective responses to alcohol in sons of alcoholics and control subjects. *Archives of General Psychiatry, 41*, 879–884.

Schuckit, M. A. (1995). A long-term study of sons of alcoholics. *Alcohol Health and Research World, 19*, 172–175.

Schuckit, M. A. (1999). New findings on the genetics of alcoholism. *Journal of the American Medical Association, 281*, 1875–1876.

Schuckit, M. A., & Smith, T. L. (1996). An 8-year followup of 450 sons of alcoholic and control subjects. *Archives of General Psychiatry, 53*, 202–210.

Schuckit, M. A., & Smith, T. L. (2000). The relationships of a family history of alcohol dependence, a low level of response to alcohol and six domains of life functioning to the development of alcohol use disorders. *Journal of Studies on Alcohol, 61*, 827–835.

Sher, K. J. (1985). Subjective effects of alcohol: The influence of setting and individual differences in alcohol expectancies. *Journal of Studies on Alcohol, 46,* 137–146.

Sher, K. J. (1991). *Children of alcoholics: A critical appraisal of theory and research.* Chicago: University of Chicago.

Sher, K. J., Bylund, D. B., Walitzer, K. S., Hartmann, J., & Ray-Prenger, C. (1994). Platelet monoamine oxidase (MAO) activity: Personality, substance use, and the stress-response-dampening effect of alcohol. *Experimental and Clinical Psychopharmacology, 2,* 53–81.

Sher, K. J., & Levenson, R. W. (1982). Risk for alcoholism and individual differences in the stress-response-dampening effect of alcohol. *Journal of Abnormal Psychology, 91,* 350–367.

Sher, K. J., & Trull, T. J. (1994). Personality and disinhibitory psychopathology: Alcoholism and antisocial personality disorder. *Journal of Abnormal Psychology, 103,* 92–102.

Sher, K. J., Trull, T. J., Bartholow, B. D., & Vieth, A. (1999). Personality and alcoholism: Issues, methods, and etiological processes. In K. E. Leonard & H. T. Blane (Eds.), *Psychological theories of drinking and alcoholism* (2nd ed., pp. 54–105). New York: Guilford.

Sher, K. J., & Walitzer, K. S. (1986). Individual differences in the stress-response-dampening effect of alcohol: A dose-response study. *Journal of Abnormal Psychology, 95,* 159–167.

Slutske, W. S., Cronk, N. J., Sher, K. J., Madden, P. A. F., Bucholz, K. K., & Heath, A. C. (2002). Genes, environment and individual differences in alcohol expectancies among female adolescents and young adults. *Psychology of Addictive Behaviors, 16,* 308–317.

Steele, C. M., & Josephs, R. A. (1990). Alcohol myopia: Its prized and dangerous effects. *American Psychologist, 45,* 921–933.

Takeshita, T., Morimoto, K., Mao, X., Hashimoto, T., & Furuyama, J. (1994). Characterization of the three genotypes of low Km aldehyde dehydrogenase in a Japanese population. *Human Genetics, 94,* 217–223.

Urschel, H. C., & Woody, G. E. (1996). Alcohol idiosyncratic intoxication: A review of the data supporting its existence. In R. L. Spitzer, M. Gibbon, A. E. Skodol, J. B. W. Williams & M. D. First (Eds.), *DSM-IV source book* (pp. 117–127). Washington, DC: American Psychiatric Press.

Vernon, P. A., Lee, D., Harris, J. A., & Jang, K. L. (1996). Genetic and environmental contributions to individual differences in alcohol expectancies. *Personality and Individual Differences, 21,* 183–187.

Vogel-Sprott, M., & Chipperfield, B. (1987). Family history of problem drinking among young male social drinkers: Behavioral effects of alcohol. *Journal of Studies on Alcohol, 48,* 430–436.

Volavka, J., Czobor, P., Goodwin, D. W., Gabrielli, W. F., Penick, E. C., Mednick, S. A. et al. (1996). The electroencephalogram after alcohol administration in high-risk men and the development of alcohol use disorders 10 years later: Preliminary findings. *Archives of General Psychiatry, 53,* 258–263.

Wall, T. L., Thomasson, H. R., Schuckit, M. A., & Ehlers, C. L. (1992). Subjective feelings of alcohol intoxication in Asians with genetic variations of ALDH2 alleles. *Alcoholism: Clinical and Experimental Research, 16,* 991–995.

Weiss, F., & Koob, G. F. (1991). The neuropharmacology of ethanol self-administration. In R. E. Meyer, G. F. Koob, M. J. Lewis, & S. M. Paul (Eds.), *Neuropharmacology of ethanol* (pp. 125–162). Boston: Birkhauser.

Zeichner, A., Edwards, P. W., & Cohen, E. (1985). Acute effects of alcohol on cardiovascular reactivity to stress in college-age Type A (coronary prone) individuals. *Journal of Psychopathology and Behavioral Assessment, 7,* 75–89.

Zeichner, A., Giancola, P. R., & Allen, J. D. (1995). Effects of hostility on alcohol stress-response-dampening. *Alcoholism: Clinical and Experimental Research, 19,* 977–983.

Zuckerman, M. (1991). *Psychobiology of personality.* Cambridge: Cambridge University.

Zuckerman, M. (1995). Good and bad humors: Biochemical bases of personality and its disorders. *Psychological Science, 6,* 325–332.

6

Ethnicity and the Subjective Effects of Alcohol

TRAVIS A. R. COOK AND TAMARA L. WALL

There are marked differences between ethnicities in both rates of substance use and substance use disorders (Bachman et al., 1991; National Institute on Drug Abuse [NIDA], 1998; Substance Abuse and Mental Health Services Administration [SAMHSA], 1998; Zhang & Snowden, 1999). For example, data from the Epidemiological Catchment Area (ECA) study indicate that in the United States, the lifetime prevalence of alcohol abuse and dependence was 7.1% for Asians, 12.7% for Whites, 12.3% for Blacks, and 16.6% for Hispanics (Zhang & Snowden, 1999). The same study reported that the lifetime prevalence of nonalcohol substance use disorders was 2.3% for Asians, 6.0% for Whites, 5.2% for Blacks, and 4.2% for Hispanics. The substantial variability between ethnic groups in the rates of substance use disorders, the findings that subjective response to alcohol is in part genetically influenced (Heath et al., 1999; Neale & Martin, 1989), and the evidence demonstrating that a low response to alcohol relates to the future development of alcohol use disorders (Heath et al., 1999; Rodriguez, Wilson, & Nagoshi, 1993; Schuckit & Smith, 1996; Volavka et al., 1996) suggest the possibility of interethnic differences in response to alcohol and possibly other drugs. Experimental evidence of such differences primarily has been found in studies evaluating response to alcohol.

The liver isoenzymes that metabolize alcohol account for a significant portion of the interethnic variability in rates of alcohol use and alcohol use disorders. Of particular relevance are the aldehyde dehydrogenase (ALDH2) and alcohol dehydrogenase (ADH2 and ADH3) isoenzymes, which are encoded by genetic polymorphisms that produce different kinetic properties (figure 6.1). Because the frequency of these polymorphisms varies across population groups, they have been suggested as candidate genes that are likely to contribute to ethnic differences in alcohol and acetaldehyde degradation, variability in both subjective and objective reactions to alcohol, and differential vulnerability for alcohol use, alcoholism, and other alcohol-related illness. The following reviews the pathway of alcohol metabolism and the associations of *ALDH2*, *ADH2*, and *ADH3* gene variations with alcohol-related behavior.

The two major enzymes involved in alcohol metabolism are ADH, which converts alcohol to acetaldehyde, and ALDH, which converts acetaldehyde to acetate. The *ALDH2* gene, located on chromosome 12, encodes the principal isoenzyme responsible for the majority of acetaldehyde oxidation and exists in two allelic forms, *ALDH2*1* and *ALDH2*2*. Isoenzymes in individuals homozygous for the *ALDH2*2* allele (*ALDH2*2/2*2* genotype) are virtually inactive, whereas isoenzymes in heterozygotes (*ALDH2*1/2*2* genotype) have measurable, though deficient, activity compared with isoenzymes in *ALDH2*1* homozygotes (*ALDH2*1/2*1* genotype; Crabb, Edenberg, Bosron, & Li, 1989).

The *ALDH2*2* allele is prevalent among East Asian populations but extremely rare in non-Asians (Goedde et al., 1992). General population

ALCOHOL	⇨	ACETALDEHYDE	⇨	ACETATE
Alcohol Dehydrogenase (ADH)		Aldehyde Dehydrogenase (ALDH)		

Polymorphic genes	ADH2*1 (ß1, low K_m, low V_{max})	ALDH2*1 (Active)
	ADH2*2 (ß2, low K_m, high V_{max})	ALDH2*2 (Inactive)
	ADH2*3 (ß3, high K_m, high V_{max})	
	ADH3*1 (γ1, low K_m, higher V_{max})	
	ADH3*2 (γ2, low K_m, lower V_{max})	

K_m refers to the Michaelis-Menten constant for alcohol. The V_{max} comparisons for the

isoenzymes indicate differences within ß or γ isoenzyme groups.

Figure 6.1 The primary pathway of alcohol metabolism by ADH and ALDH enzymes, their polymorphic gene loci, and isoenzyme properties (Crabb, 1990; Crabb, Dipple, & Thomasson, 1993)

studies indicate that the highest reported prevalence of the *ALDH2*2* allele is among Han Chinese, the majority population of China (.24–.35; C.-C. Chen et al., 1999; C.-C. Chen, Zhang, & Scott, 1992; W. J. Chen et al., 1996; Novoradovsky, Tsai, et al., 1995; Thomasson et al., 1991). *ALDH2*2* is also prevalent in Japanese (.23–.26; Higuchi, Matsushita, Murayama, Takagi, & Hayashida, 1995; Singh et al., 1989; Sun, Tsuritani, Honda, Ma, & Yamada, 1999; Takeshita & Morimoto, 1999). The prevalence of *ALDH2*2* appears to gradually diminish outward toward central and western Asia, in Koreans (.15–.16; Goedde et al., 1989; Lee et al., 1997); Mongolians (.09–.10) (S.-H. Chen, Zhang, Wang, & Scott, 1994; Shen et al., 1997); ethnic minority groups of northern and central China (.05–.09) (Cadoret, Troughton, O'Gorman, & Heywood, 1986; Shen et al., 1997); and southern Siberians (0–.02) *ALDH2*2* has been reported to be rare or absent among Filipinos, Thais, Malaysians, Papua New Guineans, Samoans, and the Maori of New Zealand (Novoradovsky, Tsai, et al., 1995).

Many studies have demonstrated that compared with those with *ALDH2*1/2*1* genotype, Chinese and Japanese with *ALDH2*2* alleles (*ALDH2*1/2*2* or *ALDH2*2/2*2* genotype) drink less alcohol (Higuchi, Matsushita, Muramatsu, Murayama, & Hayashida, 1996; Muramatsu et al., 1995; Sun et al., 1999; Takeshita & Morimoto, 1999; Takeshita, Morimoto, Mao, Hashimoto, & Furuyama, 1994) and have lower rates of alcohol dependence (C.-C. Chen et al., 1999; W. J. Chen et al., 1996; Y.-C. Chen et al., 1999; Higuchi et al., 1996; Higuchi et al., 1995; Iwahashi, 1995; Maezawa, Yamauchi, Toda, Suzuki, & Sakurai, 1995; Muramatsu et al., 1995; Nakamura et al., 1996; Shen et al., 1997; Tanaka et al., 1996; Thomasson et al., 1991). From the multiple studies conducted in Japan and China comparing *ALDH2* genotypes in alcoholics from treatment centers and controls, only one alcohol-dependent patient with *ALDH2*2/2*2* has been reported (Y.-C. Chen et al., 1999), whereas between 4 and 12% of control participants have this genotype. The one identified alcoholic who was homozygous for *ALDH2*2* had a pattern of drinking characterized by slow and prolonged alcohol consumption that was low in total overall quantity. He reportedly sipped beer almost continuously throughout the day, consuming between three and five standard drinks daily, but met six of the nine *DSM-III-R* criteria for alcohol dependence, including symptoms of tolerance and withdrawal.

*ALDH2*2* heterozygotes also have significantly lower rates of alcohol dependence than those lacking an *ALDH2*2* allele; between 6 and 21% of Chinese and Japanese alcoholics have *ALDH2*1/2*2* genotype compared with 29 to 53% of controls. In comparison to alcoholics with *ALDH2*1/2*1* genotype, there is some evidence to suggest that alcoholics with *ALDH2*1/2*2* genotype may develop alcohol dependence at lower levels of alcohol intake (Iwahashi, 1995), and their clinical course of alcohol-related life events (e.g., habitual drinking, withdrawal) is delayed between 1 and 5 years (Murayama, Matsushita, Muramatsu, & Higuchi, 1998). Moreover, in the presence of alcoholism or at lower levels of alcohol intake, *ALDH2*2* heterozygotes appear to be more vulnerable to certain alcohol-associated pathologies, including liver disease (Y.-C. Chao et al., 1994; Y.-C. Chao, Young, Tang, & Hsu, 1997; Enomoto, Takase, Takada, & Takada, 1991; Shibuya & Yoshida, 1988; Takada, Tsutsumi, & Kobayashi, 1994; Tanaka et al., 1996) and cancers (Hori, Kawano, Endo, & Yuasa, 1997; Tanabe, Ohhira, Watari, Yokota, & Kohogo, 1999; Yokoyama, Muramatsu et al., 1996; Yokoyama et al., 1998; Yokoyama, Ohmori et al., 1996). These findings are consistent with a role of acetaldehyde in the pathogenesis of organ damage (Day & Bassendine, 1992; Sorrell & Tuma, 1985).

Individuals who are homozygous for *ALDH2*2* drink little or no alcohol (Higuchi et al., 1996; Muramatsu et al., 1995; Sun et al., 1999; Takeshita & Morimoto, 1999; Takeshita et al., 1994), and only one alcoholic with this genotype has been identified (Y.-C. Chen et al., 1999). Therefore, possession of the *ALDH2*2/2*2* genotype may provide almost full protection against alcohol dependence. Alcohol use and alcoholism in *ALDH2*2* heterozygotes, however, is variable. Some drink very little; others drink heavily and develop alcohol dependence.

One possible reason for this variability is that polymorphisms in the *ADH2* and *ADH3* genes, both located on chromosome 4, further influence alcoholism risk. Based on their kinetic properties, *ADH2*2*, *ADH2*3*, and *ADH3*1* alleles should lead to more rapid production of acetaldehyde during alcohol metabolism than *ADH2*1* and *ADH3*2* alleles (Crabb, Dipple, & Thomasson, 1993). Although the effect is less robust, research among Chinese and Japanese has found that the *ADH2*2* allele is related to lower rates of alcohol dependence, independent of the *ALDH2*2* allele (C.-C. Chen et al., 1999; W. J. Chen et al., 1996; W. J. Chen, Loh, Hsu, & Cheng, 1997; Higuchi et al., 1995; Maezawa et al., 1995; Muramatsu et al., 1995; Nakamura et al., 1996; Shen et al., 1997; Tanaka et al., 1996; Thomasson et al., 1994; Thomasson et al., 1991). There is also evidence to suggest that alcoholics with *ADH2*2* alleles who consume alcohol also carry an increased risk for negative sequelae such as liver disease (Y.-C. Chao et al., 1994; Y.-C. Chao et al., 1997; Tanaka et al., 1996; Yamauchi et al., 1995). Studies of the relationship between *ADH2*2* and alcohol consumption in Asians indicate that possession of an *ADH2*2* allele is related to alcohol use, beyond that of *ALDH2*2*, only in heavier drinkers, such as men with *ALDH2*1/ 2*1* genotype (Takeshita et al., 1994) and alcoholics (Higuchi et al., 1996).

Thus, *ADH2*2* appears to exert less influence on alcohol-related behavior than *ALDH2*2*, but it is applicable to a broader range of ethnic groups. *ADH2*2* has been reported to be highly prevalent among Chinese (.68), Japanese (.59), and Koreans (.81) but rare in most Caucasians (.01–.05; Goedde et al., 1992). Recently, however, *ADH2*2* was found to have a prevalence of .41 in Russians (Ogurtsov et al., 2001) and a prevalence between .17 and .41 in individuals of Jewish descent from the United States and Israel (Hasin et al., 2002a, 2002b; Neumark, Friedlander, Thomasson, & Li, 1998; Shea, Wall, Carr, & Li, 2001). Jews, like Asians, are a population with an overall low rate of alcoholism (Levav, Kohn, Golding, & Weissman, 1997; Yeung & Greenwald, 1992), whereas Russians have high rates of heavy drinking and alcohol-related deaths (McKee, 1999). *ADH2*2* has been associated with lower rates of alcohol dependence and/or lower levels of alcohol consumption in Caucasians of European, Jewish, and Russian descent, despite its low and moderately low prevalence in these non-Asian populations (Borras et al., 2000; Hasin et al., 2002a, 2002b; Neumark et al., 1998; Ogurtsov et al., 2001; Shea et al., 2001; Whitfield et al., 1998). In addition, a study of children with fetal alcohol syndrome found a protective association of *ADH2*2* in South Africans of mixed ancestry (Viljoen et al., 2001).

A less common polymorphism of *ADH2*, the *ADH2*3* allele, is prevalent in Africans (.03–.36) and African Americans (.22–.33; Bosron, Magnes, & Li, 1983; Osier et al., 2002; Thomasson, Beard, & Li, 1993; Viljoen et al., 2001). *ADH2*3* has also been identified in low prevalence in Caucasians (0–.03) and Native Americans (.06), which could be explained by recent migration and/or admixture (Osier et al., 2002; Wall, Garcia-Andrade, Thomasson, Carr, & Ehlers, 1997). A protective association of *ADH2*3* with alcohol dependence and heavy drinking has been found in Native American Mission Indians (Wall, Carr, & Ehlers, 2003), and a protective association of *ADH2*3* with fetal alcohol syndrome has been found in African Americans (Jacobson et al., 2000; McCarver, 2001; McCarver, Thomasson, Martier, Sokol, & Li, 1997).

Some studies have reported that the *ADH3*1* allele is associated with a slightly lower risk for alcohol dependence in Chinese (W. J. Chen et al., 1996; Thomasson et al., 1991) and Japanese (Nakamura et al., 1996). Other studies reported an association between the *ADH3*1* allele and a decreased risk for alcohol use and alcoholism (Whitfield et al., 1998) and an increased risk for liver disease (Day et al., 1991) in Caucasians. Other studies, however, have failed to find a relationship between *ADH3*1* and alcohol behavior in Caucasians (Couzigou et al., 1990; Gilder, Hodgkinson, & Murray, 1993; Pares et al., 1994). Recent investigations of Chinese (C.-C. Chen et al., 1999; Osier et al., 1999) and European Caucasians (Borras et al., 2000) found that the observed differences in the frequency of *ADH3* genotypes between alcoholics and controls was accounted for by linkage disequilibrium between *ADH3*1* and *ADH2*2*. The *ADH2* and *ADH3* loci are located in close proximity on chromosome 4, and variants at these two loci do not occur independently. Thus, the effects of *ADH2*2* and *ADH3*1* on alcoholism appear to be associated. Interestingly, genome-wide scans of families of alcoholics also have found evidence suggestive of protection against alcoholism on an area of chromosome 4 that includes the ADH gene cluster in both the Collaborative Study on the Genetics of Alcoholism (COGA) (Reich et al., 1998) and a Native American Indian population (Long et al., 1998).

In summary, variations in the *ALDH2* and *ADH2* genes, and less likely the *ADH3* gene, are associated with lower risk for alcohol dependence in some Asian and non-Asian groups. Based on their kinetic properties, it is hypothesized that *ADH2*2, *ADH2*3, and *ADH3*1 lead to faster production of acetaldehyde than *ADH2*1 and *ADH3*2; and *ALDH2*2 leads to slower removal of acetaldehyde during alcohol metabolism than *ALDH2*1. It is further hypothesized that elevated levels of acetaldehyde lead to greater sensitivity to alcohol and lower levels of alcohol consumption and that this is the mechanism by which individuals with these alleles are protected against alcohol dependence.

The Subjective Effects of Alcohol in Asians

Individuals of Asian heritage constitute a diverse racial group, originating from many countries around the world. As a whole, Asians account for more than half of the world population and about 4% of the population in the United States. The use of a single category to define all Asian American subgroups disregards important cultural and genetic diversity in this population, but the large number of subgroups and their geographic dispersion create a variety of sampling problems for researchers. For this reason, most of the epidemiological research on alcohol-related behavior among Asian Americans has combined many subgroups when making comparisons to other racial and ethnic groups. Even when subgroups are aggregated, Asian Americans tend to be underrepresented in national surveys, but data indicate that lifetime alcohol use disorders for Asian Americans, as a group, are about half those of other racial and ethnic groups in the United States (Zhang & Snowden, 1999). Surveys have also shown that both Asian American youth (Adlaf, Smart, & Tan, 1989; Bachman et al., 1991; Gillmore et al., 1990; Kandel, Single, & Kessler, 1976; Newcomb & Bentler, 1986) and adults (Klatsky, Sieglaub, Landy, & Friedman, 1983) report lower levels of alcohol use than other ethnic groups. Few studies have investigated important variations between Asian American subgroups, but a large cross-national epidemiological study found substantial differences in the prevalence of alcohol use disorders between two Asian countries. Helzer and colleagues (1990) reported that the lifetime rate of alcohol abuse or dependence was 7% in Taiwan (13% for men and 0.7% for women), compared with 23% in South Korea (43% for men and 3% for women). Given the heterogeneity among Asian Americans, some investigators have argued that combining subgroups may lead to misleading conclusions (Uehara, Takeuchi, & Smukler, 1994).

Early research aimed at understanding why Asians have lower rates of alcohol use and alcoholism focused on the alcohol-induced flushing reaction that between 47 and 85% of Asians report experiencing after they drink alcohol (Chan, 1986; H. M. Chao, 1995). The flushing response is characterized by increased blood flow to the skin of the face, neck, and chest; other symptoms may include tachycardia, hypotension, headache, nausea, and vomiting. The manifestations of the flushing reaction vary widely. Some people report the full range of symptoms, whereas others report experiencing milder reactions after ingesting alcohol.

One of the earliest studies to demonstrate the flushing response in Asians reported that 83% of an Asian sample composed of Japanese, Taiwanese, and Korean adults visibly flushed after consuming a low dose of alcohol (0.11–0.24 g/kg), whereas only 3% of Caucasians visibly flushed after consuming a larger dose of alcohol (0.28–0.36 g/kg; Wolff, 1972). In addition, more Asians than Caucasians reported aversive symptoms after drinking, such as heart palpitations, tachycardia, muscle weakness, dizziness, and sleepiness. Moreover, because Asian infants flushed, but Caucasian infants did not flush, it was concluded that ethnic differences in diet or drinking practices were not responsible for the flushing response in Asians.

Another study also compared Asian participants with Caucasian participants after 0.24 or 0.32 g/kg alcohol (Ewing, Rouse, & Pellizzari, 1974). Asians experienced a higher rate of flushing and more "pounding in head" than did Caucasians, and fewer Asians reported feeling "relaxed," "confident," and "happy." Therefore, Asians in this study not only were more likely to experience negative symptoms but also were less likely to experience a variety of positive symptoms. Although Asians had both decreased diastolic blood pressure and increased heart rate compared with Caucasians, differences in absorption or metabolism of alcohol that might explain the flushing reaction were not found.

Subsequent studies examined subjective feelings of intoxication in flushing and nonflushing Asians following an alcohol challenge (Mizoi et al., 1980; Newlin, 1989; Seto, Tricomi, Goodwin, Kolodney, & Sullivan, 1978; Truitt, Rowe, & Mehl, 1987). Two initial studies (Mizoi et al., 1980; Seto et al., 1978) found that those who flushed experienced more aversive symptoms (e.g., headache, nausea, and dizziness) than those who did not flush. However, these studies did not assess positive symptoms of intoxication. Another study reported an association between flushing and increased feelings of both tension and vigor, but it did not explicitly compare flushing and nonflushing participants (Sanders, Danko, & Ching, 1980). Finally, two studies assessed both aversive and positive subjective symptoms but found no subjective differences in response to alcohol between flushing and nonflushing participants (Newlin, 1989; Truitt et al., 1987). Small sample sizes may have contributed to the failure to find differences in the latter two studies.

These early studies suggest that Asians, as a group, may be more sensitive to alcohol than Caucasians, and that Asians who experience alcohol-induced flushing may be more sensitive to alcohol than those who do not experience such flushing. The alcohol-induced flushing reaction that the majority of Asians report experiencing has now been attributed primarily to possession of an ALDH2*2 allele, which results in a deficiency in the ALDH2 isoenzyme and slower removal of acetaldehyde during alcohol metabolism. It has also been recognized that self-report of flushing among Asians is not always a valid indicator of actual observed flushing following an alcohol challenge and is not always a valid indicator of having an ALDH2*2 allele (Wall, Thomasson, & Ehlers, 1996). In addition, flushing in response to alcohol is not solely an attribute of persons of Asian heritage and may not always be associated with protection from alcoholism (Schuckit & Duby, 1982; Slutske et al., 1995). Nonetheless, possession of an ALDH2*2 allele is a specific biological factor associated with observed alcohol-induced flushing, lower levels of alcohol consumption, and decreased risk for alcoholism. These findings support the importance of using ALDH2 genotype, rather than self-report of flushing, when examining factors associated with differences in drinking behavior and response to alcohol among Asians. Therefore, more recent studies have evaluated subjective and objective response to alcohol in Asians who were genotyped at the ALDH2 locus to examine the potential mechanism by which this gene protects against alcohol dependence (Luczak, Elvine-Kreis, Shea, Carr, & Wall, 2002; Peng et al., 1999; Wall, Thomasson, Schuckit, & Ehlers, 1992).

Wall and colleagues (1992) evaluated 30 Asian American (Chinese, Japanese, and Korean) men, 15 with ALDH2*1/*, 14 with ALDH2*1/*2, and 1 with ALDH2*2/*2, following a moderate dose of alcohol (0.59 g/ kg) and placebo. A subsequent study (Luczak et al., 2002) evaluated 30 Asian American men and women, 20 with ALDH2*1/*2 and 10 with ALDH2*1/*, following a moderate dose of alcohol (dosed according to estimated body water to reach equivalent blood alcohol levels across gender) and placebo. The results from both studies suggest that there are differences in subjective and objective response to alcohol associated with ALDH2 genotype. For both men and women, findings indicated that participants with ALDH2*1/2*2 genotype subjectively experienced more intense, but not less pleasurable, reactions to alcohol than those with ALDH2*1/2*1 genotype. Despite virtually identical self-reports following placebo and equivalent blood alcohol levels following alcohol, ALDH2*2 heterozygotes subjectively rated their level of intoxication significantly higher on most, but not all, of the items from the Subjective High Assessment Scale (SHAS). Statistically significant group differences were found for positive attributes of intoxication, such as feeling "high" and "great overall," and for neutral attributes of intoxication, such as "alcohol effects," "drunk," "feelings of floating," "dizzy," "clumsy," and "muddled or confused." Although both men and women with ALDH2*1/2*2 genotype tended to rate themselves higher on negative feelings of intoxication, such as feeling "uncomfortable," "nauseated," and "terrible overall," they did not differ significantly from individuals with ALDH2*1/2*1 genotype on these SHAS items. Several objective measures of intoxication (e.g., pulse rate, observed facial flushing, cortisol levels, alcohol-related EEG, event-related potential changes, acetaldehyde levels) have corroborated the more intense subjective response to alcohol experienced by men and women with ALDH2*1/2*2 genotype compared with those with ALDH2*1/2*1 genotype (Luczak et al., 2002; Wall & Ehlers, 1995; Wall, Gallen, & Ehlers, 1993; Wall, Nemeroff, Ritchie, & Ehlers, 1994; Wall, Thomasson et al., 1996). In addition, the only participant with ALDH2*2/2*2 genotype experienced even more intense subjective and objective reactions to alcohol than participants with ALDH2*1/2*2 genotype (Wall et al., 1992). Following the alcohol beverage, this individual became tachycardic, hypotensive, and nauseated and vomited.

Peng and colleagues (1998) also evaluated subjective and objective reactions following a low dose of alcohol (0.2 g/kg) in 18 Chinese men, 6 with ALDH2*1/2*1, 6 with ALDH2*1/2*2, and 6 with ALDH2*2/2*2. Using the SHAS, the men with ALDH2*1/2*2 genotype rated themselves higher on "effects of alcohol," but they did not rate themselves higher on "terrible overall" compared with the men with the ALDH2*1/2*1 genotype. Men with the ALDH2*2/2*2 genotype rated themselves higher on "effects of alcohol" and "terrible overall" than those with the ALDH2*1/2*1 genotype. An important contribution of this study was its simultaneous evaluation of both physiological measurements, including blood alcohol and acetaldehyde levels, and subjective response to alcohol. The men who were homozygous for ALDH2*2 had higher blood alcohol levels, blood acetaldehyde levels, and faster heart rate than both other groups after drinking. The men with ALDH2*1/2*1 genotype did not show any measurable alcohol-induced changes in blood acetaldehyde levels, heart rate, or blood pressure, whereas heterozygotes showed significant increases in acetaldehyde levels that were paralleled by increased heart rate and changes in a number of other cardiovascular measures. In comparison to heterozygotes, homozygous ALDH2*2 individuals experienced even more dramatic and prolonged increases in acetaldehyde level that corresponded to the pattern of changes in cardiovascular measures.

The findings from these and other studies suggest that elevations in acetaldehyde (Enomoto, Takase, Yasuhara, & Takada, 1991; Mizoi, Yamamoto, Ueno, Fukunaga, & Harada, 1994; Takeshita & Morimoto, 2000; Wall, Peterson et al., 1997; Yoshihara et al., 2000) might mediate the enhanced sensitivity to alcohol reported and observed among persons with ALDH2*2 alleles. Enhanced sensitivity may contribute to lower alcohol intake and protection against alcoholism found among Asians with this genetic variant. Asians with ALDH2*2/2*2 genotype appear to experience dramatic increases in acetaldehyde, as well as severe subjective and objective reactions to low and moderate doses of alcohol. Such individuals usually drink little or no alcohol, and only one alcoholic with this genotype has been reported in the research literature (Y.-C. Chen et al., 1999). Asians with ALDH2*1/2*2 genotype also demonstrate elevations in blood acetaldehyde levels and more intense, but not necessarily more aversive, reactions to alcohol than Asians with ALDH2*1/2*1 genotype. As a group, heterozygotes drink less and are less likely to be alcoholic than individuals with ALDH2*1/2*1 genotype. Thus, it appears that Asians who possess one ALDH2*2 allele are less likely to develop alcoholism because they consume less alcohol due to their greater sensitivity. What appears to be important, however, is not whether the subjective response has positive or negative valence but its overall intensity.

In 1974, Ewing and colleagues were the first to relate alcohol-induced flushing and other symptoms of alcohol sensitivity among Asians with elevated acetaldehyde levels and to suggest the symptoms were similar to an alcohol-disulfiram (Antabuse) reaction. Since this report, it has been hypothesized widely that Asians who flush are protected from alcoholism because they experience unpleasant alcohol reactions. More recent evidence does not indicate that all individuals with ALDH2*1/2*2 genotype drink less because of a lack of rewarding feeling or because they experience only aversive alcohol effects. Rather, it appears that the mechanism by which the ALDH2 gene influences alcohol use and alcohol dependence is through an overall more intense response to alcohol (Luczak et al., 2002; Peng et al., 1999; Wall et al., 1992). Nevertheless, it is possible that individuals with ALDH2*2 alleles might experience greater negative subjective responses when drinking larger amounts than the low and moderate doses of alcohol administered in these studies. In addition, it is important to acknowledge that the samples who volunteered to participate in these alcohol challenge experiments may not be representative of all Asians with and without the ALDH2*2 alleles. In particular, only Asians who drank alcohol regularly were included, thereby excluding those who might experience the most adverse alcohol reactions.

Another study used the Self-Rating of the Effects of Alcohol (SRE) form to evaluate response to alcohol in Asians who were genotyped at the *ALDH2* locus (Wall et al., 1999). The SRE form is an alternative methodology for assessing variability in response to alcohol that was developed to circumvent the cost, time, and risk involved in conducting an alcohol challenge experiment (Schuckit, Tipp, Smith, Weisbeck, & Kalmijn, 1997). It is a 12–item instrument that asks participants to estimate the amount of alcohol required for four possible drug effects during three different time frames. A higher score indicates a larger number of drinks necessary to achieve intoxication and thus a low-level response to alcohol. The psychometric properties of the SRE were tested in sons of alcoholics and controls who completed the form 15 years after participating in an alcohol challenge study. SRE scores correlated with subjective reports of alcohol intoxication from the study 15 years earlier and with a current diagnosis of alcohol dependence (Schuckit et al., 1997).

Wall and colleagues (1999) evaluated SRE form scores in Asian American male and female college students and found that participants with ALDH2*1/2*1 genotype had a mean SRE score of 3.8, heterozygotes had a mean score of 2.4, and those with ALDH2*2/2*2 genotype had a mean score of 1.3. Importantly, ALDH2 status accounted for a significant amount of variability in SRE form score, after controlling for the effects of gender, body weight, and recent drinking. These results are consistent with results from alcohol challenge studies showing more intense reactions to alcohol associated with ALDH2*2 alleles (Luczak et al., 2002; Peng et al., 1999; Wall et al., 1992) and provide additional support for the SRE form as a valid instrument for measuring level of response to alcohol. In exploratory analyses, using a cutoff score of 4.5 as an indicator of a low response to alcohol, a greater proportion of those with the ALDH2*1/2*1 genotype (29%) had a low-intensity response to alcohol in comparison to heterozygotes (4%) and those with the ALDH2*2/2*2 genotype (0%). The same cutoff score revealed that significantly more Koreans (31%) than Chinese (8%) or Japanese (19%) indicated a low-intensity response. These results were particularly intriguing in light of previous research demonstrating that individuals from South Korea, particularly Korean men, have extremely high rates of alcohol abuse and dependence compared with other ethnic groups, including Taiwanese (Helzer & Canino, 1992). Korean American college students have also been found to report more than four times the rate of first-degree family history of alcohol dependence compared with Chinese American college students (17% vs. 4%; Ebberhart, Luczak, Avanecy, & Wall, in press). These findings highlight the substantial heterogeneity in vulnerability to alcohol-related problems between Asian subgroups and suggest that the differential risk may be mediated by factors associated with a family history of alcoholism, such as a low-level response to alcohol. Additional research is needed to determine whether these additional factors are genetic, environmental, or both.

In Asians, the ALDH2*2 polymorphism has the strongest protective association with alcohol dependence. Asians who are homozygous for ALDH2*2 have almost zero risk, and heterozygotes have about one third the risk for alcoholism compared with those without this allele (C.-C. Chen et al., 1999; W. J. Chen et al., 1996; Y.-C. Chen et al., 1999; Higuchi et al., 1995; Iwahashi, 1995; Maezawa et al., 1995; Muramatsu et al., 1995; Nakamura et al., 1996; Shen et al., 1997; Tanaka et al., 1996; Thomasson et al., 1991). The ADH2*2 polymorphism also has been associated with lower rates of alcohol dependence in Asians. After controlling for the effect of *ALDH2*2*, individuals with *ADH2*2* have about one third the risk for alcoholism as those without this allele (C. C. Chen et al., 1999; W. J. Chen et al., 1996; W. J. Chen et al., 1997; Higuchi et al., 1995; Maezawa et al., 1995; Muramatsu et al., 1995; Nakamura et al., 1996; Shen et al., 1997; Tanaka et al., 1996; Thomasson et al., 1994; Thomasson et al., 1991; Whitfield, 1997). Studies of the relationship between *ADH2*2* and sensitivity to alcohol indicate that after controlling for *ALDH2*2*, possession of an *ADH2*2* allele is related to self-report of alcohol-induced flushing and associated symptoms (W. J. Chen, Chen, Yu, & Cheng, 1998; Takeshita, Mao, & Morimoto, 1996). However, a relationship between *ADH2*2* and subjective and objective response to alcohol, over and above that of *ALDH2*2*, has not yet been demonstrated in Asians or Caucasians (Heath et al., 1999).

The Subjective Effects of Alcohol in Native Americans

Native Americans have the highest rates of alcohol dependence and alcohol-related mortality of all ethnic groups in the United States (Indian Health Service, 1993). Collectively, the alcohol-related death rate among Native Americans is 2.4 times greater than that for the general U.S. population (May, 1996). Using the more narrow definition of alcohol-specific deaths, which represent those deaths directly attributable to heavy alcohol consumption (e.g., alcohol-induced cirrhosis), the Native American rate is 5.3 times greater than that for the general U.S. population (May, 1996). Nevertheless, tribes vary dramatically in rates of alcohol use and alcohol-related problems, and the sheer number and diversity of ethnically distinct subgroups that are subsumed under the category Native American preclude any attempt to characterize the entire population.

A once popular theory that attempted to explain the high rates of alcohol problems among some Native American groups related to differences in response to alcohol. This theory, called the firewater myth, held that Native Americans metabolize alcohol more slowly than other ethnic groups and are more sensitive to the effects of alcohol (Leland, 1976). An initial investigation that provided support for the firewater myth reported slower metabolism of alcohol by a group of Canadian Natives and Eskimos compared with Caucasians (Fenna, Mix, Schaefer, & Gilbert, 1971). This investigation, however, suffered from methodological problems that undermine its findings (Lieber, 1972). The majority of the Native American participants were hospital patients, whereas the Caucasian participants were hospital staff members. Additionally, intravenous rather than oral administration of alcohol, and the indirect and highly variable measurement of blood alcohol levels using a Breathalyzer further hindered the interpretability of the results. Subsequent studies found either nearly equivalent metabolism of alcohol compared with Caucasians (Bennion & Li, 1976) or significantly faster metabolism in several Native American groups (Reed, Kalant, Gibbins, Kapur, & Rankin, 1976; Segal & Duffy, 1992; Zeiner, Parades, & Cowden, 1976). Two well-designed studies that controlled for the effects of gender, age, education, weight, and drinking history reported that Native Americans metabolize alcohol more quickly than Caucasians (Farris & Jones, 1978a, 1978b). Despite methodological problems and the disagreement between studies, there appears to be a small but significant difference in alcohol metabolism, with Native Americans having faster rates of alcohol elimination than Caucasians (Reed, 1978, 1985; Schaefer, 1981).

Other early research investigated the possibility that the increased rates of alcohol metabolism in Native Americans might actually confer protection against the development of alcohol problems. Following a report that 80% of a sample of 30 adult Eastern Cree flushed after consuming alcohol (Wolff, 1973), several efforts were made to determine whether the cause of this response was similar to the genetically mediated flushing response seen among Asians. Examination of ALDH2 phenotypes using electrophoretic and kinetic measurements of hair root samples (Goedde et al., 1986) suggested that approximately 40% of several groups of South American Natives demonstrated ALDH isozyme deficiency. However, only 5% of Sioux from North Dakota, 2% of Navajo from New Mexico, and 4% of Mestizo from Mexico City showed such a deficiency (Goedde et al., 1986).

More recently, the ability to determine genotypes for variations in the alcohol-metabolizing enzymes has provided no evidence of the *ALDH2*2 allele in Alaskan Eskimos; Mestizos from Mexico City; Sioux, Navajo, and Cheyenne from Colorado; Mission Indians from southern California; or other Native American tribes (Bosron, Rex, Harden, Li, & Akerson, 1988; S.-H. Chen et al., 1992; Dyck, 1993; Gill, Elk, Liu, & Deitrich, 1999; Goedde et al., 1992; Novoradovsky, Kidd, Kidd, & Goldman, 1995; Rex, Bosron, Smialek, & Li, 1985; Wall, Garcia-Andrade et al., 1997). This suggests that any flushing reaction in Native Americans is not due to polymorphism at the *ALDH2* locus.

With the exception of the study by Wolff (1973), there is scant evidence that Native Americans exhibit a flushing reaction. Gill and colleagues (1999) found that 22% of a sample composed of Sioux, Navajo, and Cheyenne Native Americans reported that they almost always or always flushed after one or two drinks, but none had an *ALDH2*2 allele. Additionally, important dimensions of response to alcohol differentiated this group of self-reported flushing Native Americans from a sample of Asian participants who also self-reported flushing. Ninety-two percent of the Asians but only 17% of the Native Americans reported facial flushing after one drink. A greater proportion of Asians (50%) than Native Americans (9%) reported that flushing was typically very unpleasant. In addition, significantly more Native Americans than

Asians reported that the flushing reaction had very little effect on the usual frequency of drinking or amount of alcohol consumed per episode. Importantly, when these Native Americans who had self-reported alcohol-induced flushing actually participated in an alcohol challenge experiment, several biological correlates of flushing failed to indicate the presence of a flushing response. Despite receiving twice the alcohol dose as the sample of Asians (0.4 vs. 0.2 g/kg), the Native Americans did not show significant elevations in heart rate, which is perhaps the most reliable biological correlate of the flushing response. These participants evinced neither decreases in diastolic blood pressure nor elevations in acetaldehyde, which is presumed to cause the flushing response.

A few studies have reported a low prevalence (0–.06) of the *ADH2*2* and/or *ADH2*3* alleles in Native American samples (Garcia-Andrade, Wall, & Ehlers, 1997; Goedde et al., 1992; Osier et al., 2002), which may be due to admixture but potentially could contribute to the faster metabolism of alcohol observed in some Native American groups. For example, Wall and colleagues (1996) evaluated Mission Indian men following a moderate (0.56 g/kg) dose of alcohol (Wall, Garcia-Andrade, Thomasson, Cole, & Ehlers, 1996). There was a nonsignificant trend for the participants with an *ADH2*3* allele to have faster alcohol elimination rates than those with only *ADH2*1* alleles. This finding was consistent with the results from a study of African Americans, where the *ADH2*3* allele was more prevalent and significantly associated with faster alcohol metabolism (Thomasson et al., 1993). Faster alcohol metabolism and accompanying rapid production of acetaldehyde, increased sensitivity to alcohol, and lower levels of alcohol consumption may serve as the mechanism for this allele's protection against alcohol dependence. Results from a sample of 340 Mission Indians support this hypothesis (Wall et al., 2003). Mission Indians with an *ADH2*3* allele were significantly less likely to be alcohol dependent and reported a lower number of maximum drinks ever consumed than those without this allele. However, there is no direct evidence, to date, that faster alcohol metabolism leads to greater production of acetaldehyde or that the *ADH2*3* is associated with greater sensitivity to alcohol.

The weight of the evidence contradicts the aspect of the firewater myth that suggests Native Americans metabolize alcohol more slowly, but there is a paucity of research addressing the idea that Native Americans might be more sensitive to the effects of alcohol. One study compared objective and subjective measures in 40 Mission Indian men who were not alcohol dependent. Analyses focused on comparing men who had less than 50% Native American heritage with men who had at least 50% Native American heritage (Garcia-Andrade et al., 1997). No significant group differences emerged on the objective measures of blood alcohol levels, diastolic or systolic blood pressure, pulse rate, or plasma cortisol levels. In contrast, significant differences emerged between groups on several subjective effects of alcohol using the SHAS. The men with at least 50% Native American heritage reported fewer effects of alcohol, including feeling less "activated," "clumsy," "confused," "dizzy," "high," "nauseated," and "terrible overall" compared with those who had less than 50% Native American heritage. In addition, Mission Indians with at least 50% Native American heritage have been found to be significantly more likely to have a lifetime diagnosis of alcohol dependence than those who had less than 50% Native American heritage (Wall et al., 2003). Taken together, these results contradict the firewater myth. Further, they are consistent with studies that have shown that groups at higher risk for alcohol use disorders, (e.g., individuals with a positive family history of alcoholism) have less intense subjective responses to alcohol (Moss, Yao, & Maddock, 1989; O'Malley & Maisto, 1985; Pollock, 1992; Pollock, Teasdale, Gabrielli, & Knop, 1986; Savoie, Emory, & Moody-Thomas, 1988; Schuckit, 1984).

The Subjective Effects of Alcohol in Jews

Jews have low rates of alcohol abuse and dependence compared with other ethnic or religious groups in the United States (Levav et al., 1997; Yeung & Greenwald, 1992). The ECA study found that the lifetime rate for DSM-III alcohol abuse or dependence in Jewish Americans was 7%, compared with 17% for non-Jews (Levav et al., 1997). Paradoxically, as many as 90% of Jews drink alcohol (Bales, 1962; Cahalan, Cisin, & Crossley, 1969; Snyder, 1958). Two cultural theories have attempted to explain the protection from alcoholism that Jews exhibit despite their low levels of abstinence (Bales, 1946; Snyder, 1958). Bales (1946, 1962) suggested that the incorporation of drinking into the rituals of Judaism fostered an ability to drink in moderation. Snyder (1958) further conjectured that sobriety is an important virtue associated with Orthodox Judaism, whereas intoxication is associated with non-Jewish culture. He therefore hypothesized that as Jews acculturated into non-Jewish societies and became less religious, rates of alcoholism would rise. Although some research supports the inverse relationship between religious orthodoxy and frequency of drinking (Kandel & Sudit, 1982), other research does not (Knupfer & Room, 1967). Further, a review of the evidence for these theories notes several methodological shortcomings (e.g., lack of appropriate control groups) that undermine these cultural explanations for the low prevalence of alcohol problems among Jews (Flasher & Maisto, 1984).

The role of biology in the protection of Jews from alcohol problems has only recently been explored. Although no studies have revealed polymorphisms at the ALDH2 locus in Jewish samples, ADH2*2 has been found to have a prevalence between .17 and .41 in individuals of Jewish descent from the United States and Israel (Hasin et al., 2002a, 2002b;

Neumark et al., 1998; Shea et al., 2001). Despite its low prevalence, ADH2*2 has been associated with lower levels of alcohol use and other alcohol-related behavior in Jews (Hasin et al., 2002a, 2002b; Neumark et al., 1998; Shea et al., 2001). Specifically, among heavy-drinking Israeli Jews, those with an ADH2*2 allele had lower mean peak weekly alcohol consumption than those without this allele (Neumark et al., 1998). Among the entire sample of Israeli Jews, the proportion of infrequent drinkers (those drinking less than once every 2 weeks during the period of heaviest consumption) was greater among those with an ADH2*2 allele than those without an ADH2*2 allele. The authors concluded,

> The aversive experience of drinking in Jews may be so subtle as to not be fully recognized by the drinker or by an outside observer, but powerful enough to provide the drinker with a physiologic cue that signals cessation of drinking at a lower level than the drinker without this allele. (Neumark et al., 1998, p. 137)

A similar study of Jewish Americans found an association between the ADH2*2 allele and fewer drinking days per month in the last 6 months (Shea et al., 2001). Another investigation examined alcohol consumption, alcohol dependence symptoms, and ADH2 polymorphism in three ethnic subgroups of Jews in Israel: Sephardics, descended primarily from North Africa and the Middle East, Ashkenazis, descended from Europe, and a group who immigrated from Russia. The three subgroups did not differ in their proportions of current drinkers, but the Russian subgroup was more likely than the other groups to demonstrate a pattern of past heavy drinking (Hasin et al., 2002b). The group from Russia also had a greater mean number of lifetime DSM-IV alcohol dependence symptoms (1.44) than the Ashkenazi (.57) or the Sephardic (.56) subgroups. Another study, a large-scale epidemiological survey conducted in Israel, found fewer Sephardics than Ashkenazis drank in the last month, drank in the last 12 months, or got drunk in the last 12 months (Aharonovich, Hasin, Rahav, & Meydan, 2001).

Preliminary evidence of protection from heavy alcohol use afforded by the ADH2*2 allele within these Jewish subgroups has also been reported (Hasin et al., 2002a). The prevalences of ADH2*2 were .17 in Russians, .20 in Ashkenazis, and .41 in Sephardics. An increasing number of ADH2*2 alleles (0, 1, or 2) was related to fewer lifetime maximum number of drinks per occasion. Perhaps due to small sample size, however, ADH2*2 was associated with fewer lifetime maximum number of drinks per occasion only among the Sephardic Jews. Although ADH2*2 was associated with fewer alcohol dependence symptoms overall (Hasin et al., 2002b), small sample size may have precluded finding significant differences in the number of symptoms by ADH2 genotype within each subgroup.

There has been little empirical evidence that Jews have either a more aversive or a more intense response to alcohol than other ethnic groups.

No studies have found evidence of a flushing response in Jews. One study used the SHAS to examine differences in response to alcohol among a group of 15 Jewish men matched on height-to-weight ratio and quantity and frequency of alcohol consumption with 15 non-Jewish Caucasian men with a family history of alcoholism (FHPs) and 15 non-Jewish Caucasian men without a family history of alcoholism (FHNs) (Monteiro, Klein, & Schuckit, 1991). The groups did not differ on blood alcohol concentrations or their expectancies about the effects of alcohol or response to placebo (both assessed by the SHAS) after consuming 0.59 g/kg of alcohol. Nevertheless, the Jewish participants demonstrated more intense responses to alcohol than the FHPs, as indicated by higher scores on "clumsy," "floating," "dizzy," "nauseated," and "drunk" and by the total SHAS score. Jewish participants also rated themselves higher than FHNs on "floating" and "dizziness." However, FHPs have been shown to have a less intense response to alcohol compared with FHNs on a variety of measures, including the SHAS (Schuckit, 1980; Schuckit & Gold, 1988). Therefore, differences in subjective response to alcohol between the Jewish participants (who were presumably FHNs) and the non-Jewish FHPs may reflect differences due to family history of alcoholism and not ethnic differences per se. Further, because ADH2 genotype was not assessed, it is not possible to determine the role of ADH2*2 in the subjective responses of the participants. Although hampered by small sample size, this study did demonstrate that Jews reported higher levels of feelings of "floating" and "dizziness" relative to non-Jewish Caucasian FHNs. Further investigation with larger samples is necessary to confirm these findings, but these subjective differences provide an indication that increased sensitivity to alcohol in Jews could prompt less heavy drinking and fewer alcohol-related problems.

A study involving 84 Ashkenazic Jewish Americans found no association between ADH2*2 genotype and self-reported subjective response to alcohol (Shea et al., 2001). Participants with ADH2*2 alleles did not report higher rates of facial flushing, sleepiness, nausea, headaches, or heart palpitations than those without ADH2*2 alleles. Nor were such participants more sensitive to alcohol as measured by the SRE form. This study did not use an actual alcohol challenge paradigm and consisted of a relatively small sample. As a result, it did not directly address the specific subjective effects found to vary by ethnicity in the prior study by Monteiro and colleagues (1991). More research is needed to explore the nature of the subjective effects of alcohol in Jews and how such effects may be associated with the low rates of alcohol abuse and dependence in this population. It is yet to be determined whether some facet of ethnicity, genetic polymorphisms, or a combination of the two creates a distinct experience associated with alcohol consumption that facilitates moderate consumption among Jews.

Genetic Associations with Other Drug Use

It is possible that the alcohol-metabolizing genes could have an indirect effect on other substance use in that individuals who drink less alcohol are also less likely to smoke cigarettes or use illicit drugs. As a means of investigating the association of *ALDH2* with the development of drug involvement, Wall and colleagues analyzed information about the onset and regular use of alcohol and other substances as reported by Asian college students (Wall, Shea, Chan, & Carr, 2001). The *ALDH2*2* allele was associated not only with lower levels of alcohol use but also with lower levels of other drug use, particularly tobacco use (Wall et al., 2001). Consistent with the hypothesis that alcohol serves as a "gateway" to other substances, analyses supported regular and heavy drinking as mediators of the association between *ALDH2* and regular smoking. In addition, recent genome scans of European Americans and African Americans have found evidence suggestive of protection against illicit substance use on the area of chromosome 4 that includes the ADH gene cluster (Uhl, Liu, Walther, Hess, & Naiman, 2001). Much of the genetic vulnerability to legal and illegal substance dependence is shared (True et al., 1999; Tsuang et al., 1998). Thus, it is possible that *ADH2* polymorphisms in individuals of European and African descent (*ADH2*2* and *ADH2*3* alleles) are associated not only with decreased risk for alcohol dependence but also with decreased risk for nicotine and illicit substance dependence.

Genetic variations in enzymes involved in other drug metabolism also exist and vary across ethnic groups. For example, many drugs of abuse, including nicotine, codeine, cocaine, and amphetamine, are known substrates or inhibitors of cytochrome P450 (CYP) enzymes (Howard, Sellers, & Tyndale, 2002). Interethnic differences in substance use and dependence appear, in part, to be due to variation in the prevalence of these CYP enzymes and the resulting variation in drug metabolism. Whether these genetic variants also exert their influence on use and dependence through subjective drug effects remains to be determined.

Conclusions

It is widely acknowledged that a myriad of factors contribute to the development of alcohol and other drug use disorders. The etiology of substance use disorders, like most other forms of psychopathology, is determined by the interplay of genetic, psychological, and social factors. Although ethnic differences in the subjective effects of drugs, primarily alcohol, had been investigated for decades, surprisingly little was known about the sources of such differences. Recent studies have shown that genetic variations in the enzymes that metabolize alcohol lead to individual differences in the subjective effects of alcohol, typically in the form of increased sensitivity to its effects. It is also recognized that these gene variations are associated with lower rates of alcohol consumption and alcohol use disorders, and possibly other substance use and substance use disorders. Causes of decreased intensity or more pleasurable effects associated with alcohol or other drug use in ethnic groups, whether such variations exist, and to what extent they are genetically and environmentally influenced remain currently unanswered questions.

It is common practice to treat ethnicity as a single independent variable on which groups meaningfully differ. In truth, the path from an individual's response to a drug to his or her likelihood of developing a substance use disorder is optimally understood within the larger social milieu. The conceptualization of ethnicity as a single independent variable obscures the many important factors that constitute it. In the end, ethnicity may be little more than an inadequate proxy for a web of interrelated biological, psychological, and social factors that are more proximally related to the behavior of interest.

This work was supported by National Institutes of Health grants T32AA013525 and K02AA00269.

References

Adlaf, E. M., Smart, R. G., & Tan, S. H. (1989). Ethnicity and drug use: A critical look. *International Journal of the Addictions, 24*, 1–18.

Aharonovich, E., Hasin, D., Rahav, G., & Meydan, J. (2001). Differences in drinking patterns among Ashkenazic and Sephardic Israeli adults. *Journal of Studies on Alcohol, 63*, 301–305.

Bachman, J. G., Wallace, J. M., O'Malley, P. M., Johnston, L. D., Kurth, C. L., & Neighbors, H. W. (1991). Racial/ethnic differences in smoking, drinking, and illicit drug use among high school seniors, 1976–1989. *American Journal of Public Health, 81*, 372–377.

Bales, R. F. (1946). Cultural differences in rates of alcoholism. *Quarterly Journal of Studies on Alcohol, 6*, 480–499.

Bales, R. F. (1962). Attitudes toward drinking in the Irish culture. In C. R. Snyder (Ed.), *Society, culture, and prinking patterns* (pp. 157–188). New York: Wiley.

Bennion, L. J., & Li, T.-K. (1976). Alcohol metabolism in American Indians and Whites: Lack of racial differences in metabolic rate and liver alcohol dehydrogenase. *New England Journal of Medicine, 294*, 9–13.

Borras, E., Coutelle, C., Rosell, A., Fernandez-Muixi, F., Broch, M., Crosas, B., et al. (2000). Genetic polymorphisms of alcohol dehydrogenase in Europeans: The ADH2*2 allele decreases the risk for alcoholism and is associated with ADH3*1. *Hepatology, 31*, 984–989.

Bosron, W. F., Magnes, L. J., & Li, T.-K. (1983). Human liver alcohol dehydrogenase: ADH Indianapolis results from genetic polymorphism at the ADH2 gene locus. *Biochemical Genetics, 21*, 735–744.

Bosron, W. F., Rex, D. K., Harden, C. A., Li, T.-K., & Akerson, R. D. (1988). Alcohol and aldehyde dehydrogenase isoenzymes in Sioux North American Indians. *Alcoholism: Clinical and Experimental Research, 12,* 454–455.

Cadoret, R. J., Troughton, E., O'Gorman, T. W., & Heywood, E. (1986). An adoption study of genetic and environmental factors on drug abuse. *Archives of General Psychiatry, 43,* 1131–1136.

Cahalan, D., Cisin, I. H., & Crossley, H. M. (1969). *American drinking practices: A national study of drinking behavior and attitudes* (Monograph No. 6). New Brunswick, NJ: Rutgers Center of Alcohol Studies.

Chan, A. W. K. (1986). Racial differences in alcohol sensitivity. *Alcohol and Alcoholism, 21,* 93–104.

Chao, H. M. (1995). Alcohol and the mystique of flushing. *Alcoholism: Clinical and Experimental Research, 19,* 104–109.

Chao, Y.-C., Liou, S.-R., Chung, Y.-Y., Tang, H.-S., Hsu, C.-T., Li, T.-K., et al. (1994). Polymorphism of alcohol and aldehyde dehydrogenase genes and alcoholic cirrhosis in Chinese patients. *Hepatology, 19,* 360–366.

Chao, Y.-C., Young, T.-H., Tang, H.-S., & Hsu, C.-T. (1997). Alcoholism and alcoholic organ damage and genetic polymorphisms of alcohol metabolizing enzymes in Chinese patients. *Hepatology, 25,* 1112–1117.

Chen, C.-C., Lu, R.-B., Chen, Y.-C., Wang, M.-F., Chang, Y.-C., Li, T.-K., et al. (1999). Interaction between the functional polymorphisms of the alcohol-metabolism genes in protection against alcoholism. *American Journal of Human Genetics, 65,* 795–807.

Chen, S.-H., Zhang, M., & Scott, C. R. (1992). Gene frequencies of alcohol dehydrogenase-2 and aldehyde dehydrogenase in Northwest Coast Amerindians. *Human Genetics, 89,* 351–352.

Chen, S.-H., Zhang, M., Wang, N.-S., & Scott, C. R. (1994). Gene frequencies of alcohol dehydrogenase 2 (ADH2) and aldehyde dehydrogenase 2 (ALDH2) in five Chinese minorities. *Human Genetics, 94,* 571–572.

Chen, W. J., Chen, C.-C., Yu, J.-M., & Cheng, A. T. A. (1998). Self-reported flushing and genotypes of ALDH2, ADH2, and ADH3 among Taiwanese Han. *Alcoholism: Clinical and Experimental Research, 22,* 1048–1052.

Chen, W. J., Loh, E. W., Hsu, Y.-P. P., Chen, C.-C., Yu, J.-M., & Cheng, A. T. A. (1996). Alcohol-metabolizing genes and alcoholism among Taiwanese Han men: Independent effect of ADH2, ADH3, and ALDH2. *British Journal of Psychiatry, 168,* 762–767.

Chen, W. J., Loh, E. W., Hsu, Y.-P. P., & Cheng, A. T. A. (1997). Alcohol dehydrogenase and aldehyde dehydrogenase and alcoholism among Taiwanese aborigines. *Biological Psychiatry, 41,* 703–709.

Chen, Y.-C., Lu, R.-B., Peng, G.-S., Wang, M.-F., Wang, H.-K., Ko, H.-C., et al. (1999). Alcohol metabolism and cardiovascular response in an alcoholic patient homozygous for the ALDH2*2 variant gene allele. *Alcoholism: Clinical and Experimental Research, 23,* 1853–1860.

Couzigou, P., Fleury, B., Groppi, A., Cassaigne, A., Begueret, J., Iron, A., et al. (1990). Genotyping study of alcohol dehydrogenase class I polymorphism in French patients with alcoholic cirrhosis. *Alcohol and Alcoholism, 25,* 623–626.

Crabb, D. W. (1990). Biological markers for increased risk for alcoholism and for quantitation of alcohol consumption. *Journal of Clinical Investigation, 85,* 311–315.

Crabb, D. W., Dipple, K. M., & Thomasson, H. R. (1993). Alcohol sensitivity, alcohol metabolism, risk for alcoholism, and the role of alcohol and aldehyde dehydrogenase genotypes. *Journal of Laboratory and Clinical Medicine, 122,* 234–240.

Crabb, D. W., Edenberg, H. J., Bosron, W. F., & Li, T.-K. (1989). Genotypes for aldehyde dehydrogenase deficiency and alcohol sensitivity: The inactive ALDH2(2) allele is dominant. *Journal of Clinical Investigations, 83,* 314–316.

Day, C. P., Bashir, R., James, O. F. W., Bassendine, M. F., Crabb, D. W., Thomasson, H. R., et al. (1991). Investigation of the role of polymorphisms at the alcohol and aldehyde dehydrogenase loci in genetic predisposition to alcohol-related end-organ damage. *Hepatology, 14,* 798–801.

Day, C. P., & Bassendine, M. F. (1992). Genetic predisposition to alcoholic liver disease. *Gut, 33,* 1444–1447.

Dyck, L. E. (1993). Absence of atypical mitochondrial aldehyde dehydrogenase (ALDH2) isoenzyme in Saskatchewan Cree Indians. *Human Heredity, 43,* 116–120.

Ebberhart, N. C., Luczak, S. E., Avanecy, N., & Wall, T. L. (in press). Family history of alcohol dependence in Asian Americans. *Journal of Psychoactive Drugs.*

Enomoto, N., Takase, S., Takada, N., & Takada, A. (1991). Alcoholic liver disease in heterozygotes of mutant and normal aldehyde dehydrogenase-2 gene. *Hepatology, 13,* 1071–1075.

Enomoto, N., Takase, S., Yasuhara, M., & Takada, A. (1991). Acetaldehyde metabolism in different aldehyde dehydrogenase-2 genotypes. *Alcoholism: Clinical and Experimental Research, 15,* 141–144.

Ewing, J. A., Rouse, B. A., & Pellizzari, E. D. (1974). Alcohol sensitivity and ethnic background. *American Journal of Psychiatry, 131,* 206–210.

Farris, J. J., & Jones, B. M. (1978a). Ethanol metabolism and memory impairments in American Indian and White women social drinkers. *Journal of Studies on Alcohol, 39,* 1975–1979.

Farris, J. J., & Jones, B. M. (1978b). Ethanol metabolism in male American Indians and Whites. *Alcoholism: Clinical and Experimental Research, 2,* 77–81.

Fenna, D., Mix, L., Schaefer, O., & Gilbert, J. A. L. (1971). Ethanol metabolism in various ethnic groups. *Canadian Medical Association Journal, 105,* 472–475.

Flasher, L. V., & Maisto, S. M. (1984). A review of theory and research on drinking patterns among Jews. *Journal of Nervous and Mental Disease, 172,* 596–603.

Garcia-Andrade, C., Wall, T. L., & Ehlers, C. L. (1997). The firewater myth and response to alcohol in Mission Indians. *American Journal of Psychiatry, 154,* 983–988.

Gilder, F. J., Hodgkinson, S., & Murray, R. M. (1993). ADH and ALDH genotype profiles in Caucasians with alcohol-related problems and controls. *Addiction, 88,* 383–388.

Gill, K., Elk, M. E., Liu, Y., & Deitrich, R. A. (1999). An examination of ALDH2 genotypes, alcohol metabolism and the flushing response in Native Americans. *Journal of Studies on Alcohol, 60,* 149–158.

Gillmore, M. R., Catalano, R. F., Morrison, D. M., Wells, E. A., Iritani, B., & Hawkins, J. D. (1990). Racial differences in acceptability and availability of drugs and early initiation of substance use. *American Journal of Drug and Alcohol Abuse, 16*, 185–206.

Goedde, H. W., Agarwal, D. P., Fritze, G., Meier-Tackmann, D., Singh, S., Beckmann, G., et al. (1992). Distribution of ADH2 and ALDH2 genotypes in different populations. *Human Genetics, 88*, 344–346.

Goedde, H. W., Agarwal, D. P., Harada, S., Whittaker, J. O., Rothhammer, F., & Lisker, R. (1986). Aldehyde dehydrogenase polymorphism in North American, South American and Mexican Indians. *American Journal of Human Genetics, 38*, 395–399.

Goedde, H. W., Singh, S., Agarwal, D. P., Fritze, G., Stapel, K., & Paik, Y. K. (1989). Genotyping of mitochondrial aldehyde dehydrogenase in blood samples using allele-specific oligonucleotides. *Human Genetics, 81*, 305–307.

Hasin, D., Aharonovich, E., Liu, X., Mamman, Z., Matseoane, K., Carr, L. G., et al. (2002a). Alcohol and ADH2 in Israel: Ashkenazis, Sephardics, and recent Russian immigrants. *American Journal of Psychiatry, 159*, 1432–1434.

Hasin, D., Aharonovich, E., Liu, X. H., Mamman, Z., Matseoane, K., Carr, L. G., et al. (2002b). Alcohol dehydrogenase symptoms and alcohol dehydrogenase 2 polymorphism: Israeli Ashkenazis, Sephardics, and recent Russian immigrants. *Alcoholism: Clinical and Experimental Research, 26*, 1315–1321.

Heath, A. C., Madden, P. A. F., Bucholz, K. K., Dinwiddie, S. H., Slutske, W. S., Bierut, L. J., et al. (1999). Genetic differences in alcohol sensitivity and the inheritance of alcoholism risk. *Psychological Medicine, 29*, 1069–1081.

Helzer, J. E., Canino, G. J., Yeh, E. K., Bland, R. C., Lee, C. K., Hwu, H. G. et al. Alcoholism–North America and Asia. *Archives of General Psychiatry, 47*, 313–319

Helzer, J. E., & Canino, G. J. (1992). *Alcoholism in North America, Europe, and Asia.* New York: Oxford University Press.

Higuchi, S., Matsushita, S., Muramatsu, T., Murayama, M., & Hayashida, M. (1996). Alcohol and aldehyde dehydrogenase genotypes and drinking behavior in Japanese. *Alcoholism: Clinical and Experimental Research, 20*, 493–497.

Higuchi, S., Matsushita, S., Murayama, M., Takagi, S., & Hayashida, M. (1995). Alcohol and aldehyde dehydrogenase polymorphisms and the risk for alcoholism. *American Journal of Psychiatry, 152*, 1219–1221.

Hori, H., Kawano, T., Endo, M., & Yuasa, Y. (1997). Genetic polymorphisms of tobacco- and alcohol-related metabolizing enzymes and human esophageal squamous cell carcinoma susceptibility. *Journal of Clinical Gastroenterology, 25*, 568–575.

Howard, L. A., Sellers, E. M., & Tyndale, R. F. (2002). The role of pharmacogenetically-variable cytochrome P450 enzymes in drug abuse and dependence. *Pharmacogenetics, 3*, 185–199.

Indian Health Service. (1993). *Trends in Indian health—1993.* Washington, DC: Department of Health and Human Services.

Iwahashi, K. (1995). Heterozygous for ALDH2 in alcohol dependence: Relationship between the ALDH2 genotype and personality disorder in alcohol dependent patients with the flushing syndrome. *Biological Psychiatry*, *37*, 137.

Jacobson, S. W., Chiodo, L., Jester, J., Carr, L., Sokol, R., Jacobson, J., et al. (2000). Protective effects of ADH2*3 in African American infants exposed prenatally to alcohol. *Alcoholism: Clinical and Experimental Research*, *24*(Suppl. 5), 28A.

Kandel, D., Single, E., & Kessler, R. C. (1976). The epidemiology of drug use among New York high school students: Distribution, trends, and change in rates of use. *American Journal of Public Health*, *66*, 43–53.

Kandel, D., & Sudit, M. (1982). Drinking practices among urban adults in Israel. *Journal of Studies on Alcohol*, *43*, 1–16.

Klatsky, A. L., Sieglaub, A. B., Landy, C., & Friedman, G. D. (1983). Racial patterns of alcoholic beverage use. *Alcoholism: Clinical and Experimental Research*, *7*, 372–377.

Knupfer, G., & Room, R. (1967). Drinking patterns and attitudes of Irish, Jewish, and White Protestant American men. *Quarterly Journal of Studies on Alcohol*, *28*, 676–699.

Lee, K.-H., Kwak, B.-Y., Kim, J.-H., Yoo, S.-K., Yum, S.-K., & Jeong, H.-S. (1997). Genetic polymorphism of cytochrome P-4502E1 and mitochondrial aldehyde dehydrogenase in a Korean population. *Alcoholism: Clinical and Experimental Research*, *21*, 953–956.

Leland, J. (1976). *Firewater myths*. New Brunswick, NJ: Journal of Studies on Alcohol.

Levav, I., Kohn, R., Golding, J. M., & Weissman, M. M. (1997). Vulnerability of Jews to affective disorders. *American Journal of Psychiatry*, *154*, 941–947.

Lieber, C. S. (1972). Metabolism of ethanol and alcoholism: Racial and acquired factors. *Annals of Internal Medicine*, *76*, 326–327.

Long, J. C., Knowler, W. C., Hanson, R. L., Robin, R. W., Urbanek, M., Moore, E., et al. (1998). Evidence for genetic linkage to alcohol dependence on chromosomes 4 and 11 from an autosome-wide scan in an American Indian population. *American Journal of Medical Genetics (Neuropsychiatric Genetics)*, *81*, 216–221.

Luczak, S. E., Elvine-Kreis, B., Shea, S. H., Carr, L. G., & Wall, T. L. (2002). Genetic risk for alcoholism relates to level of response to alcohol in Asian American men and women. *Journal of Studies on Alcohol*, *63*, 74–82.

Maezawa, Y., Yamauchi, M., Toda, G., Suzuki, H., & Sakurai, S. (1995). Alcohol-metabolizing enzyme polymorphisms and alcoholism in Japan. *Alcoholism: Clinical and Experimental Research*, *19*, 951–954.

May, P. A. (1996). Overview of alcohol abuse epidemiology for American Indian populations. In B. Cohen (Ed.), *Changing numbers, changing needs: American Indian demography and public health*. Washington, DC: National Academy Press.

McCarver, D. G. (2001). ADH2 and CYP2E1 genetic polymorphisms: Risk factors for alcohol-related birth defects. *Drug Metabolism and Disposition*, *29*, 562–565.

McCarver, D. G., Thomasson, H. R., Martier, S. S., Sokol, R. J., & Li, T.-K. (1997). Alcohol dehydrogenase-2*3 allele protects against alcohol-related birth defects among African Americans. *Journal of Pharmacology and Experimental Therapeutics*, *283*, 1095–1101.

McKee, M. (1999). Alcohol in Russia. *Alcohol and Alcoholism, 34*, 824–829.

Mizoi, Y., Hishida, S., Ijiri, I., Maruyama, J., Asakura, S., Kijima, T., et al. (1980). Individual differences in blood and breath acetaldehyde levels and urinary excretion of catecholamines after alcohol intake. *Alcoholism: Clinical and Experimental Research, 4*, 354–360.

Mizoi, Y., Yamamoto, K., Ueno, Y., Fukunaga, T., & Harada, S. (1994). Involvement of genetic polymorphism of alcohol and aldehyde dehydrogenases in individual variation of alcohol metabolism. *Alcohol and Alcoholism, 29*, 707–710.

Monteiro, M. G., Klein, J. L., & Schuckit, M. A. (1991). High levels of sensitivity to alcohol in young adult Jewish men: A pilot study. *Journal of Studies on Alcohol, 52*, 464–469.

Moss, H. B., Yao, J. K., & Maddock, J. M. (1989). Responses by sons of alcoholic fathers to alcoholic and control drinks: Perceived mood, intoxication, and plasma prolactin. *Alcoholism: Clinical and Experimental Research, 13*, 252–257.

Muramatsu, T., Wang, Z.-C., Fang, Y.-R., Hu, K.-B., Hequin, Y., Yamada, K., et al. (1995). Alcohol and aldehyde dehydrogenase genotypes and drinking behavior in Chinese living in Shanghai. *Human Genetics, 96*, 151–154.

Murayama, M., Matsushita, S., Muramatsu, T., & Higuchi, S. (1998). Clinical characteristics and disease course of alcoholics with inactive aldehyde dehydrogenase-2. *Alcoholism: Clinical and Experimental Research, 22*, 524–527.

Nakamura, K., Iwahashi, K., Matsuo, Y., Miyatake, R., Ichikawa, Y., & Suwaki, H. (1996). Characteristics of Japanese alcoholics with the atypical aldehyde dehydrogenase 2*2: A comparison of the genotypes of ALDH2, ADH2, ADH3, and cytochrome P-4502E1 between alcoholics and nonalcoholics. *Alcoholism: Clinical and Experimental Research, 20*, 52–55.

Neale, M. C., & Martin, N. G. (1989). The effects of age, sex, and genotype on self-report of drunkenness following a challenge dose of alcohol. *Behavior Genetics, 19*, 63–78.

Neumark, Y. D., Friedlander, Y., Thomasson, H. R., & Li, T.-K. (1998). Association of the ADH2*2 allele with reduced ethanol consumption in Jewish men in Israel. *Journal of Studies on Alcohol, 59*, 133–139.

Newcomb, M. D., & Bentler, P. M. (1986). Substance use and ethnicity: Differential impact of peer and adult models. *Journal of Psychology, 120*, 83–95.

Newlin, D. B. (1989). The skin-flushing response: Autonomic, self-report, and conditioned responses to repeated administration of alcohol in Asian men. *Journal of Abnormal Psychology, 98*, 421–425.

National Institute on Drug Abuse. (1998). *Drug use among racial/ethnic minorities.* Washington, DC: Author.

Novoradovsky, A., Kidd, J., Kidd, K., & Goldman, D. (1995). Apparent monomorphisms of ALDH2 in seven American Indian populations. *Alcohol, 12*, 163–167.

Novoradovsky, A., Tsai, S.-J. L., Goldfarb, L., Peterson, R., Long, J. C., & Goldman, D. (1995). Mitochondrial aldehyde dehydrogenase polymorphism in Asian and American Indian populations: Detection of new ALDH2 alleles. *Alcoholism: Clinical and Experimental Research, 19*, 1105–1110.

O'Malley, S. S., & Maisto, S. A. (1985). Effects of family drinking history and expectancies on responses to alcohol in men. *Journal of Studies on Alcohol, 46,* 289–297.

Ogurtsov, P. P., Garmush, I. V., Miandina, G. I., Guschin, A. E., Itkes, A. V., & Moiseev, V. S. (2001). Alcohol dehydrogenase ADH2-1 and ADH2-2 allelic isoforms in the Russian population correlate with type of alcoholic disease. *Addiction Biology, 6,* 377–383.

Osier, M., Pakstis, A. J., Kidd, J. R., Lee, J.-F., Yin, S.-J., Ko, H.-C., et al. (1999). Linkage disequilibrium at the ADH2 and ADH3 loci and risk for alcoholism. *American Journal of Human Genetics, 64,* 1147–1157.

Ossier, M., Pakstis, A. J., Soodyall, H., Comas, D., Goldman, D., Odunsi, A., et al. (2002). A global perspective on genetic variation at the ADH genes reveals unusual patterns of linkage disequilibrium and diversity. *American Journal of Human Genetics, 71,* 84–99.

Pares, X., Farres, J., Pares, A., Soler, X., Panes, J., Ferre, J. L., et al. (1994). Genetic polymorphism of liver alcohol dehydrogenase in Spanish subjects: Significance of alcohol consumption and liver disease. *Alcohol and Alcoholism, 29,* 701–705.

Peng, G.-S., Wang, M.-F., Chen, C. Y., Luu, S.-Y., Chau, H.-C., Li, T.-K., et al. (1999). Involvement of acetaldehyde for full protection against alcoholism by homozygosity of the variant allele of mitochondrial aldehyde dehydrogenase gene in Asians. *Pharmacogenetics, 9,* 463–476.

Pollock, V. E. (1992). Meta-analysis of subjective sensitivity to alcohol in sons of alcoholics. *American Journal of Psychiatry, 149,* 1534–1538.

Pollock, V. E., Teasdale, T. W., Gabrielli, W. F., & Knop, J. (1986). Subjective and objective measures of response to alcohol among young men at risk for alcoholism. *Journal of Studies on Alcohol, 47,* 297–304.

Reed, T. E. (1978). Racial comparisons of alcohol metabolism: Background, problems, and results. *Alcoholism: Clinical and Experimental Research, 2,* 83–87.

Reed, T. E. (1985). Ethnic differences in alcohol use, abuse, and sensitivity: A review with genetic interpretation. *Social Biology, 32,* 195–209.

Reed, T. E., Kalant, H., Gibbins, R. J., Kapur, B. M., & Rankin, J. G. (1976). Alcohol and acetaldehyde metabolism in Caucasians, Chinese and Amerinds. *Canadian Medical Association Journal, 115,* 851–855.

Reich, T., Edenberg, H. J., Goate, A., William, J. T., Rice, J. P., Van Eerdewegh, P., et al. (1998). Genome-wide search for genes affecting risk for alcohol dependence. *American Journal of Medical Genetics (Neuropsychiatric Genetics), 81,* 206–215.

Rex, D. K., Bosron, W. F., Smialek, J. E., & Li, T.-K. (1985). Alcohol and aldehyde dehydrogenase isoenzymes in North American Indians. *Alcoholism: Clinical and Experimental Research, 9,* 851–855.

Rodriguez, L. A., Wilson, J. R., & Nagoshi, C. T. (1993). Does psychomotor sensitivity to alcohol predict subsequent alcohol use? *Alcoholism: Clinical and Experimental Research, 17,* 155–161.

Substance Abuse and Mental Health Services Administration. (1998). *National Household Survey on Drug Abuse.* Rockville, MD: Author.

Sanders, B., Danko, G. P., & Ching, B. (1980). Cardiovascular responses of Oriental and Caucasian men to alcohol. *Journal of Studies on Alcohol, 41,* 496–508.

Savoie, T. M., Emory, E. K., & Moody-Thomas, S. (1988). Acute alcohol intoxication in socially drinking female and male offspring of alcoholic fathers. *Journal of Studies on Alcohol, 49,* 430–435.

Schaefer, J. M. (1981). Firewater myths revisited: Review of findings and some new directions. *Journal of Studies on Alcohol, 8,* 99–117.

Schuckit, M. A. (1980). Self-rating of alcohol intoxication by young men with and without family histories of alcoholism. *Journal of Studies on Alcohol, 41,* 242–249.

Schuckit, M. A. (1984). Subjective responses to alcohol in sons of alcoholics and control subjects. *Archives of General Psychiatry, 41,* 879–884.

Schuckit, M. A., & Duby, J. (1982). Alcohol-related flushing and the risk for alcoholism in sons of alcoholics. *Journal of Clinical Psychiatry, 43,* 415–418.

Schuckit, M. A., & Gold, E. O. (1988). A simultaneous evaluation of multiple markers of ethanol/placebo challenge in sons of alcoholics and controls. *Archives of General Psychiatry, 45,* 211–216.

Schuckit, M. A., & Smith, T. L. (1996). An 8-year follow-up of 450 sons of alcoholics and controls. *Archives of General Psychiatry, 53,* 202–210.

Schuckit, M. A., Tipp, J. E., Smith, T. L., Weisbeck, G. A., & Kalmijn, J. (1997). The relationship between self-rating of the effects of alcohol and alcohol challenge results in ninety-eight young men. *Journal of Studies on Alcohol, 58,* 397–404.

Segal, B., & Duffy, L. (1992). Ethanol elimination among different racial groups. *Alcohol, 9,* 213–217.

Seto, A., Tricomi, S., Goodwin, D. W., Kolodney, R., & Sullivan, T. (1978). Biochemical correlates of ethanol-induced flushing in Orientals. *Journal of Studies on Alcohol, 39,* 1–11.

Shea, S. H., Wall, T. L., Carr, L. G., & Li, T.-K. (2001). ADH2 and alcohol-related phenotypes in Ashkenazic Jewish American college students. *Behavior Genetics, 31,* 231–239.

Shen, Y.-C., Fan, J.-H., Edenberg, H. J., Li, T.-K., Cui, Y.-H., Wang, Y.-F., et al. (1997). Polymorphism of ADH and ALDH genes among four ethnic groups in China and effects upon the risk for alcoholism. *Alcoholism: Clinical and Experimental Research, 21,* 1272–1277.

Shibuya, A., & Yoshida, A. (1988). Genotypes of alcohol-metabolizing enzymes in Japanese with alcohol liver diseases: A strong association of the usual Caucasian-type aldehyde dehydrogenase gene (ALDH21) with the disease. *American Journal of Human Genetics, 43,* 744–748.

Singh, S., Fritze, G., Fang, B., Harada, S., Paik, Y. K., Eckey, R., et al. (1989). Inheritance of mitochondrial aldehyde dehydrogenase: Genotyping in Chinese, Japanese and South Korean families reveals a dominance of the mutant allele. *Human Genetics, 83,* 118–121.

Slutske, W. S., Heath, A. C., Madden, P. A. F., Bucholz, K. K., Dinwiddie, S. H., Dunne, M. P., et al. (1995). Is alcohol-related flushing a protective factor for alcoholism among Caucasians? *Alcoholism: Clinical and Experimental Research, 19,* 582–592.

Snyder, C. R. (1958). *Alcohol and Jews: A cultural study of drinking and sobriety.* Glencoe, IL: Free Press.

Sorrell, M. F., & Tuma, D. J. (1985). Hypothesis: Alcoholic liver injury and the covalent binding of acetaldehyde. *Alcoholism: Clinical and Experimental Research, 9,* 306–309.

Sun, F., Tsuritani, I., Honda, R., Ma, Z.-M., & Yamada, Y. (1999). Association of genetic polymorphisms of alcohol metabolizing enzymes with excessive alcohol consumption in Japanese men. *Human Genetics, 105*, 295–300.

Takada, A., Tsutsumi, M., & Kobayashi, Y. (1994). Genotypes of ALDH2 related to liver and pulmonary diseases and other genetic factors related to alcoholic liver disease. *Alcohol and Alcoholism, 29*, 719–727.

Takeshita, T., Mao, X.-Q., & Morimoto, K. (1996). The contribution of polymorphism in the alcohol dehydrogenase beta subunit to alcohol sensitivity in a Japanese population. *Human Genetics, 97*, 409–413.

Takeshita, T., & Morimoto, K. (1999). Self-reported alcohol-associated symptoms and drinking behavior in three ALDH2 genotypes among Japanese university students. *Alcoholism: Clinical and Experimental Research, 23*, 1065–1069.

Takeshita, T., & Morimoto, K. (2000). Accumulation of hemoglobin-associated acetaldehyde with habitual drinking in the atypical ALDH2 genotype. *Alcoholism: Clinical and Experimental Research, 24*, 1–7.

Takeshita, T., Morimoto, K., Mao, X. Q., Hashimoto, T., & Furuyama, J. (1994). Characterization of the three genotypes of low Km aldehyde dehydrogenase in a Japanese population. *Human Genetics, 94*, 217–223.

Tanabe, H., Ohhira, M., Watari, J., Yokota, K., & Kohogo, Y. (1999). Genetic polymorphism of aldehyde dehydrogenase 2 in patients with upper aerodigestive tract cancer. *Alcoholism: Clinical and Experimental Research, 23*, 17S–20S.

Tanaka, F., Shiratori, Y., Yokosuka, O., Imazeki, F., Tsukada, Y., & Omata, M. (1996). High incidence of ADH2*1/ALDH2*1 genes among Japanese dependents and patients with alcoholic liver disease. *Hepatology, 23*, 234–239.

Thomasson, H. R., Beard, J. D., & Li, T.-K. (1993). Faster ethanol elimination rate demonstrated in subjects with *ADH2*3* alleles. *Alcoholism: Clinical and Experimental Research, 17*, 495.

Thomasson, H. R., Crabb, D. W., Edenberg, H. J., Li, T.-K., Hwu, H.-G., Chen, C.-C., et al. (1994). Low frequency of the ADH2*2 allele among Atayal natives of Taiwan with alcohol use disorders. *Alcoholism: Clinical and Experimental Research, 18*, 640–643.

Thomasson, H. R., Edenberg, H. J., Crabb, D. W., Mai, X.-L., Jerome, R. E., Li, T.-K., et al. (1991). Alcohol and aldehyde dehydrogenase genotypes and alcoholism in Chinese men. *American Journal of Human Genetics, 48*, 667–681.

True, W. R., Xian, H., Scherrer, J. F., Madden, P. A., Bucholz, K. K., Heath, A. C., et al. (1999). Common genetic vulnerability for nicotine and alcohol dependence in men. *Archives of General Psychiatry, 56*, 655–661.

Truitt, E. B., Rowe, C. S., & Mehl, D. (1987). Aspirin attenuation of alcohol-induced flushing and intoxication in Oriental and Occidental subjects. *Alcohol and Alcoholism, 1*(Suppl.), 595–599.

Tsuang, M. T., Lyons, M. J., Meyer, J. M., Doyle, T., Eisen, S. A., Goldberg, J., et al. (1998). Co-occurrence of abuse of different drugs in men: The role of drug-specific and shared vulnerabilities. *Archives of General Psychiatry, 55*, 967–972.

Uehara, E. S., Takeuchi, D. T., & Smukler, M. (1994). Effects of combining disparate groups in the analysis of ethnic differences: Variations among

Asian American mental health service consumers in level of community functioning. *American Journal of Community Psychology, 22,* 83–99.

Uhl, G. R., Liu, Q.-R., Walther, D., Hess, J., & Naiman, D. (2001). Polysubstance abuse-vulnerability genes: Genome scans for association, using 1,004 subjects and 1,494 single-nucleotide polymorphisms. *American Journal of Human Genetics, 69,* 1290–1300.

Viljoen, D. L., Carr, L. G., Foroud, T. M., Brooke, L., Ramsay, M., & Li, T.-K. (2001). Alcohol dehydrogenase-2*2 allele is associated with decreased prevalence of fetal alcohol syndrome in the mixed-ancestry population of the Western Cape Province, South Africa. *Alcoholism: Clinical and Experimental Research, 25,* 1719–1722.

Volavka, J., Czobor, P., Goodwin, D. W., Gabrielli, W. F., Penick, E. C., Mednick, S. A., et al. (1996). The electroencephalogram after alcohol administration in high-risk men and the development of alcohol use disorders 10 years later. *Archives of General Psychiatry, 53,* 258–263.

Wall, T. L., Carr, L. G., & Ehlers, C. L. (2003). Genetic variation in alcohol dehydrogenase: A protective association with alcohol dependence in Native American Mission Indians. *American Journal of Psychiatry, 160,* 41–46.

Wall, T. L., & Ehlers, C. L. (1995). Acute effects of alcohol on P300 in Asians with different ALDH2 genotypes. *Alcoholism: Clinical and Experimental Research, 19,* 617–622.

Wall, T. L., Gallen, C. C., & Ehlers, C. L. (1993). Effects of alcohol on the EEG in Asian men with genetic variations of ALDH2. *Biological Psychiatry, 34,* 91–99.

Wall, T. L., Garcia-Andrade, C., Thomasson, H. R., Carr, L. G., & Ehlers, C. L. (1997). Alcohol dehydrogenase polymorphisms in Native Americans: Identification of the ADH2*3 allele. *Alcohol and Alcoholism, 32,* 129–132.

Wall, T. L., Garcia-Andrade, C., Thomasson, H. R., Cole, M., & Ehlers, C. L. (1996). Alcohol elimination in Native American Mission Indians: An investigation of interindividual variation. *Alcoholism: Clinical and Experimental Research, 20,* 1438–1442.

Wall, T. L., Johnson, M. L., Horn, S. M., Carr, L. G., Smith, T. L., & Schuckit, M. A. (1999). Evaluation of the self-rating of the effects of alcohol form in Asian-Americans with aldehyde dehydrogenase polymorphisms. *Journal of Studies on Alcohol, 60,* 784–789.

Wall, T. L., Nemeroff, C. B., Ritchie, J. C., & Ehlers, C. L. (1994). Cortisol responses following placebo and alcohol in Asians with different ALDH2 genotypes. *Journal of Studies on Alcohol, 55,* 207–213.

Wall, T. L., Peterson, C. M., Peterson, K. P., Johnson, M. L., Thomasson, H. R., Cole, M., et al. (1997). Alcohol metabolism in Asian-American men with genetic polymorphisms of aldehyde dehydrogenase. *Annals of Internal Medicine, 127,* 376–379.

Wall, T. L., Shea, S. H., Chan, K. K., & Carr, L. G. (2001). A genetic association with the development of alcohol and other substance use behavior in Asian Americans. *Journal of Abnormal Psychology, 110,* 173–178.

Wall, T. L., Thomasson, H. R., & Ehlers, C. L. (1996). Investigator-observed alcohol-induced flushing but not self-report of flushing is a valid predictor of ALDH2 genotype. *Journal of Studies on Alcohol, 57,* 267–272.

Wall, T. L., Thomasson, H. R., Schuckit, M. A., & Ehlers, C. L. (1992). Subjective feelings of alcohol intoxication in Asians with genetic variations of

ALDH2 alleles. *Alcoholism: Clinical and Experimental Research, 16*, 991–995.

Whitfield, J. B. (1997). Meta-analysis of the effects of alcohol dehydrogenase genotype on alcohol dependence. *Alcohol and Alcoholism, 32*, 613–619.

Whitfield, J. B., Nightingale, B. N., Bucholz, K. K., Madden, P. A. F., Heath, A. C., & Martin, N. G. (1998). ADH genotypes and alcohol use and dependence in Europeans. *Alcoholism: Clinical and Experimental Research, 22*, 1463–1469.

Wolff, P. H. (1972). Ethnic differences in alcohol sensitivity. *Science, 175*, 449–450.

Wolff, P. H. (1973). Vasomotor sensitivity to alcohol in diverse mongoloid populations. *American Journal of Human Genetics, 25*, 193–199.

Yamauchi, M., Maezawa, Y., Mizuhara, Y., Ohata, M., Hirakawa, J., Nakajima, H., et al. (1995). Polymorphisms in alcohol metabolizing enzyme genes and alcoholic cirrhosis in Japanese patients: A multivariate analysis. *Hepatology, 22*, 1136–1142.

Yeung, P. P., & Greenwald, S. (1992). Jewish Americans and mental health: Results of the NIMH Epidemiologic Catchment Area study. *Social Psychiatry and Psychiatric Epidemiology, 27*, 292–297.

Yokoyama, A., Muramatsu, T., Ohmori, T., Higuchi, S., Hayashidi, M., & Ishii, H. (1996). Esophageal cancer and aldehyde dehydrogenase-2 genotypes in Japanese males. *Cancer Epidemiology, Biomarkers and Prevention, 5*, 99–102.

Yokoyama, A., Muramatsu, T., Ohmori, T., Yokoyama, T., Okuyama, K., Takahashi, H., et al. 0(1998). Alcohol-related cancers and aldehyde dehydrogenase-2 in Japanese alcoholics. *Carcinogenesis, 19*, 1383–1387.

Yokoyama, A., Ohmori, T., Muramatsu, T., Higuchi, S., Yokoyama, T., Matsushita, S., et al. (1996). Cancer screening of upper aerodigestive tract in Japanese alcoholics with reference to drinking and smoking habits and aldehyde dehydrogenase-2 genotype. *International Journal of Cancer, 68*, 313–316.

Yoshihara, E., Ameno, K., Nakamura, K., Ameno, M., Itoh, S., Ijiri, I., et al. (2000). The effects of the ALDH2*1/2, CYP2E2E1 C1/C2 and C/D genotypes on blood ethanol elimination. *Drug and Chemical Toxicology, 23*, 371–379.

Zeiner, A. R., Parades, A., & Cowden, L. (1976). Physiologic responses to ethanol among Tarahumara Indians. *Annals of the New York Academy of Science, 273*, 151–158.

Zhang, A. Y., & Snowden, L. R. (1999). Ethnic characteristics of mental disorders in five U.S. communities. *Cultural Diversity and Ethnic Minority Psychology, 5*, 134–146.

7

Sex and Drugs

Do Women Differ From Men in Their Subjective Response to Drugs of Abuse?

SUSAN C. HAN AND SUZETTE M. EVANS

This chapter will focus primarily on studies that have administered drugs of abuse to humans and have measured subjective responses using traditional subjective effects questionnaires (described in detail later). For a comprehensive review of sex difference in drug abuse, both in animals and in humans, we refer you to Lynch, Roth, and Carroll (2002). Upon reviewing the literature for this chapter, it became clear that there is a dearth of studies that have specifically assessed differences in subjective response to drugs in males and females. Further, even though numerous studies have used mixed samples of males and females, most have not conducted separate analyses comparing males and females; therefore, those studies will not be included in this chapter. Typically the types of studies included were conducted under controlled laboratory conditions, the drugs and/or alcohol were administered under placebo-controlled, double-blind conditions, and subjective effects were measured before drug administration, as well as multiple times after drug administration. Where relevant, we will address (a) special subpopulations, either in mixed gender samples or in females, (b) the role of sex differences in drug abstinence or withdrawal, and (c) the role of the menstrual cycle in response to drugs of abuse.

Because we will be reviewing many studies that have assessed response to drugs of abuse at different phases of the menstrual cycle, a brief overview of the human menstrual cycle is warranted. The human female typically has a 28-day menstrual cycle. During the first half of the cycle, progesterone levels are minimal and estradiol levels rise gradually, peaking just before ovulation. The luteal phase begins after ovulation, and during this time progesterone levels increase, peaking 3 to 8 days after ovulation and then declining several days prior to menses. During the luteal phase, estradiol levels remain at levels similar to, or slightly higher than, those observed in the early to middle follicular phase. The menstrual cycle can be further divided into five hormonally distinct phases: menstrual or early follicular (Days 1–5, with Day 1 being the onset of menstruation); follicular (within Days 6–10); ovulatory (within 3 days after onset of the luteinizing hormone [LH] surge, i.e., when a urinary ovulation kit turns positive, generally Days 13–15); luteal (within 7–12 days after onset of the LH surge, generally Days 19–24); and late luteal (within 13–17 days after onset of the LH surge, generally Days 25–28).

Clearly, a major factor contributing to the inconsistencies across studies is the definition and measurement of menstrual cycle phase (Parlee, 1983). Even in studies that do accurately monitor the menstrual cycle, the time frame and the specific phases tested vary across studies; it is important to keep this in mind when interpreting findings related to the menstrual cycle. Unfortunately, many studies fail to provide information on how the onset of menses was determined, and often there is no verification that ovulation occurred, and hormonal levels of estradiol and progesterone are not always measured. It should be noted that normally cycling women often do not ovulate (Metcalf, 1983), and basal body temperature, used in many studies, is not precise enough for determining ovulation. Rather, a hormonal assay is necessary for accurate determination that ovulation has occurred. Further, some studies simply depend on retrospective reports for the onset of menses. We have been tracking the menstrual cycles of women for more than 8 years now, and in our experience women cannot accurately estimate the onset of their last menstruation and do not keep an accurate record of previous cycles. In the absence of prospective monitoring of the menstrual cycle and verifying that the cycles were normal ovulatory cycles using hormonal assays, scheduling women for testing at specific phases of the cycle will be unreliable. Another important criterion for menstrual cycle studies is that they use a within-subject design, rather than a between-subject design, due to the inherent variability across individuals and the small sample sizes typically employed.

Assessment of Subjective Effects

Initially, the abuse potential of drugs was assessed primarily by measuring subjective effects (see reviews by Jasinski and Henningfield, 1989;

Jaffe and Jaffe, 1989; de Wit and Griffiths, 1991; Foltin and Fischman, 1991). The profile of subjective changes produced by a drug is often measured using standardized scales that can provide information that may be relevant to likelihood of abuse. In theory, drug-related changes on these scales provide indices of reinforcing or aversive subjective effects. Although there is a strong correspondence between positive subjective effects of drugs and drug choice (de Wit and Griffiths, 1991), direct measures of reinforcement, such as self-administration and choice, are often viewed as better predictors of the abuse potential of a drug (Foltin and Fischman, 1991). In the following we briefly describe the most commonly used questionnaires for assessing the subjective effects of various drugs of abuse.

Addiction Research Center Inventory (ARCI)

The ARCI was derived by administering different classes of drugs to individuals with various histories of drug abuse and analyzing the similarity of their verbal reports compared with known drugs of abuse using 550 true-false items (Haertzen et al., 1963). The most widely used version of the ARCI consists of 49 true-false items that are factor analyzed into scales representing typical effects of various drug types (W. R. Martin, Sloan, Sapira & Jasinski, 1971). Five scales of possible relevance to abuse liability studies are the Pentobarbital-Chlorpromazine-Alcohol Group (PCAG) scale, which measures sedative effects; the Lysergic Acid (LSD) scale, which measures hallucinogenic and somatic effects and is often considered an indicator of dysphoria; the Amphetamine (A) scale and the Benzedrine Group (BG) scale, both of which measure stimulant effects; and the Morphine-Benzedrine Group (MBG) scale, which is considered to be an indicator of euphoria.

Profile of Mood States (POMS)

The POMS questionnaire can be administered either as a paper-and-pencil test or as a computerized questionnaire. Participants rate each item on a 5-point scale from 0 (*not at all*) to 4 (*extremely*). The 72-item version of the POMS includes the original 65 items (McNair, Lorr, & Droppleman, 1971) and an additional 7 items to yield scores on 8 mood subscales: Tension-Anxiety, Depression-Dejection, Anger-Hostility, Vigor, Fatigue, Confusion, Friendliness, and Elation. A 9th score, Arousal, is obtained by adding together the scores for Vigor and Tension-Anxiety and subtracting the scores for Confusion and Fatigue, and a 10th score, Positive Mood, is obtained by subtracting the Depression-Dejection score from the Elation score. The most reliable dose-related effects using the POMS are observed in individuals who use drugs only occasionally, whereas in drug-abusing populations the POMS scales have been shown to be relatively insensitive to the effects of drugs; this may be due to the fact that the POMS was developed and validated in college students and anxious patients, not substance abusers (McNair et al., 1971).

Liking Ratings

Measures of drug liking (i.e., asking the participants how much they "like" a drug's effects) have face validity for assessing likelihood of abuse and, in most instances, provide a reasonable indication of individuals' general attitude about the drug's effects. Liking measures have been used, in one form or another, in most of the laboratory studies testing the abuse liability of drugs and tend to be one of the most sensitive measures of subjective drug effect. However, despite their apparent simplicity, liking ratings deserve careful consideration. Liking scales can be either unipolar (e.g., ranging from *neutral* or *not at all* to *like very much*) or bipolar (e.g., ranging from *dislike* to *like very much*). If a unipolar scale is used, there is a risk of selectively reporting only positive drug effects and underestimating possible adverse effects. However, if a bipolar scale is used, strong negative responses by some individuals may obscure reports of positive effects by others. Further, with a bipolar scale one can detect changes on the ascending and descending limb. We generally prefer a bipolar scale because individual differences can at least be detected by inspecting the raw data.

The instructional set for a liking scale should be carefully considered because the term *liking* can be interpreted differently by different individuals. Some participants may rate their liking of a drug relative to a placebo, whereas others may rate it in relation to their prior experience with drugs of abuse outside the laboratory situation. In addition, liking ratings may be influenced by relative liking or disliking of other drugs administered in the same study (i.e., contrast effects).

As with most other measures, liking ratings are obtained repeatedly during the time course of drug effects. Liking scales can also be administered after the drug's effects have dissipated. These retrospective ratings, completed either immediately after the session or on the day following administration of the drug, have the advantage of assessing the overall drug experience under drug-free conditions that are presumably similar to those in which drugs are most frequently self-administered outside the laboratory.

A commonly used questionnaire to assess drug effects related to abuse liability is the Drug Effect Questionnaire. Participants rate "strength of the drug effect" on a 5-point scale, from 0 (*no drug effect at all*) to 4 (*very strong effect*). This questionnaire also asks participants to rate "good effects" and "bad effects" from the drug on a 5-point scale, from 0 (*no effect at all*) to 4 (*very much*), as well as the degree to which they would be "willing to take the drug again," from 0 (*not at all*) to 4 (*very much*). Finally, they rate how much they like the drug effect, either on a unipolar scale from 0 to 4 or on a bipolar 9-point scale with -4 indicating *dislike very much*, 0 indicating *feel neutral, or feel no drug effect*, and 4 indicating *like very much*. Variations of this questionnaire have been shown to be sensitive to the effects of sedatives in both drug abusers (Evans, Troisi, & Griffiths, 1994) and normal volunteers (Evans, Foltin, Levin, & Fischman, 1995).

Visual Analog Scales (VASs)

In many cases, mood states, drug liking, and side effects are assessed using VASs. Typically the participant is presented a series of 100-mm lines and instructed to indicate on the line how he or she feels. The end of each line is anchored either by opposing adjectives (e.g., tired-alert) or with labels such as "not at all" and "extremely." The number of VAS items and the exact adjectives used vary from laboratory to laboratory, but most include a range of items to detect positive subjective effects related to abuse liability (e.g., "drug liking," "high," "good drug effect"), various mood states (e.g., "drowsy," "anxious, " "depressed," "content"), as well as somatic symptoms and side effects (e.g., "dizzy," "nauseated," "headache"). Sometimes these VASs are analyzed and presented as individual items, and other times they are combined and presented as composite scales or analyzed as clusters or factors. Of course, some studies utilize the same types of questions using Likert scales rather than VASs.

Beck Depression Inventory (BDI or BDI-II)

The BDI-II (Beck, Ward, Mendelson, Mock, & Erbaugh, 1961; Beck, Steer, & Brown, 1996) is a 21-item instrument for measuring the severity of depression. Each item is rated on a 4-point scale ranging from 0 to 3. The maximum total score is 63. A score of 16 or greater is often indicative of clinical depression.

Spielberger State-Trait Anxiety Inventory

This self-report questionnaire (Spielberger, Gorsuch, & Lushene, 1970) consists of two self-rated subscales, 20 items each, with one subscale rating trait anxiety and the other state anxiety.

Other Questionnaires

Several subjective questionnaires have been used primarily to assess the effects of alcohol; these include the Biphasic Alcohol Effects Scale (BAES; C. S. Martin, Earleywine, Musty, Perrine, & Swift, 1993) and the Subjective High Assessment Scale (SHAS; Schuckit, 1980). The BAES is a 14-item self-report questionnaire consisting of adjectives rated on a scale from 0 ("not at all") to 10 ("extremely"). This scale provides a sum score, as well as two subscales, the stimulation subscale (seven adjectives such as *stimulated* and *elated*) and the sedation subscale (seven adjectives such as *sluggish, difficulty concentrating*), to measure the effects of alcohol on the ascending and descending limb. The SHAS was originally developed by Judd et al. (1977) as a 38-item adjective rating scale from 0 to 5, including positive and negative effects of alcohol. This questionnaire was modified by Schuckit (1984) to consist of 10 analog scale items on a line with 0 (*none*) to 36 (*extremely*). However, the number of SHAS items used has varied across studies (e.g., McCaul, Turkkan, Svikis, & Bigelow, 1990; Schuckit, Tipp, Smith, Wiesbeck, & Kalmijn, 1997).

In the area of nicotine research, a wide variety of questionnaires have been used, particularly to assess nicotine abstinence and withdrawal symptoms. The two most commonly used questionnaires are the Shiffman-Jarvik Withdrawal Questionnaire (Shiffman and Jarvik, 1976) and the Hughes-Hatsukami Withdrawal Scale (Hughes and Hatsukami, 1986).

Stimulants

Cocaine

Based on the National Household Survey, in 1996 almost 50% of all cocaine users were women (U.S. Department of Health and Human Services, 1996), which is a substantial increase from only 3 years earlier, when only 33% of all cocaine users were women (U.S. Department of Health and Human Services, 1993). However, relatively few studies in humans have investigated sex differences in response to cocaine administration. Several controlled studies have evaluated the direct effects of cocaine administration in men and women (Kosten et al., 1996; Lukas et al., 1996; Haney, Foltin, & Fischman, 1998; Evans, Haney, Fischman, & Foltin, 1999; Sofuoglu, Dudish-Poulsen, Nelson, Pentel, & Hatsukami, 1999), with most reporting minimal sex differences in response to cocaine. Two of these studies compared the effects of acute doses of intranasal cocaine in men and women (Kosten et al., 1996; Lukas et al., 1996). Following a single intranasal dose of approximately 2 mg/kg cocaine, no differences in ratings of "high" were observed between males and females (Kosten et al., 1996). Using a joystick device, men detected the effects of cocaine faster than women, and men tended to reported a greater number of euphoric and dysphoric responses to a single dose of 0.9 mg/kg intranasal cocaine (Lukas et al., 1996). However, that study reported no other subjective differences between males and females even though the POMS, ARCI, and a series of VASs were completed. In a study by Haney et al. (1998), although sex differences were not the focus of the study, compared with the men, women reported being less "stimulated" and reported that the cocaine dose was of lower quality following multiple doses of intravenous cocaine. As an aside, when the progressive ratio data in this study were analyzed as a function of sex, females had a larger progressive ratio breakpoint for the highest dose of cocaine. Two studies have compared the effects of smoked cocaine in males and females. In one study (Sofuoglu et al., 1999), females had lower ratings of "paranoid," "high," and "stimulated" than males. The other study (Evans et al., 1999) compared the effects of repeated doses of smoked cocaine (50 mg) in males and females. Following the first dose of cocaine, there were few differences between men and women, although women reported that they would spend significantly less for cocaine, whereas men reported being more anxious than women. During a session after repeated doses, ratings of "I want cocaine" decreased for women and increased for men. Interestingly, women achieved substantially higher cocaine plasma concentrations after repeated cocaine self-administration in this study, but they did not experience greater subjective responses to cocaine. Taken together, the limited studies comparing males and females suggest that women may actually be less sensitive than men to the subjective effects of smoked cocaine.

Cocaine and Menstrual Cycle

Recently, a number of studies have been published assessing the effects of cocaine across the menstrual cycle in women. Although Dudish, Pentel, and Hatsukami (1996) tested repeated doses of smoked cocaine in females and found that cocaine produced the typical dose-related increases in subjective effects (e.g., "high," "stimulated"), no males were tested, and the role of the menstrual cycle phase was not assessed. In a study by Lukas et al. (1996), the subjective response to intranasal cocaine did not differ as a function of menstrual cycle phase, even though a range of subjective questions sensitive to alterations in mood were measured (e.g., POMS). Also, ratings of "high" did not vary as a function of menstrual cycle phase following acute intravenous cocaine administration (Mendelson et al., 1999). In contrast, Sofuoglu et al. (1999) compared the effects of a single dose of 0.4 mg/kg smoked cocaine in women, and ratings of "high" were significantly greater in follicular phase women than in luteal phase women. Unfortunately, these two studies tested separate groups of women in each phase, making it difficult to adequately address changes in the effects of cocaine across the menstrual cycle. Another study (Evans, Haney, & Foltin, 2002) evaluated the effects of repeated doses of smoked cocaine (0, 6, 12, or 25 mg cocaine base) in women and found that cocaine administration increased several ratings such as "good drug effect," "high," and "stimulated" more in the follicular phase than in the luteal phase.

A similar profile of increased ratings during the follicular phase was observed for the "drug quality ratings" cluster (e.g., "drug liking," "drug potency," "drug quality") following repeated doses of 6 and 12 mg smoked cocaine but not following repeated doses of 25 mg smoked cocaine.

Although both the preclinical and limited clinical evidence suggests that the differential response to cocaine may be related to gonadal hormones, few studies in humans have manipulated this variable. One recent study assessed the effects of intranasal cocaine (0.9 mg/kg) or placebo in seven women on oral contraceptives during the phases of the menstrual cycle corresponding to the "follicular" and "luteal" phases (Kouri, Lundahl, Borden, McNeil, & Lukas, 2002). Using the ARCI and VAS, the subjective response to intranasal cocaine was similar regardless of when women were tested, with the exception that "desire to use cocaine" increased more rapidly in the follicular phase than in the luteal phase. In another study, oral progesterone (200 mg) or placebo was administered to five women during the follicular phase (Sofuoglu, Babb, & Hatsukami, 2002). Compared with placebo, progesterone administration decreased the subjective response (based on the average of the Cocaine Effects Questionnaire) to repeated doses of 0.4 mg/kg smoked cocaine. Taken together, these two studies in humans suggest that gonadal hormones play a role in altering the subjective effects of cocaine, with progesterone attenuating the response.

Amphetamine

Despite the many studies that have administered amphetamine to mixed-gender samples, few have actually analyzed their data using sex as a factor. In a recent study (Gabbay, 2003), the subjective response to amphetamine was compared between choosers and nonchoosers of 10–mg oral amphetamine versus placebo using a drug choice procedure. In addition to measuring drug choice, subjective responses were assessed using the ARCI, the POMS questionnaire, and a VAS of "drug liking." Out of 161 individuals, 61 (38%) were designated as choosers (choice of amphetamine on all three choice sessions), and 48 (32%) were designated as nonchoosers (choice of placebo on all three choice sessions). When the sex analysis was conducted, a significantly greater proportion of males were nonchoosers than choosers (73% vs. 46%), whereas a greater proportion of females were choosers than nonchoosers (54% vs. 27%). Despite this sex difference in amphetamine choice, there were few sex differences in subjective response. In fact, the only subjective difference between males and females was on the Anxiety scale of the POMS in that ratings of Anxiety were increased among male nonchoosers following amphetamine compared with placebo. There were no changes in ratings of Anxiety between amphetamine and placebo in choosers. Similarly, in another study (White, Justice, & de Wit,

2002), males did not differ from females tested during the follicular phase in their subjective response to 15 mg amphetamine, but when compared with females tested during the luteal phase, males had higher ratings on the Amphetamine and MBG scales of the ARCI and higher ratings of "feel drug" and "want more drug." The discrepancy between the results of these two studies may have been due to the fact that one study controlled for, and tested at, various phases of the menstrual cycle, whereas the other study did not.

Amphetamine and Menstrual Cycle

Although several studies have assessed the subjective response to oral amphetamine and placebo at different phases of the menstrual cycle in women, all these studies were conducted by the same research group, and only a single dose of oral amphetamine and placebo was tested. Several positive subjective effects (e.g., "like drug," "want more drug," "high," and "euphoria"—based on the MBG scale of the ARCI) were greater during the follicular phase than the midluteal phase following 15 mg amphetamine (Justice and de Wit, 1999; White et al., 2002). The increased response to amphetamine was found to be related to estradiol levels in the follicular phase but not in the luteal phase, whereas during the luteal phase there was no relationship between the response to amphetamine and estradiol level, progesterone level, or the ratio of estradiol to progesterone levels (Justice and de Wit, 1999). However, in a subsequent study from the same laboratory (Justice and de Wit 2000a), minimal differences in response to amphetamine between the early and late follicular phases of the menstrual cycle were observed despite significantly higher estradiol levels in the late follicular phase. Further, exogenously administered estradiol (up to levels 10 times higher than normal) during the early follicular phase produced minimal changes in the subjective response to amphetamine, with increased ratings of "pleasant stimulation" and decreased ratings of "want more" after amphetamine in the estradiol group compared with the placebo group (Justice and de Wit, 2000b). Taken together, these findings are consistent with preclinical studies suggesting that estrogen may enhance the behavioral response to a stimulant drug, whereas high levels of progesterone may mask these effects in the luteal phase.

Nicotine

Much of the research investigating sex differences between males and females in response to nicotine under controlled laboratory conditions has been conducted by Perkins and his colleagues. These researchers are unusual in that they have typically compared males and females in their studies, although overall they have found relatively subtle sex differences in response to nicotine.

When the subjective response to nicotine in nasal spray was compared between smokers and nonsmokers (Perkins, Grobe, et al., 1994), smokers showed a reduced subjective response (e.g., "head rush," "jittery, " Tension-Anxiety, Confusion-Bewilderment, and Fatigue scores of the POMS) to nicotine, although there were no differences between males and females. Similarly, when nicotine nasal spray was compared with tobacco smoking, men and women did not differ in their subjective response to the nasal spray delivery, but women reported higher ratings of "comfortable" and "relaxed" following tobacco smoking (Perkins, Sexton, et al., 1994). Consistent with these findings, after participants were allowed to smoke their normal cigarette, women reported greater reductions in "desire to smoke," "urge to smoke," "difficulty concentrating," and "anticipation of relief from withdrawal" than men (Eissenberg, Adams, Riggins, & Likness, 1999). Taken together, these studies suggest that women may be more sensitive to the subjective effects of cigarette smoking and that the sex differences in subjective response to nicotine depend on the route of nicotine administration.

When various doses of nicotine (0–30 µg/kg) were administered as a nasal spray to smokers who had been required to abstain overnight, nicotine spray decreased the desire to smoke (using the craving scale of the Shiffman-Jarvik Withdrawal Questionnaire; Shiffman and Jarvik, 1976) in a dose-related manner (Perkins, Grobe, Stiller, Fonte, & Goettler, 1992). Although no differences were observed between males and females in their self-reported desire to smoke, differences were noted in cigarette smoking behavior such that women did not reduce their cigarette smoking to the same extent as men following nicotine nasal spray. In a subsequent study, again there were no differences in subjective reports, but women tended to self-administer less nicotine in nasal spray than men (Perkins, Sanders, D'Amico, & Wilson, 1997). These data and the data presented earlier suggest that women may smoke for the nonpharmacological effects of nicotine more than men. The authors speculated that the sex differences observed with nicotine may be related to differences in the subjective response to some of the conditioned stimuli associated with tobacco smoking. To address this question, Perkins et al. (2001) assessed the role of olfactory and visual cigarette smoking stimuli on VAS measures of hedonic response to smoking in males and females. When either olfactory/taste stimuli or the combination of olfactory/taste and visual stimuli of smoking were blocked, women reported that they "liked puffs" less and found smoking less "satisfying," whereas men showed no change in subjective response to smoking when the various stimuli were blocked. These findings further support the possibility that factors other than the direct pharmacological effects of nicotine are more salient in female smokers than in male smokers. Finally, when men and women smoked their own brand, or a lower yield brand of cigarette, the subjective response (e.g., "liked puffs," "similar to own brand," "how high in nicotine") was decreased with the lower dose in men, whereas women often reported a similar subjective response to the two doses (Perkins, Jacobs, Sanders, & Cagguila, 2002). Correspondingly, men responded less to obtain puffs of the lower dose, whereas women tended to respond similarly for both doses. Thus, the dose of nicotine in cigarettes appears to influence the subjective response and the reinforcing effects of smoking less in women than in men.

Perkins and colleagues have also conducted several studies using a traditional drug discrimination procedure to train individuals to discriminate various doses of nicotine from placebo, as well as to assess subjective effects. In an early study in which participants were simply asked to identify whether they thought they had received nicotine or placebo (Perkins, 1995), male smokers were able to correctly identify various doses of nicotine from placebo, whereas female smokers performed at chance level. In subsequent studies, formal drug discrimination training was employed. One study (Perkins, DiMarco, Grobe, Scierka, & Stiller, 1994) found no differences between male and female smokers (nine in each group) in their ability to discriminate a range of nicotine doses (2–12 µg/kg) from placebo when administered as a nasal spray. Overall, there were few changes in subjective effects as a function of nicotine dose, although ratings of "dizzy" increased as a function of nicotine dose in females, but not in males. In addition, a number of other ratings ("dizzy," "jittery," "stimulated," and "head rush") were weakly correlated with nicotine-appropriate responding for women but not for men. When groups of male and female smokers and nonsmokers were trained to discriminate placebo versus a higher dose of nicotine (20 µg/kg) in a nasal spray, despite similar rates of acquiring the discrimination between males and females and smokers versus nonsmokers, female smokers reported the lowest ratings of "self-confidence" in their ability to discriminate, and they had more difficulty than males in correctly identifying placebo in nasal spray (Perkins et al., 1997). Further, the sex differences in discrimination ability appear to be related to training dose, with females maintaining less accurate placebo versus nicotine performance at lower training doses and showing a flattened dose-response function compared with males (Perkins, D'Amico, et al., 1996), but overall there were minimal sex differences on subjective measures.

Another area in which sex differences have been reported is when nicotine is administered under stressful situations. Perkins, Grobe, Fonte, and Breus (1992) compared male and female smokers, who either smoked a real cigarette or sham smoked, and nonsmokers in a high- and low-challenge task. Overall, there were few sex differences in the stress-reducing effects of smoking, and these were observed only under the high-challenge task. Specifically, stress scores (using the Stress-Arousal Checklist) were higher among female smokers who sham smoked than among female smokers who smoked, whereas there were no overall differences between male smokers and sham smokers. VAS ratings of "relaxed" increased in male smokers compared with male sham smokers, whereas among females, there were no differences between smokers and sham smokers. Another study conducted in nonsmokers (File, Fluck, & Leahy, 2001) reported that nicotine administration decreased ratings of "physical tiredness" in females but increased it in males. More important, nicotine increased several negative subjective ratings (e.g., "angry," "quarrelsome") and decreased ratings of "calm" in males after they performed a series of stressful tasks compared to placebo, whereas in females, nicotine appeared to reduce the stress-induced response of the task. While these data suggest that men may become aggressive after smoking when stressed, and women may smoke to reduce stress, this study was conducted in nonsmokers, so these findings may not be generalizable to a population of smokers. In a subsequent study (File, Dinnis, Heard, & Irvine, 2002), when smokers and nonsmokers performed stressful tasks, these sex differences were replicated; both male and female smokers reported increased ratings of aggressive mood compared with nonsmokers.

Nicotine and Menstrual Cycle

There is a growing body of literature examining the role of the menstrual cycle with respect to changes in smoking behavior, response to nicotine administration, and nicotine abstinence/withdrawal. Several studies have shown that symptoms of nicotine withdrawal are increased during the late luteal phase of the menstrual cycle (O'Hara, Portser, & Anderson, 1989; Craig, Parrott, & Coomber, 1992; Pomerleau, Garcia, Pomerleau, & Cameron, 1992; Allen, Hatsukami, Christianson, & Nelson, 1996; Allen, Hatsukami, Christianson, & Brown, 2000; DeBon, Klesges, & Klesges, 1995), although not all studies have shown changes in withdrawal symptoms as a function of menstrual cycle phase (see Allen, Hatsukami, Christianson, & Nelson, 1999). One study (O'Hara et al., 1989) showed that women who quit smoking during the luteal phase reported greater total withdrawal scores than either women who quit during the follicular phase or men. Pomerleau et al. (1992) tested 9 women during the early follicular phase, middle and late follicular phase, and the late luteal phase, with phases confirmed by hormonal assays. Unfortunately, only a small number of women were tested at the specific phases, and many effects only showed trends. For instance, there was a trend for menstrual cycle symptoms, using the Woods Menstrual Symptom Severity List, to increase during the late luteal phase during overnight abstinence. As expected, overnight abstinence increased scores on the Hughes-Hatsukami Withdrawal Scale, including "craving," but there was only a trend for withdrawal scores or craving to be highest during the late luteal phase. These findings were not replicated in a subsequent study (Pomerleau, Teuscher, Goeters, &

Pomerleau, 1994), even though a slightly larger sample of women (13) were tested; this may be due to the fact that women were tested only in the early follicular and midluteal phases or that a different withdrawal questionnaire was used. In a naturalistic study (DeBon et al., 1995), 30 females (15 smokers and 15 nonsmokers) tracked their mood daily using a modified version of the Hughes-Hatsukami Withdrawal Scale. The menstrual cycle was separated into 5 phases based on onset of menstruation and ovulation kits, but with no hormonal confirmation. Cigarette craving was greater in smokers during menses compared with the ovulatory phase, whereas the actual number of cigarettes smoked increased during the two luteal phases and menses compared with the ovulatory phase. In a study testing the effectiveness of a transdermal nicotine patch (Allen et al., 2000), premenstrual symptoms and nicotine withdrawal symptoms were greater in the late luteal phase for those with the placebo patch. Further, compared with the placebo patch, the nicotine patch decreased ratings of nicotine craving, premenstrual pain, and water retention to the greatest extent in the late luteal phase. Overall, these data suggest that withdrawal symptoms may be greatest in women during the late luteal phase of the menstrual cycle.

However, several studies have failed to report any subjective differences across the menstrual cycle after either nicotine administration, ad lib smoking, or overnight abstinence (Marks, Pomerleau, & Pomerleau, 1999; Snively, Ahijevych, Bernhard, & Wewers, 2000). No menstrual cycle differences in subjective responses to 1 mg of nicotine administered as a nasal spray were observed in 12 female smokers across four hormonally confirmed phases of the menstrual cycle (Marks et al., 1999). It should be noted that this study did not test placebo or other doses of nicotine and assessed a limited number of VASs. Snively et al. (2000) tested women in the midfollicular phase and the late luteal phase, and although there were few changes in mood (Anger-Hostility scores of the POMS tended to be increased during abstinence in the late luteal phase) or nicotine craving (measured by the Shiffman-Jarvick Tobacco Withdrawal Questionnaire), women smoked more cigarettes during the late luteal phase.

Although some studies have shown no differences across the menstrual cycle, others have shown significant differences or trends. These inconsistencies across studies could be due to a variety of factors, including the phases of the menstrual cycle tested, how these phases were determined and confirmed, the specific subjective questionnaires used, and of course the fact that almost every study had a relatively small sample size. A potential confound inherent in all these studies is the considerable overlap between nicotine withdrawal symptoms and premenstrual symptoms. However, this should not be considered a major problem given that none of these studies specifically recruited women with moderate to severe premenstrual symptoms, and several studies specifically excluded women with these symptoms. Further, among women who do not have moderate to severe premenstrual symptoms, few fluctuations in mood have been observed across the menstrual cycle when prospectively monitored on a daily basis (Evans, Levin, & Fischman, 2000; Evans and Levin, in press), suggesting that these other studies were detecting nicotine withdrawal symptoms. To our knowledge, no studies have specifically recruited women with severe premenstrual symptoms to adequately assess the role of the menstrual cycle on cigarette smoking or abstinence (but see Marks, Hair, Klock, Ginsburg, & Pomerleau, 1994). However, women with a history of major depression reported greater nicotine withdrawal symptoms during abstinence than women without a history of depression, although there were no differences based on menstrual cycle phase in either group (Pomerleau, Mehringer, Marks, Downey, & Pomerleau, 2000).

In contrast to studies described here showing that other stimulants, such as cocaine and amphetamine, tend to produce greater subjective effects in the follicular phase than the luteal phase, similar effects have not been as clearly demonstrated with nicotine. However, a recent study (Sofuoglu, Babb, & Hatsukami, 2001) showed that progesterone administration during the follicular phase decreased craving for cigarettes and reduced ratings of "good effects" while smoking, suggesting that hormones may also play a role in the response to nicotine, similar to that observed for other stimulants.

Nicotine Withdrawal and Abstinence

Several clinical trials have shown that nicotine replacement therapies are less effective for women than for men and that women are more likely to relapse than men (see review by Perkins, 1996). In addition to the studies described here, there is no consensus regarding whether there are sex differences in nicotine withdrawal symptoms. For instance, several studies found no differences between men and women, in either the number or the severity of nicotine withdrawal symptoms (Gunn, 1986; Svikis, Hatsukami, Hughes, Carroll, & Pickens, 1986). Consistent with these early findings, Perkins, Grobe, et al. (1996) reported that during initial smoking cessation, a low dose of nicotine spray was mildly effective in alleviating withdrawal symptoms to a similar extent in both males and females, although males used more nicotine spray than females. However, women, (but not men) who reported the most intense withdrawal and craving during smoking cessation had an increased chance of resuming smoking (Gunn, 1986).

Nevertheless, some studies have shown clear differences in nicotine withdrawal symptoms between males and females. When Shiffman (1979) reanalyzed tobacco withdrawal data by sex from a previous study by Guilford (1966), 13 out of 18 withdrawal symptoms were more frequently reported by women. Consistent with these findings, a more recent study showed robust differences between males and females on withdrawal symptoms following cessation of smoking while maintained on nicotine gum (Hatsukami, Skoog, Allen, & Bliss, 1995). Specifically, several withdrawal measures (e.g., "craving," "irritable-angry," "impatient") decreased as a function of nicotine gum dose in women but not in men. Further, when men were directly compared with women, women reported greater withdrawal symptoms on a number of items and showed overall greater and more sustained withdrawal symptoms, particularly when given the lower dose (2 mg) of nicotine gum. In a previous study conducted exclusively in a sample of female smokers, 2-mg nicotine gum was effective in reducing the severity and prevalence of nicotine withdrawal symptoms (Hatsukami, McBride, Pirie, Hellerstedt, & Lando, 1991). The inconsistent results with the 2-mg gum in females could be due to the large difference in sample size between the two studies, with the 1991 study having more than 200 women and the 1995 having only 19 women in the 2-mg gum condition.

Based on the findings described earlier, women may be more sensitive to the reinforcing effects of cigarette smoking, independent of the direct pharmacological effects of nicotine, and this may make it more difficult for women to stop smoking. However, the sex differences in response to nicotine clearly depend on the outcome measures assessed. In summary, these studies suggest that women should not be advised to quit smoking during the luteal phase or during menses unless they use some form of nicotine replacement, such as the patch.

Caffeine

Despite the fact that caffeine is the most commonly used drug in the world (Gilbert, 1984), the lack of studies comparing its subjective effects, or caffeine withdrawal, between males and females is remarkable given the otherwise extensive literature on caffeine. One study compared the effects of caffeine (250 mg) and placebo on pain response to a cold pressor task. Few differences in either pain measures or subjective response were noted between men and women, with the exception that women reported overall lower pain tolerance than men and, when administered placebo, felt more composed than men (Keogh and Witt, 2001). In a subsequent study, women who scored low on an Anxiety Sensitivity scale showed increased scores on "Elation" following 250 mg caffeine and increased pain threshold compared with women who scored higher on the Anxiety Sensitivity scale, but no other subjective differences were noted (Keogh & Chaloner, 2002). Finally, when caffeine was assessed in fatigued and nonfatigued individuals, the differences in subjective effects between males and females were minimal and inconsistent across experiments (Linde, 1995).

Sedatives

Alcohol

Although a number of studies have evaluated the pharmacokinetic differences between males and females following alcohol administration, we will focus only on studies that specifically assessed subjective effects following alcohol administration. In addition, we will present studies that have focused on specific subpopulations, such as individuals with family histories of alcoholism.

One major consideration in any study that compares the effects of alcohol between males and females is how the alcohol dose is calculated. Overall, men are larger and have a lower body fat content than women. Consequently, if men and women are administered the same unit dose of alcohol, women are more likely to have a greater response to alcohol that can be attributed to the fact that they have correspondingly higher breath alcohol concentrations (BACs) than men. For instance, one study that compared differences in alcohol pharmacokinetics between males and females found that women showed higher peak BACs and that these differences were due to total body water differences (Marshall, Kingstone, Boss, & Morgan, 1983). Therefore, studies involving alcohol need to make sure that similar BACs are obtained when comparing men and women. Goist and Sutker (1985) specifically compared the two dosing methods and showed that if alcohol was administered to men and women based on body weight, women had higher BACs than men, but when alcohol was administered based on estimated total body water, BACs were similar in men and women. In a relatively early study, Watson, Watson, & Batt (1980) developed separate anthropometric equations for males and females to calculate total body water volume. Despite that study, relatively few studies have used total body water estimates to calculate alcohol doses. Since then, more sophisticated methods of estimating total body water volume have been developed, such as using a body composition analyzer that determines bioelectrical impedence (Kushner, Schoeller, Fjeld, & Danford, 1992). In fact, others have suggested that this is the best indicator for determining the biological effects of consuming alcohol in an individual, either when comparing males and females or when comparing individuals of different ages (Davies & Bowen, 1999).

Several early studies that compared the effects of alcohol in males and females were inconsistent, with the strongest sex differences observed in performance impairment rather than subjective measures (e.g., Sutker, Allain, Brantley, & Randall, 1982; Wait, Welch, Thurgate, & Hineman, 1982; Mills & Bisgrove, 1983). For instance, in an early study by Logue, Gentry, Linnoila, and Erwin (1978), 10 males and 10 females were administered a range of alcohol doses (up to 1.2 g/kg); ratings of anxiety using the Spielberger State Anxiety Inventory increased as a function of alcohol dose, but there were no differences between males and females. In another study (Mills & Bisgrove, 1983), alcohol doses were adjusted to body fat based on skinfold estimates such that males and females attained similar BACs, but following a high dose of alcohol, females reported feeling less impaired than males, although they were actually more impaired on an objective performance task. In contrast, when Niaura, Nathan, Frankenstein, Shapiro, and Brick (1987) compared the effects of 0.65 mg/kg alcohol in 11 men and 13 women, they reported that women tended to show higher ratings of intoxication, although this could be attributed to the higher BACs in women. Conversely, no differences on self-reported intoxication or several other mood scales were observed between women tested in the follicular phase compared with men following alcohol administration (approximately 0.5 g/kg), even though women had higher BACs than men (Sutker, Tabakoff, Goist, & Randall, 1983).

Alcohol and Anxiety

A number of studies have assessed the effects of alcohol on anxiety, and based on a meta-analysis, alcohol consumption has been shown to decrease self-reported anxiety (Hull & Bond, 1986; but see Logue et al., 1978). In an early study by Sutker et al. (1982), males were compared with females, and the females were specifically tested during the luteal phase of the menstrual cycle, when they were expected to be most susceptible to stress. Although there were no differences between males and females in BACs or ratings of subjective intoxication, women expecting alcohol reported increased anxiety compared with women expecting placebo or with men, whereas women who were expecting placebo, but who really received alcohol, reported less anxiety than the other groups. De Boer, Schippers, and van der Staak (1993) found that alcohol reduced self-reported anxiety in both men and women, although sex differences were observed with alcohol expectancy, whereas, Schippers, De Boer, and van der Staak (1997) reported differences in self-reported anxiety between men and women as a function of alcohol expectancy and alcohol consumption. However, in a subsequent study, De Boer, Schippers, and van der Staak (1994) tested 72 women and were unable to replicate their previous findings; instead, they found that alcohol consumption increased anxiety among women with negative alcohol beliefs. Overall, the findings from studies conducted thus far attempting to demonstrate that alcohol reduces tension and anxiety indicate that there is a complex relationship between the beverage, alcohol expectancy (whether participants were told they would be receiving alcohol or placebo), and alcohol beliefs, and that the sex differences observed may be related more to the sex differences in alcohol expectancies and alcohol beliefs rather than to the pharmacological effects of alcohol itself.

Alcohol and Aggression

In studies investigating the effects of alcohol and aggression, research-ers have often used a variant of the Taylor aggression paradigm, a form of deception in which a participant engages in a computer task. Based on the speed of response, the participant either receives an electrical shock or believes he or she is administering a shock to an opponent in an adjoining room, who is actually a confederate of the experiment. Aggression is then determined by the number, intensity, and/or dura-tion of electrical shock administered. Provocation is defined as the intensity of shocks the participant received from the "opponent." Using this paradigm, researchers have investigated the effects of alcohol and sex differences on aggression. Unfortunately, many studies did not measure subjective response; therefore, we will focus primarily on those studies that also measured some form of subjective response.

Giancola and Zeichner (1995a) found that self-reported intoxication following 0.99 g/kg alcohol was similar between 30 males and 30 fe-males. Under the high-provocation condition, only males with aggres-sive personality traits and high subjective ratings of intoxication showed aggressive behavior; there was no evidence of alcohol-related aggres-sion in females. However, another study by the same group (Giancola & Zeichner, 1995b) found that both males and females who received alcohol were more aggressive than individuals in the placebo or sober groups, although for females this was evident only for indirect forms of aggression (shock duration). Giancola (2002) also studied how the effects of alcohol on aggression were influenced by certain personal-ity traits, specifically irritability, as measured by the Caprara Irritability Scale. Alcohol increased aggression among those males who scored high on irritability while intoxicated, but this was not observed in males ad-ministered placebo or in females, regardless of the beverage (Giancola, 2002). The results of these studies suggest that alcohol may increase aggressive behavior more in males than in females. In contrast, in studies where participants could make either a nonaggressive response (vibration) or an aggressive response (shock), females chose the nonaggressive method over the aggressive method regardless of whether they received alcohol or placebo (Gustafson, 1991a). Using the same procedure, males also showed no differences in aggressive responses as a function of the beverage condition (Gustafson, 1991b).

Alcohol and Social Drinkers

Social drinkers represent another population that has been studied extensively to determine their response to alcohol. Not surprisingly, many of these studies have been restricted to males (e.g., Duka, Tasker & Stephans, 1998; Bruce, Shestowsky, Mayerovitch, & Pihl, 1999), while the majority of studies include mixed samples, but data were not specifically analyzed to determine differences between males and females (e.g., de Wit & Doty, 1994; Holdstock, King, & de Wit, 2000; King, Volpicelli, Frazer, & O'Brien, 1997; King, de Wit, Holdstock, & Schuster, 2002). We were able to identify only a few studies that specifically administered alcohol to moderate/heavy drinking females. Among groups of moderate/heavy social drinkers, a preload of alcohol was found to increase alcohol craving scores in men but not in women (Willner, Field, Pitts, & Reeve, 1998). In another study (Freitag & Adesso, 1993), female heavy drinkers who were administered alcohol experienced no changes in mood across the menstrual cycle.

Alcohol and a Family History of Alcoholism

It has been relatively well established that a family history of alcoholism plays a role in the development of alcoholism in both male (Cloninger, Bohman, & Sigvardsson, 1981; Merikangas, 1990) and female offspring (Kendler, Neale, Heath, Kessler, & Eeaves, 1994). A number of laboratory studies, conducted primarily in males, have documented differences between individuals with (family history positive; FHP) and without family histories of alcoholism (family history negative; FHN) using an alcohol challenge procedure (see reviews by Newlin & Thompson, 1990; McCaul, 1998). However, the directionality of the differences between FHP and FHN individuals has been inconsistent across measures and studies. A series of studies have consistently shown that FHP *males* are less sensitive (i.e., have a low level of response) to the subjective and performance-impairing effects of alcohol (e.g., Schuckit, 1984, 1985; Pollock, Teasdale, Gabrielli, & Knop, 1986), and these results were supported by a meta-analysis of 17 independent studies (Pollock, 1992).

Relatively few studies have also assessed the behavioral response to alcohol in FHP females. In one study, ratings of "drunk" and "high" tended to be greater in FHP females than in FHN females (Lex, Lukas, Greenwald, & Mendelson, 1988) following 0.56 g/kg alcohol. However, in a subsequent study (Lex, Rhoades, Teoh, Mendelson, & Greenwald, 1994), FHP women reported a lower subjective response to alcohol (e.g., "drunk," "alcohol effects," and "high") than FHN women. It should be noted that both of these studies had a small number of participants, and the difference in subjective response to alcohol observed between FHP and FHN women in the Lex et al. (1994) study could be attributed to the fact that FHP women had lower breath alcohol levels than FHN women on the descending limb of the breath alcohol curve. In a more recent study, Evans and Levin (in press) compared the response to alcohol in 16 FHP and 16 FHN women. Following alcohol administration, FHP women tended to have higher ratings of "good drug effect," "drug liking," and "willingness to take again" than FHN women. Of note, FHP women reported more dysphoric mood on a number of the POMS scales than FHN women in the absence of alcohol administration. In that same study, there were no differences in BACs between FHN and FHP women, and FHP women were less impaired by alcohol than FHN women, as shown by Digit Symbol Substitution Test (DSST) scores and observer ratings. The results of this study suggest that FHP women may have a reduced response to alcohol on some measures, but FHP women report greater positive effects on other measures. Overall, the differences between FHP and FHN women in response to alcohol appear to be more subtle than the effects observed in previous studies in FHP men.

Similarly, only a limited number of studies have directly compared the behavioral effects of alcohol in FHP males and females. Savoie, Emory, and Moody-Thomas (1988) assessed the effects of a single dose of alcohol (approximately 0.75 g/kg, based on total body water) in FHN and FHP males and females (5–7 per group) and found that FHP males, but not FHP females or the FHN groups, showed a reduced subjective response (e.g., "light-headedness," "dizziness," "head spinning") to alcohol. Another study showed that women with a family history of alcoholism or a family history of anxiety showed a greater stress-damping response (based on heart rate and pulse transit time) following alcohol compared with those receiving placebo and compared with men, although subjective ratings of anxiety were higher in all groups of women compared with men regardless of the beverage content (Sinha, Robinson, & O'Malley, 1998). This study attempted to test women in the follicular phase of the menstrual cycle based on self-reported estimates of menstrual cycle length. However, all participants were given a dose of 0.85 mg/kg alcohol and, not surprisingly, women had significantly higher BACs than men, making it unclear how to interpret the findings. In contrast to the results by Savoie et al. (1988), Schuckit et al. (2000) reported that both FHP males and FHP females showed decreased subjective effects following a single dose of alcohol compared to FHN males, but when the FHP females in that study were compared with a small number of FHN females (11), there were no differences on subjective ratings.

Alcohol and Menstrual Cycle

Numerous studies have assessed the pharmacokinetic effects of alcohol, and the majority have found no differences in the pharmacokinetics of alcohol across the menstrual cycle (e.g., Marshall et al., 1983; Niaura et al., 1987; Freitag & Adesso, 1993; Mumenthaler, Taylor, O'Hara, & Yesavage, 1999; but see Sutker et al., 1983). In contrast, relatively few studies have assessed changes in subjective effects in response to alcohol as a function of menstrual cycle phase. An early study by Logue, Linnoila, Wallman, and Erwin (1981) administered

4 doses of alcohol to 10 women in the follicular and luteal phases of the menstrual cycle and found that State Anxiety scores increased as a function of alcohol dose during the luteal phase, but during the follicular phase, there was a biphasic effect such that the intermediate dose of alcohol decreased anxiety ratings. In contrast, Sutker, Goist, Allain, and Bugg (1987) reported sex and menstrual cycle phase differences after a moderate (0.66 ml/kg) and high (1.0 ml/kg) dose of alcohol, with women reporting greater anxiety (using the STAI) and depression (using the Depression Adjective Check List) during the early follicular phase compared with the other two phases (ovulatory and midluteal) and with men. Other studies have failed to show any differences as a function of menstrual cycle phase. For instance, Hay, Nathan, Heermans, and Frankenstein (1984) compared the effects of alcohol in 9 normally cycling women and 11 women on oral contraceptives at three phases of the menstrual cycle; they found no differences in ratings of intoxication either between the two groups or across the menstrual cycle. Holdstock and de Wit (2000) also found no significant effects of alcohol across the menstrual cycle among female light drinkers. The women were tested during the early follicular, late follicular, mid luteal, and late luteal phases; although alcohol increased a number of subjective effects such as "feel drug," "feel high," and several scales on the POMS, there were no changes in subjective effects across the menstrual cycle.

Benzodiazepines

Despite conducting extensive literature searches and contacting colleagues who assess the behavioral effects of benzodiazepines in mixed-gender samples, we were unable to find any articles that reported the presence or absence of sex differences in subjective response to benzodiazepine administration. Again, most studies have used either exclusively males or mixed samples, without analyzing for sex differences (Rush, Kelly, Fillmore, & Hays, 2003; de Wit, Pierri, & Johanson, 1989; Evans et al., 1995; Evans, Griffiths, & de Wit, 1996). However, in the past decade a few researchers have published studies using only female volunteers, and these data are summarized here.

One study reported that 1 mg of the benzodiazepine alprazolam produced greater ratings of drug liking in FHP females than in FHN females (Ciraulo et al., 1996). However, in a subsequent study by the same group (Sarid-Segal et al. 2000), ratings of drug liking following alprazolam did not differ between FHP and FHN individuals, although this study did not analyze for sex differences. Similarly, Evans et al. (2000) reported that 0.75 mg alprazolam produced more negative subjective effects in FHP women, including increased ratings of Confusion-Bewilderment (POMS), "unable to concentrate," "confused," and "unmotivated," and less positive subjective effects (e.g., "drug liking") compared with FHN women. These findings suggest that compared with FHN women, FHP women were more sensitive to the negative subjective effects of alprazolam, without any evidence of increased positive subjective effects.

To our knowledge, only one study has looked at the subjective effects of benzodiazepines in female moderate drinkers without a family history of alcoholism (Evans & Levin, 2002). In that study, light female drinkers (mean of 4.2 drinks/month) and moderate female drinkers (mean of 36 drinks/month) were administered acute doses of alprazolam and the nonbenzodiazepine anxiolytic buspirone. Overall there were few subjective differences between light and moderate drinkers following either alprazolam or buspirone. However, moderate drinkers reported greater ratings of "good drug effect" and "drug liking" than did light drinkers, but this was neither dose related nor specific to alprazolam.

Benzodiazepines and Menstrual Cycle

A few studies have specifically addressed the effects of benzodiazepines on mood in women at different phases of the menstrual cycle. When a single dose of triazolam (0.25 mg) and placebo were administered to 19 women during the follicular, ovulatory, and luteal phases of the menstrual cycle, subjective response did not vary across the three phases (Rukstalis & de Wit, 1999). However, when mood-hormone relationships were investigated specifically during the luteal phase, several correlations were observed: Estradiol levels were negatively correlated with Vigor (POMS), progesterone levels were negatively correlated with Confusion (POMS), and allopregnanolone (a metabolite of progesterone) levels were positively correlated with Fatigue and negatively correlated with Arousal (POMS) (de Wit & Rukstalis, 1997). Among women with premenstrual dysphoric disorder (PMDD), a range of doses of alprazolam did not improve negative mood during the luteal phase but rather increased negative mood in the follicular phase (Evans, Haney, Levin, Foltin, & Fischman, 1998), and there was no evidence that alprazolam increased positive subjective effects at either phase of the menstrual cycle. One interpretation of these findings is that women with PMDD are less responsive to alprazolam in the luteal phase. Similarly, Sundström and colleagues (Sundström, Ashbrook, & Bäckström, 1997; Sundstrom, Nyberg, & Bäckström, 1997) concluded that women with PMDD were less sensitive to the effects of benzodiazepines because they had lower increases in sedation ratings following intravenous challenges of either diazepam or midazolam in the luteal phase compared with women without PMDD.

Other Drugs

Opioids

Despite extensive literature searches, we found only a handful of studies that investigated sex differences in response to opioids in humans. The majority of data has been obtained by the same research group to investigate several putative kappa agonists (pentazocine, nalbuphine, and butorphanol) in people undergoing dental surgery. One of the first studies (Gordon et al., 1995) found a greater analgesic response to pentazocine in females than in males but no sex difference in response to morphine. In subsequent studies (Gear, Gordon, et al., 1996; Gear, Miaskowski, et al., 1996; Gear et al., 1999), using similar procedures, the kappa agonists have consistently prolonged the duration of analgesia in women compared with men. Such findings are intriguing, but these studies had several methodological limitations, including not controlling for differences in body weight and not measuring blood levels. Gear and colleagues (Gear, Gordon, et al., 1996; Gear, Miaskowski, et al., 1996) also attempted to evaluate the role of menstrual cycle phase and kappa analgesia, but this was done retrospectively and not confirmed with hormone levels. In another study, Sarton et al. (2000) compared the effects of intravenous morphine on experimentally induced pain and found significant differences between males and females on pain threshold and pain tolerance such that morphine was more potent in females and had a slower onset but a longer duration of action. Finally, a more recent study by Zacny (2001) retrospectively analyzed data collected in males and females following an intravenous dose of morphine (10 mg/70 kg) and saline. Females reported significantly higher ratings of "coasting," "heavy or sluggish," and "dry mouth" after morphine than did males. That study provides some evidence for sex differences in the subjective response to morphine in healthy non-drug-abusing volunteers, but only one dose of morphine was tested, and menstrual cycle phase was not assessed.

Marijuana

We could not find any studies that specifically compared the subjective effects of marijuana smoking in males and females, although we did find one study that assessed the effects of marijuana in females. In that study (Babor, Lex, Mendelson, & Mello, 1984), moderate and heavy female marijuana smokers were allowed to self-administer marijuana for 21 days. Heavy users showed increased ratings of intoxication, elation, vigor, and friendliness and decreased ratings of tension, with tolerance developing to most of these subjective effects. In contrast, moderate users appeared to develop tolerance to the intoxication effects, as well as to some of the negative subjective effects (depression and confusion).

Summary

In the process of reviewing the literature to write this chapter, it became abundantly clear that there is a lack of studies that have adequately addressed sex differences in subjective response to drugs of abuse in humans. The most data are available for the stimulants, and there seems to be sufficient evidence, particularly with cocaine and amphetamine, that there are sex differences in subjective response. Further, these sex differences in response to cocaine and amphetamine appear to be at least partly related to variations in subjective response across the menstrual cycle in women. Although the data with nicotine are less clear, there is growing evidence that women experience greater nicotine withdrawal symptoms than men, these symptoms vary across the menstrual cycle, and smoking cessation is less effective for women than for men. For other drugs of abuse, including alcohol, there appear to be limited sex differences in subjective response, although more studies are clearly needed. Unfortunately, for some drugs, such as caffeine, benzodiazepines, opioids, and marijuana, the data are insufficient to make any conclusions about sex differences.

Based on the studies that have been conducted, a number of limitations emerged. One major limitation with most of the studies has been the small sample sizes employed. Changes in subjective effects can be readily measured following adequate doses of most drugs of abuse, but difficulty arises when one wants to compare differences between two groups of individuals. Therefore, to have adequate power, a relatively large sample size is needed. Unfortunately, for controlled laboratory studies administering drugs, this poses an enormous difficulty in terms of obtaining enough eligible participants within a reasonable time frame. It is not uncommon for these types of studies to take several years to complete even 30 participants (15 of each sex). Among studies not specifically addressing sex differences, but using mixed-gender samples, a sufficient number of males and females should be included such that secondary analyses by sex can be conducted and reported. Other limitations in this body of literature include the restricted range of subjective effects measured and the failure to test more than one dose of a drug.

As summarized in this chapter, there is increasing preclinical and clinical evidence (see review by Lynch et al., 2002) that gonadal hormones play a role in the subjective effects, reinforcing effects, and other effects of abused drugs. Despite this growing evidence, most studies that include women ignore the menstrual cycle. Until more studies are conducted to provide sufficient evidence that the subjective effects of a particular drug do not vary across the menstrual cycle, studies comparing males and females need to control for menstrual cycle phase in a systematic fashion. For instance, two studies reported opposite effects in response to amphetamine; one of the primary differences was that one study controlled for menstrual cycle (White et al., 2002) and the other did not (see Gabbay, 2003). Clearly, as shown with smoking cessation, sex and menstrual cycle can play a critical role in the effectiveness of various treatments, and it is likely that this may apply to other drugs of abuse.

This research was supported by DA-09114 from the National Institute on Drug Abuse.

References

Allen, S. S., Hatsukami, D., Christianson, D., & Nelson, D. (1996). Symptomatology and energy intake during the menstrual cycle in nonsmoking women. *Journal of Substance Abuse, 8*, 303–319.

Allen, S. S., Hatsukami, D. K., Christianson, D., & Brown, S. (2000). Energy intake and energy expenditure during the menstrual cycle in short-term smoking cessation. *Addictive Behaviors, 25*, 559–572.

Allen, S. S., Hatsukami, D. K., Christianson, D., & Nelson, D. (1999). Withdrawal and pre-menstrual symptomatology during the menstrual cycle in short-term smoking abstinence: Effects of menstrual cycle on smoking abstinence. *Nicotine Tobacco Research, 1,* 129–142.

Babor, T. F., Lex, B. W., Mendelson, J. H., & Mello, N. K. (1984). Marijuana, affect and tolerance: A study of subchronic self-administration in women. In L. H. Harris (Ed.), *Problems of Drug Dependence 1983* (pp. 199–204; NIDA Research Monograph No. 49). Rockville, MD: Department of Health and Human Services, National Institute of Drug Abuse.

Beck, A. T., Steer, R. A., & Brown, G. K. (1966). *BDI-II Beck Depression Inventory Manual* (2nd ed.) San Antonio, TX: Psychological Corp.

Beck, A. T., Ward, C. H., Mendelson, M., Mock, J., & Erbaugh, J. (1961). An inventory form measuring depression. *Archives of General Psychiatry, 4*, 561–571.

Bruce, K. R., Shestowsky, J. S., Mayerovitch, J. I., & Pihl, R. O. (1999). Motivational effects of alcohol on memory consolidation and heart rate in social drinkers. *Alcoholism: Clinical and Experimental Research, 23*, 693–701.

Ciraulo, D. A., Sarid-Segal, O., Knapp, C., Ciraulo, A. M., Greenblatt, D. J., & Shader, R. I. (1996). Liability to alprazolam abuse in daughters of alcoholics. *American Journal of Psychiatry, 153*, 956–958.

Cloninger, C. R., Bohman, M., & Sigvardsson, S. (1981). Inheritance of alcohol abuse: Cross-fostering analysis of adopted men. *Archives of General Psychiatry, 38*, 861–868.

Craig, D., Parrott, A., & Coomber, J. A. (1992). Smoking cessation in women: Effects of the menstrual cycle. *International Journal of the Addictions, 27*, 697–706.

Davies, B. T., & Bowen, C. K. (1999). Total body water and peak alcohol concentration: A comparative study on young, middle-age, and older females. *Alcoholism: Clinical and Experimental Research, 23*, 969–975.

De Boer, M. C., Schippers, G. M., & van der Staak, C. P. F. (1993). Alcohol and social anxiety in women and men: Pharmacological and expectancy effects. *Addictive Behaviors, 18*, 117–126.

De Boer, M. C., Schippers, G. M., & van der Staak, C. P. F. (1994).The effects of alcohol, expectancy, and alcohol beliefs on anxiety and self-disclosure in women: Do beliefs moderate alcohol effects? *Addictive Behaviors, 19*, 509–520.

de Wit, H., & Doty, P. (1994). Preference for ethanol and diazepam in light and moderate social drinkers: A within-subject study. *Psychopharmacology, 115*, 529–538.

de Wit, H., & Griffiths, R. R. (1991). Testing the abuse liability of anxiolytic and hypnotic drugs in humans. *Drug and Alcohol Dependence, 28*, 83–111.

de Wit, H., Pierri, J., & Johanson, C. E. (1989). Reinforcing and subjective effects of diazepam in nondrug-abusing volunteers. *Pharmacology, Biochemistry and Behavior, 33*, 205–213.

de Wit, H., & Rukstalis, M. (1997). Acute effects of triazolam in women: Relationships with progesterone, estradiol and allopregnanolone. *Psychopharmacology, 130*, 69–78.

DeBon, M., Klesges, R. C., & Klesges, L. M. (1995). Symptomatology across the menstrual cycle in smoking and nonsmoking women. *Addictive Behaviors, 20*, 335–343.

Dudish, S. A., Pentel, P. R., & Hatsukami, D. K. (1996). Smoked cocaine self-administration in females. *Psychopharmacology, 123*, 79–87.

Duka, T., Tasker, R., & Stephens, D. N. (1998). Alcohol choice and outcome expectancies in social drinkers. *Behavioural Pharmacology, 9*, 643–653.

Eissenberg, T., Adams, C., Riggins, E. C., III, & Likness, M. (1999). Smokers' sex and the effects of tobacco cigarettes: Subject-rated and physiological measures. *Nicotine and Tobacco Research, 1*, 317–324.

Evans, S. M., Foltin, R. W., Levin, F. R., & Fischman, M. W. (1995). Behavioral and subjective effects of DN-2327 (Pazinaclone) and alprazolam in normal volunteers. *Behavioural Pharmacology, 6*, 176–186.

Evans, S. M., Griffiths, R. R., & de Wit, H. (1996). Preference for diazepam, but not buspirone, in moderate drinkers. *Psychopharmacology, 123*,154–163.

Evans, S. M., Haney, M., Fischman, M. W., & Foltin, R. W. (1999). Limited sex differences in response to binge smoked cocaine use in humans. *Neuropsychopharmacology, 21*, 445–454.

Evans, S. M., Haney, M., & Foltin, R. W. (2002). The effects of smoked cocaine during the follicular and luteal phases of the menstrual cycle in women. *Psychopharmacology, 159*, 397–406.

Evans, S. M., Haney, M., Levin, F. R., Foltin, R. W., & Fischman, M. W. (1998). Mood and performance changes in women with premenstrual dysphoric disorder: Acute effects of alprazolam. *Neuropsychopharmacology, 19*, 499–516.

Evans, S. M., & Levin, F. R. (2002). The effects of alprazolam and buspirone in light and moderate female social drinkers. *Behavioural Pharmacology, 13*, 427–439.

Evans, S. M., & Levin, F. R. (in press). Response to alcohol in females with a paternal history of alcoholism. *Psychopharmacology*.

Evans, S. M., Levin, F. R., & Fischman, M. W. (2000). Increased sensitivity to alprazolam in females with a paternal history of alcoholism. *Psychopharmacology, 150*, 150–162.

Evans, S. M., Troisi, J. R., & Griffiths, R. R. (1994). Tandospirone and alprazolam: Comparison of behavioral effects and abuse liability in humans. *Journal of Pharmacology and Experimental Therapeutics, 271*, 683–694.

File, S. E., Dinnis, A. K., Heard, J. E., & Irvine, E. E. (2002). Mood differences between male and female light smokers and nonsmokers. *Pharmacology, Biochemistry and Behavior, 72*, 681–689.

File, S. E., Fluck, E., & Leahy, A. (2001). Nicotine has calming effects on stress-induced mood changes in females, but enhances aggressive mood in males. *International Journal of Neuropsychopharmacology, 4*, 371–376.

Foltin, R. W., & Fischman, M. W. (1991). Methods for the assessment of abuse liability of psychomotor stimulants and anorectic agents in humans. *British Journal of the Addictions, 86*, 1633–1640.

Freitag, W. J., & Adesso, V. J. (1993). Mood effects of alcohol and expectancies across the menstrual cycle. *Alcohol, 10*, 291–298.

Gabbay, F. H. (2003). Variations in affect following amphetamine and placebo: Markers of stimulant drug preference. *Experimental and Clinical Psychopharmacology, 11*, 91–101.

Gear, R. W., Gordon, N. C., Heller, P. H., Paul, S., Miaskowski, C., & Levine, J. D. (1996). Gender differences in analgesic response to the kappa-opioid pentazocine. *Neuroscience Letters, 205*, 207–209.

Gear, R. W., Miaskowski, C., Gordon, N. C., Paul, S. M., Heller, P. H., & Levine, J. D. (1996). Kappa-opioids produce significantly greater analgesia in women than in men. *Nature Medicine, 2*, 1248–1250.

Gear, R. W., Miaskowski, C., Gordon, N. C., Paul, S. M., Heller, P. H., & Levine, J. D. (1999). The kappa opioid nalbuphine produces gender- and dose-dependent analgesia and antianalgesia in patients with postoperative pain. *Pain, 83*, 339–345.

Giancola, P. (2002). Irritability, acute alcohol consumption and aggressive behavior in men and women. *Drug and Alcohol Dependence, 68*, 263–274.

Giancola, P., & Zeichner, A. (1995a). Alcohol-related aggression in males and females: Effects of blood alcohol concentration, subjective intoxication, personality, and provocation. *Alcoholism: Clinical and Experimental Research, 19*, 130–134.

Giancola, P., & Zeichner, A. (1995b). An investigation of gender differences in alcohol-related aggression. *Journal of Studies on Alcohol, 56*, 573–579.

Gilbert, R. M. (1984). Caffeine consumption. In G. A. Spiller (Ed.), *The methylxanthine beverages and foods: Chemistry, consumption, and health effects* (185–213). New York: Liss.

Goist, K., & Sutker, P. B. (1985). Acute alcohol intoxication and body composition in women and men. *Pharmacology, Biochemistry and Behavior, 22*, 811–814.

Gordon, N. C., Gear, R. W., Heller, P. H., Paul, S., Miaskowski, C., & Levine, J. D. (1995). Enhancement of morphine analgesia by the GABA agonist baclofen. *Neuroscience, 69*, 345–349.

Guilford, J. S. (1966). *Factors related to successful abstinence from smoking.* Pittsburgh, PA: American Institutes for Research.

Gunn, R. C. (1986). Reactions to withdrawal symptoms and success in smoking cessation clinics. *Addictive Behaviors, 11,* 49–53.

Gustafson, R. (1991a). Aggressive and nonaggressive behavior as a function of alcohol intoxication and frustration in women. *Alcoholism: Clinical and Experimental Research, 15,* 886–892.

Gustafson, R. (1991b). Male physical aggression as a function of alcohol intoxication: Experimental results and methodological considerations. *Alcoholism: Clinical and Experimental Research, 15,* 158–164.

Haertzen, C. A., Hill, H. E., & Belleville, R. E. (1963). Development of the Addiction Research Center Inventory (ARCI): Selection of items that are sensitive to the effects of various drugs. *Psychopharmacologia, 4,* 155–166.

Haney, M., Foltin, R. W., & Fischman, M. W. (1998). Effects of pergolide on intravenous cocaine self-administration in men and women. *Psychopharmacology, 137,* 15–24.

Hatsukami, D., McBride, C., Pirie, P., Hellerstedt, W., & Lando, H. (1991). Effects of nicotine gum on prevalence and severity of withdrawal in female cigarette smokers. *Journal of Substance Abuse, 3,* 427–440.

Hatsukami, D., Skoog, K., Allen, S., & Bliss, R. (1995). Gender and the effects of different doses of nicotine gum on tobacco withdrawal symptoms. *Experimental and Clinical Psychopharmacology, 3,* 163–173.

Hay, W. M., Nathan, P. E., Heermans, H. W., & Frankenstein, W. (1984). Menstrual cycle, tolerance, and blood alcohol level discrimination ability. *Addictive Behaviors, 9,* 67–77.

Holdstock, L., & de Wit, H. (2000). Effects of ethanol at four phases of the menstrual cycle. *Psychopharmacology, 150,* 374–382.

Holdstock, L., King, A. C., & de Wit, H. (2000). Subjective and objective response to ethanol in moderate/heavy and light social drinkers. *Alcoholism: Clinical and Experimental Research, 24,* 789–794.

Hughes, J. R., & Hatsukami, D. K. (1986). Signs and symptoms of tobacco withdrawal. *Archives of General Psychology, 43,* 289–294.

Hull, J. G., & Bond, C. F. (1986). Social and behavioral consequences of alcohol consumption and expectancy: A meta-analysis. *Psychological Bulletin, 99,* 347–360.

Jaffe, J. H., & Jaffe, F. K. (1989). Historical perspectives on the use of subjective effects measures in assessing the abuse potential of drugs. In M. W. Fischman & N. K. Mello (Eds.), *Testing for abuse liability of drugs in humans* (pp. 43–72, NIDA Research Monograph No. 92). Rockville, MD: Department of Health and Human Services, National Institute of Drug Abuse.

Jasinski, D. R., & Henningfield, J. E. (1989). Human abuse liability assessment by measurement of subjective and physiological effects. In M. W. Fischman & N. K. Mello (Eds.), *Testing for abuse liability of drugs in humans* (pp. 73–100, NIDA Research Monograph No. 92). Rockville, MD: Department of Health and Human Services.

Judd, L. L., Hubbard, R. B., Huey, L. Y., Attewell, P. A., Janowsky, D. S., & Takahashi, K. I. (1977). Lithium carbonate and ethanol induced "highs" in normal subjects. *Archives of General Psychiatry, 34,* 463–467.

Justice, A. J. H., & de Wit, H. (1999). Acute effects of d-amphetamine during the follicular and luteal phases of the menstrual cycle in women. *Psychopharmacology, 145,* 67–75.

Justice, A. J. H., & de Wit, H. (2000a). Acute effects of d-amphetamine during the early and late follicular phases of the menstrual cycle in women. *Pharmacology, Biochemistry and Behavior, 66,* 509–515.

Justice, A. J. H., & de Wit, H. (2000b). Acute effects of estradiol pretreatment on the response to d-amphetamine in women. *Neuroendocrinology, 71,* 51–59.

Kendler, K. S., Neale, M. C., Heath, A. C., Kessler, R. C., & Eaves, L. J. (1994). A twin-family study of alcoholism in women. *American Journal of Psychiatry, 151,* 707–715.

Keogh, E., & Chaloner, N. (2002). The moderating effects of anxiety sensitivity on caffeine-induced hypoalgesia in healthy women. *Psychopharmacology, 164,* 429–431.

Keogh, E., & Witt, G. (2001). Hypoalgesic effect of caffeine in normotensive men and women. *Psychophysiology, 38,* 886–895.

King, A., Houle, T., de Wit, H., Holdstock, L., & Schuster, A. (2002). Biphasic alcohol response differs in heavy versus light drinkers. *Alcoholism: Clinical and Experimental Research, 26,* 827–835.

King, A., Volpicelli, J., Frazer, A., & O'Brien, C. (1997). Effect of naltrexone on subjective alcohol response in subjects at high and low risk for future alcohol dependence. *Psychopharmacology, 129,* 15–22.

Kosten, T. R., Kosten, T. A., McDougle, C. J., Hameedi, F. A., McCance, E. F., Rosen, M. I., et al. (1996). Gender differences in response to intranasal cocaine administration to humans. *Biological Psychiatry, 39,* 147–148.

Kouri, E. M., Lundahl, L. H., Borden, K. N., McNeil, J. F., & Lukas, S. E. (2002). Effects of oral contraceptives on acute cocaine response in female volunteers. *Pharmacology, Biochemistry and Behavior, 74,* 173–180.

Kushner, R. F., Schoeller, D. A., Fjeld, C. R., & Danford, L. (1992). Is the impedence index (ht2/R) significant in predicting total body water? *American Journal of Clinical Nutrition, 6,* 835–839.

Lex, B. W., Lukas, S. E., Greenwald, N. E., & Mendelson, J. H. (1988). Alcohol-induced changes in body sway in women at risk for alcoholism: A pilot study. *Journal of Studies on Alcohol, 49,* 346–356.

Lex, B. W., Rhoades, E. M., Teoh, S. K., Mendelson, J. H., & Greenwald, N. E. (1994). Divided attention task performance and subjective effects following alcohol and placebo: Differences between women with and without a family history of alcoholism. *Drug and Alcohol Dependence, 35,* 95–105.

Linde, L. (1995). Mental effects of caffeine in fatigued and non-fatigued female and male subjects. *Ergonomics, 38,* 864–885.

Logue, P. E., Gentry, W. D., Linnoila, M., & Erwin, C. W. (1978). Effect of alcohol consumption on state anxiety changes in male and female nonalcoholics. *American Journal of Psychiatry, 135,* 1079–1081.

Logue, P. E., Linnoila, M., Wallman, L., & Erwin, C. W. (1981). Effects of ethanol and psychomotor tests on state anxiety: Interaction with menstrual cycle in women. *Perceptual and Motor Skills, 52,* 643–648.

Lukas, S. E., Sholar, M., Hundahl, L. H., Lamas, X., Kouri, E., Wines, J. D., et al. (1996). Sex differences in plasma cocaine levels and subjective effects after acute cocaine administration in human volunteers. *Psychopharmacology, 125*, 346–354.

Lynch, W. J., Roth, M. E., & Carroll, M. E. (2002). Biological basis of sex differences in drug abuse: Preclinical and clinical studies. *Psychopharmacology, 164*, 121–137.

Marks, J. L., Hair, C. S., Klock, S. C., Ginsburg, B. E., & Pomerleau, C. S. (1994). Effects of menstrual phase on intake of nicotine, caffeine, and alcohol and nonprescribed drugs in women with late luteal phase dysphoric disorder. *Journal of Substance Abuse, 6*, 235–253.

Marks, J. L., Pomerleau, C. S., & Pomerleau, O. F. (1999). Effects of menstrual phase on reactivity to nicotine. *Addictive Behaviors, 24*, 127–134.

Marshall, A., Kingstone, D., Boss, M., & Morgan, M. (1983). Ethanol elimination in males and females: Relationship to menstrual cycle and body composition. *Hepatology, 3*, 701–706.

Martin, C. S., Earleywine, M., Musty, R. E., Perrine, M. W., & Swift, R. M. (1993). Development and validation of the Biphasic Alcohol Effects Scale. *Alcoholism: Clinical and Experimental Research, 17*, 140–146.

Martin, W. R., Sloan, J. W., Sapira, J. D., & Jasinski, D. R. (1971). Physiologic, subjective and behavioral effects of amphetamine, methamphetamine, ephedrine, phenmetrazine and methylphenidate in man. *Clinical Pharmacology and Therapeutics, 12*, 245–258.

McCaul, M. E. (1998). Substance abuse vulnerability in offspring of alcohol and drug abusers. In C. E. Wetherington & J. L. Falk (Eds), *Laboratory behavioral studies of vulnerability to drug abuse* (pp. 188–208, NIDA Research Monograph No. 169). Rockville, MD: Department of Health and Human Services, National Institute of Drug Abuse.

McCaul, M. E., Turkkan, J. S., Svikis, D. S., & Bigelow, G. E. (1990). Alcohol and secobarbital effects as a function of family alcoholism: Acute psychophysiological effects. *Alcoholism: Clinical and Experimental Research, 14*, 704–712.

McNair, D., Lorr, M., & Droppleman, L. F. (1971). *Profile of Mood States manual.* San Diego, CA: Educational and Industrial Testing Services.

Mendelson, J. H., Mello, N. K., Sholar, M. B., Siegel, A. J., Kaufman, M. J., Levin, J. M., et al. (1999). Cocaine pharmacokinetics in men and in women during the follicular and luteal phases of the menstrual cycle. *Neuropsychopharmacology, 21*, 294–303.

Merikangas, K. R. (1990). The genetic epidemiology of alcoholism. *Psychological Medicine, 20*, 11–22.

Metcalf, M. (1983). Incidence of ovulation from the menarche to the menopause: Observations of 622 New Zealand women. *New Zealand Medical Journal, 96*, 645–648.

Mills, K. C., & Bisgrove, E. Z. (1983). Body sway and divided attention performance under the influence of alcohol: Dose-response difference between males and females. *Alcoholism: Clinical and Experimental Research, 7*, 393–397.

Mumenthaler, M. S., Taylor, J. L., O'Hara, R., & Yesavage, J. A. (1999). Gender differences in moderate drinking effects. *Alcohol Research and Health, 23*, 55–64.

Newlin, D. B., & Thompson, J. B. (1990). Alcohol challenge with sons of alcoholics: A critical review and analysis. *Psychological Bulletin, 108*, 383–402.

Niaura, R. S., Nathan, P. E., Frankenstein, W., Shapiro, A. P. & Brick, J. (1987). Gender differences in acute psychomotor, cognitive, and pharmacokinetic response to alcohol. *Addictive Behaviors, 12*, 345–356.

O'Hara, P., Portser, S. A., & Anderson, B. P. (1989). The influence of menstrual cycle changes on the tobacco withdrawal syndrome in women. *Addictive Behaviors, 14*, 595–600.

Parlee, M. B. (1983). Menstrual rhythm in sensory processes: A review of fluctuations in vision, olfaction, audition, taste and touch. *Psychological Bulletin, 93*, 539–548.

Perkins, K. A. (1995). Individual variability in responses to nicotine. *Behavioral Genetics, 25*, 119–132.

Perkins, K. A. (1996). Smoking cessation in women: Special considerations. *CNS Drugs, 15*, 391–411.

Perkins, K. A., D'Amico, D., Sanders, M., Grobe, J. E., Scierka, A., & Stiller, R. L. (1996). Influence of training dose on nicotine discrimination in humans. *Psychopharmacology, 126*, 132–139.

Perkins, K. A., DiMarco, A., Grobe, J. E., Scierka, A., & Stiller, R. L. (1994). Nicotine discrimination in male and female smokers. *Psychopharmacology, 116*, 407–413.

Perkins, K. A., Gerlach, D., Vender, J., Grobe, J., Meeker, J., & Hutchinson, S. (2001). Sex differences in the subjective and reinforcing effects of visual and olfactory cigarette smoke stimuli. *Nicotine and Tobacco Research, 3*, 141–150.

Perkins, K. A., Grobe, J. E., D'Amico, D., Fonte, C., Wilson, A. S., & Stiller, R. L. (1996). Low-dose nicotine nasal spray use and effects during initial smoking cessation. *Experimental and Clinical Psychopharmacology, 4*, 157–165.

Perkins, K. A., Grobe, J. E., Fonte, C., & Breus, M. (1992b). "Paradoxical" effects of smoking on subjective stress versus cardiovascular arousal in males and females. *Pharmacology, Biochemistry and Behavior, 42*, 301–311.

Perkins, K. A., Grobe, J. E., Fonte, C., Goettler, J., Cagguila, A. R., Reynolds, W. A., et al. (1994). Chronic and acute tolerance to subjective, behavioral and cardiovascular effects of nicotine in humans. *Journal of Pharmacology and Experimental Therapeutics, 270*, 628–638.

Perkins, K. A., Grobe, J. E., Stiller, R. L., Fonte, C., & Goettler, J. (1992). Nasal spray nicotine replacement suppresses cigarette smoking desire and behavior. *Clinical Trials and Therapeutics, 52*, 627–634.

Perkins, K. A., Jacobs, L., Sanders, M., & Cagguila, A. R. (2002). Sex differences in the subjective and reinforcing effects of cigarette nicotine dose. *Psychopharmacology, 163*, 194–201.

Perkins, K. A., Sanders, M., D'Amico, D., & Wilson, A. (1997). Nicotine discrimination and self-administration in humans as a function of smoking status. *Psychopharmacology, 131*, 361–370.

Perkins, K. A., Sexton, J., Reynolds, W. A., Grobe, J. E., Fonte, C., & Stiller, R. L. (1994). Comparison of acute subjective and heart rate effects of nicotine intake via tobacco smoking versus nasal spray. *Pharmacology, Biochemistry and Behavior, 47*, 295–299.

Pollock, V. E. (1992). Meta-analysis of subjective sensitivity to alcohol in sons of alcoholics. *American Journal of Psychiatry, 149*, 1534–1538.

Pollock, V. E., Teasdale, T. W., Gabrielli, W. F., & Knop, J. (1986). Subjective and objective measures of response to alcohol among young men at risk for alcoholism. *Journal of Studies on Alcohol, 47*, 297–304.

Pomerleau, C. S., Garcia, A. W., Pomerleau, O. F., & Cameron, O. G. (1992). The effects of menstrual phase and nicotine abstinence on nicotine intake and on biochemical and subjective measures in women smokers: A preliminary report. *Psychoneuroendocrinology, 17*, 627–638.

Pomerleau, C. S., Mehringer, A. M., Marks, J. L., Downey, K. K., & Pomerleau, O. F. (2000). Effects of menstrual phase and smoking abstinence in smokers with and without a history of major depressive disorder. *Addictive Behaviors, 4*, 483–497.

Pomerleau, C. S., Teuscher, F., Goeters, S., & Pomerleau, O. F. (1994). Effects of nicotine abstinence and menstrual phase on task performance. *Addictive Behaviors, 19*, 357–362.

Rukstalis, M., & de Wit, H. (1999). Effects of triazolam at three phases of the menstrual cycle. Journal of Clinical Psychopharmacology, 19, 450–458.

Rush, C. R., Kelly, T. H., Fillmore, M. T. & Hays, L. R. (2003). Discriminative-stimulus effects of triazolam in light and moderate drinkers. *Alcoholism: Clinical and Experimental Research, 27*, 638–646.

Sarid-Segal, O., Knapp, C. M., Ciraulo, A. M., Greenblatt, D. J., Shader, R. I., & Ciraulo, D. A. (2000). Decreased EEG sensitivity to alprazolam in subjects with a paternal history of alcoholism. *Journal of Clinical Pharmacology, 40*, 84–90.

Sarton, E., Olofsen, E., Romberg, R., den Hartigh, J., Kest, B., Nieuwenhuijs, D., et al. (2000). Sex differences in morphine analgesia: An experimental study in healthy volunteers. *Anesthesiology, 93*, 1245–1254.

Savoie, T. M., Emory, E. K., & Moody-Thomas, S. (1988). Acute alcohol intoxication in socially drinking female and male offspring of alcoholic fathers. *Journal of Studies on Alcohol, 49*, 430–435.

Schippers, G. M., De Boer, M. C., & van der Staak, C. P. F. (1997). Effects of alcohol and expectancy on self-disclosure and anxiety in male and female social drinkers. *Addictive Behaviors, 22*, 305–314.

Schuckit, M. A. (1980). Self-rating alcohol intoxication by young men with and without family histories of alcoholism. *Journal of Studies on Alcohol, 41*, 242–249.

Schuckit, M. A. (1984). Subjective responses to alcohol in sons of alcoholics and control subjects. *Archives of General Psychiatry, 41*, 879–884.

Schuckit, M. A. (1985). Ethanol-induced changes in body sway in men at high alcoholism risk. *Archives of General Psychiatry, 42*, 375–379.

Schuckit, M. A., Smith, T. L., Kalmijn, J., Tsuang, J., Hesselbrock, V., & Bucholz, K. (2000). Response to alcohol in daughters of alcoholics: A pilot study and a comparison with sons of alcoholics. *Alcohol and Alcoholism, 35*, 242–248.

Schuckit, M. A., Tipp, J. E., Smith, T. L., Wiesbeck, G. A., & Kalmijn, J. (1997). The relationship between self-rating of the effects of alcohol and alcohol challenge results in ninety-eight young men. *Journal of Studies on Alcohol, 58*, 397–404.

Shiffman, S. M. (1979). *The tobacco withdrawal syndrome* (pp. 158–184, NIDA Research Monograph No. 23). Rockville, MD: Department of Health and Human Services, National Institute of Drug Abuse.

Shiffman, S. M., & Jarvik, M. E. (1976). Smoking withdrawal symptoms in two weeks of abstinence. *Psychopharmacology, 50,* 35–39.

Sinha, R., Robinson, J., & O'Malley, S. (1998). Stress response dampening: Effects of gender and family history of alcoholism and anxiety disorders. *Psychopharmacology, 137,* 311–320.

Snively, T. A., Ahijevych, K. L., Bernhard, L. A., & Wewers, M. E. (2000). Smoking behavior, dysphoric states and the menstrual cycle: Results from single smoking sessions and the natural environment. *Psychoneuroendocrinology, 25,* 677–691.

Sofuoglu, M., Babb, D. A., & Hatsukami, D.K. (2001). Progesterone treatment during the early follicular phase of the menstrual cycle: Effects on smoking behavior in women. *Pharmacology, Biochemistry and Behavior, 69,* 299–304.

Sofuoglu, M., Babb, D. A., & Hatsukami, D. K. (2002). Effects of progesterone treatment on smoked cocaine response in women. *Pharmacology, Biochemistry and Behavior, 72,* 431–435.

Sofuoglu, M., Dudish-Poulsen, S., Nelson, D., Pentel, P. R., & Hatsukami, D. K. (1999). Sex and menstrual cycle differences in the subjective effects from smoked cocaine in humans. *Experimental and Clinical Psychopharmacology, 7,* 274–283.

Spielberger, C. D., Gorsuch, R. L., & Lushene, R. E. (1970). *STAI manual for the State-Trait Anxiety Inventory ("self-evaluation questionnaire").* Palo Alto, CA: Consulting Psychologists Press.

Sundström, I., Ashbrook, D., & Bäckström, T. (1997). Reduced benzodiazepine sensitivity in patients with premenstrual syndrome: A pilot study. *Psychoneuroendocrinology, 22,* 25–38.

Sundström, I., Nyberg, S., & Bäckström, T. (1997). Patients with premenstrual syndrome have reduced sensitivity to midazolam compared to control subjects. *Neuropsychopharmacology, 17,* 370–381.

Sutker, P. B., Allain, A. N., Brantley, P. J., & Randall, C. L. (1982). Acute alcohol intoxication, negative affect, and autonomic arousal in women and men. *Addictive Behaviors, 7,* 17–25.

Sutker, P. B., Tabakoff, B., Goist, K. C. Jr., & Randall, C. L. (1983). Acute alcohol intoxication, mood states and alcohol metabolism in women and men. *Pharmacology, Biochemistry and Behavior, 18,* 349–354.

Sutker, P. B., Goist, K. C., Allain, A. N., & Bugg, F. (1987). Acute alcohol intoxication: Sex comparisons on pharmacokinetic and mood measures. Alcoholism: Clinical and Experimental Research, 11, 507–512.

Sutker, P. B., Tabakoff, B., Goist, K. C. Jr., & Randall, C. L. (1983). Acute alcohol intoxication, mood states and alcohol metabolism in women and men. *Pharmacology, Biochemistry and Behavior, 18,* 349–354.

Svikis, D. S., Hatsukami, D. K., Hughes, J. R., Carroll, K. M., & Pickens, R. W. (1986). Sex differences in tobacco withdrawal syndrome. *Addictive Behaviors, 11,* 459–462.

U.S. Department of Health and Human Services. (1993). *Preliminary estimates from the 1993 National Household Survey on Drug Abuse.* Washington, DC: Substance Abuse and Mental Health Services Administration.

U.S. Department of Health and Human Services. (1996). *Preliminary estimates from the 1996 National Household Survey on Drug Abuse.* Washington, DC: Substance Abuse and Mental Health Services Administration.

Wait, J. S., Welch, R. B., Thurgate, J. K., & Hineman, J. (1982). Drinking history and sex of subject in the effects of alcohol on perception and perceptual-motor coordination. *International Journal of the Addictions, 17*, 445–462.

Watson, P. E., Watson, I. D., & Batt, R. D. (1980). Total body water volumes for adult males and females estimated from simple anthropometric measurements. *American Journal of Clinical Nutrition, 33*, 27–29.

White, T. L., Justice, A. J. H., & de Wit, H. (2002). Differential subjective effects of d-amphetamine by gender, hormone levels and menstrual cycle phase. *Pharmacology, Biochemistry and Behavior, 73*, 729–741.

Willner, P., Field, M., Pitts, K., & Reeve, G. (1998). Mood, cue and gender influences on motivation, craving and liking for alcohol in recreational drinkers. *Behavioural Pharmacology, 9*, 631–642.

Zacny, J. P. (2001). Morphine responses in humans: A retrospective analysis of sex differences. *Drug and Alcohol Dependence, 63*, 23–28.

8

Subjective Effects of Opioids

SANDY M. COMER AND JAMES P. ZACNY

Opioids include both drugs derived from the poppy, *Papaver somniferum*, and drugs that are semisynthetic or synthetic, including hydromorphone, methadone, oxycodone, fentanyl, and butorphanol, to name but a few. Opium's active ingredients, which are responsible for analgesia and other effects, are morphine and codeine. Drugs derived from the poppy are called *opiates*. Drugs that have the same properties as opiates but are semisynthetic or synthetic are called *opioids*. In discussions of both natural opiates and opioids, the word *opioid* is used; we will follow this practice throughout this chapter.

Opioids have a fascinating history, and there is a rich literature on the many facets of these drugs. Some of those facets are briefly outlined here to put this chapter into historical context. Preserved remains of poppy seeds and pods from *Papaver somniferum* were found in Switzerland that dated to 4000 B.C.; it is thought that the opium from the pods was used for its analgesic properties and/or for religious ceremonies (Booth 1998). Hippocrates (ca. 460–377 B.C.), the father of Western medicine, used it to treat gynecological disorders but advised using it sparingly. Paracelsus, a Swiss physician-alchemist (1490–1541), is given credit for being the first to use laudanum (a pill of sorts containing opium and other psychoactive substances); Thomas Sydenham (1624–1689), an English physician regarded as the founder of clinical medicine, prepared it in a more controlled fashion, mixing a certain amount of opium with wine. Laudanum was widely used in England and America in the 1800s for both medical and nonmedical purposes and could be bought in a number of places, including pubs, bookshops, and general stores. Given its easy availability and its psychoactive properties (one of which is the subject of this chapter), not surprisingly, many people became addicted to the substance.

Friedrich Serturner, a German pharmacist's assistant, isolated morphine (named after Morpheus, the Greek god of dreams or sleep) from opium in 1805 or 1806. Morphine was used as a painkiller in several wars, including the American Civil War, and could be injected intravenously. The ability to administer the drug via this route was made possible by the invention of the hypodermic syringe in 1855 by a Scottish physician, Alexander Wood (1817–1884), and was "a turning point in not only medical but sociological history" (Booth, 1998, p. 71). One of the topics to be covered in this chapter is how the rate of onset of opioid effects can alter an opioid's abuse liability; the invention of the syringe is significant because this device provided the means to greatly increase the rate of onset of opioid effects.

Heroin was first synthesized in 1898 by the Bayer Company in Germany and was thought to be a solution to morphine addiction (known as *morphinism*). Laws were passed in the latter part of the nineteenth century and the early twentieth century in the United States (e.g., the Harrison Narcotic Act of 1914) and in other countries in an attempt to control the public health problem of widespread addiction to morphine and heroin. In the 1940s to the 1970s, studies were conducted in prisoner volunteers at the US Public Health Service Hospital's Addiction Research Center in Lexington, Kentucky, to assess abuse liability of new opioids that were being developed and being put on the market; these new opioids included methadone, meperidine, dextropropoxyphene, and others that have come to be known as mixed-action opioids. In the 1970s, the underlying mechanisms for opioid effects were first starting to be understood; during that decade opioid receptors and then the endogenous ligands that binded to the receptors were discovered. Methadone received approval from the U.S. government to be used as a pharmacotherapy for opioid addiction in the 1960s, based on the pioneering work by Vincent Dole and Marie Nyswander, but the treatment was delivered in state-run clinics and not by a doctor. In 2002, buprenorphine, a partial mu agonist, by itself or in combination with naloxone, was approved by the FDA as a pharmacotherapy that could be prescribed by a doctor.

The preceding account provides a context for understanding why it is important to study the subjective effects of opioids. Opioids, which have long been abused, are capable of producing euphoria and other "positive" subjective effects. Although the relationship between positive subjective effects and abuse of a drug is not necessarily causal, there is a predictive relationship between those drugs that produce a positive spectrum of subjective effects and their likelihood of functioning as reinforcers and being abused. A host of factors influence the subjective effects of opioids (and subsequently their abuse liability); some of the more salient ones will be covered in this chapter. We will first describe how subjective effects of opioids are measured and then discuss how such factors as dose, route of administration, rate of onset of drug effects, tolerance and dependence, and drug use history can all influence opioid subjective effects.

How Subjective Effects of Opioids Are Measured

We will briefly describe the instruments that have been and are being used to measure subjective effects of opioids. Also, we wish to refer the reader to a well-written and fascinating review article that traces the history of subjective effects testing of opioids (Jaffe & Jaffe, 1989). In the early 1900s, when new opioids were being developed, until about the early 1950s, subjective effects of opioids were largely inferred by patient studies that assessed side effects such as euphoria, nausea, pruritis, and sedation. Several experimental studies in this period examined the analgesic effects of opioids and briefly mentioned self-reports of subjects, but in a nonsystematic manner (Macht et al., 1916; Seevers & Pfeiffer, 1936; Brown, 1940; Wolff, Hardy, & Goodell, 1940; Kuhn & Bromiley, 1951; Lee & Pfeiffer, 1951; Kornetsky, Humphries, & Evarts, 1957). It is thought that one of the first questionnaires developed to assess subjective effects of opioids was by Louis Lasagna, Henry K. Beecher, and colleagues at Harvard University (Lasagna, von Felsinger, & Beecher, 1955). They used a 54-item, 7-point bipolar questionnaire with adjectives at either end of the scale, such as *sad-happy, physically energetic–physically lazy*, and *I would very much like to repeat this particular medication–I wouldn't like to go through this again*. The 54 items were grouped into three classifications: mood (which included assessment of euphoria and dysphoria), mentation, and sedation. This questionnaire or variants of it were used by this group in several other studies, but apparently it was not used by other researchers.

Another questionnaire, described in a research article by Fraser, van Horn, Martin, Wolbach, and Isbell (1961), and was called the Single Dose Questionnaire (SDQ). The SDQ was developed by Havelock F. Fraser and Harris Isbell at the Addiction Research Center in the Public Health Hospital in Lexington, Kentucky (Fraser et al., 1961). It was developed for experienced drug abusers and asked the subjects to (a) identify if they felt an effect, (b) identify the drug from a list of seven abused drugs (including the category of "other," (c) report if they experienced any of the 12 symptoms listed, and (d) rate their degree of liking for what had been administered to them on a scale of 0 (*not at all*) to 4 (*an awful lot*). This was the first subjective effects form designed to measure the abuse liability of opioids. In abuse liability testing, an opioid with unknown subjective effects is compared with a prototypic mu-opioid agonist with known abuse liability such as morphine; if the unknown opioid has the same profile and magnitude of subjective effects on the SDQ as morphine, the drug is considered to have the same degree of abuse liability (high) as morphine. There was also a form for observers to fill out at the same time subjects were filling out their questionnaire. The form was quite similar to the patient SDQ, but instead of rating "symptoms," the observers rated any observable "signs" of those symptoms. One interesting side note is that prior to the development of the SDQ, from 1948 to 1960, abuse liability studies did assess euphoria, a subjective effect that is thought to contribute to the abuse of a drug, but observers and not the subjects themselves assessed this measure. Trained observers looked for signs of euphoria, including increased talkativeness, boasting, greater ease in the experimental situation, and expression of satisfaction with the effects of the drug (Isbell, 1948). It is not clear how these behaviors were rated, but it appeared to lack the quantitative nature of the SDQ. The SDQ was widely used, and still is, often in variant form, in opioid characterization studies both in drug-abusing and in non-drug-abusing volunteers. One variant includes an adjective rating scale (Preston, Bigelow, Bickel, & Liebson, 1989) that consists of three scales: an Agonist scale (adjectives from the SDQ), an Antagonist scale (items derived from the Himmelsbach opiate withdrawal scale (Kolb & Himmelsbach, 1938), and a Mixed Agonist-Antagonist scale (describing side effects of these analgesics).

Another questionnaire designed to measure abuse liability of drugs was developed at the Addiction Research Center by Charles A. Haertzen, Harris E. Hill, and Richard E. Belleville in the early 1960s. The questionnaire, called the Addiction Research Center Inventory (ARCI), consisted of more than 500 true-false statements describing current affects, feelings, and perceptions. The statements were categorized into scales that had been empirically derived and were sensitive to the effects of various drug classes (Haertzen, Hill, & Belleville, 1963). The population used to develop the ARCI consisted of drug abusers who had extensive histories with various drugs of abuse. In 1971, Martin, Sloan, Sapira, and Jasinski published a paper in which they described a 49–item, short-form version of the ARCI consisting of six scales. Each scale was named after one or two drugs, and the statements associated with each scale were intended to reflect the effects that the drug(s) caused: Lysergic Diethylamide (LSD) scale, a measure of dysphoria and somatic and sensory disturbances; Morphine-Benzedrine Group (MBG), a measure of euphoria; Pentobarbital-Chlorpromazine-Alcohol Group (PCAG), a measure of sedation (sometimes called apathetic sedation); and two scales, the Amphetamine and Benzedrine Group scales, sensitive to stimulant effects. This short-form ARCI is widely used today in abuse liability testing.

Finally, a number of laboratories use visual analog scales (VASs), which can be either unipolar or bipolar. The particular VAS adjectives vary from laboratory to laboratory; there is no common VAS that is used in subjective effects testing of opioids.

In addition to questionnaires, another method that is increasingly used to assess the interoceptive effects of opioids in humans is the drug discrimination procedure. This procedure was initially developed in laboratory animals and has been used extensively to characterize the effects of opioid drugs. Briefly, in the drug discrimination procedure, subjects are trained to make one response following administration of drug and another response following administration of placebo. During the training period, correct responses are reinforced with either food (animals) or money (humans), and incorrect responses are not reinforced. After subjects learn the discrimination, a testing period begins, during which either a new drug or different doses of the training drug are tested. Responding under test conditions is reinforced regardless of the response that is made. Generally, drugs that produce their effects through the same receptor class as the training drug produce "drug-appropriate responding" or are identified as the training drug (refer to Preston & Bigelow, 1991, for a more in-depth discussion of the nuances of this procedure). This procedure has been a powerful tool for examining the effects of various opioids in both humans (e.g., Bickel, Bigelow, Preston, & Liebson, 1989; Preston et al., 1989; Preston & Bigelow, 2000; Oliveto, Sevarino, McCance-Katz, & Feingold, 2002) and laboratory animals (e.g., Comer et al., 1993; Butelman et al., 2001; Walker & Young, 2002; Holtzman, 2003). In humans, the discriminative stimulus effects of opioids have been demonstrated to correlate well with subjective effects (Bickel et al., 1989).

Dose

As with most psychoactive drugs, subjective responses generally increase in a linear, dose-related fashion after administration of opioid agonists. That is, the magnitude of subjective responses increases with increasing dose. However, there are some exceptions to this general finding. Some opioids, such as nalbuphine and buprenorphine, produce increases in subjective responses up to a certain dose, above which further increases in dose fail to produce further increases in subjective responses (Jasinski & Mansky, 1972; Pickworth, Johnson, Holicky, & Cone, 1993; Walsh, Preston, Stitzer, Cone, & Bigelow, 1994; Walsh, Preston, Bigelow, & Stitzer, 1995b; Comer, Collins, & Fischman, 2002; Comer & Collins, 2002). By definition, these opioids are considered to be partial agonists. They have the interesting characteristic of simultaneously producing positive subjective responses on their own and having the ability to antagonize the effects of other opioid agonists. In the case of buprenorphine, this feature serves a dual purpose in terms of its utility as a treatment medication for opioid dependence: The positive subjective responses produced by buprenorphine enhance medication compliance, but the drug's antagonist effects may contribute to its therapeutic usefulness in reducing heroin use.

Route of Administration

Like other drugs of abuse, opioids can be ingested in a variety of ways, including orally, sublingually, intranasally, intravenously, intramuscularly, and subcutaneously. Heroin vapors can also be inhaled through a heated pipe, on a cigarette, or on tinfoil (Mo & Way, 1966; Jenkins, Keenan, Henningfield, & Cone, 1994; Hendriks, van den Brink, Blanken, Bosman, & van Ree, 2001). Until recently, heroin was predominantly used intravenously in the United States, but recent increases in purity and decreases in the cost of street heroin, combined with a fear of transmitting communicable diseases through shared needles, have led to an increase in intranasal heroin use. The impact of route of administration on subjective responses can be both quantitative and qualitative. For example, in a study by Comer, Collins, MacArthur, & Fischman (1999), both intranasal and intravenous heroin produced dose-related increases in ratings of "high," "good drug effect," "quality of drug," "drug liking," "drug potency," "mellow," "sedated," and "stimulated," but the potency of heroin via the intranasal route was fourfold less than for the intravenous route. The only subjective effects for which there seemed to be qualitative differences as a function of route of administration were ratings of "nodding" and "itchy skin." For these measures, intravenous heroin produced significant increases in ratings, but intranasal heroin generally did not. Other studies comparing different routes of administration for other opioids, such as buprenorphine, have found similar quantitative differences as a function of route of administration (e.g., Jasinski, Fudala, & Johnson, 1989).

Rate of Onset of Drug Effects

Although results from the studies summarized here suggest that similar profiles of subjective effects are produced for opioids administered via different routes, one variable that has not been addressed earlier in the chapter but that is generally believed to influence the abuse liability of a drug is rate of onset of drug effects. That is, drugs or routes of drug administration that produce faster rates of onset to the brain are generally believed to have greater abuse liability. In a study designed to examine the influence of rate of onset of drug effects, Marsch et al. (2001) showed that, in normal healthy volunteers, faster infusion rates of intravenously delivered morphine resulted in greater positive subjective effects ("good drug effect," drug "liking," and "high") than did lower infusion rates. To the extent that subjective responses predict abuse liability, these results are consistent with the notion that faster rates of onset are correlated with greater abuse liability. However, some research findings are not consistent with this hypothesis. For example, Abreu, Bigelow, Fleisher, and Walsh (2001) showed that whereas the subjective effects of cocaine varied as a function of infusion duration, those of hydromorphone did not. The inconsistency between the studies conducted by Abreu et al. (2001) and Marsch et al. (2001) was possibly due to the fact that smaller differences in infusion durations (2, 15, and 60 seconds) were used by Abreu and colleagues (2001) than the infusion durations (2, 15, and 60 minutes) used by Marsch et al. (2001). Nevertheless, it is interesting that differences in subjective effects were obtained for cocaine but not for hydromorphone (Abreu et al. 2001), using the same infusion durations, suggesting that the particular drug being tested may be an important variable. Further research on the influence of rate of onset of drug effect should be conducted to more fully characterize the conditions under which this variable plays a role in the subjective effects and perhaps abuse liability of a drug.

Another variable that has recently received experimental attention is the effect of duration of action on subjective responses. Baylon, Kaplan, Somer, Busto, and Sellers (2000) compared the subjective and physiological effects of intravenously administered remifentanil and fentanyl, opioid agonists with short and longer durations of action, respectively. For the majority of subjective effects measured during the first 3 minutes after drug administration, remifentanil and fentanyl produced comparable peak ratings, up to the maximal tolerated doses of each drug. For effects measured more than 5 minutes after drug administration, fentanyl produced more robust effects than remifentanil, which is not surprising, given fentanyl's longer duration of action. Because these researchers did not ask participants which drug they preferred, and drug self-administration was not examined, it is difficult to determine from this study whether duration of action is an important variable in abuse liability. However, a study conducted by Ko, Terner, Hursh, Woods, and Winger (2002) in rhesus monkeys, comparing the reinforcing effects of remifentanil, alfentanil, and fentanyl, demonstrated that duration of action is not a critical variable in a drug's reinforcing strength.

Tolerance and Dependence

In addition to dose, route of administration, and rate of onset of drug effects, another important variable affecting the subjective effects of opioids is whether the opioid was experienced acutely or repeatedly. Tolerance, or a reduced effect after repeated administration of a given dose of drug, has been demonstrated for a variety of opioids. Tolerance is also manifested as a need for increasing doses of drug to maintain a constant level of effect. This phenomenon was demonstrated in a naturalistic study of "re-addiction" to morphine by an abstinent, formerly opioid-dependent individual who participated in the study while incarcerated in a state penitentiary (Wikler, 1952). Over the course of this study, the participant increased his daily morphine dose from 30 to 1,380 mg per day over a period of approximately 6 months. Numerous other studies have examined the effects of single versus repeated opioid administration. For example, Martin and colleagues (1973) compared the effects of single and repeated doses of methadone in individuals who were non–opioid dependent at the beginning of the study. Although single doses of methadone significantly increased positive subjective ratings, such as drug "liking," and MBG scores on the ARCI, chronic methadone administration increased negative subjective ratings, such as "lethargy," "weakness," "unmotivated," and PCAG scores on the ARCI and simultaneously decreased many positive subjective ratings. Similar results were obtained for other opioids, including morphinan, 6-methyldihydromorphine, and dihydrocodeinone (hydrocodone; Fraser & Isbell, 1950). Interestingly, at extremely high doses, chronic administration of both heroin and morphine produced reduced euphoria and increased aversive effects consistent with a histamine reaction, including severe itching, flushing, swelling, headache, pain/nausea, and general malaise, among other symptoms (Haemmig & Tschacher, 2001). These effects were much more pronounced with morphine than with heroin, which was surprising given the general belief that heroin's pharmacological effects are predominantly mediated via its metabolism to morphine. These results underscore the need for more careful evaluations and comparisons of the effects of various opioid agonists.

Following chronic administration of opioids, physical dependence develops, which is revealed following discontinuation of drug administration, a reduction in the usual dose administered, or administration of an opioid antagonist. Symptoms of opioid withdrawal have been well characterized and include sweating, runny nose, sneezing, watery eyes, nausea, vomiting, stomach pain, diarrhea, gooseflesh, hot/cold flashes, decreased appetite, increased pupil size, muscle pain, restlessness, insomnia, irritability, and anxiety (e.g., Kolb & Himmelsbach, 1938). In general, readministration of an opioid agonist can reverse the symptoms of withdrawal. When the opioid used to reverse withdrawal is different from the opioid used to maintain dependence, then cross-tolerance or cross-dependence is said to exist between the two drugs. This phenomenon has been demonstrated with a number of opioids, including morphine, hydrocodone, codoxime, morphinan, hydromorphone, levo-alpha-acetylmethadol (LAAM), and methadone (Fraser & Isbell, 1950; Houtsmuller et al., 1998; Jasinski & Martin, 1967), among others.

In addition to reversing symptoms of withdrawal, another feature of cross-tolerance/dependence is that a reduced effect is obtained when an opioid agonist, such as heroin, is administered while an individual is maintained on an opioid, such as methadone. Donny, Walsh, Bigelow, Eissenberg, and Stitzer (2002), for example, demonstrated that increasing doses of methadone maintenance (30, 60, 120 mg per day) produced dose-related decreases in heroin's subjective and physiological effects, providing an empirical demonstration of the clinical observation that high doses of methadone are needed to suppress heroin's effects. Similar results were obtained when participants were maintained on ascending doses of morphine (Schuh, Walsh, Bigelow, Preston, & Stitzer, 1996). Subjective and physiological effects were reduced in a morphine maintenance dose-related manner after acute administration of morphine.

Although full opioid agonists are generally cross-tolerant to other full opioid agonists and are able to alleviate symptoms of withdrawal in dependent individuals, the effects of partial opioid agonists, such as buprenorphine, are more variable. Several studies in opioid-dependent laboratory animals have shown that buprenorphine precipitates and/ or exacerbates withdrawal (Woods & Gmerek, 1985; Woods, France, & Winger, 1992; Yanagita, Katoh, Wakasa, & Oinuma, 1982). In humans, the ability of buprenorphine to precipitate withdrawal in opioid-dependent humans is less clear. Buprenorphine precipitates moderate to severe withdrawal in patients maintained on 60-mg methadone (Walsh, June, et al., 1995). In contrast, buprenorphine (2–8 mg s.l.) produced either no, or mild, withdrawal in patients maintained on lower doses of methadone (25–30 mg) or in heroin-dependent individuals (Kosten & Kleber, 1988; Kosten, Morgan, & Kleber, 1991; Strain, Preston, Liebson, & Bigelow, 1992; Walsh, June, et al., 1995). In fact, buprenorphine significantly increased ratings of "good effects" and feelings of "overall well-being" and decreased ratings of "overall sickness" by heroin-dependent men who received increasing doses of buprenorphine during a rapid dose induction onto buprenorphine maintenance (Johnson et al., 1989). In this study, buprenorphine was consistently identified as an opioid agonist rather than an antagonist. Intravenous administration of buprenorphine (2 mg) to heroin-dependent individuals also increased ratings of "good effects" and drug "liking," without precipitating withdrawal (Mendelson et al., 1996). Intramuscular administration of buprenorphine (6 mg) to individuals maintained on intramuscular morphine also failed to precipitate withdrawal (Schuh et al., 1996). In this study, when participants were maintained on low doses of morphine (15 or 30 mg/day), buprenorphine significantly increased ratings of "high," "good effects," and "liking." However, buprenorphine's subjective effects did not significantly differ from placebo in individuals maintained on 60 or 120 mg/day (i.m.) morphine. In addition to the maintenance drug and maintenance dose, the time since the last dose of the maintenance drug also appears to be an important factor in the ability of buprenorphine to precipitate withdrawal. Withdrawal occurred in patients maintained on 30–mg methadone when buprenorphine was administered 2 hours, but not 20 hours, after the last methadone dose (Strain et al., 1992; Strain, Preston, Liebson, & Bigelow, 1995). These studies suggest that induction onto buprenorphine from either heroin or low-dose methadone would be acceptable to most individuals. The ability of buprenorphine to precipitate withdrawal or produce opioid agonist effects depends on the buprenorphine dose, the maintenance drug (heroin/morphine versus methadone), the maintenance dose, and the time since the last maintenance dose.

In contrast to the variable effects of acute buprenorphine administration in methadone-, morphine-, or heroin-dependent individuals, maintenance on buprenorphine itself produces mostly consistent effects. That is, a variety of studies have demonstrated that buprenorphine maintenance produces a dose-related but incomplete blockade of the effects of full mu agonists, such as heroin and hydromorphone (Bickel et al., 1988; Comer et al., 2001; Greenwald, Schuh, Hopper, Schuster, & Johanson, 2002; Rosen et al., 1994). One exception to this finding is a study conducted by Mello and colleagues (Mello & Mendelson, 1980; Mello, Mendelson, & Kuehnle, 1982), who showed that intravenous heroin self-administration was almost completely blocked by buprenorphine, relative to placebo. The effects of acute administration of buprenorphine itself in buprenorphine-maintained individuals are also somewhat variable, with some studies showing that parenteral administration of buprenorphine produced typical opioid agonist effects (Strain, Walsh, Preston, Liebson, & Bigelow, 1997) and other studies showing a complete lack of reinforcing effects (Amass, Kamien, Reiber, & Branstetter, 2000).

For other partial opioid agonists, such as nalbuphine, the pharmacological profile is more straightforward. As noted earlier, nalbuphine given acutely to non-opioid-dependent individuals produces subjective and physiological effects that are less robust than morphine or other full mu agonists (Jasinski & Mansky, 1972; Preston & Bigelow, 2000; Schmidt et al., 1985). However, when given to opioid-dependent individuals, nalbuphine clearly and consistently elicits a withdrawal reaction (Schmidt et al., 1985; Jasinski & Mansky, 1972; Oliveto et al., 2002; Preston et al., 1989).

Drug Use History

Many studies have examined opioid subjective effects in opioid abusers; this is not surprising, because abuse liability testing, which includes the assessment of subjective effects, should be conducted in a population most likely to abuse opioids. However, a number of studies in the literature have also examined subjective effects of opioids in "healthy volunteers" or "normal subjects." These terms are problematic: the first category could also include opioid abusers, and the second term is pejorative. We will use the term *non-drug-abusing volunteers*. In 1955, Louis Lasagna and his colleagues conducted one of the first studies that examined the role of drug history in the subjective effects of opioids. This study is considered a classic because it used self-reports of subjects in addition to observer ratings. More recent studies also will be discussed, demonstrating the extent to which drug use history impacts on subjective effects of opioids.

After its publication and to this day (e.g., Griffiths, Bigelow, & Ator, 2003), the Lasagna et al. (1955) study has been cited as evidence that non–drug abusers do not usually feel pleasant effects from opioids. At the time of this research in 1955, the authors stated that the prevailing notion in pharmacology textbooks was that euphoria was a common side effect of opioids. In a pilot study alluded to by Lasagna et al. (1955), the authors noted a distinct absence of pleasant effects or euphoria in non-drug-abusing volunteers. The authors followed up the pilot work with the larger study that is described here. Three groups were studied: 30 drug abusers, 20 non–drug abusers, and 30 patients (all of whom had chronic pain). The reactions of the patients will be discussed briefly after describing the reactions of the other two groups. The drug abusers, all male, were studied in a group setting at the Addiction Research Center in Lexington. The non–drug abusers, all male, were studied in a solitary setting in a clinical environment in a hospital in Boston, Massachusetts. The study was a placebo-controlled, double-blind crossover trial. The drugs studied were saline, pentobarbital, amphetamine, heroin, and morphine. We will focus on placebo and the opioids that were administered subcutanously.

Two doses of heroin and morphine were studied in the non-drug-abusing and drug-abusing volunteers (doses adjusted for body weight differences); approximately half of the volunteers in each group received the lower dose, and the other half received the higher dose. Heroin doses were 2 and 4 mg in the non-drug-abusing volunteers and 4 and 6 mg in the drug-abusing volunteers. Morphine doses were 8 and 15 mg in the non-drug-abusing volunteers and 15 and 22.5 mg in the drug-abusing volunteers. A 54-item subjective effects questionnaire (described earlier) was administered at baseline and again 0.5, 1, and 2 hours after drug injection. At the end of the session, subjects were asked to write down in their own words a description of the effects of the drug and to indicate whether they would like to repeat the experience. Briefly, the authors concluded that in the non-drug-abusing volunteers, morphine and heroin were considered to be unpleasant in the majority of subjects tested, and that lower doses produced less dysphoria. In drug-abusing volunteers, morphine but not heroin was considered to be pleasant in the majority of subjects tested, and increasing the morphine and heroin doses, if anything, reduced the percentage of subjects reporting pleasant effects. There were few side effects from the opioids in this group, perhaps due to tolerance development to these effects.

The fact that the majority of subjects in the drug-abusing group did not report pleasant effects from heroin was attributed to dose (perhaps too low) and route of administration (subcutaneous vs. a preferred route, intravenous). As discussed earlier, both of these factors can indeed affect subjective effects. The rather broad conclusion that "morphine and heroin, in the described situation and doses, were not pleasant drugs to the majority of subjects" (referring to non–drug abusers) has been called into question (MacAuliffe, 1975). Briefly, the manner in which the subjective effects questionnaire data were analyzed categorized subjects as experiencing only euphoria or dysphoria or neutrality when in fact subjects could have been experiencing both pleasant and unpleasant effects during the opioid sessions. A closer look at postsession comments indicated that there were as many subjects who reported the effects of the opioids as pleasant, neutral, or a combination of pleasant and unpleasant as those who reported primarily unpleasant effects. Finally, when asked if they would like to repeat the experience, about half of the non–drug abusers reported they would like to repeat the sessions or that they were indifferent. Thus, the conclusions drawn from the Lasagna et al. (1955) study do not exactly match the results that were obtained (cf. MacAuliffe 1975). What can be said is that, especially with morphine, there was more intersubject variability in the non-drug-abusing group than in the abusing group on how many subjects found the drug effects to be pleasant.

The collection of data was less systematic in the chronic pain patient group because some individuals could not complete the questionnaire. Only a few individuals in this group reported what has come to be known as a positive euphoric reaction, and most of them reported a negative euphoric reaction. Essentially, negative euphoria is reminiscent of negative reinforcement—the drugs were perceived as pleasant because they reduced pain. Positive euphoria is measured on the MBG scale of the ARCI. The notion that patients in pain do not experience euphoria (i.e., positive euphoria) has been noted by clinicians (cf. Jaffe, 1989), but more systematic research needs to be done in this area.

The Lasagna et al. (1955) study is one of few that have examined, within the same study, the reactions of drug abusers and non–drug abusers to opioids. In a more recent study that had as its primary focus the development of acute physical dependence, 20 non–drug abusers and 20 abusers received intramuscular injections of 0.21 mg/kg morphine (Azorlosa, Stitzer, & Greenwald, 1994). Two variants of the SDQ were used to measure the subjective effects of morphine in the two groups. Opioid abusers reported higher ratings of drug liking and "good drug effect" than did non–drug abusers. Opioid abusers had lower ratings of "coasting" and "tired or sluggish" than did the non–drug abusers.

A number of studies have examined opioid effects in non–drug abusers only, and other studies have examined responses of opioid abusers. The effects of drug history can be assessed by examining such studies because they used one or more of the same subjective effects testing forms. Tables 8.1 and 8.2 show the responses of non–drug abusers and opioid abusers to several mu-opioid agonists and mixed-action opioid agonists, respectively. It should be pointed out that the non-drug-abusing studies used the intravenous route of administration and the opioid abuser studies used either the subcutaneous or intramuscular route. As discussed earlier, route of administration can be a factor in subjective effects produced by a drug. Also, the doses of a drug tested are lower in non–drug abuser studies than in opioid abuser studies. Keeping these caveats in mind, one can see that tables 8.1 and 8.2 clearly show some differences between the two groups.

With mu-opioid agonists, MBG scores were reliably increased in the opioid abuser studies, but PCAG and LSD scores showed no change relative to control conditions. In contrast, non–drug abusers rarely showed increases in scores on the MBG scale but reliably showed increases in scores on the PCAG and LSD scales. The increase in MBG scores in the morphine study was small, and in a number of subsequent studies in which 10 mg of morphine has been used as a comparator drug to another opioid, increases have not been observed on this scale (e.g., Zacny, Conley, & Marks, 1997; Zacny, Conley, & Galinkin, 1997). "Liking" scores were consistently increased in opioid abuser studies, and sometimes in non–drug abuser studies. In non–drug abusers within each of the studies, there tended to be intersubject variability on this measure, with some subjects reporting liking, some expressing neutrality, and some reporting both liking and disliking (at different times within a session). With respect to those items of the SDQ that were administered to both abusers and nonabusers, there were some differences as well as similarities between the two groups. Opioid abusers were more likely than non–drug abusers to report increases in "turning of stomach" and "skin itchy" and less likely to report increases in "sleepy" and "drunken." In both groups, there was a consistent increase in the rating of "coasting" with the four opioids tested. This term has also been defined as "spaced out" (e.g., Preston et al., 1989) in variants of the SDQ, and this is how we defined it for our nonabusing subjects. With respect to the four opioids tested, there was a similar pattern of responses, which was most apparent in the opioid abusers. The exception was with the drug meperidine. In opioid abusers, ratings of "sleepy" were increased after administration of meperidine but not after administration of the other mu-opioid agonists. This effect could be related to meperidine's anticholinergic properties (Batterman, 1943). Anticholinergics at clinically relevant doses typically produce drowsiness (e.g., Sannita, Maggi, & Rosadini, 1987).

Table 8.2 shows responses of the opioid abusers and nonabusers to four mixed-action opioid agonists. These drugs differ from mu-opioid agonists predominantly because they have lesser efficacy (on several

Table 8.1. Selected subjective effects of mu-agonist opioids in non–drug abusers and opioid abusers

Drug	Morphine		Meperidine		Hydromorphone		Fentanyl	
Volunteer status*	no ab[1]	ab[2]	no ab[3]	ab[4]	noab[5]	ab[6]	no ab[7]	ab[8]
Route of administration	iv	sc	iv	im	iv	sc	iv	im
Doses tested (mg)	2.5–10†	7.5–30	17.5–70†	75–300†	0.33–1.3†	1.5–6	0.05, 0.1†	0.4–1.6†
Subjective effect								
Drug liking	⇑⇓	⇑	⇑	⇑	⇑	⇑	⇓	⇑
ARCI								
MBG	⇑	⇑	—	⇑	—	⇑	—	NM
PCAG	⇑	—	⇑	—	⇑	—	⇑	NM
LSD	⇑	—	⇑	—	⇑	—	⇑	NM
SDQ								
Turning of stomach	—	⇑	—	⇑	—	NR	⇑	⇑
Skin itchy	—	⇑	⇑	⇑	⇑	NR	⇑	⇑
Coasting	—	⇑	⇑	⇑	—	NR	⇑	⇑
Drive	—	—	⇑	⇑	—	NR	|	—
Sleepy	—	—	⇑	⇑	⇑	NR	⇑	—
Drunken	—	—	⇑	—	⇑	NR	⇑	—

*No ab: non-drug-abusing volunteer; ab: drug-abusing volunteer.
†Doses were adjusted for body weight on a mg/kg basis; doses shown are for a 70-kg individual.
NM = not measured; short form of the ARCI had not been developed yet.
NR = not reported; only global ratings of the SDQ were reported.

[1]Zacny, Lichtor, Flemming, et al., 1994; [2]Jasinski et al., 1975; [3]Zacny et al., 1993; [4]Jasinski & Preston, 1986; [5]Hill & Zacny, 2000; [6]Jasinski et al., 1977; [7]Zacny et al., 1992; [8]Gorodetsky & Martin, 1965.

Table 8.2. Selected subjective effects of mixed-action opioids in non–drug abusers and opioid abusers

Drug	Butorphanol		Nalbuphine		Pentazocine		Buprenorphine	
Volunteer status*	no ab[1]	ab[2]	no ab[3]	ab[4]	no ab[5]	ab[6]	no ab[7]	ab[8]**
Route of administration	iv	im	iv	sc	iv	sc	iv	sc
Doses tested (mg)	0.5–2†	2–8	2.5–10†	8–72†	7.5–30†	10–60†	0.75–0.3†	0.2–2
Subjective effects								
Drug liking	⇐	⇐	⇑⇓	⇐	⇑⇓	⇐	⇑⇓	⇐
ARCI								
MBG	—	—	⇐	⇐	—	⇐	—	⇐
PCAG	⇐	⇐	⇐	⇐	⇐	⇐	⇐	—
LSD	⇐	⇐	⇐	⇐	⇐	⇐	⇐	—
SDQ								
Turning of stomach	⇐	—	—	⇐	⇐	⇐	⇐	⇐
Skin itchy	⇐	⇐	—	⇐	—	⇐	⇐	⇐
Coasting	⇐	⇐	⇐	⇐	⇐	⇐	⇐	⇐
Drive	—	—	—	—	—	—	—	—
Sleepy	⇐	⇐	⇐	⇐	⇐	⇐	⇐	—
Drunken	⇐	⇐	⇐	⇐	⇐	⇐	⇐	—

*No ab: non-drug-abusing volunteer; ab: drug-abusing volunteer.

†Doses were adjusted for body weight on a mg/kg basis; doses shown are for a 70-kg individual.

**Data are derived from two studies (Studies 1 and 4) from Jasinski et al., 1978.

[1]Zacny, Lichtor, Flemming, et al., 1994; [2]Jasinski et al., 1975; [3]Zacny Conley, & Marks, 1997a; [4]Jasinski & Mansky, 1972; [5]Zacny et al., 1998; [6]Jasinski et al., 1970; [7]Zacny Conley, & Galinkin, 1997; [8]Jasinski et al., 1978.

end points, including analgesia) at the mu receptor (some of them are known as partial mu agonists) and because some of them have agonist properties at the kappa receptor. Thus, as will be discussed shortly, one might expect differences in subjective effects between mu-opioid and mixed-action agonists. As to comparing the effects of these drugs between abusers and nonabusers, the drugs tended to produce increases in scores on the MBG scale of the ARCI (with the exception of butorphanol) in opioid abusers, and this was less likely to occur in nonabusers (with the exception of nalbuphine). Both groups tended to show increases in scores on the PCAG and LSD scales, although these scores were increased in opioid abusers only when the nalbuphine and pentazocine doses were high. There was uniform drug liking reported by opioid abusers after administration of the mixed-action agonists, but with nonabusers, the pattern of both liking and disliking was apparent. Both groups reliably reported increases in the rating of "coasting," just as with the mu-opioid agonists in table 8.1. Both abusers and nonabusers reported increases in the ratings of "sleepy" and "drunken" with butorphanol, nalbuphine, and pentazocine. "Skin itchy" ratings were increased only in opioid abusers after administration of nalbuphine and pentazocine. This difference may be a function of the higher doses tested in the opioid-abusing volunteers. When comparing the four mixed-action opioids, there was little difference between them in the opioid abusers with the exception of buprenorphine. Unlike the other mixed-action agonists, buprenorphine did not increase scores on the PCAG and LSD scales of the ARCI and did not increase SDQ ratings of "sleepy" and "drunken."

Differences in subjective effects between the two classes of opioids can be found by examining tables 8.1 and 8.2. The differences are most apparent in the responses of opioid abusers. Briefly, the mixed-action opioids, with the exception of buprenorphine, produced increases in scores on PCAG and LSD scales, as well as increases in "sleepy" ratings from the SDQ. The differences are most likely due to the kappa agonist properties of these drugs. A recent study showed that a pure kappa agonist, enadoline, produced increased scores on the PCAG and LSD scales of the ARCI (Walsh, Strain, Abreu, & Bigelow, 2001). The drug also did not increase liking scores but increased the rating of "bad effects" and produced psychotomimetic effects. At high doses, the drugs pentazocine and nalbuphine, and to a lesser extent butorphanol, have been shown to produce psychotomimetic effects in some opioid abusers (cf. Reisine & Pasternak, 1996).

Conclusions and Future Directions

The subjective effects of many parenteral opioids have been well characterized in both non–drug abusers and opioid abusers and have been

SUBJECTIVE EFFECTS OF OPIOIDS 233

shown to vary as a function of several important variables such as dose, route of administration, and state of tolerance or dependence. Less well characterized are prescription oral opioids, especially in drug abusers. Two of the more frequently abused prescription opioids are hydrocodone- and oxycodone-containing products, but to our knowledge, no published peer-reviewed studies have examined the subjective effects of these oral drugs in abusers. Such studies are important because these drugs and others (e.g., hydromorphone) are abused throughout the world, and recently the nonmedical use and abuse of prescription opioids have shown a marked increased in the United States (Zacny et al., 2003).

Another area that needs to be explored is how patients in pain experience the effects of different opioids. This is an important population to study because patients in pain are probably the largest consumers of opioids. It is unclear how the subjective effects of opioids in abusers relate to subjective effects in a patient population. Likewise, trying to generalize from studies examining opioid effects in non-drug-abusing volunteers may be inappropriate because the volunteers are not in pain. Pain may act as a "natural antagonist" of opioid subjective effects, and in fact there is evidence for such a notion (Conley, Toledano, Apfelbaum, & Zacny, 1997). Designing studies that examine subjective effects of opioids in patients will present a challenge for researchers because it may be difficult to include placebo controls, to study a range of drug doses, and to use forms that are currently used to assess subjective effects. Further, patients can be in acute pain or chronic pain, have accompanying psychiatric morbidities, and be either non-drug abusers or drug abusers. Although there are many complexities involved in conducting such research, the clinical importance of such studies necessitates the effort.

The preparation of this chapter was funded in part by USPHS grants R01 DA10909 (SDC) and R37 DA08573 (JPZ).

References

Abreu, M. E., Bigelow, G. E., Fleisher, L., & Walsh, S. L. (2001). Effect of intravenous injection. *Psychopharmacology, 154*, 76–84.

Amass, L., Kamien, J. B., Reiber, C., & Branstetter, S. A. (2000). Abuse liability of IV buprenorphine-naloxone, buprenorphine, and hydromorphone in buprenorphine-naloxone maintained volunteers. *Drug and Alcohol Dependence, 60*, S6–S7.

Azorlosa, J. L., Stitzer, M. L., & Greenwald, M. K. (1994). Opioid physical dependence development, effects of single versus repeated morphine pretreatments and of subjects' opioid exposure history. *Psychopharmacology, 114*, 71–80.

Batterman, R. C. (1943). Clinical effectiveness and safety of a new synthetic analgesic drug, demerol. *Archives of Internal Medicine, 71*, 345–356.

Baylon, G. J., Kaplan, H. L., Somer, G., Busto, U. E., & Sellers, E. M. (2000). Comparative abuse liability of intravenously administered remifentanil and fentanyl. *Journal of Clinical Psychopharmacology, 20*, 597–606.

Bickel, W. K., Bigelow, G. E., Preston, K. L., & Liebson, I. A. (1989). Opioid drug discrimination in humans, stability, specificity and relation to self-reported drug effect. *Journal of Pharmacology and Experimental Therapeutics, 251*, 1053–1063.

Bickel, W. K., Stitzer, M. L., Bigelow, G. E., Liebson, I. A., Jasinski, D. R., & Johnson, R. E. (1988). Buprenorphine, dose-related blockade of opioid challenge effects in opioid dependent humans. *Journal of Pharmacology and Experimental Therapeutics, 247*, 47–53.

Booth, M. (1998). *Opium: A history.* New York: St. Martin's.

Brown, R. R. (1940). The order of certain psycho-physiological events following intravenous injections of morphine. *Journal of General Psychology, 22*, 321–340.

Butelman, E. R., Ko, M. C., Traynor, J. R., Vivian, J. A., Kreek, M. J., & Woods, J. H. (2001). GR89,696, a potent kappa-opioid agonist with subtype selectivity in rhesus monkeys. *Journal of Pharmacology and Experimental Therapeutics, 298*, 1049–1059.

Comer, S. D., & Collins, E. D. (2002). Self-administration of intravenous buprenorphine and the buprenorphine/naloxone combination by recently detoxified heroin abusers. *Journal of Pharmacology and Experimental Therapeutics, 303*, 695–703.

Comer, S. D., Collins, E. D., & Fischman, M. W. (2001). Buprenorphine sublingual tablets, effects on IV heroin self-administration by humans. *Psychopharmacology, 154*, 28–37.

Comer, S. D., Collins, E. D., & Fischman, M. W. (2002). Intravenous buprenorphine self-administration by detoxified heroin abusers. *Journal of Pharmacology and Experimental Therapeutics, 301*, 266–276.

Comer, S. D., Collins, E. D., MacArthur, R. B. & Fischman, M. W. (1999). Comparison of intranasal and intravenous heroin self-administration by morphine-maintained humans. *Psychopharmacology, 143*, 327–338.

Comer, S. D., McNutt, R. W., Chang, K. J., De Costa, B. R., Mosberg, H. I., & Woods, J. H. (1993).Discriminative stimulus effects of BW373U86, a nonpeptide ligand with selectivity for delta opioid receptors. *Journal of Pharmacology and Experimental Therapeutics, 267*, 866–874.

Conley, K. M., Toledano, A. Y., Apfelbaum, J. L., & Zacny, J. P. (1997). The modulating effects of a cold water stimulus on opioid effects in volunteers. *Psychopharmacology, 131*, 313–320.

Donny, E. C., Walsh, S. L., Bigelow, G. E., Eissenberg, T., & Stitzer, M. L. (2002). High-dose methadone produces superior opioid blockade and comparable withdrawal suppression to lower doses in opioid-dependent humans. *Psychopharmacology, 161*, 202–212.

Fraser H, F., & Isbell, H. (1950). Addiction liabilities of morphinan, 6-methyldihydro-morphine and dihydrocodeinone. *Journal of Pharmacology and Experimental Therapeutics, 100*, 128–135.

Fraser, H. F., van Horn, G. D., Martin, W. R., Wolbach, A. B., & Isbell, H. (1961). Methods for evaluating addiction liability. (A). "Attitude" of opiate addicts toward opiate-like drugs, (B). a short-term "direct" addiction test. *Journal of Pharmacology and Experimental Therapeutics, 133*, 371–387.

Gorodetzky, C. W., & Martin, W. R. (1965). A comparison of fentanyl, droperidol, and morphine. *Clinical Pharmacology and Therapeutics, 6,* 731–739.

Greenwald, M. K., Schuh, K. J., Hopper, J. A., Schuster, C. R., & Johanson, C. E. (2002). Effects of buprenorphine sublingual tablet maintenance on opioid drug-seeking behavior by humans. *Psychopharmacology, 160,* 344–352.

Griffiths, R. R., Bigelow, G. E., & Ator, N. A. (2003). Principles of initial experimental drug abuse liability assessment in humans. *Drug and Alcohol Dependence, 70,* S41–S54.

Haemmig, R. B., & Tschacher, W. (2001). Effects of high-dose heroin versus morphine in intravenous drug users: A randomised double-blind crossover study. *Journal of Psychoactive Drugs, 33,* 105–110

Haertzen, C. A., Hill, H. E., & Belleville, R. E. (1963). Development of the Addiction Research Center Inventory (ARCI): Selection of items that are sensitive to the effects of various drugs. *Psychopharmacologia, 4,* 155–166.

Hendriks, V. M., van den Brink, W., Blanken, P., Bosman, I. J., & van Ree, J. M. (2001). Heroin self-administration by means of "chasing the dragon," pharmacodynamics and bioavailability of inhaled heroin. *European Neuropsychopharmacology, 11,* 241–252.

Hill, J. L., & Zacny, J. P. (2000). Comparing the subjective, psychomotor, and physiological effects of intravenous hydromorphone and morphine in normal volunteers. *Psychopharmacology, 152,* 31–39.

Holtzman, S. G. (2003). Discrimination of a single dose of morphine followed by naltrexone: Substitution of other agonists for morphine and other antagonists for naltrexone in a rat model of acute dependence. *Journal of Pharmacology and Experimental Therapeutics, 304,* 1033–1041.

Houtsmuller, E. J., Walsh, S. L., Schuh, K. J., Johnson, R. E., Stitzer, M. L., & Bigelow, G. E. (1998). Dose-response analysis of opioid cross-tolerance and withdrawal suppression during LAAM maintenance. *Journal of Pharmacology and Experimental Therapeutics, 285,* 387–396.

Isbell, H. (1948). Methods and results of studying experimental human addiction to the newer synthetic analgesics. *Annals of the New York Academy of Sciences, 51,* 108–122.

Jaffe, J. H. (1989). Misinformation, euphoria and addiction. In C. S. Hill & W. S. Fields, (Eds.), *Advances in Pain Research and Therapy, 11,* 163–174. Lipincott, Williams, and Wilkins: Baltimore.

Jaffe, J. H., & Jaffe, F. K. (1989). Historical perspectives on the use of subjective effects measures in assessing abuse potential of drugs. In M. W. Fischman & N. K. Mello (Eds.), *Testing for abuse liability of drugs in humans* (pp. 43–72, NIDA Research Monograph Series No. 92). Rockville, MD: Department of Health and Human Services, National Institute of Drug Abuse.

Jasinski, D. R., Fudala, P. J., & Johnson, R. E. (1989). Sublingual versus subcutaneous buprenorphine in opiate abusers. *Clinical Pharmacology and Therapeutics, 45,* 513–519.

Jasinksi, D. R., Griffith, J. D., Pevnick, J. S., & Clark, S. C. (1975). *Progress report on studies from the Clinical Research Center of the NIDA Addiction Research Center.* Washington, DC: Committee on Problems of Drug Dependence, National Research Council, National Academy of Sciences.

Jasinksi, D. R., Griffith, J. D., Pevnick, J., Gorodetzky, C., Cone, E., & Kay, D. (1977). *Progress report from the Clinical Research Center of the NIDA Ad-*

diction Research Center. Washington, DC: Committee on Problems of Drug Dependence, National Research Council, National Academy of Sciences.

Jasinski, D. R., & Mansky, P. A. (1972). Evaluation of nalbuphine for abuse potential. *Clinical Pharmacology and Therapeutics, 13,* 78–90.

Jasinski, D. R., & Martin, W. R. (1967). Assessment of the dependence-producing properties of dihydrocodeinone and codoxime. *Clinical Pharmacology and Therapeutics, 8,* 266–270.

Jasinski, D. R., Martin, W. R., & Hoeldtke, R. D. (1970). Effects of short- and long-term administration of pentazocine in man. *Clinical Pharmacology and Therapeutics, 11,* 385–403.

Jasinski, D. R., Pevnick, J. S., & Griffith, J. D. (1978). Human pharmacology and abuse potential of the analgesic buprenorphine. *Archives of General Psychiatry, 35,* 501–516.

Jasinski, D. R., & Preston, K. L. (1986). Evaluation of tilidine for morphine-like subjective effects and euphoria. *Drug and Alcohol Dependence, 18,* 273–292.

Jenkins, A. J., Keenan, R. M., Henningfield, J. E., & Cone, E. J. (1994). Pharmacokinetics and pharmacodynamics of smoked heroin. *Journal of Analytic Toxicology, 18,* 317–330.

Johnson, R. E., Cone, E. J., Henningfield, J. E., & Fudala, P. J. (1989). Use of buprenorphine in the treatment of opiate addiction. I. Physiologic and behavioral effects during a rapid dose induction. *Clinical Pharmacology and Therapeutics, 46,* 335–343.

Ko, M. C., Terner, J., Hursh, S., Woods, J. H., & Winger, G. (2002). Relative reinforcing effects of three opioids with different durations of action. *Journal of Pharmacology Experimental Therapeutics, 301,* 698–704.

Kolb, L., & Himmelsbach, C. K. (1938). Clinical studies of drug addiction. III. A critical review of the withdrawal treatments with method of evaluating abstinence syndromes. *American Journal of Psychiatry, 94,* 759–797.

Kornetsky, C., Humphries, O., & Evarts, E. (1957). Comparison of psychological effects of certain centrally acting drugs in man. *Archives of Neurological Psychiatry, 77,* 318–324.

Kosten, T. R., & Kleber, H. D. (1988). Buprenorphine detoxification from opioid dependence: A pilot study. *Life Sciences, 42,* 635–641.

Kosten, T. R., Morgan, C., & Kleber, H. D. (1991). Treatment of heroin addicts using buprenorphine. *American Journal of Drug and Alcohol Abuse, 17,* 119–128.

Kuhn, R. A., & Bromiley, R. B. (1951). Human pain thresholds determined by the radiant heat technique and the effect upon them of acetylsalicyclic acid, morphine sulfate and sodium phenobarbital. *Journal of Pharmacology and Experimental Therapeutics, 101,* 47–55.

Lasagna, L., von Felsinger, J. M., & Beecher, H. K. (1955). Drug-induced mood changes in man. 1. Observations on healthy subjects, chronically ill patients, and "postaddicts." *Journal of the American Medical Association, 157,* 1006–1020.

Lee, R. E., & Pfeiffer, C. C. (1951). Influence of analgesics, Dromoran, Nisentil and morphine, on pain thresholds in man. *Journal of Applied Physiology, 4,* 193–198.

MacAuliffe, W. E. (1975). A second look at first effects: The subjective effects of opiates on nonaddicts. *Journal of Drug Issues, 5,* 369–399.

Macht, D. I., Herman, N. B., & Levy, C. S. (1916). A quantitative study of the analgesia produced by opium alkaloids, individually and in combination with each other, in normal man. *Journal of Pharmacology and Experimental Therapeutics, 8*, 1–37.

Marsch, L. A., Bickel, W. K., Badger, G. J., Rathmell, J. P., Swedberg, M. D., Jonzon, B., & Norsten-Hoog, C. (2001). Effects of infusion rate of intravenously administered morphine on physiological, psychomotor, and self-reported measures in humans. *Journal of Pharmacology and Experimental Therapeutics, 299*, 1056–1065.

Martin, W. R., Jasinski, D. R., Haertzen, C. A., Kay, D. C., Jones, B. E., Mansky, P. A., & Carpenter, R. W. (1973). Methadone: A reevaluation. *Archives of General Psychiatry, 28*, 286–295.

Martin, W. R., Sloan, J. W., Sapira, J. D., & Jasinski, D. R. (1971). Physiologic, subjective and behavioral effects of amphetamine, methamphetamine, ephedrine, phenmetrazine, and methylphenidate in man. *Clinical Pharmacology and Therapeutics, 12*, 245–258.

Mello, N. K., & Mendelson, J. H. (1980). Buprenorphine suppresses heroin use by heroin addicts. *Science, 207*, 657–659.

Mello, N. K., Mendelson, J. H., & Kuehnle, J. C. (1982). Buprenorphine effects on human heroin self-administration: An operant analysis. *Journal of Pharmacology and Experimental Therapeutics, 223*, 30–39.

Mendelson, J., Jones, R. T., Fernandez, I., Welm, S., Melby, A. K., & Baggott, M. J. (1996). Buprenorphine and naloxone interactions in opiate-dependent volunteers. *Clinical Pharmacology and Therapeutics, 60*, 105–114.

Mo, B. P., & Way, E. L. (1966). An assessment of inhalation as a mode of administration of heroin by addicts. *Journal of Pharmacology and Experimental Therapeutics, 154*, 142–151.

Oliveto, A., Sevarino, K., McCance-Katz, E., & Feingold, A. (2002). Butorphanol and nalbuphine in opioid-dependent humans under a naloxone discrimination procedure. *Pharmacology, Biochemistry, and Behavior, 71*, 85–96.

Pickworth, W. B., Johnson, R. E., Holicky, B. A., & Cone, E. J. (1993). Subjective and physiologic effects of intravenous buprenorphine in humans. *Clinical Pharmacology and Therapeutics, 53*, 570–576.

Preston, K. L., & Bigelow, G. E. (1991). Subjective and discriminative effects of drugs. *Behavioral Pharmacology, 2*, 293–313.

Preston, K. L., & Bigelow, G. E. (2000). Effects of agonist-antagonist opioids in humans trained in a hydromorphone/not hydromorphone discrimination. *Journal of Pharmacology and Experimental Therapeutics, 295*, 114–124.

Preston, K. L., Bigelow, G. E., Bickel, W. K., & Liebson, I. A. (1989). Drug discrimination in human postaddicts, agonist-antagonist opioids. *Journal of Pharmacology and Experimental Therapeutics, 250*, 184–196.

Reisine, T., & Pasternak, G. (1996). Opioid analgesics and antagonists. In J. G. Hardman, A. G. Gilman, & L. E. Limbird (Eds.), *Goodman and Gilman's the pharmacological basis of therapeutics* (9th ed., pp. 521–555). New York: Pergamon.

Rosen, M. I., Wallace, E. A., McMahon, T. J., Pearsall, H. R., Woods, S. W., Price, L. H., et al. (1994). Buprenorphine: Duration of blockade of effects of intramuscular hydromorphone. *Drug and Alcohol Dependence, 35*, 141–149.

Sannita, W. G., Maggi, L., & Rosadini, G. (1987). Effects of scopolamine (0.25–0.75 mg i.m.) on the quantitative EEG and the neuropsychological status of healthy volunteers. *Neuropsychobiology, 17*, 199–205.

Schmidt, W. K., Tam, S. W., Shotzberger, G. S., Smith, D. H. Clark, R., & Vernier, V. G. (1985). Nalbuphine. *Drug and Alcohol Dependence, 14*, 339–362.

Schuh, K. J., Walsh, S. L., Bigelow, G. E., Preston, K. L., & Stitzer, M. L. (1996). Buprenorphine, morphine and naloxone effects during ascending morphine maintenance in humans. *Journal of Pharmacology and Experimental Therapeutics, 278*, 836–846.

Seevers, M. H., & Pfeiffer, C. C. (1936). A study of the analgesia, subjective depression, and euphoria produced by morphine, heroine, dilaudid and codeine in the normal human subject. *Journal of Pharmacology and Experimental Therapeutics, 56*, 166–187.

Strain, E. C., Preston, K. L., Liebson, I. A., & Bigelow, G. E. (1992). Acute effects of buprenorphine, hydromorphone and naloxone in methadone-maintained volunteers. *Journal of Pharmacology and Experimental Therapeutics, 261*, 985–993.

Strain, E. C., Preston, K. L., Liebson, I. A., & Bigelow, G. E. (1995). Buprenorphine effects in methadone-maintained volunteers: Effects at two hours after methadone. *Journal of Pharmacology and Experimental Therapeutics, 272*, 628–638.

Strain, E. C., Walsh, S. L., Preston, K. L., Liebson, I. A., & Bigelow, G. E. (1997). The effects of buprenorphine in buprenorphine-maintained volunteers. *Psychopharmacology, 129*, 329–338.

Walker, E. A., & Young, A. M. (2002). Clocinnamox distinguishes opioid agonists according to relative efficacy in normal and morphine-treated rats trained to discriminate morphine. *Journal of Pharmacology and Experimental Therapeutics, 302*, 101–110.

Walsh, S. L., June, H. L., Schuh, K. J., Preston, K. L., Bigelow, G. E., & Stitzer, M. L. (1995). Effects of buprenorphine and methadone in methadone-maintained subjects. *Psychopharmacology, 119*, 268–276.

Walsh, S. L., Preston, K. L., Bigelow, G. E., & Stitzer, M. L. (1995). Acute administration of buprenorphine in humans: Partial agonist and blockade effects. *Journal of Pharmacology and Experimental Therapeutics, 274*, 361–372.

Walsh, S. L., Preston, K. L., Stitzer, M. L., Cone, E. J., & Bigelow, G. E. (1994). Clinical pharmacology of buprenorphine: Ceiling effects at high doses. *Clinical Pharmacology and Therapeutics, 55*, 569–580.

Walsh, S. L., Strain, E. C., Abreu, M. E., & Bigelow, G. E. (2001). Enadoline, a selective kappa opioid agonist: Comparison with butorphanol and hydromorphone in humans. *Psychopharmacology, 157*, 151–162.

Wikler, A. (1952). A psychodynamic study of a patient during experimental self-regulated re-addiction to morphine. *Psychiatric Quarterly, 26*, 270–293.

Wolff, H. G., Hardy, J. D., & Goodell, H. (1940). Studies on pain: Measurement of the effect of morphine, codeine, and other opiates on the pain threshold and an analysis of their relationship to the pain experience. *Journal of Clinical Investigation, 19*, 659–680.

Woods, J. H., France, C. P., & Winger, G. D. (1992). *Behavioral pharmacology of buprenorphine: Issues relevant to its potential in treating drug abuse* (pp. 12–27, NIDA Research Monograph No. 121). Rockville, MD: Department of Health and Human Services, National Institute of Drug Abuse.

Woods, J. H., & Gmerek, D. E. (1985). Substitution and primary dependence studies in animals. *Drug and Alcohol Dependence, 14*, 233–247.

Yanagita, T., Katoh, S., Wakasa, Y., & Oinuma, N. (1982). *Dependence potential of buprenorphine studied in rhesus monkeys* (pp. 208–214, NIDA Research Monograph No. 41). Rockville, MD: Department of Health and Human Services, National Institute of Drug Abuse.

Zacny, J. P., Bigelow, G., Compton, P., Foley, K., Iguchi, M., & Sannerud, C. (2003). College on problems of drug dependence taskforce on prescription opioid non-medical use and abuse: Position statement. *Drug and Alcohol Dependence, 69*, 215–232.

Zacny, J. P., Conley, K., & Galinkin, J. (1997). Comparing the subjective, psychomotor, and physiological effects of buprenorphine and morphine in healthy volunteers. *Journal of Pharmacology and Experimental Therapeutics, 282*, 1187–1197.

Zacny, J. P., Conley, K., & Marks, S. (1997). Comparing the subjective, psychomotor, and physiological effects of intravenous nalbuphine and morphine in healthy volunteers. *Journal of Pharmacology and Experimental Therapeutics, 280*, 1159–1169.

Zacny, J. P., Hill, J. L., Black, M., & Sadeghi, P. (1998). Comparing the subjective, psychomotor and physiological effects of intravenous pentazocine and morphine in normal volunteers. *Journal of Pharmacology and Experimental Therapeutics 286*, 1197–1207.

Zacny, J. P., Lichtor, J. L., Binstock, W., Coalson, D. W., Cutter, T., Flemming, D. C., et al. (1993). Subjective, behavioral and physiological responses to intravenous meperidine in healthy volunteers. *Psychopharmacology, 111*, 306–314.

Zacny, J. P., Lichtor, J. L., Flemming, D., Coalson, D. W., & Thompson, W. K. (1994). A dose-response analysis of the subjective, psychomotor, and physiological effects of intravenous morphine in healthy volunteers. *Journal of Pharmacology and Experimental Therapeutics, 268*, 1–9.

Zacny, J. P., Lichtor, J. L., Thapar, P., Coalson, D. W., Flemming, D., & Thompson, W. (1994). Comparing the subjective, psychomotor, and physiological effects of intravenous butorphanol and morphine in healthy volunteers. *Journal of Pharmacology and Experimental Therapeutics, 270*, 579–588.

Zacny, J. P., Lichtor, J. L., Zaragoza, J. G., & de Wit, H. (1992). Subjective and behavioral responses to intravenous fentanyl in healthy volunteers. *Psychopharmacology, 107*, 319–326.

9

Cannabis

Attending to Subjective Effects to Improve Drug Safety

MITCH EARLEYWINE

No one has clearly delineated cannabis's subjective impact. The plant contains numerous psychoactive substances. Variation across plants is extremely dramatic, making generalizations about effects difficult. In this chapter, I will summarize previous descriptions of cannabis's subjective impact and propose a taxonomy of effects that might help distinguish among plants, predict use, and increase drug safety. My central idea is a simple one: Attending to cannabis effects and cultivating a vocabulary for describing them will, in the end, help users appreciate smaller doses and lead to increased safety.

Cannabis is not a dangerous drug for responsible adults. Its negative consequences pale in comparison to those of legal substances such as alcohol and tobacco. Despite consistent propaganda to the contrary, cannabis does not lead to aggression, reckless driving, infertility, amotivation, low grades, poor employment, mental illness, unwanted pregnancy, firearms accidents, or the use of harder drugs. A few studies do reveal pulmonary problems associated with long-term daily use, but many of these could decrease dramatically as vaporizers replace bongs, joints, and one-hitters. (A vaporizer runs hot air through cannabis so that the psychoactive cannabinoids boil off into a fine mist without generating as many burnt tars and other carcinogens.) Despite these consistent signs of safety, a percentage of regular users develop troubles with this drug, including symptoms of dependence and abuse (see Earleywine, 2002).

A taxonomy of effects could serve as an aid to cannabis drug safety in a few ways. First, users could separate plants that create the effects they desire from others. For example, medical users may want cannabis with powerful appetite enhancement but no cognitive impairment. These users might smoke relatively little of a plant that produces the effects they desire. In contrast, they may have to smoke a great deal of a plant that was not bred with their desired effects in mind. Few, if any, published studies in the mainstream pharmacological literature assess these effects in different plants. Articulating the distinctions among these effects may help researchers and users appreciate them and lead cultivators to attend to these effects as they develop new cannabis strains.

Second, articulating the effects could enhance enjoyment as well as mindfulness during the intoxication experience. By increasing the attention paid to certain effects and enhancing their enjoyment, users may decrease quantities consumed. This idea may seem counterintuitive in a culture where "more" is notoriously synonymous with "better," but a few lines of reasoning support it. People who smoke stronger cannabis tend to smoke less of it, as if an ideal intoxication level exists (Matthias, Tashkin, Marques-Magallanes, Wilkins, & Simmons, 1997). A potential parallel between cannabis users and wine drinkers may also support this idea. Wine drinkers, many of whom consider themselves connoisseurs, have developed a complex vocabulary for describing the taste of wine. If a comparable vocabulary existed for states of consciousness, cannabis users might use it to describe their intoxication. (All of us could potentially enjoy any subjective state more, too, for that matter.) Wine drinkers tend to drink less and experience fewer problems than drinkers of other alcoholic beverages, for a myriad of potential reasons (Smart & Walsh, 1999). Cannabis users who spend time describing their subjective state may also find themselves using less of the plant and enjoying it more.

In short, a vocabulary for cannabis's subjective effects could lead users to attend more to their intoxication. This increased attention could help users identify the subjective effects they appreciate most, which could help breeders create cannabis for those specific effects. In addition, the vocabulary and associated attention might lead users to reduce the quantity they consume. The idea parallels work in education that emphasizes how making distinctions enhances enjoyment. People instructed to notice novel attributes of stimuli report liking those stimuli more (Langer, Stroebe, Schut & Intoma, 2000). In addition, data on distraction-induced overeating suggest that attending to cannabis consumption might limit the amount consumed. People tend to eat more when distracted (Boon et al., 2002); perhaps cannabis users who are not mindful of their consumption smoke more as well.

Standard reinforcement theories imply that making cannabis more pleasant and mindful should increase rather than decrease the frequency of use. These theories would suggest that a more enjoyable cannabis experience would lead users to repeat it more often. Nevertheless, I argue that a more mindful and attentive intoxication experience may decrease automatic consumption. Although a great deal of drug use arises from craving, emotional distress, and physiological arousal, a great deal also stems from automatic, reflexive use that appears to begin outside of conscious awareness (see Tiffany, 1999). By making cannabis consumption and intoxication more of a conscious, mindful experience, automatic consumption may decrease. Experienced users who turn to the pipe each evening out of habit may find that a series of mindful intoxication experiences leads them to choose the drug more consciously and, in turn, choose occasions when they would prefer sobriety.

Cannabis's impact can depend dramatically on the user's state immediately prior to intoxication, as Zinberg (1984) has emphasized. Shenk (2002, p. 237) reports: "When my spirits are lifted, pot helps punctuate that. If I smoke on a downward slope or while idling, I usually experience more depression and anxiety." Attending to these state-dependent effects of cannabis could make users choosier in their consumption of the drug, potentially reserving it for enhancing mindful celebration rather than turning to the drug reflexively.

Subjective Effects

The subjective impact of cannabis is not well articulated. Thought, memory, affect, and perceptions clearly alter during intoxication. Researchers have yet to tease apart the roles of pharmacology and expectancy in these effects. Few studies have examined subjective experiences on the ascending and descending limbs of the blood-drug curve, but, like alcohol, cannabis appears to show greater sedation as time passes. In addition, most other drugs are a single psychoactive substance, like cocaine or psilocybin. Cannabis is a combination of more than 60 cannabinoids, at least 100 terpenoids, and about 20 flavonoids, making variation across plants extremely high (McPartland & Mediavilla, 2002). A great deal of research on subjective effects of drugs identifies responses in an attempt to predict subsequent use. Generally, users who report dramatic positive effects and few negative ones repeat consumption (e.g., Goldman, 2002).

Some of the most informative descriptions of cannabis intoxication appear in literature. Case studies of intoxication attempt to describe the drug's impact, too (e.g., Moreau, 1845). All studies support dramatic individual differences, as well as the importance of set and setting in the intoxication experience. Reports vary from complete paranoia and panic to utter bliss (Gautier, 1846/1966). Baudelaire (1861) described environmental and attitudinal contributors to cannabis intoxication, but Zinberg (1984) gets most of the credit for set and setting today. Most data on cannabis intoxication rely on self-reports from unintoxicated, experienced users (e.g., Adamec, Pihl, & Leiter, 1976; Halikas, Goodwin, & Guze, 1971; Tart, 1971). Laboratory administrations of cannabis or THC confirm many of these effects (e.g., Chait & Pierri, 1992). I have divided the effects into several domains.

Perceptions of Time and Space

Cannabis makes time slow, according to self-reports (Tart, 1971; Halikas et al., 1971) and laboratory studies (see Chait & Pierri, 1992, for a review). The slowing of time likely contributes to an intriguing interaction with setting. If the environment is aversive, slowing time could be a negative effect. In contrast, in a pleasant environment, slowing time may feel extremely positive. Users report deviant perceptions of space (Tart, 1971), which also have laboratory support (Bech, Rafaelsen, & Rafaelsen, 1973).

Visual Effects

Cannabis intoxication leads individuals to report enhanced visual acuity and depth perception, but laboratory studies suggest that these abilities are actually impaired. Tart's (1971) participants reported identifying patterns in meaningless visual stimuli after using cannabis, an effect that defies laboratory confirmation. Visual hallucinations, though rare, occurred in 9% of his same sample, but only at very high doses. Halikas et al. (1971) found that 4% of their sample claimed to see visions, an effect comparable to visual hallucinations and consistent with ancient Asian texts (Abel, 1980). This effect also proves difficult to investigate in the laboratory.

Although hallucinations are infrequent, perceptual aberrations are common. Gautier (1846) reported distorted visual perceptions, including a room appearing darker and more unusual after ingestion of hashish. About half of Tart's (1971) participants reported seeing auras around people's heads at high doses, but this study occurred during an era in which reading auras was part of everyday life in the counterculture. A sample of more than 200 Canadians confirms that users frequently report visual effects (Adamec et al., 1976). No laboratory work directly addresses these experiences.

The perception of colors also alters after smoking cannabis. Individuals in Tart's (1971) sample reported that they commonly saw new colors or more subtle shades of color during intoxication. Participants claimed this effect occurred when they were at least fairly high. Laboratory research reveals the opposite effect, contradicting these self-reports. After smoking marijuana, participants did a significantly poorer job of distinguishing between different hues (Adams, Brown, Haegerstrom-Portnoy, & Flom, 1976). The poorest discriminations appeared in the blue range of the spectrum. Thus, the perceived effects of marijuana on color perception do not appear to parallel the actual effects. Perhaps the drug merely makes users think that this skill has increased.

Cannabis intoxication also alters perceptions of depth. Tart's (1971) participants reported an added three-dimensional appearance to pictures. A case study confirms that cannabis helped a man learn to perceive depth (Mikulas, 1996). Nevertheless, intoxication in the laboratory actually decreases the illusion of three dimensions created by certain pictures presented with a stereoscope (Emrich et al., 1991).

Imagery

Tart's (1971) participants claim that cannabis improved their ability to imagine pictures and objects, but laboratory work does not support these reports. Participants who used imagery in a learning task reported the images they used. Judges rated the intoxicated people's descriptions as less vivid (Block & Wittenborn, 1984). Of course, marijuana intoxication may make people think they have improved their imagery ability when they have not. Nevertheless, these data also may mean that intoxicated individuals have improved imagery but a deficit in their ability to describe it.

Hearing

Cannabis alters perceptions of sound. Balzac (1900) heard music after eating hashish, but such auditory hallucinations are rare. Moreau (1845) reported increased sensitivity to and appreciation of sounds and music. Gautier (1846) claimed that after eating hashish, he heard heavenly chords that would shame the world's greatest composers. Tart's (1971) participants reported a few characteristic effects related to hearing. They claimed that notes of music sounded more distinct and rhythms seemed more clear. Nearly all (95%) of the participants reported enhanced auditory acuity. Two other large samples confirmed that users believe that the plant improves their hearing (Adamec et al., 1976; Halikas et al., 1971). Laboratory research has not addressed this effect. All three of these studies also report synesthesia at high doses, with participants reporting visual qualities associated with sound.

An additional auditory improvement reported by Tart's (1971) participants concerns greater spatial separation between sources of sound. This effect may parallel the illusion of improved depth perception. Users stated that they felt that the instruments on recordings sounded farther apart, improving stereo effects. Laboratory work has not addressed this effect. In general, appreciation for sounds also appears to increase with intoxication.

Touch

Enhanced tactile sensation is a hallmark of cannabis intoxication. Baudelaire's "The Poem of Hashish" (1861) emphasizes this effect. Most of Tart's (1971) sample (65%) reported a more exciting, more sensual sense of touch. They also reported that touch took on new qualities. Over half (55%) experienced novel tactile sensations. This finding is consistent with the recurring theme of enhanced sensations. Two other samples confirmed the perception of an improved sense of touch (Halikas, Weller, & Morse, 1982; Adamec et al., 1976). Laboratory work has neglected the thrill associated with touch, but the infamous aphrodisiac qualities associated with cannabis may relate to this experience.

Taste

Gautier (1846) claimed that the simplest water tasted like exquisite wine after eating hashish. Marijuana's legendary impact on appetite has generated many humorous depictions of "the munchies." Tart's (1971) sample reported that the drug made taste sensations take on new qualities, an effect that began even at low levels of intoxication. Other samples of experienced users also reported enhanced appreciation of tastes (Adamec et al., 1976; Halikas et al., 1982). Laboratory studies fail to reveal improvements in the ability to taste classic sour, sweet, salty, or bitter substances (Mattes, Shaw, & Engelman, 1994). Thus, intoxicated people may not actually improve their ability to taste, but their enjoyment of tastes may increase dramatically.

Tart's (1971) sample revealed a related, characteristic effect: Intoxicated individuals enjoyed eating and reported consuming large quantities of food. They also commonly craved sweets during intoxication. Both of these effects began at low levels of intoxication. In a separate sample of 100 Caucasians who had smoked cannabis at least 50 times, 72% said that the drug usually increased their hunger, and 37% said it increased their desire for sweets (Halikas et al., 1971).

A detailed laboratory study confirmed these reports. This research revealed a 40% increase in calorie consumption during intoxication. The study had six men live in a laboratory setting for 13 days. Each day they smoked four marijuana cigarettes or four placebos. They not only consumed more calories on the days that they smoked cannabis but also gained more weight than one would predict from these additional calories. This result suggests that marijuana may slow metabolism as well as increase food consumption (Foltin, Fischman, & Byrne, 1988). Results like these have inspired the medical use of cannabinoids to improve appetite for people with problematic weight loss.

Thus, reports from unintoxicated, regular users suggest that people perceive cannabis as an enhancer of the senses that alters perceptions of time and space. This deviant input creates a number of higher order effects, as summarized in the following.

Emotion

Any drug's impact on human feelings determines its potential for repeated use. Literary works devoted to cannabis frequently mention its pleasant influence on emotion. Individuals in Tart's (1971) sample reported that cannabis almost invariably improved their mood. Users also grew more relaxed during intoxication. Data from another sample of 100 people who used the drug at least 50 times revealed consistent reports of peaceful and relaxed feelings after smoking (Weller & Halikas, 1982). More than 2,500 veterans who had smoked at least 5 times also reported many pleasant effects of cannabis. More than 90% said that the drug made them feel mellow or relaxed, and more than 60% reported that the drug made them euphoric (Lyons et al., 1997). These reactions likely motivated continued consumption of the drug.

These emotional effects of cannabis are not only pharmacological; they may stem partly from expectancies. Evidence for the role of expectancies in cannabis's emotional impact comes from laboratory research. For example, people who expect to smoke hashish in the laboratory report feeling "high" even if the hash contains no THC (Cami, Guerra, Ugena, Segura, & De La Torre, 1991). Thus, part of the emotional impact of the drug arises in the user's own mind.

In addition, the idea that the drug's effect is actually pleasant may depend on expectancies. A study using synthetic THC gave the drug to two groups of people with different instructions. One group knew the drug was THC; the other group knew only that the drug was an antiemetic. People who knew that the drug was THC liked the effects more, found them more euphoric, and wanted more of the substance. People who did not know that the drug was THC were significantly less positive about it. Thus, expectations about marijuana and its effects likely contribute a great deal to its emotional impact (Kirk, Doty, & de Wit, 1998).

Tart's (1971) work documents other affective reactions, too. Participants in his sample reported that they commonly felt emotions more strongly after using cannabis. This effect did not usually begin until participants reached strong levels of intoxication. Some examples in literary works support this idea, but laboratory studies have yet to address the question. Several methods for assessing emotional reactions have developed over the years. A simple study comparing those who smoked cannabis with those who smoked placebo might elicit reactions to emotional slides or film clips. Greater reactions in the cannabis users would support this report of exaggerated emotions.

Tart (1971) also investigated emotional crises during marijuana intoxication. He used the jargon of the era, asking participants the percentage of users they had seen "freak out" or feel "catastrophic emotional upset." The vast majority of the sample (89%) estimated that this effect occurred less than 1% of the time. The actual rate of aversive reactions to marijuana is probably higher than the number reported by this sample of experienced users who clearly enjoy the drug. In fact, all these reports of positive affect come from experienced users of the drug. Clinical lore and literary work suggest that at least some people find cannabis intoxication extremely upsetting, at least on occasion. Reports of tachycardia misinterpreted as anxiety are rampant. Extreme paranoia, derealization, and anxiety also appear.

Thought

As most cognitive theories of affect would suggest, cannabis's impact on emotion may relate to some of its effects on thinking. Users report several subjective impressions about these changes in their thoughts. Individuals in Tart's (1971) sample reported that they felt that their thoughts were more "in the present" or "here and now." They found that they were more likely to have spontaneous insights about themselves, appreciate subtle humor, and accept contradictory ideas. No laboratory studies have addressed these effects directly.

Tart's (1971) participants also reported having trouble reading during intoxication, suggesting an impairment in cognitive processing. In contrast, a separate sample of 100 regular users found that 30% reported usually experiencing better concentration and improved mental powers during intoxication (Halikas et al., 1971). Laboratory studies generally contradict these impressions of cognitive improvement during intoxication. Perhaps the drug creates the illusion of improved concentration despite deficits. Perhaps some users are marijuana dependent and find that the drug improves their cognitive functions. In addition, many individuals report that the drug improves their concentration because of a mild deficit in attention. (One such user is well known as the author of a successful screenplay and two books.)

Memory

Marijuana clearly alters the ability to learn new material but does not impair memory for material learned prior to intoxication (see Earleywine, 2002). The subjective experience parallels many of the laboratory studies. Users rarely report problems remembering material learned prior to intoxication. Laboratory studies generally confirm that people can remember old material while high. In contrast, users report deficits in short-term memory during intoxication. Tart's (1971) participants characteristically forgot the topic of conversations even before they had ended. More than half of the sample stated that this forgetting of conversations occurred very often or usually. This effect began at strong or very strong levels of intoxication, as laboratory studies of memory confirm. More than 65% of the sample said that at least some of the time when they were intoxicated they could not remember the beginning of a sentence by the time they reached its end. This sort of forgetting also appeared commonly in reports from more than 200 Canadian users (Adamec et al., 1976). Users obviously have some insight into the memory deficits that appear soon after cannabis consumption.

Tart's (1971) data also revealed an intriguing and unexpected effect related to memory. Users commonly reported that they spontaneously recalled events from the distant past, including material they had not considered in many years. For example, people might recall an incident from grade school that they had not thought about for quite some time. This effect began at strong levels of intoxication for the majority of the sample. Users appear to know that their short-term memory suffers after smoking cannabis, but they also claim that spontaneous recall of distant memories improves.

Sexuality

Few topics are more controversial in American society than sex and drugs. Their combination often generates confusion and concern. Marijuana's link to sex may be as old as the drug itself. As with other effects, this one first appeared in literature. One of the tales in *The Arabian Nights*, published and popularized by 1200 B.C., mentions sexual arousal in a man who has eaten hashish. Louisa May Alcott's short story "Perilous Play" (1869) suggests that hashish may speed seduction. Harry Anslinger, the first "Drug Czar," spun tales of cannabis enhancing sexuality in his efforts to pass the Marijuana Tax Act of 1937. These reports relied on only a few cases. Larger studies confirmed the belief that marijuana alters aspects of sexuality.

The most characteristic effect related to sex for Tart's (1971) participants concerned enhanced orgasm. Users reported that they appreciated new qualities of orgasm that they did not usually experience when sober. This effect may parallel a general increase in the excitement, joy, and sensitivity of touch, which was also characteristic of intoxication in this sample. More than half of the participants reported that they were better lovers after using the drug, with many suggesting that they were more responsive and giving.

Self-report research on a separate group of 100 experienced users confirmed marijuana's impact on sex (Weller & Halikas, 1984). Two thirds of this sample, who had used the drug at least 50 times, reported that cannabis intoxication led to some form of sexual enhancement. They reported improved orgasm, a heightened sense of intimacy and closeness, and superior sexual prowess. Coincidentally, these users stayed single longer and were more likely to have sexual contact with someone of their same sex than people who did not use the drug.

Although many effects of marijuana can dissipate over time, marijuana's enhancement of sex appears to remain stable across 6 to 8 years (Halikas, Weller, Morse, & Hoffman, 1985).

Few laboratory studies have confirmed these self-reports. Studies of these sexual effects might include masturbation or intercourse after the administration of THC. Research of this type could validate reports of enhanced sexual experiences during intoxication. This work might suggest a new treatment for some sexual dysfunctions. Individuals with a relatively common and important problem, hypoactive sexual desire disorder, might benefit from marijuana. The hallmark symptom of this disorder is an extremely low sex drive. A decreased desire for sex commonly arises from medical or psychiatric conditions, as well as poor relationships. Once these potential causes have been eliminated, marijuana may prove a fruitful way to increase sexual desire.

Spirituality

Another controversial topic in American culture concerns concepts related to the divine. Scientific research on the holy, religious, sacred, or spiritual often offends some people. Empirical approaches to these topics were taboo for many years. Nevertheless, recent research documents that spirituality provides superb benefits for mental and physical health (Miller, 1999). These results are hardly news to many people leading religious lives. Nevertheless, adding illicit drugs into this sort of research remains controversial.

Several cultures view psychoactive substances as an important part of spirituality. For example, the Native American Church uses peyote as a sacrament. Members of the Coptic and Rastafarian Churches smoke cannabis as part of their religious practice, too. Certain Buddhist sects in Nepal use marijuana as a sacrament (Clarke, 1998). Thus, spiritual aspects of cannabis have inspired some investigation.

Tart's (1971) sample reported only one characteristic effect that he interpreted as potentially spiritual. This effect concerned feeling more childlike, open to experience, and filled with wonder. More than 65% of the sample experienced this effect very often or usually. Tart (1971) also asked simple yes-or-no questions about spiritual topics. A fourth of the sample reported spiritual experiences from marijuana that had a dramatic impact on them. Users described these events as moments of connection to the universe, contact with the divine, or expressions of peace and joy. These effects paralleled reports of religious ecstasy. Approximately one fifth of the sample said that intoxication had acquired religious significance for them. Contemporary authors also assert that the drug can enhance spirituality. Many encourage pensive, meditative use of the drug and deride mindless consumption (Bello, 1996). This approach may minimize the potential for negative consequences related to the drug. People who smoke cannabis in a thoughtful way and consciously attend to their experience may be less likely to show symptoms of abuse.

Sleep

Marijuana intoxication alters sleep. Dr. J. R. Reynolds, chief physician to Queen Victoria, recommended the drug for insomnia. Many early literary accounts mention sedation and dramatic dreams (Rosenthal, Gieringer, & Mikuriya, 1997). Tart's (1971) participants commonly reported that they grew drowsy, especially at strong levels of intoxication. They characteristically stated that they found falling asleep very easy, beginning at the lowest level of intoxication. They also reported improved sleep quality, especially at strong levels of intoxication.

On the other hand, a subset reported disturbed sleep, especially after very high doses. This paradoxical arousal goes against other self-report studies that confirm that marijuana relaxes people (Lyons et al., 1997; Halikas et al., 1985). Laboratory research has revealed greater sedation when participants smoke cannabis. The placebo joint did not have the same effect (Block et al., 1998). These effects have inspired cannabis use in the informal treatment of insomnia. Many other drugs have an impact on sleep, particularly the barbiturates and benzodiazepines. The barbiturates are notorious for their potential for abuse, dependence, and lethal overdose. Benzodiazepines can cause memory loss and lead to a sluggish feeling the next morning.

The drawbacks of these other insomnia drugs led a woman with multiple sclerosis to smoke marijuana before going to bed. She reported successful, restful sleep as a result (Grinspoon & Bakalar, 1997). Although THC causes many of marijuana's effects, cannabidiol appears to have the biggest impact on sleep. In one study, 15 insomniacs who received cannabidiol reported that their sleep had improved dramatically (Carlini & Cunha, 1981). Despite these encouraging data for cannabidiol, some of the best treatments for insomnia require changing behaviors rather than taking drugs. These interventions include multiple steps. People with sleep problems often benefit from retiring at the same time each night, avoiding stimulants like caffeine, and using their beds only for sleep and sex rather than other activities. This sort of good sleep hygiene may provide better rest than any medications. Nevertheless, further research on smoked marijuana and isolated cannabidiol can provide intriguing information on the role of the cannabinoids in sleep and consciousness.

Undesirable Subjective Effects

Negative feelings associated with marijuana intoxication often receive less attention than positive ones. Cannabis can create aversive reactions, particularly after extremely large doses or during the first few exposures to the drug. Literature has not neglected this distressing impact. Gautier, Ludlow, and Baudelaire all detail frightening effects. One of Louisa May Alcott's (1869, p. 72) characters describes the aversive effects as "not so pleasant, unless one likes phantoms, frenzies, and a touch of nightmare." Individuals in Tart's (1971) sample did not report many negative reactions. They claimed that they often found themselves distractible and easily sidetracked. This mental fogginess was the only characteristic negative effect. Common negative effects included an inability to think clearly, work accurately, or solve problems efficiently. Participants also said that marijuana made them feel physically weaker.

Laboratory research confirms slow and inefficient thought during intoxication. Experiments have not documented physical weakness, but reported sedation in the laboratory may reflect this feeling (Block et al., 1998). Tart's (1971) minimal reports of negative consequences such as panic or discomfort may not be typical of everyone. His participants had all smoked cannabis an average of more than 200 times. A sample of more than 2,500 people who had used cannabis at least 5 times confirmed these negative effects and suggested a few more. This study may have revealed more negative effects because it did not require as much use of the drug as Tart's (1971) research. More than half of those in his sample claimed that they could not concentrate when they were intoxicated, and nearly 40% said that the drug made them confused. Participants also reported many other undesirable reactions, including paranoia, guilt, and nausea. Some of the people in this study were twins, permitting an examination of the heritability of these effects. Analyses comparing the identical twins to the fraternal twins revealed that these negative effects were likely inherited. Positive effects, which included enhanced relaxation, creativity, energy, and euphoria, also appeared to have a heritable component (Lyons et al.,1997). These results support the idea that a biological factor contributes to cannabis's subjective effects.

Another potentially negative feeling associated with marijuana intoxication is depersonalization. Tart (1971) did not inquire about this effect. A study of 100 regular users found 12% reported usually feeling a separation from self after smoking marijuana. Almost half of this sample (49%) said they have had this experience occasionally (Weller & Halikas, 1982). Laboratory work clearly documents that cannabis heightens depersonalization (Mathew et al., 1999). This depersonalization correlated with anger, tension, and confusion, suggesting that the experience had negative components.

One of the most novel and striking undesirable reactions to cannabis illustrates the role of expectancies in drug responses. At least two individuals who smoked high doses of marijuana the first time that they tried the drug experienced Koro (Chowdhury & Bera, 1994). Koro, which means "turtle's head," is an acute state of anxiety associated with a strong fear of death. It also includes the alarming perception that one's penis has retracted into the abdomen. Thankfully, the disorder remains extremely rare. Oddly, most cases are limited to Asian countries, where the idea that anxiety might lead to penis loss is considered more tenable. In China, the disorder is known as *shook yang* (shrinking penis). The two cases associated with marijuana intoxication appeared in West Bengal, India, where a Koro epidemic had occurred in 1982 (Franzini & Grossberg, 1995). Oddly, three cases of cannabis-induced koro in Americans have also appeared. All three individuals had heard of the disorder prior to experiencing the symptoms, suggesting an odd, contagion-like expectancy effect that may contribute to this anxiety reaction to marijuana (Earleywine, 2001).

A Proposed Taxonomy of Subjective Effects

Literary examples, case studies, laboratory experiments, and reports from experienced users confirm several of cannabis's effects. Although individual reactions vary dramatically, a few key experiences appear commonly in regular users. The drug clearly alters perception. Time slows. Space appears more vast or variable. The senses generally seem more appealing and interesting despite laboratory evidence that they may actually be impaired. Visual acuity seems better. Sounds appear to take on new qualities. Touch and taste both seem more intriguing and sensual. Nevertheless, laboratory evidence does not support these enhancements.

Higher functions also change during marijuana intoxication. Emotions seem more salient or extreme. Euphoria predominates. Thoughts seem more focused on the current moment. Short-term memory clearly suffers, with users occasionally forgetting one sentence while uttering the next. Sexuality and spirituality increase. Sleep can improve at low doses or suffer at higher ones. A few negative subjective effects also seem common, including anxiety, guilt, and paranoia. Some of these effects may stem simply from expectancy, some vary with culture, and some clearly arise as part of the pharmacology of the cannabinoids. The drug's popularity may rely, in part, on its ability to create all these disparate but potentially pleasant effects.

Many experienced users suggest that this empirical and literary work is a great place to start for depicting the subjective effects of cannabis. Nevertheless, a taxonomy of effects that might aid users in giving accurate descriptions of their experiences will likely require a more extensive vocabulary. Subjective effect scales designed to assess reactions to drugs in the laboratory provide many adjectives that depict aspects of the cannabis intoxication experience. In addition, the marijuana counterculture has developed popular descriptors, including slang terms that describe aspects of intoxication that are frequently not investigated in the laboratory. Many self-report scales used in laboratory work focus on simple stimulation and sedation (Martin, Earleywine, Musty, Perrine, & Swift, 1993), drug "liking," or simple reports of feeling "high" (Henningfield, Johnson, & Jasinski, 1987). Thus, I began with laboratory research tools designed to assess marijuana intoxication but soon turned to counterculture best-sellers (King, 2001; Rosenthal, 2002) to propose the factors and items shown in tables 9.1 and 9.2.

Based on face validity, the items appear to assess 7 factors of effects: stimulating, sedating, euphoric, psychedelic, cerebral, somatic, and appetite-enhancing. Readers may disagree with my definitions of the various descriptors. That, in fact, is the point. As individual users experience the drug and attend to its effects, the meaning of each descriptor will grow more refined. The language of intoxication, and even of consciousness, could potentially grow more alive, shifting and varying with the development of new strains, new experiences, and new (articulate) users. Essentially, the experience of cannabis intoxication could grow more mindful. As users become more aware of the thoughts, feelings, and bodily sensations that accompany intoxication, their experience may change dramatically.

People might fear that a new vocabulary for intoxication could attract new users, particularly adolescents. Approximately one in three American adults has tried the drug (Substance Abuse and Mental Health Services Administration, 2002). Perhaps an articulate description of the euphoria frequently associated with cannabis would lead a larger number of people to initiate use. Nevertheless, a graphic description of intoxication might also lead many to decline the experience, particularly if an accurate depiction made the drug's effects seem like no real mystery. Given the elaborate depictions of intoxication in literature (e.g.,

Table 9.1. Factors and Items for a Taxonomy of Subjective Effects of Cannabis

Stimulating	Euphoric	Cerebral
Active	Cheerful	Clear
Alert	Giggly	Thoughtful
Energetic	Happy	Pensive
Up	Uplifting	Contemplative
		Heady
Sedating	Psychedelic	
"Couch lock"	Creative	Somatic
"Eye droop"	Psychedelic	Body high
Heavy	Psychoactive	Body stone
Lethargic	Trippy	Body rush
Mellow	Visual	Narcotic
Narcotic	Wandering mind	Physical
Relaxing		
Sleepy		Appetite Enhancing
Stoney		Munchies
		Hungry

Table 9.2. Definitions of Items for Assessing Subjective Effects of Cannabis

Active—stimulating

Alert—stimulating, with clear thoughts

Body high—a slightly arousing experience throughout the body

Body rush—a repeated, intermittent flushing sensation throughout the body

Body stone—a slightly sedating experience throughout the body

Cerebral—a thoughtful experience with potentially clear thoughts on intellectual topics

Cheerful—positive affect

Clear—thoughts appear unimpaired despite other effects

Contemplative—encouraging deep thought

Couch lock—extreme sedation despite little cognitive impairment

Creative—novel thoughts with frequent and loose associations

Energetic—stimulating

Euphoric—positive affect

Eye droop—extreme sedation accompanied by drooping eyes

Giggly—positive affect with a special sensitivity to humor

Happy—positive affect

Heady—particularly thoughtful and thought-inducing

Heavy—sedating, with a strong sense of physical relaxation

Hungry—craving food

Lethargic—sedating, with a sense of physical weakness

Mellow—mildly sedating with a sense of contentment

Munchies—increased appetite

Narcotic—dream-inducing, pain relieving

Pensive—contemplative, preoccupied with thought

Physical—primary effects involve the body

Psychedelic—comparable to the hallucinogens, involving loose associations and images present when eyes are closed

Psychoactive—cognitive changes unlike the sober state, with novel connections between ideas

Relaxing—sedating but not extremely so

Sleepy—sedating

Stoney—sedating, with slow thoughts and a somatic sense of heaviness

Trippy—loose associations with an appreciation for philosophical and potentially humorous aspects of everyday events or objects

Up—positive affect with a vigorous, energetic quality

Uplifting—positive affect and an optimistic bias

Visual—heightened sensitivity to colors and imagery

Wandering mind—looser associations and recall of distant past

Baudelaire, 1861; Gautier, 1868; Ginsberg, 1966) and popular texts (Rosenthal, 2002; King, 2001), one more description seems unlikely to add flames to this fire.

Although I have focused on potentially positive effects for experienced users, a taxonomy of negative effects is conceivable. People who react adversely to the drug report paranoia, depersonalization, derealization, painful self-consciousness, and dry eyes. Some of these effects may arise from high percentages of THC in strains with small concentrations of other cannabinoids. THC alone can create aversive, anxious effects that other cannabinoids may attenuate. In addition, medical effects, including antidepressant, anxiolytic, analgesic, and anticonvulsant effects, could receive attention on separate rating scales.

In the end, paying mindful attention to cannabis's subjective effects can lead to improved strains for medical use, the development of plants that focus on desirable aspects of intoxication, and a decrease in the quantity consumed per occasion. In addition, this work may help each of us attend more regularly to our consciousness, regardless of our state of intoxication. Few facts could be more important than a keen understanding of our own feelings. The potential of this approach requires empirical validation. Given the low priority that funding agencies give to studies of this kind, users may need to train themselves to attend to different aspects of the intoxication experience and their own consciousness. Concerted efforts will provide their own rewards.

References

Abel, E. (1980). *Marijuana: The first twelve thousand years*. New York: Plenum.

Adamec, C., Pihl, R. O., & Leiter, L. (1976). An analysis of the subjective marijuana experience. *International Journal of the Addictions, 11*, 295–307.

Adams, A. J., Brown, B., Haegerstrom-Portnoy, G., & Flom, M. C. (1976). Evidence for acute efffects of alcohol and marijuana on color discrimination. *Perception and Psychophysics, 20*, 119–124.

Alcott, L. M. (1869/1976). *Plots and counterplots: More unknown thrillers of Louisa May Alcott* (M. Stern, Ed.). New York: Morrow.

Balzac, H. (1900). *Letters to Madame Hanska*. Boston: Little, Brown.

Baudelaire, C. (1861/1989). *The flowers of evil* (M. Mathews & J. Mathews, Eds.). New York: New Directions.

Bech, P., Rafaelsen, L., & Rafaelsen, O. J. (1973). Cannabis and alcohol: Effects on estimation of time and distance. *Psychopharmacologia, 32*, 373–381.

Bello, J. (1996). *The benefits of marijuana: Physical, psychological, and spiritual*. Boca Raton, FL: Lifeservices.

Block, R. I., Erwin, W. J., Farinpour, R., & Braverman, K. (1998). Sedative, stimulant and other subjective effects of marijuana: Relationships to smoking techniques. *Pharmacology, Biochemistry and Behavior, 59*, 405–412.

Block, R. I., & Wittenborn, J. R. (1984). Marijuana effects on semantic memory: Verification of common and uncommon category members. *Psychological Reports, 55*, 503–512.

Boon, B., Stroebe, W., Schut, H. & Ijntema, R. (2002). Ironic Processes in the Eating Behavior of Restrained Eaters. *British Journal of Health Psychology, 7*, 1–10.

Cami, J., Guerra, D., Ugena, B., Segura, J., & De La Torre, R. (1991). Effects of subject expectancy on THC intoxication and disposition from smoked hashish cigarettes. *Pharmacology, Biochemistry and Behavior, 40*, 115–119.

Carlini, E. A., & Cunha, J. M. (1981). Hypnotic and antiepileptic effects of cannabidiol. *Journal of Clinical Pharmacology, 21*, 417S–427S.

Chait, L. D., & Pierri, J. (1992). Effects of smoked marijuana on human performance: A critical review. In L. Murphy & A. Bartke (Eds.), *Marijuana/cannabinoids: Neurobiology and neurophysiology* (pp. 387–423). Boca Raton, FL: CRC.

Chowdhury, A. N., & Bera, N. K. (1994). Koro following cannabis smoking: Two case reports. *Addiction, 89*, 1017–1020.

Clarke, R. C. (1998). *Hashish!* Los Angeles: Red Eye.

Earleywine, M. (2002). *Understanding Marijuana*. New York: Yale University Press.

Earleywine, M. (2001). Cannabis-induced Kora in Americans. *Addiction, 96*, 1663–1666.

Emrich, H. M., Weber, M. M., Wendl, A., Zihl, J., Von Meyer, L., & Hanishc, W. (1991). Reduced binocular depth inversion as an indicator of cannabis induced censorship impairment. *Pharmacology, Biochemistry and Behavior, 40*, 689–690.

Foltin, R. W., Fischman, M. W., & Byrne, M. F. (1988). Effects of smoked marijuana on food intake and body weight of humans living in a residential laboratory. *Appetite, 11*, 1–14.

Franzini, L. R., & Grossberg, J. M. (1995). *Eccentric and bizarre behaviors*. New York: Wiley.

Gautier, T. (1846/1966). The hashish club. In D. Solomon (Ed.), *The marijuana papers* (pp. 121–135). New York: Bobbs-Merril.

Goldman, M. (2001). Expectancy and Risk for Alcoholism. *Alcoholism: Clinical and Experimental Research, 26*, 737–746.

Ginsberg, A. (1966). First manifesto to end the bringdown. In D. Solomon (Ed.), *The marijuana papers* (pp. 183–200). New York: Bobbs-Merril.

Grinspoon, L., & Bakalar, J. B. (1997). *Marijuana, the forbidden medicine*. New Haven, CT: Yale University Press.

Halikas, J. A., Goodwin, D. W., & Guze, S. B. (1971). Marijuana effects: A survey of regular users. *Journal of the American Medical Association, 217*, 692–694.

Halikas, J. A., Weller, R. A., & Morse, C. L. (1982). Effects of regular marijuana use on sexual performance. *Journal of Psychoactive Drugs, 14*, 59–70.

Halikas, J. A., Weller, R. A., Morse, C. L., & Hoffmann, R. G. (1985). A longitudinal study of marijuana effects. *International Journal of the Addictions, 20*, 701–711.

Henningfield, J. E., Johnson, R. E., & Jasinski, D. R. (1987). Clinical procedures for the assessment of abuse potential. In M. A. Bozarth (Ed.), *Methods of assessing the reinforcing properties of abused drugs* (pp. 573–590). New York: Springer-Verlag.

King, J. (2001). *The cannabible*. Berkeley, CA: Ten Speed Press.

Kirk, J. M., Doty, P., & de Wit, H. (1998). Effects of expectancies on subjective responses to oral delta-9-tetrahydrocannabinol. *Pharmacology, Biochemistry and Behavior, 59,* 287–293.

Langer, E. (2000). Mindful learning. *Current Directions in Psychological Science. 9,* 220–223.

Lyons, M. J., Toomey, R., Meyer, J. M., Green, A. I., Eisen, S. A., Goldberg, J., et al. (1997). How do genes influence marijuana use? The role of subjective effects. *Addiction, 92,* 409–417.

Martin, C., Earleywine, M., Musty, R., Perrine, M., & Swift, R. (1993). Development and validation of the biphasic alcohol effects scale. *Alcoholism: Clinical and Experimental Research, 17,* 140–146.

McFarland, J. M., & Mediavilla, V. (2002) Non cannabinoid components. In F. Grotenhermane and E. Russo (Eds.), *Cannabis and Cannabinoids: Pharmacology, Toxicology, and Therapeutic Potential.* New York: Haworth.

Mathew, R. J., Wilson, W. H., Chiu, N. Y., Turkington, T. G., Degrado, T. R., & Coleman, R. E. (1999). Regional cerebral blood flow and depersonalization after tetrahydrocannabinol administration. *Acta Psychiatrica Scandinavica, 100,* 67–75.

Mattes, R. D., Shaw, L. M., & Engelman, K. (1994). Effects of cannabinoids (marijuana) on taste intensity and hedonic ratings and salivary flow of adults. *Chemical Senses, 19,* 125–140.

Matthias, P., Tashkin, D. P., Marques-Magallanes, J. A., Wilkins, J. N., & Simmons, M. S. (1997). Effects of varying marijuana potency on deposition of tar and delta9–THC in the lung during smoking. *Pharmacology, Biochemistry and Behavior, 58,* 1145–1150.

Mikulas, W. L. (1996). Sudden onset of subjective dimensionality: A case study. *Perceptual and Motor Skills, 82,* 852–854.

Miller, W. R. (1999). *Integrating spirituality into treatment: Resources for practitioners.* Washington, DC: American Psychological Association.

Moreau, J. J. (1845/1973). *Hashish and mental illness.* New York: Raven.

Rosenthal, E. (2001). *The Big Book of Buds.* Oakland, CA: Quick American Archives.

Rosenthal, E., Gieringer, D., & Mikuriya, T. (1997). *Marijuana medical handbook.* Oakland, CA: Quick American Archives.

Shenk, J. W. (2002). America's altered states: When does legal relief of pain become illegal pursuit of pleasure? (p. 237) In M. Gray (Ed.), *Busted: Stone cowboys, narco-lords and Washington's war on drugs.* New York: Nation Books.

Smart, R. G., & Walsh, G. (1999). Heavy drinking and problems among wine drinkers. *Journal of Studies on Alcohol, 60,* 467–471.

Tart, C. T. (1971). *On being stoned.* Palo Alto, CA: Science and Behavior Books.

Tiffany, S. T. (1999). Cognitive concepts of craving. *Alcohol Research and Health, 23,* 215–224.

Weller, R. A., & Halikas, J. A. (1982). Change in effects from marijuana: A five- to six-year follow-up. *Journal of Clinical Psychiatry, 43,* 362–365.

Weller, R. A., & Halikas, J. A. (1984). Marijuana use and sexual behavior. *Journal of Sex Research, 20,* 186–193.

Zinberg, N. E. (1984). *Drug set and setting: The basis for controlled intoxicant use.* New Haven, CT: Yale University Press.

10

Relationships Between Personality and Acute Subjective Responses to Stimulant Drugs

HARRIET DE WIT

There is a long history of research on the relationship between personality and drug use, abuse, and dependence. Individuals appear to differ in their susceptibility to develop drug abuse problems, and it is reasonable to suppose that these differences may be related to preexisting, dispositional personality factors. Although the simple idea of a unitary "addictive personality" has received little empirical support (Kerr, 1996), there is considerable evidence for associations between specific behavioral or personality traits and drug use. This support comes from a variety of sources, including studies comparing users and nonusers of drugs, laboratory-based empirical studies, and, especially, data obtained from longitudinal studies (Dawes et al., 2000; Sher, Bartholow, & Wood, 2000; Tarter, 2002). However, the specific associations between personality and drug use are still not well understood. It is not yet known how personality influences vulnerability for using drugs, including which personality traits affect drug use, or how personality interacts with any of the multiple determinants of drug use. Interestingly, recent evidence suggests that there may be neurobiological links between personality or temperament and responses to drugs. That is, the same neurobiological and genetic systems that contribute to variation in personality may also contribute to variations in responses to abused drugs. The idea that common neurobiological processes may underlie both personality and susceptibility to use drugs is likely to receive greater research attention in years to come.

Stable personality traits, defined as individual styles of behavior, cognition, and affect, could influence the development of drug use and abuse at many levels. Certain personality traits may predispose some individuals to use and experiment with drugs for the first time. For example, individuals who are more adventurous, more likely to take risks, or more susceptible to peer influence may be more likely to try drugs in the first instance (McGue, Iacono, Legrand, Malone, & Elkins, 2001). Once an individual samples a drug, his or her personality traits (such as impulsivity, or lack of constraint) may influence the ability to resist using the drug again. For example, impulsive individuals may have difficulty refraining from illicit or culturally proscribed drug use. Further, once their use of the drug has escalated to regular or problematic levels, impulsive individuals may have particular difficulty abstaining or cutting down on their drug use.

From the perspective of biological or genetic determinants of drug use, one interesting way that personality can influence drug use is through shared neurobiological processes with the direct, mood-altering, or subjective effects of drugs. It is widely assumed that people use drugs recreationally because the drugs produce feelings of well-being and euphoria. It is also recognized that individuals vary in their affective responses to drugs, in ways that may predict future drug seeking: Whereas some people experience predominantly positive subjective feelings from a drug, others experience mostly unpleasant effects. There is some evidence that these individual differences in acute mood-altering, or subjective, effects of drugs may be related to individual differences in personality. Key questions for future research will be how and why personality is related to acute drug responses. For example, the differences in self-reported subjective effects among individuals may reflect differences in the pharmacological and neurobiological responses to the drug. Alternatively, individual differences in subjective drug effects may result from differences in labeling or interpreting essentially the same neurobiological responses in different individuals. One intriguing possibility is that common neurobiological processes underlie both certain personality traits and acute subjective responses to drugs. In this chapter we will review recent studies that have examined the relationship between personality and the quality and magnitude of mood changes after acute administration of stimulant drugs, with a view to investigating the existence of common underlying brain processes.

Measuring Personality

Various personality theorists have proposed a range of core dimensions and subtraits of personality (Buss & Plomin, 1975; Cloninger, 1987; Depue & Iacono, 1989; Depue & Collins, 1999; Eysenck & Eysenck, 1968; Zuckerman, 1979, 1994). Nevertheless, experts agree that there are a small handful of core personality traits, which are probably bio-logically based. Ultimately, understanding the biological basis of these core personality traits will lead us to a clearer definition of their struc-ture and dimensions. One core trait that is particularly relevant to sub-stance abuse is a dimension related to reward, sociability, and activation. The most widely cited schema of personality traits (Cloninger, 1987; Depue 1989, 1999; Eysenck & Eysenck, 1968; Zuckerman, 1979, 1994) postulates the existence of a specific personality dimension related to reward, activation, and well-being, and there is limited evidence that this dimension is related to dopamine function. The Eysenck Personal-ity Questionnaire (EPQ; Eysenck & Eysenck, 1975) identifies three core personality dimensions: extraversion, neuroticism, and psychoticism. Extraversion, which is characterized by sociability, activity, assertiveness, sensation seeking, and dominance, is thought to be linked to dopam-ine function. In preclinical models, dopamine plays an important role in facilitating goal-directed behavior, including exploratory behavior, locomotor activity, and instrumentally reinforced behavior, sometimes referred to as *incentive motivational behavior* (Everitt, Dickinson, & Robbins, 2001). Extraversion is thought to be related to dopamine func-tion in part because the behavioral tendencies of extraverts resemble behaviors controlled by dopamine function (e.g., activation, reward, and positive affect). Genetic studies also support the idea that the core trait of extraversion is biologically based (see review by Reif & Lesch, 2003).

The Sensation Seeking Scale (SSS; Zuckerman 1979, 1994) assesses a related dimension, referred to as sensation seeking, with four subscales known as Thrill and Adventure Seeking (TAS), Experience Seeking (ES), Disinhibition (D), and Boredom Susceptibility. Several lines of evidence suggest that sensation seeking (SS) is biologically based. Twin studies comparing SS in fraternal and identical twins (Fulker, Eysenck, & Zuckerman, 1980; Tellegen et al., 1988) indicate that about 58% of the total SS trait is heritable. Further, sensation seeking is negatively cor-related with platelet monoamine oxidase levels (Zuckerman, 1994, p. 298), and one early study found that cerebrospinal fluid levels of norepinephrine were negatively correlated with SSS scores (Ballenger et al., 1983). Cloninger (1987) developed the Tridimensional Person-ality Questionnaire (TPQ) to assess three core dimensions of person-ality, Reward Dependence, Harm Avoidance, and Novelty Seeking (NS). The NS dimension is characterized by excitability, exploration, extrava-gance, and disinhibition and resembles aspects of extraversion and sensation seeking. Cloninger postulated that NS is associated with dif-ferential basal rates of dopamine activity, as well as differential reac-tivity to novel stimuli. The idea is that individuals with high basal firing of dopamine neurons have a relatively positive tonic affective state. They are thought to be relatively insensitive to novel stimuli (low NS) because of a down-regulation of postsynaptic dopamine receptors. In contrast, individuals with relatively low basal rates of dopamine activity and perhaps an upregulation of postsynaptic receptors are more sensitive to the neural effects of novel stimuli (high NS). Thus, it may be that the high NS individuals may be particularly susceptible to using mood-enhancing drugs.

Finally, Tellegen (1982) developed the Multiphasic Personality Questionnaire (MPQ), which includes the trait of Positive Emotionality, which is closely linked to extraversion. This trait is characterized by behavioral activation, arousal, sociability, positive emotions, and "positive incentive motivation." Depue and Collins (1999) suggest that this trait reflects sensitivity to reward, and, like Cloninger, they suggest that it is related to the sensitivity or reactivity of the dopamine system. Thus, they propose that extraverted individuals are more likely to use drugs because they are more sensitive to reward in general. They posit that individual differences in extraversion are related to variations in function of dopamine projections originating in the ventral tegmental area, which they argue is directly involved in the intensity of incentive motivation. Depue, Luciana, Arbisi, Collins, and Leon (1994) provided some empirical support for this link between extraversion and dopamine activity by showing that individuals who are high on the personality measure of extraversion exhibited more pronounced endocrine (prolactin) and behavioral (eye blink) responses to a dopamine receptor agonist, bromocriptine. These authors linked the trait of Positive Emotionality (MPQ) to individual differences in the rewarding effects of drugs, as follows: "Because degree of state dopamine activity affects the salience of incentive stimuli, the subjective emotional and motivational experiences that are naturally elicited by incentive stimuli and are part of extraversion—elation/euphoria, desire, incentive motivation, sense of potency or self-efficacy—will also be more enhanced in individuals high on this trait" (Depue & Collins, 1999, p. 511). This link suggests that greater reactivity of the dopamine system may underlie extraversion. Further, brain imaging studies suggest that reactivity of the dopamine system mediates the positive affective responses to acute drug administration (Breiter et al., 1997; Volkow et al., 1999).

The relationship between personality and use of nonstimulant drugs, including alcohol, will not be examined here in detail. However, it is worth noting that there is also strong evidence linking personality to use of alcohol (Cloninger, Sigvardsson, & Bohman, 1988; Sher et al., 2000; Tarter, 2002). For example, in Cloninger's (1987) schema, the traits of "reward dependence" and "novelty seeking" are linked to noradrenergic and dopaminergic function, and to genetically based individual differences in susceptibility to alcoholism. In one sample ($N = 431$) of 11–year-old Swedish children, Cloninger et al. (1988) found that high novelty seeking, together with low scores on harm avoidance, was highly predictive of alcohol abuse at age 27. At least two longitudinal studies (Gotham, Sher, & Wood, 2003; Sher et al., 2000) have linked extraversion, sensation seeking, and disinhibition to drinking (as well as use of other drugs) in college-age and younger individuals. It is likely that there are many commonalities between the risk factors for alcohol use and use of other drugs.

Models of drug use in laboratory animals support the association between reward sensitivity and susceptibility to stimulant drug use. Animals that exhibit a greater tendency to explore a novel environment are also more likely to self-administer stimulant drugs (Bardo, Donohew, & Harrington, 1996; Piazza, Deminiere, Le Moal, & Simon, 1989). In these studies, exploration of a novel environment is taken to indicate sensitivity to the rewarding effects of novel stimuli. Based on this idea, Piazza and coworkers found that rats exhibiting the most exploratory behavior in a novel environment most rapidly acquired a response to obtain injections of a self-administered stimulant drug. Since then, this finding has been extended to other drugs, other species, and other drug reward paradigms (Klebaur & Bardo, 1999). In their review of the evidence for a relation between novelty seeking and drug use, for example, Bardo et al. argue that exposure to novelty, like drugs of abuse, activates the mesolimbic dopamine system, and that individual differences in the dopamine system may account for individual differences in both novelty seeking and drug use. They review evidence that both genetic and environmental factors, such as rearing experiences and environmental enrichment, can account for individual differences in both novelty seeking and susceptibility to using drugs. Thus, several lines of evidence have tied the personality trait of extraversion or reward sensitivity to drug use, in both humans and nonhumans. Moreover, there is growing evidence that this personality dimension and perhaps other dimensions as well have a biological basis, insofar as they are genetically based and correlated to the functions of specific neurotransmitter systems. For example, there may be a common neural mechanism mediating both personality traits and the acute mood-altering effects of drugs.

Personality and Acute Subjective Drug Effects

It has long been noted that individuals vary markedly in their subjective responses to drugs (von Felsinger, Lasagna, & Beecher, 1955). Even within apparently homogeneous groups of subjects (by age, sex, weight, habitual drug use), different individuals report widely different affective and mood changes after drug administration. Individuals differ in terms of both the magnitude of effects (e.g., how strongly they feel the drug's effects; Schuckit, 1984) and the quality of the effects (e.g., whether the drug produces sedative-like effects or stimulant-like effects; de Wit, Pierri, & Johanson, 1989; de Wit, Uhlenhuth, & Johanson, 1986; Holdstock &

de Wit, 1998, 1999). In the absence of other explanations for these differences, it is not surprising that this variability has been attributed to differences in "personality." The idea that personality affects acute responses to drugs also fits with a common belief, stemming from disease models of drug abuse, that people become drug abusers because of a preexisting psychological condition or deficit (Khantzian, 1997). Although the notion that there is a single "addictive personality" that makes certain individuals uniquely vulnerable to substance abuse has been questioned (Nathan, 1988), there is empirical support for the idea that certain stable personality traits account for some of the variation in direct subjective, or mood-altering, responses to drugs. In the following we will review some of the evidence that individual differences in mood responses to drugs, especially stimulant drugs, are related to individual differences in personality. We will review data with three drugs, amphetamine, caffeine, and nicotine, which produce stimulant-like subjective effects in humans and stimulant-like behavioral effects in nonhumans. All three drugs have dependence potential, and although they have different initial actions in the brain, they all (like most other drugs of abuse) share the capacity to increase synaptic levels of dopamine (Carboni, Silvagni, Rolando, & Di Chiara, 2000; Clarke, 1990; Koob, 1992; Solinas et al., 2002).

Studies with Amphetamine

Von Felsinger et al. (1955) conducted one of the earliest systematic investigations of personality and responses to an acute dose of amphetamine. These investigators studied the mood-altering effects of 20 mg d-amphetamine in 20 healthy volunteers, under double-blind conditions. Most of the subjects reported feelings of euphoria and well-being from the drug, but 4 of the subjects experienced dysphoria. In an attempt to identify distinguishing features of the intersubject differences in responses to amphetamine, the investigators characterized the personality "traits" of their subjects based on psychiatric interviews and semiquantitative, standardized Rorschach tests conducted by psychologists who were not aware of the subjects' responses to the drug. They concluded that the 4 subjects who experienced dysphoric reactions to amphetamine displayed a lack of motivation and goal-orientedness in life, and a pervading sense of failure and inadequacy in meeting life's demands. These subjects also tended to consume more alcohol than other subjects and reported that alcohol produced a feeling of release from pressure. The Rorschach tests of these dysphoric responders revealed a fear of loss of control under any type of pressure (including, perhaps, a fear of loss of control after the drug) and high scores on anxiety-hostility. These profiles contrasted with those of the remaining subjects, who appeared well adjusted and goal oriented. The investigators also compared two other subgroups of subjects based on their responses to amphetamine: those who felt sedated by the drug (N = 5) and those who felt stimulated (N = 7). Again, based on Rorschach scores, the group that felt stimulated appeared well adjusted, responsive, and motivated, whereas the group that felt sedated by the drug exhibited a strongly negative personality profile. This negative profile, as measured by the Rorschach, included depressive tendencies, moodiness, inadequate control over emotion, and unrealistic and diffuse goals. Although now, half a century later, we can question the methods used by von Felsinger et al. to assess personality, these early findings present a vivid picture of personality differences related to qualitative differences in mood responses to amphetamine. Notably, the study utilized several currently accepted experimental methods, including double-blind administration of drugs, standardized quantitative self-ratings of the mood-altering effects of the drug, and blinded assessment of personality. This early effort provided a rich source of data that set the stage for modern human psychopharmacology studies.

In a later study, Meyer, DiMascio, and Stifler (1970) examined the relationship between personality and responses to amphetamine (10 mg) administered to subjects in a sleep-deprived state. They divided their subjects into "type A" individuals, who were extraverted and self-assertive, and "type B" individuals, who were anxious, introverted, and passive, based on a clinical interview. The researchers postulated that type A individuals would experience more discomfort from the sleep deprivation and more positive antifatigue effects from the amphetamine, compared with the type B individuals. Contrary to their hypothesis, they found that the type B individuals experienced a more positive antifatigue effect (including mood enhancement) from the amphetamine than the type A individuals. Unfortunately, these investigators did not compare the effects of amphetamine in type A and type B individuals without sleep deprivation.

In other studies, behavioral preference for amphetamine was related to the quality of subjective effects experienced from the drug, but these measures were not related to personality. We (de Wit et al., 1986) investigated the role of personality and subjective drug responses in 31 subjects who either chose or did not choose amphetamine over placebo in a choice procedure (de Wit, Uhlenhuth, & Johanson, 1985; de Wit et al., 1986). In the choice procedure, subjects first sampled 5 mg d,l-amphetamine or placebo, under double-blind conditions, and then on 5 choice sessions they chose between the amphetamine- and placebo-containing capsules. Subjects who chose amphetamine over placebo on all 5 sessions (N = 20) were compared with subjects who never chose the placebo over the amphetamine (N = 11). The subjective effects of amphetamine during the sampling sessions were markedly different in the two choice groups: In nonchoosers, amphetamine increased depression and anxiety (Profile of Mood States; McNair, Lorr, & Droppleman, 1971), whereas in choosers it increased friendliness and elation. However, subjects' drug choices (and by implication their subjective responses to the drug) were not related to personality measures, including the Taylor Manifest Anxiety Scale (Speilberger, Gorsuch, & Lushene, 1970), the SSS (Zuckerman, Kuhlman, Thornquist, & Kiers, 1991) or a measure of internal versus external locus of control. Similarly, Chait (1993) investigated the relationship between several measures of personality and acute subjective or reinforcing effects of *d*-amphetamine (7.5–20 mg) in 29 healthy volunteers and found no relationship between subjective responses to amphetamine and scores on the SSS (Zuckerman et al., 1991), the EPQ (Eysenck & Eysenck, 1975), or the TPQ (Cloninger, 1987). The relatively small numbers of subjects and the fact that individuals with any psychiatric symptoms were excluded limit the conclusions that can be drawn from these negative findings. That is, the groups may have been too small and too homogeneous to allow detection of personality-related differences.

Kavoussi and Coccaro (1993) investigated acute subjective and hormonal responses to *d*-amphetamine (0.5 mg/kg) in 11 healthy volunteers, in relation to subjects' scores on the Affective Lability Scale (ALS; Harvey, Greenberg, & Serper, 1989), a measure of emotional lability. The ALS measures the tendency toward sudden shifts in specific affect (e.g., anxiety, anger, depression). Responses to amphetamine were assessed in an in-person interview, under blinded conditions. Subjects who scored high on the ALS, especially on the anxiety and anger subscales, were more likely to report dysphoric responses (e.g., anxiety and depression) to amphetamine. However, plasma levels of HVA and MHPG, markers of monoaminergic functioning, were not related to the individual differences in mood effects of the drug. The results of this study were consistent with the previous studies indicating that mood-disordered individuals tend to experience greater dysphoric reactions to amphetamine.

Several other lines of evidence indicate that individual differences in subjective response to amphetamine have a biological basis, most likely in the dopamine system. Nurnberger et al. (1982) studied the effects of 0.3 mg/kg *d*-amphetamine in monozygotic twins, dizygotic twins, and patients with bipolar disorder. They found a strong correlation in behavioral and hormonal responses to amphetamine in monozygotic (compared with dizygotic) twins and no differential responses in the patients. This study provided strong evidence for a genetic basis for variation in behavioral excitatory effects of amphetamine, and by blocking the effects with haloperidol the authors also linked this behavioral excitation to dopamine function. Imaging studies also support a role for dopamine in the subjective effects of stimulants (Breiter et al., 1997; Volkow et al., 1999). Breiter et al. (1997) used functional magnetic resonance imaging to show that cocaine increased dopaminergic activity in the mesolimbic dopamine system, coinciding with increases in subjects' reports of feeling "high." Laruelle and colleagues (1995) found a significant relation between subjective activation after an acute dose of amphetamine and increased dopamine activity, as measured by single photon computerized tomography (SPECT) and the D2 tracer [123I] IBZM. However, this relationship between subjective experience and dopamine activity was not observed in a subsequent study (Kegeles et al., 1999). Volkow et al. (1999) used positron emission tomography (PET) with [11C]raclopride to measure D2 receptor levels at baseline and after administration of methylphenidate in healthy volunteers. They found that subjects with lower baseline D2 receptor levels liked the effects of methylphenidate more, and that reports of feeling "high" after methylphenidate were positively correlated with the level of released dopamine. These studies support the idea that stimulant drugs produce pleasurable subjective sensations through their actions on the dopamine system (although it should be noted that studies with dopamine antagonists fail to support this link; Brauer, Goudie, & de Wit, 1997; Brauer & de Wit, 1995, 1996, 1997; Wachtel, Ortengren, & de Wit, 2002).

Other studies have examined the effects of amphetamine in patients with psychiatric disorders, including major depression and borderline personality disorder. These drug challenge studies are based on the idea that responses to drugs may reveal the underlying biological dysfunction of the psychiatric disorders (Schulz et al., 1985; Schulz, Cornelius, P. M. Schulz, & Soloff, 1988; Silberman, Reus, Jimerson, Lynott, & Post, 1981). Schultz et al. (1988) found that amphetamine worsened symptoms in patients with schizotypal and borderline personality disorders but improved them in patients with only borderline personality disorder. Silberman et al. (1981) found a great deal of variability in the affective responses to amphetamine in 18 depressed patients. Although all patients experienced psychomotor activation, some patients responded with elation and others with dysphoria. However, the authors were unable to identify factors that predicted the patients' responses (including sex, initial level of depression, and order of drug and placebo administration).

Recently, Hutchinson, Wood, and Swift (1999) examined subjective and psychophysiological (startle response) measures after d-amphetamine (20 mg) in relation to scores on the TPQ (Cloninger, 1987) and the SSS (Zuckerman et al., 1991) in 36 healthy volunteers. They found that high scores on Novelty Seeking (TPQ) and Disinhibition (SSS) were correlated with greater subjective stimulation, elation, vigor, and positive affect after amphetamine. Prepulse inhibition of the startle response was related to Novelty Seeking: Amphetamine decreased percent prepulse inhibition in subjects high on Novelty Seeking but had no effect on subjects low on Novelty Seeking. This evidence suggests a link between dopaminergic sensitivity and Novelty Seeking, since prepulse inhibition is thought to be controlled in part by dopamine mechanisms (Swerdlow, Caine, Braff, & Geyer, 1992; Swerdlow, Braff, Taaid, & Geyer, 1994).

We have recently examined acute responses to d-amphetamine (0, 10, or 20 mg) in 76 healthy volunteers, in relation to the subjects' scores on a short version of the MPQ (Patrick, Curtin, & Tellegen, 2002). Normal healthy volunteers, aged 18 to 35, participated in a double-blind, laboratory-based study in which they received capsules containing d-amphetamine (10 and 20 mg) or placebo. Before and at regular intervals after ingesting the drug, they completed several self-report mood questionnaires, including visual analog ratings of how much they felt the drug effects, how much they liked the effects, and how they felt in relation to a number of adjectives describing mood states (e.g., anxious, depressed, energetic). We examined peak change in the mood and drug-liking scores after the drug, in relation to the three primary traits of the MPQ: Positive Emotionality, Negative Emotionality, and Constraint, as well as one specific subscale, Social Potency. We found that subjects' ratings of drug liking after 20 mg d-amphetamine were positively correlated with MPQ traits of Positive Emotionality ($r = .36$, $p < .001$) and Social Potency ($r = .34$, $p < .005$). In addition, subjects' ratings of Anxiety after 20 mg d-amphetamine were positively correlated with the trait of Negative Emotionality ($r = .20$, $p = .05$). These unpublished findings support previous findings that acute mood responses to stimulant drugs are related to stable personality traits. They also support the idea that there are separable components of responses to a drug (e.g., liking and anxiety) that may be associated with variability in different personality types.

Taken together, these findings with acute subjective responses to amphetamine and personality suggest that two personality factors may influence responses to amphetamine. First, the trait of extraversion and sensation seeking is associated with more positive affective effects of the drug. Conversely, the trait of neuroticism or negative affect may predispose certain individuals to experience unpleasant, anxiety-like effects from the drug. It remains to be determined whether these factors can also interact to put some individuals at especially high risk for experiencing either affectively positive or negative effects from amphetamine, and whether this affects the likelihood of future drug seeking.

Studies With Caffeine

Several studies have examined the relationship between personality and mood responses to an acute dose of caffeine, but the results have been inconsistent. Although an early study by Gilliland and Miller (1980) found that introverts reported a decrease in self-rated arousal after caffeine and extraverts reported dose-related increases in arousal, two subsequent studies (Chait, 1992 ; Liguori, Grass, & Hughes, 1999) failed to replicate this effect. Most recently, Liguori et al. (1999) compared the effects of caffeine (0, 2, or 4 mg/kg anhydrous caffeine) in introverts ($N = 17$; who scored less than 9 on the Extraversion scale of the EPQ; Eysenck & Eysenck, 1975) and extraverts ($N = 19$; who scored more than 18 on Extraversion). They found no significant differences in subjective reactions to caffeine in the two groups, although there was a nonsignificant trend for more extraverted individuals to show greater increases in vigor and happiness after caffeine. Griffiths and Woodson (1988) examined subjective responses and choice of caffeine (100–600 mg) in healthy volunteers ($N = 11$), in relation to several measures of personality. They found a negative correlation between a trait measure of anxiety (Speilberger et al., 1970) and the choice of caffeine-containing capsules. Subjects who avoided choosing the caffeine-containing capsules also reported liking the caffeine effects less and feeling less content and at ease after taking the drug.

We recently examined subjects' responses to a low dose of caffeine in relation to EPQ Extraversion and Neuroticism scores. Light caffeine users (i.e., individuals who consumed less than 3 cups per week; $N = 100$) ingested capsules containing 300 mg caffeine citrate (equivalent to about 1–2 cups of coffee) or placebo and then rated their mood and subjective states at regular intervals over the next 4 hours. In the group as a whole, caffeine produced its prototypical effects, including increased ratings of stimulation and anxiety and decreased ratings of depression and fatigue (Alsene, Deckert, & de Wit, 2003). In a separate analysis, we compared responses to caffeine in subjects who scored low or high on the trait of Extraversion (<10; $N = 22$ or >13; $N = 20$), and subjects low or high on Neuroticism (<6; $N = 22$ or >9; $N = 21$). The effects of caffeine were similar regardless of personality scores on most measures of acute drug effects, except two. Subjects high on Neuroticism reported greater increases in ratings of Anxiety (POMS) after caffeine than subjects low on Neuroticism, and subjects high on Extraversion reported greater increases in Vigor (POMS) after caffeine, compared with the low Extraversion subjects. These unpublished findings suggest that Extraversion and Neuroticism may each contribute to a separate dimension of the subjective effects experienced after an acute dose of caffeine.

Thus, there is some evidence that responses to acute doses of caffeine are related to personality. Some evidence suggests that individuals who are more extraverted may experience more positive, activational effects from caffeine, whereas individuals who are more anxious or neurotic may experience greater negative, anxiogenic effects from this drug. However, our recent analysis suggests that anxiogenic effects may be related to both neuroticism and extraversion. The differences among the studies may be related to a multitude of variables, including particularly drug dose and characteristics of the subject sample. However, the evidence suggests that more than a single personality trait can influence responses to a drug, and different traits may affect the drug response in qualitatively different ways.

Studies With Nicotine

It is recognized that nicotine dependence is strongly correlated with both personality and psychopathology (Gilbert, & Gilbert, 1995). Extraversion, neuroticism, and impulsivity have been linked to risk for smoking, and smoking is higher in patients with depression, schizophrenia, alcoholism, and other psychiatric disorders. However, the extent to which this correlation is related to individual differences in acute responses to nicotine is unclear. There is one report in which extraverts exhibited greater hormonal and EEG responses to nicotine than introverts, and individuals high on neuroticism exhibited smaller responses to nicotine (Gilbert, Meliska, Welser, & Estes, 1994). It was proposed that extraverts are more likely to smoke because they are more sensitive to the effects of nicotine, including its reinforcing effects (Pomerleau, Hariharan, Pomerleau, Cameron, & Guthrie, 1993). However, the electrophysiological differences in responses to nicotine between extraverts and introverts have been inconsistent (Gilbert, & Gilbert, 1995). Perkins, Gerlach, Broge, Grobe, and Wilson (2000) examined sensitivity to nicotine (0, 10, or 20 μg/kg in nasal spray) in relation to sensation seeking in both smokers and nonsmokers. They found that individuals who scored high on the SSS (TAS, ES, and D scales) reported stronger effects from nicotine. These effects were apparent in both smokers and nonsmokers, but they were more pronounced in nonsmokers. Thus, there is limited evidence that higher extraversion and sensation seeking, and perhaps lower neuroticism, relate to greater sensitivity to the effects of nicotine.

Other Stimulants or Dopamine Agonists

Several other studies have examined the relation between personality and acute responses to stimulant drugs. Depue et al. (1994) examined responses to bromocriptine (2.5 mg), a dopamine agonist, to the personality trait of Positive Emotionality (PE) in 11 healthy volunteers. They measured two responses that are purported to reflect dopamine function, eyeblink rate and increases in plasma level of prolactin. Bromocriptine produced no significant changes in subjective state, so that no relationship was obtained between personality and drug-induced mood in this study. In another study, Chait (1994) examined individual differences in subjective and behavioral effects of ephedrine in healthy volunteers. He found that subjects high on Harm Avoidance (TPQ) were less likely to choose ephedrine, and women, compared with men, chose ephedrine less often and experienced less positive mood effects from it.

Conclusions

We have reviewed evidence that individual differences in subjective responses to acute doses of stimulant-like drugs are related to personality. There is some evidence that the trait of extraversion/sensation seeking may be related to activating and positive affective responses to stimulant drugs, whereas the trait of neuroticism/negative emotionality may be related to dysphoric responses to these drugs. Further, there is some evidence that both extraversion and positive responses to drugs may be related to dopamine function. We do not as yet know the neurochemical basis of either the trait of neuroticism or the dysphoric responses to stimulant drugs, although they may involve either of the other two primary neurotransmitters involved in stimulant effects, norepinephrine or serotonin. We still know little about how personality or its neurobiological underpinnings affect acute subjective responses to drugs. For example, we do not know if different personality types experience basically the same pharmacological effects, differing only in how the effects are subjectively labeled and perceived. It is difficult to validate individual differences in subjective drug effects, since these are essentially private experiences. One important approach to addressing this issue is to obtain objective, physiological outcome measures as well as subjective outcome measures to characterize group differences. The possibility that behavioral styles of the individuals and their acute responses to drugs are related to differences in receptor number or function could be addressed using imaging techniques that provide a direct indicator of neurotransmitter function. Another way to investigate the mechanisms underlying the differences in drug responses is to test the effects of several drugs, with different behavioral effects and different mechanisms of action. For example, it would be important to determine whether extraverts report more positive responses to all types of drug, regardless of pharmacological class, or only to drugs that act on certain neurotransmitter systems. Finally, it will be of interest to determine whether there are genetic factors that link both personality traits and acute responses to drugs. There is good evidence that personality is strongly influenced by genetics (Reif & Lesch, 2003; Tellegen et al., 1988). We (Alsene et al., 2003) recently reported that a receptor gene polymorphism of the adenosine A2A receptor was associated with greater anxiety after administration of caffeine, and also to lower scores on the Venturesomeness scale of the EPQ (Eysenck & Eysenck, 1975). Taken together, all these lines of evidence suggest a promising new area of research linking personality and acute drug responses to underlying neural and genetic mechanisms underlying behavior and affect.

Supported by National Institute of Health grants DA02812 and DA09133. April Adams assisted in the preparation of the manuscript.

References

Alsene, K. M., Deckert, J., & de Wit, H. (2003). Increased anxiety after acute caffeine associated with adenosine A2A receptor polymorphism *Neuropsychopharmacology, 28.* 1694–1702.

Ballenger, J. C., Post, R. M, Jimerson, D. C., Lake C. R., Murphy, D. L., Zuckerman M., et al. (1983). Biochemical correlates of personality traits in normals: An exploratory study. *Personality and Individual Differences, 4*, 615–625.

Bardo, M. T., Donohew, R. L., & Harrington, N. G. (1996). Psychobiology of novelty seeking and drug seeking behavior. *Behavioral Brain Research, 77*, 23–43.

Brauer, L. H., & de Wit, H. (1995). Role of dopamine in d-amphetamine-induced euphoria in normal, healthy volunteers. *Experimental and Clinical Psychopharmacology, 3*, 371–381.

Brauer, L. H., & de Wit, H. (1996). Subjective responses to d-amphetamine alone and after pimozide pretreatment in normal healthy volunteers. *Biological Psychiatry, 39*, 26–32.

Brauer, L. H., & de Wit, H. (1997). High dose pimozide does not block amphetamine-induced euphoria in normal volunteers. *Pharmacology, Biochemistry and Behavior, 56*, 265–272.

Brauer, L. H., Goudie, A. J., & de Wit, H. (1997). Dopamine ligands and the stimulus effects of amphetamine: Animal models vs human laboratory data. *Psychopharmacology, 130*, 2–13.

Breiter, H. C., Gollub, R. L., Weisskoff, R. M., Kennedy, D. N., Makris, N., Berke, J. D., et al. (1997). Acute effects of cocaine on human brain activity and emotion. *Neuron, 19*, 591–611.

Buss, A. H., & Plomin, R. (1975). *A temperament theory of personality development*. New York: Wiley.

Carboni, E., Silvagni, A., Rolando, M. T., & Di Chiara, G. (2000). Stimulation of in vivo dopamine transmission in the bed nucleus of stria terminalis by reinforcing drugs. *Journal of Neuroscience, 20*, RC102.

Chait, L. D. (1992). Factors influencing the subjective response to caffeine. *Behavioral Pharmacology, 3*, 219–228.

Chait, L. D. (1993). Factors influencing the reinforcing and subjective effects of d-amphetamine in humans. *Behavioral Pharmacology, 4*, 191–199.

Chait, L. D. (1994). Factors influencing the reinforcing and subjective effects of ephedrine in humans. *Psychopharmacology, 113*, 381–387.

Clarke, P. B. (1990). Dopaminergic mechanisms in the locomotor stimulant effects of nicotine. *Biochemica. Pharmacology, 40*, 1427–1432.

Cloninger, C. (1987). Neurogenetic adaptive mechanisms in alcoholism. *Science, 236*, 410–416.

Cloninger, C. R., Sigvardsson, S., & Bohman, M. (1988). Childhood personality predicts alcohol abuse in young adults. *Alcoholism: Clinical and Experimental Research, 12*, 494–505.

Dawes, M. A., Antelman, S. M., Vanyukov, M. M., Giancola, P., Tarter, R. E., Susman, E. J., et al. (2000). Developmental sources of variation in liability to adolescent substance use disorders. *Drug and Alcohol Dependence, 61*, 3–14.

Depue, R. A., & Collins, P. F. (1999). Neurobiology of the structure of personality: Dopamine, facilitation of incentive motivation, and extraversion. *Behavioral and Brain Sciences, 22*, 491–569.

Depue, R. A., & Iacono, W. G. (1989). Neurobehavioral aspects of affective disorders. *Annual Review of Psychology, 40*, 457–492.

Depue, R. A., Luciana, M., Arbisi, P., Collins, P., & Leon, A. (1994). Dopamine and the structure of personality: Relation of agonist-induced dopamine activity to positive emotionality. *Journal of Personality and Social Psychology, 67*, 485–498.

de Wit, H., Pierri, J., & Johanson, C. E. (1989). Assessing individual differences in ethanol preference using a cumulative dosing procedure. *Psychopharmacology, 98*, 113–119.

de Wit, H., Uhlenhuth, E. H., & Johanson, C. E. (1985). Drug preference in normal volunteers: Effects of age and time of day. *Psychopharmacology, 87*, 186–193.

de Wit, H., Uhlenhuth, E. H., & Johanson, C. E. (1986). Individual differences in the behavioral and subjective effects of amphetamine and diazepam. *Drug and Alcohol Dependence, 16*, 341–360.

Everitt, B. J., Dickinson A., & Robbins T. W. (2001). The neuropsychological basis of addictive behaviour. *Brain Research Review, 36*, 129–138.

Eysenck, H. J., & Eysenck, S. B. G. (1968). *Eysenck Personality Inventory.* San Diego, CA: Educational and Industrial Testing Service.

Eysenck, H. J., & Eysenck, S. B. G. (1975). *Manual of the Eysenck Personality Questionnaire.* London: Hodder and Stoughton.

Fulker, D. W., Eysenck, S. B. G., & Zuckerman M. (1980). A genetic and environmental analysis of sensation seeking. *Journal of Research on Personality, 14*, 261–281.

Gilbert, D. G., & Gilbert, B. O. (1995). Personality, psychopathology, and nicotine response as mediators of the genetics of smoking. *Behavior Genetics, 2*, 133–147.

Gilbert, D. G., Meliska, C. J., Welser, R., & Estes, S. L. (1994). Depression, personality, and gender influence EEG, cortisol, beta-endorphin, heart rate, and subjective responses to smoking multiple cigarettes. *Personality and Individual Differences, 16*, 247–264.

Gilliland, L. E., & Miller, W. T. (1980). The interactive effect of introversion-extroversion with caffeine induced arousal on verbal performance. *Journal on Research in Personality, 14*, 482–492.

Gotham, H. J., Sher, K. J., & Wood, P. K. (2003). Alcohol involvement and developmental task completion during young adulthood. *Journal of Studies on Alcohol, 64*, 32–42.

Griffiths, R. R., & Woodson, P. P. (1988). Reinforcing effects of caffeine in humans. *Journal of Pharmacology and Experimental Therapeutics, 246*, 21–29.

Harvey, P. D., Greenberg, B. R., & Serper, M. R. (1989). The Affective Liability Scales: Development, reliability, and validity. *Journal of Clinical Psychology, 45*, 786–793.

Holdstock, L., & de Wit, H. (1998). Individual differences in the biphasic effects of alcohol. *Alcoholism: Clinical and Experimental Research, 22*, 1903–1911.

Holdstock, L., & de Wit, H. (1999). Individual differences in response to ethanol and triazolam. *Behavioural Pharmacology, 10*, 283–295.

Hutchinson, K. E., Wood, M. D., & Swift, R. (1999). Personality factors moderate subjective and psychophysiological responses to d-amphetamine in humans. *Experimental and Clinical Psychopharmacology, 7*, 493–501.

Kavoussi, R. J., & Coccaro, E. F. (1993). The amphetamine challenge test correlated with affective liability in healthy volunteers. *Psychiatry Research, 48*, 219–228.

Kegeles, L. S., Zea-Ponce, Y., Abi-Dargham, A., Rodenhiser, J., Wang, T., Weiss, R., Van Heertum, R. L., Mann, J. J., & Laruelle, M. (1999). Stability of [123I]IBZM SPECT measurement of amphetamine-induced striatal dopamine release in humans. *Synapse, 31*, 302–308.

Kerr, J. S. (1996). Two myths of addiction: The addictive personality and the issue of free choice. *Human Psychopharmacology, 11*, S9–S13.

Khantzian, E. J. (1997). The self-medication hypothesis of substance use disorders: A reconsideration and recent applications. *Harvard Review of Psychiatry, 4*, 231–244.

Klebaur, J. E., & Bardo, M. T. (1999). Individual differences in novelty seeking on the playground maze predict amphetamine conditioned place preference. *Pharmacology, Biochemistry and Behavior, 63*, 131–136.

Koob, G. F. (1992). Drugs of abuse: Anatomy, pharmacology and function of reward pathways. *Trends in Pharmacological Sciences, 13*, 177–184.

Laruelle, M., Abi-Dargham, A., van Dyck, C. H., Gil, R., Rosenblatt, W., Zea-Ponce, Y., et al. (1995). SPECTW imaging and striatal dopamine release after amphetamine challenge. *Journal of Nuclear Medicine, 36*, 1182–1190.

Liguori, A., Grass, J. A., & Hughes, J. R. (1999). Subjective effects of caffeine among introverts and extraverts in the morning and evening. *Experimental and Clinical Psychopharmacology, 7*, 244–249.

McGue, M., Iacono, W. G., Legrand, L. N., Malone, S., & Elkins, I. (2001). Origins and consequences of age at first drink. I. Associations with substance-use disorders, disinhibitory behavior and psychopathology, and P3 amplitude. *Alcoholism: Clinical and Experimental Research, 25*, 1156–1165.

McNair, D., Lorr, M., & Droppleman, L. (1971). *Profile of Mood States*. San Diego, CA: Educational and Industrial Testing Service.

Meyer, R. E., DiMascio, A., & Stifler, L. (1970). Personality differences in response to stimulant drugs administered during a sleep-deprived state. *Journal of Nervous and Mental Disease, 150*, 91–101.

Nathan, P. E. (1988). The addictive personality is the behavior of the addict. *Journal of Consulting and Clinical Psychology, 56*, 183–188.

Nurnberger, J. I., Gershon, E. S., Simmons, S., Ebert, M., Kessler, L. R., Dibble, E. D., et al. (1982). Biochemical and neuroendocrine responses to amphetamine in normal twins and "well-state" bipolar patients. *Psychoneuroendocrinology, 7*, 163–176.

Patrick, C. J., Curtin, J. J., & Tellegen, A. (2002). Development and validation of a brief form of the Multidimensional Personality Questionnaire. *Psychological Assessment, 14*, 150–163.

Perkins, K. A., Gerlach, D., Broge, M., Grobe, J. E., & Wilson, A. (2000). Greater sensitivity to subjective effects of nicotine in nonsmokers high in sensation seeking. *Experimental and Clinical Psychopharmacology, 8*, 462–471.

Piazza, P. V., Deminiere, J. M., Le Moal, M., & Simon, H. (1989). Factors that predict individual vulnerability to amphetamine self-administration. *Science, 245*, 1511–1513.

Pomerleau, O. F., Hariharan, M., Pomerleau, C. S., Cameron, O. G., & Guthrie, S. K. (1993). Differences between smokers and never-smokers in sensitivity to nicotine: A preliminary report. *Addiction, 88*, 113–118.

Reif, A., & Lesch, K. (2003). Toward a molecular architecture of personality. *Behavioral Brain Research, 139*, 1–20.

Schuckit, M. A. (1984). Subjective responses to alcohol in sons of alcoholics and control subjects. *Archives of General Psychiatry, 41*, 879–884.

Schulz, S. C., Cornelius, J., Schulz, P. M., & Soloff, P. H. (1988). The amphetamine challenge test in patients with borderline disorder. *American Journal of Psychiatry, 145*, 809–814.

Schulz, S. C., Schulz, P. M., Dommisse, C., Hamer, R. M., Blackard, W. G., Narasimhachari, N., et al. (1985). Amphetamine response in borderline patients. *Psychiatry Research, 15*, 97–108.

Sher, K. J., Bartholow, B. D., & Wood, M. D. (2000). Personality and substance use disorders: A prospective study. *Journal of Consulting and Clinical Psychology, 68*, 818–829.

Silberman, E. K., Reus, V. I., Jimerson, D. C., Lynott, A. M., & Post, R. M. (1981). Heterogeneity of amphetamine response in depressed patients. *American Journal of Psychiatry, 138*, 1302–1307.

Solinas, M., Ferre, S., You, Z. B., Karcz-Kubicha, M., Popoli, P., & Goldberg, S. R. (2002). Caffeine induces dopamine and glutamate release in the shell of the nucleus accumbens. *Journal of Neuroscience, 22*, 6321–6324.

Speilberger, C. D., Gorsuch, R. L., & Lushene, R. E. (1970). *STAI manual for the State-Trait Anxiety Inventory.* Palo Alto, CA: Consulting Psychologists Press.

Swerdlow, N. R., Braff, D. L., Taaid, N., & Geyer, M. A. (1994). Assessing the validity of an animal model of deficient sensorimotor gating in schizophrenic patients. *Archives of General Psychiatry, 51*, 139–154.

Swerdlow, R. R., Caine, S. B., Braff, D. L., & Geyer, M. A. (1992). The neural substrates of sensorimotor gating to study the pathophysiology and new treatments of schizophrenia. *Pharmacology, Biochemistry and Behavior, 44*, 741–744.

Tarter, R. E. (2002). Etiology of adolescent substance abuse: A developmental perspective. *American Journal of Addiction, 11*, 171–191.

Tellegen, A. (1982). *Multidimensional Personality Questionnaire Manual.* Minneapolis: University of Minnesota Press.

Tellegen, A., Lykken, D. T., Bouchard, T. J., Wilcox, K. J., Segal, N. L., & Rich, S. (1988). Personality similarity in twins reared apart and together. *Journal of Personality and Social Psychology, 54*, 1031–1039.

Volkow, N. D., Wang, G. J., Fowler, J. S., Logan, J., Gatley, S. J., Wong, C., et al. (1999). Reinforcing effects of psychostimulants in humans are associated with increases in brain dopamine and occupancy of D(2) receptors. *Journal of Pharmacology and Experimental Therapeutics, 291*, 409–415.

Von Felsinger, J. M., Lasagna, L., & Beecher, H. K. (1955). Drug-induced mood changes in man. 2. Personality and reactions to drugs. *Journal of the American Medical Association, 157*, 1113–1119.

Wachtel, S. R., Ortengren, A., & de Wit, H. (2002). The effects of acute haloperidol or risperidone on subjective respones to methamphetamine in healthy volunteers. *Drug and Alcohol Dependence, 68*, 23–33.

Zuckerman, M. (1979). *Sensation seeking: Beyond the optimal level of arousal.* Hillsdale, NJ: Erlbaum.

Zuckerman, M. (1994). *Behavioral expressions and biosocial bases of sensation seeking.* New York: Cambridge University Press.

Zuckerman, M., Kuhlman, D. M., Thornquist, M., & Kiers, H. (1991). Five (or three) robust questionnaire scale factors of personality without culture. *Personality and Individual Differences, 12*, 929–941.

11

Subjective Effects
of Methylphenidate

SCOTT KOLLINS

Methylphenidate (MPH) is one of the most widely prescribed psychotropic agents in the United States, and its increased use over the past two decades has been a source of growing controversy among scientists, clinicians, policy makers, and parents. Attention deficit/hyperactivity disorder (ADHD) has been treated with MPH for more than 40 years, and a large number of randomized clinical trials support its efficacy in children, adolescents, and adults. In spite of its documented efficacy, a number of important questions pertaining to the patterns of use, mechanisms of action, and range of effects of MPH have been raised. This chapter will highlight research and theory on the subjective effects of MPH and how their study can provide information addressing all these issues. The chapter will begin by briefly reviewing the history of the clinical use of MPH and empirical work on the recent prescription trends of this drug. The focus will then turn to the question of what kinds of information subjective effects of MPH can provide about both the clinical effects of the drug and its potential for abuse or misuse. The chapter will then review those studies that have evaluated the subjective effects of MPH in human participants, with emphasis on the methodological variation across studies in which these effects have been assessed. We will emphasize the measurement of MPH subjective effects in clinical samples of individuals with ADHD, including a recently completed study suggesting differential patterns of effects in this group versus healthy controls. Finally, the chapter will provide an overview of potential neuropharmacological mechanisms that might account for subjective effects in general and the observed differences in subjective effects of MPH between ADHD and control individuals.

Patterns of MPH Use

Stimulant medications in general and MPH specifically have long been known to exert beneficial effects on behavior problems in clinical settings (e.g., Bradley, 1950). Clinicians have used MPH since at least the 1950s with certain populations (e.g., Levy, Jones, & Croley, 1957). The first reported clinical trial of MPH for behaviorally disturbed children was in 1963 (Conners & Eisenberg, 1963). This study reported that MPH improved symptom scores and laboratory task performance in children presenting with a wide range of disruptive behavior problems. In the ensuing years, there have been several hundred well-controlled, randomized clinical trials of MPH involving several thousand school-age children, adolescents, and adults (Spencer et al., 1996). These studies have uniformly supported the safety and efficacy of the drug in managing symptoms associated with ADHD. Given substantial recent increases in the off-label use of MPH in children younger than age 6 (e.g., Zito et al., 2000), there is even a multisite study, funded by the National Institute of Mental Health, presently under way to evaluate the safety and efficacy of this compound in preschool children between 3 and 5 years old.

Studies in preadolescent, school-age children most amply demonstrate the efficacy of MPH. The Multi-Modal, Multi-Site Treatment Study of ADHD (MTA), the largest ever clinical trial of its kind, demonstrated conclusively that stimulant medication, most often MPH, was effective for reducing the core symptoms of ADHD in the school-age sample that participated (ages 7–9.9; MTA Cooperative Group, 1999). Data are more sparse but supportive of the efficacy of MPH in treating ADHD that persists into adolescence (e.g., Findling, Short, & Manos, 2001) and adulthood (e.g., Spencer, et al., 1995).

Not surprisingly given its proven efficacy, numerous sources have documented increases in the rates of MPH prescriptions in the last 10 years. A recent study reported that 4.3% of all children between the ages of 5 and 14 received a prescription for stimulant medication in the calendar year 1999, and that in certain subgroups (males between the ages of 10 and 13 years) the rates were greater than 8% (Cox, Motheral, Henderson, & Mager, 2003). These figures are comparable to other reports of MPH prevalence (2.8%, Safer, Zito, & Fine, 1996; 2.2%, Zito, Safer, dosReis, Magder, & Riddle, 1997) and may reflect an ongoing increasing trend in the rates of prescriptions for MPH. Safer et al. (1996) reported that between 1991 and 1995, there was a 2.5-fold increase in the use of MPH in children aged 5 to 18 years.

In large part because of the reported increases in the use of MPH, significant controversy has arisen about the abuse, misuse, and diversion of the drug. A number of single-case studies exist in the literature describing intranasal or intravenous use of prescribed MPH (Garland, 1998; S. L. Jaffe, 1991; Levine, Caplan, & Kaufman, 1986; Massello & Carpenter, 1999; Parran & Jasinski, 1991). Further, there are widespread reports from nonscientific media sources that MPH misuse and diversion are widespread among adolescents and college students, with the drug garnering such street names as "Vitamin R," "Skippy," and "the smart drug" (e.g., Drug Enforcement Administration, 2000; Llana & Crimson, 1999; Stepp, 1996; Vogt, 1999). The Drug Enforcement Administration (DEA) has recently expressed concern that diversion of MPH and subsequent misuse are increasing in prevalence and has suggested that rises in MPH production from 1,768 kg in 1990 to 14,957 kg in 1999 have resulted in increased illicit availability of the drug (Drug Enforcement Administration, 2000). Several indices of MPH misuse have also steadily increased in the same time frame, such as the number of reported thefts from licensed handlers of the drug and the number of young people who have reported using it without a prescription (Drug Enforcement Administration, 1995; Feussner, 1998). In recent testimony to the U.S. Congress, a DEA spokesperson cited information from case files and state investigative services suggesting that the drug has been illegally diverted in several ways, as evidenced by thefts from pharmacies and schools; ADHD "scams" in which parents obtain multiple prescriptions from different doctors and then use the drug illegally, sell, or trade it; undercover street sales; multistate distribution rings; multidrug distribution rings (along with cocaine and other substances); and smuggling from Mexico (Drug Enforcement Administration, 2000).

Empirical sources also provide support for the idea that MPH diversion and misuse are occurring at significant rates. Sixteen percent of a sample of college students reported that they had used MPH recreationally, and 12.7% of these students reported having taken the drug intranasally. These rates were comparable to those reported by the same sample for recreational use of cocaine and amphetamine (Babcock & Byrne, 2000). Another study of children and adolescents who had been prescribed MPH found that nearly one in five had been approached to sell, give away, or trade their medication at least once in the past 5 years (Musser, Ahmann, Mundt, Broste, & Mueller-Rizner, 1998). Several other studies and reviews have reported MPH abuse in specific groups of individuals (e.g., methadone maintenance patients, Raskind & Bradford, 1975) and in the general population (e.g., Crutchley & Temlett, 1999; Weiner, 2000). A recently compiled report from the Indiana Prevention Resource Center (IRPC) noted that 7.5% of Indiana high school seniors reported illicit use of MPH in their lifetime (compared with 8.4% for cocaine use and 15.6% for amphetamine use; IRPC, 1999). Data from the National Household Surveys on Drug Abuse indicate that a smaller but still substantial proportion had reported life-time recreational use of MPH (2.2% for ages 12–17 and 3.6% for ages 18–25; Substance Abuse and Mental Health Services Administration, 2000).

The significant controversy in the media and in the public regarding the abuse, misuse, and diversion of MPH does have some support from survey-based research. It is clear that nonclinical use of MPH does occur frequently in young people. These findings are related to the often negatively slanted stories on MPH in media outlets such as television magazine shows (e.g., *20/20, Dateline*) or in newspaper and magazine articles. From a scientific standpoint, however, this type of research speaks only to the patterns of misuse and diversion and says little about the actual abuse potential of the drug. Fortunately, there are well-established methods for experimentally assessing the abuse potential of different drugs, and these methods have been used in both nonhumans and human subjects to evaluate MPH in this regard.

Evaluating the Subjective Effects of MPH: What Do the Data Tell Us?

Traditionally, the subjective effects of drugs have been used in large part as an assay to evaluate the abuse potential of a compound (e.g., Fischman & Foltin, 1991; J. H. Jaffe & Jaffe, 1989). Standardized questionnaires and rating scales are typically used to measure a drug's subjective (or self-reported) effects, and the strength of these effects is inferred from the difference between ratings before and after drug administration or after drug administration compared with placebo administration. The extent to which the drug effects are associated with subjective ratings of euphoria, drug liking, or similarity to other drugs of abuse is the extent to which it is believed to have abuse potential. The Addiction Research Center Inventory (ARCI; Martin, Sloan, Sapira, & Jasinski, 1971) and the Profile of Mood States (POMS; McNair, Lorr, & Droppleman, 1971) are both standardized measures commonly used to assess the subjective effects of drugs. Other studies have used investigator-constructed instruments such as adjective rating scales and visual analog scales (e.g., Kollins, Rush, Pazzaglia, & Ali, 1998; Kollins, Shapiro, Newland, & Abramowitz, 1998; Rush, Kollins, & Pazzaglia, 1998). Drug effects on all these instruments tend to be dose dependent and pharmacologically specific. As such, subjective effects measured in this manner are believed to be strongly correlated with a drug's abuse potential (J. H. Jaffe & Jaffe, 1989; Jasinski & Henningfield, 1989).

The abuse liability of a range of clinically beneficial drugs has been assessed using subjective effects. In general, the extent to which a drug increases self-reported ratings of liking, euphoria, and willingness to take the drug again is thought to be directly related to the likelihood that it will be misused. It is certainly true that many drugs used clinically are also abused (e.g., benzodiazepines, barbiturates, analgesics). However, it is not always the case that drugs whose subjective effects profiles are indicative of high abuse potential are abused by the individuals who are most likely to receive them for clinical purposes. For example, a range of anxiolytic drugs, such as lorazepam and alprazolam, produce a pattern of subjective effects suggestive of abuse potential in healthy and drug-abusing participants (de Wit, Johanson, & Uhlenhuth, 1984; Mumford, Rush, & Griffiths, 1995; Orzack et al., 1988). However, there is evidence to suggest that in patients to whom these drugs are likely to be prescribed for clinical purposes, such as those with generalized anxiety or panic disorder, drugs such as alprazolam produce a distinct pattern of effects. Like those studies with other samples, this drug produced increased ratings of "like drug," "feel effect," and "drowsy." However, unlike other samples, in anxious patients, alprazolam does not increase scores on the POMS Elation scale significantly above those levels reported with placebo (Roache, Stanley, Creson, Shah, & Meisch, 1997).

These findings suggest that defining the abuse potential of a compound based on its subjective effects in healthy participants, or even those with histories of substance abuse, may not be telling the whole story. As such, the subjective effects of MPH in individuals diagnosed with ADHD may provide more information about clinical effects than about the drug's potential for being abused or misused. Given the lack of published studies, however, such speculation does not have a strong empirical basis. In the next section, published studies that have assessed the subjective effects of MPH are reviewed, followed by a discussion of methodological factors that may be responsible for discrepancies across the studies. We will give particular attention to the characteristics of the samples in which the subjective effects of MPH are studied.

Studies Examining the Subjective Effects of MPH

We recently completed a comprehensive review of the abuse potential of MPH, including a number of studies that have evaluated the subjective effects of the drug (Kollins, MacDonald, & Rush, 2001). Our review concluded that in most of the studies, MPH produces a pattern of subjective effects that is similar to other stimulant drugs of abuse (e.g., cocaine, d-amphetamine), although the relative potency of the drugs is different when route of administration is controlled. Here we review 28 studies (24 from the published review and 4 studies that have been published since that time) that specifically evaluated subjective effects of MPH in humans. Following this review of the studies, methodological factors that may account for variability in findings will be considered, including the dose range, statistical power, contextual factors associated with the assessment of drug effects, and sample characteristics. We will then describe in detail a recently completed study that bears on the issue of the relevance of the subjective effects of MPH to abuse potential in samples of individuals with ADHD.

Table 11.1 lists 28 published studies that have systematically assessed the subjective effects of MPH. Of the 7 studies reporting comparative data on MPH and *d*-amphetamine, all reported that MPH alone significantly increased subjective effects on POMS scales (e.g., Chait, 1994; Smith & Davis, 1977); ARCI subscales (e.g., Chait, 1994; Heishman & Henningfield, 1991; Martin et al., 1971; Rush & Baker, 2001; Rush et al., 1998); visual analog scales (VASs; e.g., Chait, 1994; Heishman & Henningfield, 1991; Rush et al., 1998); and other scales (Modified Adjective Checklist, Brown, Corriveau, & Ebert, 1978; Drug Effect Questionnaire, Rush & Baker, 2001) in orally administered doses ranging from 10 mg (Smith & Davis, 1977) to 90 mg (Rush, Essman, SImpson & Baker, 2001). Generally, these studies reported *d*-amphetamine to be more potent than MPH in producing subjective effects (e.g., Martin et al., 1971; Smith & Davis, 1977), although the pattern of effects was similar across both drugs.

There were, however, exceptions to this pattern of findings. First, one study demonstrated that *d*-amphetamine produced significantly higher magnitude subjective ratings on all the following items compared with MPH: ARCI Amphetamine, Benzedrine Group, Morphine-Benzedrine Group scales; VAS "drug liking," "stimulated," and "high" items (Chait, 1994). Another exception was from a study wherein 10 and 20 mg *d*-amphetamine produced significant changes in subjective effects associated with abuse potential (e.g., ARCI MBG scale, ratings of "High," "Good Effects"), whereas MPH did not produce effects that were different from placebo (Rush et al., 2001). This same study, however, demonstrated similar patterns of effects for the two drugs for other subjective items, such as the ARCI A scale, and ratings of "like drug" and "willing to take again" (Rush et al., 2001). Conversely, one study also reported that a high dose (60 mg) of MPH produced ratings of VAS "high" that were significantly higher than those for placebo, whereas *d*-amphetamine failed to produce such results at any dose (2.5–30 mg; Heishman & Henningfield, 1991). Finally, one study that directly compared the subjective effects of oral cocaine (50–300 mg) and MPH (15–90 mg) in human participants reported that MPH and cocaine both dose-dependently increased ratings of "drug liking" and that MPH was more potent (Rush & Baker, 2001).

Two studies have investigated the subjective effects of MPH compared with cocaine in individuals with cocaine abuse histories (Rush & Baker, 2001; Rush, Kelly, Hays, & Wooten, 2002). These studies generally showed that, compared with placebo, MPH resulted in dose-dependent increases on subjective effects such as "drug liking," "willing to pay for," and "motivated." Moreover, Rush and Baker (2001)

reported that MPH significantly elevated ratings on the ARCI Amphetamine scales significantly above levels obtained with placebo. Effects
of 50 to 300 mg oral cocaine were also compared with 15 to 90 mg
oral MPH, and no significant effect of drug or interaction of Drug ×
Dose was detected, suggesting that when the route is controlled for,
MPH and cocaine produce comparable subjective effects in these individuals with histories of cocaine abuse.

Studies that have assessed MPH in the absence of a comparison drug
or compared with other drugs have also found significant effects on
subjective ratings. In a series of studies in which intravenous MPH (0.25–
0.5 mg/kg) was administered to adult participants, the drug consistently
produced significant effects on the individual drug effect items of "high"
and "rush" without negative stimulant effects, such as "anxious" and
"restless" (Volkow et al., 1995; Volkow et al., 1996; Volkow et al., 1997;
Volkow, Wang, Fowler, Gatley, et al., 1998; Volkow, Wang, Fowler,
Gatley, et al., 1999; Fowler, Wang, Fowler, Hitzemann, et al., 1999;
Volkow, Wang, Fowler, Logan, Gatley, Wong, et al., 1999). Another
recent study reported that compared with placebo, 40 mg oral MPH
significantly increased ratings of "drug liking," "stimulated," and ARCI
A, BG, MBG, and LSD scales (Heil et al., 2002).

Six studies reported no statistically significant effects on any ARCI,
POMS, or VAS scales traditionally associated with abuse potential (Huey
et al., 1980; Miller, Taylor, & Tinklenberg, 1988; Roache et al., 2000;
Volkow, Wang, Fowler, Logan, Gatley, Gifford, et al., 1999; Walker,
Sprague, Sleator, & Ullmann, 1988), although one of these reported
significant MPH effects on observer ratings of mania, euphoria, and
arousal (Huey et al., 1980), and one reported a trend toward significant effects of MPH on VAS ratings of "feel high" (Roache et al., 2000).
For example, one study with hyperactive children reported that MPH
(0.7 mg/kg) reduced scores on the Anger/Hostility subscale of the POMS
but produced no other significant results (Walker et al., 1988). Another
study with ADHD children reported no effects of 5 to 30 mg MPH on
individual drug effect items or POMS scores (Kollins, Shapiro, et al.,
1998), and another study reported no effects in abstinent alcoholics
(10–20 mg; Miller et al., 1988). Finally, in one study in which main
effects for MPH were not reported, 12/23 healthy control adults reported
the overall effects of the drug to be "pleasant," versus 9/23 reporting
"unpleasant" effects (Volkow, Wang, Fowler, Logan, Gatley, Gifford,
et al., 1999).

A substantial proportion of all studies investigating the subjective
effects of MPH found significant effects for at least one dose of the
drug compared with baseline or placebo conditions. Visual analog scales
for the items "high" and "like drug/craving" were most often endorsed
(84.6% and 87.5% of studies, respectively), whereas ARCI and POMS
scales produced more varied results. Of the 28 studies reviewed that
investigated the subjective effects of MPH, 4 failed to report significant

Table 11.1 Summary of studies investigating the subjective effects of methylphenidate.

Study	Sample characteristics	N	Route	Subjective effects instruments used	Methylphenidate dose range tested	Other drugs tested[**]/ dose range
Brown, 1977	Healthy adult males	17	p.o.	MACL	10–20 mg	
Brown etal., 1978	Healthy adult males	59	p.o.	MACL	10–20 mg	d-amphetamine/10–20 mg
Chait, 1994	Healthy adult males and females	35	p.o.	ARCI, POMS, VAS	20–40 mg[#]	d-amphetamine[*]
Heil et al., 2002	Healthy adult males and females	16	p.o.	ARCI, VAS, ARS	20–40 mg	
Heishman & Henningfield, 1991	Adult males with significant drug use histories	8	p.o.	ARCI, VAS	7.5–60 mg	d-amphetamine/3.75–30 mg
Huey et al., 1980	Psychiatric inpatients	8	i.v.	POMS, observations	0.5 mg/kg	
Jasinski, 2000	Adult male polysubstance abusers	25	p.o.	ARCI, Drug Rating Questionnaire, Drug Identification Questionnaire, Specific Drug Effects Questionnaire	45–90 mg	
Kollins, Rush, et al., 1998	Healthy adult males and females	10	p.o.	ARCI, POMS, VAS	20–40 mg each immediate and sustained release	
Kollins, Shapiro, et at., 1998	Children diagnosed with ADHD	8	p.o.	ARCI[**]	2–30 mg[***]	
Martin et al., 1971	Male prisoners incarcerated for crimes associated with drug use	12	s.c.	ARCI	15–60 mg/70 kg	d-amphetamine/7.5–0 mg/ 70 kg
Miller et al., 1988	Males diagnosed with alcohol dependence	17	p.o.	POMS	10–20 mg	
Roache et al., 2000	Adult male and female cocaine abusers	57/12	p.o.	ARCI, POMS, VAS	20mg sustained release/5–60 mg immediate release	
Roehrs et al., 1999	Healthy adult males and females	6	p.o.	ARCI, POMS	10 mg	
Rush & Baker, 2001	Adult male cocaine abusers	6	p.o.	ARCI, DEQ, ARS, Cocaine Sensitive Adjective Scale, Pharmacological Class Questionnaire	15–90 mg	Cocaine/50-300 mg

Study	Participants	N	Route	Measures[a]	Dose	Drug/Dose[b]
Rush et al., 2001	Healthy adult males and females	8	p.o.	ARCI, DEQ	20–40 mg	d-amphetamine/10–20 mg
Rush et al., 2002	Adult males and females with recent histories of cocaine use	6	p.o.	ARCI, DEQ, Cocaine Sensitive Adjective Scale	60 mg	Cocaine/50-150 mg
Rush et al., 1998	Healthy adult males and females	5	p.o.	ARCI, POMS, VAS	5–40 mg	d-amphetamine/2.5–20 mg
Smith & Davis, 1977	Healthy adult males and females	16	p.o.	POMS	10–20 g	d-amphetamine/10–20 mg
Volkow et al., 1995	Healthy adult males	8	i.v.	VAS	0.5 mg/kg	
Volkow et al., 1996	Healthy adult males	4	i.v.	VAS	0.5 mg/kg	
Volkow et al., 1997	Adult males diagnosed with cocaine dependence, healthy controls	46	i.v.	VAS	0.5 mg/kg	
Volkow, Wang, Fowler, Gatley, et al., 1998	Healthy adult males	7	p.o.	VAS	5–60 mg varied across participants	
Volkow, Wang, Fowler, Hitzemann, et al., 1998	Healthy adult males	16	i.v.	VAS	0.25–0.5 mg/kg	
Volkow, Wang, Fowler, Logan, Gatley, Wong, et al., 1999	Healthy adult males and females	8	i.v.	VAS	0.05–0.5 mg/kg	
Volkow, Wang, Fowler, Gatley 1999	Adult males diagnosed with cocaine abuse	20	i.v.	VAS	0.25–0.5 mg/kg	
Volkow, Wang, Fowler, females Hitzemann, et al., 1999	Healthy adult males and females	14	i.v.	VAS	0.025–0.5 mg/kg	
Volkow, Wang, Fowler, Logan, Gatley, Gifford, 1999	Healthy adult males	23	i.v.	VAS	0.5 mg/kg	
Walker et al., 1998	Children diagnosed with ADHD	18	p.o.	POMS	0.3–0.7 mg/kg	

p.o. = oral; i.v. = intravenous; s.c. = subcutaneous.
[a]Lists only whether the study also tested cocaine or d-amphetamine.
[b]Only one dose ested in each participant.
[c]Compared with participants in another study; not a within-subject comparison.
[d]Only selected items from the ARCI were used in an experimenter-constructed questionnaire.
[e]Dose ranges varied across participants.

effects of MPH in the expected direction on any of the dependent measures (Kollins, Shapiro, et al., 1998; Miller et al., 1988; Roache et al., 2000; Walker et al., 1988); 1 study failed to demonstrate significant effects on one instrument (the POMS) despite significant effects on observer ratings (Huey et al., 1980); and 1 study (Volkow, Wang, Fowler, Logan, Gatley, Gifford, et al., 1999) did not report overall group effects to determine if there was a main effect of MPH on the subjective items tested. Overall, 22 out of 28 studies reviewed (78.5%) reported significant effects of at least one dose of MPH on the subjective responses of participants.

Clearly, methodological features of these studies account for at least some of the discrepant findings. Two of the studies reporting no significant effects, compared with zero studies that did report significant effects, were conducted with children. Young participants may not have developed the verbal repertoire to accurately endorse the items associated with subjective drug effects (Kollins, Shapiro, et al., 1998; Walker et al., 1988), although there were no effects for age in the 7- to 12-year-old children in one of these studies (Walker et al., 1988). Nevertheless, these findings are significant, since they were obtained with the population most likely to receive the drug for clinical purposes. Another study that failed to demonstrate significant effects on POMS scores, despite increases in observer ratings, was conducted with psychiatric inpatients, who may have also been impaired in some manner relating to the reporting of subjective effects (Huey et al., 1980). One of the studies used a relatively low dose range of MPH (10–20 mg) compared with other studies (Miller et al., 1988). Importantly, one of the studies that reported relatively weak effects of MPH on indices of abuse potential was conducted with adults who were enrolled in outpatient treatment for cocaine dependence (Roache et al., 2000). This study also reported that orally administered MPH (sustained-release dose of 20 mg; immediate-release doses of 15–60 mg) had no effects on measures of cocaine craving. Finally, one study reported MPH effects for at least a subset of individuals, but it was not clear from the analysis whether these effects resulted in group main effects (Volkow, Wang, Fowler, Logan, Gatley, Gifford, et al., 1999). In general, results from the studies examining the subjective effects of MPH suggest that the drug functions similarly to d-amphetamine in producing subjective effects (no differences between the drugs in four out of five studies comparing them) and consistently produces a constellation of effects that is associated with abuse potential of the drug. The two studies that provide comparative data on MPH and cocaine suggest that these two compounds produce similar patterns of subjective effects when orally administered, at least in the individuals with histories of cocaine abuse in whom these studies were conducted (Rush et al., 2001; Rush et al., 2002).

The literature assessing the subjective effects of MPH has used a range of doses (7.5–90 mg); across different routes of administration (e.g., intravenous, subcutaneous, oral); under different laboratory contexts (e.g., sleep deprived, inpatient settings, outpatient settings, imaging studies); and, perhaps most important, in different samples (healthy adults; alcohol, stimulant, and polysubstance abusers, children with ADHD). Given these methodological variations, the findings that MPH produces a pattern of subjective effects consistent with abuse potential in nearly four out of five studies become even more robust. We address the potential impact of each of these methodological variations in the following.

Dose Range

As with most other psychoactive drugs, the subjective effects of MPH are dose dependent. Nearly all the studies that investigated multiple doses of MPH report stronger subjective effects for the higher doses than for the lower doses. For example, Rush et al. (1998) reported that 5 and 10 mg of oral MPH did not produce results that were significantly different from placebo on subscales of the ARCI and items on a DEQ. However, both 20 and 40 mg MPH significantly increased ratings on the ARCI A scale, ratings of "vigorous," "elated," and "good effects," and 40 mg alone produced significant effects on ratings of "drug liking." Most of the studies that have used adult participants and *failed* to report significant subjective effects of MPH used relatively low doses (e.g., 10–20 mg; e.g., Brown, 1977). In reviewing the literature, it appears that, at least for adult participants, there is some threshold around 20 mg at which significant subjective effects begin to emerge. As noted, this orally administered dose produces significant effects in some studies (e.g., Rush et al., 1998) but not in others (e.g., Volkow, Wang, Fowler, Gatley, et al., 1998). It is interesting to note that this dose is sufficient to produce more than 50% blockade of the dopamine transporter (Volkow, Wang, Fowler, Gatley, et al., 1998), a level that has been suggested as necessary to produce significant subjective effects (Volkow, Fowler, Wang, Ding, & Gatley, 2002).

Statistical Power

Another methodological factor that could account for discrepancies in subjective effects across studies is sample size. It may be the case that those studies failing to report significant findings were underpowered. To empirically assess this possibility, we calculated a point-biserial correlation coefficient for studies reporting significant subjective effects ($N = 22$) and for studies failing to report significant effects ($N = 6$). This analysis was not significant ($r = .13$; $p = .49$), suggesting that sample size was not related to whether or not the study reported significant effects of any dose of MPH. Moreover, a number of the studies reporting significant effects of MPH had comparatively small numbers of participants (N = 5–6; Roehrs, Papineau, Rosenthal, & Roth, 1999; Rush et al., 1998; Rush et al., 2002; Rush & Baker, 2001). It appears, therefore, that other methodological factors are likely to account for the variability in the subjective effects of MPH.

Contextual Factors Associated With MPH Subjective Effects

Research has clearly supported the important role of contextual factors in determining a drug's effects. For example, one elegant recent study demonstrated that the subjective effects of diazepam varied within subjects as a function of what kind of activity they were in engaged in following administration of the drug (Alessi, Roll, Reilly, & Johanson, 2002). The importance of contextual factors in determining subjective effects of MPH has also been highlighted within the same study. Roehrs et al. (1999) reported that MPH produced stronger subjective effects when participants had received only 4 (vs. 8) hours of sleep the previous night. Although this finding may seem intuitive given MPH's stimulant profile, this is the only study that has experimentally manipulated context to show how subjective effects of this drug can vary as a function of the context in which it is administered.

It is likely that some of the differences across studies assessing MPH's subjective effects are attributable to the context in which the drug effects are evaluated. For example, in the Rush et al. (1998) study that produced significant subjective effects following 20 mg oral MPH, volunteers participated in pairs or larger groups and had the chance for social interaction and a range of leisure activities. On the other hand, in another study in which 20 mg oral MPH failed to produce significant effects, subjects generally participated individually and were asked to rate the effects of the drug while they were undergoing brain scans (Volkow, Wang, Fowler, Gatley, et al., 1998). These important contextual differences likely impacted the measured subjective effects, in spite of comparable doses and, presumably, comparable blood levels of the drug.

Samples Under Study

Of the 28 studies examining the subjective effects of MPH, only 2 were conducted with individuals diagnosed with ADHD and who were receiving the drug for clinical purposes (Kollins, Shapiro, et al., 1998; Walker et al., 1988). Several other subgroups of individuals were used in these studies, including healthy adult males (n = 6 studies), healthy adult males and females (n = 10), substance users of some description (n = 9), and psychiatric inpatients (n =1). As noted previously, several of the studies failing to report significant effects were conducted in comparatively unusual samples (psychiatric inpatients and children with ADHD). For healthy adults with or without a history of substance abuse or dependence, it appears that the subjective effects of MPH are even more reliable.

Certainly one facet of the controversy surrounding MPH use is related to the fact that it is prescribed so frequently to children and adolescents diagnosed with ADHD. It is not uncommon in clinical practice to encounter parents who are justifiably reluctant to have their child take a Schedule II drug for behavior problems. Playing into this concern, media reports and opponents of MPH use often highlight the behavioral and pharmacological similarities between MPH and other stimulant drugs of abuse, such as cocaine and *d*-amphetamine. The fact remains, however, that very few studies have systematically assessed the subjective effects and related abuse potential of MPH in the individuals to whom the drug is most likely to be administered for clinical purposes. As noted previously, the assessment of subjective effects provides one means of evaluating the abuse liability of the drug in these samples. Of the studies reviewed here, only two (Kollins, Shapiro, et al., 1998; Walker et al., 1988) have been conducted with individuals diagnosed with ADHD, and, as noted, none of them reported significant effects of the drug. It is not clear whether these findings are related to the age of participants (since they were all children) or their diagnostic status. In any case, these studies raise the provocative idea that perhaps MPH does not produce the same kinds of subjective effects in individuals who have ADHD and receive the drug for clinical purposes.

Subjective Effects of MPH in Children and College Students Diagnosed With ADHD

Bearing on this issue, a recently completed study suggests that there may be an important dissociation of the subjective effects and other important effects from an abuse liability standpoint. The study's primary aim was to evaluate the reinforcing effects of MPH using a choice procedure. As is typical in other studies that have used this kind of method, the subjective effects were also evaluated.

The study involved two experiments, one with school-age children ($n = 5$) and the other with college students ($n =10$). The participants for both experiments had an established diagnosis of ADHD (corroborated by rating scale scores prior to entering the study) and were currently prescribed MPH for their ADHD. All participants had been receiving MPH treatment for at least 6 months prior to selection for the study.

Procedure

In addition to a screening session in which pertinent diagnostic and background information was obtained, volunteers participated in 12 sessions. Participants and/or their parents/guardians provided informed consent to participate in the study, and all subjects received medical clearance for participation from their family physician. Individual family physicians or a collaborating physician wrote prescriptions for placebo pills and for each participant's normal dose of MPH.

All drugs were prepared in a standardized manner by a pharmacist at the University Health Center where the study took place who had experience preparing medications for other research and clinical activities in our laboratory. The participant's maintenance dose of MPH and an inert placebo were each prepared in opaque capsules (size 01) to ensure that the enclosed substance was unknown to the subject and to the researcher. Each participant's maintenance dose was encapsulated in one capsule, so that only one capsule was administered at a time. The capsules were placed in separate bottles labeled as "Bottle A" and "Bottle B," with the MPH represented by one letter (e.g., "A") and the placebo by the other (e.g., "B"). The capsule letter assignments were varied across participants. However, the participants were informed that the same-lettered capsule always contained the same substance. The general experimental procedures are outlined in the following. The specific session details varied across experiments and are described separately.

Sampling Sessions

During each experimental session, participants first completed subjective effects questionnaires. The sampling sessions were designed to allow participants to experience the effects of the two drug conditions, MPH and placebo, on the basis of which they would subsequently make a choice regarding which one they wanted to take. During the first sampling session, after completing the subjective effects questionnaire, participants received either placebo or MPH in a capsule labeled "Pill A" or "Pill B." In the second sampling session, participants received the other substance in a capsule labeled with the other letter. Participants also received a wristband or card labeled with the same letter as the pill administered as a reminder of which capsule they received that day. Participants were instructed to associate the effects of the capsule with its letter label. Capsule letter assignments varied across participants, and the order in which placebo and MPH were scheduled in the sampling sessions was counterbalanced across subjects and within subjects across weeks.

Choice Sessions

In the choice sessions, participants also completed subjective effects questionnaires at the beginning of the session. Participants were then presented with three cups: one labeled "Pill A" (or whatever letter corresponded to MPH), one labeled "Pill B" (or whatever letter corresponded to placebo), and an empty cup labeled "C." The participant chose either to ingest "Pill A," to ingest "Pill B," or to take neither capsule. This choice procedure has been used to measure the reinforcing effects of a number of drugs, in a range of contexts and with various subject populations (e.g., de Wit & Griffiths, 1991; Foltin & Fischman, 1991; Johanson & de Wit, 1989). Following each choice, the participant was presented with the appropriate letter-matched wristband (Experiment 1) or card (Experiment 2).

Dependent Measures

Drug Choice

As noted, the number of times each option (MPH, placebo, neither) was selected served as the primary dependent measure.

Subjective Effects: Experiment 1

Subjective effects in Experiment 1 conducted with school-age children were assessed before drug administration, and 1.5 hours after drug administration. The following self-report scales were used.

HOW I FEEL QUESTIONNAIRE.

This is a 28-item questionnaire adapted from the van Kammen–Murphy Mood Scale (van Kammen & Murphy, 1975). Items are rated on a 4-point scale (0 = *not at all*, 1 = *a little*, 2 = *some*, 3 = *a lot*). This adapted scale has been used with children to measure the subjective effects produced by caffeine (Elkins, et al., 1981) and *d*-amphetamine (Rapaport et al., 1980).

PROFILE OF MOOD STATES (POMS)

A short form of the POMS was used to assess mood and affective state. This version consists of 37 items that are rated on a 5-point scale (0 = *not at all*, 1 = *a little*, 2 = *moderately*, 3 = *quite a bit*, 4 = *extremely*). Compared with the original 65–item scale (McNair et al., 1971), the shortened version has been shown to have adequate psychometric properties (Shacham, 1983). This scale has been used to assess the effects of stimulants in children (Walker et al., 1988). Six scales are derived from the 37 items: Anger/Hostility, Confusion/Bewilderment, Depression/Dejection, Fatigue/Inertia, Tension/Anxiety, and Vigor/Activity.

SUBJECTIVE EFFECTS RATING SCALE (SERS)

This 22-item scale was developed by Kollins, Shapiro, et al. (1998) to assess the participant-rated effects of MPH and other stimulant medication in children and adolescents. Items from the questionnaire are rated on a 4-point scale (0 = *not at all*, 1 = *a little*, 2 = *some*, 3 = *a lot*). Items on the SERS were derived from three sources. First, stimulant-appropriate items from the Addiction Research Center Inventory (ARCI; Martin et al., 1971) were selected and changed to an age-appropriate reading level. Second, items were selected from the Side Effects Rating Scale (Barkley, 1991). Finally, items were selected based on discussions with clinicians experienced in working with children diagnosed with ADHD.

VISUAL ANALOG SCALE (VAS)

The VAS consisted of ten 100-mm horizontal lines, each labeled with a different item. Each scale was presented individually. Participants were instructed to rate each item on the basis of how they felt at the present time. Each VAS scale was anchored with "not at all" at the leftmost extreme and "very much" at the rightmost extreme. Participants were instructed to place a mark on each line indicating how they felt at the moment. The items rated included like drug, energetic, sleepy, friendly, restless, nervous, hungry, excited, happy, and feel like talking.

Subjective Effects: Experiment 2

Subjective effects in Experiment 2 conducted with college students were assessed before drug administration and 1.5 hours and 4 hours after drug administration. Different measures were used in the older sample to streamline the assessment of subjective effects and to provide the least intrusive assessment in these volunteers, since they were requested to complete these forms in their natural environment away from the laboratory.

PARTICIPANT-RATED EFFECTS SCALE (PRES)

The PRES is a 25-item scale developed for this study to assess the subjective effects of MPH in adults diagnosed with ADHD. Items from the questionnaire were rated on a 5-point scale, where each numeric value corresponded to a phrase describing the frequency or intensity of the item (1 = *not at all*, 2 = *a little bit*, 3 = *moderately*, 4 = *quite a bit*, 5 = *extremely*). Items on this form were derived from four primary sources: Addiction Research Center Inventory (ARCI; Martin et al., 1971); Profile of Mood States (POMS, McNair et al., 1971); Conners Adult ADHD Rating Scale (CAARS, Conners, Erhardt, & Sparrow, 1999); and the *DSM-IV* (APA, 1994). Items included those that had been used to measure the participant-rated effects of many drugs and are sensitive to the effects of stimulants (e.g., Heishman & Henningfield, 1991; Roache et al, 2000). The items from the CAARS and the *DSM-IV* included symptoms of ADHD and were selected because of clinical utility in determining the effects of stimulant medications in this population.

END OF THE DAY QUESTIONNAIRE

This five-item questionnaire was administered approximately 4 hours after capsule ingestion to measure the overall effect of the drug received. Participants rated "drug strength," "drug liking," "good effects," "bad effects," and "like to take again" on a 5-point scale (0 = *not at all*, 1 = *a little bit*, 2 = *moderately*, 3 = *quite a bit*, 4 = very much).

For the subjective effects in Experiment 1 (school-age children), ratings were taken before drug administration and 1.5 hours after drug administration. These ratings were obtained on MPH and Placebo sampling and choice days. The predrug ratings obtained on the questionnaires were averaged separately for MPH sampling days, Placebo sampling days, MPH choice days, Placebo choice days (when applicable), and Neither choice days (when applicable). The postdrug ratings were averaged in the same manner. In order to examine the participant rated effects, the change from baseline ([post–drug administration scores] - [pre–drug administration scores]) was computed for each questionnaire item or factor (i.e., POMS) using raw scores. Change scores for each item or factor were computed for MPH sessions, Placebo sessions, and Neither sessions. The change scores for each condition (i.e., MPH, Placebo, Neither) were averaged for each subject. The average change scores for each item were then transformed into z-scores. The differences between z-scores obtained on MPH sampling days and Placebo sampling days were computed. In addition, differences between z-scores obtained on MPH, Placebo, and Neither choice days were computed. Finally, differences between z-scores obtained on overall MPH and No Drug days (i.e., Placebo or Neither) were compared. Items that differed from the average by one standard deviation were considered to be meaningful changes.

For Experiment 2 (College Students), the subjective effects were analyzed by transforming the 25-item questionnaire into three rationally derived composite scores: ADHD composite (10 items), Mood composite (12 items), and Stimulant composite (3 items). The composite scores were averaged across "MPH", "Placebo," and "Neither" sessions for each subject at each of the three time periods (pre, 1.5 hour, 4 hour) for both Sampling and Choice sessions. A two-way analysis of variance (Time × Choice) was used to compare the participant-rated effects obtained by MPH choosers and nonchoosers.

The change from baseline ([post–drug administration scores]—[pre–drug administration scores]) was computed using raw scores for each composite for total MPH sessions, Placebo sessions, and Neither sessions, and separately for Sampling and Choice sessions. The effect size (d) was calculated by dividing the raw score difference by the standard deviation of the measure (Cohen, 1977). The effect scores obtained for the ADHD symptom composite, the Mood composite, and the Stimulant Effects composite for MPH choosers were compared with the effect scores obtained for the non-MPH choosers (i.e., placebo and nonchoosers) across Sampling Sessions.

The End of Day Questionnaire ratings were analyzed using paired t-tests to compare ratings on each item following MPH and PL across all sessions and separately across Sampling and Choice Sessions.

Results

Table 11.2 shows the results from the individual-subject analyses for participant-rated effects in Experiment 1. The patterns of responding on the participant-rated effects questionnaires were idiosyncratic, and there were no reliable increases or decreases in specific participant-rated effects across subjects.

In a similar manner, when the data for Experiment 2 were analyzed, no significant patterns were observed when comparing the participant-rated effects of all participants across sessions. Since one of the primary aims of the study was to investigate whether individuals with ADHD would choose to take MPH versus Placebo, the patterns of results were also examined for those individuals who chose MPH the majority of the time (MPH "choosers"; $n = 5$), versus those who chose Placebo or neither or who demonstrated no preference ("nonchoosers"; $n = 5$). Relative to placebo, when compared to nonchoosers, MPH choosers reported a significant decrease in ADHD symptoms (p = .001) and negative mood ($p = .055$) and an increase in stimulant effects (p = .0000). This suggests that participants who reliably chose MPH reported a decrease in ADHD symptoms, a decrease in negative mood, and an increase in stimulant drug effects, whereas nonchoosers did not report reliable changes across sessions. Results of a two-way ANOVA indicated that the effects were greatest 1.5 hours after MPH ingestion (ADHD composite, $p = .01$; Mood composite, $p = .060$; Stimulant composite, p = .000).

When comparing the difference in participant-rated effects across sampling and choice days, participants who subsequently were MPH choosers exhibited greater reduction in ADHD symptoms ($d = -0.93$) and negative mood ($d = -0.92$) and a decrease in stimulant effects (d = 1.09) at 1.5 hours after drug administration than the nonchoosers. Baseline score differences indicate that MPH choosers reported higher levels of ADHD symptoms than nonchoosers ($d = 0.76$) and higher initial

Table 11.2. Experiment I: Participant-rated effects for individual subjects

POMS Subscales	Subject 1	Subject 2	Subject 3	Subject 4	Subject 5
Tension	↓	—	↑	—	↓
Confusion	—	↑	—	—	—
Vigor	—	—	—	↓	—

How I Feel Items	Subject 1	Subject 2	Subject 3	Subject 4	Subject 5
Trouble keeping mind on things	↓	—	↓	—	—
Restless	↓	—	—	↓	—
"Funny"	↑	—	—	—	—
A lot of energy	↓	—	—	—	—
Tired and slow	↑	—	—	—	↓
Weird. "freaky"	—	—	—	—	—
No one wants to help me	—	↑	—	—	↓
Unusual thoughts	—	↑	—	—	—
Unhappy	—	—	↓	—	—
Doing a pretty good job	—	—	↑	—	↑
Something good will happen	—	—	—	↑	↑
Mad	—	—	—	—	↓
Friendly	—	—	—	—	↑
Happy	—	—	—	—	↑

SERS	Subject 1	Subject 2	Subject 3	Subject 4	Subject 5
Feel like talking	↓	—	—	—	↑
Can concentrate	↑	↓	—	—	—
Like joking	↓	↓	—	↑	—
Hungry	↓	—	—	—	—
Focused on work	—	↑	—	—	—
Popular	—	↓	↓	—	—
Get along with others	—	↓	—	—	—
Daydreamed	—	—	↓	—	—
Heart beating fast	—	—	↓	—	↑
Worked well	—	—	—	↑	—
Excited	—	—	—	↑	—

Visual Analog Scales	Subject 1	Subject 2	Subject 3	Subject 4	Subject 5
Energetic	↓	↓	—	—	—
Excited	—	↓	—	—	—
Like Drug	—	—	↑	↑	—
Sleepy	—	—	—	—	↓
Restless	—	—	—	—	↓

Note: Arrows indicate a significant deviation from the average change score across sessions. The direction of the arrows indicates the effect of MPH relative to the "no-drug" condition (i.e., placebo or neither). Dashes indicate no significant differences.

Stimulant ratings ($d = 0.94$) but did not differ significantly on the Mood composite.

Results of the pairwise t-tests examining the items on the End of Day Questionnaire indicated that, across participants, when compared with placebo, MPH was associated with higher ratings of "drug strength" ($p = .006$) and "good effects" ($p = .03$). There were no significant differences among MPH choosers and nonchoosers, or with respect to dose.

Discussion

The findings from this study raise at least two important issues with respect to the subjective effects of MPH. First, the absence of reliable subjective effects at the group level across subjects in both experiments suggests that the effects of MPH may be different when administered at clinically relevant doses to individuals with ADHD. It is relevant to note that in both experiments, participants overall chose MPH more often than Placebo or Neither, suggesting that the drug functions as a reinforcer in these individuals.

A second important point is that, within subjects, the pattern of subjective effects varied as a function of whether or not the drug was chosen reliably. In Experiment 2, when the subjective effects were examined across those individuals who were MPH choosers versus nonchoosers, it became clear that those individuals who chose the drug more often also reported significant subjective effects. It is likely that this pattern of effects was driving the choice patterns to some extent. In any case, it supports the idea that the subjective effects of a drug are driven, in part, by the context in which the drug is taken, even in clinical settings. As noted, the MPH choosers who reported more significant subjective effects were also those individuals who reported higher baseline levels of ADHD symptoms.

Continued research examining the conditions associated with the subjective and reinforcing effects of MPH may also be important from the standpoint of assessing the abuse potential of MPH. The subjective and reinforcing effects of a substance are typically used to assess its abuse potential. In addition, recent media attention has focused on the misuse and abuse of MPH among adolescents, college students, and parents of children with prescriptions for MPH for the treatment of ADHD (e.g., Drug Enforcement Administration, 2000; Llana & Crimson, 1999; Popper, 1995; Safer, 2000).

Most research asserts that if a drug functions as a reinforcer and produces a pattern of positive subjective effects, it is considered to have considerable abuse liability (Fischman & Mello, 1989). Yet, as discussed by Roache, Stanley, Creson, Shah, and Meisch (1997), drug effects in clinical populations are not always indicative of abuse potential in the same manner as drug effects in drug abusers or other nonclinical samples. Drug abuse refers to a repeated pattern of self-administration that results in functional impairment for the individual taking the drugs (APA, 1994). The subjective and reinforcing effects of clinically used agents may necessitate a different conceptualization of such drug-taking behavior. In these situations, the choice of drug over placebo may be reinforced by the consequences of eliminating aversive stimuli (e.g., anxiety; Roache et al., 1997) or by more positive consequences, such as being able to work more efficiently, receiving greater praise from teachers and peers, or getting better grades (as may be the case with ADHD).

In the present experiments, the subjective and reinforcing effects of MPH were associated with a reduction in seemingly aversive symptoms (e.g., inattention, anxiety, sadness) and an increase in positive symptoms (e.g., "good effects," happiness). This suggests that choosing to ingest MPH is associated with clinical efficacy; thus, perhaps MPH is not producing significant clinical effects in nonchoosers. Again, future work that examines MPH in a context where there are measurable clinical changes will be important to help clarify the functional role of the subjective and reinforcing effects of the drug in this and other samples. Specifically, it is suggested that future studies examine the subjective effects of MPH in diagnosed and nondiagnosed populations to further explore the role of clinical effects in moderating the effects of this drug.

Mechanisms Underlying the Subjective Effects of MPH in ADHD and Non-ADHD Samples

As noted, the finding that the subjective effects of MPH may differ between individuals with ADHD and those who are not so diagnosed has a number of implications. One important consideration has to do with what these differences might tell us about the underlying neuropharmacological mechanisms associated with ADHD. That MPH is reliably chosen by individuals with ADHD but does not produce the same constellation of subjective effects is consistent with recent evidence from several recent lines of neuroimaging research.

To begin with, a number of converging lines of evidence support the idea that there are important neuropharmacological differences between individuals with ADHD and nondiagnosed controls. These differences pertain primarily to alterations in dopaminergic functioning in individuals with ADHD. For example, molecular genetic studies have consistently identified associations between ADHD and genes associated with dopamine receptors. A recent meta-analysis found strong support for the involvement of genes associated with dopamine transporter (DAT), dopamine D4 (DRD4), and dopamine D5 (DRD5) in individuals with ADHD (Maher, Marazita, Ferrell, & Vanyukov, 2002). Such differences form the basis for hypotheses about differential abuse potential of MPH in individuals with ADHD.

Several recent studies report that adults with ADHD differ from nondiagnosed controls in DAT density in striatal regions. Using SPECT imaging techniques, one study reported that ADHD patients had 70% greater density of DAT, primarily in the striatum (Dougherty et al., 1999). These findings were replicated in a larger sample, although the magnitude of the difference was not as great (Dresel et al., 2000). Importantly, both of these studies used patients who either were drug naive (i.e., had never taken medication for ADHD) or had not taken any medication for the past month. Although these findings have not been universally replicated (e.g., van Dyck et al., 2002), they suggest a possible neuropharmacological basis both for the symptoms observed in ADHD and for the mechanism of stimulant drug action in treating these symptoms. For example, problems with excessive motor activity, attentional deficits, organization, and working memory are all believed to have substrates in the circuits between the prefrontal cortex and striatum. These regions and circuits are also known to be richly innervated with dopaminergic neurons (Solanto, 2002; Solanto, Arnsten, & Castellanos, 2001). As such, the therapeutic action of MPH is believed to be mediated, in part, by the effects of the drug on dopaminergic functioning in these regions.

Specifically, it has been hypothesized that the increases in DAT density in ADHD patients results in overall reductions in extracellular dopamine in the striatal regions, which, through frontostriatal circuits are associated with attentional control and motor activity. MPH functions, then, to bind to DAT in these regions, thus increasing the levels of extracellular dopamine and enhancing attention and decreasing distractibility (Volkow et al., 2002).

As noted earlier, the observed differences in dopamine function in general, and in DAT density specifically, are likely to play a key role in the expression of ADHD symptoms and the effects of MPH and other stimulant medication in the treatment of the disorder. Data from a number of other neuroimaging studies suggest how these differences might also lead to differential abuse potential of MPH between ADHD and nondiagnosed individuals. Volkow and colleagues (2002) have demonstrated that DAT blockage is essential to produce the accompanying reports of "high" with MPH and cocaine in healthy adults. One study demonstrated that intravenous MPH and cocaine both produced significant reports of "high" by participants only when the dose was high enough to achieve 50% blockage of the DAT, and that the greater blockage of the transporter, the more intense the reports of "high" (Volkow et al., 1997; Volkow, Wang, Fowler, Gatley, et al., 1999). Volkow, Wang, Fowler, Gatley, et al. (1998) have also reported a relative lack of subject-rated effects of "high" when MPH was administered orally, even at doses that resulted in greater than 50% blockade of DAT (20 mg). It is important to note that other studies of the subjective effects of oral administration with healthy adults have shown significant effects at this dose (e.g., Kollins, Rush, et al., 1998; Rush et al., 1998). Studies have also shown a direct relation between the extracellular dopamine concentration following intravenous MPH administration and subjective ratings of "high" in healthy control adults (r = .78; Volkow, Wang, Fowler, Logan, Gatley, Wong, et al., 1999).

The imaging studies of Volkow and colleagues clearly establish that the subjective effects of MPH and, by extension, the abuse potential of the drug are associated with at least two primary factors: the extent of DAT blockade of the drug and the amount of extracellular dopamine released following drug administration. Based on the findings that individuals with ADHD have increased density of DAT (e.g., Dougherty et al., 1999; Dresel et al., 2000), it would be expected that DAT binding would be lower for ADHD patients than for controls at a given dose of MPH. Also, since the increases in DAT density would result in a net decrease in extracellular MPH concentration, MPH would be expected to increase extracellular dopamine concentrations to a greater extent in control subjects than in individuals with ADHD. These findings, then, provide a neuropharmacological basis for predicting lower abuse potential of MPH in individuals with ADHD than in nondiagnosed controls.

Conclusions

Based on the findings reviewed here, several conclusions are warranted. MPH produces a reliable pattern of subjective effects in healthy adults and those with histories of substance use and abuse. The profile is generally consistent with other drugs of abuse (e.g., cocaine and d-amphetamine), is dose dependent, and is significantly associated with the route of administration. Studies of intravenous administration report subjective effects that are higher in magnitude than studies using the oral route (e.g., Volkow, Wang, Fowler, Gatley, et al., 1998; Volkow, Wang, Fowler, Hitzemann, et al., 1998). Moreover, studies have shown that the faster the absorption of a drug, the greater the subjective effects (e.g., Kollins, Rush, et al., 1998).

The subjective effects of MPH are not well characterized in individuals diagnosed with ADHD who are prescribed the drug for clinical purposes. Some data suggest that the drug may function differently in these individuals. Such a finding, if replicated, is very important from a public health perspective because it suggests that MPH's abuse potential is lower in the people actually receiving it for clinical purposes. There may still be cause for concern about the drug's diversion and misuse in nondiagnosed individuals.

The differences in subjective effects of this drug between ADHD and non-ADHD individuals provide potentially important information about the neuropharmacological mechanisms of the drug, as well as potential baseline differences in individuals with and without ADHD. These differences suggest that the overall level of dopamine transporter occupancy of MPH may be lower in individuals with ADHD following a given dose of MPH compared with non-diagnosed individuals. Lower DAT occupancy, in turn, may be related to lower overall DAT density in these patients compared with controls.

A number of questions will be important to address through subsequent research:

What is the profile of MPH subjective effects in children and adolescents compared with in adults?

What is the role of context in determining the subjective effects of MPH? Do different kinds of tasks result in different patterns of subjective effects for a given dose of MPH?

Is the pattern of subjective effects truly different in individuals with ADHD versus controls (or other clinical samples, for that matter)?

References

Alessi, S. M., Roll, J. M., Reilly, M. P., & Johanson, C. E. (2002). Establishment of a diazepam preference in human volunteers following a differential-conditioning history of placebo versus diazepam choice. *Experimental and Clinical Psychopharmacology, 10,* 77–83.

American Psychiatric Association. (1994). *Diagnostic and statistical manual of mental disorders* (4th ed.). Washington, DC: Author.

Babcock, Q., & Byrne, T. (2000). Student perceptions of methylphenidate abuse at a public liberal arts college. *Journal of American College Health, 49,* 143–145.

Barkley, R. A. (1991). *The hyperactive child: A handbook for diagnosis and treatment.* New York: Guilford.

Bradley, C. (1950). Benzedrine® and dexedrine® in the treatment of children's behavior disorders. *Pediatrics, 5,* 24–37.

Brown, W. A.(1977). Psychologic and neuroendocrine response to methylphenidate. *Archives of General Psychiatry, 34,* 1103–1108.

Brown, W. A., Corriveau, D. P., & Ebert, M. H. (1978). Acute psychologic and neuroendocrine effects of dextroamphetamine and methylphenidate. *Psychopharmacology, 58,* 189–195.

Chait, L. D. (1994). Reinforcing and subjective effects of methylphenidate in humans. *Behavioral Pharmacology, 5,* 281–288.

Cohen, J. (1977). Statistical power analysis for the behavioral sciences (rev. ed.). New York: Academic Press.

Conners, C.,K., & Eisenberg, L. (1963). The effects of methylphenidate on symptomatology and learning in disturbed children. *American Journal of Psychiatry, 120,* 458–464.

Conners, C. K., Erhardt, D., & Sparrow, E. (1999). Conners's Adult ADHD Rating Scales (CAARS). North Tonawanda, NY: Multi-Health Systems.

Cox, E. R., Motheral, B. R., Henderson, R. R., & Mager, D. (2003). Geographic variation in the prevalence of stimulant medication use among children 5 to 14 years old: Results from a commercially insured US sample. *Pediatrics, 111,* 237–243.

Crutchley, A., & Temlett, J. A. (1999). Methylphenidate (Ritalin) use and abuse. *South African Medical Journal, 89,* 1076–1079.

de Wit, H., & Griffiths, R. R. (1991). Testing the abuse liability of anxiolytics and hypnotic drugs in humans. *Drug and Alcohol Dependence, 28,* 83–111.

de Wit, H., Johanson, C. E., & Uhlenhuth, E. H. (1984). *Drug preference in humans: Lorazepam* (pp. 227–232, NIDA Research Monograph No. 49). Rockville, MD: Department of Health and Human Services, National Institute of Drug Abuse.

Dougherty, D. D., Bonab, A. A., Spencer, T. J., Rauch, S. L., Madras, B. K., & Fischman, A. J. (1999). Dopamine transporter density in patients with attention deficit hyperactivity disorder. *Lancet, 354,* 2132–2133.

Dresel, S., Krause, J., Krause, K. H., LaFougere, C., Brinkbaumer, K., Kung, H. F., et al. (2000). Attention deficit hyperactivity disorder: Binding of [99mTc]TRODAT-1 to the dopamine transporter before and after methylphenidate treatment. *European Journal of Nuclear Medicine, 27,* 1518–1524.

Drug Enforcement Administration. (2000). DEA Congressional Testimony by Terrance Woodworth before the Committee on Education and the Workforce: Subcommittee on Early Childhood, Youth and Families. Retrieved May 16, 2000, from http://www.usdoj.gov/dea/pubs/cngrtest/ct051600.htm.

Drug Enforcement Administration. (1995). Office of Diversion Control, Methylphenidate review: *Eight factor analysis.* Author: Washington, DC..

Elkins, R., Rapoport, J., Zahn, T. P., Buchsbaum, M. S., Weingartner, H., Kopin, I. J., et al. (1981). Acute effects of caffeine in normal prepuberal boys. *American Journal of Psychiatry, 138,* 178–183.

Feussner, G. (1998, November). Diversion, trafficking, and abuse of methylphenidate. Proceedings of: *Diagnosis and Treatment of Attention Deficit Hyperactivity Disorder.* National Institutes of Health Consensus Conference, Bethesda, MD.

Findling, R. L., Short, E. J., & Manos, M. J. (2001). Developmental aspects of psychostimulant treatment in children and adolescents with attention-deficit/hyperactivity disorder. *Journal of the American Academy of Child and Adolescent Psychiatry, 40,* 1441–1447.

Fischman, M. W., & Mello, N. K. (1989). *Testing for abuse liability of drugs in humans.* NIDA Monograph No. 92. Department of Health and Human Services Publication No. (ADM) 1989; 89–1613. Washington, DC: U.S. Government Printing Office.

Foltin, R. W., & Fischman, M. W. (1991). Methods for the assessment of abuse liability of psychomotor stimulants and anorectic agents in humans. *British Journal of the Addictions, 86,* 1633–1640.

Garland, E. J. (1988). Intranasal abuse of prescribed methylphenidate. *Journal of the American Academy of Child and Adolescent Psychiatry, 37,* 573–574.

Heil, S. H., Holmes, H. W., Bickel, W. K., Higgins, S. T., Badger, G. J., Laws, H. F., et al. (2002). Comparison of the subjective, physiological, and psychomotor effects of atomoxetine and methylphenidate in light drug users. *Drug and Alcohol Dependence, 67*, 149–156.

Heishman, S. J., & Henningfield, J. E. (1991). Discriminative stimulus effects of *d*-amphetamine, methylphenidate and diazepam in humans. *Psychopharmacology, 103*, 436–442.

Huey, L. Y., Janowsky, D. S., Judd, L. L., Roitman, N. A., Clopton, P. L., Segal, D., et al. (1980). The effects of naloxone on methylphenidate-induced mood and behavioral changes: A negative study. *Psychopharmacology, 67*, 125–130.

Indiana Resource Prevention Center. (1999). *Alcohol, tobacco, and other drug use by Indiana children and adolescents.* Bloomington, IN: Institute for Drug Abuse Prevention. Also available: *http://www.drugs.indiana.edu/drug_stats/youth99/*

Jaffe, J. H., & Jaffe, F. K. (1989). Historical perspectives on the use of subjective effects measures in assessing the abuse potential of drugs. In M. W. Fishman & N. K. Mello (Eds.), *Testing for abuse liability of drugs in humans* (pp. 43–72, NIDH Monograph No. 92). Department of Health and Human Services Publication No. (ADM)89–1613. Washington, DC: U.S. Government Printing Office.

Jaffe, S. L. (1991). Intranasal abuse of prescribed methylphenidate by an alcohol and drug abusing adolescent with ADHD. *Journal of the American Academy of Child and Adolescent Psychiatry, 30*, 773–775.

Jasinski, D. R. (2000). An evaluation of the abuse potential of modafinil using methylphenidate as a reference. *Journal of Psychopharmacology, 14*, 53–60.

Jasinski, D. R., & Henningfield, J. E. (1989). Human abuse liability assessment by measurement of subjective and physiological effects. In M. W. Fishman & N. K. Mello (Eds.), *Testing for abuse liability of drugs in humans* (pp. 73–100). NIDA Monograph No. 92. Washington, DC: U.S. Government Printing Office.

Johanson, C. E., & deWit, H. (1989). The use of choice procedures for assessing the reinforcing properties of drugs in humans. In M. W. Fischman & N. K. Mello (Eds.), *Testing for abuse liability of drugs in humans* (pp. 148–171). (NIDA Research Monograph No. 92). Washington, DC: U.S. Government Printing Office.

Johanson, C. E., & Uhlenhuth, E. H.(1980). Drug preference and mood in humans: *d*-Amphetamine. *Psychopharmacology, 72*, 275–279.

Kollins, S. H., MacDonald, E. K., & Rush, C. R. (2001). Assessing the abuse potential of methylphenidate in nonhuman and human subjects: A review. *Pharmacology, Biochemistry and Behavior, 68*, 611–627.

Kollins, S. H., Rush, C. R., Pazzaglia, P. J., & Ali, J. A. (1998). Comparison of acute behavioral effects of sustained-release and immediate-release methylphenidate. *Experimental and Clinical Psychopharmacology, 6*, 367–374.

Kollins, S. H., Shapiro, S. K., Newland, M. C., & Abramowitz, A.(1998). Discriminative and participant-rated effects of methylphenidate in children diagnosed with attention deficit hyperactivity disorder (ADHD). *Experimental and Clinical Psychopharmacology, 6*, 1–15.

Levine, B., Caplan, Y. H., & Kaufman, G. (1986). Fatality resulting from methylphenidate overdose. *Journal of Analytical Toxicology, 10*, 209–210.

Levy, J. M., Jones, B. E., & Croley, H. T. (1957). Effects of methylphenidate (Ritalin) on drug-induced drowsiness in mentally retarded patients. *American Journal of Mental Deficiency, 62,* 284–287.

Llana, M. E., & Crismon, M. L. (1999). Methylphenidate: Increased abuse or appropriate use? *Journal of the American Pharmaceutical Association, 39,* 526–530.

Maher, B. S., Marazita, M. L., Ferrell, R. E., & Vanyukov, M. M. (2002). Dopamine system genes and attention deficit hyperactivity disorder: A meta-analysis. *Psychiatric Genetics, 12,* 207–215.

Martin, W. R., Sloan, J. W., Sapira, J. D., & Jasiniski, D. R. (1971). Physiologic, subjective and behavioral effects of amphetamine, methamphetamine, ephedrine, phenmetrazine and methylphenidate in man. *Clinical Pharmacology and Therapeutics, 12,* 245–258.

Massello, W., III, & Carpenter, D. A. (1999). A fatality due to the intranasal abuse of methylphenidate (Ritalin). *Journal of Forensic Science, 44,* 220–221.

McNair, D. M., Lorr, M., & Droppleman, L. F. (1971). *Profile of Mood States (Manual).* San Diego, CA: Educational and Industrial Testing Services.

Miller, T. P., Taylor, J. L., & Tinklenberg, J. R. (1988). A comparison of assessment techniques measuring the effects of methylphenidate, secobarbital, diazepam, and diphenhydramine in abstinent alcoholics. *Neuropsychobiology, 19,* 90–96.

MTA Cooperative Group. (1999). A 14–month randomized clinical trial of treatment strategies for attention-deficit/hyperactivity disorder. The MTA Cooperative Group. Multimodal Treatment Study of Children with ADHD. *Archives of General Psychiatry, 56,* 1073–1086.

Mumford, G. K., Rush, C. R., & Griffiths, R. R. (1995). Abecarnil and alprazolam in humans: Behavioral, subjective and reinforcing effects. *Journal of Pharmacology and Experimental Therapeutics, 272,* 570–580.

Musser, C. J., Ahmann, F. W., Mundt, P., Broste, S. K., & Mueller-Rizner, N. (1998). Stimulant use and the potential for abuse in Wisconsin as reported by school administrators and longitudinally followed children. *Journal of Developmental and Behavioral Pediatrics, 19,* 187–192.

Orzack, M. H., Friedman, L., Dessain, E., Bird, M., Beake, B., McEachern, J., et al. (1988). Comparative study of the abuse liability of alprazolam, lorazepam, diazepam, methaqualone, and placebo. *International Journal of the Addictions, 23,* 449–467.

Parran, T. V., Jr., & Jasinski, D. R. (1991). Intravenous methylphenidate abuse: Prototype for prescription drug abuse. *Archives of Internal Medicine, 151,* 781–783.

Popper, C. W. (1995). Combining methylphenidate and clonidine: Pharmacologic questions and news reports about sudden death. *Journal of Child and Adolescent Psychopharmacology, 5,* 157–166.

Rapoport, J. L., Buchsbaum, M. S., Weingartner, H., Zahn, T. P., Ludlow, C., & Mikkelsen, E. J. (1980). Dextroamphetamine: Its cognitive and behavioral effects in normal and hyperactive boys and normal men. *Archives of General Psychiatry, 37,* 933–943.

Raskind, M., & Bradford, T. (1975). Methylphenidate (Ritalin) abuse and methadone maintenance. *Disorders of the Nervous System, 36,* 9–12.

Roache, J. D., Grabowski, J., Schmitz, J. M., Creson, D. L., & Rhoades, H. M. (2000). Laboratory measures of methylphenidate effects in cocaine-dependent patients receiving treatment. *Journal of Clinical Psychopharmacology, 20,* 61–68.

Roache, J. D., Stanley, M. A., Creson, D. R., Shah, N. N., & Meisch, R. A. (1997). Alprazolam-reinforced medication use in outpatients with anxiety. *Drug and Alcohol Dependence, 45,* 143–155.

Roehrs, T., Papineau, K., Rosenthal, L., & Roth, T. (1999). Sleepiness and the reinforcing and subjective effects of methylphenidate. *Experimental and Clinical Psychopharmacology, 7,* 145–150.

Rush, C. R., & Baker, R. W. (2001). Human behavioral pharmacology of oral cocaine: Discriminative-stimulus, subject-rated and reinforcing effects. *Experimental and Clinical Psychopharmacology, 9,* 59–73.

Rush, C. R., Essman, W. D., Simpson, C. A., & Baker, R. W. (2001). Reinforcing and subject-rated effects of methylphenidate and *d*-amphetamine in non-drug abusing humans. *Journal of Clinical Psychopharmacology, 21,* 273–286.

Rush, C. R., Kelly, T. H., Hays, L. R., & Wooten, A. F. (2002). Discriminative-stimulus effects of modafinil in cocaine-trained humans. *Drug and Alcohol Dependence, 67,* 311–322.

Rush, C. R., Kollins, S. H., & Pazzaglia, P. J. (1998). Discriminative-stimulus and participant-rated effects of methylphenidate, bupropion, and triazolam in *d*-amphetamine-trained humans. *Experimental and Clinical Psychopharmacology, 6,* 32–44.

Safer, D. J. (2000). Are stimulants overprescribed for youths with ADHD? *Annals of Clinical Psychiatry, 12,* 55–62.

Safer, D. J., Zito, J. M., & Fine, E. M. (1996). Increased methylphenidate usage for attention deficit disorder in the 1990s. *Pediatrics, 98,* 1084–1088.

Shacham, S. (1983). A shortened version of the Profile of Mood States. *Journal of Personality Assessment, 47,* 305–306.

Smith, R. C., & Davis, J. M. (1977). Comparative effects of *d*-amphetamine, l-amphetamine, and methylphenidate in man. *Psychopharmacology, 53,* 1–12.

Solanto, M. V. (2002). Dopamine dysfunction in ADHD: Integrating clinical and basic neuroscience research. *Behavioural Brain Research, 130,* 65–71.

Solanto, M. V., Arnsten, A. F. T., & Castellanos, F. X. (2001). The neuroscience of stimulant drug action in ADHD. In M. V. Solanto, A. F. T. Arnsten, & F. X. Castellanos (Eds.), *Stimulant drugs and ADHD: Basic and clinical neuroscience.* New York: Oxford University Press.

Spencer, T., Biederman, J., Wilens, T., Harding, M., O'Donnell, D. & Griffin, S. (1996). Pharmacotherapy of attention-deficit hyperactivity disorder across the life cycle. *Journal of the American Academy of Child and Adolescent Psychiatry, 35,* 409–432.

Spencer, T., Wilens, T., Biederman, J., Faraone, S. V., Ablon, J. S., & Lapey, K. . (1995). A double-blind, crossover comparison of methylphenidate and placebo in adults with childhood-onset attention-deficit hyperactivity disorder. *Archives of General Psychiatry, 52,* 434–443.

Stepp, L. S. (1996, February 5). A wonder drug's worst side effect; Kids turning to easy-to-get Ritalin for a quick—and sometimes deadly—high. *The Washington Post,* p. A1.

Substance Abuse and Mental Health Services Administration. (2002). *Results from the 2001 National Household Survey on Drug Abuse: Vol. 1. Summary of national findings* (Office of Applied Studies, NHSDA Series H-17, DHHS Publication No. SMA 02–3758). Rockville, MD.

van Dyck, C. H., Quinlan, D. M., Cretella, L. M., Staey, J. K., Malison, R. T., Baldwin, R. M., et al. (2002). Unaltered dopamine transporter availability in adult attention deficit hyperactivity disorder. *American Journal of Psychiatry, 159*, 309–312.

Van Kammen, D. P., & Murphy, D. L. (1975). Attentuation of the euphoriant and activating effects of d- and l-amphetamine by lithium carbonate treatment. *Psychopharmacologia, 44*, 215–224.

Vogt, A. (1999, January 22). Teens find high in Ritalin, experts say; Suburban schools lock up drug after break-ins. *The Chicago Tribune*, p.1.

Volkow, N. D., Ding, Y. S., Fowler, J. S., Wang, G. J., Logan, J., Gatley, J. S., et al. (1995). Is methylphenidate like cocaine? Studies on their pharmacokinetics and distribution in the human brain. *Archives of General Psychiatry, 52*, 456–463.

Volkow, N.,D. Fowler, J. S., Wang, G. J., Ding, Y. S., & Gatley, J. S. (2002). Role of dopamine in the therapeutic and reinforcing effects of methylphenidate in humans: Results from imaging studies. *European Neuropsychopharmacology, 12*, 557–566.

Volkow, N. D., Wang, G. J., Fowler, J. S., Gatley, S. J., Logan, J., Ding, Y. S., et al. (1999). Blockade of striatal dopamine transporters by intraveneous methylphenidate is not sufficient to induce self-reports of "high." *Journal of Pharmacology and Experimental Therapeutics, 288*, 14–20.

Volkow, N. D., Wang, G. J., Fowler, J. S., Gatley, S. J., Logan, J., Ding, Y. S., et al. (1998). Dopamine transporter occupancies in the human brain induced by therapeutic doses or oral methylphenidate. *American Journal of Psychiatry, 155*, 1325–1331.

Volkow, N. D., Wang, G. J., Fowler, J. S., Hitzemann, R., Angrist, B., Gatley, S. J., et al. (1999). Association of methylphenidate-induced craving with changes in right striato-orbitofrontal metabolism in cocaine abusers: Implications in addiction. *American Journal of Psychiatry, 156*, 19–26.

Volkow, N. D., Wang, G. J., Fowler, J. S., Hitzemann, R., Gatley, J., Ding, Y. S., et al. (1998). Differences in regional brain metabolic responses between single and repeated doses of methylphenidate. *Psychiatric Research: Neuroimaging, 83*, 29–36.

Volkow, N. D., Wang, G. J., Fowler, J. S., Logan, J., Gatley, S. J., Wong, C., et al. (1999). Reinforcing effects of psychostimulants in humans are associated with increases in brain dopamine and occupancy of D_2 receptors. *Journal of Pharmacology and Experimental Therapeutics, 291*, 409–415.

Volkow, N. D., Wang, G. J., Fowler, J. S., Logan, J., Gatley, S. J., Gifford, A., et al. (1999). Prediction of reinforcing responses to psychostimulants in humans by brain dopamine D_2 receptor levels. *American Journal of Psychiatry, 156*, 1440–1443.

Volkow, N. D., Wang, G. J., Fowler, J. S., Logan, J., Gatley, S. J., Hitzemann, R., et al. (1997). Decreased striatal dopaminergic responsiveness in detoxified cocaine-dependent subjects. *Nature, 386*, 830–833.

Volkow, N. D., Wang, G. J., Gatley, S. J., Fowler, J. S., Ding, Y. S., Logan, J., et al. (1996). Temporal relationships between the pharmacokinetics of methylphenidate in the human brain and its behavioral and cardiovascular effects. *Psychopharmacology, 123*, 26–33.

Walker, M. K., Sprague, R. L., Sleator, E. K., & Ullmann, R. K. (1988). Effects of methylphenidate hydrochloride on the subjective reporting of mood in children with attention deficit disorder. *Issues in Mental Health Nursing, 9*, 373–385.

Weiner, A. L. (2000). Emerging drugs of abuse in Connecticut. *Connecticut Medicine, 64*, 19–23.

Zito, J. M., Safer, D. J., dosReis, S., Gardner, J. F., Boles, M., & Lynch, F. (2000). Trends in the prescribing of psychotropic medications to preschoolers. *Journal of the American Medical Association, 283*, 1059–1060.

Zito, J. M., Safer, D. J., dosReis, S., Magder, L. S., & Riddle, M. A. (1997). Methylphenidate patterns among Medicaid youths. *Psychopharmacology Bulletin, 33*, 143–147.

12

Subjective Effects of Nitrous Oxide (N₂O)

DIANA J. WALKER AND JAMES P. ZACNY

Nitrous oxide (N₂O) is a gas at room temperature and pressure. It is used primarily for anesthesia but is also used as a propellant for whipped cream or to boost octane levels in racing cars (U.S. Department of Health and Human Services, 2000). It is thought to have been discovered in 1772 by the chemist Joseph Priestley, who christened the gas "dephlogisticated nitrous air" (Smith, 1982). Shortly after, the Medical Pneumatic Institution was established in Bristol, England, to examine the therapeutic effects of inhalation of various gases. It was here that N₂O was extensively studied by Sir Humphrey Davy, who presented a detailed description of his subjective experiences under the influence of N₂O, as well as self-reports by friends and colleagues of their own experiences while inhaling the gas (Davy, 1800). Sir Davy's treatise was a thorough, systematic, and extensive characterization of N₂O and was a foreshadowing of two centuries of research to follow, which will be presented in this chapter. Sir Davy's and subsequent research consisted of the dose-response assessment of subjective effects of acute and repeated N₂O administration, examination of individual differences, and the study of environmental and organismic determinants/modulators of N₂O effects. This chapter will present the results of such experiments in a chronological framework and will attempt to detail the various characterizations of N₂O across the years since its discovery.

Researches, Chemical and Philosophical;
Chiefly Concerning Nitrous Oxide

In 1800, Sir Humphrey Davy presented his extensive treatise on "chemical and philosophical" research on N_2O respiration. Davy first assessed the safety of N_2O inhalation, using himself as the subject. He reported making one inspiration of "pure" N_2O, with no ill effects on the lungs or glottis. He then "breathed three quarts of nitrous oxide from and into a silk bag for more than half a minute" and reported giddiness, fullness of the head, intoxication, and a quicker pulse. Davy then began to increase the concentration of N_2O (i.e., the number of quarts breathed from and into the silk bag) and the duration of breathing bouts (to minutes, rather than seconds), in effect constructing a dose-response curve of N_2O effects, including the time course of those effects. In these longer bouts, the initial giddiness and fullness of the head diminished after half a minute or so and were replaced by a "highly pleasurable thrilling," which increased across the inhalation and was followed by "an irresistible propensity to action," including "various and violent" motions. As the dose increased, certain effects diminished (e.g., pleasure, violent muscular motions), suggesting a bitonic, or inverted-U-shaped, dose-response function for those effects. That is, certain drug effects increased from small to intermediate doses, then began to decrease as the dose was increased further. Subsequent to Davy's research, inverted-U-shaped dose-response functions have been observed for behavioral effects of numerous drug classes (Branch, 1991; Carlton, 1983), including N_2O (Walker & Zacny, 2003).

Davy found that he could breathe 9 quarts of N_2O for 3 minutes and 12 quarts for more than 4 minutes but could breathe no quantity of N_2O for 5 minutes. He reported that "the pleasurable thrilling, at its height about the middle of the experiment, gradually diminished" until at some point the inhalation necessarily ceased, either because he could no longer breathe the mixture or because he had lost consciousness. Later in his treatise Davy reported having developed a breathing box in order to assess the effects of the highest dose possible that would not result in death during prolonged (e.g., 30 minutes) inhalation. The breathing box was big enough for him to enter completely, and 20 quarts of N_2O at a time were "thrown in" in order to assess the effects of prolonged inhalation of increasing doses. The concentrations actually inhaled by Davy and his subjects (his friends and colleagues, see later in this chapter) were not specifically identified when administered via silk bag or breathing box. Nor did they remain constant across the inhalation, as in research today in which a constant, precise concentration can be administered without being diluted by respiration by the subject. Regardless of the lack of specific identification of the actual N_2O concentrations being inhaled, Davy's self-experiments and his experiments on his friends and colleagues amounted to systematic, controlled dose-response studies that approached the scientific rigor of N₂O studies today.

Following Davy's self-reports of N₂O effects are descriptions by his friends and colleagues of their own experiences while inhaling the gas. Among these friends were Roget (of *Roget's Thesaurus*), Coleridge (author of *The Rime of the Ancient Mariner*), and Beddoes (leader of the Medical Pneumatic Institution). Many inhalations were conducted with Davy as the experimenter and his friends and colleagues as the subjects. When this was the case, the studies were frequently single blind (the subject was unaware of the dose being administered) and placebo controlled (air was administered instead of N₂O without the subject's knowledge). Within-subject dose-response functions, including replication of some doses, were constructed, and the role of modulating variables, such as subject characteristics, was also examined. For example, poor health in one subject was associated with increased sensitivity to N₂O effects, relative to effects when that subject was healthy. In addition, some subjects with "delicate and irritable constitutions" who were prone to hysteria (i.e., "delicate females"—remember, the year was 1800) were found to be overly sensitive to the drug. However, other subjects with such "fragile constitutions" reacted similarly to the drug as most people with more "normal" dispositions, especially in their enjoyment of N₂O's effects. Thus, intersubject variability in sensitivity to N₂O, as well as in the extent of enjoyment of N₂O's effects, was noted by Davy, even in a class of people with similar personality characteristics.

Davy also assessed potential modulators of N₂O effects through self-experimentation. Time of day was found to modulate N₂O effects: Davy found N₂O to be less pleasurable in the evening than during the day, a result that he discovered while examining the effects of N₂O on sleep (he found no effect). Repeated exposure to N₂O (6–9 quarts) between May and July, ranging from four to five exposures per week to three to four times per day for a week, was examined by Davy. No tolerance developed to subjective effects, but intrasubject variability was observed; according to Davy, "Effects appeared undiminished by habit and were hardly ever exactly similar (p. 462)." Davy's (1800) observation of inter- and intrasubject variability in N₂O effects has been replicated (e.g., Walker & Zacny, 2001).

Table 12.1 shows N₂O effects reported by Davy and his subjects.

Many of the subjective effects listed in table 12.1 might be considered pleasant in nature or indicative of the potential for abuse (e.g., euphoria, craving, desire to continue inhaling the drug). Such subjective effects are consistent with the fact that N₂O is a known drug of abuse (U.S. Department of Health and Human Services, 2000). In addition, certain aspects of the subjective experience of N₂O inhalation were difficult to describe and may not be conveyed in a list of subjective effects. This "ineffability" was noted by Davy following a relatively

Table 12.1. Self-Reported Effects of N₂O (Davy, 1800)

- giddiness
- fullness of the head
- intoxication
- quicker pulse
- analgesia
- excitement equal in duration and superior in intensity to opium or alcohol
- energy
- craving induced by the sight of another person inhaling or by the paraphernalia used to inhale it
- vivid sensations and ideas
- dazzling objects increased sense of power
- cheer
- sense of freedom
- delight
- liking of drug effects
- stimulant properties
- strong desire to continue the inspiration
- sensations superior to any before experienced
- recurrence of previously experienced pain
- anesthesia/narcosis at high doses
- increase in perceived strength or muscular power
- psychotherapeutic efficacy
- thrill/warmth in chest
- like alcohol but without unpleasant effects

- fast recovery
- more acute hearing
- sweet taste, agreeable odor
- intense intoxication with little pleasure
- stammering, difficulty pronouncing words
- involuntary laughter
- unpleasant effects
- disinhibition (described as engaging in behavior that would normally be constrained by social conventions)
- increased propensity to action, exercise, or muscular movements
- ineffability/indescribability
- increased awareness of bodily sensations
- dizziness
- vertigo
- drowsiness
- delirium
- disposition to muscular motion and merriment
- light-headedness
- musical ("I felt like the sound of a harp")
- no "hangover" effects
- distortions in time perception (time appeared longer than by a watch)
- glow in cheeks
- some amnesia for specific details of the experience
- pleasant sensations
- tingling

prolonged inhalation of N₂O in his "breathing box" apparatus. In one experiment Davy entered the box, and 20 quarts of N₂O were added (the resulting concentration was estimated to be about 25% N₂O by Smith, 1982). Davy recorded his body temperature and heart rate and noted subjective effects as 20 quarts were added every 3 to 4 minutes. After the third 20 quarts had been added, Davy began to have difficulty breathing and left the box, immediately inhaling 20 quarts of "fresh" N₂O. The subjective effects described following this sequence of events foreshadowed the "anesthetic revelation" that will be described in the next section. Davy reported "sensations similar to no others" that were consequently "indescribable." He wrote,

> Trains of vivid visible images rapidly passed through my mind, and were connected with words in such a manner, as to produce perceptions perfectly novel. I existed in a world of newly connected and newly

modified ideas. I theorised—I imagined that I made discoveries. . . . I felt an inclination to communicate the discoveries I had made during the experiment. I endeavoured to recall the ideas, . . . "Nothing exists but thoughts!—the universe is composed of impressions, ideas, pleasures and pains!" (p. 488–489).

The experience described here may be difficult to imagine, especially for those who are "N₂O-naive." Such open-ended introspections provided the bulk of the information on subjective effects of N₂O until the 1950s, when more standardized assessment of subjective effects began to evolve (Steinberg, 1956).

The Anesthetic Revelation: 1800 to Early 1900s

In the early 1800s, N₂O was used "as laughing gas for the purpose of creating a little scientific amusement" (O. Atkinson, 1873, p. 106). This use of N₂O is consistent with the fact that several of Davy's subjects reported "involuntary laughter" induced by N₂O (table 12.1). There were lectures and side shows on laughing gas, demonstrating N₂O's effects on volunteers from the audience (e.g., Thomas, 1814). It was not until 1844 that N₂O began to be used medically, as an analgesic/anesthetic in dental and other types of surgery (Kaufman, Galili, Furer, & Steiner, 1990; Sigerist, 1933), even though Davy had described the analgesic effects of the gas in 1800. In the 150 years or so following Davy's treatise, most of the published reports on N₂O were self-reports of effects experienced during N₂O anesthesia by patients or self-reports by dentists who wanted to experience the effects themselves before administering the gas to patients (Evans, 1943; Jacobson, 1911; MacFarlane, 1913; Richardson, 1873; Seldin, 1937; Talbot, 1915). These self-reports emphasized the "revelatory" effects of N₂O, typically experienced right before the loss of consciousness during anesthesia or upon emerging from unconsciousness after anesthesia (although one early report warned about the "ill effects" of N₂O, such as "pain in the head" and "giddiness" [Brande, 1827, p. 458]). In 1874, Benjamin Blood wrote "The Anaesthetic Revelation and the Gist of Philosophy," which was reviewed by William James in 1874. The experiences of Blood, James, and the various patients and dentists who wrote about N₂O effects in the late 1800s and early 1900s were remarkably similar to Davy's experiences in 1800.

Blood described the revelations induced by N₂O anesthesia in terms of philosophy, which he considered "the desire for truth" (Blood, 1874, p. 4). After 14 years of self-experimenting with N₂O, Blood concluded that when emerging from N₂O anesthesia, "the genius of being is revealed; but because it cannot be remembered in the normal condition it is lost altogether . . . and buried, amid the hum of returning common sense" (p. 34). Blood stated that surgeons and dentists reported that their patients, too, seemed to experience revelations about the "Secret of Life" but failed in their attempts to describe their discoveries. For Blood the anesthetic revelation was worthwhile, transforming, religious, and philosophical. James (1874, 1882) agreed and, like Blood, lamented the fact that the insight quickly faded as the drug effect dissipated and could not be conveyed effectively to an outside observer:

> With me, as with every other individual of whom I have heard, the keynote of the experience is the tremendously exciting sense of an intense metaphysical illumination. Truth lies open to the view in depth beneath depth of almost blinding evidence. The mind sees all the logical relations of being with an apparent subtlety and instantaneity to which its normal consciousness offers no parallel; only as sobriety returns, the feeling of insight fades, and one is left staring vacantly at a few disjointed words or phrases. (James, 1882, p. 206)

Early Studies of N₂O in Healthy, Normal Volunteers: 1920s to 1950s

Following the "anesthetic revelation," published reports of the subjective effects of N_2O began to evolve from self-experimentation and patient self-reports toward the more formal, controlled experiments conducted today. Davidson (1925) was the first to characterize the effects of precisely controlled, specific N_2O concentrations in a healthy volunteer. Recall that Davy (1800) could not control the actual concentration (%) of N_2O being inhaled by himself or his friends and colleagues due to rebreathing from the silk bag or breathing box. For Davidson, however, "no re-breathing occurred in any of the experiments," and "since a constant partial pressure of the gas could be maintained in the lungs for a definite time, the effect of a definite concentration in the blood could be investigated" (p. 92). Using controlled N_2O dosing procedures, then, Davidson tested the effects of N_2O concentrations ranging from subanesthetic to anesthetic doses (4–75% N_2O in an air, oxygen, and nitrogen mixture).

> Further, in order to maintain the conditions as uniform as possible, one individual, who volunteered for the purpose, was used throughout the experiments . . . a healthy man . . . of studious habit and good intelligence, with medical training and unaccustomed to alcohol or other narcotics. (p. 92)

In effect, the study was a within-subject design using one volunteer (N = 1) who appeared to have no physical or mental health problems and no history of drug dependence.

Although the main focus of Davidson's (1925) study was to characterize the psychomotor impairment that occurs during N_2O intoxication, subjective effects were noted, as well as objective effects that were presumably related to subjective effects. These effects and the concentrations of N$_2$O at which they occurred (in parentheses) included feeling lightheaded (4%), feeling intoxicated and impaired (10–20%), and muscular incoordination and lack of attention (30%). There was "difficulty of concentrating the mind on the work to be performed" (40%, p. 93); excitement, laughter, talkativeness, and noisy speech (50%); marked muscular incoordination, aggression, and emotionality (60%); and more marked muscular incoordination and maudlin speech (65%). Unconsciousness occurred 6 minutes into the inhalation of 70% N$_2$O and 4 minutes into the inhalation of 75% N$_2$O. "The onset of unconsciousness was usually preceded by unintelligible speech, a lull in conversation and activity, and loss of sight before hearing and touch" (p. 93). Davidson's subject himself later wrote of his experiences while participating in the study (Marshall, 1938). That report agrees with Davidson's; in addition, Marshall reported a sense of omniscience and exaggerated estimates of his abilities during inhalation of 50% N$_2$O.

Besides testing precise N$_2$O concentrations that remained constant throughout a prolonged inhalation, Davidson's (1925) study had other notable features. For example, Davidson tested the effects of varying concentrations of N$_2$O administered within the same session, in both ascending and descending order. Results showed that the effects of a particular concentration varied, depending on whether it had been preceded by a lower or a higher concentration. Another determinant of N$_2$O effects was the environmental conditions surrounding the inhalation. "When experiments involving concentration of effort were made during the inhalation of 50 per cent nitrous oxide, talkativeness and laughter were generally absent" (pp. 93–94). Finally, Davidson also examined the effects of brief inhalation of pure (100%) N$_2$O for varying numbers of inspirations (0–5). Only objective effects were reported, from which one could infer potential subjective effects. These objective effects included laughter, increased talking, apparently purposeless movements of the head and arms, followed by restlessness (observed after four inhalations, which took 25–40 seconds) and volubility, excitation, aggression, and difficulty articulating (observed after five inspirations, which took 40–45 seconds). These research questions are still relevant today. Recent studies have compared ascending versus descending within-session dosing procedures (T. J. Martin, Walker, Sizemore, Smith, & Dworkin, 1996) or examined the effects of task requirements on drug effects (Comer, Haney, Foltin, & Fischman, 1996; Silverman, Kirby, & Griffiths, 1994). The effects of brief inhalation of 100% N$_2$O have also been examined recently because this method of self-administration is common in N$_2$O abuse (Zacny, Lichtor, Coalson, Apfelbaum, et al., 1994; Zacny, Lichtor, et al., 1996). Although research today would certainly include more than one subject in a published report, and although Davidson failed to mention whether she included a placebo control, the precise administration of N_2O, the within-subject replication of different dose conditions, and the systematic examination of various doses and dosing procedures make this early characterization of N_2O effects in a healthy volunteer an impressive one.

Two other early studies examined the analgesic effects of sub-anesthetic doses of N_2O in healthy volunteers, noting subjective effects reported by the subjects after the inhalations were complete (Chapman, Arrowood, & Beecher, 1943; Seevers, Bennett, Pohle, & Reinardy, 1937). Both studies used healthy male volunteers between 18 and 35 years old. Specific N_2O concentrations were carefully administered and maintained across the inhalations, and both air and 100% O_2 were administered as controls. Subjects in the Chapman et al. study were blind to the dose and drug being administered. Seevers et al. did not state specifically that subjects were blind; however, the use of the air and O_2 controls suggests that they were. Subjective effects reported by Seevers et al. (1937) included tingling of the extremities at low concentrations that produced insignificant analgesia (15–20%) and generalized tingling, numbness in the extremities, perspiration, a sense of sinking in the stomach, distortions of auditory and sometimes visual perception, and mental dullness at higher concentrations that produced significant analgesia (20–40% and higher). Subjects described experiencing an "initial 'jolt'" (p. 296) from analgesic concentrations of N_2O that occurred 1 to 3 minutes into the inhalation. This initial jolt was interpreted by some subjects as euphoria and by others as an impending loss of consciousness. "Unrestrained hilarity" was also reported by Seevers et al. (p. 299), as was substantial intersubject variability in the concentrations that induced unconsciousness. Chapman et al. reported similar effects: spontaneous laughter, euphoria, light-headedness, and intersubject variability in the doses that produced unconsciousness. In these two studies subjective effects were still being assessed via open-ended introspective self-reports that were obtained after the inhalation was over (retrospectively). Notable features of these studies are the inclusion of two placebo controls (air and O_2) and the fact that subjects were blind to the drug and dose being administered.

Steinberg and colleagues conducted several experiments on N_2O in the 1950s, examining its subjective effects (Steinberg, 1956; Wilson, Crockett, Exton-Smith, & Steinberg, 1950) and its effects on cognitive performance (Steinberg, 1954), time perception (Steinberg, 1955), and stress (Russell & Steinberg, 1955; Steinberg & Russell, 1957). All studies were group designs: A control group (subjects who inhaled placebo [O_2 or air]) was compared with an experimental group (subjects who inhaled a specific concentration of N_2O mixed with O_2). The studies were single-blind or double-blind, and both N_2O and placebo were scented with lavender to disguise any odor N_2O might produce. The concentrations of N_2O being delivered were estimated to be accurate to within 2%.

In the first of these studies, Wilson et al. (1950) tested the effects of 40% and 50% N_2O on sensory-motor coordination in medical students. Students worked in pairs, with one student receiving the drug or placebo and the other acting as experimenter; both were blind to the drug being administered. At the end of the experiment, subjects were asked to describe their experiences while inhaling the gas. These retrospective self-reports included a "general muzziness" (p. 487), feeling vague, dreamy, distant, giggly, and/or talkative; having difficulty concentrating; enjoying the experience; and a sense that time was "dragging." A comment by one subject was reminiscent of the "anesthetic revelation" (though his experience was perhaps less euphoric than those of Davy, Blood, and James): "I've just had the most frightening dream about relativity I've ever had" (p. 487). In the study of time perception conducted with 30% N_2O, Steinberg (1955) reported that "the drug induced subjective impressions of changes in the rate at which time was passing in a substantial proportion of subjects, some of whom reported apparent quickening and a smaller number apparent slowing" (p. 278). The studies on stress showed that 30% N_2O abolished the impairing effects of stress on learning, suggesting an anxiolytic effect of N_2O (Russell & Steinberg, 1955; Steinberg & Russell, 1957). According to Russell and Steinberg (1955), "While efficiency in the performance of a wide variety of tasks deteriorated under its influence, the subject's general behaviour tended to be characterized by euphoria, i.e., 'elation,' 'optimism,' and a general reduction of anxiety and tension" (p. 67).

Steinberg (1956) examined the subjective effects of N_2O in healthy volunteers under the hypothesis that the effects induced by N_2O resemble psychiatric symptoms. Fifty students inhaled 30% N_2O in O_2 through a lavender-scented face mask for approximately 30 minutes (experimental group), and 50 students matched for age and sex inhaled air through a lavender-scented mask (control group). Subjects performed cognitive tasks during the inhalation (those results are reported in Steinberg, 1954):

> The experimenter: (i) recorded any incidental behaviour, including verbal behaviour, in shorthand; (ii) obtained a written introspective account as soon as the inhalation was over; and then (iii) presented orally to each subject a prepared check-list mentioning some sixteen psychological and physiological symptoms commonly encountered with this and similar drugs (p. 184)

Thus, to our knowledge, this study was the first that did not rely exclusively on open-ended self-reports to characterize the subjective effects of N_2O; rather, information was obtained on the occurrence of "experimenter-specified" subjective effects. Table 12.2 shows the symptoms that constituted the 16-item checklist and the percentage of subjects who reported experiencing each symptom, in response to the checklist and/or in the open-ended written self-report.

Table 12.2. Percentage of Subjects Reporting Symptoms in Steinberg (1956)

Symptom	Experimental Group (30% N_2O)	Control Group (Air)
"Compulsive" laughter	20	0
Unsteadiness of finer movements	80	24
Impaired control over grosser movements	46	4
Tingling	68	4
Numbness	50	2
Visual disturbances	38	6
Auditory disturbances	52	14
"Dreaminess"	86	24
Difficulty in concentrating	92	34
Difficulty in talking	34	4
Difficulty in writing	50	6
Impaired control over whole situation	68	16
Memory disturbances	62	24
General effect of inhalation		
Pleasant	44	22
Unpleasant	32	8
Neutral	20	40
Pleasant and unpleasant	2	0
Euphoria	72	14
Dizziness	52	12

It is interesting to note that not all subjects appeared to like N_2O: 44% reported that the general effect of the inhalation was pleasant, whereas 32% reported that it was unpleasant. Given that the majority of open-ended self-reports published in the nineteenth century described pleasant subjective effects of N_2O, this result is surprising. One reason may be that subjects were required to perform several cognitive/psychomotor tasks during Steinberg's (1956) study (described in Steinberg, 1954). Recall that Davidson (1925) found less talkativeness and laughter "when experiments involving concentration of effort were made during the inhalation" (p. 93). In addition, a recent study has suggested that work requirements can decrease the pleasantness of N_2O inhalation (Block, Ghoneim, Kumar, & Pathak, 1990, below). Other potential reasons for the lesser pleasant effects have also been offered by R. M. Atkinson, Morozumi, Green, & Kramer, (1977, below).

Steinberg (1956) pointed out the similarity of several symptoms to the symptoms of psychopathology and emphasized the existence of individual differences in N_2O's effects. "Abnormal" behaviors induced by N_2O were classified by Steinberg as "illusions and hallucinations" (p. 187), "irrelevant or exaggerated thoughts and emotions" (p. 188), "perseverations" (p. 188), or "dissociated states" (p. 189). Detailed examples of "abnormal" behavior induced by N_2O included auditory hallucinations (musical or paranoid), visual hallucinations/distortions, and the sensation of dental pain induced by the similarity of the experimental situation to the subject's last visit to the dentist. Steinberg's classification of "abnormal" behavior included examples of effects that Blood and James might label as "revelatory" rather than psychotic. Although subjects in Steinberg's study reported more pleasant than unpleasant effects of N$_2$O, "a very few subjects were visibly distressed and anxious during inhalation and one said he felt 'panicky'" (p. 188). Thus, individual differences were observed in this study, and such results have been replicated numerous times with various drug classes (cf. de Wit, 1998), including N$_2$O (Walker & Zacny, 2001).

The reader may have noticed that the "violent muscular motions," "disinhibition," and "increased propensity to action, exercise, or muscular movements" reported by Davy and colleagues (and by some patients and dentists in early papers) were rarely reported in more recent studies. This difference is probably due to the difference in dosing procedures. Beginning with Davidson (1925), the concentration of N$_2$O and, perhaps more important, the concentration of O$_2$ were held constant across the inhalation, whereas earlier, rebreathing continuously altered the concentrations of gases being inhaled. Bennett and Seevers (1937) tested 30% N$_2$O in gas mixtures that contained one of three concentrations of O$_2$: 21%, 9%, or 6% O$_2$. Healthy volunteers showed restlessness and muscular phenomena as a result of O$_2$ deprivation, supporting the hypothesis that rebreathing, which decreased the O$_2$ concentration, may have been responsible for the muscular phenomena observed by Davy and others but that were absent in studies that maintained sufficient O$_2$ concentrations throughout the inhalation. Lehmann and Bos (1947) agreed that the hypoxia associated with N$_2$O anesthesia is responsible for the excitement/muscular effects. However, Parbrook (1967) reported the possibility of involuntary movement in the absence of hypoxia between 66% and 85% N$_2$O. Involuntary movement is considered a characteristic of "Stage 2 anesthesia," which occurs after sedation (Stage 1) and before surgical anesthesia (Stage 3; Stanski, 2000). The muscular movement reported by the early self-experimenters may have reflected O$_2$ deprivation or Stage 2 anesthesia or both (and, indeed, the two are not mutually exclusive). Regardless, such excitement/ disinhibition is less likely in studies that test subanesthetic doses of N$_2$O delivered in combination with a constant, sufficient O$_2$ concentration.

Toward Quantifying the Subjective Effects of N$_2$O: 1960s to Early 1970s

Steinberg (1956) ended her paper by suggesting the need for the development of "appropriate measuring instruments" (p. 193). This section will focus on the various instruments used for measuring subjective effects of N$_2$O in the 1960s to early 1970s and how those instruments evolved over that time. In a study assessing a range of doses of N$_2$O

(0–40%), Parkhouse, Henrie, Duncan, and Rome (1960) used "a carefully prepared sheet . . . provided with headings designed to extract as much spontaneous information as possible from the subject with regard to his mental and physical sensations while he was breathing the gas . . . All leading questions were avoided" (p. 46). Although the study did not quantify subjective effects, it did assess dose-response relationships by assessing the number of subjects reporting different effects as a function of dose: Dose-related increases in the number of subjects reporting paresthesias, cold, nausea, auditory sensations, visual sensations, sweating, sleepiness, light-headedness, and impaired memory were observed. A second study by the same group required subjects to complete an introspection sheet similar to the one used by Parkhouse et al. (1960), except that subjects were asked to rate the effects that they had experienced as minimal, mild, moderate, or severe (Henrie, Parkhouse, & Bickford, 1961). Subjective effects were similar to those reported by Parkhouse et al. (1960). This study was a step toward quantifying subjective effects; unfortunately, however, because only one dose of N_2O (30%) was tested, the possibility of dose-related increases in the magnitude of symptoms could not be assessed.

In 1962, Frankenhaeuser and Järpe conducted an experiment in order "to try out a direct subjective scaling method for measuring subjective intoxication at various dose levels" (p. 171). They borrowed the method of magnitude estimation from perceptual research, in which a standard stimulus is assigned a numerical value (usually 10), and comparison stimuli are rated based on their intensity/magnitude relative to the standard. Because the authors were attempting to measure subjective intoxication, the standard had to be some level of intoxication. This standard had to remain constant throughout the entire experiment; therefore, the standard level of intoxication was defined outside the experimental situation, based on previous experience. The standard level of intoxication was defined as "a little high" and was given a value of 10, and subjects were asked to rate their level of intoxication relative to the standard and to keep the same standard throughout the experiment.

Twelve male medical students between 21 and 26 years old were divided into four groups of three volunteers each. During sessions one volunteer served as subject and inhaled a dose of N_2O or placebo (100% O_2), and two volunteers served as observers and estimated the subject's level of intoxication based on his performance on various tasks. This procedure was repeated twice during a session, so that each volunteer served as subject once and observer twice during each session. Six sessions were conducted; the doses tested were 10%, 16%, 22%, 28%, and 34% N_2O in O_2, as well as 100% O_2 (placebo). The doses were administered to each subject in randomized order, each subject inhaled each concentration once, and subjects did not know what concentration they were inhaling. Both the subject and the observers estimated the level of intoxication while the subject was inhaling the drug, using the subjective scaling method described earlier in this chapter. Thus, this study was the first of its kind to measure subjective effects of N_2O while subjects were inhaling the drug. A final questionnaire—a 40–item symptom checklist adapted from Steinberg (1956)—was completed during inhalation of placebo and 28% N_2O. Subjects drew two tick marks next to a symptom if they definitely felt that effect at that moment, one tick mark if they possibly felt that effect at that moment, or a mark through the word if that symptom definitely did not apply. Thus, this study not only examined "experimenter-specified" subjective effects but also obtained quantitative data (0–2 tick marks) on those effects.

Results showed that subject- and observer-rated estimates of the level of intoxication increased with increasing dose of N_2O; therefore, the subjective scaling method appeared effective for estimating drug-induced intoxication. The symptoms on the checklist that were affected to the greatest extent by 28% N_2O relative to placebo included ratings of feeling carefree, elated, foggy, happy, jolly, and talkative. Frankenhaeuser and Järpe (1962) concluded that subjective scaling may be useful for measuring other subjective effects besides level of intoxication. Because several items on the checklist were sensitive in detecting effects of N_2O, a second study was conducted to characterize quantitatively those subjective effects by applying the method of subjective scaling to items on the checklist (Frankenhaeuser, 1963). The same doses were tested as in the previous study, and 12 different medical students (21–33 years old) participated. Two differences between the two studies were (a) the checklist was administered during all dose conditions (rather than just during placebo and 28% N_2O), and (b) the checklist was rated using the subjective scaling method (rather than the tick-mark method). In Frankenhaeuser's (1963) study, too, the subjective scaling method was effective: Dose-related increases in subject-rated estimates of intoxication and of feeling hazy and tired were observed, and ratings of feeling talkative, elated, and happy increased at the highest concentration only. Interestingly, Frankenhaeuser (1963) noted that subject estimates of intoxication were consistently lower than in the 1962 study; she attributed that difference to the more "stiff and formal social situation . . . [which] would tend to reduce the feeling of intoxication" (p. 42). More recent studies have also hypothesized that setting is an important determinant of N_2O effects (e.g., Block et al., 1988; Block, Ghoneim, Kumar, & Pathak, 1990).

In a further move toward quantifying experimenter-specified subjective effects, Lader and Norris (1969) obtained quantitative self-reports from 12 healthy volunteers while they inhaled N_2O concentrations of 0%, 12.5%, and 25% N_2O (in O_2). Twelve minutes into the inhalation, subjects placed a mark on each of two 100–mm lines, one anchored on the left (at 0 mm) with "drowsy" and on the right (at 100 mm) with "alert," the other anchored with "relaxed" (0 mm) and "tense" (100 mm).

Dose-related decreases in the number of millimeters from the 0–mm point on the line were observed, indicating that subjects became more drowsy/less alert and more relaxed/less tense with increasing doses of N_2O. In a follow-up study Jarvis and Lader (1971) replicated these results. To our knowledge, these studies were the first to use a visual analog scale (VAS) to assess subjective effects of N_2O. Their VAS was bipolar, as opposed to specifying a drug effect and having subjects rate that effect from "not at all" (0 mm) to "extremely" (100 mm), a method that is common in drug research today. The VAS is now a mainstay in subjective drug-effects research, and the continuum, which can range from 0 to 100, results in a subjective-effects measure that is sensitive to subtle changes in dose and environmental variables (Brady, Lydiard, & Brady, 2003).

N_2O as an Abused, "Psychedelic" Drug: 1960s to 1990

On the Dangers of N_2O Abuse: 1960s to 1970s

By the late 1960s and early 1970s, much of the research on subjective effects of N_2O had evolved into the quantification of experimenter-specified subjective effects while subjects were inhaling the drug and/or shortly thereafter. Around this time the recreational use of N_2O was becoming a concern of the medical and scientific communities, and reports began to warn about the dangers of N_2O abuse. In one early article Danto (1964) reported that one of his patients had described an "addiction activity" involving "a two-and-a-half inch, gray metal cartridge containing nitrous oxide gas. The cartridge was inserted into an oxygen inhaler or re-breathing type bag device purchased at a medical supply house," and the gas was inhaled "for party 'kicks'" (p. 612). The patient reported that people at the party were happy and giddy and experienced compulsive laughter, sexual excitement, and no ill effects. Danto felt that "although this type of drug-induced acute brain syndrome delight appears to be devoid of any ominous properties [e.g., it was not highly explosive], physicians should be alerted to the potential addiction aspect of this nitrous gas party fad" (p. 613). Other potential dangers of N_2O use noted by Danto included neurotoxic effects, memory impairment, asphyxiation, brain damage, psychosis, impaired respiratory and circulatory functioning, elevated blood pressure, nausea, and vomiting. Another article in that same period described a man who had been reported to have had nine automobile accidents while inhaling N_2O (Dillon, 1967). These articles were among the first to warn doctors of the potential adverse effects of the nonmedical use of N_2O, including its abuse potential. According to Helisten (1975), other "problems arising from the non-medical use of the drug can include frozen lips and throat, oxygen deprivation, nausea, vomiting, disorientation, depersonalization, and occasionally death" (p. 2). Besides these potentially dangerous acute effects, subsequent case reports described actual accounts of adverse effects associated with prolonged nonmedical use of N_2O that Danto (1964) had warned about 10 to 15 years earlier, including N_2O-induced psychosis, cerebral dysfunction, and neurotoxicity (e.g., Brodsky & Zuniga, 1975; Layzer, Fishman, & Schafer, 1978; Paulson, 1979). By 1979, then, N_2O was a known drug of abuse, and the extent of its abuse and reports of adverse effects resulting from such abuse were increasing (H. Rosenberg, Orkin, & Springstead, 1979; Sharp, 1979).

Characterizing the Effects of "Naturalistic" N_2O Inhalation in the Laboratory: Early 1970s

Presumably, N_2O was being abused for its subjective effects, and research was conducted in an effort to characterize those effects for which recreational users/abusers were inhaling the drug. In the early 1970s, Lynn, Harris, and colleagues (Lynn, James, Dendy, Harris, & Walter, 1971; Lynn, Walter, Harris, Dendy, & James, 1972; Harris, Zucker, & Lynn, 1974) conducted controlled studies on N_2O as it would be inhaled in actual abuse settings, claiming that the little research that had been conducted on N_2O had taken place in unnatural settings (laboratories) under unnatural conditions (N_2O-O_2 mixtures that were administered via medical equipment). In the Lynn et al. (1972) study, healthy volunteers were told that they would be inhaling N_2O. In the first part of the study, 5 subjects with no previous drug experience besides alcohol or prescription drugs were categorized as "straights," and 5 subjects with prior drug experience, including marijuana, LSD, mescaline, heroin, and so forth, were categorized as "freaks." (In a preliminary report, these groups were referred to as "naives" and "sophisticates" [Lynn et al., 1971]; we will use this terminology in the remainder of this section.) These 10 subjects inhaled 100% N_2O from a balloon, taking as deep a breath as possible and holding it for varying lengths of time, sometimes rebreathing from the balloon. Latency to become "high" and subjects' remarks were recorded. In the second part of the study, 24 other subjects (12 naives and 12 sophisticates) also inhaled 100% N_2O in this manner and completed an open-ended questionnaire, after which their psychomotor skills were tested. Later these 24 subjects were given a full balloon to breathe as desired and a semistructured questionnaire to complete after they had had their fill of the balloon. The questionnaire asked subjects about "anticipation, drug effects, adverse reactions, residual effects, beneficial effects, motivation, and whether or not they would be willing to participate in further research using nitrous oxide" (Lynn et al., 1972, p. 3).

In both parts of the study by Lynn et al. (1972), "all subjects reported a pleasant experience (calm, euphoria, relaxation, orgasm-like) which seemed to heighten or be prolonged in most cases with repeated exposure. The duration of the peak effects of N_2O were from 20 seconds to 3 minutes for both [sophisticates] and [naives]" (p. 6). Analgesia and relief of depression were reported, as were "tingling or warmth around the face and head and auditory illusory or hallucinatory phenomena" (p. 4). The researchers also reported that a state of well-being continued for 30 minutes to several hours afterward. During the second part of the study, in which questionnaires were administered, 4 naives and 3 sophisticates reported a lessening of preexisting dysphoric sensations, and 11 naives and 10 sophisticates were willing to participate in further research involving N_2O. Similar numbers of naives and sophisticates reported auditory sensations, numbness, tingling, and liking of the drug. In contrast, drug-naive subjects tended to report somatic and dysphoric sensations (warmth, light-headedness, dizziness, floating, motion, unpleasantness, nausea, decreased sense of control, suspiciousness) more than did drug-sophisticated subjects, who tended to describe more "psychedelic" effects (see the next section for a more detailed description of psychedelic drug effects). These results suggested that drug use history influences the subjective effects of N_2O.

Quantification of N_2O's "Psychedelic" Effects: 1977 to 1990

From 1977 to 1990, two groups of researchers sought to characterize objectively the profile of typical subjective effects of subanesthetic doses of N_2O. A major component of their research was the use of questionnaires that quantitatively measured potential subjective effects that were specified by the experimenter. The first group published four articles on the subjective effects of N_2O (R. M. Atkinson, 1979; R. M. Atkinson et al. 1977; R. M. Atkinson, Green, Chenoweth, & Atkinson, 1979; R. M. Atkinson & Green, 1983); we will describe one of these articles in detail to illustrate that group's contribution to the characterization of N_2O's subjective effects.

As already mentioned, the goal of the study was to develop a profile of typical N_2O subjective effects. To achieve this goal, the authors administered the Subjective Drug Effects Questionnaire (SDEQ), which can differentiate among various classes of drugs, including lysergic acid diethylamide (LSD), the prototypical psychedelic drug; amphetamine, a stimulant; chlorpromazine, a tranquilizer; and placebo (Katz, Waskow, & Olsson, 1968). The SDEQ consists of 190 items assessing physical, emotional, cognitive, and perceptual effects of drugs. The inclusion of so many items that measured such a myriad of possible drug effects allowed Atkinson et al. (1977) to develop an extensive profile of typical N_2O effects. For example, some drugs produce opposite effects that seem mutually exclusive (e.g., feeling bad and good at the same time); the SDEQ allows subjects to report such contradictory or paradoxical effects, in contrast to other subjective-effects questionnaires, such as bipolar VASs, which do not.

In the first experiment, 26 males (21–30 years old) inhaled 10% N_2O and 40% N_2O for 20 minutes in separate sessions. Twenty minutes after the inhalation was over, subjects completed the SDEQ, basing their responses on their recollection of effects during the inhalation. Subjects were also asked to rate their overall experience as pleasant or unpleasant and to state whether they would like to inhale N_2O again. The authors developed a profile of typical N_2O effects by defining "common effect items" as those items from the SDEQ that were endorsed by at least half the subjects for 40% N_2O and that were endorsed by a significantly greater number of subjects in the 40% N_2O condition than in the 10% N_2O condition. The 40 items that met these criteria are shown in table 12.3 under the first six headings (the headings correspond to six scales of a questionnaire that evolved from this study and will be described later). Twenty-nine of these items fell into five of eight categories of putative psychedelic (i.e., LSD-like) effects that had been described by Barber (1970). These five categories are the first five headings shown in table 12.3. In addition to the putative psychedelic effects, a group of 13 SDEQ items that were face-valid indicators of "unpleasant or distressing" effects were endorsed by 3–33% of subjects (see table 12.3, Adverse, dysphoric changes). The authors noted that N_2O failed to produce some effects characteristic of LSD, including visual and other special sensory effects and sympathetic autonomic effects. The conclusion, therefore, was that N_2O produces "a moderate but 'incomplete' psychedelic experience" (R. M. Atkinson et al., 1977, p. 324).

The purpose of the second experiment conducted by Atkinson et al. (1977) was to extend the database on effects of 40% N_2O. Sixty-two males (21–30 years old) inhaled 40% N_2O for 20 minutes and completed subjective-effects questionnaires 20 minutes after the inhalation was over, as in Experiment 1. A major difference between the two experiments was that subjects in the first experiment were instructed not to talk during the inhalation, whereas in Experiment 2 subjects were prompted by the research assistant 14 minutes into the inhalation to describe "any interesting or dramatic life experience" (p. 320). These speech reports were recorded and scored using Gottschalk-Gleser Verbal Content Scales (Gottschalk & Gleser, 1969), and scores on these scales were correlated with the written self-reports obtained 20 minutes after the inhalation, in an attempt to determine whether retrospective self-reports of drug effects corresponded with the actual drug effects experienced. Scores on 7 Gottschalk scales were correlated with scores on 10 SDEQ scales, each scale representing a positive or negative affect. Of the 70 possible correlations, 58 were in the predicted direction, and 18 of those were statistically significant. Such results support the hypothesis that retrospective self-reports are valid descriptions of drug effects; that is, verbal samples reflecting affect that were obtained during the inhalation were concordant with subjective effects of affect reported after the inhalation.

Subjective effects of 40% N_2O were similar in the two experiments. For example, in both experiments, few subjects endorsed the 13 items representing adverse, dysphoric effects, and most subjects rated the N_2O experience as being pleasant (80%) and said they would inhale it again (81%). Although most of the subjective-effects results were similar to those of Steinberg (1956), fewer subjects in the earlier study rated the effects as being pleasant (44%). Atkinson et al. (1977) attributed this difference to the use of 40% rather than 30% N_2O, to the use of all male subjects (P. Rosenberg, 1974, had shown that males were more likely to report pleasant effects of N_2O than females), or, perhaps most interestingly, to the possibility of experimenter bias. That is, Steinberg had characterized the behavior induced by N_2O as abnormal and likened the symptoms of N_2O intoxication to psychopathology, whereas Atkinson et al. (1977) took a psychedelic, nonpsychopathological approach. Whether or not this difference in approach contributed to the difference in results, such disparate approaches surely influence how studies are designed and what measurement tools are used and, therefore, what results are obtained.

The second group of researchers who sought to identify the protypical effects of N_2O was Block, Ghoneim, and colleagues. Ghoneim, Mewaldt, and Peterson (1981) used 16 bipolar VASs, anchored at each end with opposite extremes of the effect to be rated, to assess mental and physical sedation, tranquilization, and attitudes/feelings induced by N_2O. These subjective-effects measures, which had been shown to be sensitive in detecting tranquilizers, sedatives, narcotics, and stimulants, were relatively insensitive to N_2O, even though subjects reported substantial effects of N_2O at the end of the study. The authors took this result to mean that N_2O's effects are distinct from the effects of these classes of drugs, and Block and colleagues (Block et al., 1988; Block et al., 1990) incorporated into their studies the 40 common effects from Atkinson et al. (1977), as well as the 13 adverse effects reported by at least one subject in that study. Subjects rated each drug effect relative to what they normally felt on a typical day, from 1 (*no drug effect*) to 7 (*strong drug effect*). The 1988 study assessed the effects of 30% N_2O or placebo (100% O_2) on memory in a group design: 16 healthy volunteers (18–33 years old) inhaled N_2O, and 16 others inhaled placebo for 99 minutes. The effects of Atkinson et al. were replicated, except that scores on the scale of happy, euphoric mood changes were higher in the previous study, and ratings of adverse effects were less common in that study than in Block et al. (1988). The authors concluded that "Atkinson's volunteers had a better time than ours" (p. 264) and suggested that the difference in results could have been due to the higher concentration (40% N$_2$O), the shorter duration of gas inhalation (20 minutes), or the absence of performance tests in the previous study. The authors reached another conclusion that has become clear in the course of this chapter: that N$_2$O produces a rich and diverse set of drug effects that is difficult to characterize by the use of a limited set of subjective-effects questionnaires. One must include a diverse set of items in the subjective-effects assessment to obtain a picture of N$_2$O's effects. "If one only assesses sedation, one will not find anything else. However obvious, this seems worth mentioning, since many experimental studies of drugs include very limited assessments of subjective effects" (Block et al., 1988, p. 264).

Following up on the hypotheses that the weaker euphoric effects and the stronger dysphoric effects observed by Block et al. (1988) relative to Atkinson et al. (1977) were due to the longer inhalation duration and/or the inclusion of performance tests, Block et al. (1990) systematically replicated their earlier procedure, shortening the inhalation duration to 30 minutes and replacing memory tests with measurements of skin conductance obtained during the inhalation. Subjective effects were assessed 40 minutes after the inhalation ended. In support of their hypotheses, euphoric effects were greater and dysphoric effects were lesser than in the 1988 study. Recall that Davidson (1925) observed less laughter when her subject was completing tasks that required concentration, and that Steinberg (1956), who required subjects to perform several cognitive tasks, found only 44% of subjects reporting a pleasant experience from N$_2$O. (For more recent studies on the effects of work requirements on drug effects, see Comer et al., 1996; Silverman et al., 1994.) With respect to the possibility that longer inhalations produce less pleasant overall effects than shorter inhalations, other recent studies showed that initially high ratings of drug liking during a 120-minute inhalation of 30% to 40% N$_2$O tended to decrease as the inhalation progressed (Zacny, Cho, et al., 1996; Yajnik et al., 1996).

The appendix of Block et al. (1990) lists individual items that constitute the five psychedelic-effects scales, other common effects, and adverse effects that were observed in that study and by Atkinson et al (1977). These items and scales are listed in table 12.3. Our laboratory currently uses this questionnaire in our studies of N$_2$O and other inhaled drugs; we have labeled it the "Inhalant Drug Effects Checklist."

Recent Research on the Subjective Effects of N$_2$O:
1990s to Present

Recent research on N$_2$O's subjective effects includes dose-response characterization studies, effects of repeated exposure, and potential mediators and modulators of N$_2$O effects.

Table 12.3. Inhalant Drug Effects checklist (from Atkinson et al., 1977; Block et al., 1990)

Changes in body awareness and image (8 items)
- Been noticing the way your body feels more than you usually do
- Arms or legs felt more numb
- Arms or legs felt tingling
- Hands or feet felt funny or strange
- Skin felt tingling
- Felt as if you are floating
- Body felt heavier
- Skin felt funny

Alterations of time perception (2 items)
- Been losing your sense of time
- Time seemed to be going faster

Experiences of a dreamy, detached reverie state (4 items)
- Had a weird feeling
- Imagination been more lively than usual
- Felt as if you were in a dream
- Things seemed more unreal than usual

Sense of diminished cognitive-motor proficiency (5 items)
- Felt you have less control over your body
- Felt it's harder to talk
- Seemed harder than usual to describe in words how you feel
- Movements seemed slower
- Felt that you have less control over your thoughts

Happy, euphoric mood changes (10 items)
- Felt high
- Felt better than usual
- Felt less irritable
- Things seemed more pleasing than usual
- Felt happier
- Felt more excited

- Felt extreme well-being
- Felt sillier
- Felt like laughing
- Felt as if you see the comical side of things more

Other common effects (now called "Changes in sensation/perception") (11 items)
- Felt not a care in the world
- Felt more free than usual
- Sounds seemed closer
- Body felt lighter
- Felt dizzy
- Lips felt more sensitive
- Eyesight been worse, more blurred than usual
- Felt as if you have less control over your feelings
- Been more aware of your skin
- Been noticing things around you less
- Thinking seemed clearer

Adverse, dysphoric changes (13 items)
- Felt afraid of losing control over your thoughts
- Felt afraid of losing control over your feelings
- Felt extreme anxiety
- Felt sick to your stomach (nauseous)
- Felt worse than usual
- Felt more afraid
- Been afraid of losing control over your body
- Felt more irritable
- Head been aching
- Had a greater feeling of dislike for others
- Felt angrier
- Felt like crying
- Felt sadder

Subjective Effects of N₂O: Dose-Response Studies

Several studies by Dohrn, Zacny, and colleagues assessed the subjective effects of various doses of N_2O using standardized, validated questionnaires. In the first, Dohrn et al. (1992) conducted a within-subject dose-response assessment of the effects of N_2O in six male and six female healthy volunteers who were 21 to 35 years old. The study was double blind, and the order of drug conditions was randomized. Each subject participated in five sessions, during which one dose of N_2O or one placebo was administered through a face mask for 30 minutes. The inhalation followed a baseline period (subjects inhaled compressed air through the mask) and preceded a recovery period (mask off). The placebo conditions were 100% O_2 and compressed air, and the active drug conditions were 10%, 20%, and 40% N_2O.

Several standardized subjective-effects questionnaires were administered, including the Addiction Research Center Inventory (ARCI). The ARCI consisted of 53 items describing potential drug effects, which were grouped to form six subscales corresponding to six types of drug effect: sedation, stimulation-psychomotor, stimulation-euphoria, somatic/dysphoric effects (LSD scale), euphoria (MBG scale), and marijuana-like effects (Chait, Fischman, & Schuster, 1985; Haertzen, 1966; W. R. Martin, Sloan, Sapira, & Jasinski, 1971). The VAS questionnaire consisted of eight 100-mm lines, each labeled with an adjective (*stimulated, high, anxious, sick, happy, sedated, down,* and *hungry*) and anchored on the left (0 mm) by *not at all* and on the right (100 mm) by *extremely*. These two tests were administered during the baseline period, 15 minutes into the inhalation period, and 5, 30, and 60 minutes into the recovery period. The VAS was also administered 2 minutes into the inhalation period to determine initial effects of N_2O. The End-of-Session questionnaire asked subjects to rate retrospectively the intensity of the drug effect at its peak from 1 ("no effect") to 5 ("very strong effect") and the extent to which they liked the drug effects on a 100-mm line, from 0 mm ("dislike a lot") through 50 mm ("neutral") to 100 mm ("like a lot"). Subjects were also asked to state whether they thought they had received a drug and, if so, whether it was sedative-like or stimulant-like.

Scores on the ARCI scales measuring sedation, dysphoria, psychomotor stimulation, euphoria, and marijuana-like effects, as well as VAS ratings of high, stimulated, and sedated, increased in a dose-related manner during the inhalation period, then decreased during recovery. End-of-session ratings of the intensity of the drug effect also increased in a dose-related manner. End-of-session ratings of drug liking did not show statistically significant effects, probably because of the extent of between-subject variability. For example, 8 subjects liked the effects of 40% N_2O, 1 subject reported neutrality toward this dose, and 3 subjects disliked the effects. The number of subjects reporting that they believed they had received active drug increased as a function of dose (10%: $n = 7$, 20%: $n = 10$, 40%: $n = 11$), as did the number of subjects reporting that the drug was sedative-like. There was no difference between the effects of compressed air and those of 100% O_2, indicating that both are appropriate placebo control conditions for use in studies on inhaled drugs. These results replicated those of other studies described earlier in this chapter, including increases in euphoria, dysphoria, and LSD-like drug effects and variability in extent of drug liking/pleasant effects (e.g., R. M. Atkinson et al., 1977; Block et al., 1990;

Steinberg, 1956). Finally, females had higher scores on the LSD and marijuana scales of the ARCI and reported that they felt more "high" than males, and the three subjects who did not like 40% N_2O were female. Rosenberg (1974) also found sex differences in N_2O effects, with females tending to evaluate the N_2O experience as less pleasant than males.

Zacny, Lichtor, et al. (1996) systematically replicated the study by Dohrn et al. (1992), including reinforcing effects (choice) of N_2O as an additional dependent variable. Procedures were similar to those used by Dohrn et al. (1992), with some exceptions, including the assessment of a dose of N_2O and placebo within the same session, the use of a 21-item (rather than 8–item) VAS questionnaire, and the assessment of drug effect intensity and drug liking occurring during (rather than after) the inhalation. Dose-related increases in ratings of drug-effect strength and drug liking, scores on the LSD and euphoria scales of the ARCI, and ratings of 13 VAS items (carefree, coasting, confused, difficulty concentrating, dizzy, drunk, elated, high, having pleasant thoughts, having pleasant bodily sensations, sedated, stimulated, tingling) were observed. There were dose-related decreases in ratings of three VAS items (hungry, in control of body, in control of thoughts). VAS ratings of feeling anxious, down, or nauseated and of having unpleasant thoughts and unpleasant bodily sensations were not affected by N_2O. Thirty-eight percent, 44%, 44%, and 50% of subjects chose to inhale 10, 20, 30, and 40% N_2O, respectively, rather than placebo, during the choice period. Importantly, this study found no carryover effects from the first "sampling" trial to the second, indicating that more than one dose of N_2O could be tested in the same session. Previously, Tiplady, Sinclair, and Morrison (1992) had drawn this same conclusion, and Cheam, Dob, Skelly, and Lockwood (1995) had constructed a full dose-response function of N_2O effects within a single session. Given the necessity of including a range of doses when characterizing the effects of a drug, combined with the difficulty of conducting prolonged studies with human volunteers, these results were significant and continue to be influential in the design of dose-response studies of N_2O today.

Two other dose-response studies by the Zacny group examined the effects of 0%, 10%, 20%, 30%, and 40% N_2O (Yajnik et al., 1996; Zacny, Cho, et al., 1996). The purpose was to determine whether acute tolerance developed to the effects of N_2O when it was inhaled for a prolonged period (120 minutes). Similar procedures were used as in the study by Dohrn et al. (1992). Yajnik et al. (1996) found that ratings of drug liking tended to decrease as the inhalation progressed, but virtually no other evidence of acute tolerance was observed, even though previous studies had found acute tolerance to the anesthetic and analgesic effects of N_2O (Ramsay, Brown, & Woods, 1992; Ruprecht et al., 1985; Whitwam et al., 1976). For this reason, Zacny, Cho, et al. (1996) systematically replicated the study by Yajnik et al., including analgesia (as measured by pain ratings during immersion of the forearm in ice-cold water) as a dependent variable. They found acute tolerance to analgesia, as well as to ratings of feeling carefree and elated, of having pleasant thoughts and pleasant bodily sensations, and of drug liking. The results of these studies suggest that N_2O initially produces pleasant subjective effects but that these effects tend to decrease during prolonged inhalation of the drug. Such results are reminiscent of those observed by Block and colleagues, which found greater euphoric and lesser dysphoric effects during a 30-minute inhalation of N_2O (Block et al., 1990) than during a 99-minute inhalation (Block et al., 1988).

Another pair of studies by the Dohrn-Zacny group assessed the subjective effects of different doses of N_2O administered via brief inhalations of the drug, a common method among recreational N_2O users (Dohrn, Lichtor, Coalson, Flemming, & Zacny, 1993; Zacny, Lichtor, Coalson, Apfelbaum, et al., 1994). In the first study, 12 healthy volunteers (21–35 years old) participated in four sessions in which placebo (100% O_2) or a dose of N_2O (20%, 40%, or 80% N_2O in O_2) was inhaled for 45 seconds (Dohrn, Lichtor, Coalson, Flemming, et al., 1993). Subjective effects were assessed immediately after the inhalation and at multiple times thereafter, except for the Inhalant Drug Effects Checklist (table 12.3), which was administered retrospectively at the end of the session. Ratings of drug-effect strength increased as a function of dose immediately after the inhalation and had already begun to decline after 2 minutes. Drug liking varied substantially across subjects: Some subjects showed dose-related increases in liking, others showed dose-related decreases in liking, and others reported liking 40% but not 80% N_2O (i.e., bitonic dose-response function). VAS ratings of feeling high, tingling, stimulated, sedated, coasting, confused, and dizzy at the 3-minute assessment increased as a function of dose; ratings decreased rapidly and returned to baseline levels by 13 minutes. Similar effects were observed by Zacny, Lichtor, Coalson, Apfelbaum, et al. (1994) when 40%, 60%, and 80% N_2O were compared with placebo (100% O_2), all within the same session. Dohrn, Lichtor, Coalson, Flemming, et al. (1993) found no effect on the LSD or MBG scale of the ARCI, but scores on all scales of the Inhalant Drug Effects Checklist, except Changes in Time Perception and Adverse, Dysphoric Effects, were increased in a dose-related manner. The euphoric and psychedelic effects observed by Dohrn et al. replicated results of previous studies on both extended (e.g., R. M. Atkinson et al., 1977; Block et al., 1990; Dohrn et al., 1992; Zacny, Lichtor, et al., 1996) and brief (Lynn et al., 1971; Lynn et al., 1972) inhalations of N_2O.

Several other studies by Zacny and colleagues have examined both the subjective and reinforcing effects of extended or brief inhalations of N_2O, where reinforcing effects were indicated by the extent of choice of N_2O over placebo (Dohrn, Lichtor, Coalson, Flemming, & Zacny, 1993a; Dohrn, Lichtor, Coalson, Uitvlugt, et al., 1993; Walker & Zacny,

2001, 2002, 2003; Zacny, Klafta, et al., 1996). In general, subjective effects were similar across all studies (e.g., dose-related increases in ratings of drug-effect strength, between-subject variability in ratings of drug liking and other measures indicative of a pleasant experience, and psychedelic effects as measured by the Inhalant Drug Effects Checklist). In addition, choice was typically related to subjective effects (e.g., positive correlations between choice and "pleasant" subjective effects, negative correlations between choice and "unpleasant" subjective effects, group differences in subjective effects between choosers and nonchoosers of the drug). These studies illustrate the reliability of subjective effects of N$_2$O under various experimental conditions. In addition, the fact that N$_2$O self-administration is related to the subjective effects of the drug provides support for the idea that the assessment of N$_2$O's subjective effects can contribute to our understanding of N$_2$O abuse.

Other studies that determined dose-response functions for N$_2$O's subjective effects were conducted by Fagan, Paul, Tiplady, and Scott (1994) and Armstrong, Morton, Sinclair, and Tiplady (1995). These studies found effects similar to those reported by the Zacny group and by Cheam et al. (1995), such as dose-related increases in feeling drowsy, dizzy, euphoric, ill, lethargic, unpleasant, warm, abnormal, drunk, and muzzy. Armstrong et al. studied low doses of N$_2$O (0%, 3%, 5%, 7%, 10%, and 15% N$_2$O in O$_2$) to determine the threshold dose at which detectable impairment occurs. Dizziness did not appear until 7% N$_2$O, and other subjective effects did not appear until 15% N$_2$O had been administered. These recent dose-response studies by other researchers illustrate the reliability of N$_2$O effects across different studies using different methods of assessing similar subjective effects. They also illustrate the continued interest in quantifying subjective effects of various doses of subanesthetic N$_2$O.

Effects of Repeated Exposure to N$_2$O

Hamilton, Laliberté, and Heslegrave (1992) administered 30% N$_2$O (in O$_2$) and room air for 30 minutes each to 11 healthy volunteers (24–35 years old) on 5 successive days. The purpose of the study was to determine whether "adaptation" occurs to nitrogen narcosis, which is experienced by divers at certain depths. Nitrous oxide had been used to simulate nitrogen narcosis in previous studies (Biersner, 1972, 1987; Biersner, Edwards, & Bailey, 1974); in these studies divers likened the effects of N$_2$O to those experienced during nitrogen narcosis. Hamilton et al. found that global estimates of narcosis decreased across exposures, as did ratings of inability to think clearly and of feeling dizzy, elated, hazy, light-headed, numb, tingling, and uninhibited. Other items were sensitive to N$_2$O but did not adapt across sessions: ability to concentrate, ability to work hard, feeling alert, businesslike, carefree, cautious, defiant, dependable, detached, dreamy, efficient, fuzzy, indifferent, intoxicated, reckless, and self-confident. Because psychomotor performance did not show adaptation in that study, the authors concluded that "subjective adaptation to narcosis may occur without corresponding performance improvement" (p. 867); therefore, "care should be exercised when using one's perception of the subjective state to estimate performance capability" (p. 868). Walker and Zacny (2001) systematically replicated that study, including reinforcing effects (choice) as a dependent variable. They found quantitative but not qualitative variability in subjective effects across sessions, but that variability was unsystematic; that is, effects neither decreased (adaptation/tolerance) nor increased (sensitization) across sessions but, rather, fluctuated unsystematically. In contrast, reinforcing effects were remarkably stable across sessions within-subject. The failure to replicate the "adaptation" in subjective effects observed by Hamilton et al. may have been due to the fact that sessions were not conducted on successive days but were separated by at least 2 days.

Potential Pharmacological Mechanisms of Action of N₂O's Effects

In an attempt to determine the receptor mechanisms responsible for the subjective effects of N_2O, three studies by the Zacny group were conducted to determine whether the administration of a receptor antagonist during N_2O inhalation would block the effects of N_2O. Presumably, the blocking or attenuation of a drug effect by an antagonist that produces little or no effects of its own can be considered evidence that the receptor system that has been antagonized plays a role in that drug effect. Zacny and colleagues (Zacny, Coalson, et al., 1994; Zacny et al., 1999) examined the effects of naloxone, an opioid antagonist, on the subjective effects of 30% N_2O; Zacny et al. (1999) also included analgesia as a dependent variable. Neither study found convincing evidence of antagonism of subjective or analgesic effects, even though numerous studies of nonhumans had suggested that N_2O has opioid actions. Zacny et al. (1995) assessed the effects of flumazenil, a benzodiazepine antagonist, on N_2O effects. They found that N_2O-induced increases in VAS ratings of feeling high were decreased significantly by a supratherapeutic dose of flumazenil. Similar, nonsignificant trends were observed for ratings of drug liking and VAS ratings of feeling drunk and elated. This study, therefore, provided evidence of "partial antagonism" of N_2O's subjective effects. All three studies included a range of doses of the antagonist but only one dose of N_2O (30%). The question of opioid and benzodiazepine system involvement in the mediation of N_2O effects should be examined further (Quock, Emmanouil, Vaughn, & Pruhs, 1992; Curtis, Reynolds, & Mueller, 1993).

Various Studies on Potential Modulators of the Subjective Effects of N_2O

CURRENT DRUG USAGE

Two studies examined the effects of current patterns of drug use on the subjective and reinforcing effects of N_2O. Yajnik, Thapar, Lichtor, Patterson, and Zacny (1994) found that choice of 40% N_2O did not differ between current marijuana users versus nonusers, but some subjective effects were greater in marijuana users (VAS ratings of coasting, high, and carefree, scores on the euphoria scale of the Inhalant Drug Effects questionnaire). In contrast, Cho et al. (1997) found that moderate drinkers (mean drinks per week = 11.4) chose 10% to 40% N_2O more than did light drinkers (mean drinks per week = 0.8). In addition, VAS ratings of feeling drunk and nauseated, and scores on three scales of the Inhalant Drug Effects questionnaire (Diminished Cognitive-Motor Proficiency, Changes in Sensation/Perception, and Adverse, Dysphoric Effects) were higher for light than for moderate drinkers.

PAIN, ANXIETY, INFORMATION, AND RESTING STATE

In a study designed to test the hypothesis that N_2O inhaled in the context of pain produces less pleasant effects than when it is inhaled in a pain-free state, Pirec et al. (1995) found that ratings of drug-effect strength and of feeling high and elated were lower in the presence of pain than in its absence. Examining the effect of level of anxiety on the effects of N_2O in dental patients, two studies found that treatment with N_2O during dental procedures decreased anxiety in patients with both low and high dental anxiety (Goodall, File, Sanders, & Skelly, 1994; Zacny, Hurst, Graham, & Janiszewski, 2002), but the level of dental anxiety did not modulate the positive effects of N_2O; rather, both groups reported a similar magnitude of pleasant subjective effects during N_2O treatment (Zacny et al., 2002). Zacny et al. (1997) hypothesized that subjects who were told that they were inhaling N_2O and were informed of N_2O's prototypical effects would choose to inhale N_2O more than subjects who were blind to the drug and given no information about its prototypical effects. In fact, that was the result they found, although subjective effects of the drug did not differ for the two groups. Finally, Mathew, Wilson, Humphreys, and Lowe (1997) found that 40% N_2O increased ratings of dizziness when it was inhaled while volunteers were standing but not while they were reclining.

These studies are consistent with a number of other studies reviewed in this chapter demonstrating that the subjective effects of N_2O can be influenced by a variety of factors. The systematic evaluation of such factors will increase our understanding of N_2O effects, including effects related to N_2O abuse.

Conclusions

Nitrous oxide produces a complex spectrum of interesting and diverse subjective effects that can vary substantially across subjects and can be difficult to describe in words or to quantify via standardized questionnaires. Two questionnaires, however, have been shown to be particularly useful for measuring subjective effects of N_2O. One, the Inhalant Drug Effects questionnaire, is uniquely relevant to the study of N_2O subjective effects because it was developed specifically for that purpose using data from many subjects. The other, the VAS questionnaire, can be used to measure any potential drug effect specified by the experimenter, and the magnitude of that effect can range from 0 to 100, allowing quantitative differences to be observed as a function of changes in dose or other independent variables. We believe that N_2O should continue to be studied using these and other questionnaires. Specifically, because N_2O is believed to be a moderate but incomplete psychedelic drug, other subjective-effects instruments that putatively measure psychedelic effects could be utilized, such as the Hallucinogen Rating Scale, which was developed by Strassman, Qualls, Uhlenhuth, and Kellner (1994) to assess the effects of psychedelic drugs.

The characterizations of N_2O effects have changed over the years. Such characterizations depend on the instruments used to measure subjective effects. As we have noted, the selection of these instruments varies over time, due to cultural factors (e.g., the psychedelic drug culture of the 1970s), as well as scientific factors (e.g., the development or improvement of techniques/questionnaires). Currently, N_2O is not typically identified as a psychedelic drug in the scientific literature but, rather, as an anesthetic, a sedative drug used in dental procedures, or an inhaled drug of abuse. The need for research on inhalant abuse, including N_2O, is clear (Balster, 1998). Much research remains to be conducted on the subjective effects of N_2O, such as improved studies on potential pharmacological mechanisms of action, sex differences in psychedelic and other effects, and further examination of environmental and organismic variables that may modulate N_2O's effects. The continued study of N_2O has the potential to prove as interesting and informing as Davy's research was more than 200 years ago.

References

Armstrong, P. J., Morton, C., Sinclair, W., & Tiplady, B. (1995). Effects of nitrous oxide on psychological performance: A dose-response study using inhalation of concentrations up to 15%. *Psychopharmacology, 117*, 486–490.

Atkinson, O. (1873). Nitrous oxide gas. *British Journal of Dental Science, 16*, 106.

Atkinson, R. M. (1979). Measurement of subjective effects of nitrous oxide: Validation of post-drug questionnaire responses by verbal content analysis of speech samples collected during drug intoxication. In L. A. Gottschalk

(Ed.), *The content analysis of verbal behavior: Further studies* (pp. 335–347). New York: Spectrum.

Atkinson, R. M., & Green, J. D. (1983). Personality, prior drug use, and introspective experience during nitrous oxide intoxication. *International Journal of the Addictions, 18,* 717–738.

Atkinson, R. M., Green, J. D., Chenoweth, D. E., & Atkinson, J. H. (1979). Subjective effects of nitrous oxide: Cognitive, emotional, perceptual and transcendental experiences. *Journal of Psychedelic Drugs, 11,* 317–330.

Atkinson, R. M., Morozumi, P., Green, J. D., & Kramer, J. C. (1977). Nitrous oxide intoxication: Subjective effects in healthy young men. *Journal of Psychedelic Drugs, 9,* 317–328.

Balster, R. L. (1998). Neural basis of inhalant abuse. *Drug and Alcohol Dependence, 51,* 207–214.

Barber, T. X. (1970). *LSD, marijuana, yoga, and hypnosis.* Chicago: Aldine.

Bennett, J. H., & Seevers, M. H. (1937). The effect of anoxia on the action of nitrous oxide in the normal human subject. *Journal of Pharmacology and Experimental Therapeutics, 61,* 459–463.

Biersner, R. J. (1972). Selective performance effects of nitrous oxide. *Human Factors, 14,* 187–194.

Biersner, R. J. (1987, January). Emotional and physiological effects of nitrous oxide and hyperbaric air narcosis. *Aviation, Space, and Environmental Medicine,* 34–38.

Biersner, R. J., Edwards, D., & Bailey, L. W. (1974). Effects of N$_2$O on responses of divers to personality tests. *Perceptual and Motor Skills, 38,* 1091–1097.

Block, R. I., Ghoneim, M. M., Hinrichs, J. V., Kumar, V., & Pathak, D. (1988). Effects of a subanaesthetic concentration of nitrous oxide on memory and subjective experience: Influence of assessment procedures and types of stimuli. *Human Psychopharmacology, 3,* 257–265.

Block, R. I., Ghoneim, M. M., Kumar, V., & Pathak, D. (1990). Psychedelic effects of a subanesthetic concentration of nitrous oxide. *Anesthesia Progress, 37,* 271–276.

Blood, B. P. (1874). *The anaesthetic revelation and the gist of philosophy.* New York: Amsterdam.

Brady, K. T., Lydiard, R. B., & Brady, J. V. (2003). Assessing abuse liability in clinical trials. *Drug and Alcohol Dependence, 70,* S87–S95.

Branch, M. N. (1991). Behavioral pharmacology. In I. H. Iversen & K. A. Lattal (Eds.), *Experimental analysis of behavior, Part 2* (pp. 21–77). Amsterdam: Elsevier.

Brande, W. T. (1827). Lectures on chemistry: Lecture XVII. On muriatic acid, hydriodic acid, and nitrous oxide. *Lancet, 1,* 455–461.

Brodsky, L., & Zuniga, J. (1975). Nitrous oxide: A psychotogenic agent. *Comprehensive Psychiatry, 16,* 185–187.

Carlton, P. L. (1983). *A primer of behavioral pharmacology.* New York: Freeman.

Chait, L. D., Fischman, M. W., & Schuster, C. R. (1985). "Hangover" effects the morning after marijuana smoking. *Drug and Alcohol Dependence, 15,* 229–238.

Chapman, W. P., Arrowood, J. G., & Beecher, H. K. (1943). The analgetic effects of low concentrations of nitrous oxide compared in man with morphine sulfate. *Journal of Clinical Investigation, 22,* 871–875.

Cheam, E. W. S., Dob, D. P., Skelly, A. M., & Lockwood, G. G. (1995). The effect of nitrous oxide on the performance of psychomotor tests. *Anaesthesia, 50,* 764–768.

Cho, A. M., Coalson, D. W., Klock, P. A., Klafta, J. M., Marks, S., Toledano, A. Y., et al. (1997). The effects of alcohol history on the reinforcing, subjective and psychomotor effects of nitrous oxide in healthy volunteers. *Drug and Alcohol Dependence, 45,* 63–70.

Comer, S. D., Haney, M., Foltin, R. W., & Fischman, M. W. (1996). Amphetamine self-administration by humans: Modulation by contingencies associated with task performance. *Psychopharmacology, 127,* 39–46.

Danto, B. L. (1964). A bag full of laughs. *American Journal of Psychiatry, 121,* 612–613.

Davidson, B. M. (1925). Studies of intoxication. I. The action of nitrous oxide. *Journal of Pharmacology and Experimental Therapeutics, 25,* 91–118.

Davy, H. (1800). *Researches, chemical and philosophical, chiefly concerning nitrous oxide, or dephlogisticated nitrous air, and its respiration.* London: J. Johnson.

de Wit, H. (1998). *Individual differences in acute effects of drugs in humans: Their relevance to risk for abuse* (pp. 176–187, NIDA Research Monograph No. 169). Rockville, MD: Department of Health and Human Services, National Institute of Drug Abuse.

Dillon, J. B. (1967). Nitrous oxide inhalation as a fad: Dangers in uncontrolled sniffing for psychedelic effect. *California Medicine, 106,* 444–446.

Dohrn, C. S., Lichtor, J. L., Coalson, D. W., Flemming, D., & Zacny, J. P. (1993). Reinforcing effects of extended inhalation of a low nitrous oxide concentration in humans. *Pharmacology, Biochemistry and Behavior, 46,* 927–932.

Dohrn, C. S., Lichtor, J. L., Coalson, D. W., Flemming, D., & Zacny, J. P. (1993). Subjective and psychomotor effects of bolus doses of nitrous oxide in humans. *Human Psychopharmacology, 8,* 97–106.

Dohrn, C. S., Lichtor, J. L., Coalson, D. W., Uitvlugt, A., de Wit, H., & Zacny, J. P. (1993). Reinforcing effects of extended inhalation of nitrous oxide in humans. *Drug and Alcohol Dependence, 31,* 265–280.

Dohrn, C. S., Lichtor, J. L., Finn, R. S., Uitvlugt, A., Coalson, D. W., Rupani, G., et al. (1992). Subjective and psychomotor effects of nitrous oxide in healthy volunteers. *Behavioural Pharmacology, 3,* 19–30.

Evans, D. I. (1943). A layman's account of "going under." *British Journal of Anaesthesia, 18,* 119–125.

Fagan, D., Paul, D. L., Tiplady, B., & Scott, D. B. (1994). A dose-response study of the effects of inhaled nitrous oxide on psychological performance and mood. *Psychopharmacology, 116,* 333–338.

Frankenhaeuser, M. (1963). Effects of nitrous oxide on subjective and objective variables. *Scandinavian Journal of Psychology, 4,* 37–43.

Frankenhaeuser, M., & Järpe, G. (1962). Subjective intoxication induced by nitrous oxide in various concentrations. *Scandinavian Journal of Psychology, 3,* 171–176.

Ghoneim, M. M., Mewaldt, S. P., & Peterson, R. C. (1981). Subanesthetic concentration of nitrous oxide and human memory. *Progress in Neuro-Psychopharmacology, 5,* 395–402.

Goodall, E., File, S. E., Sanders, F. L., & Skelly, A. M. (1994). Self-ratings by phobic patients during dental treatment: Greater improvement with nitrous oxide than midazolam. *Human Psychopharmacology, 9*, 203–209.

Gottschalk, L. A., & Gleser, G. C. (1969). *The measurement of psychological states through the content analysis of verbal behavior.* Berkeley: University of California Press.

Haertzen, C. A. (1966). Development of scales based on patterns of drug effects, using the Addiction Research Center Inventory (ARCI). *Psychological Reports, 18*, 163–194.

Hamilton, K., Laliberté, M.-F., & Heslegrave, R. (1992, October). Subjective and behavioral effects associated with repeated exposure to narcosis. *Aviation, Space, and Environmental Medicine*, 865–869.

Harris, L., Zucker, R. A., & Lynn, E. J. (1974). Some effects of nitrous oxide on fear. *Journal of Psychedelic Drugs, 6*, 29–41.

Helisten, C. (1975). Nitrous oxide's a gas. *PharmChem Newsletter, 4*. 1–2.

Henrie, J. R., Parkhouse, J., & Bickford, R. G. (1961). Alteration of human consciousness by nitrous oxide as assessed by electroencephalography and psychological tests. *Anesthesiology, 22*, 247–259.

Jacobson, E. (1911). Consciousness under anaesthetics. *American Journal of Psychology, 22*, 333–345.

James, W. (1874). Review of "The Anaesthetic Revelation and the Gist of Philosophy." *Atlantic Monthly, 33*, 627–628.

James, W. (1882). On some Hegelisms. *Mind, 7*, 186–208.

Jarvis, M. J., & Lader, M. H. (1971). The effects of nitrous oxide on the auditory evoked response in a reaction time task. *Psychopharmacologia, 20*, 201–212.

Katz, M. M., Waskow, I. E., & Olsson, J. (1968). Characterizing the psychological state produced by LSD. *Journal of Abnormal Psychology, 73*, 1–14.

Kaufman, E., Galili, D., Furer, R., & Steiner, J. (1990). Sensory experience induced by nitrous oxide analgesia. *Anesthesia Progress, 37*, 282–285.

Lader, M., & Norris, H. (1969). The effects of nitrous oxide on the human auditory evoked response. *Psychopharmacologia, 16*, 115–127.

Layzer, R. B., Fishman, R. A., & Schafer, J. A. (1978). Neuropathy following abuse of nitrous oxide. *Neurology, 28*, 594–597.

Lehmann, H., & Bos, C. (1947). The advantages of nitrous oxide inhalation in psychiatric treatment. *American Journal of Psychiatry, 104*, 164–170.

Lynn, E. J., James, M., Dendy, R., Harris, L. A., & Walter, R. G. (1971, March). Non-medical use of nitrous oxide: A preliminary report. *Michigan Medicine*, 203–204.

Lynn, E. J., Walter, R. G., Harris, L. A., Dendy, R., & James, M. (1972). Nitrous oxide: It's a gas. *Journal of Psychedelic Drugs, 5*, 1–7.

MacFarlane, W. I. (1913). My experience with nitrous oxide and oxygen. *Dental Digest, 20*, 16–19.

Marshall, C. R. (1938). The threshold of unconsciousness. *British Journal of Psychology, 28*, 424–429.

Martin, T. J., Walker, L. E., Sizemore, G. M., Smith, J. E., & Dworkin, S. I. (1996). Within-session determination of dose-response curves for heroin self-administration in rats: Comparison with between-session determination and effects of naltrexone. *Drug and Alcohol Dependence, 41*, 93–100.

Martin, W. R., Sloan, J. W., Sapira, J. D., & Jasinski, D. R. (1971). Physiologic, subjective, and behavioral effects of amphetamine, methamphetamine, ephedrine, phenmetrazine, and methylphenidate in man. *Clinical Pharmacology and Therapeutics, 12,* 245–258.

Mathew, R. J., Wilson, W. H., Humphreys, D., & Lowe, J. V. (1997). Effect of nitrous oxide on cerebral blood velocity while reclining and standing. *Biological Psychiatry, 41,* 979–984.

Parbrook, G. D. (1967). The levels of nitrous oxide analgesia. *British Journal of Anaesthesia, 39,* 974–982.

Parkhouse, J., Henrie, J. R., Duncan, G. M., & Rome, H. P. (1960). Nitrous oxide analgesia in relation to mental performance. *Journal of Pharmacology and Experimental Therapeutics, 128,* 44–54.

Paulson, G. W. (1979). "Recreational" misuse of nitrous oxide. *Journal of the American Dental Association, 98,* 410–411.

Pirec, V., Coalson, D. W., Lichtor, J. L., Klafta, J., Young, C., Rupani, G., et al. (1995). Cold water immersion modulates the reinforcing effects of nitrous oxide in healthy volunteers. *Experimental and Clinical Psychopharmacology, 3,* 148–155.

Quock, R. M., Curtis, B. A., Reynolds, B. J., & Mueller, J. L. (1993). Dose-dependent antagonism and potentiation of nitrous oxide antinociception by naloxone in mice. *Journal of Pharmacology and Experimental Therapeutics, 267,* 117–122.

Quock, R. M., Emmanouil, D. E., Vaughn, L. K., & Pruhs, R. J. (1992). Benzodiazepine receptor mediation of behavioral effects of nitrous oxide in mice. *Psychopharmacology* (Berlin), *107,* 310–314.

Ramsay, D. S., Brown, A. C., & Woods, S. C. (1992). Acute tolerance to nitrous oxide in humans. *Pain, 51,* 367–373.

Richardson, J. (1873). Personal experiences under nitrous oxide. *British Journal of Dental Science, 16,* 102–106.

Rosenberg, H., Orkin, F. K., & Springstead, J. (1979). Abuse of nitrous oxide. *Anesthesia and Analgesia, 58,* 104–106.

Rosenberg, P. (1974). The effect of N_2O-oxygen inhalation on subjective experiences of healthy young adults. *Annales Chirurgiae et Gynaecologiae Fenniae, 63,* 500–504.

Ruprecht, J., Dworacek, B., Bonke, B., Dzoljic, M. R., van Eijndhoven, J. H., & de Vlieger, M. (1985). Tolerance to nitrous oxide in volunteers. *Acta Anaesthesiologia Scandinavia, 29,* 635–638.

Russell, R. W., & Steinberg, H. (1955). Effects of nitrous oxide on reactions to "stress." *Quarterly Journal of Experimental Psychology, 6,* 67–73.

Seevers, M. H., Bennett, J. H., Pohle, H. W., & Reinardy, E. W. (1937). The analgesia produced by nitrous oxide, ethylene and cyclopropane in the normal human subject. *Journal of Pharmacology and Experimental Therapeutics, 59,* 291–300.

Seldin, H. M. (1937). Nitrous oxide-oxygen analgesia from the viewpoint of the dentist and the patient. *Anesthesia and Analgesia, 16,* 74–77.

Sharp, C. W. (1979). It's no laughing matter: Editorial. *Anesthesia and Analgesia, 58,* 73–75.

Shedlin, M., Wallechinsky, D., & Salyer, S. (Eds.). (1992). *Laughing gas: Nitrous oxide.* Berkeley, CA: Ronin.

Sigerist, H. E. (1933). A collection of nineteenth century autographs: Being a contribution to the history of anesthesia. *Bulletin of the History of Medicine, 1,* 107–117.

Silverman, K., Kirby, K. C., & Griffiths, R. R. (1994). Modulation of drug reinforcement by behavioral requirements following drug ingestion. *Psychopharmacology, 114,* 243–247.

Smith, W. D. A. (1982). *Under the influence: A history of nitrous oxide and oxygen anaesthesia.* Park Ridge, IL: Wood Library Museum of Anesthesiology.

Stanski, D. R. (2000). Monitoring depth of anesthesia. In R. D. Miller (Ed.), *Anesthesia* (5th ed., Vol. 1, pp. 1087–1116). Philadelphia: Churchill Livingstone.

Steinberg, H. (1954). Selective effects of an anaesthetic drug on cognitive behaviour. *Quarterly Journal of Experimental Psychology, 6,* 170–180.

Steinberg, H. (1955). Changes in time perception induced by an anaesthetic drug. *British Journal of Psychology, 46,* 273–279.

Steinberg, H. (1956). "Abnormal behaviour" induced by nitrous oxide. *British Journal of Psychology, 47,* 183–194.

Steinberg, H., & Russell, R. W. (1957). Transfer effects in reactions to "stress." *Quarterly Journal of Experimental Psychology, 9,* 215–220.

Strassman, R. J., Qualls, C. R., Uhlenhuth, E. H., & Kellner, R. (1994). Dose-response study of N,N-dimethyltryptamine in humans. II. Subjective effects and preliminary results of a new rating scale. *Archives of General Psychiatry, 51,* 98–108.

Talbot, F. (1915). Psychic disturbances in nitrous oxide analgesia. *British Dental Journal, 36,* 668–670.

Thomas, M. (1814). A Cursory Glimpse of the State of the Nation, on the Twenty-Second of February, 1814, being the Eighty-First Anniversary of the Birth of Washington; or a Physico-Politico-Theologico, Lucubration upon the Wonderful Properties of Nitrous Oxide, or the Newly Discovered Exhilarating Gas, in its effects upon the Human Mind, and Body; as they were exhibited, by actual experiment; on the evening of the twenty-third instant. Reprinted in full in M. Shedlin, D. Wallechinsky, & S. Salyer (Eds.), *Laughing gas: Nitrous oxide* (pp. 82–89). Berkeley, CA: Ronin.

Tiplady, B., Sinclair, W. A., & Morrison, L. M. M. (1992). Effects of nitrous oxide on psychological performance. *Psychopharmacology Bulletin, 28,* 207–211.

U.S. Department of Health and Human Services. (2000). *Inhalant abuse* (National Institute on Drug Abuse Research Report Series 3, NIH Publication No. 00-3818). Washington, D. C.: Author.

Walker, D. J., & Zacny, J. P. (2001). Within- and between-subject variability in the reinforcing and subjective effects of nitrous oxide in healthy volunteers. *Drug and Alcohol Dependence, 64,* 85–96.

Walker, D. J., & Zacny, J. P. (2002). Analysis of the reinforcing and subjective effects of different doses of nitrous oxide using a free-choice procedure. *Drug and Alcohol Dependence, 66,* 93–103.

Walker, D. J., & Zacny, J. P. (2003). Bitonic dose-response functions for reinforcing and self-reported effects of nitrous oxide in humans. *Pharmacology, Biochemistry and Behavior, 74,* 851–857.

Whitwam, J. G., Morgan, M., Hall, G. M., & Petrie, A. (1976). Pain during continuous nitrous oxide administration. *British Journal of Anaesthesia, 48,* 425–429.

Wilson, A., Crockett, G. S., Exton-Smith, A. N., & Steinberg, H. (1950). Clinical evaluation of effects of drugs on medical students as a teaching method. *British Medical Journal, 2*, 484–488.

Yajnik, S., Thapar, P., Lichtor, J. L., Patterson, T., & Zacny, J. P. (1994). Effects of marijuana history on the subjective, psychomotor, and reinforcing effects of nitrous oxide in humans. *Drug and Alcohol Dependence, 36*, 227–236.

Yajnik, S., Zacny, J. P., Young, C. J., Lichtor, J. L., Rupani, G., Klafta, J. M., et al. (1996). Lack of acute tolerance development to the subjective, cognitive, and psychomotor effects of nitrous oxide in healthy volunteers. *Pharmacology, Biochemistry and Behavior, 54*, 501–508.

Zacny, J. P., Cho, A. M., Coalson, D. W., Rupani, G., Young, C. J., Klafta, J. M., et al. (1996). Differential acute tolerance development to effects of nitrous oxide in humans. *Neuroscience Letters, 209*, 73–76.

Zacny, J. P., Cho, A. M., Toledano, A. Y., Galinkin, J., Coalson, D. W., Klock, P. A., et al. (1997). Effects of information on the reinforcing, subjective, and psychomotor effects of nitrous oxide in healthy volunteers. *Drug and Alcohol Dependence, 48*, 85–95.

Zacny, J. P., Coalson, D. W., Lichtor, J. L., Yajnik, S., & Thapar, P. (1994). Effects of naloxone on the subjective and psychomotor effects of nitrous oxide in humans. *Pharmacology Biochemistry and Behavior, 49*, 573–578.

Zacny, J. P., Conran, A., Pardo, H., Coalson, D. W., Black, M., Klock, P. A., et al. (1999). Effects of naloxone on nitrous oxide actions in healthy volunteers. *Pain, 83*, 411–418.

Zacny, J. P., Hurst, R. J., Graham, L., & Janiszewski, D. J. (2002). Preoperative dental anxiety and mood changes during nitrous oxide inhalation. *Journal of the American Dental Association, 133*, 82–88.

Zacny, J. P., Klafta, J. M., Coalson, D. W., Marks, S., Young, C. J., Klock, P. A., et al. (1996). The reinforcing effects of brief exposures to nitrous oxide in healthy volunteers. *Drug and Alcohol Dependence, 42*, 197–200.

Zacny, J. P., Lichtor, J. L., Coalson, D. W., Alessi, R., Goldsher, G., Young, C. J., et al. (1996). Examining the subjective, psychomotor and reinforcing effects of nitrous oxide in healthy volunteers: A dose-response analysis. *Behavioural Pharmacology, 7*, 194–199.

Zacny, J. P., Lichtor, J. L., Coalson, D. W., Apfelbaum, J. L., Flemming, D., & Foster, V. (1994). Time course of effects of brief inhalations of nitrous oxide in normal volunteers. *Addiction, 89*, 831–839.

Zacny, J. P., Lichtor, J. L., Coalson, D. W., Flemming, D., Apfelbaum, J. L., & Foster, V. (1994). Time course of effects of brief inhalations of nitrous oxide in normal volunteers. *Addiction, 89*, 831–840.

Zacny, J. P., Yajnik, S., Coalson, D., Lichtor, J. L., Apfelbaum, J. L., Rupani, G., et al. (1995). Flumazenil may attenuate some subjective effects of nitrous oxide in humans: A preliminary report. *Pharmacology, Biochemistry and Behavior, 51*, 815–819.

13

Corporate Highs, Corporeal Lows

DAVID LENSON

There is no more depressing family of drugs than the antidepressants. They are the children of an unexamined malaise in the lives of the prosperous nations. Their widespread proscription has utterly obviated the need for any explanation, any diagnosis, any etiology. A script closes off further inquiry. One rip of the pad, and there's nothing else to say.

But there should be. To explain so much misery in terms of chemical imbalance alone is like explaining poverty with statistics. The cultural questions go begging. For example: Why is there a culture of depression, so deeply rooted that, as any depressed person will tell you, it feels like a worldview, like realism, like a principled position? How is it that the lower you feel, the higher the moral ground?

Or: Is someone making us depressed in order to sell more antidepressants? Is a depressed and then medicated population easier to control than one made unpredictable by wild happiness? Has the compulsory happiness depicted as a government strategy by Aldous Huxley in *Brave New World* been superseded by compulsory hopelessness, from which no resistance can come? Is depression a form of crowd control?

There is cold comfort in Consumerism, a metaphysic that promises satisfaction with the next purchase, when in fact all that happens when you acquire the first thing on the to-buy list is that the second item moves up in priority. Thus millions live the torment of King Tantalus in Hades, reaching for nourishment that is always snatched away. And there is no escape, as every space of consciousness becomes commercial, from the street to the classroom to the art museum to the kitchen. So what comes to save us? Another product! To assuage Consumerist despair we must make an additional purchase: a bottle of pills. If they have their intended effect, we can return to the normal state of affairs feeling nothing, like Tantalus after centuries, no longer giving a damn.

My own unwelcome encounter with these drugs came after my own true and righteous depression caused trouble in my marriage. Having already huffed and puffed my way through years of talk therapy, eaten buckets of St. John's Wort, and exercised and self-medicated myself half to death, I was finally driven to consult the one person I'd never thought to ask: my physician. I figured he would have only one suggestion, and I'd wind up a Stepford wife. My doctor was concerned, since I'd managed to keep from mentioning my lunacy to him for our first 20 years together, and I left his office with the anticipated Prozac prescription—along with the hep C diagnosis they throw in gratis with every visit these days, the way they used to give away decongestant samples. This latter misfortune was, I thought, unrelated to my original complaint. But, as you'll see, I was wrong about that.

I skulked off to fill the prescription, feeling the irony of it all, since I'd spilt a good bit of ink making fun of Prozac, without having tried it. I found Peter D. Kramer's *Listening to Prozac* very interesting back in 1993, but I was suspicious. It seemed like a death knell for humanistic psychology, but at the same time it smacked of something else, something a little like marketing. And I believe that the way a drug—any drug—is sold is an integral part of its character. In my book *On Drugs*, I'd noted the chemical resemblance of MDMA to fluoxetine.

The competition between MDMA (Ecstasy) and Prozac also illustrates the new competition between pharmaceutical corporations and illegal chemists. There is no doubt that these drugs are trying to reach the same clientele, even though the former is sold as a sex and love drug and the latter as a preparation for almost any psychiatric diagnosis.[1]

Some of my bias against Prozac was therefore related to my feelings about Ecstasy, a drug I dislike because I never know where I'm at with it. One second it seems quite transparent, and the next quite trippy, but I never quite know which quite it's in. Somehow my body senses MDMA's origin in amphetamine and wants it to be speed. This is frustrating, because it's not speed. Plus X makes my back hurt. If I don't enjoy it, illegal aura around it and all, why should I like a time-release version from a pharmaceutical corporation?

There's also a theoretical objection: Everyone knows that Prozac stops working after a while. The reason, I had supposed, is that instead of giving the body raw material for manufacturing new serotonin, Prozac just keeps recirculating the same old stuff. For this reason 5-HTP or tryptophan would seem to be a better bet. But my physician countered by saying that serotonin derived from those precursors goes all over the place, not specifically to the brain, so that you might end up with serotonin in places you don't want it. I shuddered, thinking where exactly that might be. So my doctor chose the drug "with the best track record," that is, the most tiresome, predictable, cliché-ridden script on the planet. A script I filled out of town rather than come clean with the neighborhood pharmacist.

Here, then, was a test for my theory of user construction, a hypothesis derived from Timothy Leary's set and setting, which claims that almost all drug experience is predetermined by the expectations of the user. I had worked this out at great length for marijuana and psychedelics, but my unwelcome dose-to-be presented a new methodological question: Do the principles of user construction apply when the user doesn't want the drug he's about to take?

My doctor himself set out to help me preconstruct the experience. He told me that Prozac would not squelch my emotions but would enable me to step away from them, permitting a space of deliberation. He assured me it would not affect my performances as lecturer and saxophonist. He predicted a loss of libido and a delay in achieving orgasm. And he told me not to read the list of side effects in any of my reference books.

For good reason. For when I peeked, after being on the drug for a couple of weeks, here's what I found:

> The most common side effects of fluoxetine are headache, anxiety, nervousness, sleeplessness, drowsiness, tiredness, weakness, tremors, sweating, dizziness, light-headedness, dry mouth, upset or irritated stomach, appetite loss, nausea, vomiting, diarrhea, stomach gas, rash, and itching.
>
> Less common side effects include changes in sex drive, abnormal ejaculation, impotence, abnormal dreams, difficulty concentrating, increased appetite, acne, hair loss, dry skin, chest pains, allergy, runny nose, bronchitis, abnormal heart rhythms, bleeding, blood pressure changes, fainting when suddenly rising from a sitting position, bone pain, bursitis, twitching, breast pain, fibrocystic disease of the breast, cystitis, urinary pain, double vision, eye or ear pain, conjunctivitis, anemia, swelling, low blood-sugar, and low thyroid activity.

Many other side effects affecting virtually every body system have been reported by people taking this medicine.[2]

Had I used this resource in my construction of the Prozac experience, I probably wouldn't be able to write this. Or else I'd never have taken a single dose of the stuff in the first place. There are questions raised by this battle of information. First of all, the notion of user construction assumes rather naively that the user creates the high purely from internal sources. But isn't the raw material of user construction in some sense *cultural*? Isn't it impacted by external sources of "facts" and subjectivities? My doctor wanted to limit my sources of information. He wanted his view of the situation to inform my own, for my own good. He was right. But this heterogeneous information engulfs the planet like a gas. Is it possible to pick what components of the air you breathe—no thanks, I'm cutting down on nitrogen? Construction of street-drug experience is based largely on hearsay, the accounts of other users. But prescription drugs are constructed on the basis of corporate hearsay: We tell you this stuff is good. And why believe the sellers over the users?

Information tainted by ulterior motives is spurious, viral disinformation. The soundest user constructions are the ones made before a second administration: I felt this, therefore I will feel that. The empirical fallacy. But what determines the construction of the first time? Or the motivation of it? One of the great behavioral mysteries is why anyone would take the first drag on a cigarette. So, too, why smoke *Salvia divinorum* for the first time? Haven't you got enough problems and interests? What do you think you're going to get out of it? What are its promises? What are its dreams? What does it want for you, and what do you want from it? It can only be that you hear this from other people, from prior users.

But how do I know that my doctor is a prior user? I don't. He never said he was. Why am I accepting his street cred? If he's recommending a drug he's never used, he must be endorsing it on somebody else's say-so. But whose? Oh, crap, could it be I was right when I suggested, so snottily and so long ago, that doctors are turning into drug dealers?[3] That they get their marketing "information" from the drug producers themselves?

Prozac exhibits the same "flicker" that MDMA does, an oscillation between opposite polarities. Either you don't know you're on it, or down it comes with every side effect known to medicine. But with the list of side effects unknown to me at the time, and with the bland reassurances of transparency offered by my physician, my construction of the drug (partly my low expectations for its efficacy) allowed me to benefit from it in exactly the way I needed. For a while, anyway.

However uninteresting it all proved to be after the drama of its prescription, people close to me observed a difference. Traffic jams used to drive me to a frenzy of rage, but no more. Now I just sat sheepily like everybody else. I used to feel overwhelmed with commitments at work, but now I'd blow things off or be late. I went from unreasonable expectations to no expectations. I became, so they said, easier to live with.

Which complicates the whole notion of transparency. The classic transparent drug, nicotine, which is quite invisible to a habituated user, becomes opaque only during the process of giving it up. Yet its use is anything but transparent to those who observe the user, thus leading to the astonishingly successful public health campaign to delimit the spatial boundaries within which its use is permitted. Low doses of stimulants are also nearly transparent to the user but perhaps opaque to observers. My previous phenomenologies of drug use had been grounded solely in the experience of the user, but there may also have to be a phenomenology of *observed* drug use. This, too, would be constructed by a cultural apparatus, as so recently we have seen the once positive associations with tobacco quite utterly reversed. What I took to be Prozac's very marginal result was noted approvingly by others as evidence the drug was "working." They were now able to reconstruct me as a saner and more reliable person, even as I saw myself becoming less motivated, and therefore less reliable, professionally anyway.

But what did it feel like, apart from all this worry about construction? On the one hand, it felt like nothing. But on the other hand, like nothingness. I had blackouts as if from alcohol, unable to remember what was for dinner last night. I began taking careful notes on evening phone calls, knowing I'd never recollect them in the morning. I was ashamed of this, the way I'd be abashed about a drunken amnesia. Conversations with family members often had to be repeated later. Yet long-term, general memory, the kind you need for teaching, was undisturbed. All of this was depressing but, because of the drug, not depressing enough.

And then there's the famous death of interest in sex. It wasn't physical impotence but the eradication of an entire category of interest. Kramer's accounts of mousy people turning polygamous or polyandrous struck me as preposterous. Intellectually I knew that I was missing an essential part of being human, but I didn't care. When my doctor asked me if it bothered me, I said no. I told him the story of Sophocles, who, when he became impotent in his 90s, was asked how he felt about it. He replied, "I feel as if a great weight has been lifted from my shoulders."

After 7 months, it just occurred to me, fingers pinched around a greenwhite pill a trice above my larynx, not to drop it. I didn't ask the doctor. Slowly the withered libido grew back, the testicles swollen by disuse receded.

That would have been it between me and antidepressants, except for the aforementioned hep C diagnosis. I appeared to be a candidate for the brutal interferon/Ribovirin therapy that is all allopathy has to offer at the moment. But given what was now easily referred to as "my history," I was informed that I'm *required* to be on some such drug, since interferon has driven hundreds of people to suicide. So I put in a request for Wellbutrin (Zyban), a "broad-spectrum" antidepressant that makes you forget your cigarettes everywhere. I thought that "broad spectrum" might include a dopamine boost like the one you get from speed or cocaine. Being an augmenter rather than diminisher by temperament, I'd rather get above than below the depression.

I got this script with a false promise that I'd use it to quit smoking, a feint that pleased my by now multiple doctors, who were all avid to detox me before their intended retoxification of my body. And the street news on Wellbutrin was very good. One junkie of my acquaintance said it was "kind of sweet." And a poet friend who used it to quit smoking became so devoted to it that she now scores it on the black market, just for the lucid and lurid dreams it gives her, with poems ensuing. And it lacked the hee-hee stigma of Prozac, so that I was able to bring it to the local druggist and not have to face the lines of golems at the CVS prescription pickup.

After the concerted blandness of Prozac and its gray pharmacogenic world, I was utterly unprepared for the express journey to hell that Wellbutrin booked for me. I got the dreams all right, pretty for the first two nights, then turning to a rigorously scheduled train of nightmares that would come at half past each even-numbered hour. Here I was pursued by zombies, trolls, and my mother, confronted imminent nuclear war, appeared in front of enormous lecture halls with no pants on and nothing to say, tried to get to hopelessly disorganized gigs by incomprehensible spiderwebs of highways, only to find upon arriving that I'd forgotten my saxophone and had to drive back after it. After each of these Technicolor thrillers I paced around the kitchen for about an hour, smoking twice as much as usual, then went back to bed to face the same thing all over again. After 6 days of this I gave the pills to the poet and did yardwork in 90-degree heat till I sweated it all away.

Another challenge to user construction. All the preparation from the doctors and the streets was in concert: You're gonna love this. Was this hopeful intelligence countered by an unconscious desire to resist, to preserve my apparent freedom even if led to despair? As Mustapha Mond says to John Savage in *Brave New World*, a book I've taught perhaps once too often:

> "In fact," said Mustapha Mond, "you're claiming the right to be unhappy."
> "All right then," said the Savage defiantly, "I'm claiming the right to be unhappy."
> "Not to mention the right to grow old and ugly and impotent; the right to have syphilis and cancer; the right to have too little to eat; the right to be lousy; the right to live in constant apprehension of what may happen tomorrow; the right to catch typhoid; the right to be tortured by unspeakable pains of every kind." There was a long silence.
> "I claim them all," said the Savage at last.[4]

"What a bummer," my doctor said when he called me back. And so it was, a bummer in the real sixties sense of the word, a pleasant anticipation gone suddenly and unexpectedly sour. When I tried to quit smoking via the patch shortly thereafter, I had a horrible Wellbutrin flashback. If I'd bought this purple pill from someone in the street, I'd go back and punch him out.

So now the hit parade continues with Effexor, and if that doesn't do it, then Errexor or Erasor or whatever. It is a curious inversion of the usual gap between user construction and observer construction, where the drug feels good to the user but makes her look like an ass to the observer. With antidepressants the observer may like what's going on better than the user does. Yet there are conditions, like mine, where these psychotropics are all but compulsory. What if this were the case with street drugs? You *must* try this and then that, or we'll have you die a gruesome death? Down the gavel would come, the long mandatory minimum sentence recited grim-faced from the bench. But who will say the sentence when the surly local thug is supplanted by a global corporation, nowhere and everywhere? Perhaps this is the real objective of the War on Drugs—to put the small-time dealer out of business like the family farm and the mom-and-pop store. I can still refuse to fill my prescriptions at CVS, but I can't refuse third-rate corporate highs, for that is all that they are selling.

Notes

1. David Lenson, *On drugs* (Minneapolis: University of Minnesota Press, 1995), 187.

2. Harold M. Silverman, ed., *The pill book* (New York: Bantam Books, 1994), 396.

3. "The addition of products like Rogaine and Prozac to the prescription lists reinforces the notion that the pharmaceutical companies are trying to invade the markets previously served by quacks and outlaw dealers. Soon everyone may be engaging in the same *bricolage* of the body that the illicit user always has. But the new and expanded medical corporations are calling on the state to help them get their share of the interdicted markets. This would be the effect of 'legalization,' which would be little more than a recognition that there is a lot of money to be made in euphorics and herbal remedies, and that the 'legitimate' health care establishment wants its share of it." Lenson, *On drugs*, 193.

4. Aldous Huxley, *Brave new world* (New York: Harper and Row, 1969), 163.

14

The Subjective Response
to Neurofeedback

SIEGFRIED OTHMER, VICKI POLLOCK,
AND NORMAN MILLER

What Is Neurofeedback?

> Measurements of the electrical activity of brains show that
> dynamical states of Neuroactivity emerge like vortices in a
> weather system, triggered by physical energies impinging on
> sensory receptors, drifting in time, and changing with the context
> of subjects. These dynamical states determine the structures of
> intentional actions and the patterns constructed . . . [in accord
> with] the three basic properties of intentionality: to stretch forth
> and modify the self in conformance with the world; to seek
> wholeness in growth; and to maintain the unity of self.
> —Walter J. Freeman, *Societies of Brains*, p. 111

Neurofeedback is a rapidly emerging technique of biofeedback that is
based on brain activity directly rather than on peripheral measures.
These body measures have historically been used to reveal disregulation
of the autonomic nervous system, and as such biofeedback has generally focused on the autonomic disregulation that attends various psychological and psychiatric conditions. Bringing such disregulations under
better self-regulatory control not only helps with symptom reduction
but also may ameliorate the underlying condition. This has led to a
more general disregulation hypothesis in which psychopathologies are
seen as involving deficits in central nervous system regulatory function.

Biofeedback in general and neurofeedback in particular are then seen as a strategy to restore effective regulation.

The electroencephalogram (EEG) directly reflects the quality of brain self-regulation, and by training the EEG in specific ways, one is able to coax the brain toward more effective states of functioning. Also known as *EEG biofeedback* or *EEG operant conditioning*, neurofeedback also improves autonomic regulation and thus covers a lot of the same bases that have historically been covered by conventional biofeedback. If that were all, however, neurofeedback might not have gotten off the ground. Neurofeedback addresses itself to a variety of brain-based functional disorders, and even to the domain of optimum functioning.

Neurofeedback has grown largely through being adopted by an increasing body of clinicians populating a variety of disciplines, including in particular psychology, social work, rehabilitation medicine, family therapy, psychiatry, and even neurology. In all these venues, the focus is on the remediation of manifest deficits. From a narrow research base in the control of seizures and attention deficit disorder (ADD), the field has grown largely through empirical observation of clinical benefit for a broad range of conditions. Whereas this is extremely satisfying, and portends a significant role for neurofeedback in the future of mental health, it may obscure the possibly even larger potential of neurofeedback to impinge upon the "normal" range of human functioning. This aspect of neurofeedback can be likened to the field of education. Insofar as education involves the development of new skills, we do not model it as the remediation of deficits. Likewise, neurofeedback can be viewed as promoting a wider range of brain functional competences. This is brain learning at the level of brain functional mechanisms rather than of information content.

At first blush it may seem surprising that such a simple feedback mechanism can induce significant change in brain function. However, the brain is largely organized around feedback mechanisms, and neurofeedback can be regarded as simply the addition of one more—in this case external—feedback loop. If we were to monitor closely the state of our autonomic nervous system as we meet the demands of our day, it would quickly become clear that our nervous system manages these functions exquisitely and with exceedingly short delays. The observed fluctuations in EEG measures are likely connected with functional demands. The biofeedback is therefore done under circumstances in which the person is minimally challenged, that is to say, under conditions of maximal physiological quiescence. Under these conditions, it is more likely that the observed fluctuations are connected with disregulation. These residual fluctuations in relevant brain activity are rendered observable instrumentally, and the feedback signal assumes a dominant place in the person's attentions. Gradually the reinforcement brings about an adjustment in regulatory ambients and in signal variability.

Description of the Method

Neurofeedback involves the detection of some aspect of the EEG that is particularly relevant to a clinical issue or training objective, and the conversion of that signal into one that is suitable for feedback to the individual. The trainee simply wishes for the feedback signal to first reach criterion and then to maintain criterion over time. We generally have no sensation with respect to the regulatory brain processes and thus must depend on making the relevant information visible and tangible through overt instrumental feedback.

Feedback can be provided visually or through auditory or tactile means. Visual feedback is usually predominant and is now typically provided via computer screens, so that the feedback signal can be embedded in visually engaging media. Eyes-closed training is also done, in which case auditory feedback predominates. Tactile feedback is perhaps the easiest to employ because it involves the least amount of decoding by the brain. It is therefore usable even with the extremely cognitively compromised brain.

Sessions are typically 30 to 50 minutes, although customary applications differ greatly in the particulars among clinicians. The neurofeedback training can be done with a clinician standing by to optimize the training parameters, but it can also be done in a home training context after it has been established what training a person requires. The number of sessions necessary to induce reliable change in behavior depends on the specific symptom, disorder, or goal targeted for treatment, but generally 20 to 40 sessions are considered a minimum (Othmer, Othmer, & Kaiser, 1999).

Historical Development

There have been two main thrusts within the field of neurofeedback, with entirely independent historical roots. The first involved training of the famous alpha rhythm, and the second involved training the higher frequencies, what Hans Berger called beta. Alpha training got its start with Joe Kamiya at the University of Chicago, and the higher-frequency training originated with Barry Sterman at the Sepulveda Veterans Administration Hospital and the UCLA School of Medicine.

Joe Kamiya (1969) was interested in the physiological observables that track man's mental and emotional states. He found it possible for people to become aware of aspects of their own EEG through the associated feeling states, and he found the alpha rhythm of the EEG to be trainable. The EEG alpha training caught the public fancy in the late 1960s and unfortunately got caught up in the excesses of the psychedelic age. Here was a nondrug means of accessing a variety of brain states, and there was no price to be paid in terms of withdrawal or dependence. Officialdom, however, lumped the two technologies together and took a dim view of our younger generation escaping into altered states by either means. The popular takeover of this field also made it more difficult for serious scientists to take up this area of study or to obtain funding to pursue more fundamental research.

Barry Sterman (e.g., Sterman, Howe, & Macdonald, 1970) discovered neurofeedback at the higher frequencies in the course of animal research. While in a resting but wakeful state, cats exhibited a certain dominant brain rhythm of 12 to 15 Hz (cycles per second) that was subsequently called the *sensorimotor rhythm*, or SMR. This rhythm was similar to the alpha rhythm but at a slightly higher frequency. It has come to be seen as the resting rhythm of the motor system just as the alpha appears to be the resting rhythm of the visual system. Overt reinforcement of the SMR rhythm resulted in change in sleep properties of the cats (Sterman et al., Macdonald, 1970). This was enough to entertain animal researchers, but what really caused a stir was the finding that such EEG training could also raise the seizure threshold in cats for well-calibrated, chemically induced seizures (for review and summary, see Sterman, 2000).

This was a completely fortuitous finding in the course of an investigation of a toxic substance, monomethylhydrazine, which is a common constituent of rocket fuel. Two sets of cats, one trained to produce SMR and one trained to suppress it, were subjected to the toxin, and the trained cats showed much greater tolerance. This was perhaps the biological analog of the Schroedinger cat experiment. Is the cat alive or dead as a result of the toxin? Just check the records. If some months prior the cat had SMR training, then it was alive. If not, then it would behave classically, exhibiting a seizure within an hour and possibly succumbing to it (Sterman, LoPresti, & Fairchild, 1975).

This started a flurry of research on the method. Joel Lubar (Lubar & Shouse, 1976) investigated the technique for attention deficit disorder, although it was still called hyperactivity at the time. Sterman continued his work with seizures. Eventually the SMR training was used with a variety of conditions, including sleep disorders, depression, and traumatic brain injury. Government funding of this research continued until 1985. One suspects that politics was behind the abrupt cessation in funding that occurred at that time. In any event, the work continued mainly under the sponsorship of individual clinicians who had been exposed to the method. The learning curve continued upward in a chaotic way, with each clinician developing his or her own particular style of training, and with little or no contact with any other therapist working away in another part of the country. This was before the Internet.

The original discovery of neurofeedback, called EEG biofeedback at the time, also caused enough excitement in the professional world to kindle the formation of the Biofeedback Society in 1969 in Santa

Monica. This meeting drew together the two camps, one concerned with lower frequency training and altered states, and one concerned with the higher frequency training and normalization of function. The scientists and the meditators, the suits and the saffron robes, eyed each other with suspicion at this conference, and the cultural divide has continued at some level to this day.

By the mid-1970s, the field of low-frequency EEG training was under siege. The nascent field of biofeedback took refuge in peripheral physiology and turned to the training of autonomic regulation using bodily measures. It was not until 1993 that two conferences were held to draw the clinical and research communities back together in the field of neurofeedback. This meeting of the minds caused practitioners to realize the breadth of applicability of what each of us had stumbled into, and of the range of thinking that clinical experience had brought about. By the mid-1990s, EEG biofeedback was the largest interest group within the Association for Applied Psychophysiology and Biofeedback (AAPB), which is what the old Biofeedback Society had morphed into.

Range of Current Practice

With the continued development of the field, neurofeedback has come to be used with the entire range of psychopathologies and as training for enhanced performance. Both involve training higher frequencies, but the low-frequency training, too, has found clinical application to addiction, to recovery from psychological trauma, to the relief of anxiety conditions, and to optimum performance.

To date, the predominant applications of neurofeedback have been to the anxiety-depression spectrum, to the attentional and behavioral problems of children, to sleep disorders, to pain syndromes, to brain injuries, and to developmental disorders among children, as well as degenerative conditions among the aged.

The best way to look at this breadth of applications, however, is not in terms of specific diagnoses but in terms of broader classifications. Regardless of what is done in practice, the technique does not appear to be narrowly targeted, even though it can have very specific effects. The best way to view this is to think of neurofeedback as impinging on brain regulatory mechanisms in some generality.

The Clinical Neighborhood of Neurofeedback

Neurofeedback does not stand alone. As a clinical technique, it is second cousin to rhythmic stimulation techniques called "light and sound," to the use of binaural beats, to magnetic stimulation methods such as repetitive Transcranial Magnetic Stimulation (rTMS), to eye movement desensitization and reprocessing (EMDR; Shapiro, 2001), and to hypnotherapy, holotropic breathwork, and sensory deprivation. *All these techniques either directly or indirectly depend on the frequency basis of organization of brain activity.* Even acupuncture may be included in this listing, in that successful acupuncture treatment is often accompanied by profound changes in the EEG. With each of these techniques a particular appeal is made to one or another aspect of brain function. With neurofeedback, a single technique can cover all the bases.

Brain Model Underlying Neurofeedback

Neurofeedback addresses those mechanisms by which the brain organizes synaptic transport of information. Such information is typically the property of ensembles, rather than that of specific, individual neural events (e.g., Freeman, 1995). The organization of information is therefore a matter of organizing ensembles. It is such collective, ensemble activity that shows up in the EEG. Hence, the EEG reflects to us the instantaneous state of regulation of the system.

The regulation of brain states involves bringing certain functions on-line and taking them off-line as required. We are therefore talking about the activation-relaxation dynamics of brain networks, processes that are reflected in the amplitude and frequency distributions of the EEG at various points on the scalp. Subjecting these signals to reinforcement at first elicits a change in brain state and at the same time mobilizes the brain's resources to reestablish the equilibrium the brain had intended for itself. The brain will not allow its state to be changed arbitrarily. The continual practice of this action-reaction couple seems to eventuate in enhanced capacities for self-regulation in the brain.

Recent insights into network relations reveal that the human brain is perhaps the best exemplar of what is known as a *small-world model* (e.g., Barabasi, 2002; Granovetter, 1973). That is to say, the human cortex is strongly interconnected, so that even distant regions are in intimate communication. In fact, the human cortex is more intimately interconnected than any other known network, biological or otherwise. It is estimated that on average it takes only three synaptic junctions to get from any point on the cortex to any other. This means that our cortex must be largely understandable in terms of group properties. Neurofeedback happens to measure, and thus impinge directly upon, such properties. The ensemble behavior in turn must be understandable as a composite of individual firing events. These are thought to obey simple rules, but the translation is not straightforward from the smooth and somewhat predictable time course of ensemble properties to the erratic, grainy, staccato, drunken-sailor properties of the individual firing neuron.

Ultimately, the action is all at the synapse, and there it lacks subtlety. Either an action potential is generated in the target neuron or it is not. This all depends on a conspiracy of events at the synapse that has a timing sensitivity of 10 ms. The integrity of brain function is therefore contingent on cortical organization at the 10-millisecond level, and one may readily conjecture that the brain may suffer a variety of ills when such timing integrity is poorly maintained. Such is most likely the story of traumatic brain injury, of dementia, and of the various conditions involving demyelinization of the white matter. The typically positive impact of neurofeedback on these conditions, which are not generally responsive to medication, makes the more general case for the timing model of neurofeedback: that the training tends to normalize timing relationships in brain networks.

Who Comes for Neurofeedback?

In these early phases of the development of the field of neurofeedback, those who come and stay tend to fall into three groups. The first group consists of those who have essentially run the gauntlet of everything that Big Medicine has to offer and are now looking for something else. They include the more challenging clinical conditions: severe behavioral disorders in children; bipolar disorder; the autistic spectrum; pervasive developmental delay; cerebral palsy; brain trauma; multiple sclerosis; and the dementias.

The second group consists of those who are already acquainted with alternative modalities. They are already used to a nonauthoritarian way of working, one that places a considerable part of the responsibility on the client not only in terms of commitment to the training but also with respect to good reporting and follow-up.

The third group consists of high achievers who are looking for an edge. They trust themselves to figure this technique out and to be able to judge readily whether it is helping them or not. If it does so, they know it could make the difference in terms of their professional success and even distinction. We include in this group the seekers who are interested in enlarging their own awareness and in accessing a greater variety of brain states, but they wish to do so under professional supervision so that they do not do anything foolish or can be rescued when they inadvertently stray into uncomfortable domains.

Neurofeedback and Placebo

The response to neurofeedback training turns out to have a lot to do with expectations, on the one hand, and with persistence, on the other. The relationship with expectancy factors in neurofeedback has not been as systematically studied in conjunction with the placebo effect as it has in drug research. It seems likely that, as has been observed in research on drugs and placebos (e.g., Kleijnen, de Craen, van Everdingen, & Krol, 1994), expectancies on the part of the client as well as the health care provider probably mediate some outcomes. It is, however, difficult to attribute some of the documented changes that occur after neurofeedback, such as increased IQ scores (Othmer et al., 1999) solely to expectancies.

The other factor bearing on success is persistence. The cumulative import of all the work in the field is that more training sessions result in better outcomes, and that is also in accord with common sense. On the other hand, it is also apparent that if there is a bias in outcome data, then it goes in the same direction, insofar as those who continue to progress in training will be more compellingly motivated to continue in search of greater gains. Moreover, there has not been intensive research effort devoted to assessing the role of conditioning contexts and schedules as components of the placebo response in relation to outcome in neurofeedback treatment. Disentangling the role of conditioning achieved via neurofeedback as opposed to the unique role conditioning contexts and schedules might play in the placebo response (Ader, 1985) poses serious empirical challenges. *It is, however, of particular interest because a central hypothesis that could account for placebo effects generally is that they are mediated by a reorganization of brain timing.* Basic research on reinforcement schedules, in conjunction with different neurofeedback training protocols, is needed to address this possibility.

Despite the fact that paradigms such as the balanced placebo design have not been widely used in the evaluation of neurofeedback, results of clinical research studies suggest it is unlikely that placebo responding alone mediates the outcomes. In studies of seizures, for example, symptom alleviation appears to occur specifically under conditions of neurofeedback using reinforcement of specific frequencies (Sterman, 2000) but not under conditions of random (Quy, Hutt, & Forrest 1979), noncontingent (Kuhlman, 1978), or EMG (Wyler, Lockard, & Ward, 1976) feedback. Moreover, in research on attention deficits, reversal designs have been used. These results demonstrate that statistically significant changes in behavior are observed as a function of neurofeedback training at specific reinforcement frequencies (Shouse & Lubar, 1978, 1979). In other words, it appears that neurofeedback can be used to alleviate behavioral symptoms—and, it can be used to reelicit them.

Subjective Response to Neurofeedback

With this background, we now address the main topic of this chapter: the subjective response that is variously reported for neurofeedback.

People's experience is very different for the two kinds of training, the higher-frequency training done under eyes-open conditions, and the lower-frequency training done mostly under eyes-closed conditions. We therefore discuss these separately.

HigherFrequency Neurofeedback: SMR-beta Training

One of my dreams is to find all the ways that you can use the plasticity processes of the brain to drive correction. My belief is that this sort of thing will be part of a normal future life. It will be understood that you have to exercise your brain and that there are specific things you have to do.
—Michael M. Merzenich, *Scientific American*,
September 2003, p. 80

Higher frequency training typically refers to reinforcing the sensorimotor (SMR) rhythm (i.e., 12–15 Hz), and/or beta frequencies in the range 15 to 18 Hz. In SMR-beta training the first objective is typically to normalize the person's functioning in terms of arousal level. This is a function of frequency, with higher frequencies taking one to high arousal and ultimately agitation. Lower frequencies progressively make for calmness, drowsiness, somnolence, and transition to sleep. If training finds one in the optimal state of functioning, there is no particular feeling attached to that. It is when one moves either toward higher or lower arousal that one becomes aware of either agitation or pressure, on the one hand, or mental disengagement and drowsiness, on the other. The result is that when training parameters are properly selected, the trainee actually does not feel profoundly moved by the experience.

Goals of Training

The first objective of SMR-beta training is symptom alleviation. Subjective experiences reported by people undertaking this kind of training generally relate to the symptoms they bring to the experience or to symptom vulnerability they may have. The training changes one's pain threshold, for example. In this regard, the training has an effect on the system like that of a stimulant. It can also impinge directly on headaches or other pain syndromes, and that would be very apparent to the trainee. It should be noted, however, that most people do not seem particularly skillful at noticing the disappearance of a symptom. Often when clients are queried about their headache at the end of the session they will act surprised. "Oh, I guess it's all gone."

A second major objective of SMR-beta training is to improve attention and cognitive function. The training of attentional networks, however, does not seem to be accompanied by a lot of subjective cues.

Formal assessment of attention is therefore conducted before and after several sessions of SMR-beta training to track enhancements. However, people are aware of mental clutter, of multiple thoughts pressing in on them, of discontinuities in thinking or poor memory access, of rumination, perseveration, or obsessive thinking. And when these aspects of mental functioning change, there is typically an awareness of the shift having occurred. This is particularly true if the change is rapid, as is sometimes the case. When changes occur slowly over time, they may still be noted, but they are less clearly attributable to neurofeedback by the client.

A third major objective of SMR-beta training is to improve emotional regulation. In this domain we address the anxiety-depression spectrum in its affective dimension. This has an obvious subjective component. The anxiety response is used to determine the optimum training frequency in the session. Over time, as anxiety normalizes, there may be an increasing tolerance to a broader range of training frequencies.

Although a number of studies have evaluated SMR-beta in clinical populations, and they yield outcomes that attest to its utility in alleviating symptoms and improving attention (for reviews, see Sterman, 2000, on epilepsy; see Nash, 2000, on attention deficit disorder), very few studies have explored the possibility that such training might enhance function in normal adults. Gruzelier and colleagues, however, have recently examined this issue (Egner & Gruzelier, 2001; Vernon et al., 2003). The outcomes provide empirical evidence that healthy adults show significant increases on scores indexing attention and memory in as few as eight SMR sessions, as compared to control groups (Vernon et al., 2003).

Subjective Experiences During Training

Most of the subjective reports from actual sessions relate to deviations of the training from the ideal, or to the kindling of one symptom or another from the client's inventory. Good neurofeedback is a little bit like good acting. At its best, you do not really know that it is being done. There is no feeling component to good brain self-regulation, so subjective experiences tend to relate to the changes in state from what the person is used to, or to the appearance or disappearance of symptoms with the challenge of training.

With neurofeedback we generally experience the disappearance of symptoms, and it has already been alluded to that in general we are not very sensitive to the disappearance of symptoms. A fresh toothache draws our immediate attention, but when it goes away over a period of time, there is no particular moment that calls attention to itself. Subjective experiences in the high-frequency training therefore tend to relate to specific responses of individuals because of the peculiarities of their situation rather than to generic aspects of the neurofeedback training.

One woman exclaimed at the end of a training session, "I feel holy." The training had given her a very complete, integrated feeling in which she was not only at one with herself but at peace with the outside world. It was a boundary-less and exalted feeling that for her was the essence of a religious or spiritual experience. This was unusual, to say the least. After thousands of clients, we have never had another such ecstatic report as this in connection with the high-frequency training.

Another woman, after completing her first session, pronounced that she felt better than she ever had before in her life. When she did not show up for her subsequent sessions, we were puzzled and eventually called her. She again confirmed that she had had a wonderful experience in the session. As a very religious person, however, she did not think that she was meant to feel that good, or at least not by artificial means. She had related the neurofeedback to the closest thing in her experience, which was the euphoria of an illicit drug, and decided that she did not wish to be tempted further.

These examples are unusual in the sense that the high-frequency training rarely evokes an overwhelming euphoric response. The training is more about normalization of function than of mobilizing a peak emotional experience. However, the particulars of a situation may take individuals there or elsewhere if their brain predisposes them to it.

ALEXITHYMIA

Where the training does open up an entirely new domain of emotional responding is in the case of alexithymia. People with this condition tend to navigate through their lives in a somewhat unattached way. They have few friends or close contacts. Their families have typically become somewhat distant and irrelevant. One key aspect of the condition is that one is not particularly aware of the deficit, so there is usually no strong motivation to see it resolved. Nevertheless, we sometimes see these people in training, and it can be rewarding to see them start to reach out to others. There must be a subjective awareness that attends such initial impulses toward bonding. Remarkably, however, these changes in behavior always appear to be more obvious to others than to the person themselves. Somehow the current behavior must feel "natural," as if the situation itself demanded it, just as the earlier period of detachment felt natural.

ANGER

An even better example of this is anger. Neurofeedback deals exquisitely with propensities toward anger, yet to the actor it must always feel that the situation deserves his or her anger. The problem is "out there," and their visceral reaction is thought to be situationally appropriate. When the tendency to anger is dealt with in training, the world simply no longer deserves their anger to the same degree. The change in internal state will not necessarily be apparent to the person, although it may be obvious to others.

Another illustration of this dilemma is the following: A very driven professional came for training for his "adult ADD." Anger was one issue, but another was the fact that the rest of the world was just too slow for him. People were always in his way and holding him up. We offered neurofeedback. "But how is *that* going to solve the problem?" he wondered. This is not going to make the world any faster. Well, if we could train everybody it might well do so, but at the moment we had only him to work with. We left the matter hanging, but soon enough he did get the point: His sense of time urgency was resolved, and the rest of the world looked a lot better to him.

On another occasion, we worked with a problem of road rage. Within just a session or two, the client reported that his road rage had completely disappeared. That was in fact the first time we heard about the road rage at all—when it had gone away. And he had made the observation himself, in that he usually drove to work alone. His wife also reported, however, that he seemed less irritable at home. In both instances we have here the disappearance of subjective experience with the training.

ATTACHMENT AND RELATEDNESS

Another important area where we see an augmentation of emotional responding is in the whole domain of the autistic spectrum and of attachment disorder. The EEG training seems to break through the disconnectedness of autistic responding and bring about more appropriate interpersonal relating. And it seems to stabilize emotional responding in attachment disorder. This whole process must be attended by an increasing richness of subjective experience within the person. But we often do not learn this directly because we are dealing with children who also have language problems. As in the other cases already mentioned, outsiders typically notice the change.

It is when we see these folks as adults that we find out more about the change in their internal milieu. The training of an adult case of attachment disorder, a successful executive who was skirting the edge of full-blown sociopathy, led to his observation at one point that throughout his life he had had no real understanding of what being in love meant. As he experienced the shift within himself, he became profoundly grateful to his wife for hanging in there all those years with his more distant self.

And then there is the case of a young adult who was trained for reactive attachment disorder. She had been brought from China and delivered to foster parents at the age of 11 months. She was so tiny at that point she could have fit in a shoebox. Now in her 20s, and having experienced a gradual recovery from a horrific mental life with more than 150 neurofeedback training sessions, she reported to her therapist at one point, "I have never been more myself, and yet I have never known less who I am." This puts exquisitely well the dichotomy that we confront in neurofeedback between the physiological and the psychodynamic realms. The brain had been stabilized to the point where she could now function, but the encounter with self had yet to unfold. For the first time, there was a real prospect of conducting fruitful psychotherapy. Neurofeedback had prepared the ground.

FEAR

It appears that the SMR-beta neurofeedback protocols are particularly helpful in reducing fear. We refer here to a generalized state of physiological arousal characterized by hypervigilance and chronic apprehension and anxiety. Clients often report a profound calming with the neurofeedback training, even though they may not have been aware of symptoms indicative of high arousal. Such chronic elevations of arousal levels are behaviorally costly and yet unproductive. When arousal levels are reduced, the person subjectively experiences significant relief and calmness. Some specific training protocols have been found that are particularly applicable to calming excessive fears. These can have a tangible effect in a matter of 1 to 6 minutes.

Fear is a case in point of a general truth about SMR-beta training. Many symptoms that are impacted are not necessarily salient at the time of the neurofeedback session. Sleep disorders are the most obvious example. Seizures are another. With successful neurofeedback training, sleep quality improves and seizures are reduced. What is being trained in neurofeedback is brain self-regulation, and that can be done under any circumstances. The most benign circumstances turn out to be the most propitious, as the person's attentions can be entirely devoted to the task of learning and are not distracted or compromised by prevailing symptoms. When training occurs under such relatively benign circumstances, there may be very little in terms of subjective experience to be reported.

Lower Frequency Neurofeedback: Alpha-Theta Training

Mystical states indeed wield no authority due simply to their being mystical states. But the higher ones among them point in directions to which the religious sentiments even of non-mystical men incline. They tell of the supremacy of the ideal, of vastness, of union, of safety, and of rest. They offer us hypotheses, hypotheses which we may voluntarily ignore, but which as thinkers we cannot possibly upset. The

> supernaturalism and optimism to which they would persuade
> us may, interpreted in one sense or another, be after all the
> truest of insights into the meaning of this life.
> —William James, *Varieties of Religious Experience*, 1902, p. 420

Whereas higher frequency training targets the mechanics of brain functioning, alpha-theta training is oriented almost entirely to the experiential realm. It is not particularly about brain training at all. Rather, it has to do with accessing brain states in which internally generated experience dominates consciousness.

As the reward frequency is lowered in EEG-reinforcement paradigms, the person is gradually shifted from external focus to internal engagement. The transition occurs around the alpha frequency. The presence of alpha in the visual cortex is a signature of a state of visual disengagement. Such a state is most readily attained under eyes-closed conditions, although staring at a bland scene will also do nicely. Consistent with the objective, the low-frequency training is usually conducted under eyes-closed conditions with auditory or tactile feedback.

Two reward bands are used, with one centered on the alpha band (nominally, 8–11 Hz) and one on the theta band (nominally, 5 to 8 Hz). It appears that these bands of activity are associated with very different qualities of consciousness. In an alpha-dominant state visual imagery still has the quality of appropriate sequencing, of following a story line, and of a more obvious connectedness with real-world experience. Imagery in a theta-dominant state, on the other hand, is more disconnected and disjointed, occasionally bizarre and not of this world, but perhaps even more closely evocative of core experiences.

By rewarding the person subtly and gently for entering either state, the brain seems to end up doing a kind of random walk through the unconscious, but since the person is in fact in a wakeful state, this material can be consciously experienced and even appraised. One could think of this by analogy to the traditional process of getting water out of a deep well with a bucket on a rope. Deeply buried material is unearthed in the theta state. It then sloshes over into the alpha state, where one's more organized consciousness can access it. Somewhat chaotically, this process repeats many times during a session as the person shifts back and forth between theta-dominant and alpha-dominant states.

Research on the subjective states elicited by alpha and theta is extremely limited. It has been reported, however, that subjective states of euphoria elicited by acute alcohol intoxication are temporally associated with transient alpha bursts (e.g., Lukas & Mendelson, 1988). Others have suggested that the theta state is likely to be the key mediator of meaningful changes in consciousness (Green & Green, 1989). To our knowledge, there are no systematic studies that address the issue of differences in states of consciousness as a function of reinforcement band. Nor is it known whether reinforcement of particular frequencies within the alpha, theta, or delta bands can reliably elicit changes in subjective state in a between-subject design.

Nonetheless, one interesting caveat to emerge from early clinical experience with the alpha-theta protocol was that training theta at 4 to 7 Hz, rather that 5 to 8 Hz, more often elicited troublesome changes in subjective state. By troublesome, we refer to subjective, abreactive experiences that startled and upset the person undergoing the training. It is for this reason that a slightly higher reinforcement range in theta is more typically used in clinical practice today.

Characteristics of Alpha-Theta

The principal qualities of consciousness that characterize the alpha-theta states are those of "mystical states" that have been characterized by William James as having a number of defining features. First, many persons describe them as ineffable: "No adequate report of its content can be given in words" (James, 1902, p. 371). Second, alpha-theta states are typically described as having a noetic quality: They are utterly compelling and convincing from a subjective stance.

Many persons who have undergone a series of alpha-theta sessions feel that they have transformed their lives. Often such transformative events can even be localized to a brief moment of time. This recalls James's third attribute of mystical states, namely, that of transience: "Mystical states cannot be sustained for long...but when they recur it is recognized; and from one recurrence to another it is susceptible of continuous development in what is felt as inner richness and importance" (James, 1902, p. 372). During the alpha-theta training, there can be complete loss of a sense of time. The sessions themselves, however, do not typically exceed 45 to 90 minutes, and clinical experience suggests that the emergence of unusual states of clarity that sometimes characterize the alpha-theta experience may not last more than a few minutes at most. Also, it is typical that the unusual event takes much longer to describe than to experience in the session.

In his final criterion, that of passivity, James comments that "the mystic feels as if his own will were in abeyance, and indeed, sometimes as if he were grasped and held by a superior power" (James, 1890, p. 372). Many persons who have had unusual experiences during alpha-theta sessions focus less on this aspect than on the joy, warmth, and beauty inherent in it. The attempt is often made to revisit an experience from a prior alpha-theta session, but such striving is nearly always disappointed. Moreover, such attempts at revisiting are likely to disrupt a productive alpha-theta session. But in keeping with James's notion, an element of passivity seems to characterize the unusual subjective experience of alpha-theta, in that it is most definitely not under the ordinary control of one's will. Rather, it has a quality of simply "happening" and of being "seized" by the experience.

The process is not as random as might appear to the external observer, in that the brain tends to access material that matters to the person. The brain itself is in charge of the pacing, so the process is not forced by an energetic or goal-oriented therapist. The self-governance of this process is perhaps its most outstanding virtue. The process is self-limiting, in that if the person is unable to handle the material accessed, he or she simply emerges from the alpha and theta states into the normal censorious consciousness.

This is in contrast to the other techniques that attempt to navigate in this terrain: hypnotherapy, EMDR, holotropic breathwork (Grof, 1986), and the use of rhythmic light and sound at the same low frequencies. In all these other cases, the brain is moved more compellingly and ineluctably to low-frequency states, and the person has fewer options of escape if there is discomfort.

The second principal virtue of this technique is that the process is essentially nonverbal. This is particularly appropriate, since our earliest experiences, and our deepest emotions, are encoded nonverbally. As discussed more fully in what follows, clinical case material provides evidence of the resolution of deep emotional trauma with relatively little verbal intervention by the therapist. This should not be ignored. The third virtue is that because induction into deep states occurs via EEG reinforcement, it becomes possible to observe the details of the process and ultimately to use more refined EEG information to fine-tune the process. When experienced trainees enter these deep states, they are characterized by elevated low-frequency activity over broad regions of cortex. We may think of this in terms of these same regions being brought into simultaneous awareness. In particular, we are tempted to think of this experience as bringing together the disparate "realities" that reside in our two hemispheres. After all, information is encoded very differently in the two hemispheres (e.g., Gazzaniga, 1985). Apparently, the low-frequency state brings the two back into more harmonious communication.

It is important to emphasize that alpha-theta does not reliably elicit a single subjective state or even a reproducible sequence of them: a single alpha-theta experience can be quite different from another experienced by the same person. Indeed, from clinical vignettes and descriptions encountered thus far, it appears most likely that the cultivation of these states leads one to encounter not only elements of personal memories and unconscious material but also higher states, in which a unity of the sense of self and world are experienced. Contemporary phenomenological descriptions of states of consciousness that seem to be accessed through alpha-theta do not provide an adequate theoretical framework from which to develop a model here. But meditative traditions, such as yoga and Zen (Austin, 1998), offer some insights concerning how we might begin to conceptualize these processes.

The points that deserve emphasis are that the alpha-theta training seems to elicit encounters with one's own personal unconscious; that people seem to possess the potential to access nonordinary states of consciousness; and, that although most experiences reported by individuals are good in the sense that they lead persons to experience a richer and deeper sense of fulfillment in their lives, abreactions can occur among those with a trauma history. For this reason, clinicians often approach this work with caution for the very clients who are most in need of it.

Also, many practitioners incorporate scripts developed by clients that are used to guide the alpha-theta sessions. The purpose and development of such scripts are beyond the scope of this work. Suffice it to say that they are used either within the contexts of peak performance training or in the attempt to resolve trauma or to address a life issue. New research, however, suggests that alpha-theta training itself, even without such scripts, can benefit a musician's quality of performance (Egner & Gruzelier, 2003).

Subjective Experience During Alpha-Theta

It is in the realm of alpha-theta training that the entire phenomenology concerns subjective experience, its evocation and processing. As already pointed out, these experiences can be very idiosyncratic and individual. A person with a deep spiritual consciousness or religious orientation can have an experience that is filled with familiar iconic imagery that arises out of his religious tradition. He may be left profoundly moved, shaken to his foundation.

The person with a trauma history may well encounter the self at a younger age, sitting alone at the shore or in an abandoned house. Variants of the imagery may recur in subsequent sessions. The imagery is not just passive. People report interacting with a baby or young child, picking it up, and soothing it. Even within the session, there is an awareness that they are encountering their own younger self. One person used these sessions to construct a mother who actually loved her. Another person constructed a different relationship with her sister, which allowed her to forgive her flesh-and-blood sister. One woman reported excitedly that she had visited the house where she grew up, but she did so as an eagle, flying over the neighborhood. She flew higher and higher, eventually seeing the earth as a ball and flying off even farther into the stars. Her problems shrank along with the perspective of the disappearing earth. Eventually she swooped back down, ending up in her childhood yard. Her relationship to her family was altered from that moment on, and her life satisfactions were curiously much greater.

One observation often made by therapists in connection with alpha-theta training is that a critical, gully-washing, bench-clearing, shaken-to-one's-roots transformative event can often be identified. The person in retrospect recognizes this as the signal event in the whole healing process. We normally recommend a sequence of 40 sessions, but progress in those sessions is more commonly fitful and episodic rather than linear. This is in contrast to our experience with SMR-beta training, where progress is usually gradual and progressive.

Another person found help with a number of life crises that impinged on him within a short space of time. An athletic man, his knees were giving out and required surgery. His mother had suddenly died just shortly before this time. His mother-in-law, with whom he was close, had sunk into the oblivion of Alzheimer's disease and no longer recognized him. And his father was succumbing to Parkinson's disease but was declining the help that the son offered. He felt himself slipping back into a major depression such as he had lived through much earlier. The alpha-theta training restored equanimity to his life. There was a greater level of acceptance of these situations, and the depressive cloud was banished. Then followed an intensive 1-week program of alpha training with Jim Hardt, one of the pioneers of the field and an early graduate student of Joe Kamiya. During the training there were several episodes in which there was compelling imagery of black regions. As he entered these black regions, to which he was strangely drawn, they eventually yielded to the emergence of bright light, first at a distance and then totally enveloping. The training in this case was being done in 3-minute epochs. Amazingly, each of these sequences had to have occurred in that short space of time. The cumulative impact of such an intensive immersion in the alpha training was profound.

TRAUMA AND ADDICTION

The most obvious application of low-frequency EEG work relates to the recovery from deep emotional trauma and from addiction—fields in which empirical research has been reported and controversy has flourished (see Trudeau, 2000, for an overview). But the research does not address the fact that a very large percentage of people feel themselves profoundly moved by undergoing an alpha-theta training sequence (by which we mean more than exposure to a single session). It is likely that the alpha-theta training loosens the grip of adverse experiences that essentially everyone must have had in the course of growing up, even when these events do not rise to the level of what we now call trauma. It seems that alpha-theta work allows the deeply imbedded experiences to be revisited with an adult consciousness and thus reframed.

Despite the dramatic quality of these reports, it is also true that progress in trauma recovery, in the healing of addictions, and in therapy with other crises does not require a singular transformative event. Progress can also be gradual and almost imperceptible.

A professor who came because he was suffering unremitting depression following the death of his wife experienced a whole host of beneficial life changes. During the time he was undergoing neurofeedback, he was diagnosed as having a brain tumor. The prognosis was poor. Also, at the time of his initial visit, he was not well liked by his students, and his reputation as brusque and unapproachable was well known on campus. Over the course of training, this all changed, and the professor was able to confront his own mortality with equanimity. By the time he died, he left a retinue of people who genuinely mourned his passing.

It appears that alpha-theta training accomplishes cortical quieting, which in turn disinhibits subcortical activity. This allows the easier surfacing of traumatic material and the expression of nonverbally encoded emotional resonance. It is possible that by the repetitive juxtaposition in-session of the most troublesome material with the most benign of physiological resting states, we are setting the stage for the healing of the deepest wounds and for the amelioration of the most intractable of psychological disturbances.

Summary

Neurofeedback, by giving us access to mental states in all their specificity and variety, opens the door to new treatment options for the psychologist that are congenial with, and complementary to, existing psychotherapeutic methods. By relying so strongly on the client's own resources, and by drawing benignly on the client's experiential repertoire, the prospects for therapeutic success are enhanced. Almost beneath notice, the client's resources for recovery are reinforced. Through the higher frequency training, the physiological underpinnings are strengthened and stability is enhanced, whereas through the lower frequency sessions, the psychological reserves are replenished and impediments to healthy functioning are allowed to subside. Neurofeedback also obscures the boundary between a deficit focus and the emerging thrust toward the enhancement of resilience and toward positive psychology. Finally, it provides a sanctuary for the healthy spiritual yearnings and transcendent aspirations of our clients in a nonprescriptive and nondoctrinaire way. Throughout this process, the subjective experiences attendant to it reinforce the impression that the client is on a trajectory toward greater health, personal autonomy, and capacity for relationship.

References

Ader, R. (1985). Conditioned immunopharmacological effects in animals: Implications for a conditioning model of pharmacotherapy. In L. White, B. Tursky, & G. Schwartz (Eds.), *Placebo: Theory, research, and mechanisms* (pp. 306–323). New York: Guilford.

Austin, J. H. (1998). *Zen and the brain.* Cambridge, MA: MIT Press.

Barabasi, A. L. (2002) *Linked: The new science of networks.* Cambridge, MA: Perseus.

Egner, T., & Gruzelier, J. (2001). Learned self-regulation of EEG frequency components affects attention and event-related brain potentials in humans. *Neuroreport, 12,* 4155–4159.

Egner, T., & Gruzelier, J. (2003). Ecological validity of neurofeedback: Modulation of slow wave EEG enhances musical performance. *Neuroreport, 14,* 1221–1224.

Freeman, W. J. (1995). *Societies of brains: A study in the neuroscience of love and hate.* Hillsdale, NJ: Erlbaum.

Freeman, W. J. (2000). *Neurodynamics: An exploration in mesoscopic brain dynamics.* London: Springer-Verlag.

Gazzaniga, M. S. (1985). *The social brain: Discovering the networks of mind.* New York: Basic Books.

Granovetter, M. S. (1973). The strength of weak ties. *American Journal of Sociology, 78,* 1360–1380.

Green, E., & Green, A. (1989). *Beyond biofeedback.* New York: Knoll.

Grof, S. (1986). *Beyond the brain.* Albany, NY: State University of New York Press.

James, W. (1902). *Varieties of religious experience.* New York: Modern Library.

Kamiya, J. (1969). Operant control of the EEG alpha rhythm and some of its reported effects on consciousness. In C. Tart (Ed.), *Altered states of consciousness* (3rd ed., pp. 600–611). San Francisco: Harper.

Kleijnen, J., de Craen, A. J. M., van Everdingen, J., & Krol, L. (1994). Placebo effect in double-blind clinical trials: A review of interactions with medications. *Lancet, 344,* 1347–1349.

Kuhlman, W. N. (1978). EEG feedback training of epileptic patients: Clinical and electroencephalographic analysis. *Electoencephalgraphy and Clinical Neurophysiology, 45,* 699–710.

Lukas, S. E. & Mendelson, J. H. (1988) Electroencephalographic activity and plasma ACTH during ethanol-induced euphoria. *Biological Psychiatry, 23,* 141–148.

Lubar, J. F., & Shouse, M. N. (1976). Use of biofeedback in the treatment of seizure disorders and hyperactivity. *Advances in Clinical Child Psychology, 1,* 203–265.

Merzenich, M. (2003, September). The mutable brain. *Scientific American,* 80

Nash, J. K. (2000). Treatment of attention deficit hyperactivity disorder with neurotherapy. *Clinical Electroencephalography, 31,* 30–37.

Othmer, S., Othmer, S. F., & Kaiser, D. A. (1999). EEG biofeedback: An emerging model for its global efficacy. In J. R. Evans & A. Abarbanel (Eds.), *Introduction to quantitative EEG and neurofeedback* (pp. 243–310). New York: Academic Press.

Peniston, E. G., & Kulkosky, P. J. (1989). Alpha-theta brainwave training and beta-endorphin levels in alcoholics. *Alcohol: Clinical and Experimental Research, 13,* 271–279.

Quy, R. J., Hutt, S. J., & Forrest, S. (1979). Sensorimotor rhythm feedback training and epilepsy: Some methodological and conceptual issues. *Biological Psychology, 9,* 129–149.

Shapiro, F. (2001). *Eye movement desensitization and reprocessing (EMDR): Basic principles, protocols, and procedures* (2nd ed.). New York: Guilford.

Shouse, M. N., & Lubar, J. F. (1978). Physiological bases of hyperkinesis treated with methylphenidate. *Pediatrics, 12,* 343–351.

Shouse, M. N., & Lubar, J. F. (1979). Sensorimotor rhythm (SMR) operant conditioning and methylphenidate in the treatment of hyperkinesis. *Biofeedback and Self-Regulation, 4,* 299–311.

Sterman, M. B. (2000). Basic concepts and clinical findings in the treatment of seizure disorders with EEG operant conditioning. *Clinical Electroencephalography, 31,* 45–55.

Sterman, M. B., Howe, R. D., & Macdonald, L. R. (1970). Facilitation of spindle-burst sleep by conditioning of electroencephalographic activity while awake. *Science, 167,* 1146–1148.

Sterman, M. B., LoPresti, R. W., & Fairchild, M. D. (1975). *Effects of monomethylhydrazine on thalamocortical excitability and patterns of sleep in the cat* (Technical Report AMRL-TR-75–34 (AD A014817), Wright-Patterson Air Force Base, Ohio, Aerospace Medical Research Laboratory).

Trudeau, D. L. (2000). The treatment of addictive disorders by brain wave biofeedback: A review and suggestions for future research. *Clinical Electroencephalography, 31,* 13–22.

Vernon, D., Egner, T., Cooper, N., Compton, T., Neilands, C., Sheri, A., et al. (2003). The effect of training distinct neurofeedback protocols on aspects of cognitive performance. *International Journal of Psychophysiology, 47,* 75–85.

Ward, L. M. (2002). *Dynamical cognitive science.* Cambridge, MA: MIT Press.

Wyler, A. R., Lockard, J. S., & Ward, A. A. (1976). Conditioned EEG desynchronization and seizure occurrence in patients. *Electoencephalgraphy and Clinical Neurophysiology, 41,* 501–512.

Author Index

Subject Index

Page references followed by "f" indicate figures; page references followed by "t" indicate tables.